THE RISE

OF THE

DUTCH REPUBLIC.

A History.

BY JOHN LOTHROP MOTLEY.

IN THREE VOLUMES.

VOL. III.

NEW YORK:
HARPER & BROTHERS,
329 & 331 PEARL STREET.
1861.

THE

RISE OF THE DUTCH REPUBLIC.

CHAPTER III.

Latter days of the Blood Council—Informal and insincere negotiations for peace—Characteristics of the negotiators and of their diplomatic correspondence—Dr. Junius—Secret conferences between Dr. Leoninus and Orange—Steadfastness of the Prince—Changes in the internal government of the northern provinces—Generosity and increasing power of the municipalities—Incipient jealousy in regard to Orange rebuked—His offer of resignation refused by the Estates—His elevation to almost unlimited power—Renewed mediation of Maximilian—Views and positions of the parties—Advice of Orange—Opening of negotiations at Breda—Propositions and counter-propositions—Adroitness of the plenipotentiaries on both sides—Insincere diplomacy and unsatisfactory results—Union of Holland and Zealand under the Prince of Orange—Act defining his powers—Charlotte de Bourbon—Character, fortunes, and fate of Anna of Saxony—Marriage of Orange with Mademoiselle de Bourbon—Indignation thereby excited—Horrible tortures inflicted upon Papists by Sonoy in North Holland—Oudewater and Schoonoven taken by Hierges—The isles of Zealand—A submarine expedition projected—Details of the adventure—Its entire success—Death of Chiappin Vitelli—Deliberations in Holland and Zealand concerning the renunciation of Philip's authority—Declaration at Delft—Doubts as to which of the Great Powers the sovereignty should be offered—Secret international relations—Mission to England—Unsatisfactory negotiations with Elizabeth—Position of the Grand Commander—Siege of Zierickzee—Generosity of Count John—Desperate project of the Prince—Death and character of Requesens.

THE Council of Troubles, or, as it will be for ever denominated in history, the Council of Blood, still existed, although the Grand Commander, upon his arrival in the Netherlands, had advised his sovereign to consent to the immediate abolition of so odious an institution.* Philip accepting the advice of his governor and his cabinet, had accordingly authorized him by a letter of the 10th of March, 1574, to take that step if he continued to believe it advisable.†

Requesens had made use of this permission to extort money from the obedient portion of the provinces. An assembly of deputies was held at Brussels on the 7th of June, 1574, and there was a tedious interchange of protocols, reports, and remonstrances.‡ The estates, not satisfied with the extinction of a tribunal which had at last worn itself out by its own violence, and had become inactive through lack of victims, insisted on greater concessions. They demanded the departure of the Spanish troops, the establishment of a council of Netherlanders in Spain for Netherland affairs, the restoration to offices in the provinces, of natives and natives only;§ for these drawers of documents thought it possible, at that epoch, to recover by pedantry what their brethren of Holland and Zealand were maintaining with the sword. It was not the moment for historical disquisition, citations from Solomon, nor chopping of logic; yet with such lucubrations were reams of paper filled, and days and weeks occupied.‖ The result was what might have been expected. The Grand Commander obtained but little money; the estates obtained none of their demands; and the Blood Council remained, as it were, suspended in mid-air. It continued to transact business at intervals during the administration of Requesens,¶ and at last, after nine years of existence, was destroyed by the violent imprisonment of the Council of State at Brussels. This event, however, belongs to a subsequent page of this history.

Noircarmes had argued, from the tenor of Saint Aldegonde's letters, that the Prince would be ready to accept his pardon

---

* Lettre de Requesens à Philippe II., Dec. 30, 1673, apud Gachard, Notice, etc., 24.

† Gachard, Notice, etc., 24, 26.

‡ Bor, viii. 517–523, seq.

§ Ibid.

‖ Vide Bor, vii. 517–523, seq.

¶ Gachard, Notice, etc., 27, 28, and note, p. 27.

upon almost any terms.* Noircarmes was now dead,† but Saint Aldegonde still remained in prison, very anxious for his release, and as well disposed as ever to render services in any secret negotiation. It will be recollected that, at the capitulation of Middelburg, it had been distinctly stipulated by the Prince that Colonel Mondragon should at once effect the liberation of Saint Aldegonde, with certain other prisoners, or himself return into confinement. He had done neither the one nor the other. The patriots still languished in prison, some of them being subjected to exceedingly harsh treatment, but Mondragon, although repeatedly summoned as an officer and a gentleman, by the Prince, to return to captivity, had been forbidden by the Grand Commander to redeem his pledge.‡

Saint Aldegonde was now released from prison upon parole, and despatched on a secret mission to the Prince and estates.§ As before, he was instructed that two points were to be left untouched—the authority of the King and the question of religion.‖ Nothing could be more preposterous than to commence a negotiation from which the two important points were thus carefully eliminated. The King's authority and the question of religion covered the whole ground upon which the Spaniards and the Hollanders had been battling for six years, and were destined to battle for three-quarters of a century longer. Yet, although other affairs might be discussed, those two points were to be reserved for the more conclusive arbitration of gunpowder. The result of negotiations upon such a basis was easily to be foreseen. Breath, time, and paper were profusely wasted and nothing gained. The Prince assured his friend, as he had done secret agents previously sent to him,

---

* Correspondance de Guillaume le Tacit., iii. 369–373.

† He died March 4th, 1574, at Utrecht, of poison, according to suspicion.—Bor, vii. 492.

‡ Vide Gachard, Correspondance de Guillaume le Tacit., iii. DXLIII. DXLIV. DLXV.—Compare Groen van Prinst., Archives, etc., v. 71, 72.

§ Bor, vii. 534. Gachard, Correspondance de Guillaume le Tacit., iii. 400, seq.

‖ Ibid. Ibid.

that he was himself ready to leave the land, if by so doing he could confer upon it the blessing of peace ;* but that all hopes of reaching a reasonable conclusion from the premises established was futile. The envoy treated also with the estates, and received from them in return an elaborate report, which was addressed immediately to the King.† The style of this paper was bold and blunt, its substance bitter and indigestible. It informed Philip what he had heard often enough before, that the Spaniards must go and the exiles come back, the inquisition be abolished and the ancient privileges restored, the Roman Catholic religion renounce its supremacy, and the Reformed religion receive permission to exist unmolested, before he could call himself master of that little hook of sand in the North Sea. With this paper, which was entrusted to Saint Aldegonde, by him to be delivered to the Grand Commander, who was, after reading it, to forward it to its destination, the negotiator returned to his prison.‡ Thence he did not emerge again till the course of events released him, upon the 15th of October, 1574.§

This report was far from agreeable to the Governor, and it became the object of a fresh correspondence between his confidential agent, Champagny, and the learned and astute Junius de Jonge, representative of the Prince of Orange and Governor of Veere.|| The communication of De Jonge consisted of a brief note and a long discourse. The note was sharp and stinging, the discourse elaborate and somewhat pedantic. Unnecessarily historical and unmercifully extended, it was yet bold, bitter, and eloquent. The presence of foreigners was proved to have been, from the beginning of Philip's reign, the curse of the country. Doctor Sonnius, with

* "Quant à luy il étoit content, si ceulx là le treuvoient bon de se retirer du pays, afin que tant mieulx ilz puissent parvenir à ce que dessus," etc.—Gachard, Guillaume le Tacit., iii. 400.

† Bor, vii. 535.

‡ See the "Vertooning" in Bor, vii. 535, seq.

§ Gachard, Guillaume le Tacit., iii. 101. Bor, vii.

|| See the Correspondence in Bor, vii. 535, 536.

his batch of bishops, had sowed the seed of the first disorder. A prince, ruling in the Netherlands, had no right to turn a deaf ear to the petitions of his subjects. If he did so, the Hollanders would tell him, as the old woman had told the Emperor Adrian, that the potentate who had no time to attend to the interests of his subjects, had not leisure enough to be a sovereign. While Holland refused to bow its neck to the Inquisition, the King of Spain dreaded the thunder and lightning of the Pope. The Hollanders would, with pleasure, emancipate Philip from his own thraldom, but it was absurd that he, who was himself a slave to another potentate, should affect unlimited control over a free people. It was Philip's councillors, not the Hollanders, who were his real enemies; for it was they who held him in the subjection by which his power was neutralized and his crown degraded.*

It may be supposed that many long pages, conceived in this spirit and expressed with great vigor, would hardly smooth the way for the more official negotiations which were soon to take place, yet Doctor Junius fairly and faithfully represented the sentiment of his nation.

Towards the close of the year, Doctor Elbertus Leoninus, professor of Louvain, together with Hugo Bonte, ex-pensionary of Middelburg, was commissioned by the Grand Commander to treat secretly with the Prince.† He was, however, not found very tractable when the commissioners opened the subject of his own pardon and reconciliation with the King, and he absolutely refused to treat at all except with the co-operation of the estates.‡ He, moreover, objected to the use of the word "pardon" on the ground that he had never done anything requiring his Majesty's forgiveness. If adversity should visit him, he cared but little for it; he had lived long enough, he said, and should die with some glory, regretting

---

* See the discourse of Junius in Bor, vii. 536–544.

† The letters and documents concerning this secret negotiation are published in Gachard, Guillaume le Tacit., iii. 403—430. See also Bor, vii. 585.

‡ See the account by Bonte, in Gachard. Correspondance de Guillaume le Tacit., iii. 378, 379.

the disorders and oppressions which had taken place, but conscious that it had not been in his power to remedy them. When reminded by the commissioners of the King's power, he replied that he knew his Majesty to be very mighty, but that there was a King more powerful still—even God the Creator, who, as he humbly hoped, was upon his side.*

At a subsequent interview with Hugo Bonte, the Prince declared it almost impossible for himself or the estates to hold any formal communication with the Spanish government, as such communications were not safe. No trust could be reposed either in safe conducts or hostages. Faith had been too often broken by the administration. The promise made by the Duchess of Parma to the nobles, and afterwards violated, the recent treachery of Mondragon, the return of three exchanged prisoners from the Hague, who died next day of poison administered before their release, the frequent attempts upon his own life—all such constantly recurring crimes made it doubtful, in the opinion of the Prince, whether it would be possible to find commissioners to treat with his Majesty's government. All would fear assassination, afterwards to be disavowed by the King and pardoned by the Pope.† After much conversation in this vein, the Prince gave the Spanish agents warning that he might eventually be obliged to seek the protection of some foreign power for the provinces. In this connection he made use of the memorable metaphor, so often repeated afterwards, that "the country was a beautiful damsel, who certainly did not lack suitors able and willing to accept her and defend her against the world."‡ As to the matter of religion, he said he was willing to leave it to be settled by the estates-general; but doubted whether anything short of entire liberty of worship would ever satisfy the people.§

Subsequently there were held other conferences, between the

* See the account by Bonte, in Gachard.—Correspondance de Guillaume le Tacit., iii. 378, 379, 380.

† Ibid., 383.

‡ Ibid., 387.—Compare Bor, viii. 613.

§ Correspondance de Guillaume le Tacit., iii. 387.—Compare Bor, viii. 613.

Prince and Doctor Leoninus, with a similar result, all attempts proving fruitless to induce him to abandon his position upon the subject of religion, or to accept a pardon on any terms save the departure of the foreign troops, the assembling of the estates-general, and entire freedom of religion. Even if he were willing to concede the religious question himself, he observed that it was idle to hope either from the estates or people a hand's-breadth of concession upon that point. Leoninus was subsequently admitted to a secret conference with the estates of Holland, where his representations were firmly met by the same arguments as those already used by the Prince.*

These proceedings on the part of Saint Aldegonde, Champagny, Junius, and Elbertus Leoninus extended through the whole summer and autumn of 1574, and were not terminated until January of the following year.

Changes fast becoming necessary in the internal government of the provinces, were also undertaken during this year. Hitherto the Prince had exercised his power under the convenient fiction of the King's authority, systematically conducting the rebellion in the name of his Majesty, and as his Majesty's stadholder. By this process an immense power was lodged in his hands; nothing less, indeed, than the supreme executive and legislative functions of the land; while since the revolt had become, as it were, perpetual, ample but

* Gachard, Correspondance de Guillaume le Tacit, iii. 403–430. Bor, vii. 565, seq.—Compare Hoofd, ix. 400, 401; Wagenaer, d. vii. 25–27. See also a very ample memoir of the distinguished scholar and diplomatist, Albert de Leeuw (or Elbertus Leoninus), by J. P. Van Cappelle. Bijdragen tot de Ges. d. Nederl., 1–204. He began his active life as law professor at Louvain, in which city he married Barbara de Haze, with whom he lived more than fifty-two years. The lady, however, seems not to have pined away after the termination of this wedlock of more than half a century; for she survived her husband *thirty-six years.* The biographer shrewdly suspects, therefore, that she must have been a "*very young miss when she was married.*" "Dit meisje moet nog seer jong zijn geweest, toen Leoninus zich met haar in het huwelijk begaf."—V. d. Cappelle, 93, note 8. He was born at Bommel, in 1519 or 1520, and died in 1598, full of years and honours. His public services, on various important occasions, will be often alluded to in subsequent pages.

anomalous functions had been additionally thrust upon him by the estates and by the general voice of the people.

The two provinces, even while deprived of Harlem and Amsterdam, now raised two hundred and ten thousand florins monthly,* whereas Alva had never been able to extract from Holland more than two hundred and seventy-one thousand florins yearly. They paid all rather than pay a tenth. In consequence of this liberality, the cities insensibly acquired a greater influence in the government. The coming contest between the centrifugal aristocratic principle, represented by these corporations, and the central popular authority of the stadholder, was already foreshadowed, but at first the estates were in perfect harmony with the Prince. They even urged upon him more power than he desired, and declined functions which he wished them to exercise. On the 7th of September, 1573, it had been formally proposed by the general council to confer a regular and unlimited dictatorship upon him,† but in the course of a year from that time, the cities had begun to feel their increasing importance.‡ Moreover, while growing more ambitious, they became less liberal.

The Prince, dissatisfied with the conduct of the cities, brought the whole subject before an assembly of the estates of Holland on the 20th October, 1574. He stated the inconveniences produced by the anomalous condition of the government. He complained that the common people had often fallen into the error that the money raised for public purposes had been levied for his benefit only, and that they had, therefore, been less willing to contribute to the taxes. As the only remedy for these evils, he tendered his resignation of all the powers with which he was clothed, so that the estates might then take the government, which they could exercise without conflict or control. For himself, he had never desired power, except as a means of being useful to his country, and he did not

* Resol. Holl., Mar. 15 und 17, 1576, bl. 16, 19.

† Kluit, Hist. Holl. Staatsreg., dl. i. 86.

‡ Kluit, i. 78, et seq. Wagenaer, vii. 5, 6.

offer his resignation from unwillingness to stand by the cause, but from a hearty desire to save it from disputes among its friends. He was ready, now as ever, to shed the last drop of his blood to maintain the freedom of the land.*

This straightforward language produced an instantaneous effect. The estates knew that they were dealing with a man whose life was governed by lofty principles, and they felt that they were in danger of losing him through their own selfishness and low ambition. They were embarrassed, for they did not like to relinquish the authority which they had begun to relish, nor to accept the resignation of a man who was indispensable. They felt that to give up William of Orange at that time was to accept the Spanish yoke for ever. At an assembly held at Delft on the 12th of November, 1574, they accordingly requested him "to continue in his blessed government, with the council established near him,"† and for this end, they formally offered to him, "under the name of Governor or Regent," absolute power, authority, and sovereign command. In particular, they conferred on him the entire control of all the ships of war, hitherto reserved to the different cities, together with the right to dispose of all prizes and all monies raised for the support of fleets. They gave him also unlimited power over the domains; they agreed that all magistracies, militia bands, guilds, and communities, should make solemn oath to contribute taxes and to receive garrisons, exactly as the Prince, with his council, should ordain; but they made it a condition that the estates should be convened and consulted upon requests, impositions, and upon all changes in the governing body. It was also stipulated that the judges of the supreme court and of the exchequer, with other high officers, should be appointed by and with the consent of the estates.‡

---

* Resol. Holl., Oct. 20, Nov. 1, bl. 148–176. Kluit, d. i. 96, 97. Wagenaer, vii. 10, 11.

† Resol. Holl., Nov., 1574, bl. 178. Wagenaer, vii. 11, 12, 13. Kluit, 97, 98, d. i.

‡ Resol. Holl. Kluit, Wagenaer, ubi sup. Groen v. Prinst., Archives, etc., v. 90–94.

The Prince expressed himself willing to accept the government upon these terms. He, however, demanded an allowance of forty-five thousand florins monthly for the army expenses and other current outlays.* Here, however, the estates refused their consent. In a mercantile spirit, unworthy the occasion and the man with whom they were dealing, they endeavoured to chaffer where they should have been only too willing to comply, and they attempted to reduce the reasonable demand of the Prince to thirty thousand florins.† The Prince, who had poured out his own wealth so lavishly in the cause—who, together with his brothers, particularly the generous John of Nassau, had contributed all which they could raise by mortgage, sales of jewellery and furniture, and by extensive loans, subjecting themselves to constant embarrassment, and almost to penury, felt himself outraged by the paltriness of this conduct. He expressed his indignation, and denounced the niggardliness of the estates in the strongest language, and declared that he would rather leave the country for ever, with the maintenance of his own honor, than accept the government upon such disgraceful terms.‡ The estates, disturbed by his vehemence, and struck with its justice, instantly, and without further deliberation, consented to his demand. They granted the forty-five thousand florins monthly, and the Prince assumed the government, thus remodelled.§

During the autumn and early winter of the year 1574, the Emperor Maximilian had been actively exerting himself to bring about a pacification of the Netherlands. He was certainly sincere, for an excellent reason. "The Emperor

---

* Resol. Holl., Nov. 13 und 25, 1574, bl. 196, 207, 208. Kluit, i. 101, 102.

† Resol. Holl., Nov. 25, 1574, bl. 207, 208.

‡ Resol. Holl., Nov. 25, 1574, bl. 208.

§ They made the offer of thirty thousand in the morning, and granted the whole demand in the afternoon of the 25th Nov.—Resol. Holl., Nov. 25, 1574, bl. 196–208. Kluit, Holl. Staatsreg., i. 102. Wagenaer, vii. 13, 14. Groen v. Prinst., Archives, etc., v. 90–94.

maintains," said Saint Goard, French ambassador at Madrid, "that if peace is not made with the Beggars, the Empire will depart from the house of Austria, and that such is the determination of the electors."* On the other hand, if Philip were not weary of the war, at any rate his means for carrying it on were diminishing daily. Requesens could raise no money in the Netherlands;† his secretary wrote to Spain, that the exchequer was at its last gasp, and the cabinet of Madrid was at its wits' end, and almost incapable of raising ways and means. The peace party was obtaining the upper hand; the fierce policy of Alva regarded with increasing disfavor. "The people here," wrote Saint Goard from Madrid, "are completely desperate, whatever pains they take to put a good face on the matter. They desire most earnestly to treat, without losing their character." It seemed, nevertheless, impossible for Philip to bend his neck. The hope of wearing the Imperial crown had alone made his bigotry feasible. To less potent influences it was adamant; and even now, with an impoverished exchequer, and, after seven years of unsuccessful warfare, his purpose was not less rigid than at first. "The Hollanders demand liberty of conscience," said Saint Goard, "to which the King will never consent, or I am much mistaken."‡

As for Orange, he was sincerely in favor of peace—but not a dishonorable peace, in which should be renounced all the objects of the war. He was far from sanguine on the subject, for he read the signs of the times and the character of Philip too accurately to believe much more in the success of the present than in that of the past efforts of Maximilian. He was pleased that his brother-in-law, Count Schwartzburg, had been selected as the Emperor's agent in the affair, but expressed his doubts whether much good would come of the proposed negotiations. Remembering the many traps which

---

* Archives et Correspondance, v. 81.

† Ibid., v. 28–32.

‡ Ibid., v. 83.

in times past had been set by Philip and his father, he feared that the present transaction might likewise prove a snare. "We have not forgotten the words 'ewig' and 'einig' in the treaty with Landgrave Philip," he wrote; "at the same time we beg to assure his Imperial Majesty that we desire nothing more than a good peace, tending to the glory of God, the service of the King of Spain, and the prosperity of his subjects."*

This was his language to his brother, in a letter which was meant to be shown to the Emperor. In another, written on the same day, he explained himself with more clearness, and stated his distrust with more energy. There were no papists left, except a few ecclesiastics, he said, so much had the number of the Reformers been augmented, through the singular grace of God. It was out of the question to suppose, therefore, that a measure, dooming all who were not Catholics to exile, could be entertained. None would change their religion, and none would consent, voluntarily, to abandon for ever their homes, friends, and property. "Such a peace," he said, "would be poor and pitiable indeed."†

These, then, were the sentiments of the party now about to negotiate. The mediator was anxious for a settlement, because the interests of the Imperial house required it. The King of Spain was desirous of peace, but was unwilling to concede a hair. The Prince of Orange was equally anxious to terminate the war, but was determined not to abandon the objects for which it had been undertaken. A favorable result, therefore, seemed hardly possible. A whole people claimed the liberty to stay at home and practice the Protestant religion, while their King asserted the right to banish them for ever, or to burn them if they remained. The parties seemed too far apart to be brought together by the most elastic compromise. The Prince addressed an earnest appeal

* Archives et Correspondance, v. 61–65.

† Ibid., v. 73, 74.

to the assembly of Holland, then in session at Dort, reminding them that, although peace was desirable, it might be more dangerous than war, and entreating them, therefore, to conclude no treaty which should be inconsistent with the privileges of the country and their duty to God.*

It was now resolved that all the votes of the assembly should consist of five : one for the nobles and large cities of Holland, one for the estates of Zealand, one for the small cities of Holland, one for the cities Bommel and Buren, and the fifth for William of Orange.† The Prince thus effectually held in his hands three votes : his own, that of the small cities, which through his means only had been admitted to the assembly, and thirdly, that of Buren, the capital of his son's earldom. He thus exercised a controlling influence over the coming deliberations. The ten commissioners, who were appointed by the estates for the peace negotiations, were all his friends. Among them were Saint Aldegonde, Paul Buis, Charles Boisot, and Doctor Junius. The plenipotentiaries of the Spanish government were Leoninus, the Seigneur de Rassinghem, Cornelius Suis, and Arnold Sasbout.‡

The proceedings were opened at Breda upon the 3rd of March, 1575.§ The royal commissioners took the initiative, requesting to be informed what complaints the estates had to make, and offering to remove, if possible, all grievances which they might be suffering. The states' commissioners replied that they desired nothing, in the first place, but an answer to the petition which they had already presented to the King. This was the paper placed in the hands of Saint Aldegonde during the informal negotiations of the preceding year. An answer was accordingly given, but couched in such vague and general language as to be quite without meaning. The estates then demanded a categorical reply to the two principal demands in the peti-

* Bor, viii. 595, 596. Resol. Holl., Feb. 6, 1575.

† Resol. Holl., Feb. 5, 6, 7, 1575, bl. 47, 51, 52. Wagenaer, vii. 29.

‡ Resol. Holl., Feb. 12, 1575, bl. 49–59.

§ Bor, viii. 597.

tion, namely, the departure of the foreign troops and the assembling of the states-general. They were asked what they understood by foreigners and by the assembly of states-general. They replied that by foreigners they meant those who were not natives, and particularly the Spaniards. By the estates-general they meant the same body before which, in 1555, Charles had resigned his sovereignty to Philip. The royal commissioners made an extremely unsatisfactory answer, concluding with a request that all cities, fortresses, and castles, then in the power of the estates, together with all their artillery and vessels of war, should be delivered to the King. The Roman Catholic worship, it was also distinctly stated, was to be re-established at once exclusively throughout the Netherlands; those of the Reformed religion receiving permission, *for that time only*, to convert their property into cash within a certain time, and to depart the country.*

Orange and the estates made answer on the 21st March. It could not be called hard, they said, to require the withdrawal of the Spanish troops, for this had been granted in 1559, for less imperious reasons. The estates had, indeed, themselves made use of foreigners, but those foreigners had never been allowed to participate in the government. With regard to the assembly of the states-general, that body had always enjoyed the right of advising with the Sovereign on the condition of the country, and on general measures of government. Now it was only thought necessary to summon them, in order that they might give their consent to the King's "requests." Touching the delivery of cities and citadels, artillery and ships, the proposition was pronounced to resemble that made by the wolves to the sheep, in the fable—that the dogs should be delivered up, as a preliminary to a lasting peace. It was unreasonable to request the Hollanders to abandon their religion or their country. The reproach of heresy was unjust,

---

* Resol. Holl., Maart 7, 1575, bl. 121, 122, 123, 125. Maart 17, 1575, bl. 158, et seq. Bor, viii. 597, sqq. Wagenaer, vii. 31.

for they still held to the Catholic Apostolic Church, wishing only to purify it of its abuses. Moreover, it was certainly more cruel to expel a whole population than to dismiss three or four thousand Spaniards who for seven long years had been eating their fill at the expense of the provinces. It would be impossible for the exiles to dispose of their property, for all would, by the proposed measure, be sellers, while there would be no purchasers.*

The royal plenipotentiaries, making answer to this communication upon the 1st of April, signified a willingness that the Spanish soldiers should depart, if the states would consent to disband their own foreign troops. They were likewise in favor of assembling the states-general, but could not permit any change in the religion of the country. His Majesty had sworn to maintain the true worship at the moment of assuming the sovereignty. The dissenters might, however, be allowed a period of six months in which to leave the land, and eight or ten years for the sale of their property. After the heretics had all departed, his Majesty did not doubt that trade and manufactures would flourish again, along with the old religion. As for the Spanish inquisition, there was not, and there never had been, any intention of establishing it in the Netherlands.†

No doubt there was something specious in this paper. It appeared to contain considerable concessions. The Prince and estates had claimed the departure of the Spaniards. It was now promised that they should depart. They had demanded the assembling of the states-general. It was now promised that they should assemble. They had denounced the inquisition. It was now averred that the Spanish inquisition was not to be established.

Nevertheless, the commissioners of the Prince were not

---

* Resol. Holl., Maart 21, 1575, bl. 166. Bor, viii. 599. Wagenaer, vii. 34–39.

† Resol. Holl., Apl. 1575, bl. 202. Bor, viii. 602.

deceived by such artifices. There was no parity between the cases of the Spanish soldiery and of the troops in service of the estates. To assemble the estates-general was idle, if they were to be forbidden the settlement of the great question at issue. With regard to the Spanish inquisition, it mattered little whether the slaughter-house were called Spanish or Flemish, or simply the Blood-Council. It was, however, necessary for the states' commissioners to consider their reply very carefully; for the royal plenipotentiaries had placed themselves upon specious grounds. It was not enough to feel that the King's government was paltering with them; it was likewise necessary for the states' agents to impress this fact upon the people.

There was a pause in the deliberations. Meantime, Count Schwartzburg, reluctantly accepting the conviction that the religious question was an insurmountable obstacle to a peace, left the provinces for Germany.* The last propositions of the government plenipotentiaries had been discussed in the councils of the various cities,† so that the reply of the Prince, and estates was delayed until the 1st of June. They admitted, in this communication, that the offer to restore ancient privileges had an agreeable sound; but regretted that if the whole population were to be banished, there would be but few to derive advantage from the restoration. If the King would put an end to religious persecution, he would find as much loyalty in the provinces as his forefathers had found. It was out of the question, they said, for the states to disarm and to deliver up their strong places, before the Spanish soldiery had retired, and before peace had been established. It was their wish to leave the question of religion, together with all other disputed matters, to the decision of the assembly. Were it possible, in the meantime, to devise any effectual method for restraining hostilities, it would gladly be embraced.‡

---

* Bor, viii. 604, 506.

† Wagenaer, vii. 43.

‡ Resol. Holl., Apl. 19, 1575, bl. 240; May 20, 23, 1575; Jun. 5. 1575, bl. 240, 305, 314, 316, 355. Bor, viii. 605–608.

On the 8th of July, the royal commissioners inquired what guarantee the states would be willing to give, that the decision of the general assembly, whatever it might be, should be obeyed. The demand was answered by another, in which the King's agents were questioned as to their own guarantees. Hereupon it was stated that his Majesty would give his word and sign manual, together with the word and signature of the Emperor into the bargain. In exchange for these promises, the Prince and estates were expected to give their own oaths and seals, together with a number of hostages. Over and above this, they were requested to deliver up the cities of Brill and Enkhuizen, Flushing and Arnemuyde.* The disparity of such guarantees was ridiculous. The royal word, even when strengthened by the imperial promise, and confirmed by the autographs of Philip and Maximilian, was not so solid a security, in the opinion of Netherlanders, as to outweigh four cities in Holland and Zealand, with all their population and wealth. To give collateral pledges and hostages upon one side, while the King offered none, was to assign a superiority to the royal word, over that of the Prince and the estates which there was no disposition to recognize. Moreover, it was very cogently urged that to give up the cities was to give as security for the contract, some of the principal contracting parties.†

This closed the negotiations. The provincial plenipotentiaries took their leave by a paper dated 13th July, 1575, which recapitulated the main incidents of the conference. They expressed their deep regret that his Majesty should insist so firmly on the banishment of the Reformers, for it was unjust to reserve the provinces to the sole use of a small number of Catholics. They lamented that the proposition which had been made, to refer the religious question to the estates, had neither been loyally accepted, nor candidly refused. They inferred, therefore, that the object of the royal government

* Resol. Holl., July 8, 1575, bl. 47.

† Resol. Holl., July 8, 16, 1575, bl. 478, 506. Wagenaer, vii. 49.

had been to amuse the states, while time was thus gained for reducing the country into a slavery more abject than any which had yet existed.* On the other hand, the royal commissioners as solemnly averred that the whole responsibility for the failure of the negotiations belonged to the estates.†

It was the general opinion in the insurgent provinces that the government had been insincere from the beginning, and had neither expected nor desired to conclude a peace. It is probable, however, that Philip was sincere; so far as it could be called sincerity to be willing to conclude a peace, if the provinces would abandon the main objects of the war.‡ With his impoverished exchequer, and ruin threatening his whole empire, if this mortal combat should be continued many years longer, he could have no motive for further bloodshed, provided all heretics should consent to abandon the country. As usual, however, he left his agents in the dark as to his real intentions. Even Requesens was as much in doubt as to the King's secret purposes as Margaret of Parma had ever been in former times.§ Moreover, the Grand Commander and the

* Resol. Holl. July 16, bl. 506. Wagenaer, vii. 49, 50. Bor, viii. 610.

† Resol. Holl. July 16, 1575, bl. 512. Bor, viii. 612.

‡ See Kluit, Hist. der Holl. Staatsreg., i. 90, 91, note 34.—Compare the remarks of Groen v. Prinst., Archives, etc., v. 259–262; Bor, viii. 606, 615; Meteren, v. 100; Hoofd, x. 410.—Count John of Nassau was distrustful and disdainful from the beginning. Against his brother's loyalty and the straightforward intentions of the estates, he felt that the whole force of the Macchiavelli system of policy would be brought to bear with great effect. He felt that the object of the King's party was to temporize, to confuse, and to deceive. He did not believe them capable of conceding the real object in dispute, but he feared lest they might obscure the judgment of the plain and well meaning people with whom they had to deal. Alluding to the constant attempts made to poison himself and his brother, he likens the pretended negotiations to Venetian drugs, by which eyesight, hearing, feeling, and intellect were destroyed. Under this pernicious influence, the luckless people would not perceive the fire burning around them, but would shrink at a rustling leaf. Not comprehending then the tendency of their own acts, they would "lay bare their own backs to the rod, and bring faggots for their own funeral pile."—Archives, etc., v. 131–137.

§ Vigl. ad Hopp., ep. 253.

government had, after all, made a great mistake in their diplomacy. The estates of Brabant, although strongly desirous that the Spanish troops should be withdrawn, were equally stanch for the maintenance of the Catholic religion, and many of the southern provinces entertained the same sentiments. Had the Governor, therefore, taken the states' commissioners at their word, and left the decision of the religious question to the general assembly, he might perhaps have found the vote in his favor.* In this case, it is certain that the Prince of Orange and his party would have been placed in a very awkward position.†

The internal government of the insurgent provinces had remained upon the footing which we have seen established in the autumn of 1574, but in the course of this summer (1575), however, the foundation was laid for the union of Holland and Zealand, under the authority of Orange. The selfish principle of municipal aristocracy, which had tended to keep asunder these various groups of cities, was now repressed by the energy of the Prince and the strong determination of the people.

In April, 1575, certain articles of union between Holland and Zealand were proposed, and six commissioners appointed to draw up an ordinance for the government of the two provinces. This ordinance was accepted in general assembly of both.‡ It was in twenty articles. It declared that, during the war, the Prince, as sovereign, should have absolute power in all matters concerning the defence of the country. He was to appoint military officers, high and low, establish and remove garrisons, punish offenders against the laws of war. He was to regulate the expenditure of all money voted by the

* See Wagenaer, vii. 52.

† Besides the Resolutions of the estates of Holland, already cited, see for the history of these negotiations; Meteren, v. 96–100; Bor, viii. 595–615. Groen v. Prinst., Archives, v. 69, et seq.; Hoofd, x. 400, 411.—Compare Bentivoglio, ib. ix. 157–161; Mendoza, xiii. 269, 270.

‡ Resol. Holl., May 17, 18, 1575, bl. 291, 294. Wagenaer vii. 15–18.

estates. He was to maintain the law, in the King's name, as Count of Holland, and to appoint all judicial officers upon nominations by the estates. He was, at the usual times, to appoint and renew the magistracies of the cities, according to their constitutions. He was to protect the exercise of the Evangelical Reformed religion, *and to suppress the exercise of the Roman religion,** without permitting, however, that search should be made into the creed of any person. A deliberative and executive council, by which the jealousy of the corporations had intended to hamper his government, did not come into more than nominal existence.†

The articles of union having been agreed upon, the Prince, desiring an unfettered expression of the national will, wished the ordinance to be laid before the people in their primary assemblies. The estates, however, were opposed to this democratic proceeding. They represented that it had been customary to consult, after the city magistracies, only the captains of companies and the deans of guilds on matters of government. The Prince, yielding the point, the captains of companies and deans of guilds accordingly alone united with the aristocratic boards in ratifying the instrument by which his authority over the two united provinces was established. On the 4th of June this first union was solemnized.‡

Upon the 11th of July, the Prince formally accepted the government.§ He, however, made an essential change in a very important clause of the ordinance. In place of the words, the "Roman religion," he insisted that the words, "religion at variance with the Gospel," should be substituted

---

* Ook de oefening der Evangelische Gereformeerde Religie handhaaven, doende de oefeninge der Romische Religie ophouden."—Resol. Holl., ubi sup.

† Wagenaer, vii. 19, 22, 23, 25.—Compare Groen v. Prinst., Archives, v. 268–272.—See Resol. Holl., June 10, 21, 23, 1575, bl. 381, 414, 420.

‡ Wagenaer, vii. 19. Resol. Holl., May 21, 1575, bl. 311, 313. June 4, 1575, bl. 359.—Compare Groen v. Prinst., Archives, etc., v. 271, 272.

§ Resol. Holl., July 12, 15, 18, 19, 20, 1575, bl. 487, 501, 514, 516, 520. Bor, viii. 641–643. Hoofd, x. 420, 421.

in the article by which he was enjoined to prohibit the exercise of such religion.* This alteration rebuked the bigotry which had already grown out of the successful resistance to bigotry, and left the door open for a general religious toleration.

Early in this year the Prince had despatched Saint Aldegonde on a private mission to the Elector Palatine. During some of his visits to that potentate he had seen at Heidelberg the Princess Charlotte of Bourbon. That lady was daughter of the Duc de Montpensier, the most ardent of the Catholic Princes of France, and the one who at the conferences of Bayonne had been most indignant at the Queen Dowager's hesitation to unite heartily with the schemes of Alva and Philip for the extermination of the Huguenots. His daughter, a woman of beauty, intelligence, and virtue, forced before the canonical age to take the religious vows, had been placed in the convent of Joüarrs, of which she had become Abbess. Always secretly inclined to the Reformed religion, she had fled secretly from her cloister, in the year of horrors 1572, and had found refuge at the court of the Elector Palatine, after which step her father refused to receive her letters, to contribute a farthing to her support, or even to acknowledge her claims upon him by a single line or message of affection.†

Under these circumstances the outcast princess, who had arrived at years of maturity, might be considered her own mistress, and she was neither morally nor legally bound, when her hand was sought in marriage by the great champion of the Reformation, to ask the consent of a parent who loathed her religion and denied her existence. The legality of the divorce from Anne of Saxony had been settled by a full expression of the ecclesiastical authority which she most respected ;‡

* Resol. Holl., July 22, 30, 1575, bl. 528, 542. Wagenaer, vii. 22.—Compare Groen v. Prinst., Archives, v. 272; Kluit, Holl. Staatsreg., i. 116, 117, note 55.

† Archives et Corresp., v. 113.

‡ Acte de cinq Ministres du St. Evangile par lequel ils declarent le mariage du Prince d'Orange être legitime."—Archives, etc., v. 216–226.

the facts upon which the divorce had been founded having been proved beyond peradventure.

Nothing, in truth, could well be more unfortunate in its results than the famous Saxon marriage, the arrangements for which had occasioned so much pondering to Philip, and so much diplomatic correspondence on the part of high personages in Germany, the Netherlands, and Spain. Certainly, it was of but little consequence to what church the unhappy Princess belonged, and they must be slightly versed in history or in human nature who can imagine these nuptials to have exercised any effect upon the religious or political sentiments of Orange. The Princess was of a stormy, ill-regulated nature; almost a lunatic from the beginning. The dislike which succeeded to her fantastic fondness for the Prince, as well as her general eccentricity, had soon become the talk of all the court at Brussels. She would pass week after week without emerging from her chamber, keeping the shutters closed and candles burning, day and night.* She quarrelled violently with Countess Egmont for precedence, so that the ludicrous contentions of the two ladies in antechambers and doorways were the theme and the amusement of society.† Her insolence, not only in private but in public, towards her husband became intolerable. "I could not do otherwise than bear it with sadness and patience," said the Prince, with great magnanimity, "hoping that with age would come improvement." Nevertheless, upon one occasion, at a supper party, she had used such language in the presence of Count Horn and many other nobles, "that all wondered that he could endure the abusive terms which she applied to him."‡

When the clouds gathered about him, when he had become an exile and a wanderer, her reproaches and her violence increased. The sacrifice of their wealth, the mortgages and sales

* Groen v. Prinst., Archives, i. 386.

† Papiers d'Etat, vii. 452.

‡ Letter to the Elector Augustus.—Groen v. Prinst., Archives, ii. 31, 32.

which he effected of his estates, plate, jewels, and furniture, to raise money for the struggling country, excited her bitter resentment. She separated herself from him by degrees, and at last abandoned him altogether. Her temper became violent to ferocity. She beat her servants with her hands and with clubs; she threatened the lives of herself, of her attendants, of Count John of Nassau, with knives and daggers, and indulged in habitual profanity and blasphemy, uttering frightful curses upon all around. Her original tendency to intemperance had so much increased, that she was often unable to stand on her feet. A bottle of wine, holding more than a quart, in the morning, and another in the evening, together with a pound of sugar, was her usual allowance. She addressed letters to Alva, complaining that her husband had impoverished himself "in his good-for-nothing Beggar war," and begging the Duke to furnish her with a little ready money and with the means of arriving at the possession of her dower.*

---

* "Derhalben auch die Princessin sich dermassen ertzurnedt, das sie ihr der frawen man und die fraw midt einem scheidtholltz gleichfalls auch mit feusten geschlagen und sehr ubel gescholten hab," etc.—Summarische Verreichnisz und Protocolle der Abgesandten, 85–120. Act. der Fr. Princessin zu Uranien vorgefliche vorhandlung belangnt, A°. 1572.—MS., Dresden Archives.

"Habe darnach des Abends, als sie gahr und also beweindt gewesen das sie nicht stehen können, ein schreibmesserlein in den rechten ermel zu sich gestegkt, vorhabens Graf Johann wan er zu ihr kumen wehre, sollchs in den halsz zu stossen —— gleichfolls habe sie ein briefstecher bekhumen und sollchen, alls sie auch etwas zuviel getrunken, zu ihrem Haupt ins bedt gelegt, etc., etc. —— Es las ihr auch die Fr. Prinzessin offtmals eyer gahr hardt im salltz sieden, darauf, tringkt sie dan edtwan zuvil und werde ungedultig, fluche alle bösze flueche, und werfe die speisze und schussel und allem von tisch von sich," etc., etc.—MS., Dresden Archives, dict. act.

"Und die Fr. Prinzessin, wie sie es genant, *den tollen man*, nemlich ein guedte flasche weins morgens und abermals ein guedte flasche zu abendtszeidt mehr dan ein masz haltend bekumen, welches ir sambt einem Pfundt Zugkers bei sich zu nemen nicht zu vil sey," etc., etc.—Ibid.

"Der man sich verweigert hat einen brief so sie an den Duca de Alba geschrieben gen Cölln zu tragen und daselbst ferner zu uberschigken.——Der Innhalt solches Briefs sei ungeverlich gewesen, das sie sich beclagdt, wie man sie alhie so gahr ubel tractir—das guedt, so ihr auf des Könings anordnung gehandtraicht habe sollen werden, entwendt und es *ihrem herrn zu seinem un-*

An illicit connexion with a certain John Rubens, an exiled magistrate of Antwerp, and father of the celebrated painter, completed the list of her delinquencies, and justified the marriage of the Prince with Charlotte de Bourbon.* It was therefore determined by the Elector of Saxony and the Landgrave William to remove her from the custody of the Nassaus. This took place with infinite difficulty, at the close of the year 1575. Already, in 1572, Augustus had proposed to the Landgrave that she should be kept in solitary confinement, and that a minister should preach to her daily through the grated aperture by which her food was to be admitted. The Landgrave remonstrated at so inhuman a proposition, which was, however, carried into effect. The wretched Princess, now completely a lunatic, was imprisoned in the electoral palace, in a chamber where the windows were walled up and a small grating let into the upper part of the door. Through this wicket came her food, as well as the words of the holy man appointed to preach daily for her edification.†

Two years long, she endured this terrible punishment, and died mad,‡ on the 18th of December, 1577. On the following

nutzen Goesen Kriegk zu gebrauchen zugestellt haben. Bidte das der *Duca de Alba wölle vor sie schreiben* an das Cammergericht umb Mandat, das sie von Gf. Johanns gefengknisz ledig unnd zu Spier vor recht gestellt werden möge. Auch das er, der von Alba, ir die *nechste Mesz etwas von geldt* und dabei einen gesandten mit mundlicher werbung zuschigken wolle. Sey der Brief zwei Bogen lank," etc.—MS., Dresden Archives, dict. act.

* Acta: Der. Fran Princessin zu Uranien, etc.—Abschriften von F. Annen, Ehestifftung, etc.—Schickung an Joh. G. tzu Nass. Abholung der Princessin und todtlichen Abgang.—MS., Dresd. Arch., 1575–1579, passim. Bakhuyzen v. d. Brinck. Het Huwelijk van W. v. Oranje, 133, sqq.

† "Seindt auch der endlichen meinung, wan sie also in geheim vorwahret und ein Predicant verordnet, der sie teglich durch ein fensterlein do ir die speys und tranck gericht werde Irer begangenen sunde mit Vleiss erinnere."—Letter of Elector Augustus to Landgrave William, July 9, 1572.—MS., Dresd. Arch. "Ganz gestöaten Geistes."—Ibid.

§ "Desgleichen, habe ich auch angeordnet," writes Secretary Hans Jenitz immediately after the decease of the Princess, "dasz *die Fenster durch die Maurer*, welche sie *zuvor zugemauert*, wiederum ausgebrochen werden und sol der Bettmeister mit *Reinigung derselben Stube und Kammer* sich E. F. G. befehl nach verhalten. E. F. G. kann ich auch unterthänigst nicht verhalten, dasz keine neue Thür vor solche stube gemaecht worden —— sondern man hat

day, she was buried in the electoral tomb at Meissen; a pompous procession of "school children, clergy, magistrates, nobility, and citizens" conducting her to that rest of which she could no longer be deprived by the cruelty of man nor her own violent temperament.*

So far, therefore, as the character of Mademoiselle de Bourbon and the legitimacy of her future offspring were concerned, she received ample guarantees. For the rest, the Prince, in a simple letter, informed her that he was already past his prime, having reached his forty-second year, and that his fortune was encumbered not only with settlements for his children by previous marriages, but by debts contracted in the cause of his oppressed country.† A convention of doctors and bishops of France, summoned by the Duc de Montpensier, afterwards confirmed the opinion that the conventual vows of the Princess Charlotte had been conformable neither to the laws of France nor to the canons of the Trent Council.‡ She was conducted to Brill by Saint Aldegonde, where she was

---

durch die alte Thure in dem obern Felde nur *ein vier eckicht Loch ausgeschnitten und von starkem eisernen Blech* ein *enges Gitter dafur gemacht* dasz man auswendig auf *dem Saal auch verschliessen* kann.——Es steht auch zu E. F. G. Gefallen, ob man die *grosse eiserne bande* mit den Vorlege *schlossern, damit die Thuere von aussen verwart* gewesen, also daran bleiben lassen, oder wieder aus dem stein aushauen und abfeilen lassen wolle, aber die gegitter vor den Fenstern können meines Bedünckens wohl bleiben. Hans Jenitz an Churfürstin Anna Acta: Inventarium über F. Annen, p. 3. Uranien Vorlassenschaft, etc., A°. 1577.—MS., Dresden Archives.

* Dict. Act.—MS., Dresden Archives.

It can certainly be considered no violation of the sanctity of archives to make these slender allusions to a tale, the main features of which have already been published, not only by MM. Groen v. Prinsterer and Bakhuyzen, in Holland, but by the Saxon Professor Böttiger, in Germany. It is impossible to understand the character and career of Orange, and his relations with Germany, without a complete view of the Saxon marriage. The extracts from the "geomantic letters" of Elector Augustus, however, given in Böttiger (Hist. Taschenb. 1836, p. 169–173), with their furious attacks upon the Prince and upon Charlotte of Bourbon, seem to us too obscene to be admitted, even in a note to these pages, and in a foreign language.

† "Memoire pour le Comte de Hohenlo allant de la part du Prince d'Orange vers le Comte J. de Nassau, l'Electeur Palatin, et son épouse, Mlle. de Bourbon." —Arch. etc., v. 189–192. ‡ Apologie du Prince d'Orange.—Ed. Sylvius, 37, 38.

received by her bridegroom, to whom she was united on the 12th of June. The wedding festival was held at Dort with much revelry and holiday making, "but without dancing."*

In this connexion, no doubt the Prince consulted his inclination only. Eminently domestic in his habits, he required the relief of companionship at home to the exhausting affairs which made up his life abroad. For years he had never enjoyed social converse, except at long intervals, with man or woman; it was natural, therefore, that he should contract this marriage. It was equally natural that he should make many enemies by so impolitic a match. The Elector Palatine, who was in place of guardian to the bride, decidedly disapproved, although he was suspected of favoring the alliance.† The Landgrave of Hesse for a time was furious; the Elector of Saxony absolutely delirious with rage.‡ The Diet of the Empire was to be held within a few weeks at Frankfort, where it was very certain that the outraged and influential Elector would make his appearance, overflowing with anger, and determined to revenge upon the cause of the Netherland Reformation the injury which he had personally received. Even the wise, considerate, affectionate brother, John of Nassau, considered the marriage an act of madness. He did what he could, by argument and entreaty, to dissuade the Prince from its completion;§ although he afterwards voluntarily confessed that the Princess Charlotte had been deeply calumniated, and was an inestimable treasure to his brother.‖ The French government made use of the circumstance to justify itself in a still further alienation from the cause of the Prince than it had hitherto manifested, but this was rather pretence than reality.

It was not in the nature of things, however, that the Saxon and Hessian indignation could be easily allayed. The Land-

---

* Archives et Corresp., v. 226. Bor, viii. 644. Meteren, v. 100.

† Archives et Correspondance, v. 300.

‡ Ibid.

§ Ibid., v. 203, 204.

‖ Ibid., v. 312, 313.

grave was extremely violent. "Truly, I cannot imagine," he wrote to the Elector of Saxony, "*quo consilio* that wiseacre of an Aldegonde, and whosoever else has been aiding and abetting, have undertaken this affair. *Nam si pietatem respicias*, it is to be feared that, considering she is a Frenchwoman, a nun, and moreover a fugitive nun, about whose chastity there has been considerable question, the Prince has got out of the frying-pan into the fire. *Si formam* it is not to be supposed that it was her beauty which charmed him, since, without doubt, he must be rather frightened than delighted, when he looks upon her. *Si spem prolis*, the Prince has certainly only too many heirs already, and ought to wish that he had neither wife nor children. *Si amicitiam*, it is not to be supposed, while her father expresses himself in such threatening language with regard to her, that there will be much cordiality of friendship on his part. Let them look to it, then, lest it fare with them no better than with the Admiral, at his Paris wedding; for those gentlemen can hardly forgive such injuries, *sine mercurio et arsenico sublimato*."*

The Elector of Saxony was frantic with choler, and almost ludicrous in the vehemence of its expression. Count John was unceasing in his exhortations to his brother to respect the sensitiveness of these important personages, and to remember how much good and how much evil it was in their power to compass, with regard to himself and to the great cause of the Protestant religion. He reminded him, too, that the divorce had not been, and would not be considered impregnable as to form, and that much discomfort and detriment was likely to grow out of the whole proceeding, for himself and his family.† The Prince, however, was immovable in his resolution, and from the whole tone of his correspondence and deportment it was obvious that his marriage was one rather of inclination than of

* Archives et Correspondance, v. 227, 228.

† See the letter of Count John to Prince of Orange, Archives, v. 208–213.

policy. "I can assure you, my brother," he wrote to Count John, "that my character has always tended to this—to care neither for words nor menaces in any matter where I can act with a clear conscience, and without doing injury to my neighbour. Truly, if I had paid regard to the threats of princes, I should never have embarked in so many dangerous affairs, contrary to the will of the King, my master, *in times past*, and even to the advice of many of my relatives and friends."*

The evil consequences which had been foreseen were not slow to manifest themselves. There was much discussion of the Prince's marriage at the Diet of Frankfort, and there was even a proposition, formally to declare the Calvinists excluded in Germany from the benefits of the Peace of Passau. The Archduke Rudolph was soon afterwards elected King of the Romans and of Bohemia, although hitherto, according to the policy of the Prince of Orange, and in the expectation of benefit to the cause of the Reformation in Germany and the Netherlands, there has been a strong disposition to hold out hopes to Henry the Third, and to excite the fears of Maximilian.†

While these important affairs, public and private, had been occurring in the south of Holland and in Germany, a very nefarious transaction had disgraced the cause of the patriot party in the northern quarter. Diedrich Sonoy, governor of that portion of Holland, a man of great bravery but of extreme ferocity of character, had discovered an extensive conspiracy among certain of the inhabitants, in aid of an approaching Spanish invasion. Bands of land-loupers had been employed, according to the intimation which he had received or affected to have received, to set fire to villages and towns in every direction, to set up beacons, and to conduct a series of signals by which the expeditions about to be organized were to be furthered in their objects.‡ The Governor, determined

* See the letter, Archives, etc., 244–252.

† Vide Groen v. Prinst., Archives, v. 299, 300.

‡ Bor, viii. 623, sqq. Hoofd, x. 411, 412. Wagenaer, vii. 54, et seq.

to show that the Duke of Alva could not be more prompt nor more terrible than himself, improvised, of his own authority, a tribunal in imitation of the infamous Blood-Council. Fortunately for the character of the country, Sonoy was not a Hollander, nor was the jurisdiction of this newly established court allowed to extend beyond very narrow limits. Eight vagabonds were, however, arrested and doomed to tortures the most horrible, in order to extort from them confessions implicating persons of higher position in the land than themselves. Seven, after a few turns of the pulley and the screw, confessed all which they were expected to confess, and accused all whom they were requested to accuse. The eighth was firmer, and refused to testify to the guilt of certain respectable householders, whose names he had, perhaps, never heard, and against whom there was no shadow of evidence. He was, however, reduced by three hours and a half of sharp torture to confess, entirely according to their orders, so that accusations and evidence were thus obtained against certain influential gentlemen of the province, whose only crime was a secret adherence to the Catholic Faith.*

The eight wretches who had been induced by promises of unconditional pardon upon one hand, and by savage torture on the other, to bear this false witness, were condemned to be burned alive, and on their way to the stake, they all retracted the statements which had only been extorted from them by the rack. Nevertheless, the individuals who had been thus designated, were arrested. Charged with plotting a general conflagration of the villages and farmhouses, in conjunction with an invasion by Hierges and other Papist generals, they indignantly protested their innocence; but two of them, a certain Kopp Corneliszoon, and his son, Nanning Koppezoon, were selected to undergo the most cruel torture which had yet been practised in the Netherlands.† Sonoy, to his eternal shame, was disposed to prove that human

* Bor, viii. 623, seq. Hoofd, x. 412.

† Bor, viii. 626, seq. Hoofd, x. 413, seq.

ingenuity to inflict human misery had not been exhausted in the chambers of the Blood Council, for it was to be shown that Reformers were capable of giving a lesson even to inquisitors in this diabolical science. Kopp, a man advanced in years, was tortured during a whole day. On the following morning he was again brought to the rack, but the old man was too weak to endure all the agony which his tormentors had provided for him. Hardly had he been placed upon the bed of torture than he calmly expired, to the great indignation of the tribunal.* "The Devil has broken his neck and carried him off to hell," cried they ferociously. "Nevertheless, that shall not prevent him from being hung and quartered." This decree of impotent vengeance was accordingly executed.† The son of Kopp, however, Nanning Koppezoon, was a man in the full vigor of his years. He bore with perfect fortitude a series of incredible tortures, after which, with his body singed from head to heel, and his feet almost entirely flayed, he was left for six weeks to crawl about his dungeon on his knees. He was then brought back to the torture-room, and again stretched upon the rack, while a large earthen vessel, made for the purpose, was placed, inverted, upon his naked body. A number of rats were introduced under this cover, and hot coals were heaped upon the vessel, till the rats, rendered furious by the heat, gnawed into the very bowels of the victim, in their agony to escape.‡ The holes thus torn in his

---

* Bor, viii. 627, 628. Hoofd, x. 413.

† Hoofd, x. 413.

‡ Bor (viii. 628) conscientiously furnishes diagrams of the machinery by aid of which this devilish cruelty was inflicted. The rats were sent by the Governor himself.—Vide Letter of the Commissioners to Sonoy, apud Bor, viii. 640, 641. The whole letter is a wonderful monument of barbarity. The incredible tortures to which the poor creatures had been subjected are detailed in a business-like manner, as though the transactions were quite regular and laudable. The Commissioners conclude with pious wishes for the Governor's welfare: "Noble, wise, virtuous, and very discreet sir," they say, "we have wished to apprise you of the foregoing, and we now pray that God Almighty may spare you in a happy, healthy and long-continued government."—It will be seen, however, that the "wise, virtuous, and very discreet" Governor, who thus caused his fellow-citizen's bowels to be gnawed by rats, was not allowed to remain much longer in his "happy and healthy government."

bleeding flesh were filled with red-hot coals. He was afterwards subjected to other tortures too foul to relate ; nor was it till he had endured all this agony, with a fortitude which seemed supernatural, that he was at last discovered to be human. Scorched, bitten, dislocated in every joint, sleepless, starving, perishing with thirst, he was at last crushed into a false confession, by a promise of absolute forgiveness. He admitted everything which was brought to his charge, confessing a catalogue of contemplated burnings and beacon firings of which he had never dreamed, and avowing himself in league with other desperate Papists, still more dangerous than himself.

Notwithstanding the promises of pardon, Nanning was then condemned to death. The sentence ordained that his heart should be torn from his living bosom, and thrown in his face, after which his head was to be taken off and exposed on the church steeple of his native village. His body was then to be cut in four, and a quarter fastened upon different towers of the city of Alkmaar, for it was that city, recently so famous for its heroic resistance to the Spanish army, which was now sullied by all this cold-blooded atrocity. When led to execution, the victim recanted indignantly the confessions forced from him by weakness of body, and exonerated the persons whom he had falsely accused. A certain clergyman, named Jurian Epeszoon, endeavored by loud praying to drown his voice, that the people might not rise with indignation, and the dying prisoner with his last breath solemnly summoned this unworthy pastor of Christ to meet him within three days before the judgment-seat of God. It is a remarkable and authentic fact, that the clergyman thus summoned, went home pensively from the place of execution, sickened immediately and died upon the appointed day.*

Notwithstanding this solemn recantation, the persons accused were arrested, and in their turn subjected to torture,

* Bor, viii. 628, et seq. Hoofd, x. 414. Wagenaer, vii. 58. Brandt, Hist. Ref. i. 563. Velius Horn, bl. 440.

but the affair now reached the ears of Orange. His peremptory orders, with the universal excitement produced in the neighbourhood, at last checked the course of the outrage, and the accused persons were remanded to prison, where they remained till liberated by the Pacification of Ghent. After their release they commenced legal proceedings against Sonoy, with a view of establishing their own innocence, and of bringing the inhuman functionary to justice. The process languished, however, and was finally abandoned, for the powerful Governor had rendered such eminent service in the cause of liberty, that it was thought unwise to push him to extremity. It is no impeachment upon the character of the Prince that these horrible crimes were not prevented. It was impossible for him to be omnipresent. Neither is it just to consider the tortures and death thus inflicted upon innocent men an indelible stain upon the cause of liberty. They were the crimes of an individual who had been useful, but who, like the Count De la Marck, had now contaminated his hand with the blood of the guiltless. The new tribunal never took root, and was abolished as soon as its initiatory horrors were known.*

On the 19th of July, Oudewater, entirely unprepared for such an event, was besieged by Hierges, but the garrison and the population, although weak, were brave. The town resisted eighteen days, and on the 7th of August was carried by assault,† after which the usual horrors were fully practised, after which the garrison was put to the sword, and the townspeople fared little better. Men, women, and children were murdered in cold blood, or obliged to purchase their lives by heavy ransoms, while matrons and maids were sold by auction to the soldiers at two or three dollars each.‡ Almost every house in the city was burned to the ground, and these horrible but very customary scenes having been enacted, the army of

* Bor, viii. 628–641. Hoofd, x. 415–419.

† Bor, viii. 646. Meteren, v. 100. ‡ Bor, viii. 646. Hoofd, x. 424, 425.

Hierges took its way to Schoonhoven. That city, not defending itself, secured tolerable terms of capitulation, and surrendered on the 24th of August.*

The Grand Commander had not yet given up the hope of naval assistance from Spain, notwithstanding the abrupt termination to the last expedition which had been organized. It was, however, necessary that a foothold should be recovered upon the seaboard, before a descent from without could be met with proper co-operation from the land forces within, and he was most anxious, therefore, to effect the reconquest of some portion of Zealand. The island of Tholen was still Spanish, and had been so since the memorable expedition of Mondragon to South Beveland. From this interior portion of the archipelago the Governor now determined to attempt an expedition against the outer and more important territory. The three principal islands were Tholen, Duiveland, and Schouwen. Tholen was the first which detached itself from the continent. Next, and separated from it by a bay two leagues in width, was Duiveland, or the Isle of Doves. Beyond, and parted by a narrower frith, was Schouwen, fronting directly upon the ocean, fortified by its strong capital city, Zierickzee, and containing other villages of inferior consequence.†

Requesens had been long revolving in his mind the means of possessing himself of this important island. He had caused to be constructed a numerous armada of boats and light vessels of various dimensions, and he now came to Tholen to organize the expedition. His prospects were at first not flattering, for the gulfs and estuaries swarmed with Zealand vessels, manned by crews celebrated for their skill and audacity. Traitors, however, from Zealand itself now came forward to teach the Spanish Commander how to strike at the heart of their own country. These refugees explained

* Bor, viii. 447. Meteren, v. 100.

† Bor, viii. 648–650. Hoofd, x. 426, 427. Meteren, v. 101, 102. Mendoza, xiv. 281. Bentivoglio, ix. 164, et seq.

to Requesens that a narrow flat extended under the sea from Philipsland, a small and uninhabited islet situate close to Tholen, as far as the shore of Duiveland. Upon this submerged tongue of land the water, during ebb-tide, was sufficiently shallow to be waded, and it would therefore be possible for a determined band, under cover of the night, to make the perilous passage. Once arrived at Duiveland, they could more easily cross the intervening creek to Schouwen, which was not so deep and only half as wide, so that a force thus sent through these dangerous shallows, might take possession of Duiveland and lay siege to Zierickzee, in the very teeth of the Zealand fleet, which would be unable to sail near enough to intercept their passage.*

The Commander determined that the enterprise should be attempted. It was not a novelty, because Mondragon, as we have seen, had already most brilliantly conducted a very similar expedition. The present was, however, a much more daring scheme. The other exploit, although sufficiently hazardous, and entirely successful, had been a victory gained over the sea alone. It had been a surprise, and had been effected without any opposition from human enemies. Here, however, they were to deal, not only with the ocean and darkness, but with a watchful and determined foe. The Zealanders were aware that the enterprise was in contemplation, and their vessels lay about the contiguous waters in considerable force.† Nevertheless, the determination of the Grand Commander was hailed with enthusiasm by his troops. Having satisfied himself by personal experiment that the enterprise was possible, and that therefore his brave soldiers could accomplish it, he decided that the glory of the achievement should be fairly shared, as before, among the different nations which served the King.

After completing his preparations, Requesens came to

---

* Bor, ubi sup. Hoofd, x. 426. Mendoza, xiv. 282. Bentivoglio, ix. 165.

† Bentivoglio, ix. 165. Hoofd, x. 428. Bor, viii. 648–650. Mendoza, xiv. 283.

Tholen, at which rendezvous were assembled three thousand infantry, partly Spaniards, partly Germans, partly Walloons. Besides these, a picked corps of two hundred sappers and miners was to accompany the expedition, in order that no time might be lost in fortifying themselves as soon as they had seized possession of Schouwen. Four hundred mounted troopers were, moreover, stationed in the town of Tholen, while the little fleet, which had been prepared at Antwerp, lay near that city ready to co-operate with the land force as soon as they should complete their enterprise. The Grand Commander now divided the whole force into two parts. One half was to remain in the boats, under the command of Mondragon; the other half, accompanied by the two hundred pioneers, were to wade through the sea from Philipsland to Duiveland and Schouwen. Each soldier of this detachment was provided with a pair of shoes, two pounds of powder, and rations for three days in a canvas bag suspended at his neck. The leader of this expedition was Don Osorio d'Ulloa, an officer distinguished for his experience and bravery.*

On the night selected for the enterprise, that of the 27th September, the moon was a day old in its fourth quarter, and rose a little before twelve. It was low water at between four and five in the morning. The Grand Commander, at the appointed hour of midnight, crossed to Philipsland, and stood on the shore to watch the setting forth of the little army. He addressed a short harangue to them, in which he skilfully struck the chords of Spanish chivalry and the national love of glory,† and was answered with loud and enthusiastic cheers. Don Osorio d'Ulloa then stripped and plunged into the sea immediately after the guides. He was followed by the Spaniards, after whom came the Germans and then the Walloons. The two hundred sappers and miners came next, and Don Gabriel Peralta, with his Spanish com-

* Bentivoglio, ix. 166. Hoofd, x. 427, 428. Mendoza, xiv. 283.

† Hoofd, x. 428. Bor, viii. 648–650. Mendoza, xiv. 283, 284.

pany, brought up the rear. It was a wild night. Incessant lightning alternately revealed and obscured the progress of the midnight march through the black waters, as the anxious Commander watched the expedition from the shore, but the soldiers were quickly swallowed up in the gloom.* As they advanced cautiously, two by two, the daring adventurers found themselves soon nearly up to their necks in the waves, while so narrow was the submerged bank along which they were marching, that a misstep to the right or left was fatal. Luckless individuals repeatedly sank to rise no more. Meantime, as the sickly light of the waning moon came forth at intervals through the stormy clouds, the soldiers could plainly perceive the files of Zealand vessels through which they were to march, and which were anchored as close to the flat as the water would allow. Some had recklessly stranded themselves, in their eagerness to interrupt the passage of the troops, and the artillery played unceasingly from the larger vessels. Discharges of musketry came continually from all, but the fitful lightning rendered the aim difficult and the fire comparatively harmless,† while the Spaniards were, moreover, protected, as to a large part of their bodies, by the water in which they were immersed.

At times, they halted for breath, or to engage in fierce skirmishes with their nearest assailants. Standing breast-high in the waves, and surrounded at intervals by total darkness, they were yet able to pour an occasional well-directed volley into the hostile ranks. The Zealanders,

---

* Bor, viii. 648–650. Hoofd, x. 428. Bentivoglio, ix. 167.—According to Mendoza, the sky was full of preternatural appearances on that memorable night; literally,

"The exhalations whizzing through the air
Gave so much light that one might read by them."

Julius Cæsar.

"Viendose *en aqual punto cometas y señales en el cielo de grande claridad y tanta que se leian cartas como si fuera de dia,* quo ponia admiracion el verlas; juzgando los mas ser cosa fuera del curso natural," etc.: xiv. 284.—Compare Strada, viii. 398.

† Bentivoglio, ix. 167. Hoofd, x. 429. Wagenaer, vii. 71.

however, did not assail them with fire-arms alone. They transfixed some with their fatal harpoons ; they dragged others from the path with boathooks ; they beat out the brains of others with heavy flails.* Many were the mortal duels thus fought in the darkness, and, as it were, in the bottom of the sea ; many were the deeds of audacity which no eye was to mark save those by whom they were achieved. Still, in spite of all impediments and losses, the Spaniards steadily advanced. If other arms proved less available, they were attacked by the fierce taunts and invectives of their often invisible foes, who reviled them as water-dogs, fetching and carrying for a master who despised them ; as mercenaries who coined their blood for gold, and were employed by tyrants for the basest uses. If stung by these mocking voices, they turned in the darkness to chastise their unseen tormentors, they were certain to be trampled upon by their comrades, and to be pushed from their narrow pathway into the depths of the sea. Thus many perished.

The night wore on, and the adventurers still fought it out manfully, but very slowly, the main body of Spaniards, Germans, and Walloons, soon after daylight, reaching the opposite shore, having sustained considerable losses, but in perfect order. The pioneers were not so fortunate. The tide rose over them before they could effect their passage, and swept nearly every one away.† The rear-guard, under Peralta, not surprised, like the pioneers, in the middle of their passage, by the rising tide, but prevented, before it was too late, from advancing far beyond the shore from which they had departed, were fortunately enabled to retrace their steps.‡

---

* "Ne bastara a nemici di travagliargli solamente co i moschetti, e con gli archibugi, ma piu d'appresso con uncini di ferro, con legni maneggiabili a molti doppi, é con altsi istromenti," etc.—Bentivoglio, ix. 167. "Llegavan á herir á los nuestros con unos instrumentos de lamanera que los con que bateren el trigo para sacar el grano de la paja."—Mendoza, xiv. 285.

† Hoofd, x. 429.—"Donde vays malaventurados, que os haren ser perros de agua," etc., etc.—Mendoza, ubi sup. Bentivoglio, ix. 168. Hoofd, x. 429. Mendoza, xiv. 285.

‡ Mendoza, xiv. 285. Bentivoglio, Hoofd, Bor, ubi sup.

Don Osorio, at the head of the successful adventurers, now effected his landing upon Duiveland. Reposing themselves but for an instant after this unparalleled march through the water, of more than six hours, they took a slight refreshment, prayed to the Virgin Mary and to Saint James, and then prepared to meet their new enemies on land. Ten companies of French, Scotch, and English auxiliaries lay in Duiveland, under the command of Charles Van Boisot. Strange to relate, by an inexplicable accident, or by treason, that general was slain by his own soldiers, at the moment when the royal troops landed. The panic created by this event became intense, as the enemy rose suddenly, as it were, out of the depths of the ocean to attack them. They magnified the numbers of their assailants, and fled terror-stricken in every direction. Some swam to the Zealand vessels which lay in the neighbourhood; others took refuge in the forts which had been constructed on the island, but these were soon carried by the Spaniards, and the conquest of Duiveland was effected.*

The enterprise was not yet completed, but the remainder was less difficult and not nearly so hazardous, for the creek which separated Duiveland from Schouwen was much narrower than the estuary which they had just traversed. It was less than a league in width, but so encumbered by rushes and briers that, although difficult to wade, it was not navigable for vessels of any kind.† This part of the expedition was accomplished with equal resolution, so that, after a few hours' delay, the soldiers stood upon the much-coveted island of Schouwen. Five companies of states' troops, placed to oppose their landing, fled in the most cowardly manner at the first discharge of the Spanish muskets,‡ and took refuge

* Hoofd, x. 429. Bor, viii. 649. Mendoza, xiv. 286.—The officer, whose career was thus unfortunately closed, was a brother of the famous Admiral Boisot, had himself rendered good service to the cause of his country, and was Governor of Walcheren at the time of his death.—Archives et Corresp., v. 283.

† Mendoza, xiv. 286. Bentivoglio (ix. 168) says, "poco men d'una lengua." —Compare Bor, viii. 649. Hoofd, x. 429.

‡ Mendoza, xiv. 287. Hoofd, x. 429. Bentivoglio, ix. 168.

in the city of Zierickzee, which was soon afterwards beleaguered.

The troops had been disembarked upon Duiveland from the armada, which had made its way to the scene of action, after having received, by signal, information that the expedition through the water had been successful. Brouwershaven, on the northern side of Schouwen, was immediately reduced, but Bommenede resisted till the 25th of October, when it was at last carried by assault, and delivered over to fire and sword. Of the whole population and garrison not twenty were left alive. Siege was then laid to Zierickzee, and Colonel Mondragon was left in charge of the operations. Requesens himself came to Schouwen to give directions concerning this important enterprise.*

Chiapin Vitelli also came thither in the middle of the winter, and was so much injured by a fall from his litter, while making the tour of the island, that he died on shipboard during his return to Antwerp.† This officer had gained his laurels upon more than one occasion, his conduct in the important action near Mons, in which the Huguenot force under Genlis was defeated, having been particularly creditable. He was of a distinguished Umbrian family, and had passed his life in camps, few of the generals who had accompanied Alva to the Netherlands being better known or more odious to the inhabitants. He was equally distinguished for his courage, his cruelty, and his corpulence. The last characteristic was so remarkable that he was almost monstrous in his personal appearance. His protuberant stomach was always supported in a bandage suspended from his neck, yet in spite of this enormous impediment, he was personally active on the battle-field, and performed more service, not only as a commander but as a subaltern, than many a younger and lighter man.‡

* Mendoza, xiv. 287–293, seq. Bentivoglio, ix. 169, 170. Bor, viii, 652. seq. Hoofd, x. 431.

† Meteren, v. 103. Strada, viii. 403.

‡ Strada, viii. 404.—Vitelli seems to have been unpopular with the Span-

The siege of Zierickzee was protracted till the following June, the city holding out with firmness. Want of funds caused the operations to be conducted with languor, but the same cause prevented the Prince from accomplishing its relief. Thus the expedition from Philipsland, the most brilliant military exploit of the whole war, was attended with important results. The communication between Walcheren and the rest of Zealand was interrupted, the province cut in two; a foothold on the ocean, for a brief interval at least, acquired by Spain. The Prince was inexpressibly chagrined by these circumstances, and felt that the moment had arrived when all honorable means were to be employed to obtain foreign assistance. The Hollanders and Zealanders had fought the battles of freedom alone hitherto, and had fought them well, but poverty was fast rendering them incapable of sustaining much longer the unequal conflict. Offers of men, whose wages the states were to furnish, were refused, as worse than fruitless. Henry of Navarre, who perhaps deemed it possible to acquire the sovereignty of the provinces by so barren a benefit, was willing to send two or three thousand men, but not at his own expense. The proposition was respectfully declined.* The Prince and his little country were all alone. "Even if we should not only see ourselves deserted by all the world, but also all the world against us," he said, "we should not cease to defend ourselves even to the last man. Knowing the

---

iards also, and Mendoza does not even allude to his death. The Netherlanders hated him cordially. His name, which afforded the materials for a pun, was, of course, a whetstone for their wits. They improved his death by perpetrating a multitude of epigrams, of which the following may serve as a sample:—

EPITAPHIUM CHIAP. VITELLI, MARCHIONIS CETONIS, ETC.

"O Deus omnipotens crassi miserere Vitelli,
Quem mors proveniens non sinit esse bovem.
Corpus in Italia est, tenet intestina Brabantus,
Ast animam nemo, cur? quia non habuit.

—Vide Meteren, v. 103b.

His death occurred towards the end of February (1576), a few days before that of the Grand Commander.

* Wagenaer, vii. 88. Resol. Holl., Mart. 15, 1576.

justice of our cause, we repose entirely in the mercy of God."* He determined, however, once more to have recourse to the powerful of the earth, being disposed to test the truth of his celebrated observation, that "there would be no lack of suitors for the bride that he had to bestow." It was necessary, in short, to look the great question of formally renouncing Philip directly in the face.

Hitherto the fiction of allegiance had been preserved, and, even by the enemies of the Prince, it was admitted that it had been retained with no disloyal intent.† The time, however, had come when it was necessary to throw off allegiance, provided another could be found strong enough and frank enough to accept the authority which Philip had forfeited. The question was, naturally, between France and England, unless the provinces could effect their re-admission into the body of the Germanic Empire. Already in June the Prince had laid the proposition formally before the states, "whether they should not negotiate with the Empire on the subject of their admission, with maintenance of their own constitutions," but it was understood that this plan was not to be carried out, if the protection of the Empire could be obtained under easier conditions.‡

Nothing came of the proposition at that time. The nobles and the deputies of South Holland now voted, in the beginning of the ensuing month, "that it was their duty to abandon the King, as a tyrant who sought to oppress and destroy his subjects; and that it behoved them to seek another protector." This was while the Breda negotiations were still pending, but when their inevitable result was very visible. There was still a reluctance at taking the last and decisive step in the rebellion, so that the semblance of loyalty was still

---

* Archives de la Maison d'Orange, v. 281. Letter to Count John.

† See the remarks of Groen v. Prinsterer on a passage in a letter of the Council of State to Requesens.—Archives, etc., v. 273. See also the letter in Bor, viii. 613.

‡ Resol. Holl., June 6, 1575, bl. 363. Wagenaer, vii. 78.

retained; that ancient scabbard, in which the sword might yet one day be sheathed. The proposition was not adopted at the diet. A committee of nine was merely appointed to deliberate with the Prince upon the "means of obtaining foreign assistance, without accepting foreign authority, or severing their connexion with his Majesty." The estates were, however, summoned a few months later, by the Prince, to deliberate on this important matter at Rotterdam. On the 1st of October he then formally proposed, either to make terms with their enemy, and that the sooner the better, or else, once for all, to separate entirely from the King of Spain, and to change their sovereign, in order, with the assistance and under protection of another Christian potentate, to maintain the provinces against their enemies. Orange, moreover, expressed the opinion that upon so important a subject it was decidedly incumbent upon them all to take the sense of the city governments. The members for the various municipalities acquiesced in the propriety of this suggestion, and resolved to consult their constituents, while the deputies of the nobility also desired to consult with their whole body. After an adjournment of a few days, the diet again assembled at Delft, and it was then *unanimously* resolved by the nobles and the cities, "*that they would forsake the King* and seek foreign assistance; referring the choice to the Prince, who, in regard to the government, was to take the opinion of the estates."*

Thus, the great step was taken, by which two little provinces declared themselves independent of their ancient master. That declaration, although taken in the midst of doubt and darkness, was not destined to be cancelled, and the germ of a new and powerful commonwealth was planted. So little, however, did these republican fathers foresee their coming republic, that the resolution to renounce one king was combined with a proposition to ask for the authority of another. It was not

* Resol. Holl., Jul. 7, 1575, bl. 474. Jul. 9, 1575, bl. 482. Oct. 3, 1575, bl. 668, 669. Oct. 13, 1575, bl. 692. Bor, viii. 651. Wagenaer, vii. 81.

imagined that those two slender columns, which were all that had yet been raised of the future stately peristyle, would be strong enough to stand alone. The question now arose, to what foreign power application should be made. But little hope was to be entertained from Germany, a state which existed only in name, and France was still in a condition of religious and intestine discord. The attitude of revolt maintained by the Duc d'Alençon seemed to make it difficult and dangerous to enter into negotiations with a country where the civil wars had assumed so complicated a character, that a loyal and useful alliance could hardly be made with any party. The Queen of England, on the other hand, dreaded the wrath of Philip, by which her perpetual dangers from the side of Scotland would be aggravated, while she feared equally the extension of French authority in the Netherlands, by which increase her neighbour would acquire an overshadowing power. She was also ashamed openly to abandon the provinces to their fate, for her realm was supposed to be a bulwark of the Protestant religion. Afraid to affront Philip, afraid to refuse the suit of the Netherlands, afraid to concede an aggrandizement to France, what course was open to the English Queen? That which, politically and personally, she loved the best—a course of barren coquetry. This the Prince of Orange foresaw; and although not disposed to leave a stone unturned in his efforts to find assistance for his country, he on the whole rather inclined for France. He, however, better than any man, knew how little cause there was for sanguine expectation from either source.*

It was determined, in the name of his Highness and the estates, first to send a mission to England, but there had already been negotiations this year of an unpleasant character with that power. At the request of the Spanish envoy, the foremost Netherland rebels, in number about fifty, including by

* De Thou, tom. vii. liv. 61. See Wagenaer, vii. 81.

name the Prince of Orange, the Counts of Berg and Culemburg, with Saint Aldegonde, Boisot, Junius, and others, had been formally forbidden by Queen Elizabeth to enter her realm.* The Prince had, in consequence, sent Aldegonde and Junius on a secret mission to France,† and the Queen, jealous and anxious, had thereupon sent Daniel Rogers secretly to the Prince.‡ At the same time she had sent an envoy to the Grand Commander, counselling conciliatory measures, and promising to send a special mission to Spain with the offer of her mediation, but it was suspected by those most in the confidence of the Spanish government at Brussels, that there was a great deal of deception in these proceedings.§ A truce for six months having now been established between the Duc d'Alençon and his brother, it was supposed, that an alliance between France and England, and perhaps between Alençon and Elizabeth, was on the carpet, and that a kingdom of the Netherlands was to be the wedding present of the bride to her husband. These fantasies derived additional color from the fact that, while the Queen was expressing the most amicable intentions towards Spain, and the greatest jealousy of France, the English residents at Antwerp and other cities of the Netherlands had received private instructions to sell out their property as fast as possible, and to retire from the country.‖ On the whole, there was little prospect either of a final answer, or of substantial assistance from the Queen.

The envoys to England were Advocate Buis and Doctor Francis Maalzon, nominated by the estates, and Saint Aldegonde, chief of the mission, appointed by the Prince. They arrived in England at Christmas-tide. Having represented to the Queen the result of the Breda negotiations, they stated

---

† Resol. Holl., Jul. 13, 1575, bl. 492. Meteren, v. 100, 101.

† Bor, viii. 641.

‡ Wagenaer, vii. 83.

§ Letter from Morillon to Cardinal Granvelle, of date Dec. 11, 1575.—Archives et Corresp., v. 325, 326.

‖ Letter of Morillon, ubi sup.

that the Prince and the estates, in despair of a secure peace, had addressed themselves to her as an upright protector of the Faith, and as a princess descended from the blood of Holland. This allusion to the intermarriage of Edward III. of England with Philippa, daughter of Count William III. of Hainault and Holland, would not, it was hoped, be in vain. They furthermore offered to her Majesty, in case she were willing powerfully to assist the states, the sovereignty over Holland and Zealand, under certain conditions.*

The Queen listened graciously to the envoys, and appointed commissioners to treat with them on the subject. Meantime, Requesens sent Champagny to England, to counteract the effect of this embassy of the estates, and to beg the Queen to give no heed to the prayers of the rebels, to enter into no negotiations with them, and to expel them at once from her kingdom.†

The Queen gravely assured Champagny "that the envoys were no rebels, but faithful subjects of his Majesty."‡ There was certainly some effrontery in such a statement, considering the solemn offer which had just been made by the envoys. If to renounce allegiance to Philip and to propose the sovereignty to Elizabeth did not constitute rebellion, it would be difficult to define or to discover rebellion anywhere. The statement was as honest, however, as the diplomatic grimace with which Champagny had reminded Elizabeth of the ancient and unbroken friendship which had always existed between herself and his Catholic Majesty. The attempt of Philip to procure her dethronement and assassination but a few years before was, no doubt, thought too trifling a circumstance to have for a moment interrupted those harmonious relations. Nothing came of the negotiations on either side. The Queen coquetted, as was her custom. She could not

* Bor, viii. 660, 661. Resol. Holl., Nov. 14, 1575, bl. 730.

† Bor, viii. 661. Vigl. Epist. Select. No. 177, p. 407.

‡ Bor, viii. 661.

accept the offer of the estates; she could not say them nay. She would not offend Philip; she would not abandon the provinces; she would therefore negotiate—thus there was an infinite deal of diplomatic nothing spun and unravelled, but the result was both to abandon the provinces and to offend Philip.

In the first answer given by her commissioners to the states' envoys, it was declared, "that her Majesty considered it too expensive to assume the protection of both provinces. She was willing to protect them in name, but she should confer the advantage exclusively on Walcheren in reality. The defence of Holland must be maintained at the expense of the Prince and the estates.*

This was certainly not munificent, and the envoys insisted upon more ample and liberal terms. The Queen declined, however, committing herself beyond this niggardly and inadmissible offer. The states were not willing to exchange the sovereignty over their country for so paltry a concession. The Queen declared herself indisposed to go further, at least before consulting parliament.† The commissioners waited for the assembling of parliament. She then refused to lay the matter before that body, and forbade the Hollanders taking any steps for that purpose.‡ It was evident that she was disposed to trifle with the provinces, and had no idea of encountering the open hostility of Philip. The envoys accordingly begged for their passports. These were granted in April, 1576, with the assurance on the part of her Majesty that "she would think more of the offer made to her after she had done all in her power to bring about an arrangement between the provinces and Philip."§

After the result of the negotiations of Breda, it is difficult to imagine what method she was likely to devise for accomplishing such a purpose. The King was not more disposed than during the preceding summer to grant liberty of religion,

* Bor, viii. 661–663. Wagenaer, vii. 85.

† Wagenaer, vii. 85, 86. Bor, ubi sup.

‡ Wagenaer, ubi sup.

§ Bor, viii. 663. Wagenaer, vii. 86.

nor were the Hollanders more ready than they had been before to renounce either their faith or their fatherland. The envoys, on parting, made a strenuous effort to negotiate a loan, but the frugal Queen considered the proposition quite inadmissible. She granted them liberty to purchase arms and ammunition, and to levy a few soldiers with their own money, and this was accordingly done to a limited extent. As it was not difficult to hire soldiers or to buy gunpowder anywhere, in that warlike age, provided the money were ready, the states had hardly reason to consider themselves under deep obligation for this concession. Yet this was the whole result of the embassy. Plenty of fine words had been bestowed, which might or might not have meaning, according to the turns taken by coming events. Besides these cheap and empty civilities, they received permission to defend Holland at their own expense, with the privilege of surrendering its sovereignty, if they liked, to Queen Elizabeth—and this was all.

On the 19th of April, the envoys returned to their country, and laid before the estates the meagre result of their negotiations.* Very soon afterwards, upon an informal suggestion from Henry III. and the Queen Mother, that a more favorable result might be expected, if the same applications were made to the Duc d'Alençon which had been received in so unsatisfactory a manner by Elizabeth, commissioners were appointed to France.† It proved impossible, however, at that juncture, to proceed with the negotiations, in consequence of the troubles occasioned by the attitude of the Duke. The provinces were still, even as they had been from the beginning, entirely alone.

Requesens was more than ever straitened for funds, wringing, with increasing difficulty, a slender subsidy, from time to time, out of the reluctant estates of Brabant, Flanders, and the other obedient provinces. While he was still at

---

* Bor, viii. 661–663. Hoofd, x. 434, 435. Meteren, v. 101. Resol. Holl., Apr. 19, 1576, bl. 42.

† Ever. Reid. Ann., lib. i. 18.

Duiveland, the estates-general sent him a long remonstrance against the misconduct of the soldiery, in answer to his demand for supplies. "Oh, these estates! these estates!" cried the Grand Commander, on receiving such vehement reproaches instead of his money; "may the Lord deliver me from these estates!"* Meantime, the important siege of Zierickzee continued, and it was evident that the city must fall. There was no money at the disposal of the Prince. Count John, who was seriously embarrassed by reason of the great obligations in money which he, with the rest of his family, had incurred on behalf of the estates, had recently made application to the Prince for his influence towards procuring him relief. He had forwarded an account of the great advances made by himself and his brethren in money, plate, furniture, and endorsements of various kinds, for which a partial reimbursement was almost indispensable to save him from serious difficulties.† The Prince, however, unable to procure him any assistance, had been obliged once more to entreat him to display the generosity and the self-denial which the country had never found wanting at his hands or at those of his kindred. The appeal had not been in vain; but the Count was obviously not in a condition to effect anything more at that moment to relieve the financial distress of the states. The exchequer was crippled.‡ Holland and Zealand were cut in twain by the occupation of Schouwen and the approaching fall of its capital. Germany, England, France, all refused to stretch out their hands to save the heroic but exhaustless little provinces. It was at this moment that

---

* "Dios nos libera de estos Estados."—Meteren, v. 103b.

† Archives et Correspondance, v. 301–304.

‡ The contributions of Holland and Zealand for war expenses amounted to one hundred and fifty thousand florins monthly. The pay of a captain was eighty florins monthly; that of a lieutenant, forty; that of a corporal, fifteen; that of a drummer, fifer, *or minister*, twelve; that of a common soldier, seven and a half. A captain had also one hundred and fifty florins each month to distribute among the most meritorious of his company. Each soldier was likewise furnished with food, bedding, fire, light, and washing.—Renom de France MS., vol. ii. c. 46.

a desperate but sublime resolution took possession of the Prince's mind. There seemed but one way left to exclude the Spaniards for ever from Holland and Zealand, and to rescue the inhabitants from impending ruin. The Prince had long brooded over the scheme, and the hour seemed to have struck for its fulfilment. His project was to collect all the vessels, of every description, which could be obtained throughout the Netherlands. The whole population of the two provinces, men, women, and children, together with all the moveable property of the country, were then to be embarked on board this numerous fleet, and to seek a new home beyond the seas. The windmills were then to be burned, the dykes pierced, the sluices opened in every direction, and the country restored for ever to the ocean, from which it had sprung.*

It is difficult to say whether the resolution, if Providence had permitted its fulfilment, would have been, on the whole, better or worse for humanity and civilization. The ships which would have borne the heroic Prince and his fortunes might have taken the direction of the newly-discovered Western hemisphere. A religious colony, planted by a commercial and liberty-loving race, in a virgin soil, and directed by patrician but self-denying hands, might have preceded, by half a century, the colony which a kindred race, impelled by similar motives, and under somewhat similar circumstances and conditions, was destined to plant upon the stern shores of New England. Had they directed their course to the warm and fragrant islands of the East, an independent Christian commonwealth

---

* Bor relates that this plan had been definitely formed by the Prince. His authority is "a credible gentleman of quality" (een geloofswaerdig edelmann van qualiteit) who, at the time, was a member of the estates and government of Holland.—viii. 664. Groen v. Prinsterer, however, rejects the tale as fabulous; or believes, at any rate, that the personage alluded to by Bor took the Prince's words too literally. It is probable that the thought was often in the Prince's mind, and found occasional expression, although it had never been actually reduced to a scheme. It is difficult to see that it was not consistent with his character, supposing that there had been no longer any room for hope. Hoofd, x. 443, adopts the story without hesitation. Wagenaer, vii. 88, 89, alludes to it as a matter of current report.—Compare Van Wyn op Wagen. vii. 33–35.

might have arisen among those prolific regions, superior in importance to any subsequent colony of Holland, cramped from its birth by absolute subjection to a far distant metropolis.

The unexpected death of Requesens suddenly dispelled these schemes. The siege of Zierickzee had occupied much of the Governor's attention, but he had recently written to his sovereign, that its reduction was now certain. He had added an urgent request for money, with a sufficient supply of which he assured Philip that he should be able to bring the war to an immediate conclusion. While waiting for these supplies, he had, contrary to all law or reason, made an unsuccessful attempt to conquer the post of Embden, in Germany. A mutiny had, at about the same time, broken out among his troops in Harlem, and he had furnished the citizens with arms to defend themselves, giving free permission to use them against the insurgent troops. By this means the mutiny had been quelled, but a dangerous precedent established. Anxiety concerning this rebellion is supposed to have hastened the Grand Commander's death. A violent fever seized him on the 1st, and terminated his existence on the 5th of March, in the fifty-first year of his life.*

It is not necessary to review elaborately his career, the chief incidents of which have been sufficiently described. Requesens was a man of high position by birth and office, but a thoroughly commonplace personage. His talents either for war or for civil employments were not above mediocrity. His friends disputed whether he were greater in the field or in the council, but it is certain that he was great in neither. His bigotry was equal to that of Alva, but it was impossible to rival the Duke in cruelty. Moreover, the condition of the country, after seven years of torture under his predecessor, made it difficult for him, at the time of his arrival, to imitate the severity which had made the name of Alva infamous. The Blood Council had been re-

---

* Bor, viii. 663, 665. Hoofd, x. 436–437. Vigl. Epist. Select., Ep. Card. Granv., No. 178, p. 408.

tained throughout his administration, but its occupation was gone, for want of food for its ferocity. The obedient provinces had been purged of Protestants; while crippled, too, by confiscation, they offered no field for further extortion. From Holland and Zealand, whence Catholicism had been nearly excluded, the King of Spain was nearly excluded also. The Blood Council which, if set up in that country, would have executed every living creature of its population, could only gaze from a distance at those who would have been its victims. Requesens had been previously distinguished in two fields of action: the Granada massacres and the carnage of Lepanto. Upon both occasions he had been the military tutor of Don John of Austria, by whom he was soon to be succeeded in the government of the Netherlands. To the imperial bastard had been assigned the pre-eminence, but it was thought that the Grand Commander had been entitled to a more than equal share of the glory. We have seen how much additional reputation was acquired by Requesens in the provinces. The expedition against Duiveland and Schouwen, was, on the whole, the most brilliant feat of arms during the war, and its success reflects an undying lustre on the hardihood and discipline of the Spanish, German, and Walloon soldiery. As an act of individual audacity in a bad cause, it has rarely been equalled. It can hardly be said, however, that the Grand Commander was entitled to any large measure of praise for the success of the expedition. The plan was laid by Zealand traitors. It was carried into execution by the devotion of the Spanish, Walloon, and German troops, while Requesens was only a spectator of the transaction. His sudden death arrested, for a moment, the ebb-tide in the affairs of the Netherlands, which was fast leaving the country bare and desolate, and was followed by a train of unforeseen transactions, which it is now our duty to describe.

CHAPTER IV.

Assumption of affairs by the state council at Brussels—Hesitation at Madrid—Joachim Hopper—Mal-administration—Vigilance of Orange—The provinces drawn more closely together—Inequality of the conflict—Physical condition of Holland—New act of Union between Holland and Zealand—Authority of the Prince defined and enlarged—Provincial polity characterized—Generous sentiments of the Prince—His tolerant spirit—Letters from the King—Attitude of the great powers towards the Netherlands—Correspondence and policy of Elizabeth—Secret negotiations with France and Alençon—Confused and menacing aspect of Germany—Responsible and laborious position of Orange—Attempt to relieve Zierickzee—Death of Admiral Boisot—Capitulation of the city upon honourable terms—Mutiny of the Spanish troops in Schouwen—General causes of discontent—Alarming increase of the mutiny—The rebel regiments enter Brabant—Fruitless attempts to pacify them—They take possession of Alost—Edicts, denouncing them, from the state council—Intense excitement in Brussels and Antwerp—Letters from Philip brought by Marquis Havré—The King's continued procrastination—Ruinous royal confirmation of the authority assumed by the state council—United and general resistance to foreign military oppression—The German troops and the Antwerp garrison, under Avila, join the revolt—Letter of Verdugo—A crisis approaching—Jerome de Roda in the citadel—The mutiny universal.

THE death of Requesens, notwithstanding his four days' illness, occurred so suddenly, that he had not had time to appoint his successor. Had he exercised this privilege, which his patent conferred upon him, it was supposed that he would have nominated Count Mansfeld to exercise the functions of Governor-General, until the King should otherwise ordain.*

 * Bor, viii. 663. Meteren, v. 104ᵃ.

In the absence of any definite arrangement, the Council of State, according to a right which that body claimed from custom, assumed the reins of government. Of the old board, there were none left but the Duke of Aerschot, Count Berlaymont, and Viglius. To these were soon added, however, by royal diploma, the Spaniard, Jerome de Roda, and the Netherlanders, Assonleville, Baron Rassenghiem and Arnold Sasbout. Thus, all the members, save one, of what had now become the executive body, were natives of the country. Roda was accordingly looked askance upon by his colleagues. He was regarded by Viglius as a man who desired to repeat the part which had been played by Juan Vargas in the Blood Council, while the other members, although stanch Catholics, were all of them well-disposed to vindicate the claim of Netherland nobles to a share in the government of the Netherlands.

For a time, therefore, the transfer of authority seemed to have been smoothly accomplished. The Council of State conducted the administration of the country. Peter Ernest Mansfeld was entrusted with the supreme military command, including the government of Brussels; and the Spanish commanders, although dissatisfied that any but a Spaniard should be thus honored, were for a time quiescent.* When the news reached Madrid, Philip was extremely disconcerted. The death of Requesens excited his indignation. He was angry with him, not for dying, but for dying at so very inconvenient a moment. He had not yet fully decided either upon his successor, or upon the policy to be enforced by his successor. There were several candidates for the vacant post; there was a variety of opinions in the cabinet as to the course of conduct to be adopted.† In the impossibility of

---

* Bor, Meteren, ubi sup. Viglii Epist. Select. ad Diversos, No. 179, p. 409. Vigl. Epist., ubi sup. Hoofd, xi. 438. Bor, ix. 663. Wagenaer (vii. 91), however, states that Mansfeld was entrusted simply with the government of Brussels, and that it is an error to describe him as invested with the supreme military command.

† Letter of Philip (March 24, 1576) to states general, in Bor, ix. 663.

instantly making up his mind upon this unexpected emergency, Philip fell, as it were, into a long reverie, than which nothing could be more inopportune. With a country in a state of revolution and exasperation, the trance, which now seemed to come over the government, was like to be followed by deadly effects. The stationary policy, which the death of Requesens had occasioned, was allowed to prolong itself indefinitely,* and almost for the first time in his life, Joachim Hopper was really consulted about the affairs of that department over which he imagined himself, and was generally supposed by others, to preside at Madrid. The creature of Viglius, having all the subserviency, with none of the acuteness of his patron, he had been long employed as chief of the Netherland bureau, while kept in profound ignorance of the affairs which were transacted in his office. He was a privy councillor, whose counsels were never heeded, a confidential servant in whom the King reposed confidence, only on the ground that no man could reveal secrets which he did not know. This deportment of the King's showed that he had accurately measured the man, for Hopper was hardly competent for the place of a chief clerk. He was unable to write clearly in any language, because incapable of a fully developed thought upon any subject. It may be supposed that nothing but an abortive policy, therefore, would be produced upon the occasion thus suddenly offered. "'Tis a devout man, that poor Master Hopper," said Granvelle, "but rather fitted for platonic researches than for affairs of state."†

It was a proof of this incompetency, that now, when really called upon for advice in an emergency, he should recommend a continuance of the interim. Certainly nothing worse could be devised. Granvelle recommended a reappointment of the Duchess Margaret.‡ Others suggested Duke Eric of Brunswick, or an Archduke of the Austrian house; although the opinion

* Strada, viii. 407, 408. Hoofd, xi. 438. Bor, viii. 663, sqq. V. d. Vynckt, ii. 176, et sqq., etc.

† Archives et Correspondance, v. 374.

‡ MS. cited by Groen v. Prinst. v. 331.

held by most of the influential councillors was in favor of Don John of Austria.* In the interests of Philip and his despotism, nothing, at any rate, could be more fatal than delay. In the condition of affairs which then existed, the worst or feeblest governor would have been better than none at all. To leave a vacancy was to play directly into the hands of Orange, for it was impossible that so skilful an adversary should not at once perceive the fault, and profit by it to the utmost. It was strange that Philip did not see the danger of inactivity at such a crisis. Assuredly, indolence was never his vice, but on this occasion indecision did the work of indolence. Unwittingly, the despot was assisting the efforts of the liberator. Viglius saw the position of matters with his customary keenness, and wondered at the blindness of Hopper and Philip. At the last gasp of a life, which neither learning nor the accumulation of worldly prizes and worldly pelf could redeem from intrinsic baseness, the sagacious but not venerable old man saw that a chasm was daily widening, in which the religion and the despotism which he loved might soon be hopelessly swallowed. "The Prince of Orange and his Beggars do not sleep," he cried, almost in anguish; "nor will they be quiet till they have made use of this interregnum to do us some immense grievance."†

Certainly the Prince of Orange did not sleep upon this nor any other great occasion of his life. In his own vigorous language, used to stimulate his friends in various parts of the country, he seized the swift occasion by the forelock. He opened a fresh correspondence with many leading gentlemen in Brussels and other places in the Netherlands; persons of influence, who now, for the first time, showed a disposition to side with their country against its tyrants.‡ Hitherto the land had been

* MS. cited by Groen v. Prinst. v. 331.—Compare Bor, viii. 663, and the letters of Philip to State Council, in Bor, ubi sup; letters which Cabrera characterizes as "amorosas, suaves enlas razones fraternales," and in which "dezia los amaba como a hijos!!" These letters distinctly indicated Don John as the probable successor of Requesens.—Cabrera, Vita de Felipe II., xi. 845.

† Vigl. Epist. ad Joach. Hopperum, ep. 265, p. 863.

‡ De Thou, liv. 62, t. vii. 368, 369. Wagenaer, vii. 104, 105, sqq.

divided into two very unequal portions. Holland and Zealand were devoted to the Prince; their whole population, with hardly an individual exception, converted to the Reformed religion. The other fifteen provinces were, on the whole, loyal to the King; while the old religion had, of late years, taken root so rapidly again, that perhaps a moiety of their population might be considered as Catholic.* At the same time, the reign of terror under Alva, the paler, but not less distinct tyranny of Requesens, and the intolerable excesses of the foreign soldiery, by which the government of foreigners was supported, had at last maddened all the inhabitants of the seventeen provinces. Notwithstanding, therefore, the fatal difference of religious opinion, they were all drawn into closer relations with each other; to regain their ancient privileges, and to expel the detested foreigners from the soil, being objects common to all. The provinces were united in one great hatred and one great hope.

The Hollanders and Zealanders, under their heroic leader, had well nigh accomplished both tasks, so far as those little provinces were concerned. Never had a contest, however, seemed more hopeless at its commencement. Cast a glance at the map. Look at Holland—not the Republic, with its sister provinces beyond the Zuyder Zee—but Holland only, with the Zealand archipelago. Look at that narrow tongue of half-submerged earth. Who could suppose that upon that slender sand-bank, one hundred and twenty miles in length, and varying in breadth from four miles to forty, one man, backed by the population of a handful of cities, could do battle nine years long with the master of two worlds, the "Dominator of Asia, Africa, and America"—the despot of the fairest realms of Europe—and conquer him at last. Nor was William even entirely master of that narrow shoal where clung the survivors of a great national shipwreck. North and South Holland were cut in two by the loss of Harlem, while the enemy was in possession of the natural capital of the little country,

* Groen v. Prinst., Archives, v. 381--385.—Compare de Thou, liv. 62.

Amsterdam. The Prince affirmed that the cause had suffered more from the disloyalty of Amsterdam than from all the efforts of the enemy.

Moreover, the country was in a most desolate condition. It was almost *literally* a sinking ship. The destruction of the bulwarks against the ocean had been so extensive, in consequence of the voluntary inundations which have been described in previous pages, and by reason of the general neglect which more vital occupations had necessitated, that an enormous outlay, both of labor and money, was now indispensable to save the physical existence of the country. The labor and the money, notwithstanding the crippled and impoverished condition of the nation, were, however, freely contributed; a wonderful example of energy and patient heroism was again exhibited. The dykes which had been swept away in every direction were renewed at a vast expense.* Moreover, the country, in the course of recent events, had become almost swept bare of its cattle, and it was necessary to pass a law forbidding, for a considerable period, the slaughter of any animals, "oxen, cows, calves, sheep, or poultry."† It was, unfortunately, not possible to provide by law against that extermination of the human population which had been decreed by Philip and the Pope.

Such was the physical and moral condition of the provinces of Holland and Zealand. The political constitution of both assumed, at this epoch, a somewhat altered aspect. The union between the two states, effected in June, 1575, required improvement. The administration of justice, the conflicts of laws, and more particularly the levying of monies and troops in equitable proportions, had not been adjusted with perfect smoothness. The estates of the two provinces, assembled in congress at Delft, concluded, therefore, a new act of union, which was duly signed upon the 25th of April, 1576.‡ Those

* The work was, however, not fairly taken in hand until the spring of 1577.—Wagenaer, vii. 158, sqq. Bor, x. 819.

† Resol. Holl. Feb. 28, 1575, bl. 97. Van Wyn op Wagenaer, vii. 26.

‡ Bor, ix. 668. Kluit, Hist. Holl. Reg., i. 115, et sqq. Wagenaer, vii. 94.

estates, consisting of the knights and nobles of Holland, with the deputies from the cities and countships of Holland and Zealand, had been duly summoned by the Prince of Orange.* They as fairly included all the political capacities, and furnished as copious a representation of the national will, as could be expected, for it is apparent upon every page of his history, that the Prince, upon all occasions, chose to refer his policy to the approval and confirmation of as large a portion of the people as any man in those days considered capable or desirous of exercising political functions.

The new union consisted of eighteen articles. It was established that deputies from all the estates should meet, when summoned by the Prince of Orange or otherwise, on penalty of fine, and at the risk of measures binding upon them being passed by the rest of the Congress.† Freshly arising causes of litigation were to be referred to the Prince.‡ Free intercourse and traffic through the united provinces was guaranteed.§ The confederates were mutually to assist each other in preventing all injustice, wrong, or violence, even towards an enemy.‖ The authority of law and the pure administration of justice were mutually promised by the contracting states.¶ The common expenses were to be apportioned among the different provinces, "as if they were all included in the republic of a single city."** Nine commissioners, appointed by the Prince on nomination by the estates, were to sit permanently, as his advisers, and as assessors and collectors of the taxes.†† The tenure of the union was from six months to six months, with six weeks' notice.‡‡

The framers of this compact having thus defined the general outlines of the confederacy, declared that the government, thus constituted, should be placed under a single head. They

* Bor, ix. 668. Wagenaer, vii. 93. Kluit, i. 115, sqq.

† Art. 3. The document is given in full by Bor, ix. 668, sqq.

‡ Article 4.

§ Article 5.

‖ "Hoewel ook vijand."—Article 7.

¶ Article 7.

** Article 10.

†† Article 11.

‡‡ Article 17, 18.

accordingly conferred supreme authority on the Prince,* defining his powers in eighteen articles. He was declared chief commander by land and sea. He was to appoint all officers, from generals to subalterns, and to pay them at his discretion.† The whole protection of the land was devolved upon him. He was to send garrisons or troops into every city and village at his pleasure, without advice or consent of the estates, magistrates of the cities, or any other persons whatsoever.‡ He was, in behalf of the King as Count of Holland and Zealand, to cause justice to be administered by the supreme court.§ In the same capacity he was to provide for vacancies in all political and judicial offices of importance,‖ choosing, *with the advice of the estates*, one officer for each vacant post out of three candidates nominated to him by that body.¶ He was to appoint and renew, at the usual times, the magistracies in the cities, according to the ancient constitutions. He was to make changes in those boards, if necessary, at unusual times, with consent of the majority of those representing the great council and *corpus* of the said cities.** He was to uphold the authority and pre-eminence of all civil functionaries, and to prevent governors and military officers from taking any cognizance of political or judicial affairs. With regard to religion, he was to maintain the practice of the Reformed Evangelical religion, and to *cause to surcease* the exercise of all other religions *contrary to the Gospel*. He was, however, not to permit that *inquisition should be made into any man's belief or conscience*, or *that any man by cause thereof should suffer trouble, injury, or hindrance.*††

The league thus concluded was a confederation between a

---

* Articles of Union, Bor, ix. 620. † Articles 1 and 2. ‡ Articles 3–7.

§ Article 8. ‖ Compare Kluit, Holl. Staatsreg., i. 121, 122.

¶ Article 10.—See Kluit's Commentary on this article.—Holl. Staatsreg., i. 121, 122.

** Article 13.

†† Article 15.—"Sonder dat syne E. sal toelaten dat men op jemands geloof op conscientie sal inquireren of dat jemand ter cause van die eenige moeyenis, injurie, of letsel angedaen sal worden, etc., etc.

group of virtually independent little republics. Each municipality, was, as it were, a little sovereign, sending envoys to a congress to vote and to sign as plenipotentiaries. The vote of each city was, therefore, indivisible, and it mattered little, practically, whether there were one deputy or several. The nobles represented not only their own order, but were supposed to act also in behalf of the rural population. On the whole, there was a tolerably fair representation of the whole nation. The people were well and worthily represented in the government of each city, and therefore equally so in the assembly of the estates.* It was not till later that the corporations, by the extinction of the popular element, and by the usurpation of the right of self-election, were thoroughly stiffened into fictitious personages which never died, and which were never thoroughly alive.

At this epoch the provincial liberties, so far as they could maintain themselves against Spanish despotism, were practical and substantial. The government was a representative one,† in which all those who had the inclination possessed, in one mode or another, a voice. Although the various members of the confederacy were locally and practically republics or self-governed little commonwealths, the general government which they established was, in form, monarchical. The powers conferred upon Orange constituted him a sovereign *ad interim*, for while the authority of the Spanish monarch remained suspended, the Prince was invested, not only with the whole executive and appointing power, but even with a very large share in the legislative functions of the state.‡

The whole system was rather practical than theoretical, without any accurate distribution of political powers. In living, energetic communities, where the blood of the body politic circulates swiftly, there is an inevitable tendency of the different organs to sympathize and commingle more closely than

* Compare Kluit, Holl., Staatsreg., i. 130.

† Kluit, 129, 130.

‡ Kluit, i. 125.

à priori philosophy would allow. It is usually more desirable than practicable to keep the executive, legislative, and judicial departments entirely independent of each other.*

Certainly, the Prince of Orange did not at that moment indulge in speculations concerning the nature and origin of government. The Congress of Delft had just clothed him with almost regal authority. In his hands were the powers of war and peace, joint control of the magistracies and courts of justice, absolute supremacy over the army and the fleets. It is true that these attributes had been conferred upon him *ad interim*, but it depended only upon himself to make the sovereignty personal and permanent.† He was so thoroughly absorbed in his work, however, that he did not even see the diadem which he put aside. It was small matter to him whether they called him stadholder or guardian, prince or king. He was the father of his country and its defender. The people, from highest to lowest, called him "Father William," and the title was enough for him. The question with him was, not what men should call him, but how he should best accomplish his task.

So little was he inspired by the sentiment of self-elevation, that he was anxiously seeking for a fitting person—strong, wise, and willing enough—to exercise the sovereignty which was thrust upon himself, but which he desired to exchange against an increased power to be actively useful to his country. To expel the foreign oppressor; to strangle the Inquisition; to maintain the ancient liberties of the nation;—here was labor enough for his own hands. The vulgar thought of carving a throne out of the misfortunes of his country seems not to have entered his mind. Upon one point, however, the Prince had been peremptory. He would have no persecution of the opposite creed. He was requested to suppress the Catholic religion, in terms. As we have seen, he caused the expression to be exchanged for the words, "religion at vari-

* Compare Guizot, du Système Representatif, t. i.

† Compare Groen v. Prinst., Archives et Correspondance, v. 340–342.

ance with the Gospel." He resolutely stood out against all meddling with men's consciences, or inquiring into their thoughts. While smiting the Spanish Inquisition into the dust, he would have no Calvinist inquisition set up in its place. Earnestly a convert to the Reformed religion, but hating and denouncing only what was corrupt in the ancient Church, he would not force men, with fire and sword, to travel to heaven upon his own road. Thought should be toll-free. Neither monk nor minister should burn, drown, or hang his fellow-creatures, when argument or expostulation failed to redeem them from error. It was no small virtue, in that age, to rise to such a height. We know what Calvinists, Zwinglians, Lutherans, have done in the Netherlands, in Germany, in Switzerland, and almost a century later in New England. It is, therefore, with increased veneration that we regard this large and *truly catholic* mind. His tolerance proceeded from no indifference. No man can read his private writings, or form a thorough acquaintance with his interior life, without recognizing him as a deeply religious man. He had faith unfaltering in God. He had also faith in man and love for his brethren. It was no wonder that in that age of religious bigotry he should have been assaulted on both sides. While the Pope excommunicated him as a heretic, and the King set a price upon his head as a rebel, the fanatics of the new religion denounced him as a godless man. Peter Dathenus, the unfrocked monk of Poperingen, shrieked out in his pulpit that the "Prince of Orange cared nothing either for God or for religion."*

The death of Requesens had offered the first opening through which the watchful Prince could hope to inflict a wound in the vital part of Spanish authority in the Netherlands. The languor of Philip and the procrastinating counsel of the dull Hopper unexpectedly widened the opening. On the 24th of March letters were written by his Majesty to the states-general, to the provincial estates, and to the courts of

* Brandt, Hist. der Ref., t. i. b. xi. 607.

justice, instructing them that, until further orders, they were all to obey the Council of State. The King was confident that all would do their utmost to assist that body in securing the holy Catholic Faith and the implicit obedience of the country to its sovereign. He would, in the meantime, occupy himself with the selection of a new Governor-General, who should be of his family and blood. This uncertain and perilous condition of things was watched with painful interest in neighbouring countries.

The fate of all nations was more or less involved in the development of the great religious contest now waging in the Netherlands. England and France watched each other's movements in the direction of the provinces with intense jealousy. The Protestant Queen was the natural ally of the struggling Reformers, but her despotic sentiments were averse to the fostering of rebellion against the Lord's anointed. The thrifty Queen looked with alarm at the prospect of large subsidies which would undoubtedly be demanded of her. The jealous Queen could as ill brook the presence of the French in the Netherlands as that of the Spaniards whom they were to expel. She therefore embarrassed, as usual, the operations of the Prince by a course of stale political coquetry. She wrote to him, on the 18th of March, soon after the news of the Grand Commander's death,* saying that she could not yet accept the offer which had been made to her, to take the provinces of Holland and Zealand under her safe keeping, to assume, as Countess, the sovereignty over them, and to protect the inhabitants against the alleged tyranny of the King of Spain. She was unwilling to do so until she had made every effort to reconcile them with that sovereign. Before the death of Requesens she had been intending to send him an envoy, proposing a truce, for the purpose of negotiation. This purpose she still retained. She should send commissioners to the Council of State and to the new Governor, when he should arrive. She should also send a special envoy to the King of

* Bor, ix. 667.

Spain. She doubted not that the King would take her advice, when he heard her speak in such straightforward language. In the meantime, she hoped that they would negotiate with no other powers.*

This was not very satisfactory. The Queen rejected the offers to herself, but begged that they might, by no means, be made to her rivals. The expressed intention of softening the heart of Philip by the use of straightforward language seemed but a sorry sarcasm. It was hardly worth while to wait long for so improbable a result. Thus much for England at that juncture. Not inimical, certainly; but over-cautious, ungenerous, teasing, and perplexing, was the policy of the maiden Queen. With regard to France, events there seemed to favor the hopes of Orange. On the 14th of May, the "Peace of *Monsieur*," the treaty by which so ample but so short-lived a triumph was achieved by the Huguenots, was signed at Paris.† Everything was conceded, but nothing was secured. Rights of worship, rights of office, political and civil, religious enfranchisement, were recovered, but not guaranteed.‡ It seemed scarcely possible that the King could be in earnest then, even if a Medicean Valois could ever be otherwise than treacherous. It was almost, certain, therefore, that a reaction would take place; but it is easier for us, three centuries after the event, to mark the precise moment of reaction, than it was for the most far-seeing contemporary to foretell how soon it would occur. In the meantime, it was the Prince's cue to make use of this sunshine while it lasted. Already, so soon as the union of 25th of April had been concluded between Holland and Zealand, he had forced the estates to open negotiations with France.§ The provinces, although desirous to confer sovereignty upon him, were indisposed to renounce their old allegiance to their King in order to place it at the disposal of

---

* Letter of Queen Elizabeth, March 16, 1576, in Bor, ix. 667.—Compare Groen v. Prinst., v. 332, 333.

† De Thou, t. vii. l. lxii. 418.

‡ De Thou, vii. 413–418.—Compare Groen v. Prinst., v. 349–351.

§ Resol. v. Holl., 64, 65. Groen v. Prinst., v. 341.

a foreigner. Nevertheless, a resolution, at the reiterated demands of Orange, was passed by the estates, to proceed to the change of master, and, for that purpose, to treat with the King of France, his brother, or any other foreign potentate, who would receive these provinces of Holland and Zealand under his government and protection.* Negotiations were accordingly opened with the Duke of Anjou, the *dilettante* leader of the Huguenots at that remarkable juncture. It was a pity that no better champion could be looked for among the anointed of the earth than the false, fickle, foolish Alençon, whose career, everywhere contemptible, was nowhere so flagitious as in the Netherlands. By the fourteenth article of the Peace of Paris, the Prince was reinstated and secured in his principality of Orange, and his other possessions in France.† The best feeling, for the time being, was manifested between the French court and the Reformation.‡

Thus much for England and France. As for Germany, the prospects of the Netherlands were not flattering. The Reforming spirit had grown languid, from various causes. The self-seeking motives of many Protestant princes had disgusted the nobles. Was that the object of the bloody wars of religion, that a few potentates should be enabled to enrich themselves by confiscating the broad lands and accumulated treasures of the Church? Had the creed of Luther been embraced only for such unworthy ends? These suspicions chilled the ardor of thousands, particularly among the greater ones of the land. Moreover, the discord among the Reformers themselves waxed daily, and became more and more mischievous. Neither the people nor their leaders could learn that, not a new doctrine, but a wise toleration for all Christian doctrines was wanted. Of new doctrines there was no lack. Lutherans, Calvinists, Flaccianists, Majorists, Adiaphorists,

* Resol. v. Holl., 64, 65. Groen v. Prinst., v. 341.

† Bor, ix. 684.

‡ The Edict, or Peace of Paris, in sixty-three articles, is published at length, by Bor, ix. 683–690.—Comparé Groen v. Prinst., v. 349–351. De Thou, t. v. l. vii. 413–418.

Brantianists, Ubiquitists, swarmed and contended pell-mell.* In this there would have been small harm, if the Reformers had known what reformation meant. But they could not invent or imagine toleration. All claimed the privilege of persecuting. There were sagacious and honest men among the great ones of the country, but they were but few. Wise William of Hesse strove hard to effect a *concordia* among the jarring sects; Count John of Nassau, though a passionate Calvinist, did no less; while the Elector of Saxony, on the other hand, raging and roaring like a bull of Bashan, was for sacrificing the interest of millions on the altar of his personal spite. Cursed was his tribe if he forgave the Prince. He had done what he could at the Diet of Ratisbon to exclude all Calvinists from a participation in the religious peace of Germany,† and he redoubled his efforts to prevent the extension of any benefits to the Calvinists of the Netherlands. These determinations had remained constant and intense.

On the whole, the political appearance of Germany was as menacing as that of France seemed for a time favorable to the schemes of Orange. The quarrels of the princes, and the daily widening schism between Lutherans and Calvinists, seemed to bode little good to the cause of religious freedom. The potentates were perplexed and at variance, the nobles lukewarm and discontented. Among the people, although subdivided into hostile factions, there was more life. Here, at least, were heartiness of love and hate, enthusiastic conviction, earnestness and agitation. "The true religion," wrote Count John, "is spreading daily among the common men. Among the powerful, who think themselves highly learned, and who sit in roses, it grows, alas, little. Here and there a Nicodemus or two may be found, but things will hardly go better here than in France or the Netherlands."‡

Thus, then, stood affairs in the neighbouring countries. The

* See in particular a letter of Count John of Nassau to the Prince of Orange, dated Dillemberg, May 9, 1576.—Archives de la Maison d'Orange, v. 349–358

† Groen v. Prinst., Archives, etc., v. 229, 230.

‡ Archives, etc., de la Maison d'Orange, v. 346, 347.

prospect was black in Germany, more encouraging in France, dubious, or worse, in England. More work, more anxiety, more desperate struggles than ever, devolved upon the Prince. Secretary Brunynck wrote that his illustrious chief was tolerably well in health, but so loaded with affairs, sorrows, and travails, that, from morning till night, he had scarcely leisure to breathe.* Besides his multitudinous correspondence with the public bodies, whose labors he habitually directed ; with the various estates of the provinces, which he was gradually moulding into an organised and general resistance to the Spanish power ; with public envoys and with secret agents to foreign cabinets, all of whom received their instructions from him alone ; with individuals of eminence and influence, whom he was eloquently urging to abandon their hostile position to their fatherland, and to assist him in the great work which he was doing ; besides these numerous avocations, he was actively and anxiously engaged during the spring of 1576, with the attempt to relieve the city of Zierickzee.†

That important place, the capital of Schouwen, and the key to half Zealand, had remained closely invested since the memorable expedition to Duiveland. The Prince had passed much of his time in the neighbourhood, during the month of May, in order to attend personally to the contemplated relief, and to correspond daily with the beleaguered garrison.‡ At last, on the 25th of May, a vigorous effort was made to throw in succor by sea. The brave Admiral Boisot, hero of the memorable relief of Leyden, had charge of the expedition. Mondragon had surrounded the shallow harbor with hulks and chains, and with a loose submerged dyke of piles and rubbish. Against this obstacle Boisot drove his ship, the 'Red Lion,' with his customary audacity, but did not succeed in cutting it through. His vessel, the largest of the fleet, became entangled : he was, at the same time, attacked

* Archives, etc., de la Maison d'Orange, v. 365.

† Bor, ix. 667, sqq. Meteren, v. 102, 103.

‡ Archives, etc., de la Maison d'Orange, v. 358, 359.

from a distance by the besiegers. The tide ebbed and left his ship aground, while the other vessels had been beaten back by the enemy. Night approached, and there was no possibility of accomplishing the enterprise. His ship was hopelessly stranded. With the morning's sun his captivity was certain. Rather than fall into the hands of his enemy, he sprang into the sea, followed by three hundred of his companions, some of whom were fortunate enough to effect their escape. The gallant Admiral swam a long time, sustained by a broken spar. Night and darkness came on before assistance could be rendered, and he perished.* Thus died Louis Boisot, one of the most enterprising of the early champions of Netherland freedom—one of the bravest precursors of that race of heroes, the commanders of the Holland navy. The Prince deplored his loss deeply as that of a "valiant gentleman, and one well affectioned to the common cause."† His brother, Charles Boisot, as will be remembered, had perished by treachery at the first landing of the Spanish troops, after their perilous passage from Duiveland. Thus both the brethren had laid down their lives for their country, on this its outer barrier, and in the hour of its utmost need. The fall of the beleaguered town could no longer be deferred. The Spaniards were, at last, to receive the prize of that romantic valor which had led them across the bottom of the sea to attack the city. Nearly nine months had, however, elapsed since that achievement; and the Grand Commander, by whose orders it had been undertaken, had been four months in his grave. He was permitted to see neither the long-delayed success which crowned the enterprise, nor the procession of disasters and crimes which were to mark it as a most fatal success.

On the 21st of June, 1576, Zierickzee, instructed by the

* Bor, ix. 678. Hoofd, x. 440. Archives de la Maison d'Orange, v. 364–368. Meteren, v. 102.—The last historian erroneously gives the 12th of June instead of the 25th of May as the date of the unfortunate adventure. Cabrera, xi. 846, who states the loss of the Orangists at eight hundred and upwards.

† Archives, etc. v. 367.

Prince of Orange to accept honorable terms, if offered, agreed to surrender. Mondragon, whose soldiers were in a state of suffering, and ready to break out in mutiny, was but too happy to grant an honorable capitulation. The garrison were allowed to go out with their arms and personal baggage. The citizens were permitted to retain or resume their privileges and charters, on payment of two hundred thousand guldens. Of sacking and burning there was, on this occasion, fortunately, no question; but the first half of the commutation money was to be paid in cash. There was but little money in the impoverished little town, but mint-masters were appointed by the magistrates to take their seats at once in the Hotel de Ville. The citizens brought their spoons and silver dishes, one after another, which were melted and coined into dollars and half-dollars, until the payment was satisfactorily adjusted. Thus fell Zierickzee, to the deep regret of the Prince. "Had we received the least succor in the world from any side," he wrote, "the poor city should never have fallen. I could get nothing from France or England, with all my efforts. Nevertheless, we do not lose courage, but hope that, although abandoned by all the world, the Lord God will extend His right hand over us."*

The enemies were not destined to go farther. From their own hand now came the blow which was to expel them from the soil which they had so long polluted. No sooner was Zierickzee captured than a mutiny broke forth among several companies of Spaniards and Walloons, belonging to the army in Schouwen.† A large number of the most influential officers had gone to Brussels, to make arrangements, if possible, for the payment of the troops. In their absence there was more scope for the arguments of the leading

* Bor, ix. 681. Hoofd, x. 440, 441. Meteren, v. 102, 103. Archives de la Maison d'Orange, v. 372, 373. Letter of 16th July, 1576, in Archives de la Maison d'Orange, v. 379–381.

† Bor, ix. 681, 692, sqq. Meteren, vi. 106. Hoofd, x. 443. Groen v. Prinst. v. 381, sqq.

mutineers ;—arguments assuredly, not entirely destitute of justice or logical precision. If ever laborers were worthy of their hire, certainly it was the Spanish soldiery. Had they not done the work of demons for nine years long ? Could Philip or Alva have found in the wide world men to execute their decrees with more unhesitating docility, with more sympathizing eagerness ? What obstacle had ever given them pause in their career of duty ? What element had they not braved ? Had not they fought within the bowels of the earth, beneath the depths of the sea, within blazing cities, and upon fields of ice ? Where was the work which had been too dark and bloody for their performance ? Had they not slaughtered unarmed human beings by townfuls, at the word of command ? Had they not eaten the flesh, and drank the hearts' blood of their enemies ? Had they not stained the house of God with wholesale massacre ? What altar and what hearthstone had they not profaned ? What fatigue, what danger, what crime, had ever checked them for a moment ? And for all this obedience, labor, and bloodshed, were they not even to be paid such wages as the commonest clown, who only tore the earth at home, received ? Did Philip believe that a few thousand Spaniards were to execute his sentence of death against three millions of Netherlanders, and be cheated of their pay at last ?

It was in vain that arguments and expostulations were addressed to soldiers who were suffering from want, and maddened by injustice. They determined to take their cause into their own hand, as they had often done before. By the 15th of July, the mutiny was general on the isle of Schouwen.* Promises were freely offered, both of pay and pardon ; appeals were made to their old sense of honor and loyalty ; but they had had enough of promises, of honor, and of work. What they wanted now were shoes and jerkins, bread and meat, and money. Money they would have, and that at once. The

* Hoofd, x. 443, sqq. Bor, ix. 692. Meteren, vi. 106. Mendoza, xv. 298, sqq. Cabrera, xi. 848, sqq.

King of Spain was their debtor. The Netherlands belonged to the King of Spain. They would therefore levy on the Netherlands for payment of their debt. Certainly this was a logical deduction. They knew by experience that this process had heretofore excited more indignation in the minds of the Netherland people than in that of their master. Moreover, at this juncture, they cared little for their sovereign's displeasure, and not at all for that of the Netherlanders. By the middle of July, then, the mutineers, now entirely beyond control, held their officers imprisoned within their quarters at Zierickzee. They even surrounded the house of Mondragon, who had so often led them to victory, calling upon him with threats and taunts to furnish them with money.* The veteran, roused to fury by their insubordination and their taunts, sprang from his house into the midst of the throng. Baring his breast before them, he fiercely invited and dared their utmost violence. Of his life-blood, he told them bitterly, he was no niggard, and it was at their disposal. His wealth, had he possessed any, would have been equally theirs.† Shamed into temporary respect, but not turned from their purpose by the choler of their chief, they left him to himself. Soon afterwards, having swept Schouwen island bare of every thing which could be consumed, the mutineers swarmed out of Zealand into Brabant, devouring as they went.‡

It was their purpose to hover for a time in the neighbourhood of the capital, and either to force the Council of State to pay them their long arrears, or else to seize and sack the richest city upon which they could lay their hands. The compact, disciplined mass, rolled hither and thither, with uncertainty of purpose, but with the same military precision of movement which had always characterized these remarkable mutinies. It gathered strength daily. The citizens of Brussels contemplated with dismay the eccentric

* Hoofd, x. 443, 444.

† Ibid., x. 444.—Compare Cabrera, xi. 848.

‡ Bor, ix. 692. Cabrera, xi. 848, sqq. Mendoza, xv. 300.

and threatening apparition. They knew that rapine, murder, and all the worst evils which man can inflict on his brethren were pent within it, and would soon descend. Yet, even with all their past experience, did they not foresee the depth of woe which was really impending. The mutineers had discarded such of their officers as they could not compel to obedience, and had, as usual, chosen their Eletto. Many straggling companies joined them as they swept to and fro. They came to Herenthals, where they were met by Count Mansfeld, who was deputed by the Council of State to treat with them, to appeal to them, to pardon them, to offer them everything but money. It may be supposed that the success of the commander-in-chief was no better than that of Mondragon and his subalterns. They laughed him to scorn when he reminded them how their conduct was tarnishing the glory which they had acquired by nine years of heroism. They answered with their former cynicism, that glory could be put neither into pocket nor stomach. They had no use for it ; they had more than enough of it. Give them money, or give them a city ;* these were their last terms.

Sorrowfully and bodingly Mansfeld withdrew to consult again with the State Council. The mutineers then made a demonstration upon Mechlin, but that city having fortunately strengthened its garrison, was allowed to escape. They then hovered for a time outside the walls of Brussels. At Grimsberg, where they paused for a short period, they held a parley with Captain Montesdocca, whom they received with fair words and specious pretences. He returned to Brussels with the favourable tidings, and the mutineers swarmed off to Assche. Thither Montesdocca was again despatched, with the expectation that he would be able to bring them to terms, but they drove him off with jeers and threats, finding that he brought neither money nor the mortgage of a populous city. The next day, after a feint or two in a different direction, they made a sudden swoop

* Bor, ix. 692. Meteren, vi. 106. Hoofd, x. 444. Mendoza, xv. 300

upon Alost, in Flanders. Here they had at last made their choice, and the town was carried by storm. All the inhabitants who opposed them were butchered, and the mutiny, at last established in a capital, was able to treat with the State Council upon equal terms. They were now between two and three thousand strong, disciplined, veteran troops, posted in a strong and wealthy city. One hundred parishes belonged to the jurisdiction of Alost, all of which were immediately laid under contribution.*

The excitement was now intense in Brussels. Anxiety and alarm had given place to rage, and the whole population rose in arms to defend the capital, which was felt to be in imminent danger. This spontaneous courage of the burghers prevented the catastrophe, which was reserved for a sister city. Meantime, the indignation and horror excited by the mutiny were so universal that the Council of State could not withstand the pressure. Even the women and children demanded daily in the streets that the rebel soldiers should be declared outlaws. On the 26th of July, accordingly, the King of Spain was made to pronounce his Spaniards traitors and murderers. All men were enjoined to slay one or all of them, wherever they should be found; to refuse them bread, water, and fire, and to assemble at sound of bell, in every city, whenever the magistrates should order an assault upon them.† A still more stringent edict was issued on the 2nd of August,‡ and so eagerly had these degrees been expected, that they were published throughout Flanders and Brabant almost as soon as issued. Hitherto the leading officers of the Spanish army had kept aloof from the insurgents, and frowned upon their proceedings. The Spanish member of the State Council, Jerome de Roda, had joined without opposition in the edict. As, however, the mutiny gathered strength on the outside, the indignation waxed daily within the capital. The citizens

---

* Bor, ix. 693. Meteren, vi. 106. Bentivoglio, ix. 173. Hoofd, x. 445.

† See the Edict, in Bor, ix. 693.

‡ Hoofd, x. 445.

of Brussels, one and all, stood to their arms. Not a man could enter or leave without their permission. The Spaniards who were in the town, whether soldiers or merchants, were regarded with suspicion and abhorrence. The leading Spanish officers, Romero, Montesdocca, Verdugo, and others, who had attempted to quell the mutiny, had been driven off with threats and curses, their soldiers defying them and brandishing their swords in their very faces. On the other hand, they were looked upon with ill-will by the Netherlanders. The most prominent Spanish personages in Brussels were kept in a state of half-imprisonment.* Romero, Roda, Verdugo, were believed to favor at heart the cause of their rebellious troops, and the burghers of Brabant had come to consider all the King's army in a state of rebellion. Believing the State Council powerless to protect them from the impending storm, they regarded that body with little respect, keeping it, as it were, in durance, while the Spaniards were afraid to walk the streets of Brussels for fear of being murdered. A retainer of Roda, who had ventured to defend the character and conduct of his master before a number of excited citizens, was slain on the spot.†

In Antwerp, Champagny, brother of Granvelle, and governor of the city, was disposed to cultivate friendly relations with the Prince of Orange. Champagny hated the Spaniards, and the hatred seemed to establish enough of sympathy between himself and the liberal party to authorize confidence in him. The Prince dealt with him, but regarded him warily.‡ Fifteen companies of German troops, under Colonel Altaemst, were suspected of a strong inclination to join the mutiny. They were withdrawn from Antwerp, and in their room came Count Oberstein, with his regiment, who swore to admit no suspicious person inside the gates, and in all things to obey the orders of Champagny.§ In the citadel, however,

* Bor, ix. 692, 693. Cabrera, xi. 849. Hoofd, x. 445.

† Bor, ix. 693. Meteren, vi. 106.

‡ Archives de la Maison d'Orange, v. 487, 488. Cabrera, xi. 863.—"Pero el Champaigne estaba convenido con los Estados y con le Principe de Orange su grande amigo.

§ Bor, ix. 694. Hoofd, x. 447.

matters were very threatening. Sancho d'Avila, the governor, although he had not openly joined the revolt, treated the edict of outlawry against the rebellious soldiery with derision. He refused to publish a decree which he proclaimed infamous, and which had been extorted, in his opinion, from an impotent and trembling council.* Even Champagny had not desired or dared to publish the edict within the city. The reasons alleged were his fears of irritating and alarming the foreign merchants, whose position was so critical and friendship so important at that moment.† On the other hand, it was loudly and joyfully published in most other towns of Flanders and Brabant. In Brussels there were two parties, one holding the decree too audacious for his Majesty to pardon ; the other clamoring for its instantaneous fulfilment. By far the larger and more influential portion of the population favored the measure, and wished the sentence of outlawry and extermination to be extended at once against all Spaniards and other foreigners in the service of the King. It seemed imprudent to wait until all the regiments had formally accepted the mutiny, and concentrated themselves into a single body.‡

At this juncture, on the last day of July, the Marquis of Havré, brother to the Duke of Aerschot, arrived out of Spain.§ He was charged by the King with conciliatory but unmeaning phrases to the estates. The occasion was not a happy one. There never was a time when direct and vigorous action had been more necessary. It was probably the King's desire then, as much as it ever had been his desire at all, to make up the quarrel with his provinces. He had been wearied with the policy which Alva had enforced, and for which he endeavoured at that period to make the Duke appear responsible. The barren clemency which the Grand Commander had been instructed to affect, had deceived but few persons, and had produced but small results. The King was, perhaps, really

---

* Mendoza, xv. 301. Cabrera, xi. 849.

† Bor, ix. 694.

‡ Ibid., 694, sqq. Hoofd, x. 447, sqq.

§ Bor, ix. 704.

inclined at this juncture to exercise clemency—that is to say, he was willing to pardon his people for having contended for their rights, provided they were now willing to resign them for ever. So the Catholic religion and his own authority were exclusively and inviolably secured, he was willing to receive his disobedient provinces into favor. To accomplish this end, however, he had still no more fortunate conception than to take the advice of Hopper. A soothing procrastination was the anodyne selected for the bitter pangs of the body politic—a vague expression of royal benignity the styptic to be applied to its mortal wounds. An interval of hesitation was to bridge over the chasm between the provinces and their distant metropolis. "The Marquis of Havré has been sent," said the King, "that he may expressly witness to you of our good intentions, and of our desire, with the grace of God, to bring about a pacification."* Alas, it was well known whence those pavements of good intentions had been taken, and whither they would lead. They were not the material for a substantial road to reconciliation. "His Majesty," said the Marquis, on delivering his report to the State Council, "has long been pondering over all things necessary to the peace of the land. His Majesty, like a very gracious and bountiful Prince, has ever been disposed, in times past, to treat these, his subjects, by the best and sweetest means."† There being, however, room for an opinion that so bountiful a prince might have discovered sweeter means, by all this pondering, than to burn and gibbet his subjects by thousands, it was thought proper to insinuate that his orders had been hitherto misunderstood. Alva and Requesens had been unfaithful agents, who did not know their business, but it was to be set right in future. "As the good-will and meaning of his Majesty has by no means been followed," continued the envoy, "his Majesty has determined to send Councillor Hopper, keeper of the privy seal, and myself, hitherwards, to execute the resolutions of his Majesty."‡ Two such

* See the letter, in Bor, ix. 704.

† Report of Marquis of Havré, in Bor, ix. 704.

‡ Ibid.

personages as poor, plodding, confused, time-serving Hopper, and flighty, talkative* Havré, whom even Requesens despised, and whom Don John, while shortly afterwards *recommending him for a state councillor*, characterized to Philip as "a very great scoundrel,"† would hardly be able, even if royally empowered, to undo the work of two preceding administrations. Moreover, Councillor Hopper, on further thoughts, was not despatched at all to the Netherlands.

The provinces were, however, assured by the King's letters to the Brabant estates, to the State Council, and other public bodies, as well as by the report of the Marquis, that efficacious remedies were preparing in Madrid. The people were only to wait patiently till they should arrive.‡ The public had heard before of these nostrums, made up by the royal prescriptions in Spain ; and were not likely to accept them as a panacea for their present complicated disorders. Never, in truth, had conventional commonplace been applied more unseasonably. Here was a general military mutiny flaming in the very centre of the land. Here had the intense hatred of race, which for years had been gnawing at the heart of the country, at last broken out into most malignant manifestation. Here was nearly the whole native population of every province, from grand seigneur to plebeian, from Catholic prelate to Anabaptist artisan, exasperated alike by the excesses of six thousand foreign brigands, and united by a common hatred, into a band of brethren. Here was a State Council too feeble to exercise the authority which it had arrogated, trembling between the wrath of its sovereign, the menacing cries of the Brussels burghers, and the wild threats of the rebellious army, and held virtually captive in the capital which it was supposed to govern.

Certainly, the confirmation of the Council in its authority,

---

* "Loquillo y insubstancial."—Letter of Requesens to Philip, cited by Gachard, Corresp. Guillaume le Tacit., iii. 130, n. 1.

† "Muy grandissimo vellacho."—Letter of Don John to Philip, cited by Gachard, ubi sup.

‡ Report of Marq. Havré, etc., Bor, ix. 705.

for an indefinite, even if for a brief period, was a most unlucky step at this juncture. There were two parties in the provinces, but one was far the most powerful upon the great point of the Spanish soldiery. A vast majority were in favor of a declaration of outlawry against the whole army, and it was thought desirable to improve the opportunity by getting rid of them altogether. If the people could rise *en masse*, now that the royal government was in abeyance, and, as it were, in the nation's hands, the incubus might be cast off for ever. If any of the Spanish officers had been sincere in their efforts to arrest the mutiny, the sincerity was not believed. If any of the foreign regiments of the King appeared to hesitate at joining the Alost crew, the hesitation was felt to be temporary. Meantime, the important German regiments of Fugger, Fronsberger, and Polwiller, with their colonels and other officers, had openly joined the rebellion,* while there was no doubt of the sentiments of Sancho d'Avila and the troops under his command.† Thus there were two great rallying-places for the sedition, and the most important fortress of the country, the key which unlocked the richest city in the world, was in the hands of the mutineers. The commercial capital of Europe, filled to the brim with accumulated treasures, and with the merchandize of every clime, lay at the feet of this desperate band of brigands. The horrible result was but too soon to be made manifest.

Meantime, in Brussels, the few Spaniards trembled for their lives. The few officers shut up there were in imminent danger. "As the Devil does not cease to do his work," wrote Colonel Verdugo,‡ "he has put it into the heads of the Brabanters to rebel, *taking for a pretext* the mutiny of the Spaniards. The Brussels men have handled their weapons so well *against those who were placed there to protect them*, that they have begun to kill the Spaniards, threatening likewise the

* Bor, ix. 711, 712. Hoofd, x. 448.

† Meteren, vi. 107. Mendoza, xv. 303, sqq. Cabrera, xi. 849, sqq.

‡ This letter of Verdugo to his Lieutenant De la Margella is published by Bor, ix. 702, and by Groen, v. Prinsterer, Archives, v. 387–389.

Council of State. Such is their insolence, that they care no more for these great lords than for so many varlets." The writer, who had taken refuge, together with Jerome de Roda and other Spaniards, or "Hispaniolized" persons, in Antwerp citadel, proceeded to sketch the preparations which were going on in Brussels, and the counter measures which were making progress in Antwerp. "The states," he wrote, "are enrolling troops, saying 'tis to put down the mutiny; but I assure you 'tis to attack the army indiscriminately. To prevent such a villanous undertaking, *troops of all nations are assembling here*, in order to march straight upon Brussels, there to enforce everything which my lords of the State Council shall ordain." Events were obviously hastening to a crisis—an explosion, before long, was inevitable. "I wish I had my horses here," continued the Colonel, "and must beg you to send them. I see a black cloud hanging over our heads. I fear that the Brabantines will play the beasts so much, that they will have all the soldiery at their throats."*

Jerome de Roda had been fortunate enough to make his escape out of Brussels,† and now claimed to be sole Governor of the Netherlands, as the only remaining representative of the State Council. His colleagues were in durance at the capital. Their authority was derided. Although not yet actually imprisoned, they were in reality bound hand and foot, and compelled to take their orders either from the Brabant estates or from the burghers of Brussels. It was not an illogical proceeding, therefore, that Roda, under the shadow of the Antwerp citadel, should set up his own person as all that remained of the outraged majesty of Spain. Till the new Governor, Don Juan, should arrive, whose appointment the King had already communicated to the government, and who might be expected in the Netherlands before the close of the autumn, the solitary councillor claimed to embody the whole Council.‡ He caused a new seal to be struck—a pro-

---

* Letter of Verdugo.

† Bor, ix. 705. Hoofd, x. 449.

‡ Bor, Hoofd, ubi sup.

ceeding very unreasonably charged as forgery by the provincials—and forthwith began to thunder forth proclamations and counter-proclamations in the King's name and under the royal seal.* It is difficult to see any technical crime or mistake in such a course. As a Spaniard, and a representative of his Majesty, he could hardly be expected to take any other view of his duty. At any rate, being called upon to choose between rebellious Netherlanders and mutinous Spaniards, he was not long in making up his mind.

By the beginning of September the mutiny was general. All the Spanish army, from general to pioneer, were united. The most important German troops had taken side with them. Sancho d'Avila held the citadel of Antwerp, vowing vengeance, and holding open communication with the soldiers at Alost.† The Council of State remonstrated with him for his disloyalty. He replied by referring to his long years of service, and by reproving them for affecting an authority which their imprisonment rendered ridiculous.‡ The Spaniards were securely established. The various citadels which had been built by Charles and Philip to curb the country now effectually did their work. With the castles of Antwerp, Valenciennes, Ghent, Utrecht, Culemburg, Viane, Alost, in the hands of six thousand veteran Spaniards, the country seemed chained in every limb. The foreigner's foot was on its neck. Brussels was almost the only considerable town out of Holland and Zealand which was even temporarily safe. The important city of Maestricht was held by a Spanish garrison, while other capital towns and stations were in the power of the Walloon and German mutineers.§ The depredations committed in the villages, the open country, and the cities were incessant—the Spaniards treating every Netherlander as their foe. Gentleman and peasant, Protestant and Catholic, priest and layman, all were plundered, maltreated, outraged. The

---

* Bor, ix. 712. Hoofd, x. 449.

† Mendoza, xv. 301, sqq. Cabrera, xi. 864, sqq. ‡ Mendoza, ubi sup.

§ Bor, ix. 715. Mendoza, xv. 303.

indignation became daily more general and more intense.* There were frequent skirmishes between the soldiery and promiscuous bands of peasants, citizens, and students; conflicts in which the Spaniards were invariably victorious. What could such half-armed and wholly untrained partisans effect against the bravest and most experienced troops in the whole world? Such results only increased the general exasperation, while they impressed upon the whole people the necessity of some great and general effort to throw off the incubus.

---

* Meteren, vi. 107. Hoofd, x. 450–453.

CHAPTER V.

Religious and political sympathies and antipathies in the seventeen provinces—Unanimous hatred for the foreign soldiery—Use made by the Prince of the mutiny — His correspondence — Necessity of Union enforced — A congress from nearly all the provinces meets at Ghent—Skirmishes between the foreign troops and partisan bands—Slaughter at Tisnacq—Suspicions entertained of the State-Council—Arrest of the State-Council—Siege of Ghent citadel — Assistance sent by Orange — Maestricht lost and regained — Wealthy and perilous condition of Antwerp—Preparations of the mutineers under the secret superintendence of Avila—Stupidity of Oberstein—Duplicity of Don Sancho—Reinforcements of Walloons under Havré, Egmont, and others, sent to Antwerp—Governor Champagny's preparations for the expected assault of the mutineers—Insubordination, incapacity, and negligence of all but him—Concentration of all the mutineers from different points, in the citadel—The attack—the panic—the flight—the massacre—the fire—the sack—and other details of the "Spanish Fury"—Statistics of murder and robbery—Letter of Orange to the states-general—Surrender of Ghent citadel—Conclusion of the "Ghent Pacification"—The treaty characterized—Forms of ratification—Fall of Zierickzee and recovery of Zealand.

MEANTIME, the Prince of Orange sat at Middelburg,* watching the storm. The position of Holland and Zealand with regard to the other fifteen provinces was distinctly characterized. Upon certain points there was an absolute sympathy, while upon others there was a grave and almost fatal difference. It was the task of the Prince to deepen the sympathy, to extinguish the difference.

In Holland and Zealand, there was a warm and nearly uni-

* Bor, ix. 694, sqq.

versal adhesion to the Reformed religion, a passionate attachment to the ancient political liberties. The Prince, although an earnest Calvinist himself, did all in his power to check the growing spirit of intolerance toward the old religion, omitted no opportunity of strengthening the attachment which the people justly felt for their liberal institutions.

On the other hand, in most of the other provinces, the Catholic religion had been regaining its ascendency. Even in 1574, the estates assembled at Brussels declared to Requesens "that they would rather die the death than see any change in their religion."* That feeling had rather increased than diminished. Although there was a strong party attached to the new faith, there was perhaps a larger, certainly a more influential body, which regarded the ancient Church with absolute fidelity. Owing partly to the persecution which had, in the course of years, banished so many thousands of families from the soil, partly to the coercion, which was more stringent in the immediate presence of the Crown's representative, partly to the stronger infusion of the Celtic element, which from the earliest ages had always been so keenly alive to the more sensuous and splendid manifestations of the devotional principle—owing to these and many other causes, the old religion, despite of all the outrages which had been committed in its name, still numbered a host of zealous adherents in the fifteen provinces. Attempts against its sanctity were regarded with jealous eyes. It was believed, and with reason, that there was a disposition on the part of the Reformers to destroy it root and branch. It was suspected that the same enginery of persecution would be employed in its extirpation, should the opposite party gain the supremacy, which the Papists had so long employed against the converts to the new religion.

As to political convictions, the fifteen provinces differed much less from their two sisters. There was a strong attachment to their old constitutions; a general inclination to

* "Datse liever willen sterven de dood, dan te sien eenige veranderinge in de Religie," etc.—Remonstrance, etc., in Bor, viii. 518b.

make use of the present crisis to effect their restoration. At the same time, it had not come to be the general conviction, as in Holland and Zealand, that the maintenance of those liberties was incompatible with the continuance of Philip's authority. There was, moreover, a strong aristocratic faction which was by no means disposed to take a liberal view of government in general, and regarded with apprehension the simultaneous advance of heretical notions both in church and state. Still there were, on the whole, the elements of a controlling constitutional party throughout the fifteen provinces. The great bond of sympathy, however, between all the seventeen was their common hatred to the foreign soldiery. Upon this deeply imbedded, immovable fulcrum of an ancient national hatred, the sudden mutiny of the whole Spanish army served as a lever of incalculable power. The Prince seized it as from the hand of God. Thus armed, he proposed to himself the task of upturning the mass of oppression under which the old liberties of the country had so long been crushed. To effect this object, adroitness was as requisite as courage. Expulsion of the foreign soldiery, union of the seventeen provinces, a representative constitution, according to the old charters, by the states-general, under an hereditary chief, a large religious toleration, suppression of all inquisition into men's consciences—these were the great objects to which the Prince now devoted himself with renewed energy.

To bring about a general organization and a general union, much delicacy of handling was necessary. The sentiment of extreme Catholicism and Monarchism was not to be suddenly scared into opposition. The Prince, therefore, in all his addresses and documents was careful to disclaim any intention of disturbing the established religion, or of making any rash political changes. "Let no man think," said he, to the authorities of Brabant, "that, against the will of the estates, we desire to bring about any change in religion. Let no one suspect us capable of prejudicing the rights of any man. We have long since taken up arms to maintain a legal and constitutional freedom, founded upon law. God forbid that we should now attempt to introduce novelties, by which the face of liberty should be defiled."*

In a brief and very spirited letter to Count Lalain, a Catholic and a loyalist, but a friend of his country and fervent hater of foreign oppression, he thus appealed to his sense of chivalry and justice: "Although the honorable house from which you spring," he said, "and the virtue and courage of your ancestors have always impressed me with the conviction that you would follow in their footsteps, yet am I glad to have received proofs that my anticipations were correct. I cannot help, therefore, entreating you to maintain the same high heart, and to accomplish that which you have so worthily begun. Be not deluded by false masks, mumming faces, and borrowed titles, which people assume for their own profit, persuading others that the King's service consists in the destruction of his subjects."†

While thus careful to offend no man's religious convictions, to startle no man's loyalty, he made skillful use of the general indignation felt at the atrocities of the mutinous army. This chord he struck boldly, powerfully, passionately, for he felt sure of the depth and strength of its vibrations. In his address to the estates of Gelderland,‡ he used vigorous language, inflaming and directing to a practical purpose the just wrath which was felt in that, as in every other province. "I write to warn you," he said, "to seize this present opportunity. Shake from your necks the yoke of the godless Spanish tyranny, join yourselves at once to the lovers of the fatherland, to the defenders of freedom. According to the example of your own ancestors and ours, redeem for the country its ancient laws, traditions, and privileges. Permit no longer, to your shame and ours, a band of Spanish landloupers and other foreigners, together with three or four self-seeking enemies of their own land, to keep their feet upon our necks. Let them no longer, in the very wantonness of tyranny, drive

---

* Letter to States of Brabant, in Bor, ix. 695.

† The letter to Lalain is published by Bor, ix. 696.

‡ Address to the Estates of Gelderland, apud Bor, ix. 702.

us about like a herd of cattle—like a gang of well-tamed slaves."

Thus, day after day, in almost countless addresses to public bodies and private individuals, he made use of the crisis to pile fresh fuel upon the flames. At the same time, while thus fanning the general indignation, he had the adroitness to point out that the people had already committed themselves. He represented to them that the edict, by which they had denounced his Majesty's veterans as outlaws, and had devoted them to the indiscriminate destruction which such brigands deserved, was likely to prove an unpardonable crime in the eyes of majesty. In short, they had entered the torrent. If they would avoid being dashed over the precipice, they must struggle manfully with the mad waves of civil war into which they had plunged. "I beg you, with all affection," he said to the states of Brabant,* "to consider the danger in which you have placed yourselves. You have to deal with the proudest and most overbearing race in the world. For these qualities they are hated by all other nations. They are even hateful to themselves. 'Tis a race which seeks to domineer wheresoever it comes. It particularly declares its intention to crush and to tyrannize you, my masters, and all the land. They have conquered you already, as they boast, for the crime of lese-majesty has placed you at their mercy. I tell you that your last act, by which you have declared this army to be rebels, is decisive. You have armed and excited the whole people against them, even to the peasants and the peasants' children, and the insults and injuries thus received, however richly deserved and dearly avenged, are all set down to your account. Therefore, 'tis necessary for you to decide now, whether to be utterly ruined, yourselves and your children, or to continue firmly the work which you have begun boldly, and rather to die a hundred thousand deaths than to make a treaty with them, which can only end in your ruin. Be assured that the measure dealt to you will be ignominy as

* In Bor, ix. 694–696.

well as destruction. Let not your leaders expect the honorable scaffolds of Counts Egmont and Horn. The whipping-post and then the gibbet will be their certain fate."*

Having by this and similar language, upon various occasions, sought to impress upon his countrymen the gravity of the position, he led them to seek the remedy in audacity and in union. He familiarized them with his theory, that the legal, historical government of the provinces belonged to the states-general, to a congress of nobles, clergy, and commons, appointed from each of the seventeen provinces.† He maintained, with reason, that the government of the Netherlands was a representative constitutional government, under the hereditary authority of the King.‡ To recover this constitution, to lift up these down-trodden rights, he set before them most vividly the necessity of union. "'Tis impossible," he said, "that a chariot should move evenly having its wheels unequally proportioned; and so must a confederation be broken to pieces, if there be not an equal obligation on all to tend to a common purpose."§ Union, close, fraternal, such as became provinces of a common origin and with similar laws, could alone save them from their fate. Union against a common tyrant to save a common fatherland. Union, by which differences of opinion should be tolerated, in order that a million of hearts should beat for a common purpose, a million hands work out, invincibly, a common salvation. "'Tis hardly necessary," he said,‖ "to use many words in recommendation of union. Disunion has been the cause of all our woes. There is no remedy, no hope, save in the bonds of friendship. Let all particular disagreements be left to the decision of the states-general, in order that with one heart and one will we may seek the disenthralment of the fatherland from the tyranny of strangers."

* "Aen de galge of kake," etc. Address to the Estates of Brabant, etc., Bor, ubi sup.

† Missive of Prince of Orange to States-general, in Bor, x. 747–749.

‡ Missive, etc., Bor, ubi sup.

§ Gachard, Correspondance de Guillaume le Tacit., iii. 140–154.

‖ Address to Estates of Brabant, apud Bor, ix. 694–696.

The first step to a thorough union among all the provinces was the arrangement of a closer connection between the now isolated states of Holland and Zealand on the one side, and their fifteen sisters on the other. The Prince professed the readiness of those states which he might be said to represent in his single person, to draw as closely as possible the bonds of fellowship. It was almost superfluous for him to promise his own ready co-operation. "Nothing remains to us," said he, "but to discard all jealousy and distrust. Let us, with a firm resolution and a common accord, liberate these lands from the stranger. Hand to hand let us accomplish a just and general peace. As for myself, I present to you, with very good affection, my person and all which I possess, assuring you that I shall regard all my labors and pains in times which are past, well bestowed, if God now grant me grace to see the desired end. That this end will be reached, if you hold fast your resolution and take to heart the means which God presents to you, I feel to be absolutely certain."*

Such were the tenor and the motives of the documents which he scattered broadcast at this crisis. They were addressed to the estates of nearly every province. Those bodies were urgently implored to appoint deputies to a general congress, at which a close and formal union between Holland and Zealand with the other provinces might be effected. That important measure secured, a general effort might, at the same time, be made to expel the Spaniard from the soil. This done, the remaining matters could be disposed of by the assembly of the estates-general. His eloquence and energy were not without effect. In the course of the autumn, deputies were appointed from the greater number of the provinces, to confer with the representatives of Holland and Zealand, in a general congress.† The place appointed for the deliberations was the city of Ghent. Here, by the middle of October, a large number of delegates were already assembled.‡

Events were rapidly rolling together from every quarter, and

* Letter to Estates of Brabant, Bor, ix. 694–696.

† Bor, ix. 703, 718, 719.

‡ Ibid., ix. 719, sqq. Meteren, vi. 111.

accumulating to a crisis. A congress—a rebellious congress, as the King might deem it—was assembling at Ghent; the Spanish army, proscribed, lawless, and terrible, was strengthening itself daily for some dark and mysterious achievement; Don John of Austria, the King's natural brother, was expected from Spain to assume the government, which the State Council was too timid to wield and too loyal to resign, while, meantime, the whole population of the Netherlands, with hardly an exception, was disposed to see the great question of the foreign soldiery settled, before the chaos then existing should be superseded by a more definite authority. Everywhere, men of all ranks and occupations—the artisan in the city, the peasant in the fields—were deserting their daily occupations to furbish helmets, handle muskets, and learn the trade of war.* Skirmishes, sometimes severe and bloody, were of almost daily occurrence. In these the Spaniards were invariably successful, for whatever may be said of their cruelty and licentiousness, it cannot be disputed that their prowess was worthy of their renown. Romantic valor, unflinching fortitude, consummate skill, characterized them always. What could half-armed artisans achieve in the open plain against such accomplished foes? At Tisnacq, between Louvain and Tirlemont, a battle was attempted by a large miscellaneous mass of students, peasantry, and burghers, led by country squires.† It soon changed to a carnage, in which the victims were all on one side. A small number of veterans, headed by Vargas, Mendoza, Tassis, and other chivalrous commanders, routed the undisciplined thousands at a single charge. The rude militia threw away their arms, and fled panic-struck in all directions, at the first sight of their terrible foe. Two Spaniards lost their lives and two thousand Netherlanders.‡ It was natural that these consummate warriors

---

* Strada.

† Bor, ix. 715, 716. Hoofd, x. 450. Mendoza, xv. 305–308.

‡ Hoofd, x. 450.—"Bet dan twee duizent man, wil man dat er het leeven liet," etc., etc.—"Dit geluk hadden de Spangaerds zonder booven twee man te verliezen," etc. This is Dutch authority. Mendoza, one of the chief com-

should despise such easily slaughtered victims. A single stroke of the iron flail, and the chaff was scattered to the four winds ; a single sweep of the disciplined scythe, and countless acres were in an instant mown. Nevertheless, although beaten constantly, the Netherlanders were not conquered. Holland and Zealand had read the foe a lesson which he had not forgotten, and although on the open fields, and against the less vigorous population of the more central provinces, his triumphs had been easier, yet it was obvious that the spirit of resistance to foreign oppression was growing daily stronger, notwithstanding daily defeats.

Meantime, while these desultory but deadly combats were in daily progress, the Council of State was looked upon with suspicion by the mass of the population. That body, in which resided provisionally the powers of government, was believed to be desirous of establishing relations with the mutinous army. It was suspected of insidiously provoking the excesses which it seemed to denounce. It was supposed to be secretly intriguing with those whom its own edicts had outlawed. Its sympathies were considered Spanish. It was openly boasted by the Spanish army that, before long, they would descend from their fastnesses upon Brussels, and give the city to the sword. A shuddering sense of coming evil pervaded the population, but no man could say where the blow would first be struck. It was natural that the capital should be thought exposed to imminent danger. At the same time, while every man who had hands was disposed to bear arms to defend the city, the Council seemed paralyzed. The capital was insufficiently garrisoned, yet troops were not enrolling for its pro-

---

manders in the affair, says no Spaniard was killed, and that but one was wounded, slightly, in the foot, but he does not give the number of the states, troops, students, and burghers slain.—Mendoza, xv. 308. Cabrera, xi. 856, states the number at two thousand. That bitter Walloon, Renom de France, who saw the states' force pass through Louvain, on their way to the encounter, exults, as usual, over the discomfiture of his own countrymen. "The Spaniards cut them all to pieces," he observes, "teaching these pedants and schoolboys that war was a game in which they had no skill."—Histoire des Causes des Révoltes, etc.—MS., iii. c. xii.

tection. The state councillors obviously omitted to provide for defence, and it was supposed that they were secretly assisting the attack. It was thought important, therefore, to disarm, or, at least, to control this body which was impotent for protection, and seemed powerful only for mischief. It was possible to make it as contemptible as it was believed to be malicious.

An unexpected stroke was therefore suddenly levelled against the Council in full session. On the 5th of September,* the Seigneur de Héze, a young gentleman of a bold, but unstable character, then entertaining close but secret relations with the Prince of Orange, appeared before the doors of the palace. He was attended by about five hundred troops, under the immediate command of the Seigneur de Glimes, bailiff of Walloon Brabant. He demanded admittance, in the name of the Brabant estates, to the presence of the State Council, and was refused. The doors were closed and bolted. Without further ceremony the soldiers produced iron bars brought with them for the purpose, forced all the gates from the hinges, entered the hall of session, and at a word from their commander, laid hands upon the councillors, and made every one prisoner.† The Duke of Aerschot, President of the Council, who was then in close alliance with the Prince, was not present at the meeting, but lay, forewarned, at home, confined to his couch by a sickness assumed for the occasion. Viglius, who rarely participated in the deliberations of the board, being already afflicted with the chronic malady under which he was ere long to succumb, also escaped the fate of his fellow-senators.‡ The others were carried into

---

* Bor, ix. 712, Meteren, vi. 197, fix the date of this important transaction at the 14th September. A letter of William of Orange to Count John of 9th September states that it occurred on the 5th September.—Archives de la Maison d'Orange, etc., v. 408, and note 1. Tassis gives the same date, iii. 207, 208.

† Gachard, Correspondance de Guillaume le Tacit., iii. 106—note 1. Bor, ubi sup. Hoofd, x. 448. Meteren, vi. 107. I. B. de Tassis, Comm. de Tum. Belg., l. iii. 207, 208.

‡ Ibid. There is, however, considerable doubt upon this point. Viglius was ill and confined to his bed at the time of the Grand Commander's death, in

confinement. Berlaymont and Mansfeld were imprisoned in the Brood-Huys,* where the last mortal hours of Egmont and Horn had been passed. Others were kept strictly guarded in their own houses. After a few weeks, most of them were liberated. Councillor Del Rio was, however, retained in confinement, and sent to Holland, where he was subjected to a severe examination by the Prince of Orange, touching his past career, particularly concerning the doings of the famous Blood Council.† The others were set free, and even permitted to resume their functions, but their dignity was gone, their authority annihilated. Thenceforth the states of Brabant and the community of Brussels were to govern for an interval, for it was in their name that the daring blow against the Council had been struck. All individuals and bodies, however, although not displeased with the result, clamorously disclaimed responsi-

March. He ceased to write letters to Hopper in April. The arrest of the State Council took place in September, and Viglius died on the 8th of May of the following year (1577). It seems highly probable, therefore, that Tassis is correct in his statement, that Viglius was kept at home by the illness "quæ erat ei continua." The historians, however, Meteren (vi. 107), Bor (ix. 712), Bentivoglio (lib. ix. 176), Strada (viii. 414), Hoofd (x. 448), De Thou (lib. 64, vii. 534), all mention the name of President Viglius among those of the councillors arrested. The Prince of Orange (Archives, etc., v. 408) also mentions him as having been arrested and imprisoned with the rest. De Thou (ubi sup.) gives an account of a visit which he paid to him in the following spring, at which time the aged president seems to have been under arrest, although "il n'étoit pas gardé fort étroitement."—Some writers mention him as among those who were detained, while others of the arrested were released, (Meteren, Hoofd, Bor, etc.), —others, as Cabrera, (who is, however, no authority in such matters), mention him as one of those who were immediately set at liberty, in order that the Council might have an appearance of power. (Don Felipe II., xi. 853). On the whole, it seems most probable that he was arrested after the seizure of the Council, but that he was kept confined in a nominal durance, which the infirmities of illness and age rendered quite superfluous. It is almost unquestionable that De Thou visited him at his own house in Brussels, and not at any state prison. Wagenaer, vii. 106, says that Viglius was released in October, and quotes Langueti, ep., lib. i. (ii.), ep. 93, p. 289.—Compare Groen v. Prinst., Archives, etc., v. 404, sqq.; and Hoynk van Papendrecht, Not. ad Vit. Viglii., Analect. Belg., 192, 193, and Not. ad Comm., I. R. de Tassis, iii. 208.

* Van der Vynckt, ii. 188.

† Archives et Correspondance, v. 406. Extracts from the confessions of Del Rio have been given in the first volume of this history.

bility for the deed. Men were appalled at the audacity of the transaction, and dreaded the vengeance of the King. The Abbot Van Perch, one of the secret instigators of the act, actually died of anxiety for its possible consequences.* There was a mystery concerning the affair. They in whose name it had been accomplished, denied having given any authority to the perpetrators. Men asked each other what unseen agency had been at work, what secret spring had been adroitly touched. There is but little doubt, however, that the veiled but skilful hand which directed the blow, was the same which had so long been guiding the destiny of the Netherlands.†

It had been settled that the congress was to hold its sessions in Ghent, although the citadel commanding that city was held by the Spaniards. The garrison was not very strong, and Mondragon, its commander, was absent in Zealand,‡ but the wife of the veteran ably supplied his place, and stimulated the slender body of troops to hold out with heroism, under the orders of his lieutenant, Avilos Maldonado.§ The mutineers, after having accomplished their victory at Tisnacq, had been earnestly solicited to come to the relief of this citadel. They had refused and returned to Alost.‖ Meantime, the siege was warmly pressed by the states. There being, however, a deficiency of troops, application for assistance was formally made to the Prince of Orange. Count Reulx, governor of Flanders, commissioned the Seigneur d'Haussy, brother of Count Bossu, who, to obtain the liberation of that long-imprisoned and distinguished nobleman, was about visiting the Prince in Zealand, to make a request for an auxiliary force.¶ It was, however, stipulated that care should be taken lest any prejudice should be done to the Roman Catholic

---

* Hoofd, x. 448. Ev. Reid. Ann., lib. ii. 20.

† Wagenaer, vii. 105. Langueti Epist., lib. i. (ii.) ep. 87, p. 230.—Declaration of the Brussels Deputies in 1584. Bor, xix. 20 (477).—Compare Groen v. Prinst., Archives, etc., v. 404–407.

‡ Bor, ix. 726, 727.

§ Bor, ix. 727. Hoofd, xi. 470.—Compare Meteren, vi. 108.

‖ Hoofd, xi. 450, 451. Bor, ix. 716.

¶ Bor, ix. 716.

religion or the authority of the King. The Prince readily acceded to the request, and agreed to comply with the conditions under which only it could be accepted.* He promised to send twenty-eight companies. In his letter announcing this arrangement, he gave notice that his troops would receive strict orders to do no injury to person or property, Catholic or Protestant, ecclesiastic or lay, and to offer no obstruction to the Roman religion or the royal dignity.† He added, however, that it was not to be taken amiss, if his soldiers were permitted to exercise their own religious rites, and to sing their Protestant hymns within their own quarters.‡ He moreover, as security for the expense and trouble, demanded the city of Sluys.§ The first detachment of troops, under command of Colonel Vander Tympel, was, however, hardly on its way, before an alarm was felt among the Catholic party at this practical alliance with the rebel Prince. An envoy, named Ottingen, was despatched to Zealand, bearing a letter from the estates of Hainault, Brabant, and Flanders, countermanding the request for troops, and remonstrating categorically upon the subject of religion and loyalty.‖ Orange deemed such tergiversation paltry, but controlled his anger. He answered the letter in liberal terms, for he was determined that by no fault of his should the great cause be endangered. He reassured the estates as to the probable behaviour of his troops. Moreover, they had been already admitted into the city, while the correspondence was proceeding. The matter of the psalm-singing was finally arranged to the satisfaction of both parties, and it was agreed that Niewport, instead of Sluys, should be given to the Prince as security.¶

The siege of the citadel was now pressed vigorously, and

---

* Bor, ix. 716.

† See the letter in Bor, ix. 716, 717.—Compare Groen v. Prinst., Archives, etc., 420, 421.

‡ Letter of Prince of Orange, in Bor, ix. 716, 717.

§ Bor, ix. 717.

‖ Bor, ix. 717, 718.

¶ Bor, ubi sup.—Compare Groen v. Prinst. Archives, etc., 420, 421. Meteren, vi. 108.

the deliberations of the congress were opened under the incessant roar of cannon. While the attack was thus earnestly maintained upon the important castle of Ghent, a courageous effort was made by the citizens of Maestricht to wrest their city from the hands of the Spaniards. The German garrison having been gained by the burghers, the combined force rose upon the Spanish troops, and drove them from the city.* Montesdocca, the commander, was arrested and imprisoned, but the triumph was only temporary. Don Francis d'Ayala, Montesdocca's lieutenant, made a stand, with a few companies, in Wieck, a village on the opposite side of the Meuse, and connected with the city by a massive bridge of stone.† From this point he sent information to other commanders in the neighbourhood. Don Ferdinand de Toledo soon arrived with several hundred troops from Dalem. The Spaniards, eager to wipe out the disgrace to their arms, loudly demanded to be led back to the city. The head of the bridge, however, over which they must pass, was defended by a strong battery, and the citizens were seen clustering in great numbers to defend their firesides against a foe whom they had once expelled. To advance across the bridge seemed certain destruction to the little force. Even Spanish bravery recoiled at so desperate an undertaking, but unscrupulous ferocity supplied an expedient where courage was at fault. There were few fighting men present among the population of Wieck, but there were many females. Each soldier was commanded to seize a woman, and, placing her before his own body, to advance across the bridge.‡ The column, thus bucklered, to the shame of Spanish chivalry, by female bosoms, moved in good order toward the battery. The soldiers levelled their muskets with steady aim over the shoulders or under the arms of the women whom they thus held before them.§ On the other hand, the citizens dared not discharge their cannon at their own townswomen, among whose numbers

* Strada, viii. 416. Hoofd, xi. 454.

† Strada, Hoofd, ubi sup.

‡ Strada, viii. 416.

§ Ibid.

many recognized mothers, sisters, or wives.* The battery was soon taken, while at the same time Alonzo Vargas, who had effected his entrance from the land side by burning down the Brussels gate, now entered the city at the head of a band of cavalry. Maestricht was recovered, and an indiscriminate slaughter instantly avenged its temporary loss. The plundering, stabbing, drowning, burning, ravishing, were so dreadful that, in the words of a cotemporary historian, "the burghers who had escaped the fight had reason to think themselves less fortunate than those who had died with arms in their hands."†

This was the lot of Maestricht on the 20th of October. It was instinctively felt to be the precursor of fresh disasters. Vague, incoherent, but widely disseminated rumors had long pointed to Antwerp and its dangerous situation. The Spaniards, foiled in their views upon Brussels, had recently avowed an intention of avenging themselves in the commercial capital. They had waited long enough, and accumulated strength enough. Such a trifling city as Alost could no longer content their cupidity, but in Antwerp there was gold enough for the gathering. There was reason for the fears of the inhabitants, for the greedy longing of their enemy. Probably no city in Christendom could at that day vie with Antwerp in wealth and splendor. Its merchants lived in regal pomp and luxury. In its numerous, massive warehouses were the treasures of every clime. Still serving as the main entrepôt of the world's traffic, the Brabantine capital was the centre of that commercial system which was soon to be superseded by a larger international life. In the midst of the miseries which had so long been raining upon the Netherlands, the stately and egotistical city seemed to have taken stronger root and to flourish more freshly than ever. It was not wonderful that its palaces and its magazines,

---

* Strada, viii. 416.

† Bor, ix. 725.—Compare Strada, Hoofd, ubi sup. Meteren, vi. 109.

glittering with splendor and bursting with treasure, should arouse the avidity of a reckless and famishing soldiery. Had not a handful of warriors of their own race rifled the golden Indies? Had not their fathers, few in number, strong in courage and discipline, revelled in the plunder of a new world? Here were the Indies in a single city.* Here were gold and silver, pearls and diamonds, ready and portable; the precious fruit dropping, ripened, from the bough. Was it to be tolerated that base, pacific burghers should monopolize the treasure by which a band of heroes might be enriched?

A sense of coming evil diffused itself through the atmosphere. The air seemed lurid with the impending storm, for the situation was one of peculiar horror. The wealthiest city in Christendom lay at the mercy of the strongest fastness in the world; a castle which had been built to curb, not to protect, the town. It was now inhabited by a band of brigands, outlawed by government, strong in discipline, furious from penury, reckless by habit, desperate in circumstance—a crew which feared not God, nor man, nor Devil. The palpitating quarry lay expecting hourly the swoop of its trained and pitiless enemy, for the rebellious soldiers were now in a thorough state of discipline. Sancho d'Avila, castellan of the citadel, was recognized as the chief of the whole mutiny, the army and the mutiny being now one. The band, entrenched at Alost, were upon the best possible understanding with their brethren in the citadel, and accepted without hesitation the arrangements of their superior. On the side of the Scheld, opposite Antwerp, a fortification had been thrown up by Don Sancho's orders, and held by Julian Romero. Lier, Breda, as well as Alost, were likewise ready to throw their reinforcements into the citadel at a moment's warning. At the signal of their chief, the united bands might sweep from their impregnable castle with a single impulse.†

---

* "—— queste Indie d'una cittá."—Bentivoglio, ix. 181.

† Meteren, vi. 107. Bor, ix. 727, sqq. Mendoza, xv. 303, sqq.

The city cried aloud for help, for it had become obvious that an attack might be hourly expected. Meantime an attempt, made by Don Sancho d'Avila to tamper with the German troops stationed within the walls, was more than partially successful. The forces were commanded by Colonel Van Ende and Count Oberstein. Van Ende, a crafty traitor to his country, desired no better than to join the mutiny on so promising an occasion, and his soldiers shared his sentiments. Oberstein, a brave but blundering German, was drawn into the net of treachery* by the adroitness of the Spaniard and the effrontery of his comrade. On the night of the 29th of October, half-bewildered and half-drunk, he signed a treaty with Sancho d'Avila† and the three colonels—Fugger, Frondsberger, and Polwiller. By this unlucky document, which was of course subscribed also by Van Ende, it was agreed that the Antwerp burghers should be forthwith disarmed; that their weapons should be sent into the citadel; that Oberstein should hold the city at the disposition of Sancho d'Avila; that he should refuse admittance to all troops which might be sent into the city, excepting by command of Don Sancho, and that he should decline compliance with any orders which he might receive from individuals calling themselves the council of state, the states-general, or the estates of Brabant. This treaty was signed, moreover, by Don Jeronimo de Roda, then established in the citadel, and claiming to represent exclusively his Majesty's government.‡

Hardly had this arrangement been concluded than the Count saw the trap into which he had fallen. Without intending to do so, he had laid the city at the mercy of its foe, but the only remedy which suggested itself to his mind was an internal resolution not to keep his promises. The burghers were suffered to retain their arms, while, on the other hand, Don Sancho lost no time in despatching messages to Alost,

---

* Bor, ix. 727, sqq.

† Ibid. Hoofd, xi. 455, 456.

‡ See the Articles in Bor, ix. 728.—Compare Meteren, v. 109, 110; Hoofd, xi. 455, 456.

to Lier, to Breda, and even to Maestricht, that as large a force as possible might be* assembled for the purpose of breaking immediately the treaty of peace which he had just concluded. Never was a solemn document regarded with such perfectly bad faith by all its signers as the accord of the 29th of October.

Three days afterwards, a large force of Walloons and Germans was despatched from Brussels to the assistance of Antwerp. The command of these troops was entrusted to the Marquis of Havré, whose brother, the Duke of Aerschot, had been recently appointed chief superintendent of military affairs by the deputies assembled at Ghent.† The miscellaneous duties comprehended under this rather vague denomination did not permit the Duke to take charge of the expedition in person, and his younger brother, a still more incompetent and unsubstantial character, was accordingly appointed to the post. A number of young men, of high rank but of lamentably low capacity, were associated with him. Foremost among them was Philip, Count of Egmont, a youth who had inherited few of his celebrated father's qualities, save personal courage and a love of personal display. In character and general talents he was beneath mediocrity. Beside these were the reckless but unstable De Héze, who had executed the *coup d'état* against the State Council, De Berselen, De Capres, D'Oyngies, and others, all vaguely desirous of achieving distinction in those turbulent times, but few of them having any political or religious convictions, and none of them possessing experience or influence enough to render them useful at the impending crisis.‡

On Friday morning, the 2nd of November,§ the troops

---

* Mendoza, xv. 303. Cabrera, xi. 862, 863, sqq. Strada, viii. 417.

† Bor, ix. 719.

‡ Bor, ix. 728, 729. Cabrera, xi. 863. Mendoza, xv. 313. Meteren, vi. 109.

§ Bor, ix. 728. Meteren, vi. 109. Hoofd, xi. 457, and not the 3rd of October as stated by Mendoza, xv. 313, and by Cabrera, xi. 863, following Mendoza.

appeared under the walls of Antwerp. They consisted of twenty-three companies of infantry and fourteen of cavalry, amounting to five thousand foot and twelve hundred horse. They were nearly all Walloons, soldiers who had already seen much active service, but unfortunately of a race warlike and fiery indeed, but upon whose steadiness not much more dependence could be placed at that day than in the age of Civilis. Champagny, brother of Granvelle, was Governor of the city. He was a sincere Catholic, but a still more sincere hater of the Spaniards. He saw in the mutiny a means of accomplishing their expulsion, and had already offered to the Prince of Orange his eager co-operation towards this result. In other matters there could be but small sympathy between William the Silent and the Cardinal's brother ; but a common hatred united them, for a time at least, in a common purpose.

When the troops first made their appearance before the walls, Champagny was unwilling to grant them admittance. The addle-brained Oberstein had confessed to him the enormous blunder which he had committed in his midnight treaty, and at the same time ingenuously confessed his intention of sending it to the winds.* The enemy had extorted from his dulness or his drunkenness a promise, which his mature and sober reason could not consider binding. It is needless to say that Champagny rebuked him for signing, and applauded him for breaking the treaty. At the same time its ill effects were already seen in the dissensions which existed among the German troops. Where all had been tampered with, and where the commanders had set the example of infidelity, it would have been strange if all had held firm. On the whole, however, Oberstein thought he could answer for his own troops. Upon Van Ende's division, although the crafty colonel dissembled his real intentions, very little reliance was placed.† Thus there was distraction within the

* Bor, ix. 729. Hoofd, xi. 457.

† Bor, ix. 729, sqq. Hoofd, xi. 457, sqq.—Compare Strada, viii. 117; Mendoza, xv. 313. Cabrera, xi. 863, et al.

walls. Among those whom the burghers had been told to consider their defenders, there were probably many who were ready to join with their mortal foes at a moment's warning. Under these circumstances, Champagny hesitated about admitting these fresh troops from Brussels. He feared lest the Germans, who knew themselves doubted, might consider themselves doomed. He trembled, lest an irrepressible outbreak should occur within the walls, rendering the immediate destruction of the city by the Spaniards from without inevitable. Moreover, he thought it more desirable that this auxiliary force should be disposed at different points outside, in order to intercept the passage of the numerous bodies of Spaniards and other mutineers, who from various quarters would soon be on their way to the citadel. Havré, however, was so peremptory, and the burghers were so importunate, that Champagny was obliged to recede from his opposition before twenty-four hours had elapsed. Unwilling to take the responsibility of a farther refusal, he admitted the troops through the Burgherhout gate, on Saturday, the 3rd of November, at ten o'clock in the morning.*

The Marquis of Havré, as commander-in-chief, called a council of war. It assembled at Count Oberstein's quarters, and consulted at first concerning a bundle of intercepted letters which Havré had brought with him. These constituted a correspondence between Sancho d'Avila with the heads of the mutiny at Alost, and many other places. The letters were all dated subsequently to Don Sancho's treaty with Oberstein, and contained arrangements for an immediate concentration of the whole available Spanish force at the citadel.†

The treachery was so manifest, that Oberstein felt all self-reproach for his own breach of faith to be superfluous. It was however evident that the attack was to be immediately expected. What was to be done? All the officers counselled the immediate erection of a bulwark on the side of the city

* Bor, ix. 729. Hoofd, xi. 457. Meteren, vi. 110.

† Bor, ix. 730. Hoofd, xi. 457, 458.

exposed to the castle, but there were no miners nor engineers. Champagny, however, recommended a skilful and experienced engineer to superintend the work in the city; and pledged himself that burghers enough would volunteer as miners. In less than an hour, ten or twelve thousand persons, including multitudes of women of all ranks, were at work upon the lines marked out by the engineer. A ditch and breast-work extending from the gate of the Beguins to the street of the Abbey Saint Michael, were soon in rapid progress. Meantime, the newly arrived troops, with military insolence, claimed the privilege of quartering themselves in the best houses which they could find. They already began to insult and annoy the citizens whom they had been sent to defend; nor were they destined to atone, by their subsequent conduct in the face of the enemy, for the brutality with which they treated their friends. Champagny, however, was ill-disposed to brook their licentiousness. They had been sent to protect the city and the homes of Antwerp from invasion. They were not to establish themselves at every fireside on their first arrival. There was work enough for them out of doors, and they were to do that work at once. He ordered them to prepare for a bivouac in the streets, and flew from house to house, sword in hand, driving forth the intruders at imminent peril of his life. Meantime, a number of Italian and Spanish merchants fled from the city, and took refuge in the castle. The Walloon soldiers were for immediately plundering their houses, as if plunder had been the object for which they had been sent to Antwerp. It was several hours before Champagny, with all his energy, was able to quell these disturbances.*

In the course of the day, Oberstein received a letter from Don Sancho d'Avila, calling solemnly upon him to fulfil his treaty of the 29th of October.† The German colonels from the

---

* Bor, ix. 730. Hoofd, xi. 458. Meteren, vi. 110. Cabrera, xi. 864. Strada, viii. 417.—A remarkable pamphlet, published by Champagny in 1578, entitled "Recueil d'Arétophile" (Lyon. Guerin, 1578), is the best authority for many striking details of this memorable affair.

† Bor, ix. 729.

citadel had, on the previous afternoon, held a personal interview with Oberstein beneath the walls, which had nearly ended in blows, and they had been obliged to save themselves by flight from the anger of the Count's soldiers, enraged at the deceit by which their leader had been so nearly entrapped.* This summons of ridiculous solemnity to keep a treaty which had already been torn to shreds by both parties, Oberstein answered with defiance and contempt. The reply was an immediate cannonade from the batteries of the citadel, which made the position of those erecting the ramparts excessively dangerous. The wall was strengthened with bales of merchandise, casks of earth, upturned wagons, and similar bulky objects, hastily piled together. In some places it was sixteen feet high; in others less than six. Night fell before the fortification was nearly completed. Unfortunately it was bright moonlight. The cannon from the fortress continued to play upon the half-finished works. The Walloons, and at last the citizens, feared to lift their heads above their frail rampart. The senators, whom Champagny had deputed to superintend the progress of the enterprise, finding the men so ill disposed, deserted their posts. They promised themselves that, in the darkest hour of the following night, the work should be thoroughly completed.† Alas! all hours of the coming night were destined to be dark enough, but in them was to be done no manner of work for defence. On Champagny alone seemed devolved all the labor and all the responsibility. He did his duty well, but he was but one man. Alone, with a heart full of anxiety, he wandered up and down all the night.‡ With his own hands, assisted only by a few citizens and his own servants, he planted all the cannon with which they were provided, in the "Fencing Court," at a point where the battery might tell upon the castle. Unfortunately,

* Hoofd, xi. 457, 458.

† Bor, ix. 729, sqq. Meteren, vi. 110. Hoofd, xi. 458–460.

‡ Recueil d'Arétophile.

the troops from Brussels had brought no artillery with them, and the means of defence against the strongest fortress in Europe were meagre indeed. The rampart had been left very weak at many vital points. A single upturned wagon was placed across the entrance to the important street of the Beguins. This negligence was to cost the city dear. At daybreak, there was a council held in Oberstein's quarters. Nearly all Champagny's directions had been neglected. He had desired that strong detachments should be posted during the night at various places of security on the outskirts of the town, for the troops which were expected to arrive in small bodies at the citadel from various parts, might have thus been cut off before reaching their destination. Not even scouts had been stationed in sufficient numbers to obtain information of what was occurring outside. A thick mist hung over the city that eventful morning. Through its almost impenetrable veil, bodies of men had been seen moving into the castle, and the tramp of cavalry had been distinctly heard, and the troops of Romero, Vargas, Oliveira, and Valdez had already arrived from Lier, Breda, Maestricht, and from the forts on the Scheld.*

The whole available force in the city was mustered without delay. Havré had claimed for his post the defence of the lines opposite the citadel, the place of responsibility and honor. Here the whole body of Walloons were stationed, together with a few companies of Germans. The ramparts, as stated, were far from impregnable, but it was hoped that this living rampart of six thousand men, standing on their own soil, and in front of the firesides and altars of their own countrymen, would prove a sufficient bulwark even against Spanish fury. Unhappily, the living barrier proved more frail than the feeble breastwork which the hands of burghers and women

---

* Meteren, vii. 110. Recueil d'Arétophile. Hoofd, xi. 460. Bor, ix. 730. Cabrera, xi. 864. Mendoza, xv. 315.

† Hoofd, xi. 458, 459. Recueil d'Arétophile.

had constructed. Six thousand men were disposed along the side of the city opposite the fortress. The bulk of the German troops was stationed at different points on the more central streets and squares. The cavalry was posted on the opposite side of the city, along the Horse-market, and fronting the "New-town." The stars were still in the sky when Champagny got on horseback and rode through the streets, calling on the burghers to arm and assemble at different points. The principal places of rendezvous were the Cattle-market and the Exchange. He rode along the lines of the Walloon regiments, conversing with the officers, Egmont, De Héze, and others, and encouraging the men, and went again to the Fencing Court, where he pointed the cannon with his own hand, and ordered their first discharge at the fortress. Thence he rode to the end of the Beguin street, where he dismounted and walked out upon the edge of the esplanade which stretched between the city and the castle. On this battle-ground a combat was even then occurring between a band of burghers and a reconnoitring party from the citadel. Champagny saw with satisfaction that the Antwerpers were victorious. They were skirmishing well with their disciplined foe, whom they at last beat back to the citadel. His experienced eye saw, however, that the retreat was only the signal for a general onslaught, which was soon to follow; and he returned into the city to give the last directions.*

At ten o'clock, a moving wood was descried, approaching the citadel from the south-west. The whole body of the mutineers from Alost, wearing green branches in their helmets,† had arrived under command of their Eletto, Navarrete. Nearly three thousand in number, they rushed into the castle, having accomplished their march of twenty-four miles

---

* Recueil d'Arétophile. Meteren, vi. 110[b]. Hoofd, xi. 458, 460, 461. Brantome, Hommes Illust., ii. 201 (Sanc. d'Av.)

† Ibid., 113.

since three o'clock in the morning.* They were received with open arms. Sancho d'Avila ordered food and refreshments to be laid before them, but they refused everything but a draught of wine. They would dine in Paradise, they said, or sup in Antwerp.† Finding his allies in such spirit, Don Sancho would not balk their humor. Since early morning, his own veterans had been eagerly awaiting his signal, "straining upon the start." The troops of Romero, Vargas, Valdez, were no less impatient. At about an hour before noon, nearly every living man in the citadel was mustered for the attack, hardly men enough being left behind to guard the gates. Five thousand veteran foot soldiers, besides six hundred cavalry, armed to the teeth, sallied from the portals of Alva's citadel.‡ In the counterscarp they fell upon their knees, to invoke, according to custom, the blessing of God§ upon the Devil's work, which they were about to commit. The Eletto bore a standard, one side of which was emblazoned with the crucified Saviour, and the other with the Virgin Mary.‖ The image of Him who said, "Love your enemies," and the gentle face of the Madonna, were to smile from heaven upon deeds which might cause a shudder in the depths of hell. Their brief orisons concluded, they swept forward to the city. Three thousand Spaniards, under their Eletto, were

* Mendoza, xv. 314, 315.

† Mendoza, xiv. 315.—" Respondieron el estar resueltos de comer en el Parayso ó cenar en la villa de Anvers."—Bor, ix. 730. Hoofd, xi. 461. Cabrera, xi. 864, et al.

‡ Hoofd gives the numbers as two thousand from Alost, five hundred under Romero, five hundred under Valdez, one thousand under the German colonels, and one thousand cavalry under Vargas, in all, five thousand.—xi. 461. Mendoza states the whole attacking force at two thousand two hundred Spanish infantry, eight hundred Germans, and five hundred cavalry, in all, three thousand five hundred.—xv. 315. Cabrera, following Mendoza as usual, estimates the number at a little more than three thousand.—xi. 864.

§ Mendoza, xv. 315. Hoofd, xi. 461.

‖ "Con la figura de Jesu Cristo cruzificado en la una faz, i en la otra la de su Madre Santissima manifestando iban a vengar la magestad divina ofendida de la eregia depravada."—Cabrera, xi. 864. Mendoza, xv. 315. Hoofd, xi. 431.

to enter by the street of Saint Michael; the Germans, and the remainder of the Spanish foot, commanded by Romero, through that of Saint George. Champagny saw them coming, and spoke a last word of encouragement to the Walloons. The next moment the compact mass struck the barrier, as the thunderbolt descends from the cloud. There was scarcely a struggle. The Walloons, not waiting to look their enemy in the face, abandoned the posts which they had themselves claimed. The Spaniards crashed through the bulwark, as though it had been a wall of glass. The Eletto was first to mount the rampart; the next instant he was shot dead, while his followers, undismayed, sprang over his body, and poured into the streets. The fatal gaps, due to timidity and carelessness, let in the destructive tide. Champagny, seeing that the enemies had all crossed the barrier, leaped over a garden wall, passed through a house into a narrow lane, and thence to the nearest station of the German troops. Hastily collecting a small force, he led them in person to the rescue. The Germans fought well, died well, but they could not reanimate the courage of the Walloons, and all were now in full retreat, pursued by the ferocious Spaniards.* In vain Champagny stormed among them; in vain he strove to rally their broken ranks. With his own hand he seized a banner from a retreating ensign,† and called upon the nearest soldiers to make a stand against the foe. It was to bid the flying clouds pause before the tempest. Torn, broken, aimless, the scattered troops whirled through the streets before the pursuing wrath. Champagny, not yet despairing, galloped hither and thither, calling upon the burghers everywhere to rise in defence of their homes, nor did he call in vain. They came forth from every place of rendezvous, from every alley, from every house. They fought as men fight to defend their hearths and altars,

---

* Recueil d'Arétophile. Meteren, vi. 110c. Mendoza, xv. 316. Hoofd, xi. 461. Bor, ix. 731.

† Meteren, vi. 110c. Hoofd, 461.

but what could individual devotion avail, against the compact, disciplined, resistless mass of their foes? The order of defence was broken, there was no system, no concert, no rallying point, no authority. So soon as it was known that the Spaniards had crossed the rampart, that its six thousand defenders were in full retreat, it was inevitable that a panic should seize the city.*

Their entrance once effected, the Spanish force had separated, according to previous arrangement, into two divisions, one half charging up the long street of Saint Michael, the other forcing its way through the street of Saint Joris.† "Santiago, Santiago! España, España! á sangre, á carne, á fuego, á sacco!" Saint James, Spain, blood, flesh, fire, sack!!—such were the hideous cries which rang through every quarter of the city, as the savage horde advanced.‡ Van Ende, with his German troops, had been stationed by the Marquis of Havré to defend the Saint Joris gate, but no sooner did the Spaniards under Vargas present themselves, than he deserted to them instantly with his whole force.§ United with the Spanish cavalry, these traitorous defenders of Antwerp dashed in pursuit of those who had only been fainthearted. Thus the burghers saw themselves attacked by many of their friends, deserted by more. Whom were they to trust? Nevertheless, Oberstein's Germans were brave and faithful, resisting to the last, and dying every man in his harness.‖ The tide of battle flowed hither and thither, through every street and narrow lane. It poured along the magnificent Place de Meer, where there was an obstinate contest. In front of the famous Exchange, where in peaceful hours, five thousand merchants¶ met daily, to arrange the commercial affairs of Christendom, there was a determined rally, a savage slaughter. The citizens and faithful Germans, in this

* Hoofd, xi. 461.

† Hoofd, xi. 461. Mendoza, xv. 315.

‡ Brantome, Hommes Illustres, etc., ii. 203. Mendoza, xv. 315.

§ Hoofd, xi. 461. Mendoza, xv. 316.

‖ Bor, ix. 730. Hoofd, xi. 465.

¶ Guicciardini, Belg. Descript.

broader space, made a stand against their pursuers. The tesselated marble pavement, the graceful, cloister-like arcades ran red with blood. The ill-armed burghers faced their enemies clad in complete panoply, but they could only die for their homes. The massacre at this point was enormous, the resistance at last overcome.*

Meantime, the Spanish cavalry had cleft its way through the city. On the side farthest removed from the castle, along the Horse-market, opposite the New-town, the states dragoons and the light horse of Beveren had been posted, and the flying masses of pursuers and pursued swept at last through this outer circle. Champagny was already there. He essayed, as his last hope, to rally the cavalry for a final stand, but the effort was fruitless. Already seized by the panic, they had attempted to rush from the city through the gate of Eeker. It was locked; they then turned and fled towards the Red-gate, where they were met face to face by Don Pedro Tassis, who charged upon them with his dragoons. Retreat seemed hopeless. A horseman in complete armor, with lance in rest, was seen to leap from the parapet of the outer wall into the moat below, whence, still on horseback, he escaped with life. Few were so fortunate. The confused mob of fugitives and conquerors, Spaniards, Walloons, Germans, burghers, struggling, shouting, striking, cursing, dying, swayed hither and thither like a stormy sea. Along the spacious Horse-market, the fugitives fled onward towards the quays. Many fell beneath the swords of the Spaniards, numbers were trodden to death by the hoofs of horses, still greater multitudes were hunted into the Scheld. Champagny, who had thought it possible, even at the last moment, to make a stand in the New-town, and to fortify the Palace of the Hansa, saw himself deserted. With great daring and presence of mind, he effected his escape to the fleet of the Prince of Orange in the river.† The Marquis of Havré, of whom no

---

* Hoofd, xi. 460–465. Bor, ix. 731. Mendoza, xv. 315. Meteren, vi. 110.

† Bor, ix. 731. Hoofd, xi. 462. Rec. d'Arétophile. Mendoza, xv. 336. Cabrera, xi. 865.

deeds of valor on that eventful day have been recorded, was equally successful. The unlucky Oberstein, attempting to leap into a boat, missed his footing, and oppressed by the weight of his armor, was drowned.*

Meantime, while the short November day was fast declining, the combat still raged in the interior of the city. Various currents of conflict, forcing their separate way through many streets, had at last mingled in the *Grande Place*. Around this irregular, not very spacious square, stood the gorgeous Hotel de Ville, and the tall, many storied, fantastically gabled, richly decorated palaces of the guilds. Here a long struggle took place. It was terminated for a time by the cavalry of Vargas, who, arriving through the streets of Saint Joris, accompanied by the traitor Van Ende, charged decisively into the mêlée. The masses were broken, but multitudes of armed men found refuge in the buildings, and every house became a fortress. From every window and balcony a hot fire was poured into the square, as, pent in a corner, the burghers stood at last at bay. It was difficult to carry the houses by storm, but they were soon set on fire. A large number of sutlers and other varlets had accompanied the Spaniards from the citadel, bringing torches and kindling materials for the express purpose of firing the town. With great dexterity, these means were now applied, and in a brief interval, the City-hall, and other edifices on the square were in flames. The conflagration spread with rapidity, house after house, street after street, taking fire. Nearly a thousand buildings, in the most splendid and wealthy quarter of the city, were soon in a blaze, and multitudes of human beings were burned with them.† In the City-hall many were consumed, while others leaped from the windows to renew the

---

* Bor, ix. 731. Hoofd, xi. 462. Mendoza, xv. 316.

† Hoofd, xi. 462. Mendoza, xv. 316. Strada, viii. 419.—According to Meteren (vi. 110) the whole town was on fire, and five hundred houses entirely consumed. According to the contemporary manuscript of De Weerdt, who was a citizen of Antwerp, one thousand houses were burned to the ground.—Chronyke oft Journael, MS., p. 83.

combat below. The many tortuous streets which led down a slight descent from the rear of the Town-house to the quays were all one vast conflagration. On the other side, the magnificent cathedral, separated from the *Grande Place* by a single row of buildings, was lighted up, but not attacked by the flames. The tall spire cast its gigantic shadow across the last desperate conflict. In the street called the *Canal au Sucre,* immediately behind the Town-house, there was a fierce struggle, a horrible massacre. A crowd of burghers, grave magistrates, and such of the German soldiers as remained alive, still confronted the ferocious Spaniards. There, amid the flaming desolation, Goswyn Verreyck, the heroic margrave of the city, fought with the energy of hatred and despair. The burgomaster, Van der Meere, lay dead at his feet; senators, soldiers, citizens, fell fast around him, and he sank at last upon a heap of slain. With him effectual resistance ended. The remaining combatants were butchered, or were slowly forced downward to perish in the Scheld.* Women, children, old men, were killed in countless numbers, and still, through all this havoc, directly over the heads of the struggling throng, suspended in mid-air above the din and smoke of the conflict, there sounded, every half-quarter of every hour, as if in gentle mockery, from the belfry of the cathedral, the tender and melodious chimes.

Never was there a more monstrous massacre, even in the blood-stained history of the Netherlands. It was estimated that, in the course of this and the two following days, not less than eight thousand human beings were murdered.† The Spaniards seemed to cast off even the vizard of humanity. Hell

---

* Mendoza, xv. 316. Bor, ix. 731. Hoofd, xi. 463.

† This is the estimate of Mendoza; viz. two thousand five hundred slain with the sword, and double that number burned and drowned.—xv. 317. Cabrera puts the figures at seven thousand and upwards.—xi. 865[b]. Bor and Hoofd give the same number of dead bodies, actually found in the streets, viz. two thousand five hundred; and estimating the drowned at as many more, leave the number of the burned to conjecture. Meteren (vi. 110), who on all occasions seeks to diminish the number of his countrymen slain in battle or massacre,

seemed emptied of its fiends. Night fell upon the scene before the soldiers were masters of the city; but worse horrors began after the contest was ended. This army of brigands had come thither with a definite, practical purpose, for it was not blood-thirst, nor lust, nor revenge, which had impelled them, but it was avarice, greediness for gold. For gold they had waded through all this blood and fire. Never had men more simplicity of purpose, more directness in its execution. They had conquered their India at last; its golden mines lay all before them, and every sword should open a shaft. Riot and rape might be deferred; even murder, though congenial to their taste, was only subsidiary to their business. They had come to take possession of the city's wealth, and they set themselves faithfully to accomplish their task. For gold, infants were dashed out of existence in their mothers' arms; for gold, parents were tortured in their children's presence; for gold, brides were scourged to death before their husbands' eyes.* Wherever treasure was suspected, every expedient which ingenuity, sharpened by greediness, could suggest, was employed to extort it from its possessors. The fire, spreading more extensively and more rapidly than had been desired through the wealthiest quarter of the city, had unfortunately devoured a vast amount of property. Six millions,† at least,

---

while he magnifies the loss of his opponents, admits that from four to five thousand were slain; adding, however, that but fifteen hundred bodies were found, which were all buried together in two great pits. He thus deducts exactly one thousand from the number of counted corpses, as given by every other authority, Spanish or Flemish. Strada (viii. 422) gives three thousand as the number of those slain with the sword.—Compare De Thou, vii. 383-390, (l. 62.) The letter of Jerome de Roda to the King, written from the citadel of Antwerp upon the 6th November, when the carnage was hardly over, estimates the number of the slain at eight thousand, and one thousand horses. This authority, coming from the very hour and spot, and from a man so deeply implicated, may be considered conclusive.—See the Letter of Roda, in Bor, ix. 737, 738.

* Bor, ix. 731, sqq. Hoofd, xi. 462, sqq.

† Hoofd, xi. 462. Bor's estimate is three millions, ix. 731. The property consumed, says Meteren, was equal in value to that which was obtained in the plundering afterwards by the soldiery. This he estimates at more than four millions in cash, not counting jewellery and other merchandise, vi. 110.

had thus been swallowed ; a destruction by which no one had profited. There was, however, much left. The strong boxes of the merchants, the gold, silver, and precious jewelry, the velvets, satins, brocades, laces, and similar well concentrated and portable plunder, were rapidly appropriated. So far the course was plain and easy, but in private houses it was more difficult. The cash, plate, and other valuables of individuals were not so easily discovered. Torture was, therefore, at once employed to discover the hidden treasures. After all had been given, if the sum seemed too little, the proprietors were brutally punished for their poverty or their supposed dissimulation.* A gentlewoman, named Fabry,† with her aged mother and other females of the family, had taken refuge in the cellar of her mansion. As the day was drawing to a close, a band of plunderers entered, who, after ransacking the house, descended to the cellarage. Finding the door barred, they forced it open with gunpowder. The mother, who was nearest the entrance, fell dead on the threshold. Stepping across her mangled body, the brigands sprang upon her daughter, loudly demanding the property which they believed to be concealed. They likewise insisted on being informed where the master of the house had taken refuge. Protestations of ignorance as to hidden treasure, or the whereabouts of her husband, who, for aught she knew, was lying dead in the streets, were of no avail. To make her more communicative, they hanged her on a beam in the cellar, and after a few moments cut her down before life was extinct. Still receiving no satisfactory reply, where a satisfactory reply was impossible, they hanged her again. Again, after another brief interval, they gave her a second release, and a fresh interrogatory. This barbarity they repeated several times, till they were satisfied that there was nothing to be gained by it, while, on the other hand, they were losing much valuable time. Hoping to be more successful elsewhere, they left her hanging

* Hoofd, xi. 463.

† Ibid., xi. 463.—The lady was grandmother of the historian's wife.

for the last time, and trooped off to fresher fields. Strange to relate, the person thus horribly tortured, survived. A servant in her family, married to a Spanish soldier, providentially entered the house in time to rescue her perishing mistress. She was restored to existence, but never to reason. Her brain was hopelessly crazed, and she passed the remainder of her life wandering about her house, or feebly digging in her garden for the buried treasure which she had been thus fiercely solicited to reveal.*

A wedding-feast was rudely interrupted. Two young persons, neighbours of opulent families, had been long betrothed, and the marriage day had been fixed for Sunday, the fatal 4th of November. The guests were assembled, the ceremony concluded, the nuptial banquet in progress, when the horrible outcries in the streets proclaimed that the Spaniards had broken loose. Hour after hour of trembling expectation succeeded. At last, a thundering at the gate proclaimed the arrival of a band of brigands. Preceded by their captain, a large number of soldiers forced their way into the house, ransacking every chamber, no opposition being offered by the family and friends, too few and powerless to cope with this band of well-armed ruffians. Plate chests, wardrobes, desks, caskets of jewelry, were freely offered, eagerly accepted, but not found sufficient, and to make the luckless wretches furnish more than they possessed, the usual brutalities were employed. The soldiers began by striking the bridegroom dead. The bride fell shrieking into her mother's arms, whence she was torn by the murderers, who immediately put the mother to death, and an indiscriminate massacre then followed the fruitless attempts to obtain by threats and torture treasure which did not exist. The bride, who was of remarkable beauty, was carried off to the citadel.† Maddened by this last outrage, the father, who was the only man of the party left alive, rushed upon the Spaniards. Wresting a sword from one of the crew, the old man dealt with it so fiercely, that he stretched more than one enemy

* Hoofd, xi. 463, 464.

† Bor, ix. 731. Hoofd, xi. 464.

dead at his feet, but it is needless to add that he was soon despatched. Meantime, while the party were concluding the plunder of the mansion, the bride was left in a lonely apartment of the fortress. Without wasting time in fruitless lamentation, she resolved to quit the life which a few hours had made so desolate. She had almost succeeded in hanging herself with a massive gold chain which she wore, when her captor entered the apartment. Inflamed, not with lust, but with avarice, excited not by her charms, but by her jewelry, he rescued her from her perilous position. He then took possession of her chain and the other trinkets with which her wedding-dress was adorned, and caused her to be entirely stripped of her clothing. She was then scourged with rods till her beautiful body was bathed in blood, and at last alone, naked, nearly mad, was sent back into the city. Here the forlorn creature wandered up and down through the blazing streets, among the heaps of dead and dying, till she was at last put out of her misery by a gang of soldiers.*

Such are a few isolated instances, accidentally preserved in their details, of the general horrors inflicted on this occasion. Others innumerable have sunk into oblivion. On the morning of the 5th of November, Antwerp presented a ghastly sight. The magnificent marble Town-house, celebrated as a "world's wonder,"† even in that age and country, in which so much splendour was lavished on municipal palaces, stood a blackened ruin—all but the walls destroyed, while its archives, accounts, and other valuable contents, had perished. The more splendid portion of the city had been consumed; at least five hundred palaces, mostly of marble or hammered stone, being a smouldering mass of destruction.‡ The dead bodies of those fallen in the massacre were on every side, in greatest profusion around the Place de Meer, among the Gothic pillars of the

---

* Bor, ix. 731. Hoofd, xi. 465.

† "Het welk man mocht tellen onder de wonderen der wereld."—Address of the States of Brabant to the States-General, in Bor, ix. 734.

‡ Hoofd, xi. 462. Meteren, vi. 110ª.

Exchange, and in the streets near the Town-house. The German soldiers lay in their armor, some with their heads burned from their bodies, some with legs and arms consumed by the flames through which they had fought.* The Margrave Goswyn Verreyck, the burgomaster Van der Meere, the magistrates Lancelot Van Urselen, Nicholas Van Boekholt, and other leading citizens, lay among piles of less distinguished slain.† They remained unburied until the overseers of the poor, on whom the living had then more importunate claims than the dead, were compelled by Roda to bury them out of the pauper fund.‡ The murderers were too thrifty to be at funeral charges for their victims. The ceremony was not hastily performed, for the number of corpses had not been completed. Two days longer the havoc lasted in the city. Of all the crimes which men can commit, whether from deliberate calculation or in the frenzy of passion, hardly one was omitted, for riot, gaming, rape, which had been postponed to the more stringent claims of robbery and murder, were now rapidly added to the sum of atrocities.§ History has recorded the account indelibly on her brazen tablets; it can be adjusted only at the judgment-seat above.

Of all the deeds of darkness yet compassed in the Netherlands, this was the worst. It was called The Spanish Fury,‖ by which dread name it has been known for ages. The city, which had been a world of wealth and splendor, was changed to a charnel-house, and from that hour its commercial prosperity was blasted. Other causes had silently girdled the yet green and flourishing tree, but the Spanish Fury was the fire which consumed it to ashes. Three thousand dead bodies were discovered in the streets, as many more were estimated to have perished in the Scheld, and nearly an equal number were burned or destroyed in other

* Bor, ix. 732. Hoofd, xi. 465.

† Bor, ix. 731. Hoofd, xi. 463.

‡ Hoofd, xi. 466.

§ Remonstrance of the States of Brabant to the States-General.—Bor, ix. 733, 734.

‖ Bor, ix. 732. Hoofd, xi. 462. Meteren, vi. 111. Wagenaer, vii. 115, et mult. al.

ways. Eight thousand persons undoubtedly were put to death. Six millions of property were destroyed by the fire, and at least as much more was obtained by the Spaniards.* In this enormous robbery no class of people was respected. Foreign merchants, living under the express sanction and protection of the Spanish monarch, were plundered with as little reserve as Flemings. Ecclesiastics of the Roman Church were compelled to disgorge their wealth as freely as Calvinists. The rich were made to contribute all their abundance, and the poor what could be wrung from their poverty. Neither paupers nor criminals were safe. Captain Caspar Ortis made a brilliant speculation by taking possession of the *Stein*, or city prison, whence he ransomed all the inmates who could find means to pay for their liberty. Robbers, murderers, even Anabaptists, were thus again let loose.† Rarely has so small a band obtained in three days' robbery so large an amount of wealth. Four or five millions divided among five thousand soldiers made up for long arrearages, and the Spaniards had reason to congratulate themselves upon having thus taken the duty of payment into their own hands. It is true that the wages of iniquity were somewhat unequally distributed, somewhat foolishly squandered. A private trooper was known to lose ten thousand crowns in one day in a gambling transaction at the Bourse,‡ for the soldiers, being thus handsomely in funds, became desirous of aping the despised and plundered merchants, and resorted daily to the Exchange, like men accustomed to affairs. The dearly purchased gold was thus lightly squandered by many, while others, more prudent, melted their portion into sword-hilts, into scabbards, even into whole suits of armor, darkened, by

---

* The estimate of Meteren is, that four millions, in hard cash alone, were obtained by the soldiery, exclusively of precious stones, other articles of jewelry, laces, brocades, embroidery, and similar property of a portable and convertible character.—Meteren, vi. 111[a]. The estimates of Hoofd and Bor do not materially differ. In single houses as much as 300,000 guldens were found; over 90,000 in the dwelling of a widow.—Meteren, ubi sup.

† Bor, ix. 732. Hoofd, xi. 465. Meteren, vi. 111.

‡ Hoofd, xi. 466. Bor, ix. 732. Meteren, vi. 111.

precaution, to appear made entirely of iron. The brocades, laces, and jewelry of Antwerp merchants were converted into coats of mail for their destroyers. The goldsmiths, however, thus obtained an opportunity to outwit their plunderers, and mingled in the golden armor which they were forced to furnish much more alloy than their employers knew. A portion of the captured booty was thus surreptitiously redeemed.*

In this Spanish Fury many more were massacred in Antwerp than in the Saint Bartholomew at Paris.† Almost as many living human beings were dashed out of existence now as there had been statues destroyed in the memorable image-breaking of Antwerp, ten years before, an event which had sent such a thrill of horror through the heart of Catholic Christendom. Yet the Netherlanders and the Protestants of Europe may be forgiven, if they regarded this massacre of their brethren with as much execration as had been bestowed upon that fury against stocks and stones. At least, the image-breakers had been actuated by an idea, and their hands were polluted neither with blood nor rapine. Perhaps the Spaniards had been governed equally by religious fanaticism. Might not they believe they were meriting well of their Mother Church while they were thus disencumbering infidels of their wealth and earth of its infidels? Had not the Pope and his cardinals gone to church in solemn procession, to render thanks unto God for the massacre of Paris?‡ Had not cannon thundered and beacons blazed to commemorate that auspicious event? Why should not the Antwerp executioners claim equal commendation? Even if in their delirium they had confounded friend with foe, Catholic with Calvinist, and church property with lay, could they not point to an

* Bor, Hoofd, Meteren, ubi sup. Strada, viii. 421.

† Nearly three times as many, if the estimate of De Thou as to the number of Huguenots slain, three thousand, be correct.—De Thou, liv. 53, vi. 443. Many contemporary writers have, however, placed the number of the Paris victims as high as ten thousand.

‡ De Thou, vi. 442.

equal number of dead bodies, and to an incredibly superior amount of plunder?

Marvellously few Spaniards were slain in these eventful days. Two hundred killed is the largest number stated.*

---

* Bor's estimate is two hundred Spaniards killed and four hundred wounded, ix. 731. Hoofd, xi. 463, gives the same. Mendoza allows only fourteen Spaniards to have been killed, and rather more than twenty wounded. Meteren, as usual, considering the honor of his countrymen at stake, finds a grim consolation in adding a few to the number of the enemies slain, and gives a total of three hundred Spaniards killed.—vi. 110. Strada (viii. 422) gives the two extremes; so that it is almost certain that the number was not less than fourteen nor more than two hundred. These statistics are certainly curious, for it would seem almost impossible that a force numbering between thirty-five hundred and five thousand men (there is this amount of discrepancy in the different estimates) should capture and plunder, with so little loss to themselves, a city of two hundred thousand souls, defended by an army of at least twelve thousand, besides a large proportion of burghers bearing weapons. No wonder that the chivalrous Brantome was in an ecstasy of delight at the achievement (Hom. Illust., etc., ii. 204), and that the Netherlanders, seeing the prowess and the cruelty of their foes, should come to doubt whether they were men or devils. This disproportion between the number of Spaniards and States' soldiers slain was the same in all the great encounters, particularly in those of the period which now occupies us. In the six months between the end of August, 1576, and the signing of the perpetual edict on the 17th of February, 1577, the Spaniards killed twenty thousand, by the admission of the Netherlanders themselves, and acknowledged less than six slain on their own side! Mendoza, xvi. 335. —Compare Cabrera, xi. 866; Meteren, vi. 120. So much for the blood expended annually or monthly by the Netherlanders in defence of liberty and religion. As for the money consumed, the usual estimate of the expense of the States' army was from 800,000 to one million guldens monthly. (Meteren, viii. 138[d] and 144.) The same historian calculates the expense of Philip's army at forty-two millions of crowns for the nine years from 1567 to 1576, which would give nearly 400,000 dollars monthly, half of which, he says, came from Spain. The Netherlanders, therefore, furnished the other half, so that 200,000 dollars, equal to 500,000 guldens, monthly, were to be added to the million required for their own war department. Here then was a tax of one and a half millions monthly, or eighteen millions yearly, simply for the keeping of the two armies on foot to destroy the Netherlanders and consume their substance. The frightful loss by confiscations, plunderings, brandschettings, and the sackings of cities and villages innumerable, was all in addition, of course, but that enormous amount defies calculation. The regular expense in money which they were to meet, if they could, for the mere pay and provision of the armies, was as above, and equal to at least sixty millions yearly, to-day, making the common allowance for the difference in the value of money. This was certainly sufficient for a population of three millions. Their frequent promise to maintain their liberty with their "goods

The discrepancy seems monstrous, but it is hardly more than often existed between the losses inflicted and sustained by the Spaniards in such combats. Their prowess was equal to their ferocity, and this was enough to make them seem endowed with preterhuman powers. When it is remembered, also, that the burghers were insufficiently armed, that many of their defenders turned against them, that many thousands fled in the first moments of the encounter—and when the effect of a sudden and awful panic is duly considered, the discrepancy between the number of killed on the two sides will not seem so astonishing.

A few officers of distinction were taken alive and carried to the castle. Among these were the Seigneur de Capres and young Count Egmont. The councillor Jerome de Roda was lounging on a chair in an open gallery when these two gentlemen were brought before him, and Capres was base enough to make a low obeisance to the man who claimed to represent the whole government of his Majesty.* The worthy successor of Vargas replied to his captive's greeting by a "kick in his stomach," adding, with a brutality which his prototype might have envied, "*Ah puto tradidor,*"—whoreson traitor—"let me have no salutations from such as you."† Young Egmont, who had been captured, fighting bravely at the head of coward troops, by Julian Romero, who nine years before had stood on his father's scaffold, regarded this brutal scene with haughty indignation. This behaviour had more effect upon Roda than the suppleness of Capres. "I am sorry for your misfortune, Count," said the councillor, without however rising from his chair; "such is the lot of those who

---

and their blood" was no idle boast; three thousand men and one and a hall million florins being consumed monthly.

* Bor, ix. 731. Hoofd, xi. 412. Meteren, vi. 110. "——pour certaines bonnes considérations j'ay prins mon logis en ce chasteau, qu'est la maison royalle de sa Maj^{te}, pour d'icy pourveoir et ordonner toutes les choses de son service, jusques les seigneurs du conseil soyent remis en leur entière liberté," etc.—Letter of Jerome de Roda to the authorities of Antwerp, Sept. 8, 1576. III. Register der Dolianten van Brabant, A°. 1576, f. 203. MS., Hague Archives.

† Bor, ix. 731. Hoofd, xi. 462. Meteren, vi. 110.

take arms against their King."* This was the unfortunate commencement of Philip Egmont's career, which was destined to be inglorious, vacillating, base, and on more than one occasion unlucky.

A shiver ran through the country as the news of the horrible crime was spread, but it was a shiver of indignation, not of fear. Already the negotiations at Ghent between the representatives of the Prince and of Holland and Zealand with the deputies of the other provinces were in a favorable train, and the effect of this event upon their counsels was rather quickening than appalling. A letter from Jerome de Roda to the King was intercepted, giving an account of the transaction. In that document the senator gave the warmest praise to Sancho d'Avila, Julian Romero, Alonzo de Vargas, Francis Verdugo, as well as to the German colonels Fugger, Frondsberger, Polwiller, and others who had most exerted themselves in the massacre. "I wish your Majesty much good of this victory," concluded the councillor, "'tis a very great one, and the damage to the city is enormous."† This cynical view was not calculated to produce a soothing effect on the exasperated minds of the people. On the other hand, the estates of Brabant addressed an eloquent appeal to the states-general, reciting their wrongs, and urging immediate action. "'Tis notorious," said the remonstrants, "that Antwerp was but yesterday the first and principal ornament of all Europe; the refuge of all the nations of the world; the source and supply of countless treasure; the nurse of all arts and industry; the protectress of the Roman Catholic religion; the guardian of science and virtue; and, above all these pre-eminences, more than faithful and obedient to her sovereign prince and lord. The city is now changed to a gloomy cavern, filled with robbers and murderers, enemies of God, the King, and all good subjects."‡ They then proceeded to recite the story of the massacre, "whereof the memory shall be abominable so long as the

---

* Bor, Hoofd, Meteren, ubi sup. Strada, viii. 418.

† Letter of Roda, apud Bor, ix. 737, 738.

‡ Remonstrance of the States of Brabant, in Bor, ix. 733.

world stands,"* and concluded with an urgent appeal for redress. They particularly suggested that an edict should forthwith be passed, forbidding the alienation of property and the exportation of goods in any form from Antwerp, together with concession of the right to the proprietors of reclaiming their stolen property summarily, whenever and wheresoever it might be found. In accordance with these instructions, an edict was passed, but somewhat tardily, in the hope of relieving some few of the evil consequences by which the Antwerp Fury had been attended.†

At about the same time the Prince of Orange addressed a remarkable letter‡ to the states-general then assembled at Ghent, urging them to hasten the conclusion of the treaty. The news of the massacre, which furnished an additional and most vivid illustration of the truth of his letter, had not then reached him at Middelburg, but the earnestness of his views, taken in connexion with this last dark deed, exerted a powerful and indelible effect. The letter was a masterpiece, because it was necessary, in his position, to inflame without alarming; to stimulate the feelings which were in unison, without shocking those which, if aroused, might prove discordant. Without, therefore, alluding in terms to the religious question, he dwelt upon the necessity of union, firmness, and wariness. If so much had been done by Holland and Zealand, how much more might be hoped when all the provinces were united? "The principal flower of the Spanish army has fallen," he said, "without having been able to conquer one of those provinces from those whom they call, in mockery, poor beggars; yet what is that handful of cities compared to all the provinces which might join us in the quarrel?"§ He

---

* "Waer van de memorie is en sal abominabel wesen so lang als de wereld staet," etc.—Remonstrance, etc. Bor, ubi sup.

† Bor, ix. 736, 737.

‡ The letter is published by Gachard, Correspondance de Guillaume le Tacit., iii. 140–154.

§ Gachard, Corresp., etc., iii. 147, 148.

warned the states of the necessity of showing a strong and united front; the King having been ever led to consider the movement in the Netherlands a mere conspiracy of individuals. "The King told me himself, in 1559," said Orange, "that if the estates had no pillars to lean upon, they would not talk so loud." It was, therefore, necessary to show that prelates, abbots, monks, seigniors, gentlemen, burghers, and peasants, the whole people in short, now cried with one voice, and desired with one will. To such a demonstration the King would not dare oppose himself. By thus preserving a firm and united front, sinking all minor differences, they would, moreover, inspire their friends and foreign princes with confidence. The princes of Germany, the lords and gentlemen of France, the Queen of England, although sympathizing with the misfortunes of the Netherlanders, had been unable effectually to help them, so long as their disunion prevented them from helping themselves; so long as even their appeal to arms seemed merely "a levy of bucklers, an emotion of the populace, which, like a wave of the sea, rises and sinks again as soon as risen."*

While thus exciting to union and firmness, he also took great pains to instil the necessity of wariness. They were dealing with an artful foe. Intercepted letters had already proved that the old dissimulation was still to be employed; that while Don John of Austria was on his way, the Netherlanders were to be lulled into confidence by glozing speeches. Roda was provided by the King with a secret programme of instructions for the new Governor's guidance, and Don Sancho d'Avila, for his countenance to the mutineers of Alost, had been applauded to the echo in Spain.† Was not this applause a frequent indication of the policy to be adopted by Don John, and a thousand times more significative one than the unmeaning phrases of barren benignity with

* Gachard, Corresp., etc., iii. 152.

† Ibid., iii. 129.

which public documents might be crammed? "The old tricks are again brought into service," said the Prince; "therefore 'tis necessary to ascertain your veritable friends, to tear off the painted masks from those who, under pretence of not daring to displease the King, are seeking to swim between two waters. 'Tis necessary to have a touchstone; to sign a declaration in such wise that you may know whom to trust, and whom to suspect."

The massacre at Antwerp and the eloquence of the Prince produced a most quickening effect upon the Congress at Ghent. Their deliberations had proceeded with decorum and earnestness, in the midst of the cannonading against the citadel, and the fortress fell on the same day which saw the conclusion of the treaty.*

This important instrument, by which the sacrifices and exertions of the Prince were, for a brief season, at least, rewarded, contained twenty-five articles.† The Prince of Orange, with the estates of Holland and Zealand, on the one side, and the provinces signing, or thereafter to sign the treaty, on the other, agreed that there should be a mutual forgiving and forgetting, as regarded the past. They vowed a close and faithful friendship for the future. They plighted a mutual promise to expel the Spaniards from the Netherlands without delay. As soon as this great deed should be done, there was to be a convocation of the states-general, on the basis of that assembly before which the abdication of the Emperor had taken place. By this congress, the affairs of religion in Holland and Zealand should be regulated, as well as the surrender of fortresses and other places belonging to his Majesty. There was to be full liberty of communication and

* Bor, ix. 727. Hoofd, xi. 470.—The final and decisive assault was made upon the 8th; the articles of surrender were arranged, and the castle was evacuated upon the 11th of November.—Meteren, vi. 113. Mendoza, xvi. 326. Archives. etc., v. 525.

† See them in Bor, ix. 738–741; Hoofd, xi. 467 and 470; Mendoza, xvi. 320–326; Meteren, vi. 112, sqq. et al.

traffic between the citizens of the one side and the other. It should not be legal, however, for those of Holland and Zealand to attempt anything outside their own territory against the Roman Catholic religion, nor for cause thereof to injure or irritate any one, by deed or word. All the placards and edicts on the subject of heresy, together with the criminal ordinances made by the Duke of Alva, were suspended, until the states-general should otherwise ordain. The Prince was to remain lieutenant, admiral, and general for his Majesty in Holland, Zealand, and the associated places, till otherwise provided by the states-general, after the departure of the Spaniards. The cities and places included in the Prince's commission, but not yet acknowledging his authority, should receive satisfaction from him, as to the point of religion and other matters, before subscribing to the union. All prisoners, and particularly the Comte de Bossu, should be released without ransom. All estates and other property not already alienated should be restored, all confiscations since 1566 being declared null and void. The Countess Palatine, widow of Brederode, and Count de Buren, son of the Prince of Orange, were expressly named in this provision. Prelates and ecclesiastical persons, having property in Holland and Zealand, should be reinstated, if possible; but in case of alienation, which was likely to be generally the case, there should be reasonable compensation. It was to be decided by the states-general whether the provinces should discharge the debts incurred by the Prince of Orange in his two campaigns. Provinces and cities should not have the benefit of this union until they had signed the treaty, but they should be permitted to sign it when they chose.*

This memorable document was subscribed at Ghent, on the 8th of November, by Saint Aldegonde, with eight other commissioners appointed by the Prince of Orange and the estates of Holland on the one side, and by Elbertus Leoninus and other deputies appointed by Brabant, Flanders, Artois, Hain-

* See particularly Arts. 1, 2, 4, 5, 7, 8, 10, and 25.

ault, Valenciennes, Lille, Douay, Orchies, Namur, Tournay, Utrecht, and Mechlin on the other side.*

The arrangement was a masterpiece of diplomacy on the part of the Prince, for it was as effectual a provision for the safety of the Reformed religion as could be expected under the circumstances. It was much, considering the change which had been wrought of late years in the fifteen provinces, that they should consent to any treaty with their two heretic sisters. It was much more that the Pacification should recognize the new religion as the established creed of Holland and Zealand, while at the same time the infamous edicts of Charles were formally abolished. In the fifteen Catholic provinces, there was to be no prohibition of private Reformed worship, and it might be naturally expected that with time and the arrival of the banished religionists, a firmer stand would be taken in favor of the Reformation. Meantime, the new religion was formally established in two provinces, and tolerated, in secret, in the other fifteen ; the Inquisition was for ever abolished, and the whole strength of the nation enlisted to expel the foreign soldiery from the soil. This was the work of William the Silent,† and the great Prince thus saw the labor of years crowned with, at least, a momentary success. His satisfaction was very great when it was announced to him, many days before the exchange of the signatures, that the treaty had been concluded. He was desirous that the Pacification should be referred for approval, not to the municipal magistrates only, but to the people itself.‡ In all great emergencies, the man who, in his whole character, least resembled

* Bor, ix. 741.

† There is no mention in the Resolutions of Holland, from the 25th of April to the 8th of November, 1576, of any draughts for a treaty, or of any preparations for, or deliberations concerning, such a document. The inference of Kluit (i. 146, 147) is that the Prince, with his council and nine commissioners, managed the whole negotiation; such was the confidence reposed in him by the two provinces.

‡ Two commissioners were, in fact, despatched to each city of Holland, to lay the treaty before the respective governments, and obtain their signatures.—Kluit, Holl., Staatsreg., i. 148.

a demagogue, either of antiquity or of modern times, was eager for a fresh expression of the popular will. On this occasion, however, the demand for approbation was superfluous. The whole country thought with his thoughts, and spoke with his words, and the Pacification, as soon as published, was received with a shout of joy.* Proclaimed in the market-place of every city and village, it was ratified, not by votes, but by hymns of thanksgiving, by triumphal music, by thundering of cannon, and by the blaze of beacons, throughout the Netherlands. Another event added to the satisfaction of the hour. The country so recently, and by deeds of such remarkable audacity, conquered by the Spaniards in the north, was recovered almost simultaneously with the conclusion of the Ghent treaty. It was a natural consequence of the great mutiny. The troops having entirely deserted Mondragon, it became necessary for that officer to abandon Zierickzee, the city which had been won with so much valor. In the beginning of November, the capital, and with it the whole island of Schouwen, together with the rest of Zealand, excepting Tholen, was recovered by Count Hohenlo, lieutenant-general of the Prince of Orange, and acting according to his instructions.†

Thus, on this particular point of time, many great events had been crowded. At the very same moment Zealand had been redeemed, Antwerp ruined, and the league of all the Netherlands against the Spaniards concluded. It now became known that another and most important event had occurred at the same instant. On the day before the Antwerp massacre, four days before the publication of the Ghent treaty, a foreign cavalier, attended by a Moorish slave and by six men-at-arms, rode into the streets of Luxemburg.‡ The cavalier was Don

* Bor, ix. 740. Wagenaer, vii. 117.—"—— avecq une si grande joie et contentement du peuple, de toutes les provinces en général et en particulier, qu'il n'est mémoire d'homme qui puisse se souvenir d'une pareille. Un chascun se peult souvenir des promesses mutuelles d'amitié qui y sont compris," etc. —Apologie du P. d'Orange, p. 95.

† Bor, ix. 727. Hoofd, xi. 470.

‡ Bor, ix. 742. Hoofd, xi. 472.

Ottavio Gonzaga, brother of the Prince of Melfi. The Moorish slave was Don John of Austria, the son of the Emperor, the conqueror of Granada, the hero of Lepanto.* The new Governor-general had traversed Spain and France in disguise with great celerity, and in the romantic manner which belonged to his character. He stood at last on the threshold of the Netherlands, but with all his speed he had arrived a few days too late.

* Strada, ix. 423. Cabrera, xi. 874.

PART V.

DON JOHN OF AUSTRIA.

1576—1578.

CHAPTER I.

Birth and parentage of Don John—Barbara Blomberg—Early education and recognition by Philip—Brilliant military career—Campaign against the Moors—Battle of Lepanto—Extravagant ambition—Secret and rapid journey of the new Governor to the Netherlands—Contrast between Don John and William of Orange—Secret instructions of Philip and private purposes of the Governor—Cautious policy and correspondence of the Prince—Preliminary negotiations with Don John at Luxemburg characterized—Union of Brussels—Resumption of negotiations with the Governor at Huy—The discussions analyzed and characterized—Influence of the new Emperor Rudolph II. and of his envoys—Treaty of Marche en Famine, or the Perpetual Edict, signed—Remarks upon that transaction—Views and efforts of Orange in opposition to the treaty—His letter, in name of Holland and Zealand, to the States-General—Anxiety of the royal government to gain over the Prince—Secret mission of Leoninus—His instructions from Don John—Fruitless attempts to corrupt the Prince—Secret correspondence between Don John and Orange—Don John at Louvain—His efforts to ingratiate himself with the Netherlanders—His incipient popularity—Departure of the Spanish troops—Duke of Aerschot appointed Governor of Antwerp citadel—His insincere character.

Don John of Austria was now in his thirty-second year, having been born in Ratisbon on the 24th of February, 1545.* His father was Charles the Fifth, Emperor of Germany, King of Spain, Dominator of Asia, Africa, and America; his mother was Barbara Blomberg, washerwoman of Ratisbon. Introduced to the Emperor, originally, that she might alleviate his melancholy by her singing,† she soon exhausted all that was harmonious in her nature, for never was a more uncomfortable,

---

* Strada, x. 506.

† Ibid.—Compare Brantome, ii. 149.

unmanageable personage than Barbara in her after life. Married to one Pyramus Kegell, who was made a military commissary in the Netherlands, she was left a widow in the beginning of Alva's administration. Placed under the especial superintendence of the Duke, she became the torment of that warrior's life. The terrible Governor, who could almost crush the heart out of a nation of three millions, was unable to curb this single termagant. Philip had expressly forbidden her to marry again, but Alva informed him that she was surrounded by suitors. Philip had insisted that she should go into a convent, but Alva, who, with great difficulty, had established her quietly in Ghent, assured his master that she would break loose again at the bare suggestion of a convent. Philip wished her to go to Spain, sending her word that Don John was mortified by the life his mother was leading, but she informed the Governor that she would be cut to pieces before she would go to Spain. She had no objection to see her son, but she knew too well how women were treated in that country. The Duke complained most pathetically to his Majesty of the life they all led with the ex-mistress of the Emperor. Never, he frequently observed, had woman so terrible a head.* She was obstinate, reckless, abominably extravagant. She had been provided in Ghent with a handsome establishment: "with a duenna, six other women, a major domo, two pages, one chaplain, an almoner, and four men-servants, and this seemed a sufficiently liberal scheme of life for the widow of a commissary. Moreover, a very ample allowance had been made for the education of her only legitimate son, Conrad, the other having perished by an accident on the day of his father's death. While Don John of Austria was gathering laurels in Granada, his half-brother, Pyramus junior, had been ingloriously drowned in a cistern at Ghent.

Barbara's expenses were exorbitant ; her way of life scandalous. To send her money, said Alva, was to throw it into

* Correspondance de Philippe II., 884, 912, 960, 969, 984, 987, 1025, 1054.

the sea. In two days she would have spent in dissipation and feasting any sums which the King might choose to supply. The Duke, who feared nothing else in the world, stood in mortal awe of the widow Kegell. "A terrible animal, indeed, is an unbridled woman," wrote secretary Cayas, from Madrid, at the close of Alva's administration, for, notwithstanding every effort to entice, to intimidate, and to kidnap her from the Netherlands, there she remained, through all vicissitudes, even till the arrival of Don John. By his persuasions or commands she was, at last, induced to accept an exile for the remainder of her days, in Spain, but revenged herself by asserting that he was quite mistaken in supposing himself the Emperor's child; a point, certainly, upon which her authority might be thought conclusive. Thus there was a double mystery about Don John. He might be the issue of august parentage on one side; he was, possibly, sprung of most ignoble blood. Base-born at best, he was not sure whether to look for the author of his being in the halls of the Cæsars or the booths of Ratisbon mechanics.*

Whatever might be the heart of the mystery, it is certain that it was allowed to enwrap all the early life of Don John. The Emperor, who certainly never doubted his responsibility

---

* Corresp. de Philippe II., 1025. "Lo tiene banqueteado"——"Quan terribile animal es una muger des énfrenada."—Ibid., ii. 1255. Meteren, vi. 119d.—Compare Van der Hammen y Leon: Don Juan de Austria; Historia, Madrid, 1627, vi. 294. Strada, Brantome.—Compare V. d. Vynckt, ii. 218.—"Wie Zijne ware moeder geweest zii, is een raadsal gebleeven, dat nooit volkomen opgelost is," etc. etc.—Cabrera, xii. 1009. An absurd rumor had existed that Barbara Blomberg had only been employed to personate Don John's mother. She died at an estate called Arronjo de Molinos, four leagues from Madrid, some years after the death of Don John.—Cabrera, xii. 1009. The following squib, taken from a MS. collection of pasquilles of the day, shows what was a very general opinion in the Netherlands concerning the parentage of Don John and the position of Barbara Blomberg. The verses are not without ingenuity:—

"ECHO.

'——sed at Austriacum nostrum redeamus—eamus
Hunc Cesaris filium esse satis est notum—nothum
Multi tamen de ejus patre dubitavere—*vere*
Cujus ergo filium eum dicunt Itali—*Itali*

for the infant's existence, had him conveyed instantly to Spain, where he was delivered to Louis Quixada, of the Imperial household, by whom he was brought up in great retirement at Villa-garcia. Magdalen Ulloa, wife of Quixada, watched over his infancy with maternal and magnanimous care, for her husband's extreme solicitude for the infant's welfare had convinced her that he was its father. On one occasion, when their house was in flames, Quixada rescued the infant before he saved his wife, "although Magdalen knew herself to be dearer to him than the apple of his eye." From that time forth she altered her opinion, and believed the mysterious child to be of lofty origin. The boy grew up full of beauty, grace, and agility, the leader of all his companions in every hardy sport. Through the country round there were none who could throw the javelin, break a lance, or ride at the ring like little Juan Quixada. In taming unmanageable horses he was celebrated for his audacity and skill. These accomplishments, however, were likely to prove of but slender advantage in the ecclesiastical profession, to which he had been destined by his Imperial father. The death of Charles occurred before clerical studies had been commenced, and Philip, to whom the secret had been confided at the close of the Emperor's life, prolonged the delay thus interposed.* Juan had already reached his fourteenth year, when one day his supposed father Quixada invited him to ride towards Valladolid to see the royal hunt. Two horses stood at the

---

Verum mater satis est nota in nostrâ republicâ—*publica*
Imo hactenus egit in Brabantiâ ter voere—hoere
Crimen est ne frui amplexu unius Cesaris tam generosi—osi
Pluribus ergo usa in vitâ est—ita est
Seu post Cesaris congressum non vere ante—ante
Tace garrula ne tale quippiam loquare—quare?
Nescis quâ pœna afficiendum dixerit Belgium insigne—igne,"
etc. etc. etc.

Vers Satiriques contra Dom Jean d'Autriche, MS., Bibl. de Bourg., 17,524.

* Strada, x. 506, 507. Cabrera, xi. 874.

door—a splendidly caparisoned charger and a common hackney. The boy naturally mounted the humbler steed, and they set forth for the mountains of Toro, but on hearing the bugles of the approaching huntsmen, Quixada suddenly halted, and bade his youthful companion exchange horses with himself. When this had been done, he seized the hand of the wondering boy and kissing it respectfully, exclaimed, "Your Highness will be informed as to the meaning of my conduct by his Majesty, who is even now approaching." They had proceeded but a short distance before they encountered the royal hunting party, when both Quixada and young Juan dismounted, and bent the knee to their monarch. Philip, commanding the boy to rise, asked him if he knew his father's name. Juan replied, with a sigh, that he had at that moment lost the only father whom he had known, for Quixada had just disowned him. "You have the same father as myself," cried the King; "the Emperor Charles was the august parent of us both." Then tenderly embracing him, he commanded him to remount his horse, and all returned together to Valladolid, Philip observing with a sentimentality that seems highly apocryphal, that he had never brought home such precious game from any hunt before.*

This theatrical recognition of imperial descent was one among the many romantic incidents of Don John's picturesque career, for his life was never destined to know the commonplace. He now commenced his education, in company with his two nephews, the Duchess Margaret's son, and Don Carlos, Prince-royal of Spain. They were all of the same age, but the superiority of Don John was soon recognized. It was not difficult to surpass the limping, malicious, Carlos, either in

* "Nunquam se jucundiorem venando prædam quam eo die retulisse domum."—Strada, x. 508. It must be borne in mind that the legends of Don John's boyhood have passed through the busy and inventive brain of Father Strada. Placed in a severe crucible, much of the romantic filigree would perhaps disappear, but the substance of his narrative is genuine.—Compare V. d. Vynckt, ii. 219.

physical graces or intellectual accomplishments; but the graceful, urbane, and chivalrous Alexander, destined afterwards to such wide celebrity, was a more formidable rival, yet even the professed panegyrist of the Farnese family, exalts the son of Barbara Blomberg over the grandson of Margaret Van Geest.*

Still destined for the clerical profession, Don John, at the age of eighteen, to avoid compliance with Philip's commands, made his escape to Barcelona. It was his intention to join the Maltese expedition. Recalled peremptorily by Philip, he was for a short time in disgrace, but afterwards made his peace with the monarch by denouncing some of the mischievous schemes of Don Carlos. Between the Prince-royal and the imperial bastard, there had always been a deep animosity, the Infante having on one occasion saluted him with the most vigorous and offensive appellation which his illegitimate birth could suggest. "Base-born or not," returned Don John, "at any rate I had a better father than yours."† The words were probably reported to Philip and doubtless rankled in his breast, but nothing appeared on the surface, and the youth rose rapidly in favor. In his twenty-third year, he was appointed to the command of the famous campaign against the insurgent Moors of Granada. Here he reaped his first laurels, and acquired great military celebrity. It is difficult to be dazzled by such glory. He commenced his operations by the expulsion of nearly all the Moorish inhabitants of Granada, bed-ridden men, women, and children, together, and the cruelty inflicted, the sufferings patiently endured in that memorable deportation, were enormous.† But few of the many thousand exiles survived the horrid march, those who were so unfortunate as to do so being sold into slavery by their captors.‡ Still a few Moors held out in

---

* Strada, x. 509.

† "Hijo de puta." The anecdote is related by V. der Vynckt (ii. 220) on the authority of Amelot de la Houssaie. "Yo soy hijo de mejor padre."—Ibid.

‡ Strada, 509. De Thou, liv. vi. 72, sqq. (tom. vi.)

their mountain fastnesses, and two years long the rebellion of this handful made head against the power of Spain. Had their envoys to the Porte succeeded in their negotiation, the throne of Philip might have trembled ; but Selim hated the Republic of Venice as much as he loved the wine of Cyprus. While the Moors were gasping out their last breath in Granada and Ronda, the Turks had wrested the island of Venus from the grasp of the haughty Republic. Famagosta had fallen ; thousands of Venetians had been butchered with a ferocity which even Christians could not have surpassed ; the famous General Bragadino had been flayed, stuffed, and sent hanging on the yard-arm of a frigate, to Constantinople, as a present to the Commander of the Faithful ; and the mortgage of Catherine Cornaro, to the exclusion of her husband's bastards, had been thus definitely cancelled. With such practical enjoyments, Selim was indifferent to the splendid but shadowy vision of the Occidental caliphate—yet the revolt of the Moors was only terminated, after the departure of Don John, by the Duke of Arcos.

The war which the Sultan had avoided in the West, came to seek him in the East. To lift the Crucifix against the Crescent, at the head of the powerful but quarrelsome alliance between Venice, Spain, and Rome, Don John arrived at Naples.† He brought with him more than a hundred ships and twenty-three thousand men, as the Spanish contingent. Three months long the hostile fleets had been cruising in the same waters without an encounter ; three more were wasted in barren manœuvres. Neither Mussulman nor Christian had much inclination for the conflict, the Turk fearing the consequences of a defeat, by which gains already secured might be forfeited ; the allies being appalled at the possibility of their own triumph. Nevertheless, the Otto-

---

* De Thou, liv. xlviii., vi. 212–215, (liv. xlix).—Compare Cabrera, liv. vii. c. 21, seq.

† Cabrera, ix. 675[a]. De Thou, vi. 226.

mans manœuvred themselves at last into the gulf of Lepanto, the Christians manœuvred themselves towards its mouth as the foe was coming forth again. The conflict thus rendered inevitable, both Turk and Christian became equally eager for the fray, equally confident of victory. Six hundred vessels of war met face to face. Rarely in history had so gorgeous a scene of martial array been witnessed. An October sun gilded the thousand beauties of an Ionian landscape. Athens and Corinth were behind the combatants, the mountains of Alexander's Macedon rose in the distance; the rock of Sappho and the heights of Actium were before their eyes. Since the day when the world had been lost and won beneath that famous promontory, no such combat as the one now approaching had been fought upon the waves. The chivalrous young commander despatched energetic messages to his fellow chieftains, and now that it was no longer possible to elude the encounter, the martial ardor of the allies was kindled. The Venetian High-Admiral replied with words of enthusiasm. Colonna, lieutenant of the league, answered his chief in the language of St. Peter; "Though I die, yet will I not deny thee."*

The fleet was arranged in three divisions. The Ottomans, not drawn up in crescent form, as usual, had the same triple disposition. Barbarigo and the other Venetians commanded on the left, John Andrew Doria on the right, while Don John himself and Colonna were in the centre, Crucifix in hand, the High-Admiral rowed from ship to ship exhorting generals and soldiers to show themselves worthy of a cause which he had persuaded himself was holy.† Fired by

* De Thou, vi. liv. l. 226, et seq. Cabrera, ix. cap. 24, 25. Brantome, ii. 119, et seq. See the statements of Al-Hamet, after the battle, to the Conqueror. —Navarrete, Documentos Inéditos, iii. 249–251. Total number of Christian ships, three hundred and thirty-six; of Turkish, two hundred and eighty-three.—Relacion cierta y verdadera, Documentos Inéditos, iii. 255–256. "Etiamsi oporteat me mori, non te negabo."—Brantome, Hommes Illust., ii. 122.

† Relacion cierta y verdadera, Documentos Inéditos, iii. 243. Ibid.—Compare de Thou, vi. 239–243. Brantome, ii. 124.

his eloquence and by the sight of the enemy, his hearers answered with eager shouts, while Don John returned to his ship, knelt upon the quarter-deck, and offered a prayer. He then ordered the trumpets to sound the assault, commanded his sailing-master to lay him alongside the Turkish Admiral, and the battle began. The Venetians, who were first attacked, destroyed ship after ship of their assailants after a close and obstinate contest, but Barbarigo fell dead ere the sunset, with an arrow through his brain. Meantime the action, immediately after the first onset, had become general. From noon till evening the battle raged, with a carnage rarely recorded in history. Don John's own ship lay yard-arm and yard-arm with the Turkish Admiral, and exposed to the fire of seven large vessels besides. It was a day when personal audacity, not skilful tactics, was demanded, and the imperial bastard showed the metal he was made of. The Turkish Admiral's ship was destroyed, his head exposed from Don John's deck upon a pike, and the trophy became the signal for a general panic and a complete victory. By sunset the battle had been won.*

Of nearly three hundred Turkish galleys, but fifty made their escape. From twenty-five to thirty thousand Turks were slain, and perhaps ten thousand Christians. The galley-slaves on both sides fought well, and the only beneficial result of the victory was the liberation of several thousand Christian captives. It is true that their liberty was purchased with the lives of a nearly equal number of Christian soldiers, and by the reduction to slavery of almost as many thousand Mussulmen,† duly distributed among the Christian

---

* Relacion cierta y verdadera, 244. Cabrera, ix., cap. 25. De Thou, vi. 242, sqq. Brantome, ii. 126, sqq.

† Cabrera says that thirty thousand Turks were slain, ten thousand made prisoners, ten thousand Christians killed, and fifteen thousand Christian prisoners liberated, ix. 693. De Thou's estimate is twenty-five thousand Turks killed, three thousand prisoners, and ten thousand Christians killed, vi. 247. Brantome states the number of Turks killed at thirty thousand, *without counting* those who were drowned or who died afterwards of their wounds; six

victors. Many causes contributed to this splendid triumph. The Turkish ships, inferior in number, were also worse manned than those of their adversaries, and their men were worse armed. Every bullet of the Christians told on muslin turbans and embroidered tunics, while the arrows of the Moslems fell harmless on the casques and corslets of their foes. The Turks, too, had committed the fatal error of fighting upon a lee shore. Having no sea room, and being repelled in their first onset, many galleys were driven upon the rocks, to be destroyed with all their crews.*

But whatever the cause of the victory, its consequence was to spread the name and fame of Don John of Austria throughout the world. Alva wrote, with enthusiasm, to

---

thousand prisoners, twelve thousand Christian prisoners liberated, and ten thousand Christians killed. Hoofd, vi. 214, gives the figures at twenty-five thousand Turks and ten thousand Christians slain. Bor, v. 354[a], (t. i.) makes a minute estimate, on the authority of Pietro Contareno, stating the number of Christians killed at seven thousand six hundred and fifty, that of Turks at twenty-five thousand one hundred and fifty, Turkish prisoners at three thousand eight hundred and forty-six, and Christians liberated at twelve thousand; giving the number of Turkish ships destroyed at eighty, captured fifty. According to the "Relacion cierta y verdadera," (which was drawn up a few days after the action,) the number of Turks slain was "thirty thousand and upwards, besides many prisoners," that of Christians killed was seven thousand, of Christian slaves liberated twelve thousand, of Ottoman ships taken or destroyed two hundred and thirty. Documentos Inéditos, iii. 249. Philip sent an express order, forbidding the ransoming of even the captive officers (Carta de F. II. à D. I. de Zuñiga. Documentos Inéditos, iii. 236). The Turkish slaves were divided among the victors in the proportion of one-half to Philip and one-half to the Pope and Venice. The other booty was distributed on the same principle. Out of the Pope's share Don John received, as a present, one hundred and seventy-four slaves (Documentos Inéditos, iii. 229). Alexander of Parma received thirty slaves; Requesens thirty. To each general of infantry was assigned six slaves; to each colonel four; to each ship's captain one. The number of "slaves in chains" (esclavos de cadena) allotted to Philip was thirty-six hundred (Documentos Inéditos, 257). Seven thousand two hundred Turkish slaves, therefore, at least, were divided among Christians. This number of wretches, who were not fortunate enough to die with their twenty-five thousand comrades, must be set off against the twelve thousand Christian slaves liberated, in the general settlement of the account with Humanity.

* De Thou, vi. 245, 246, 247.

congratulate him ; pronouncing the victory the most brilliant one ever achieved by Christians, and Don John the greatest general since the death of Julius Cæsar. At the same time, with a sarcastic fling at the erection of the Escorial, he advised Philip to improve this new success in some more practical way than by building a house for the Lord and a sepulchre for the dead. "If," said the Duke, "the conquests of Spain be extended in consequence of this triumph, then, indeed, will the Cherubim and Seraphim sing glory to God."* A courier, despatched post haste to Spain, bore the glorious news, together with the sacred standard of the Prophet, the holy of holies, inscribed with the name of Allah twenty-eight thousand nine hundred times, always kept in Mecca during peace, and never since the conquest of Constantinople lost in battle before. The King was at vespers in the Escorial. Entering the sacred precincts, breathless, travel-stained, excited, the messenger found Philip impassible as marble to the wondrous news. Not a muscle of the royal visage was moved, not a syllable escaped the royal lips, save a brief order to the clergy to continue the interrupted vespers. When the service had been methodically concluded, the King made known the intelligence and requested a Te Deum.†

The youthful commander-in-chief obtained more than his full meed of glory. No doubt he had fought with brilliant courage, yet in so close and murderous a conflict, the valor of no single individual could decide the day, and the result was due to the combined determination of all. Had Don John remained at Naples, the issue might have easily been the same. Barbarigo, who sealed the victory with his blood ; Colonna, who celebrated a solemn triumph on his return to Rome ; Parma, Doria, Giustiniani, Venieri, might each as well have claimed a monopoly of the glory, had not the Pope, at

* Parabien del Duque de Alba, Documentos Inéditos, iii. 270–287.

† Relacion por Luis del Marmol, Documentos Inéditos, iii. 270–573.

Philip's entreaty, conferred the baton of command upon Don John.* The meagre result of the contest is as notorious as the victory. While Constantinople was quivering with apprehension, the rival generals were already wrangling with animosity. Had the Christian fleet advanced, every soul would have fled from the capital, but Providence had ordained otherwise, and Don John sailed westwardly with his ships. He made a descent on the Barbary coast, captured Tunis, destroyed Biserta, and brought King Amidas and his two sons prisoners to Italy. Ordered by Philip to dismantle the fortifications of Tunis, he replied by repairing them thoroughly, and by placing a strong garrison within the citadel. Intoxicated with his glory, the young adventurer already demanded a crown, and the Pope was disposed to proclaim him King of Tunis, for the Queen of the Lybian seas was to be the capital of his Empire, the new Carthage which he already dreamed.

Philip thought it time to interfere, for he felt that his own crown might be insecure, with such a restless and ambitious spirit indulging in possible and impossible chimeras. He removed John de Soto, who had been Don John's chief councillor and emissary to the Pope, and substituted in his place the celebrated and ill-starred Escovedo.† The new secretary, however, entered as heartily but secretly into all these romantic schemes. Disappointed of the Empire which he had contemplated on the edge of the African desert, the champion of the Cross turned to the cold islands of the

* De Thou, vi. 243.—Compare Cabrera, ix. 689[b]. Brantome, ii. 133. Even Don John's favorite monkey distinguished himself in the action. The creature is reported to have picked up a shell, which had fallen upon a holy shrine, close at its master's feet, and to have thrown it overboard.—Van der Hammen y Leon, iii. 180.

† De Thou, Brantome, Cabrera in locis citatis. Strada, x. 510. De Thou, vii. 112. Van der Vynckt, ii. 221. Bor, xi. 840, 841. Memorial de Ant. Perez Obras y Relaciones, Geneva, 1644, p. 297.

‡ Bor, xi. 840, 841. Strada, x. 510. De Thou, vii. 112. Memorial de Antonio Perez, Obras y Relaciones, p. 298, 299.

northern seas. There sighed, in captivity, the beauteous Mary of Scotland, victim of the heretic Elizabeth. His susceptibility to the charms of beauty—a characteristic as celebrated as his courage—was excited, his chivalry aroused. What holier triumph for the conqueror of the Saracens than the subjugation of these northern infidels? He would dethrone the proud Elizabeth; he would liberate and espouse the Queen of Scots, and together they would reign over the two united realms. All that the Pope could do with bulls and blessings, letters of excommunication, and patents of investiture, he did with his whole heart. Don John was at liberty to be King of England and Scotland as soon as he liked;* all that was left to do was to conquer the kingdoms.

Meantime, while these schemes were flitting through his brain, and were yet kept comparatively secret by the Pope, Escovedo, and himself, the news reached him in Italy that he had been appointed Governor-General of the Netherlands.† Nothing could be more opportune. In the provinces were ten thousand veteran Spaniards, ripe for adventure, hardened by years of warfare, greedy for gold, audacious almost beyond humanity, the very instruments for his scheme. The times were critical in the Netherlands, it was true; yet he would soon pacify those paltry troubles, and then sweep forward to his prize. Yet events were rushing forward with such feverish rapidity, that he might be too late for his adventure. Many days were lost in the necessary journey from Italy into Spain to receive the final instructions of the King. The news from the provinces grew more and more threatening.

---

* Strada, x. 511. Bor, xi. 840, 841. V. d. Vynckt, ii. 221. De Thou, vii. 549.—"Y dixo le el nuncio que havia tenido un despacho de Roma, en que le avisa haver llegado alta otro, del Senor Don Juan en çifra sobre lo de Inglaterra pidiendo á su sanctidad favor para alto de persona (y aun con la investidura del Reyno en la persona de Don Juan como se entendió despues), bullas, breves, dinero, y que assy se le havia embiado persona con todo ello."—Memorial de Antonio Perez. Obras y Relaciones, p. 303.

† Strada, x. 510. De Thou, vii. 391.

With the impetuosity and romance of his temperament, he selected his confidential friend Ottavio Gonzaga, six men-at-arms, and an adroit and well-experienced Swiss courier, who knew every road of France.* It was no light adventure for the Catholic Governor-General of the Netherlands to traverse the kingdom at that particular juncture. Staining his bright locks and fair face to the complexion of a Moor, he started on his journey, attired as the servant of Gonzaga. Arriving at Paris, after a rapid journey, he descended at a hostelry opposite the residence of the Spanish ambassador, Don Diego de Cuñiga. After nightfall he had a secret interview with that functionary, and learning, among other matters, that there was to be a great ball that night at the Louvre, he determined to go thither in disguise. There, notwithstanding his hurry, he had time to see and to become desperately enamored of "that wonder of beauty," the fair and frail Margaret of Valois, Queen of Navarre. Her subsequent visit to her young adorer at Namur, to be recorded in a future page of this history, was destined to mark the last turning point in his picturesque career. On his way to the Netherlands he held a rapid interview with the Duke of Guise, to arrange his schemes for the liberation and espousal of that noble's kinswoman, the Scottish Queen; and on the 3rd of November he arrived at Luxemburg.†

There stood the young conqueror of Lepanto, his brain full of schemes, his heart full of hopes, on the threshhold of the Netherlands, at the entrance to what he believed the most brilliant chapter of his life—schemes, hopes, and visions, doomed speedily to fade before the cold reality with which he was to be confronted. Throwing off his disguise after reaching Luxemburg, the youthful paladin stood confessed. His appearance was as romantic as his origin and his exploits. Every contemporary chronicler, French, Spanish, Italian, Flemish, Roman, have dwelt upon his personal beauty and the

* Brantome, ii. 137. Strada, ix. 423. Cabrera, xi. 874.

† Cabrera, xi. 874. Strada, ix. 423. V. d. Vynckt, ii. 222. Bor, ix. 742. Brantome, ii. 137, 138. Hoofd, xi. 472.

singular fascination of his manner.* Symmetrical features, blue eyes of great vivacity, and a profusion of bright curling hair, were combined with a person not much above middle height, but perfectly well proportioned. Owing to a natural peculiarity of his head, the hair fell backward from the temples, and he had acquired the habit of pushing it from his brows. The custom became a fashion among the host of courtiers, who were but too happy to glass themselves in so brilliant a mirror. As Charles the Fifth, on his journey to Italy to assume the iron crown, had caused his hair to be clipped close, as a remedy for the headaches with which, at that momentous epoch, he was tormented, bringing thereby close shaven polls into extreme fashion; so a mass of hair pushed backward from the temples, in the style to which the name of John of Austria was appropriated, became the prevailing mode wherever the favorite son of the Emperor appeared.

Such was the last crusader whom the annals of chivalry were to know; the man who had humbled the crescent as it had not been humbled since the days of the Tancreds, the Baldwins, the Plantagenets—yet, after all, what was this brilliant adventurer when weighed against the tranquil Christian champion whom he was to meet face to face? The contrast was striking between the real and the romantic hero. Don John had pursued and achieved glory through victories with which the world was ringing; William was slowly compassing a country's emancipation through a series of defeats. He moulded a commonwealth and united hearts with as much contempt for danger as Don John had exhibited in scenes of slave driving and carnage. Amid fields of blood, and through webs of tortuous intrigue, the brave and subtle son of the Emperor pursued only his own objects. Tawdry schemes of personal ambition, conquests for his own benefit, impossible crowns for his own wearing, were the motives which impelled

---

* Meteren, vi. 119. Bentivoglio, etc., 218. Brantome, ii. 150. Strada, x. 509. J. R. Tassis, iv. 326.

† Strada, x. 513, 514.

him, and the prizes which he sought. His existence was feverish, fitful, and passionate. "Tranquil amid the raging billows," according to his favorite device, the father of his country waved aside the diadem which for him had neither charms nor meaning. Their characters were as contrasted as their persons. The curled darling of chivalry seemed a youth at thirty-one. Spare of figure, plain in apparel, benignant, but haggard of countenance, with temples bared by anxiety as much as by his helmet, earnest, almost devout in manner, in his own words, "Calvus et Calvinista,"* William of Orange was an old man at forty-three.

Perhaps there was as much good faith on the part of Don John, when he arrived in Luxemburg, as could be expected of a man coming directly from the cabinet of Philip. The King had secretly instructed him to conciliate the provinces, but to concede nothing,† for the Governor was only a new incarnation of the insane paradox that benignity and the system of Charles the Fifth were one. He was directed to restore the government to its state during the imperial epoch.‡ Seventeen provinces, in two of which the population were all dissenters, in all of which the principle of mutual toleration had just been accepted by Catholics and Protestants, were now to be brought back to the condition according to which all Protestants were beheaded, burned, or buried alive. So that the Inquisition, the absolute authority of the monarch, and the exclusive worship of the Roman Church were preserved intact, the King professed himself desirous of "extinguishing the fires of rebellion, and of saving the people from the last desperation." With these slight exceptions, Philip was willing to be very benignant. "More than this," said he,

---

* Gachard, Corresp. Guillaume le Tacit., iii., pref. lxiii. and note.—Compare Strada, ix. 44,—"Areschoti Duci —— nudato capite subridens, Vides inquit hoc calvitum, scito me non magis capite quam corde calvum esse."—Strada, ix. 434, 435.

† Instruccion Secreta qu' el Rey D. Felipe II., diò al Son. D. J. de Austria, escrivio la de mano propria. Bibl. de Bourgogne, MS., No. xvii. 385.

‡ "Que se vuelvan las cosas al govierno y pie antiguo del tiempo del Emperador," etc.—Instruccion Secreta, MS.

"cannot and ought not be conceded."* To these brief but pregnant instructions was added a morsel of advice, personal in its nature, but very characteristic of the writer. Don John was recommended to take great care of his soul, and also to be very cautious in the management of his amours.†

Thus counselled and secretly directed, the new Captain-General had been dismissed to the unhappy Netherlands. The position, however, was necessarily false. The man who was renowned for martial exploits, and notoriously devoured by ambition, could hardly inspire deep confidence in the pacific dispositions of the government. The crusader of Granada and Lepanto, the champion of the ancient Church, was not likely to please the rugged Zealanders who had let themselves be hacked to pieces rather than say one Paternoster, and who had worn crescents in their caps at Leyden, to prove their deeper hostility to the Pope than to the Turk. The imperial bastard would derive but slight consideration from his paternal blood, in a country where illegitimate birth was more unfavorably regarded than in most other countries, and where a Brabantine edict, recently issued in name of the King, deprived all political or civil functionaries not born in wedlock, of their offices.‡ Yet he had received instructions, at his departure, to bring about a pacification, if possible, always maintaining, however, the absolute authority of the crown and the exclusive exercise of the Catholic religion. How the two great points of his instructions were to be made entirely palatable, was left to time and chance. There was a vague notion that with the new Governor's fame, fascinating manners, and imperial parentage, he might accomplish a result which neither fraud nor force—not the arts of Granvelle, nor

* "—— Salvando la Religion y mi obediencia, quanto se puede llegando las cosas a estos terminos presupuestos que conviene atajar este fuego y no dexar llegar aquella gente a la ultima desperacion. Y con ello se cierre todo que se deve conceder," etc.—Instruccion Secreta, MS.

† "—— Lo de la quenta con su alma——Andar con tiento en los amores," etc., etc.—Instruccion Secreta, MS.

‡ Bor, ix. 673. The edict was dated 26th of March, 1576.

the atrocity of Alva, nor the licentiousness of a buccaneering soldiery had been able to effect. As for Don John himself, he came with no definite plans for the Netherlanders, but with very daring projects of his own, and to pursue these misty visions was his main business on arriving in the provinces. In the meantime he was disposed to settle the Netherland difficulty in some showy, off-hand fashion, which should cost him but little trouble, and occasion no detriment to the cause of Papacy or absolutism. Unfortunately for these rapid arrangements, William of Orange was in Zealand, and the Pacification had just been signed at Ghent.

It was, naturally, with very little satisfaction that the Prince beheld the arrival of Don John. His sagacious combinations would henceforth be impeded, if not wholly frustrated. This he foresaw. He knew that there could be no intention of making any arrangement in which Holland and Zealand could be included. He was confident that any recognition of the Reformed religion was as much out of the question now as ever. He doubted not that there were many Catholic magnates, wavering politicians, aspirants for royal favor, who would soon be ready to desert the cause which had so recently been made a general cause, and who would soon be undermining the work of their own hands. The Pacification of Ghent would never be maintained in letter and spirit by the vicegerent of Philip ; for however its sense might be commented upon or perverted, the treaty, while it recognized Catholicism as the state religion, conceded, to a certain extent, liberty of conscience. An immense stride had been taken, by abolishing the edicts, and prohibiting persecution. If that step were now retraced, the new religion was doomed, and the liberties of Holland and Zealand destroyed. "If they make an arrangement with Don John, it will be for us of the religion to run," wrote the Prince to his brother, "for their intention is to suffer no person of that faith to have a fixed domicile in the Netherlands."* It was, therefore, with a

* Archives de la Maison d'Orange, v. 544.

calm determination to counteract and crush the policy of the youthful Governor that William the Silent awaited his antagonist. Were Don John admitted to confidence, the peace of Holland and Zealand was gone. Therefore it was necessary to combat him both openly and secretly—by loud remonstrance and by invisible stratagem. What chance had the impetuous and impatient young hero in such an encounter with the foremost statesman of the age? He had arrived, with all the self-confidence of a conqueror; he did not know that he was to be played upon like a pipe—to be caught in meshes spread by his own hands—to struggle blindly—to rage impotently—to die ingloriously.

The Prince had lost no time in admonishing the states-general as to the course which should now be pursued. He was of opinion that, upon their conduct at this crisis depended the future destinies of the Netherlands. "If we understand how to make proper use of the new Governor's arrival," said he, "it may prove very advantageous to us; if not, it will be the commencement of our total ruin."* The spirit of all his communications was to infuse the distrust which he honestly felt, and which he certainly took no pains to disguise; to impress upon his countrymen the importance of improving the present emergency by the enlargement, instead of the threatened contraction of their liberties, and to enforce with all his energy the necessity of a firm union. He assured the estates that Don John had been sent, in this simple manner, to the country, because the King and cabinet had begun to despair of carrying their point by force. At the same time he warned them that force would doubtless be replaced by fraud. He expressed his conviction that so soon as Don John should attain the ascendency which he had been sent to secure, the gentleness which now smiled upon the surface would give place to the deadlier purposes which lurked below. He went so far as distinctly to recommend the seizure of Don John's person. By so doing, much bloodshed might be saved; for such was the

* Archives et Correspondance, v. 495.

King's respect for the Emperor's son that their demands would be granted rather than that his liberty should be permanently endangered.* In a very striking and elaborate letter which he addressed from Middelburg to the estates-general, he insisted on the expediency of seizing the present opportunity in order to secure and to expand their liberties, and urged them to assert broadly the principle that the true historical polity of the Netherlands was a representative, constitutional government. Don John, on arriving at Luxemburg, had demanded hostages for his own security, a measure which could not but strike the calmest spectator as an infraction of all provincial rights. "He asks you to disarm," continued William of Orange; "he invites you to furnish hostages, but the time has been when the lord of the land came unarmed and uncovered, before the estates-general, and swore to support the constitutions before his own sovereignty could be recognized."

He reiterated his suspicions as to the honest intentions of the government, and sought, as forcibly as possible, to infuse an equal distrust into the minds of those he addressed. "Antwerp," said he, "once the powerful and blooming, now the most forlorn and desolate city of Christendom, suffered because she dared to exclude the King's troops. You may be sure that you are all to have a place at the same banquet. We may forget the past, but princes never forget, when the means of vengeance are placed within their hands. Nature teaches them to arrive at their end by fraud, when violence will not avail them. Like little children, they whistle to the birds they would catch. Promises and pretences they will furnish in plenty."†

He urged them on no account to begin any negotiation with the Governor, except on the basis of the immediate departure of the soldiery. "Make no agreement with him, unless the Spanish and other foreign troops have been sent away beforehand; beware, meantime, of disbanding your own,

---

* Archives et Correspondance, v. 496.

† Letter to the states-general, 30th of November, 1576, in Bor, 747, 748, 749.

for that were to put the knife into his hands to cut your own throats withal."* He then proceeded to sketch the outlines of a negotiation, such as he could recommend. The plan was certainly sufficiently bold, and it could hardly cause astonishment, if it were not immediately accepted by Don John, as the basis of an arrangement. "Remember *this is not play*," said the Prince, "and that you have to choose between the two, either total ruin or manly self-defence. Don John must command the immediate departure of the Spaniards. All our privileges must be revised, and an oath to maintain them required. New councils of state and finance must be appointed by the estates. The general assembly ought to have power to come together twice or thrice yearly, and, indeed, as often as they choose. The states-general must administer and regulate all affairs. The citadels must be demolished everywhere. No troops ought to be enlisted, nor garrisons established, without the consent of the estates."†

In all the documents, whether public memorials or private letters, which came at this period from the hand of the Prince, he assumed, as a matter of course, that in any arrangement with the new Governor the Pacification of Ghent was to be maintained. This, too, was the determination of almost every man in the country. Don John, soon after his arrival at Luxemburg, had despatched messengers to the states-general, informing them of his arrival. It was not before the close of the month of November that the negotiations seriously began. Provost Fonck, on the part of the Governor, then informed them of Don John's intention to enter Namur, attended by fifty mounted troopers.‡ Permission, however, was resolutely refused, and the burghers of Namur were forbidden to render oaths of fidelity until the Governor should have complied with the preliminary demands of the estates.§ To enunciate these demands categorically, a deputation of the estates-general

* "Het ware hem het mes in de hand gegeven daer mede hy u den hals soude afsnyden," etc.—Ibid., p. 748.

† Letter to states-general, etc.

‡ Bor, x. 761.

§ Ibid.

came to Luxemburg.* These gentlemen were received with courtesy by Don John, but their own demeanour was not conciliatory. A dislike to the Spanish government; a disloyalty to the monarch with whose brother and representative they were dealing, pierced through all their language. On the other hand, the ardent temper of Don John was never slow to take offence. One of the deputies proposed to the Governor, with great coolness, that he should assume the government in his own name, and renounce the authority of Philip. Were he willing to do so, the patriotic gentleman pledged himself that the provinces would at once acknowledge him as sovereign, and sustain his government. Don John, enraged at the insult to his own loyalty which the proposition implied, drew his dagger and rushed towards the offender. The deputy would, probably, have paid for his audacity with his life had there not been by-standers enough to prevent the catastrophe. This scene was an unsatisfactory prelude to the opening negotiations.†

On the 6th of December the deputies presented to the Governor at Luxemburg a paper, containing their demands, drawn up in eight articles, and their concessions in ten.‡ The states insisted on the immediate removal of the troops, with the understanding that they were never to return, but without prohibition of their departure by sea; they demanded the immediate release of all prisoners; they insisted on the main-

---

* Bor, x. 762.

† Strada, x. 512. The anecdote is, however, related differently by other historians, according to some of whom the intimation was made indirectly on the part of the Prince of Orange, through Elbertus Leoninus to Don John, that if he chose to assume the sovereignty himself, he might rely on the support of the Protestants and patriot party. According to the same authorities, Don John neither accepted nor rejected the offer.—See Ev. Reid, ann. ii. 27; Wagenaer, vii. 237.—Compare V. d. Vynckt, who relates the circumstance much in the same manner as Strada. V. d. Vynckt, ii. 227, 228.—Also Tassis, iii. 241, who states that the Governor was so angry with the deputy—"ut punire audaciam propriis manibus vix abstinuerit."—Compare J. P. Van Capelle, Elb. Leoninus in Bijdragen tot de Gesch. der Ned., 47–49. The story of Reid is entirely improbable, and is consistent with the character of neither of the principal personages implicated.

‡ See the articles in Bor, x. 762, 763.

tenance of the Ghent treaty, *there being nothing therein* which did not tend to the *furtherance* of the *Catholic* religion; they claimed an act of amnesty; they required the convocation of the states-general, on the basis of that assembly before which took place the abdication of Charles the Fifth; they demanded an oath, on the part of Don John, to maintain all the charters and customs of the country.

Should these conditions be complied with, the deputies consented on the part of the estates, that he should be acknowledged as Governor, and that the Catholic religion and the authority of his Majesty should be maintained. They agreed that all foreign leagues should be renounced, their own foreign soldiery disbanded, and a guard of honor, native Netherlanders, such as his Majesty was contented with at his "Blythe Entrance," provided. A truce of fifteen days, for negotiations, was furthermore proposed.*

Don John made answers to these propositions by adding a brief comment, as apostille,† upon each of the eighteen articles, in succession. He would send away the troops, but, at the same time, the states must disband their own. He declined engaging himself not to recal his foreign soldiery, should necessity require their service. With regard to the Ghent Pacification, he professed himself ready for a general peace negotiation, on condition that the supremacy of the Catholic Church and the authority of his Majesty were properly secured. He would settle upon some act of amnesty after due consultation with the State Council. He was willing that the states should be convoked in general assembly, provided sufficient security were given him that nothing should be there transacted prejudicial to the Catholic religion and the King's sovereignty. As for their privileges, he would govern as had been done *in the time of his imperial father*. He expressed his satisfaction with most of the promises offered by the estates, particularly with their expression in favor of the

---

* See the articles in Bor, x. 762, 763.

† Bor, x. 762, 763.

Church and of his Majesty's authority; the two all-important points to secure which he had come thither unattended, at the peril of his life, but he received their offer of a body-guard, by which his hirelings were to be superseded, with very little gratitude. He was on the point, he said, of advancing as far as Marche en Famine, and should take with him as strong a guard as he considered necessary, and composed of such troops as he had at hand.* Nothing decisive came of this first interview. The parties had taken the measures of their mutual claims, and after a few days, fencing with apostilles, replies, and rejoinders, they separated, their acrimony rather inflamed than appeased.

The departure of the troops and the Ghent treaty were the vital points in the negotiation. The estates had originally been content that the troops should go by sea. Their suspicions were, however, excited by the pertinacity with which Don John held to this mode of removal. Although they did not suspect the mysterious invasion of England, a project which was the real reason why the Governor objected to their departure by land,† yet they soon became aware that he had been secretly tampering with the troops at every point. The effect of these secret negotiations with the leading officers of the army was a general expression of their unwillingness, on account of the lateness of the season, the difficult and dangerous condition of the roads and mountain-passes, the plague in Italy, and other pretexts, to undertake so long a journey by land.‡ On the other hand, the states, seeing the anxiety and the duplicity of Don John upon this particular point, came to the resolution to thwart him at all hazards, and insisted on the land journey. Too long a time, too much money, too many ships would be necessary, they said, to forward so large a force by sea, and in the meantime it would be necessary to permit them to live for another indefinite period at the charge of the estates.§

---

* Bor, x. 762, 763.

† Bor, x. 765. Hoofd, xi. 479.—Compare Strada, ix. 429.

‡ Bor, x. 765, 766.

§ Bor, x. 766. Hoofd, 479, 480.

With regard to the Ghent Pacification, the estates, in the course of December, procured an express opinion from the eleven professors of theology, and doctors *utriusque juris* of Louvain, that the treaty contained nothing which conflicted with the supremacy of the Catholic religion.* The various bishops, deacons, abbots, and pastors of the Netherlands made a similar decision.† An elaborate paper, drawn up by the State-Council, at the request of the states-general, declared that there was nothing in the Pacification derogatory to the supreme authority of his Majesty.‡ Thus fortified with opinions which, it must be confessed, were rather dogmatically than argumentatively drawn up, and which it would have been difficult very logically to defend, the states looked forward confidently to the eventual acceptance by Don John of the terms proposed. In the meantime, while there was still an indefinite pause in the negotiations, a remarkable measure came to aid the efficacy of the Ghent Pacification.

Early in January, 1577, the celebrated "Union of Brussels" was formed.§ This important agreement was originally signed by eight leading personages, the Abbot of Saint Gertrude, the Counts Lalain and Bossu, and the Seigneur de Champagny being among the number. Its tenor was to engage its signers to compass the immediate expulsion of the Spaniards and the execution of the Ghent Pacification, to maintain the Catholic religion and the King's authority, and to defend the fatherland and all its constitutions. Its motive was to generalize the position assumed by the Ghent treaty. The new act was to be signed, not by a few special deputies alone, like a diplomatic convention, but by all the leading individuals of all the provinces, in order to exhibit to Don John such an array of united strength that he would find himself forced to submit to the demands of the estates.‖ The

---

* See the document in Bor, x. 766. † Ibid.

‡ Bor, x. 768. Opinion of the State Council.

§ De Jonghe, De Unie van Brussel. Dewez Hist. gen. de la Belg., vi. 58, 59. Gr. v. Prinsterer, v. 589, sqq. Bor, x. 769.

‖ Bor, x. 769, 770, and Meteren, vi. 116, 117.

tenor, motive, and effect were all as had been proposed and foreseen. The agreement to expel the Spaniards, under the Catholic and loyal manifestations indicated, passed from hand to hand through all the provinces. It soon received the signature and support of all the respectability, wealth, and intelligence of the whole country. Nobles, ecclesiastics, citizens, hastened to give to it their adhesion. The states-general had sent it, by solemn resolution, to every province, in order that every man might be forced to range himself either upon the side of the fatherland or of despotism. Two copies of the signatures procured in each province were ordered, of which one was to be deposited in its archives, and the other forwarded to Brussels. In a short time, every province, with the single exception of Luxemburg, had loaded the document with signatures. This was a great step in advance. The Ghent Pacification, which was in the nature of a treaty between the Prince and the estates of Holland and Zealand on the one side, and a certain number of provinces on the other, had only been signed by the envoys of the contracting parties. Though received with deserved and universal acclamation, it had not the authority of a popular document. This, however, was the character studiously impressed upon the "Brussels Union." The people, subdivided according to the various grades of their social hierarchy, had been solemnly summoned to council, and had deliberately recorded their conviction. No restraint had been put upon their freedom of action, and there was hardly a difference of opinion as to the necessity of the measure.*

A rapid revolution in Friesland, Groningen, and the dependencies, had recently restored that important country to the national party. The Portuguese De Billy had been deprived of his authority as King's stadholder, and Count Hoogstraaten's brother, Baron de Ville, afterwards as Count

* De Jonghe, De Unie van Brussel. Hoofd, xi. 479, 480. Meteren, vi. 116. Dewez Hist. Gen. de la Belgique, vi., c. ix. 56–68.—Compare Groen v. Prinst., Archives, etc., v. 589, sqq.

Renneberg infamous for his treason to the cause of liberty, had been appointed by the estates in his room.* In all this district the "Union of Brussels" was eagerly signed by men of every degree. Holland and Zealand, no less than the Catholic provinces of the south willingly accepted the compromise which was thus laid down, and which was thought to be not only an additional security for the past, not only a pillar more for the maintenance of the Ghent Pacification, but also a sure precursor of a closer union in the future. The Union of Brussels became, in fact, the stepping-stone to the "Union of Utrecht," itself the foundation-stone of a republic destined to endure more than two centuries. On the other hand, this early union held the seed of its own destruction within itself. It was not surprising, however, that a strong declaration in favor of the Catholic religion should be contained in a document intended for circulation through all the provinces. The object was to unite as large a force, and to make as striking a demonstration before the eyes of the Governor-General as was practicable under the circumstances. The immediate purpose was answered, temporary union was formed, but it was impossible that a permanent crystallization should take place where so strong a dissolvent as the Catholic clause had been admitted. In the sequel, therefore, the union fell asunder precisely at this fatal flaw. The next union† was that which definitely separated the provinces into Protestant and Catholic, into self-governing republics, and the dependencies of a distant despotism. The immediate effect, however, of the "Brussels Union" was to rally all lovers of the fatherland and haters of a foreign tyranny upon one vital point—the expulsion of the stranger from the land. The foot of the Spanish soldier should no longer profane their soil. All men were forced to pronounce themselves boldly and unequivocally,

* Bor, x. 750–752. Hoofd, xi. 473–475.

† The "new or closer Union of Brussels," however admirable as a manifestation, and important as an example, cannot, from its very brief duration, be considered as anything but an unsuccessful attempt at union.

in order that the patriots might stand shoulder to shoulder, and the traitors be held up to infamy. This measure was in strict accordance with the advice given more than once by the Prince of Orange, and was almost in literal fulfilment of the Compromise, which he had sketched before the arrival of Don John.*

The deliberations were soon resumed with the new Governor, the scene being shifted from Luxemburg to Huy.† Hither came a fresh deputation from the states-general—many signers of the Brussels Union among them—and were received by Don John with stately courtesy. They had, however, come, determined to carry matters with a high and firm hand, being no longer disposed to brook his imperious demeanour, nor to tolerate his dilatory policy. It is not surprising, therefore, that the courtesy soon changed to bitterness, and that attack and recrimination usurped the place of the dignified but empty formalities which had characterized the interviews at Luxemburg.‡

The envoys, particularly Sweveghem and Champagny, made no concealment of their sentiments towards the Spanish soldiery and the Spanish nation, and used a freedom of tone and language which the petulant soldier had not been accustomed to hear. He complained, at the outset, that the Netherlanders seemed new-born—that instead of bending the knee, they seemed disposed to grasp the sceptre. Insolence had taken the place of pliancy, and the former slave now applied the chain and whip to his master. With such exacerbation of temper at the commencement of negotiations, their progress was of necessity stormy and slow.§

The envoys now addressed three concise questions to the Governor. Was he satisfied that the Ghent Pacification contained nothing conflicting with the Roman religion and the

---

* Avis du Prince d'Orange, etc., Archives, etc., v. 437, sqq.

† Bor, x. 771.

‡ Bor, x. 772, 773. Tassis, iii. 246.

§ "—— Austriacum non lenibus nec modestis modis sed loris ac fustibus ut servum ad suam voluntatem adigere," etc.—Tassis, iii. 246.

King's authority? If so, was he willing to approve that treaty in all its articles? Was he ready to dismiss his troops at once, and by land, the sea voyage being liable to too many objections?*

Don John answered these three questions—which, in reality, were but three forms of a single question—upon the same day, the 24th of January. His reply was as complex as the demand had been simple. It consisted of a proposal in six articles, and a requisition in twenty-one, making in all twenty-seven articles. Substantially he proposed to dismiss the foreign troops—to effect a general pacification of the Netherlands—to govern on the basis of the administration in his imperial father's reign—to arrange affairs in and with regard to the assembly-general as the King should judge to be fitting—to forgive and forget past offences—and to release all prisoners. On the other hand he required the estates to pay the troops before their departure, and to provide ships enough to transport them, as the Spaniards did not choose to go by land, and as the deputies at Luxemburg had consented to their removal by sea. Furthermore, he demanded that the states should dismiss their own troops. He required ecclesiastical authority to prove the Ghent Pacification not prejudicial to the Catholic religion; legal authority that it was not detrimental to his Majesty's supremacy; and an oath from the states-general to uphold both points inviolably, and to provide for their maintenance in Holland and Zealand. He claimed the right to employ about his person soldiers and civil functionaries of any nation he might choose, and he exacted from the states a promise to prevent the Prince of Orange from removing his son, Count van Buren, forcibly or fraudulently, from his domicile in Spain.†

The deputies were naturally indignant at this elaborate trifling. They had, in reality, asked him but one question, and that a simple one—Would he maintain the

* Bor, x. 773.

† Articles in Bor, x. 772, 773

treaty of Ghent? Here were twenty-seven articles in reply, and yet no answer to that question. They sat up all night, preparing a violent protocol, by which the Governor's claims were to be utterly demolished. Early in the morning, they waited upon his Highness, presented the document, and at the same time asked him plainly, by word of mouth, did he or did he not intend to uphold the treaty. Thus pressed into a corner in presence of the deputies, the members of the State Council who were in attendance from Brussels, and the envoys whom the Emperor had recently sent to assist at these deliberations, the Governor answered, No. He would not and could not maintain the treaty, because the Spanish troops were in that instrument denounced as rebels, because he would not consent to the release of Count Van Buren—and on account of various other reasons not then specified.* Hereupon ensued a fierce debate, and all day long the altercation lasted, without a result being reached. At ten o'clock in the evening, the deputies having previously retired for a brief interval, returned with a protest† that they were not to be held responsible for the termination of the proceedings, and that they washed their hands of the bloodshed which might follow the rupture. Upon reading this document, Don John fell into a blazing passion. He vehemently denounced the deputies as traitors. He swore that men who came to him thus prepared with ready-made protests in their pockets, were rebels from the commencement, and had never intended any agreement with him. His language and gestures expressed unbounded fury. He was weary of their ways, he said. They had better look to themselves, for the King would never leave their rebellion unpunished. He was ready to draw the sword at once—not his own, but his Majesty's, and they might be sure that the war which they were thus provoking, should be the fiercest ever waged.‡ More abusive language in this strain

* Bor, x. 772, 774.

† See the protest in Bor, x. 774, 775.

‡ Bor, x. 775.

was uttered, but it was not heard with lamb-like submission. The day had gone by when the deputies of the states-general were wont to quail before the wrath of vicarious royalty. The fiery words of Don John were not oil to troubled water, but a match to a mine. The passions of the deputies exploded in their turn, and from hot words they had nearly come to hard blows. One of the deputies replied with so much boldness and vehemence that the Governor, seizing a heavy silver bell which stood on the table, was about to hurl it at the offender's head, when an energetic and providential interference on the part of the imperial envoys, prevented the unseemly catastrophe.*

The day thus unprofitably spent, had now come to its close, and the deputies left the presence of Don John with tempers as inflamed as his own. They were, therefore, somewhat surprised at being awakened in their beds, after midnight, by a certain Father Trigoso, who came to them with a conciliatory message from the Governor. While they were still rubbing their eyes with sleep and astonishment, the Duke of Aerschot, the Bishop of Liege, and several councillors of state, entered the room. These personages brought the news that Don John had at last consented to maintain the Pacification of Ghent, as would appear by a note written in his own hand, which was then delivered. The billet was eagerly read, but unfortunately did not fulfil the anticipations which had been excited. "I agree," said Don John, "to approve the peace made between the states and the Prince of Orange, on condition that nothing therein may seem detrimental to the authority of his Majesty and the supremacy of the Catholic religion, and also with reservation of the points mentioned in my last communication."†

Men who had gone to bed in a high state of indignation were not likely to wake in much better humour, when suddenly aroused in their first nap, to listen to such a message as this. It seemed only one piece of trifling the more. The deputies had

* Tassis, iii. 246.

† Bor, x. 775.

offered satisfactory opinions of divines and jurisconsults, as to the two points specified which concerned the Ghent treaty. It was natural, therefore, that this vague condition concerning them, the determination of which was for the Governor's breast alone, should be instantly rejected, and that the envoys should return to their disturbed slumbers with an increase of ill-humour.

On the morrow, as the envoys, booted and spurred, were upon the point of departure for Brussels, another communication was brought to them from Don John.* This time, the language of the Governor seemed more to the purpose. "I agree," said he, "to maintain the peace concluded between the states and the Prince of Orange, on condition of receiving from the ecclesiastical authorities, and from the University of Louvain, satisfactory assurance that the said treaty contains nothing derogatory to the Catholic religion—and similar assurance from the State Council, the Bishop of Liege, and the imperial envoys, that the treaty is in no wise prejudicial to the authority of his Majesty." Here seemed, at last, something definite. These conditions could be complied with. They had, in fact, been already complied with. The assurances required as to the two points had already been procured, as the deputies and as Don John well knew. The Pacification of Ghent was, therefore, virtually admitted. The deputies waited upon the Governor accordingly, and the conversation was amicable. They vainly endeavoured, however, to obtain his consent to the departure of the troops by land—the only point then left in dispute. Don John, still clinging to his secret scheme, with which the sea voyage of the troops was so closely connected, refused to concede. He reproached the envoys, on the contrary, with their importunity in making a fresh demand, just as he had conceded the Ghent treaty, upon his entire responsibility and without instructions. Mentally resolving that this point should still be wrung from the Governor, but not suspecting his secret motives for resisting

* Bor, x. 775.

it so strenuously, the deputies took an amicable farewell of the Governor, promising a favorable report upon the proceedings, so soon as they should arrive in Brussels.*

Don John, having conceded so much, was soon obliged to concede the whole. The Emperor Rudolph had lately succeeded his father, Maximilian.† The deceased potentate, whose sentiments on the great subject of religious toleration were so much in harmony with those entertained by the Prince of Orange, had, on the whole, notwithstanding the ties of relationship and considerations of policy, uniformly befriended the Netherlands, so far as words and protestations could go, at the court of Philip. Active co-operation, practical assistance, he had certainly not rendered. He had unquestionably been too much inclined to accomplish the impossibility of assisting the states without offending the King—an effort which, in the homely language of Hans Jenitz, was "like wishing his skin washed without being wet."‡ He had even interposed many obstacles to the free action of the Prince, as has been seen in the course of this history, but nevertheless, the cause of the Netherlands, of religion, and of humanity had much to lose by his death. His eldest son and successor, Rudolph the second, was an ardent Catholic, whose relations with a proscribed prince and a reformed population could hardly remain long in a satisfactory state. The New Emperor had, however, received the secret envoys of Orange with bounty,§ and was really desirous of accomplishing the pacification of the provinces. His envoys had assisted at all the recent deliberations between the estates and Don John, and their vivid remonstrances removed, at this juncture, the last objection on the part of the Governor-General. With a secret sigh, he deferred the darling and mysterious hope which had lighted him to the Netherlands, and consented to the departure of the troops by land.||

---

* Bor, x. 775.

† The Emperor Maximilian died on the 12th of October, 1576.

‡ "——und gehts nach dem sprichwort, wasche mir den beltz und mache mir ihn nicht nasz."—MS. cited by Groen v. Prinst., Archives, etc., v. 725.

§ Archives, etc., v. 426.

|| Bor, x. 786.

All obstacles having been thus removed, the memorable treaty called the Perpetual Edict was signed at Marche en Famine on the 12th, and at Brussels on the 17th of February, 1577.* This document, issued in the name of the King, contained nineteen articles. It approved and ratified the Peace of Ghent, in consideration that the prelates and clergy, with the doctors *utriusque juris* of Louvain, had decided that nothing in that treaty conflicted either with the supremacy of the Catholic Church or the authority of the King, but, on the contrary, that it advanced the interests of both.† It promised that the soldiery should depart "freely, frankly, and without delay, by land,‡ never to return except in case of foreign war"—the Spaniards to set forth within forty days, the Germans and others so soon as arrangements had been made by the states-general for their payment. It settled that all prisoners, on both sides, should be released, excepting the Count Van Buren, who was to be set free so soon as the states-general having been convoked, the Prince of Orange should have fulfilled the resolutions to be passed by that assembly. It promised the maintenance of all the privileges, charters, and constitutions of the Netherlands. It required of the states an oath to maintain the Catholic religion. It recorded their agreement to disband their troops. It settled that Don John should be received as Governor-General, immediately upon the departure of the Spaniards, Italians, and Burgundians from the provinces.§

These were the main provisions of this famous treaty, which was confirmed a few weeks afterwards by Philip, in a letter addressed to the states of Brabant, and by an edict issued at Madrid.|| It will be seen that everything required by the envoys of the states, at the commencement of their ne-

---

* Bor, x. 786–789. Hoofd, xi. 485–487. Meteren, vi. f. 117–119. Cabrera, xi. 901, 902. Strada, ix. 430. Bor and Meteren publish the treaty in full.

† Art. 2—"Niet nadelig maer ter contrarie tot vordering van de selve," etc.

‡ Art. 3—"Te lande, vry, vrank en onbelet," etc.

§ See in particular Articles 8, 10, 11, and 16.

|| Bor, x. 789, 790. V. d. Vynckt, ii. 232.

gotiations, had been conceded by Don John. They had claimed the departure of the troops, either by land or sea. He had resisted the demand a long time, but had at last consented to despatch them by sea. Their departure by land had then been insisted upon. This again he had most reluctantly conceded. The ratification of the Ghent treaty, he had peremptorily refused. He had come to the provinces, at the instant of its conclusion, and had, of course, no instructions on the subject. Nevertheless, slowly receding, he had agreed, under certain reservations, to accept the treaty. Those reservations relating to the great points of Catholic and royal supremacy, he insisted upon subjecting to his own judgment alone. Again he was overruled. Most unwillingly he agreed to accept, instead of his own conscientious conviction, the dogmas of the State Council and of the Louvain doctors. Not seeing very clearly how a treaty which abolished the edicts of Charles the Fifth and the ordinances of Alva—which removed the religious question in Holland and Zealand from the King's jurisdiction to that of the states-general—which had caused persecution to surcease—had established toleration—and which moreover, had confirmed the arch rebel and heretic of all the Netherlands in the government of the two rebellious and heretic provinces, as stadholder for the King—not seeing very clearly how such a treaty was "advantageous rather than prejudicial to royal absolutism and an exclusive Catholicism," he naturally hesitated at first.

The Governor had thus disconcerted the Prince of Orange, not by the firmness of his resistance, but by the amplitude of his concessions. The combinations of William the Silent were, for an instant, deranged. Had the Prince expected such liberality, he would have placed his demands upon a higher basis, for it is not probable that he contemplated or desired a pacification. The Duke of Aerschot and the Bishop of Liege in vain essayed to prevail upon his deputies at Marche en Famine, to sign the agreement of the 27th January, upon which was founded the Perpetual Edict.* They refused to do so without consulting

* Bor, x. 786.

the Prince and the estates. Meantime, the other commissioners forced the affair rapidly forward. The states sent a deputation to the Prince to ask his opinion, and signed the agreement before it was possible to receive his reply.* This was to treat him with little courtesy, if not absolutely with bad faith. The Prince was disappointed and indignant. In truth, as appeared from all his language and letters, he had no confidence in Don John. He believed him a consummate hypocrite, and as deadly a foe to the Netherlands as the Duke of Alva, or Philip himself. He had carefully studied twenty-five intercepted letters from the King, the Governor, Jerome de Roda, and others, placed recently in his hands by the Duke of Aerschot,† and had found much to confirm previous and induce fresh suspicion. Only a few days previously to the signature of the treaty, he had also intercepted other letters from influential personages, Alonzo de Vargas and others, disclosing extensive designs to obtain possession of the strong places in the country, and then to reduce the land to absolute subjection.‡ He had assured the estates, therefore, that the deliberate intention of the Government, throughout the whole negotiation, was to deceive, whatever might be the public language of Don John and his agents. He implored them, therefore, to have "pity upon the poor country," and to save the people from falling into the trap which was laid for them. From first to last, he had expressed a deep and wise distrust, and justified it by ample proofs. He was, with reason, irritated, therefore, at the haste with which the states had concluded the agreement with Don John—at the celerity with which, as he afterwards expressed it, "they had rushed upon the boar-spear of that sanguinary heart."§ He believed that everything had been signed and sworn by the Governor, with the mental reservation that such agreements were valid only until he should repent

* Archives et Corresp., v. 629. Bor, x. 791. Letter of Estates of Holland.

† Archives et Corresp., v. 588, sqq. Apologie du Prince d'Orange, p. 97.

‡ Letter of Orange to the States-General, 2nd of February, 1577, Acta Statuum Belgii, i. f. 258. MS., Hague Archives.

§ Apologie du Prince d'Orange, p. 98.

having made them. He doubted the good faith and the stability of the grand seigniors. He had never felt confidence in the professions of the time-serving Aerschot, nor did he trust even the brave Champagny, notwithstanding his services at the sack of Antwerp. He was especially indignant that provision had been made, not for demolishing but for restoring to his Majesty those hateful citadels, nests of tyranny, by which the flourishing cities of the land were kept in perpetual anxiety. Whether in the hands of King, nobles, or magistrates, they were equally odious to him, and he had long since determined that they should be razed to the ground. In short, he believed that the estates had thrust their heads into the lion's mouth, and he foresaw the most gloomy consequences from the treaty which had just been concluded. He believed, to use his own language, "that the only difference between Don John and Alva or Requesens was, that he was younger and more foolish than his predecessors, less capable of concealing his venom, more impatient to dip his hands in blood."*

In the Pacification of Ghent, the Prince had achieved the prize of his life-long labors. He had banded a mass of provinces by the ties of a common history, language, and customs, into a league against a foreign tyranny. He had grappled Holland and Zealand to their sister provinces by a common love for their ancient liberties, by a common hatred to a Spanish soldiery. He had exorcised the evil demon of religious bigotry by which the body politic had been possessed so many years ; for the Ghent treaty, largely interpreted, opened the door to universal toleration. In the Perpetual Edict the Prince saw his work undone. Holland and Zealand were again cut adrift from the other fifteen provinces, and war would soon be let loose upon that devoted little territory. The article stipulating the maintenance of the Ghent treaty he regarded as idle wind ; the solemn saws of the State Council

* Letter of Prince of Orange and the States of Holland, Bor, x. 791.—Compare Groen v. Prinst., Archives, etc., v. 559, sqq., and "Instruction from le Sieur de Haultain," etc. Archives, etc., v. 579, sqq. Apologie du Prince d'Orange, 97.

and the quiddities from Louvain being likely to prove but slender bulwarks against the returning tide of tyranny. Either it was tacitly intended to tolerate the Reformed religion, or to hunt it down. To argue that the Ghent treaty, loyally interpreted, strengthened ecclesiastical or royal despotism, was to contend that a maniac was more dangerous in fetters than when armed with a sword; it was to be blind to the difference between a private conventicle and a public scaffold. The Perpetual Edict, while affecting to sustain the treaty, would necessarily destroy it at a blow, while during the brief interval of repose, tyranny would have renewed its youth like the eagles. Was it possible, then, for William of Orange to sustain the Perpetual Edict, the compromise with Don John? Ten thousand ghosts from the Lake of Harlem, from the famine and plague-stricken streets of Leyden, from the smoking ruins of Antwerp, rose to warn him against such a composition with a despotism as subtle as it was remorseless.

It was, therefore, not the policy of William of Orange, suspecting, as he did, Don John, abhorring Philip, doubting the Netherland nobles, confiding only in the mass of the citizens, to give his support to the Perpetual Edict. He was not the more satisfied because the states had concluded the arrangement without his sanction, and against his express advice.* He refused to publish or recognize the treaty in Holland and Zealand.† A few weeks before, he had privately laid before the states of Holland and Zealand a series of questions, in order to test their temper, asking them, in particular, whether they were prepared to undertake a new and sanguinary war for the sake of their religion, even although their other privileges should be recognised by the new government, and a long and earnest debate had ensued, of a satisfactory nature, although no positive resolution was passed upon the subject.‡ As soon as the Perpetual Edict had been signed, the states-

* Apologie du Prince d'Orange, p. 98.

† Letter of Prince of Orange and the States of Holland, Bor, x. 791-973.

‡ Bor, x. 776.

general had sent to the Prince, requesting his opinion and demanding his sanction.* Orange, in the name of Holland and Zealand, instantly returned an elaborate answer,† taking grave exceptions to the whole tenor of the Edict. He complained that the constitution of the land was violated, because the ancient privilege of the states-general to assemble at their pleasure, had been invaded, and because the laws of every province were set at nought by the continued imprisonment of Count Van Buren, who had committed no crime, and whose detention proved that no man, whatever might be promised, could expect security for life or liberty. The ratification of the Ghent treaty, it was insisted, was in no wise distinct and categorical, but was made dependent on a crowd of deceitful subterfuges.‡ He inveighed bitterly against the stipulation in the Edict, that the states should pay the wages of the soldiers, whom they had just proclaimed to be knaves and rebels, and at whose hands they had suffered such monstrous injuries. He denounced the cowardice which could permit this band of hirelings to retire with so much jewelry, merchandize, and plate, the result of their robberies. He expressed, however, in the name of the two provinces, a willingness to sign the Edict, provided the states-general would agree solemnly beforehand, in case the departure of the Spaniards did not take place within the stipulated time, to abstain from all recognition of, or communication with, Don John, and themselves to accomplish the removal of the troops by force of arms.§

Such was the first and solemn manifesto made by the Prince in reply to the Perpetual Edict; the states of Holland and Zealand uniting heart and hand in all that he thought, wrote,

---

* Bor, x. 790. Hoofd, xii. 490.

† The letter is published at length in Bor, x. 790–792.—Compare Wagenaer, vii. 144, 145. Meteren, vi. 119. Cabrera, xi. 902, 903.

‡ Letter of Prince of Orange and the Estates, Bor, ubi sup.—"Tot een ontalligkheid van bedreegelijke uitvluchten," etc.

§ Letter of Prince of Orange, etc.

and said. His private sentiments were in strict accordance with the opinions thus publicly recorded. "Whatever appearance Don John may assume to the contrary," wrote the Prince to his brother, "'tis by no means his intention to maintain the Pacification, and less still to cause the Spaniards to depart, with whom he keeps up the most strict correspondence possible."*

On the other hand, the Governor was most anxious to conciliate the Prince. He was most earnest to win the friendship of the man without whom every attempt to recover Holland and Zealand, and to re-establish royal and ecclesiastical tyranny, he knew to be hopeless. "This is the pilot," wrote Don John to Philip, "who guides the bark. He alone can destroy or save it. The greatest obstacles would be removed if he could be gained." He had proposed, and Philip had approved the proposition, that the Count Van Buren should be clothed with his father's dignities, on condition that the Prince should himself retire into Germany.† It was soon evident, however, that such a proposition would meet with little favor, the office of father of his country and protector of her liberties not being transferable.

While at Louvain, whither he had gone after the publication of the Perpetual Edict, Don John had conferred with the Duke of Aerschot, and they had decided that it would be well to send Doctor Leoninus on a private mission to the Prince. Previously to his departure on this errand, the learned envoy had therefore a full conversation with the Governor. He was charged to represent to the Prince the dangers to which Don John had exposed himself in coming from Spain to effect the pacification of the Netherlands. Leoninus was instructed to give assurance that the treaty just concluded should be maintained, that the Spaniards should depart, that all other promises should be inviolably kept, and that the Governor would take up arms against all who should oppose the fulfilment of

* Archives, etc., v. 111.

† Ext. from MS. letter, 16th of March, 1577, in Gachard; preface to vol. iii. Corresp. Guillaume le Tacit., p. li.

his engagements. He was to represent that Don John, in proof of his own fidelity, had placed himself in the power of the states. He was to intimate to the Prince that an opportunity was now offered him to do the crown a service, in recompence for which he would obtain, not only pardon for his faults, but the favor of the monarch, and all the honors which could be desired; that by so doing he would assure the future prosperity of his family; that Don John would be his good friend, and, as such, would do more for him than he could imagine.* The envoy was also to impress upon the Prince, that if he persisted in his opposition every man's hand would be against him, and the ruin of his house inevitable. He was to protest that Don John came but to forgive and to forget, to restore the ancient government and the ancient prosperity, so that, if it was for those objects the Prince had taken up arms, it was now his duty to lay them down, and to do his utmost to maintain peace and the Catholic religion. Finally, the envoy was to intimate that if he chose to write to Don John, he might be sure to receive a satisfactory answer. In these pacific instructions and friendly expressions, Don John was sincere. "The name of your Majesty," said he, plainly, in giving an account of this mission to the King, "is as much abhorred and despised in the Netherlands as that of the Prince of Orange is loved and feared. I am negotiating with him, and giving him every security, for I see that the establishment of peace, as well as the maintenance of the Catholic religion, and the obedience to your Majesty, depend now upon him. Things have reached that pass that 'tis necessary to make a virtue of necessity. If he lend an ear to my proposals, it will be only *upon very advantageous conditions*, but to these it will be necessary to submit, rather than to lose everything.†

Don John was in earnest; unfortunately he was not aware that the Prince was in earnest also. The crusader, who had

---

* Gachard, Corresp. Guillaume le Tacit., iii., preface lii.

† "El nombre y servicio de V. M[d]. estan aborrecido y poco estimado cuanto temido y amado el del Principe de Oranges," etc.—Ibid.

sunk thirty thousand paynims at a blow, and who was dreaming of the Queen of Scotland and the throne of England, had not room in his mind to entertain the image of *a patriot.* Royal favors, family prosperity, dignities, offices, orders, advantageous conditions, these were the baits with which the Governor angled for William of Orange. He did not comprehend that attachment to a half-drowned land and to a despised religion, could possibly stand in the way of those advantageous conditions and that brilliant future. He did not imagine that the rebel, once assured not only of pardon but of advancement, could hesitate to refuse the royal hand thus amicably offered. Don John had not accurately measured his great antagonist.

The results of the successive missions which he despatched to the Prince were destined to enlighten him.* In the course of the first conversation between Leoninus and the Prince at Middelburg, the envoy urged that Don John had entered the Netherlands without troops, that he had placed himself in the power of the Duke of Aerschot, that he had since come to Louvain without any security but the promise of the citizens and of the students ; and that all these things proved the sincerity of his intentions. He entreated the Prince *not to let slip so favorable an opportunity for placing his house above the reach of every unfavorable chance,* spoke to him of Marius, Sylla, Julius Cæsar, and other promoters of civil wars, and on retiring for the day, begged him to think gravely on what he had thus suggested, and to pray that God might inspire him with good resolutions.

Next day, William informed the envoy that, having prayed to God for assistance, he was more than ever convinced of his obligation to lay the whole matter before the states, whose servant he was. He added, that he could not forget the

* Full details of the mission of Leoninus are given in the preface to Gachard's 3rd volume of the Corresp. de Guillaume le Tacit., pages liv., sqq. That distinguished publicist has condensed them from a MS. relation made by Leoninus, on his return to Louvain, a narrative, of which a Spanish translation was found by M. Gachard in the archives of Simancas.

deaths of Egmont and Horn, nor the manner in which the promise made to the confederate nobles by the Duchess of Parma had been visited, nor the conduct of the French monarch towards Admiral Coligny. He spoke of information which he had received from all quarters, from Spain, France, and Italy, that there was a determination to make war upon him and upon the states of Holland and Zealand. He added that they were taking their measures in consequence, and that they were well aware that a Papal nuncio had arrived in the Netherlands, to intrigue against them.* In the evening, the Prince complained that the estates had been so precipitate in concluding their arrangement with Don John. He mentioned several articles in the treaty which were calculated to excite distrust; dwelling particularly on the engagement entered into by the estates to maintain the Catholic religion. This article he declared to be in direct contravention to the Ghent treaty, by which this point was left to the decision of a future assembly of the estates-general. Leoninus essayed, as well as he could, to dispute these positions. In their last interview, the Prince persisted in his intention of laying the whole matter before the states of Holland and Zealand. Not to do so, he said, would be to expose himself to ruin on one side, and on the other, to the indignation of those who might suspect him of betraying them. The envoy begged to be informed if any hope could be entertained of a future arrangement. Orange replied that he had no expectation of any, but advised Doctor Leoninus to be present at Dort when the estates should assemble.

Notwithstanding the unfavorable result of this mission, Don John did not even yet despair of bending the stubborn character of the Prince. He hoped that, if a personal interview between them could be arranged, he should be able to remove many causes of suspicion from the mind of his adversary. "In such times as these," wrote the Governor

* Gachard, Correspondance de Guillaume le Tacit, iii. lvi

† Ibid., lviii. sqq.

to Philip, "we can make no election, nor do I see any remedy to preserve the state from destruction, save to gain over this man, who has so much influence with the nation."* The Prince had, in truth, the whole game in his hands. There was scarcely a living creature in Holland and Zealand who was not willing to be bound by his decision in every emergency. Throughout the rest of the provinces, the mass of the people looked up to him with absolute confidence, the clergy and the prominent nobles respecting and fearing him, even while they secretly attempted to thwart his designs. Possessing dictatorial power in two provinces, vast influences in the other fifteen, nothing could be easier for him than to betray his country. The time was singularly propitious. The revengeful King was almost on his knees to the denounced rebel. Everything was proffered: pardon, advancement, power. An indefinite vista was opened. "You cannot imagine," said Don John, "how much it will be within my ability to do for you." The Governor was extremely anxious to purchase the only enemy whom Philip feared. The Prince had nothing personally to gain by a continuance of the contest. The ban, outlawry, degradation, pecuniary ruin, assassination, martyrdom—these were the only guerdons he could anticipate. He had much to lose: but yesterday loaded with dignities, surrounded by pomp and luxury, with many children to inherit his worldly gear, could he not recover all, and more than all, to-day? What service had he to render in exchange? A mere nothing. He had but to abandon the convictions of a lifetime, and to betray a million or two of hearts which trusted him.

As to the promises made by the Governor to rule the country with gentleness, the Prince could not do otherwise than commend the intention, even while distrusting the fulfilment. In his reply to the two letters of Don John, he thanked his Highness, with what seemed a grave irony, for the benign courtesy and signal honor which he had manifested

---

* Gachard, Correspondance, etc., p. lx., MS. letter of the 16th of March, 1577.

to him, by inviting him so humanely and so carefully *to a tranquil life,* wherein, according to his Highness, consisted the perfection of felicity in this mortal existence, and by promising him so liberally favor and grace.* He stated, however, with earnestness, that the promises in regard to the pacification of the poor Netherland people were much more important. He had ever expected, he said, beyond all comparison, the welfare and security of the public before his own ; "having always placed his particular interests under his foot, even as he was still resolved to do, as long as life should endure."†

Thus did William of Orange receive the private advances made by the government towards himself. Meantime, Don John of Austria came to Louvain.‡ Until the preliminary conditions of the Perpetual Edict had been fulfilled, and the Spanish troops sent out of the country, he was not to be received as Governor-General, but it seemed unbecoming for him to remain longer upon the threshold of the provinces. He therefore advanced into the heart of the country, trusting himself without troops to the loyalty of the people, and manifesting a show of chivalrous confidence which he was far from feeling. He was soon surrounded by courtiers, time-servers, noble office-seekers. They who had kept themselves invisible, so long as the issue of a perplexed negotiation seemed doubtful, now became obsequious and inevitable as his shadow. One grand seignior wanted a regiment, another a government, a third a chamberlain's key ; all wanted titles, ribbons, offices, livery, wages. Don John distributed favors and promises with vast liberality.§ The object with which Philip had sent him to the Netherlands, that he might conciliate the hearts of its inhabitants by the personal graces which he had inherited from his imperial father, seemed

---

* Letter of the Prince of Orange to Don John of Austria, May 24, 1577, in Gachard, Correspondance de Guillaume le Tacit., iii. 289–291.

† Ibid., 290.—"Aiant, tousjours mis dessoubz les pieds mon regard particulier, ainsi que suis encore résolu de faire, tant que la vie me demeurera."

‡ Bor, x. 804. Hoofd, xi. 493.

§ Bor, Hoofd, ubi sup. Tassis, iii. 257, sqq. Cabrera, xi. 904.

in a fair way of accomplishment, for it was not only the venal applause of titled sycophants that he strove to merit, but he mingled gaily and familiarly with all classes of citizens.* Everywhere his handsome face and charming manner produced their natural effect. He dined and supped with the magistrates in the Town-house, honored general banquets of the burghers with his presence, and was affable and dignified, witty, fascinating, and commanding, by turns. At Louvain, the five military guilds held a solemn festival. The usual invitations were sent to the other societies, and to all the martial brotherhoods, the country round. Gay and gaudy processions, sumptuous banquets, military sports, rapidly succeeded each other. Upon the day of the great trial of skill, all the high functionaries of the land were, according to custom, invited, and the Governor was graciously pleased to honor the solemnity with his presence. Great was the joy of the multitude when Don John, complying with the habit of imperial and princely personages in former days, enrolled himself, cross-bow in hand, among the competitors. Greater still was the enthusiasm, when the conqueror of Lepanto brought down the bird, and was proclaimed king of the year, amid the tumultuous hilarity of the crowd. According to custom, the captains of the guild suspended a golden popinjay around the neck of his Highness, and placing themselves in procession, followed him to the great church. Thence, after the customary religious exercises, the multitude proceeded to the banquet, where the health of the new king of the cross-bowmen was pledged in deep potations.† Long and loud was the merriment of this initiatory festival, to which many feasts succeeded during those brief but halcyon days, for the good-natured Netherlanders already believed in the blessed advent of peace. They did not dream that the war, which had been consuming the marrow of their commonwealth for ten flaming years, was but in its infancy, and that neither they nor their children were destined to see its close.

* Bor, Hoofd, Tassis, ubi sup.

† Tassis, iii. 257, 258. Van Wyn op Wagenaer, vii. 50.

For the moment, however, all was hilarity at Louvain. The Governor, by his engaging deportment, awoke many reminiscences of the once popular Emperor. He expressed unbounded affection for the commonwealth, and perfect confidence in the loyalty of the inhabitants. He promised to maintain their liberties, and to restore their prosperity. Moreover, he had just hit the popinjay with a skill which his imperial father might have envied, and presided at burgher banquets with a grace which Charles could have hardly matched. His personal graces, for the moment, took the rank of virtues. "Such were the beauty and vivacity of his eyes," says his privy councillor, Tassis, "that with a single glance he made all hearts his own,"* yet, nevertheless, the predestined victim secretly felt himself the object of a marksman who had no time for painted popinjays, but who rarely missed his aim. "The whole country is at the devotion of the Prince, and nearly every one of its inhabitants;"† such was his secret language to his royal brother, at the very moment of the exuberant manifestations which preceded his own entrance to Brussels.

While the Governor still tarried at Louvain, his secretary, Escovedo, was busily engaged in arranging the departure of the Spaniards,‡ for, notwithstanding his original reluctance and the suspicions of Orange, Don John loyally intended to keep his promise. He even advanced twenty-seven thousand florins towards the expense of their removal,§ but to raise the whole amount required for transportation and arrears, was a difficult matter. The estates were slow in providing the one hundred and fifty thousand florins which they had stipulated to furnish. The King's credit, moreover, was at a very low ebb. His previous bonds had not been duly honored, and there had even been instances of royal repudiation, which by

* Tassis, iv. 326.

† Letter of Don John to Philip, April 7, 1577, in the appendix to the intercepted letters, Discours Sommier des Justes Causes, etc. Qui ont contrainct les Estats-Generaux de pourveoir a leur defence contre le Seign^r. D. Jehan d'Austrice, p. 41—Ed. G. Sylvius, Anvers., 1577.

‡ Letter of Escovedo, Discours Sommier, etc., p. 24, sqq. § Bor, x. 806, 807.

no means lightened the task of the financier, in effecting the new loans required.* Escovedo was very blunt in his language upon this topic, and both Don John and himself urged punctuality in all future payments. They entreated that the bills drawn in Philip's name upon Lombardy bankers, and discounted at a heavy rate of interest, by the Fuggers of Antwerp, might be duly provided for at maturity. "I earnestly beg," said Escovedo, "that your Majesty will see to the payment of these bills, at all events;" adding, with amusing simplicity, "this will be a means of recovering your Majesty's credit, and as for my own, I don't care to lose it, small though it be." Don John was even more solicitous. "For the love of God, Sire," he wrote, "do not be delinquent now. You must reflect upon the necessity of recovering your credit. If this receives now the final blow, all will desert your Majesty, and the soldiers too will be driven to desperation."†

By dint of great diligence on the part of Escovedo, and through the confidence reposed in his character, the necessary funds were raised in the course of a few weeks. There was, however, a difficulty among the officers, as to the right of commanding the army on the homeward march. Don Alonzo de Vargas, as chief of the cavalry, was appointed to the post by the Governor, but Valdez, Romero, and other veterans, indignantly refused to serve under one whom they declared their inferior officer. There was much altercation and heartburning, and an attempt was made to compromise the matter by the appointment of Count Mansfeld to the chief command. This was, however, only adding fuel to the flames. All were dissatisfied with the superiority accorded to a foreigner, and Alonzo de Vargas, especially offended, addressed most insolent language to the Governor.‡ Nevertheless, the arrangement was

* See the letters of Escovedo in the intercepted letters, Discours Sommier, etc., passim.

† Letter of Escovedo to the King, 6 Avril, 1577, in Discours Sommier, etc., p. 11. Letter of Don John to the King, Discours Sommier, etc., p. 34, appendix.

‡ Bor, x. 807, Hoofd, xii. 495.

maintained, and the troops finally took their departure from the country, in the latter days of April.* A vast concourse of citizens witnessed their departure, and could hardly believe their eyes, as they saw this incubus at last rolling off, by which the land had so many years been crushed.† Their joy, although extravagant, was, however, limited by the reflection that ten thousand Germans still remained in the provinces, attached to the royal service, and that there was even yet a possibility that the departure of the Spaniards was a feint. In truth, Escovedo, although seconding the orders of Don John, to procure the removal of these troops, did not scruple to express his regret to the King, and his doubts as to the result. He had been ever in hopes that an excuse might be found in the condition of affairs in France, to justify the retention of the forces near that frontier. He assured the King that he felt very doubtful as to what turn matters might take, after the soldiers were gone, seeing the great unruliness which even their presence had been insufficient completely to check.‡ He had hoped that they might be retained in the neighbourhood, ready to seize the islands at the first opportunity. "For my part," he wrote, "I care nothing for the occupation of places within the interior, but the islands must be secured. To do this," he continued, with a deceitful allusion to the secret projects of Don John, "is, in my opinion, more difficult than to effect the scheme upon England. If the one were accomplished, the other would be easily enough managed, and would require but moderate means. Let not your Majesty suppose that I say this as favoring the plan of Don John, for this I put entirely behind me."§

---

* Bor, x. 807. Hoofd, xii. 496. Strada, ix. 433.

† Among the many witticisms perpetrated upon this occasion, the following specimen may be thought worth preserving:—

"Boetica gens Abiit: cur ploras Belgica? dicam
A quod in O non est litera versa queror."

Bor, x. 807. Hoofd, xii. 496.

‡ Letter of Escovedo to the King, 6 Abril, 1577, in Discours Sommier, etc., p. 16, appendix.

§ Letter of Escovedo, 9 April, 1577, Discours Sommier, p. 50.

Notwithstanding these suspicions on the part of the people, this reluctance on the part of the government, the troops readily took up their line of march, and never paused till they reached Lombardy.* Don John wrote repeatedly to the King, warmly urging the claims of these veterans, and of their distinguished officers, Romero, Avila, Valdez, Montesdocca, Verdugo, Mondragon, and others, to his bountiful consideration. They had departed in very ill humour, not having received any recompense for their long and arduous services. Certainly, if unflinching endurance, desperate valor, and congenial cruelty, could atone in the monarch's eyes for the mutiny, which had at last compelled their withdrawal, then were these laborers worthy of their hire. Don John had pacified them by assurances that they should receive adequate rewards on their arrival in Lombardy, and had urged the full satisfaction of their claims and his promises in the strongest language. Although Don Alonzo de Vargas had abused him "with flying colors,"† as he expressed himself, yet he hastened to intercede for him with the King in the most affectionate terms. "His impatience has not surprised me," said the Governor, "although I regret that he has been offended, for I love and esteem him much. He has served many years with great distinction, and I can certify that his character for purity and religion is something extraordinary."‡

The first scene in the withdrawal of the troops had been the evacuation of the citadel of Antwerp, and it had been decided that the command of this most important fortress should be conferred upon the Duke of Aerschot.§ His claims as commander-in-chief, under the authority of the State Council, and as chief of the Catholic nobility, could hardly be passed over, yet he was a man whom neither party trusted. He was too

---

* Mendoza, xvi. 336. Van. d. Vynckt, ii. 233. Strada, ix. 433.

† Letter of Don John to the King, 7 Abríl, 1577, in Discours Sommier, p. 29, appendix.—"Y quexase tan a banderas desplegadas de mi."

‡ Ibid.

§ Bor, x. 805. Cabrera, xi. 907. Meteren, vi. 119.

visibly governed by interested motives. Arrogant where he felt secure of his own, or doubtful as to another's position, he could be supple and cringing when the relations changed. He refused an interview with William of Orange before consulting with Don John, and solicited one afterwards when he found that every effort was to be made to conciliate the Prince.* He was insolent to the Governor-General himself in February, and respectful in March. He usurped the first place in the church,† before Don John had been acknowledged Governor, and was the first to go forth to welcome him after the matter had been arranged. He made a scene of virtuous indignation in the State Council,‡ because he was accused of place-hunting, but was diligent to secure an office of the highest dignity which the Governor could bestow. Whatever may have been his merits, it is certain that he inspired confidence neither in the adherents of the King nor of the Prince; while he by turns professed the warmest regard both to the one party and the other. Spaniards and patriots, Protestants and Catholics, suspected the man at the same moment, and ever attributed to his conduct a meaning which was the reverse of the apparent.§ Such is often the judgment passed upon those who fish in troubled waters only to fill their own nets.

The Duke, however, was appointed Governor of the citadel. Sancho d'Avila, the former constable, refused, with Castillian haughtiness, to surrender the place to his successor, but appointed his lieutenant, Martin d'Oyo, to perform that ceremony.‖ Escovedo, standing upon the drawbridge with Aerschot, administered the oath: "I, Philip, Duke of Aerschot," said the new constable, "solemnly swear to hold this

---

* Gachard, Correspondance de Guillaume le Tacit., iii., Preface, p. lv. and note 1.

† Tassis, iii. 241.—Compare Van d. Vynckt, ii. 228.

‡ Archives et Correspondance, vi. 66.

§ Ibid., vi. 66, 67.—Compare letter of Escovedo, Discours Sommier, p. 13, appendix.

‖ Bor, x. 805. Meteren, vi. 119. Hoofd, xii. 494. Cabrera, xi. 907.

castle for the King, and for no others." To which Escovedo added, "God help you, with all his angels, if you keep your oath; if not, may the Devil carry you away, body and soul." The few by-standers cried Amen; and with this hasty ceremony, the keys were delivered, the prisoners, Egmont, Capres, Goignies, and others, liberated, and the Spaniards ordered to march forth.*

* Bor, Meteren, Hoofd, ubi sup. Mendoza, xvi. 325, 326. Cabrera, xi. 908.

CHAPTER II.

Triumphal entrance of Don John into Brussels—Reverse of the picture—Analysis of the secret correspondence of Don John and Escovedo with Antonio Perez—Plots against the Governor's liberty—His desponding language and gloomy anticipations—Recommendation of severe measures—Position and principles of Orange and his family—His private views on the question of peace and war—His toleration to Catholics and Anabaptists censured by his friends—Death of Viglius—New mission from the Governor to Orange—Details of the Gertruydenberg conferences—Nature and results of these negotiations—Papers exchanged between the envoys and Orange—Peter Panis executed for heresy—Three parties in the Netherlands—Dissimulation of Don John—His dread of capture.

As already narrated, the soldiery had retired definitely from the country at the end of April, after which Don John made his triumphal entrance into Brussels on the 1st of May. It was long since so festive a May-day had gladdened the hearts of Brabant. So much holiday magnificence had not been seen in the Netherlands for years. A solemn procession of burghers, preceded by six thousand troops, and garnished by the free companies of archers and musketeers, in their picturesque costumes, escorted the young prince along the streets of the capital. Don John was on horseback, wrapped in a long green cloak, riding between the Bishop of Liege and the Papal nuncio.* He passed beneath countless triumphal

* Bor, x. 811. Meteren, vi. 120. Hoofd, xii. 500, sqq. Van d. Vynckt, ii. 233. Strada, ix. 433. Lettre de Barthelemi Liebart (avocat et bailli General de Tournay) 3me Mai, 1577.—"Estant le Sr. Dom Jean affublé d'un manteau de drap de couleur verd," etc. The Duke of Aerschot was magnificent as usual—

arches. Banners waved before him, on which the battle of Lepanto, and other striking scenes in his life, were emblazoned. Minstrels sang verses, poets recited odes, rhetoric clubs enacted fantastic dramas in his honor, as he rode along. Young virgins crowned him with laurels. Fair women innumerable were clustered at every window, roof, and balcony, their bright robes floating like summer clouds above him. "Softly from those lovely clouds," says a gallant chronicler, "descended the gentle rain of flowers."* Garlands were strewed before his feet, laurelled victory sat upon his brow. The same conventional enthusiasm and decoration which had characterized the holiday marches of a thousand conventional heroes were successfully produced. The proceedings began with the church, and ended with the banquet, the day was propitious, the populace pleased, and after a brilliant festival, Don John of Austria saw himself Governor-General of the provinces.

Three days afterwards, the customary oaths, to be kept with the customary conscientiousness, were rendered at the Town House,† and for a brief moment all seemed smiling and serene.

There was a reverse to the picture. In truth, no language can describe the hatred which Don John entertained for the Netherlands and all the inhabitants. He had come to the country only as a stepping-stone to the English throne, and he never spoke, in his private letters, of the provinces or the people but in terms of abhorrence. He was in a "Babylon of disgust," in a "Hell," surrounded by "drunkards," "wine-skins," "scoundrels," and the like. From the moment of his arrival he had strained every nerve to retain the Spanish troops, and to send them away by sea when it should be no longer feasible to keep them. Escovedo shared in the sentiments and entered fully into the schemes of his chief. The

---

"Vestu d'un collet de velours rouge cremoisy brodé d'or," etc., etc.—Ibid., apud Gachard, Documens Inédits concernant l'Histoire de la Belgique (Bruxelles, 1833), i. 362–364.

* "Een lieflyke reeghen uit zoo heldere wolken."—Hoofd, xii. 500.

† Bor, x. 812. Meteren, vi. 120.

plot, the secret enterprise, was the great cause of the advent of Don John in the uncongenial clime of Flanders. It had been, therefore, highly important, in his estimation, to set, as soon as possible, about the accomplishment of this important business. He accordingly entered into correspondence with Antonio Perez, the King's most confidential Secretary of State at that period. That the Governor was plotting no treason is sufficiently obvious from the context of his letters. At the same time, with the expansiveness of his character, when he was dealing with one whom he deemed his close and trusty friend, he occasionally made use of expressions which might be made to seem equivocal. This was still more the case with poor Escovedo. Devoted to his master, and depending most implicitly upon the honor of Perez, he indulged in language which might be tortured into a still more suspicious shape, when the devilish arts of Perez and the universal distrust of Philip were tending steadily to that end. For Perez—on the whole, the boldest, deepest, and most unscrupulous villain in that pit of duplicity, the Spanish court—was engaged at that moment with Philip, in a plot to draw from Don John and Escovedo, by means of this correspondence, the proofs of a treason which the King and minister both desired to find. The letters from Spain were written with this view—those from Flanders were interpreted to that end. Every confidential letter received by Perez was immediately laid by him before the King, every letter which the artful demon wrote was filled with hints as to the danger of the King's learning the existence of the correspondence, and with promises of profound secrecy upon his own part, and was then immediately placed in Philip's hands, to receive his comments and criticisms, before being copied and despatched to the Netherlands.* The

* Many of these letters are contained in a very valuable MS. collection belonging to the royal library at the Hague, and entitled "Cartas qu'el Señor Don Juan de Austria y el Secretario Joan de Escobedo, descifradas, escribieron à Su. Mag^d. y Antonio Perez, desde Flandes." It is probable that these copies were made by the direction of Perez himself, when obliged to deposit the originals before the judges of Aragon.—Vide Gachard, Notice sur un Manuscrit de la Bibliothèque Royale de la Haye, etc. Bullet. Com. Roy. xiii.

minister was playing a bold, murderous, and treacherous game, and played it in a masterly manner. Escovedo was lured to his destruction, Don John was made to fret his heart away, and Philip—more deceived than all—was betrayed in what he considered his affections, and made the mere tool of a man as false as himself and infinitely more accomplished.

Almost immediately after the arrival of Don John in the Netherlands, he had begun to express the greatest impatience for Escovedo, who had not been able to accompany his master upon his journey, but without whose assistance the Governor could accomplish none of his undertakings. "Being a man, not an angel, I cannot do all which I have to do," said he to Perez, "without a single person in whom I can confide."* He protested that he could do no more than he was then doing. He went to bed at twelve and rose at seven, without having an hour in the day in which to take his food regularly; in consequence of all which he had already had three fevers. He was plunged into a world of distrust. Every man suspected him, and he had himself no confidence in a single individual throughout that whole Babylon of disgusts. He observed to Perez that he was at liberty to show his letters to the King, or to read them in the Council, as he meant always to speak the truth in whatever he should write. He was sure that Perez would do all for the best; and there is something touching in these expressions of an honest purpose towards Philip, and of generous confidence in Perez, while the two were thus artfully attempting to inveigle him into damaging revelations. The Netherlanders certainly had small cause to love or trust their new Governor, who very sincerely detested and suspected them, but Philip had little reason to complain of his brother. "Tell me if my letters are read in Council, and what his Majesty says about them," he wrote; "and, above all, send money. I am driven to desperation at finding myself *sold to this people*, utterly unprovided as I am,

* Cartas del Señor Don J. d'Austria y el Señor Escobedo, MS., f. 1–4, 21 Dic., 1576.

and knowing the slow manner in which all affairs are conducted in Spain."*

He informed the King that there was but one man in the Netherlands, and that he was called the Prince of Orange. To him everything was communicated, with him everything was negotiated, opinions expressed by him were implicitly followed. The Governor vividly described the misgivings with which he had placed himself in the power of the states by going to Louvain, and the reluctance with which he had consented to send away the troops. After this concession, he complained that the insolence of the states had increased. "They think that they can do and undo what they like, now that I am at their mercy," he wrote to Philip. "Nevertheless, I do what you command without regarding *that I am sold,* and that I am in great danger of losing my liberty, a loss which I dread more than anything in the world, for I wish to remain justified before God and men."† He expressed, however, no hopes as to the result. Disrespect and rudeness could be pushed no further than it had already gone, while the Prince of Orange, the actual governor of the country, considered his own preservation dependent upon maintaining things as they then were. Don John, therefore, advised the King steadily to make preparations for "a rude and terrible war,"‡ which was not to be avoided, save by a miracle, and which ought not to find him in this unprepared state. He protested that it was impossible to exaggerate the boldness which the people felt at seeing him thus defenseless. "They say publicly," he continued, "that your Majesty is not to be feared, not being capable of carrying on a war, and having consumed and exhausted every resource. One of the greatest injuries ever inflicted upon us was by Marquis Havré, who, after his return from Spain, went about publishing everywhere the poverty of the royal exchequer. This has emboldened them to rise, for they believe that, whatever the

* Cartas del Señor Don J. d'Austria y el Señor Escobedo, MS. f. 1–4, 21 Dic., 1576.

† Cartas del S. Don Joan, etc., MS., f. 4–12, 2 Jan., 1577.

‡ "Una cruda y terible guerra."—Ibid.

disposition, there is no strength to chastise them. They see a proof of the correctness of their reasoning in the absence of new levies, and in the heavy arrearages due to the old troops."*

He protested that he desired, at least, to be equal to the enemy, without asking, as others had usually done, for double the amount of the hostile force. He gave a glance at the foreign complications of the Netherlands, telling Philip that the estates were intriguing both with France and England. The English envoy had expressed much uneasiness at the possible departure of the Spanish troops from the Netherlands by sea, coupling it with a probable attempt to liberate the Queen of Scots. Don John, who had come to the provinces for no other purpose, and whose soul had been full of that romantic scheme, of course stoutly denied and ridiculed the idea. "Such notions," he had said to the envoy, "were subjects for laughter. If the troops were removed from the country, it was to strengthen his Majesty's force in the Levant."† Mr. Rogers, much comforted, had expressed the warm friendship which Elizabeth entertained both for his Majesty and his Majesty's representative; protestations which could hardly seem very sincere, after the series of attempts at the Queen's life, undertaken so recently by his Majesty and his Majesty's former representative. Nevertheless, Don John had responded with great cordiality, had begged for Elizabeth's portrait, and had expressed the intention, if affairs went as he hoped, to go privately to England for the purpose of kissing her royal hand.‡ Don John further informed the King, upon the envoy's authority, that Elizabeth had refused assistance to the estates, saying, if she stirred it would be to *render aid to Philip*, especially if France should meddle in the matter. As to France, the Governor advised Philip to hold out hopes to Alençon of espousing the Infanta, but by no means ever to

* Cartas del S. Don Joan, etc., MS., f. 4–12, 2 Jan., 1577. † Ibid.

‡ "—— y yo compedirle su retrato y diciendo que si las cossas de aqui tomassen assiento come esperava, hiria prividamente a besar la las *manos*."—Ibid. Upon this passage in his brother's letter, Philip made the pithy annotation, "*Mucho decir fue esto*; that was saying a good deal."—Ibid.

fulfil such a promise, as the Duke, "besides being the shield of heretics, was unscrupulously addicted to infamous vices."*

A month later, Escovedo described the downfall of Don John's hopes and his own in dismal lauguage.—"You are aware," he wrote to Perez, "*that a throne*—a chair with a canopy—is our intention and our appetite, and all the rest is good for nothing. Having failed in our scheme, we are desperate and like madmen. All is now weariness and death."† Having expressed himself in such desponding accents, he continued, a few days afterwards, in the same lugubrious vein, "I am ready to hang myself," said he, "and I would have done it already, if it were not for keeping myself as executioner for those who have done us so much harm. Ah, Senor Antonio Perez!" he added, "what terrible pertinacity have those devils shown in making us give up our plot. It seems as though Hell were opened and had sent forth heaps of demons to oppose our schemes."‡ After these vigorous ejaculations he proceeded to inform his friend that the English envoy and the estates, governed by the Prince of Orange, in whose power were the much-coveted ships, had prevented the departure of the troops by sea. "These devils complain of the expense," said he; "but we would willingly swallow the cost if we could only get the ships." He then described Don John as so cast down by his disappointment as to be fit for nothing, and most desirous of quitting the Netherlands as soon as possible. He had no disposition to govern these wine-skins.§ Any one who ruled in the provinces was obliged to

---

* "Porque de mas de ser este el escudo de los hereges, se tiene entendido que no hace escrupulo del pecado nefando."—Ibid.

† Cartas, etc., MS., f. 12, 3 Feb., 1577.—"Vin se prevenga y crea que silla y cortina es nuestro intento y apetito, y que todo lo demas es ymproprio y que abiendose caydo la traça de aquel amigo con loqual estamos desperados y como locos; todo a de ser cansancio y muerte."

‡ Cartas, etc., MS., f. 12-16, 7 Feb., 1577.—"Estoy por aorcarme, ya lo habia hecho sino me guardase para verdugo de quien tanto mal nos hace. A! Señor Antonio Perez y que pertinacia y terribilidad a sido la desos demonios en quitarnos nuestra traça: el ynfierno parece que sea abierto y que enbian de allà gentes a montones à este efeto."

§ "Y para gobiernar estos cueros realmente no lo quiere."—Ibid.

do exactly what they ordered him to do. Such rule was not to the taste of Don John. Without any comparison, a woman would answer the purpose better than any man, and Escovedo accordingly suggested the Empress Dowager, or Madame de Parma, or even Madame de Lorraine. He further recommended that the Spanish troops, thus forced to leave the Netherlands by land, should be employed against the heretics in France. This would be a salvo for the disgrace of removing them.* "It would be read in history," continued the Secretary, "that the troops went to France in order to render assistance in a great religious necessity; while, at the same time, they will be on hand to chastise these drunkards, if necessary.† To have the troops in France is almost as well as to keep them here." He begged to be forgiven if he spoke incoherently. 'T was no wonder that he should do so, for his reason had been disordered by the blow which had been received. As for Don John, he was dying to leave the country, and although the force was small for so great a general, yet it would be well for him to lead these troops to France in person. "It would sound well in history," said poor Escovedo, who always thought of posterity, without ever dreaming that his own private letters would be destined, after three centuries, to comment and earnest investigation; "it would sound well in history, that Don John went to restore the French kingdom and to extirpate heretics, with six thousand foot and two thousand horse. 'Tis a better employment, too, than to govern such vile creatures as these."‡

If, however, all their plans should fail, the Secretary suggested to his friend Antonio, that he must see and make courtiers of them. He suggested that a strong administration might be formed in Spain, with Don John, the Marquis de Los Velez, and the Duke of Sesa. "With such chiefs, and with Anthony and John§ for acolytes," he was of opinion that much

* Cartas, etc., MS., f. 12–16, 7 Feb., 1577.

† "Y tanbien servirá esto de refrenar estos borrachos."—Ibid.

‡ "Se olgará mas de servir en esto que no en govierno de tan ruin gente."—Ibid.

§ Viz., John of Escovedo and Antony Perez.

good work might be done, and that Don John might become "the staff for his Majesty's old age."* He implored Perez, in the most urgent language, to procure Philip's consent that his brother should leave the provinces. "Otherwise," said he, "we shall see the destruction of the friend whom we so much love! He will become seriously ill, and if so, good night to him!† His body is too delicate." Escovedo protested that he would rather die himself. "In the catastrophe of Don John's death," he continued, "adieu the court, adieu the world!" He would incontinently bury himself among the mountains of San Sebastian, "preferring to dwell among wild animals than among courtiers." Escovedo accordingly, not urged by the most disinterested motives certainly, but with as warm a friendship for his master as princes usually inspire, proceeded to urge upon Perez the necessity of aiding the man who was able to help them. The first step was to get him out of the Netherlands. That was his constant thought, by day and night. As it would hardly be desirable for him to go alone, it seemed proper that Escovedo should, upon some pretext, be first sent to Spain. Such a pretext would be easily found, because, as Don John had accepted the government, "it would be necessary for him to do all which the rascals bade him."‡ After these minute statements, the Secretary warned his correspondent of the necessity of secrecy, adding that he especially feared "all the court ladies, great and small, but that he in *everything confided entirely in Perez.*"

Nearly at the same time, Don John wrote to Perez in a similar tone. "Ah, Señor Antonio," he exclaimed, "how certain is my disgrace and my misfortune. Ruined is our enterprise, after so much labor and such skilful management."§ He was to have commenced the work with the very Spanish

* "El baculo por su bexez."—Cartas, etc., MS., 12–16, 7 Feb., 1577.

† "Y es de cuerpo tan delicado que lo temo dexarnos hia a buenas noches."—Ibid.

‡ "Porque recebido el gobierno a de acer lo que le aconsejaren estos bellacos."—Ibid.

§ Cartas, etc., MS., 16 Feb., 1577, f. 16–18.—"A, Señor Antonio y cuan cierto es de mi desgracia y desdicha—la quiebra do nostro designio tras muy trabajado y bien guiado que se tenia."

soldiers who were now to be sent off by land, and he had nothing for it but to let them go, or to come to an open rupture with the states. "The last, his conscience, his duty, and the time, alike forbade."* He was therefore obliged to submit to the ruin of his plans, and "could think of nothing save to turn hermit, a condition in which a man's labors, being spiritual, might not be entirely in vain."† He was so overwhelmed by the blow, he said, that he was constantly thinking of an anchorite's life. That which he had been leading had become intolerable. He was not fitted for the people of the Netherlands, nor they for him. Rather than stay longer than was necessary in order to appoint his successor, there was no resolution he might not take, even to leaving everything and coming upon them when they least expected him, although he were to receive a bloody punishment in consequence. He, too, suggested the Empress, who had all the qualities which he lacked himself, or Madame de Parma, or Madame de Lorraine, as each of them was more fit to govern the provinces than he pretended to be. "The people," said he, plainly, "*are beginning to abhor me, and I abhor them already.*"‡ He entreated Perez to get him out of the country by fair means or foul, "*per fas aut per nefas.*"§ His friends ought to procure his liberation, if they wished to save him from the sin of disobedience, and even of infamy. He expressed the most unbounded confidence in the honor of his correspondent, adding that if nothing else could procure his release, the letter might be shown to the King. In general, the Governor was always willing that Perez should make what changes he thought advisable in the letters for his Majesty, altering or softening whatever seemed crude or harsh, provided always the main point—that of procuring his recal—were steadily kept in view, In this, said the Governor, vehemently, my life, my honor,

---

* Cartas, etc., MS., 16 Feb., 1577, f. 16–18.

† "Pues no sé en que pensar sino en una hermita y donde no sera en vano lo que el hombre trabaja se con el espiritu."—Ibid.

‡ "Por lo que me enpieçan avorrecer y por lo que yo les aborresco."—Ibid.

§ Ibid.

and my soul are all at stake; for as to the two first, I shall forfeit them both certainly, and, in my desperate condition, I shall run great risk of losing the last.*

On the other hand, Perez was profuse in his professions of friendship both to Don John and to Escovedo; dilating in all his letters upon the difficulty of approaching the King upon the subject of his brother's recal, but giving occasional information that an incidental hint had been ventured which might not remain without effect. All these letters were, however, laid before Philip, for his approval, before being despatched, and the whole subject thoroughly and perpetually discussed between them, about which Perez pretended that he hardly dared breathe a syllable to his Majesty. He had done what he could, he said, while reading, piece by piece, to the King, during a fit of the gout, the official despatches from the Netherlands, to insinuate such of the arguments used by the Governor and Escovedo as might seem admissible, but it was soon obvious that no impression could be made upon the royal mind. Perez did not urge the matter, therefore, "because," said he, "if the King should suspect that we had any other object than his interests, *we should all be lost*."† Every effort should be made by Don John and all his friends to secure his Majesty's entire confidence, since by that course more progress would be made in their secret plans, than by proceedings concerning which the Governor wrote "with such fury and anxiety of heart."‡ Perez warned his correspondent, therefore, most solemnly, against the danger of "striking the blow without hitting the mark," and tried to persuade him that his best interests required him to protract his residence in the provinces for a longer period. He informed Don John that his disappointment as to the English scheme had met with the warmest sympathy of the King, who had wished his brother

* Cartas, etc., MS., 1 Marzo, 1577, f. 18–19.—"Que en hacerlo me va la vida y onra y alma, porque las dos primeras partes perderé cierto—— y la tercera de puro desperado hira a gran riesgo."

† Cartas, etc., MS., f. 20–24.

‡ Ibid.—"Con tanta furia y cuidado de coraçon."

success. "I have sold to him, at as high a price as I could," said Perez, "the magnanimity with which your Highness had sacrificed, on that occasion, a private object to his service."*

The minister held the same language, when writing, in a still more intimate and expansive style, to Escovedo. "We must avoid, by a thousand leagues, the possibility of the King's thinking us influenced by private motives," he observed; "for we know the King and the delicacy of these matters. The only way to gain the good-will of the man is carefully to accommodate ourselves to his tastes, and to have the appearance of being occupied solely with his interests."† The letter, like all the rest, being submitted to "the man" in question before being sent, was underlined by him at this paragraph and furnished with the following annotation:—"but you must enlarge upon the passage which I have marked—say more, even if you are obliged to copy the letter, in order that we may see the *nature of the reply*."‡

In another letter to Escovedo, Perez enlarged upon the impropriety, the impossibility of Don John's leaving the Netherlands at that time. The King was so resolute upon that point, he said, that 'twas out of the question to suggest the matter. "We should, by so doing, only lose all credit with him in other things. You know what *a terrible man* he is; if he should once suspect us of having a private end in view, we should entirely miss our mark."§ Especially the secretary was made acquainted with the enormous error which would be committed by Don John in leaving his post.

* "Su Mag[d]. ha manifestado gran deseo de que se hubiera podido executar en esta occasion; y yo le he vendido quan caro he savido el aber pospuesto V. A[a] su particular servicio."—Cartas, etc., MS., 20–24.

† Cartas, etc., MS., f. 24–27.—"Me parece que hemos de huir mil leguas de que piense el rey que tratamos tan de proposito de lo que toca al Señor Don Juan —— pues conocemos al rey y cuan delicadas materias de estado son estas, pues por el mismo caso no nos fiara nada y el camino *para ganar este hombre la voluntad* no a de ser sino tratar solamente de su negocio y accomodalle los estados y los negocios a su gusto."

‡ "Mas os aviades de alargar en lo que yo rayo. Decid mas aunque se copie la carta, para ver el animo de la respuesta."—Ibid.

§ Cartas, etc., MS., f. 27–32.—"Porque no perdemos el credito con el para otras cosas, que como Vm. sabe es terribile hombre," etc., etc.

Perez "had ventured into the water" upon the subject, he said, by praising the Governor warmly to his Majesty. The King had responded by a hearty eulogium, adding that the greatest comfort in having such a brother was, that he might be where his Majesty could not be. Therefore, it was out of the question for Don John to leave the provinces. The greatest tact was necessary, urged Perez, in dealing with the King. If he should once "suspect that we have a private purpose, we are lost, and no Demosthenes or Cicero would be able to influence him afterwards."* Perez begged that his ardent attachment to Don John might be represented in the strongest colors to that high personage, who was to be assured that every effort would be made to place him at the head of affairs in Spain, according to the suggestion of Escovedo. "It would never do, however," he continued, "*to let our man see* that we desire it, for then we should never succeed. The only way to conquer him is to make him believe that things are going on *as he wishes*, not as his Highness may desire, and that we have none of us any will but the King's."† Upon this passage the "terrible man" made a brief annotation: "this paragraph does admirably," he said, adding, with characteristic tautology, "*and what you say in it is also excellent.*"‡

"Therefore," continued the minister, "God forbid, Master Escovedo, that you should come hither now; for we should all be lost. In the English matter, I assure you that his Majesty was extremely anxious that the plan should succeed, either through the Pope, or otherwise. That puts me in mind," added Perez, "to say, body of God! Señor Escovedo! how the devil came you to send that courier to Rome about the English plot without giving me warning?"§ He then

* "Porque la ora que lleguemos a esto somos perdidos, y no abra Demosthenes ni Ciceron qui le persuada despues."—Cartas, etc., MS., 27–32.

† "Pero no lo mostremos a este ombre jamas que lo deseamos porque nunca lo veramos," etc.—Ibid.

‡ "Este capitulo va muy bien, y lo que decis en el tanbien."—Ibid.

§ "Cuerpo de Dios, Señor Escobedo, como diablos despacharon el correo a Roma sobre esto de Inglaterra," etc.—Ibid. Upon this passage the King has also noted with his own hand: "and this paragraph is even still more to the purpose, ("Y este capitulo va aun mejor al proposito.")—Ibid.

proceeded to state that the papal nuncio in Spain had been much troubled in mind upon the subject, and had sent for him. "I went," said Perez, "and after he had closed the door, and looked through the keyhole to see that there were no listeners, he informed me that he had received intelligence from the Pope as to the demands made by Don John upon his Holiness for bulls, briefs, and money to assist him in his English scheme, and that eighty thousand ducats had already been sent to him in consequence." Perez added that the nuncio was very anxious to know how the affair should best be communicated to the King, without prejudice to his Highness. He had given him the requisite advice, he continued, and had himself subsequently told the King that, no doubt, letters had been written by Don John to his Majesty, communicating these negotiations at Rome, but that probably the despatches had been forgotten. Thus, giving himself the appearance of having smoothed the matter with the King, Perez concluded with a practical suggestion of much importance—the necessity, namely, of procuring the assassination of the Prince of Orange as soon as possible. "Let it never be absent from your mind," said he, "that a good occasion must be found *for finishing Orange*, since, besides the service which will thus be rendered *to our master*, and to the states, it will be worth *something to ourselves.*"*

No apology is necessary for laying a somewhat extensive analysis of this secret correspondence before the reader. If there be any value in the examples of history, certainly few chronicles can furnish a more instructive moral. Here are a despotic king and his confidential minister laying their heads together in one cabinet ; the viceroy of the most important provinces of the realm, with his secretary, deeply conferring in another, not as to the manner of advancing the great

* "Ojo que no dexe Vm. de llevar en su pensamiento para si conviniesse y se pudiesse en ocasion pero compuesto todo de los estados a *acavar a Oranxe*, que demas del servicio que se ara a nuestro Señor y bien a esos estados *nos valdria algo*, y crea me que le digo la verdad y creame le digo otra vez."—Cartas, etc., MS., f. 27–32.

interests, moral or material, of the people over whom God has permitted them to rule, but as to the best means of arranging conspiracies against the throne and life of a neighboring sovereign, with the connivance and subsidies of the Pope. In this scheme, and in this only, the high conspirators are agreed. In every other respect, mutual suspicion and profound deceit characterize the scene. The Governor is filled with inexpressible loathing for the whole nation of "drunkards and wine-skins" who are at the very moment strewing flowers in his path, and deafening his ears with shouts of welcome; the king, while expressing unbounded confidence in the viceroy, is doing his utmost, through the agency of the subtlest intriguer in the world, to inveigle him into confessions of treasonable schemes, and the minister is filling reams of paper with protestations of affection for the governor and secretary, with sneers at the character of the King, and with instructions as to the best method of deceiving him, and then laying the despatches before his Majesty for correction and enlargement. To complete the picture, the monarch and his minister are seen urging the necessity of murdering the foremost man of the age upon the very dupe who, within a twelvemonth, was himself to be assassinated by the self-same pair; while the arch-plotter who controls the strings of all these complicated projects is equally false to King, Governor, and Secretary, and is engaging all the others in these blind and tortuous paths, for the accomplishment of his own secret and most ignoble aims.

In reply to the letters of Perez, Don John constantly expressed the satisfaction and comfort which he derived from them in the midst of his annoyances. "He was very disconsolate," he said, "to be in that hell, and to be obliged to remain in it,"* now that the English plot had fallen to the ground, but he would nevertheless take patience, and wait for a more favorable conjuncture.

* Cartas, etc., MS., 26 Màyo, 1577, f. 32–34.—"Tiene me muy desconsolado por que estar en este ynfierno y aver destar."

Escovedo expressed the opinion, however, notwithstanding all the suggestions of Perez, that the presence of Don John in the provinces had become entirely superfluous. "An old woman with her distaff," suggested the Secretary, "would be more appropriate; for there would be nothing to do, if the states had their way, save to sign everything which they should command."* If there should be war, his Highness would, of course, not abandon his post, even if permitted to do so; but otherwise, nothing could be gained by a prolonged residence. As to the scheme of assassinating the Prince of Orange, Escovedo prayed Perez to believe him incapable of negligence on the subject. "You know that the *finishing of Orange* is very near my heart," wrote the poor dupe to the man by whom he was himself so soon to be finished. "You may believe that I have never forgotten it, and never will forget it, until it be done. Much, and very much artifice is, however, necessary to accomplish this object. A proper person to undertake a task fraught with such well-known danger, is hard to find. Nevertheless, I will not withdraw my attention from the subject till such a person be procured, and the deed be done."†

A month later, Escovedo wrote that he was about to visit Spain. He complained that he required rest in his old age, but that Perez could judge how much rest he could get in such a condition of affairs. He was, unfortunately, not aware, when he wrote, how soon his correspondent was to give him a long repose. He said, too, that the pleasure of visiting his home was counterbalanced by the necessity of travelling back to the Netherlands;‡ but he did not know that Perez was to

* Cartas, etc., MS., 29 Màyo, 1577, f. 33–37.—"El Señor Don Juan no sera menester sino una dueña con su rueca que firme lo quellos quisieren."

† "Ya Vm. save cuanto que tengo en el pensamiento *el acavar a Oranxe* pues bien crera que no se me a *olvidado ni olvidara hasta acerlo;* que es menester mucho y muy mucho artificio y *persona tal que se encargue* del casso que como trae consigo tan conocido peligro no acavo de allarla aunque la he buscado. *No perdere al cuidado della asta ver lo hecho.*"—Ibid.

‡ Cartas, etc., MS., 21 Jùnio, 1577, f. 36–37.

spare him that trouble, and to send him forth upon a much longer journey.

The Governor-General, had, in truth, not inspired the popular party or its leader with confidence, nor did he place the least reliance upon them. While at Louvain, he had complained that a conspiracy had been formed against his life and liberty. Two French gentlemen, Bonnivet and Bellangreville, had been arrested on suspicion of a conspiracy to secure his person, and to carry him off a prisoner to Rochelle. Nothing came of the examination which followed; the prisoners were released, and an apology was sent by the states-general to the Duke of Alençon, as well for the indignity which had been offered to two of his servants, as for the suspicion which had been cast upon himself.* Don John, however, was not satisfied. He persisted in asserting the existence of the conspiracy, and made no secret of his belief that the Prince of Orange was acquainted with the arrangement.† As may be supposed, nothing was discovered in the course of the investigation to implicate that astute politician. The Prince had indeed secretly recommended that the Governor should be taken into custody on his first arrival, not for the purpose of assassination or personal injury, but in order to extort better terms from Philip, through the affection or respect which he might be supposed to entertain for his brother. It will be remembered that unsuccessful attempts had also been made to capture the Duke of Alva and the Commander Requesens. Such achievements comported with the spirit of the age, and although it is doubtful whether any well-concerted plot existed against the liberty of the Governor, it is certain that he entertained no doubt on the subject himself.‡

* Bor, x. 805. Hoofd, xi. 493.

† Cabrera asserts that Count Lalain, with other deputies of the estates, had conspired ("por persuasion del Princîpe de Orange y orden del Duque de Alençon") to make the capture of Don John's person; adding that the confession would have been extorted from them upon the rack, there being sufficient proofs of their guilt, but the affair was hushed up.—xi. 909[a] and [b].

‡ See the remarks of Groen van Prinsterer, Archives, etc., vi. 42, 43.

In addition to these real or suspected designs, there was an ever-present consciousness in the mind of Don John that the enthusiasm which greeted his presence was hollow, that no real attachment was felt for his person, that his fate was leading him into a false position, that the hearts of the people were fixed upon another, and that they were never to be won by himself. Instinctively he seemed to feel a multitude of invisible threads twining into a snare around him, and the courageous heart and the bounding strength became uneasily conscious of the act in which they were to be held captive till life should be wasted quite away.

The universal affection for the rebel Prince, and the hopeless abandonment of the people to that deadliest of sins, the liberty of conscience, were alike unquestionable. "They mean to remain free, sire," wrote Escovedo to Philip, "and to live as they please. To that end they would be willing that the Turk should come to be master of the country. By the road which they are travelling, however, it will be the Prince of Orange—which comes to quite the same thing."* At the same time, however, it was hoped that something might be made of this liberty of conscience. All were not equally sunk in the horrible superstition, and those who were yet faithful to Church and King might be set against their besotted brethren. Liberty of conscience might thus be turned to account. While two great parties were "by the ears, and pulling out each other's hair, all might perhaps be reduced together."† His Majesty was warned, nevertheless, to expect the worst, and to believe that the country could only be cured with fire and blood.‡ The position of the Governor was painful and perplexing. "Don John," said Escovedo, "*is thirty years old.* I promise your Majesty nothing, save that

* Letter of Escovedo to the King, March 27, 1577, Discours Sommier, etc., p. 4, appendix.

† Letter of Escovedo, etc., Discours Sommier, p. 16.

‡ "Este negocio no esta para curarse con buenas razones, sino con fuego y con sangre."—Ibid.

if he finds himself without requisite assistance, he will take himself off when your Majesty is least thinking of such a thing."*

Nothing could be more melancholy than the tone of the Governor's letters. He believed himself disliked, even in the midst of affectionate demonstrations. He felt compelled to use moderate counsels, although he considered moderation of no avail. He was chained to his post, even though the post could, in his opinion, be more advantageously filled by another. He would still endeavour to gain the affections of the people, although he believed them hopelessly alienated. If patience would cure the malady of the country, he professed himself capable of applying the remedy, although the medicine had so far done but little good, and although he had no very strong hopes as to its future effects.† "Thus far, however," said he, "I am but as one crying in the wilderness."‡ He took occasion to impress upon his Majesty, in very strong language, the necessity of money. Secret agents, spies, and spies upon spies, were more necessary than ever, and were very expensive portions of government machinery. Never was money more wanted. Nothing could be more important than to attend faithfully to the financial suggestions of Escovedo, and Don John, therefore, urged his Majesty, again and again, not to dishonor their drafts. "Money is the gruel," said he, "with which we must cure this sick man;"§ and he therefore prayed all those who wished well to his efforts, to see that his Majesty did not fail him in this important matter. Notwithstanding, however, the vigor of his efforts, and the earnestness of his intentions, he gave but little hope to his Majesty of any valuable fruit from the pacification just concluded. He saw the Prince of Orange strengthening himself, "with great

* Letter of Escovedo, Discours Sommier, appendix, p. 16.

† Letter of Don John to the King, 7 Abríl, 1577, Discours Sommier, p. 27.

‡ "Pero veo que hasta agora es todo predicar en desierto."—Letter of Don John, 7 Abríl, 1577, Discours Sommier, etc., appendix, p. 36.

§ "—— en materia de dinero: porque este es el pisto con que a de bolver en si este enformo," etc.—Letter of Don John to Perez, Discours Sommier, p. 44.

fury," in Holland and Zealand;* he knew that the Prince was backed by the Queen of England, who, notwithstanding her promises to Philip and himself, had offered her support to the rebels in case the proposed terms of peace were rejected in Holland, and he felt that "nearly the whole people was at the devotion of the Prince."†

Don John felt more and more convinced, too, that a conspiracy was on foot against his liberty. There were so many of the one party, and so few of the other, that if he were once fairly "trussed," he affirmed that not a man among the faithful would dare to budge an inch.‡ He therefore informed his Majesty that he was secretly meditating a retreat to some place of security; judging very properly that, if he were still his own master, he should be able to exert more influence over those who were still well disposed, than if he should suffer himself to be taken captive. A suppressed conviction that he could effect nothing, except with his sword, pierced through all his more prudent reflections. He maintained that, after all, there was no remedy for the body but to cut off the diseased parts at once,§ and he therefore begged his Majesty for the means of performing the operation handsomely. The general expressions which he had previously used in favor of broths and mild treatment hardly tallied with the severe amputation thus recommended. There was, in truth, a constant struggle going on between the fierceness of his inclinations and the shackles which had been imposed upon him. He already felt entirely out of place, and although he scorned to fly from his post so long as it seemed the post of danger, he was most anxious that the King should grant him his dismissal, so soon as his presence should no longer be imperiously required. He was sure that the people would never believe

* "El Principe de Oranges continue el fortificar á gran fuia en Olanda y Zelanda."—Letter of Don John to the King, Discours Sommier, p. 35.

† Ibid., p. 36.—"La mayor parte de las estados esta a su devocion y casi todo el pueblo," etc.

‡ Ibid., p. 36.

§ "Pues no tiene este cuerpo otro remedio que el cortar lo dañado del: lo qual se a de hazer ajora haziendo la provision que suplico de nuevo," etc., etc.—Ibid., p. 38.

in his Majesty's forgiveness until the man concerning whom they entertained so much suspicion should be removed; for they saw in him only the "thunderbolt of his Majesty's wrath."* Orange and England confirmed their suspicions, and sustained their malice. Should he be compelled, against his will, to remain, he gave warning that he might do something which would be matter of astonishment to everybody.†

Meantime, the man in whose hands really lay the question of war and peace, sat at Middelburg, watching the deep current of events as it slowly flowed towards the precipice. The whole population of Holland and Zealand hung on his words. In approaching the realms of William the Silent, Don John felt that he had entered a charmed circle, where the talisman of his own illustrious name lost its power, where his valor was paralyzed, and his sword rusted irrevocably in its sheath. "The people here," he wrote, "are *bewitched* by the Prince of Orange. They love him, they fear him, and wish to have him for their master. They inform him of everything, and take no resolution without consulting him."‡

While William was thus directing and animating the whole nation with his spirit, his immediate friends became more and more anxious concerning the perils to which he was exposed. His mother, who had already seen her youngest-born, Henry, her Adolphus, her chivalrous Louis, laid in their bloody graves for the cause of conscience, was most solicitous for the welfare of her "heart's-beloved lord and son," the Prince of Orange. Nevertheless, the high-spirited old dame was even more alarmed at the possibility of a peace in which that religious liberty for which so much dear blood had been poured forth should be inadequately secured. "My heart longs for certain tidings from my lord," she wrote to William,

---

* Letter of Don John to Philip, Discours Sommier, p. 44.

† "Seré forçado á hazer alguna cosa que de mucho que maravillar á todos," etc.—Letter to Perez, Discours Sommier, p. 45.

‡ "—— los tiene encantados porque le aman y temen y quieren por Señor. Ellos le avisan de todo y sin el no resuelven cosa."—Extract of MS. letter in Gachard, Correspondance de Guillaume le Tacit., iii., preface, lxiii., note 3.

"for methinks the peace now in prospect will prove but an oppression for soul and conscience. I trust my heart's dearly-beloved lord and son will be supported by Divine grace to do nothing against God and his own soul's salvation. 'Tis better to lose the temporal than the eternal."* Thus wrote the mother of William, and we can feel the sympathetic thrill which such tender and lofty words awoke in his breast. His son, the ill-starred Philip, now for ten years long a compulsory sojourner in Spain, was not yet weaned from his affection for his noble parent, but sent messages of affection to him whenever occasion offered, while a less commendable proof of his filial affection he had lately afforded, at the expense of the luckless captain of his Spanish guard. That officer having dared in his presence to speak disrespectfully of his father, was suddenly seized about the waist by the enraged young Count, hurled out of the window, and killed stone-dead upon the spot.† After this exhibition of his natural feelings, the Spanish government thought it necessary to take more subtle means to tame so turbulent a spirit. Unfortunately they proved successful.

Count John of Nassau, too, was sorely pressed for money. Six hundred thousand florins, at least, had been advanced by himself and brothers to aid the cause of Netherland freedom.‡ Louis and himself had, unhesitatingly and immediately, turned into that sacred fund the hundred thousand crowns which the King of France had presented them for their personal use,§ for it was not the Prince of Orange alone who had consecrated his wealth and his life to the cause, but the members of his family, less immediately interested in the country, had thus furnished what may well be called an enormous subsidy, and one most disproportioned to their means. Not only had they given all the cash which they could com-

---

* Groen v. Prinsterer, Archives, etc., vi. 49, 50.

† De la Pise, p. 603. Groen v. Prinsterer, Archives, etc., vi. 102.

‡ Archives et Correspondance, vi. 95, sqq.

§ Ibid.

mand by mortgaging their lands and rents, their plate and furniture, but, in the words of Count John himself, "they had taken the chains and jewels from the necks of their wives, their children, and their mother, and had hawked them about, as if they had themselves been traders and hucksters."* And yet, even now, while stooping under this prodigious debt, Count John asked not for present repayment. He only wrote to the Prince to signify his extreme embarrassment, and to request some obligation or recognition from the cities of Holland and Zealand, whence hitherto no expression of gratitude or acknowledgment had proceeded.†

The Prince consoled and assured, as best he could, his mother, son, wife, and brother, even at the same moment that he comforted his people. He also received at this time a second and more solemn embassy from Don John.‡ No sooner had the Governor exchanged oaths at Brussels, and been acknowledged as the representative of his Majesty, than he hastened to make another effort to conciliate the Prince. Don John saw before him only a grand seignior of lofty birth and boundless influence, who had placed himself towards the Crown in a false position, from which he might even yet be rescued; for to sacrifice the whims of a reforming and transitory religious fanaticism, which had spun itself for a moment about so clear a brain, would, he thought, prove but a trifling task for so experienced a politician as the Prince. William of Orange, on the other hand, looked upon his young antagonist as the most brilliant impersonation which had yet been seen of the foul spirit of persecution.

It will be necessary to follow, somewhat more in detail than is usually desirable, the interchange of conversations, letters, and protocols, out of which the brief but important administration of Don John was composed; for it was exactly in such manifestations that the great fight was really proceeding.

---

* Archives et Correspondance, vi. 95, sqq. † Ibid.

‡ Bor, x. 814. Meteren, vii. 121.

Don John meant peace, wise William meant war, for he knew that no other issue was possible. Peace, in reality, was war in its worst shape. Peace would unchain every priestly tongue, and unsheath every knightly sword in the fifteen provinces against little Holland and Zealand. He had been able to bind all the provinces together by the hastily forged chain of the Ghent treaty, and had done what he could to strengthen that union by the principle of mutual religious respect. By the arrival of Don John that work had been deranged. It had, however, been impossible for the Prince thoroughly to infuse his own ideas on the subject of toleration into the hearts of his nearest associates. He could not hope to inspire his deadly enemies with a deeper sympathy. Was he not himself the mark of obloquy among the Reformers, because of his leniency to Catholics? Nay more, was not his intimate councillor, the accomplished Saint Aldegonde, in despair because the Prince refused to exclude the Anabaptists of Holland from the rights of citizenship? At the very moment when William was straining every nerve to unite warring sects, and to persuade men's hearts into a system by which their consciences were to be laid open to God alone—at the moment when it was most necessary for the very existence of the fatherland that Catholic and Protestant should mingle their social and political relations, it was indeed a bitter disappointment for him to see wise statesmen of his own creed unable to rise to the idea of toleration. "The affair of the Anabaptists," wrote Saint Aldegonde, "has been renewed. The Prince objects to exclude them from citizenship. He answered me sharply, that their yea was equal to our oath, and that we should not press this matter, unless we were *willing to confess that it was just for the Papists to compel us* to a divine service which was against our conscience." It seems hardly credible that this sentence, containing so sublime a tribute to the character of the Prince, should have been indited as a bitter censure, and that, too, by an enlightened and accomplished Protestant. "In short," continued Saint Aldegonde, with increasing vexation, "I don't see how we can accomplish our wish in this matter. The Prince has uttered reproaches to me that our clergy are striving to obtain a mastery over consciences. He praised lately the saying of a monk who was not long ago here, that our pot had not gone to the fire as often as that of our antagonists, but that when the time came it would be black enough. In short, the Prince fears that after a few centuries the clerical tyranny on both sides will stand in this respect on the same footing."*

Early in the month of May, Doctor Leoninus and Caspar Schetz, Seigneur de Grobbendonck, had been sent on a mission from the states-general to the Prince of Orange.† While their negotiations were still pending, four special envoys from Don John arrived at Middelburg. To this commission was informally adjoined Leoninus, who had succeeded to the general position of Viglius. Viglius was dead.‡ Since the memorable arrest of the State Council, he had not appeared on the scene of public affairs. The house-arrest, to which he had been compelled by a revolutionary committee, had been indefinitely prolonged by a higher power, and after a protracted illness he had noiselessly disappeared from the stage of life. There had been few more learned doctors of both laws than he. There had been few more adroit politicians, considered from his point of view. His punning device was "*Vita mortalium vigilia*,"§ and he acted accordingly, but with a narrow interpretation. His life had indeed been a vigil, but it must be confessed that the vigils had been for Viglius. The weather-beaten Palinurus, as he loved to call himself, had conducted his own argosy so warily that he had saved his whole cargo,

* See the letter of Saint Aldegonde in Brandt, Hist. der Reformatie, i. b. xi. 588, 589.

† Bor, x. 814. Hoofd, xii. 501.

‡ He died May 8, 1577.—Bor, x. 812. Hoofd, xii. 501.

§ Bor, x. 812. Meteren, vi. 120.—Another motto of his was, "*En groot Jurist een booser Christ*;" that is to say, A good lawyer is a bad Christian.—Meteren, vi. 120. Unfortunately his own character did not give the lie satisfactorily to the device.

and perished in port at last, while others, not sailing by his compass, were still tossed by the tempest.

The agents of Don John were the Duke of Aerschot, the Seigneur de Hierges, Seigneur de Willerval, and Doctor Meetkercke, accompanied by Doctor Andrew Gaill, one of the imperial commissioners.* The two envoys from the states-general, Leoninus and Schetz, being present at Gertruydenberg were added to the deputation.† An important conference took place, the details of which have been somewhat minutely preserved.‡ The Prince of Orange, accompanied by Saint Aldegonde and four other councillors, encountered the seven champions from Brussels in a long debate, which was more like a passage of arms or a trial of skill than a friendly colloquy with a pacific result in prospect; for it must be remembered that the Prince of Orange did not mean peace. He had devised the Pacification of Ghent as a union of the other provinces with Holland and Zealand, against Philip. He did not intend that it should be converted into a union of the other provinces with Philip, against Holland and Zealand.

Meetkercke was the first to speak. He said that the Governor had despatched them to the Prince, to express his good intentions, to represent the fidelity with which his promises had thus far been executed, and to entreat the Prince, together with the provinces of Holland and Zealand, to unite with their sister provinces in common allegiance to his Majesty. His Highness also proposed to advise with them concerning the proper method of convoking the states-general.§ As soon as Meetkercke had finished his observations, the Prince

---

* Bor, x. 814. Hoofd, xii. 502.

† Bor, x. 816. Hoofd, xii. 502.

‡ By the learned and acute Gachard, to whom the history of the Netherlands is under such great obligations. Vide Correspondance de Guillaume le Tacit., iii. preface, lxii. lxiii., and appendice, pp. 447–459, where is to be found the "Vraye Narration des Propos da Costé et d'aultre tenuz entre des Deputez d'Hollande et de Zelande á Gheertrudenbergh au mois de May, 1577." "On reconnait," says Mr. Gachard, "en lisant cette curieuse relation, qu'elle fut l'ouvrage d'un des conseillers du Prince, peut-être l'auteur en est il Philippe de Marnix (St. Aldegonde) lui-même."—Note to p. 447, Guillaume le Tacit., iii.

§ Vraye Narration, etc., 447, 448.

demanded that the points and articles should be communicated to him in writing. Now this was precisely what the envoys preferred to omit. It was easier, and far more agreeable to expatiate in a general field of controversy, than to remain tethered to distinct points. It was particularly in these confused conferences, where neither party was entirely sincere, that the volatile word was thought preferable to the permanent letter. Already so many watery lines had been traced, in the course of these fluctuating negotiations, that a few additional records would be, if necessary, as rapidly effaced as the rest.

The commissioners, after whispering in each other's ears for a few minutes, refused to put down anything in writing. Protocols, they said, only engendered confusion.

"No, no," said the Prince, in reply, "we will have nothing except in black and white. Otherwise things will be said on both sides, which will afterwards be interpreted in different ways. Nay, it will be denied that some important points have been discussed at all. We know that by experience. Witness the solemn treaty of Ghent, which ye have tried to make fruitless, under pretence that some points, arranged by word of mouth, and not stated particularly in writing, had been intended in a different sense from the obvious one. Governments given by royal commission, for example; what point could be clearer? Nevertheless, ye have hunted up glosses and cavils to obscure the intention of the contracting parties. Ye have denied my authority over Utrecht, because not mentioned expressly in the treaty of Ghent."*

"But," said one of the envoys, interrupting at this point, "neither the Council of State nor the Court of Mechlin consider Utrecht as belonging to your Excellency's government."†

"Neither the Council of State," replied the Prince, "nor the Court of Mechlin have anything to do with the matter. 'Tis in my commission, and all the world knows it."‡ He added that instead of affairs being thrown into confusion by

* Vraye Narration, etc., 449, 450.

† See details of Conferences at Gertruydenberg, preserved by Bor, x. 819.

‡ Bor, x. 819. Hoofd, xii. 504.

being reduced to writing, he was of opinion, on the contrary, that it was by that means alone they could be made perfectly clear.

Leoninus replied, good naturedly, that there should be no difficulty upon that score, and that writings should be exchanged. In the meantime, however, he expressed the hope that the Prince would honor them with some preliminary information as to the points in which he felt aggrieved, as well as to the pledges which he and the states were inclined to demand.

"And what reason have we to hope," cried the Prince, "that your pledges, if made, will be redeemed? That which was promised so solemnly at Ghent, and ratified by Don John and his Majesty, has not been fulfilled."*

"Of what particular point do you complain?" asked Schetz. "Wherein has the Pacification been violated?"

Hereupon the Prince launched forth upon a flowing stream of invective. He spoke to them of his son detained in distant captivity—of his own property at Breda withheld—of a thousand confiscated estates—of garrisons of German mercenaries—of ancient constitutions annihilated—of the infamous edicts nominally suspended, but actually in full vigor. He complained bitterly that the citadels, those nests and dens of tyranny, were not yet demolished. "Ye accuse me of distrust," he cried; "but while the castles of Antwerp, Ghent, Namur, and so many more are standing, 'tis yourselves who show how utterly ye are without confidence in any permanent and peaceful arrangement."†

"And what," asked a deputy, smoothly, "is the point which touches you most nearly? What is it that your Excellency most desires? By what means will it be possible for the government fully to give you contentment?"‡

"I wish," he answered, simply, "the full execution of the

* Vraye Narration, etc. Gachard, Guillaume le Tacit., iii. 450.

† Bor, x. 819. Hoofd, xii. 504. Compare Cabrera, xi. 913, 914.

‡ Bor, x. 819. Hoofd, xii. 504.

Ghent Pacification. If you regard the general welfare of the land, it is well, and I thank you. If not, 'tis idle to make propositions, for I regard my country's profit, not my own."* Afterwards, the Prince simply repeated his demand that the Ghent treaty should be executed ; adding, that after the states-general should have been assembled, it would be time to propose the necessary articles for mutual security.

Hereupon Doctor Leoninus observed that the assembly of the states-general could hardly be without danger. He alluded to the vast number of persons who would thus be convoked, to the great discrepancy of humors which would thus be manifested. Many men would be present neither discreet nor experienced. He therefore somewhat coolly suggested that it might be better to obviate the necessity of holding any general assembly at all. An amicable conference, for the sake of settling doubtful questions, would render the convocation superfluous, and save the country from the dangers by which the step would be attended. The Doctor concluded by referring to the recent assemblies of France, the only result of which had been fresh dissensions.† It thus appeared that the proposition on the part of Don John meant something very different from its apparent signification. To advise with the Prince as to the proper method of assembling the estates really meant, to advise with him as to the best means of preventing any such assembly. Here, certainly, was a good reason for the preference expressed by the deputies, in favor of amicable discussions over formal protocols. It might not be so easy in a written document to make the assembly, and the prevention of the assembly, appear exactly the same thing.

The Prince replied that there was a wide difference between the condition of France and of the Netherlands. Here, was one will and one intention. There, were many factions, many partialities, many family intrigues. Since it had been agreed

* Bor, x. 819. Hoofd, xii. 504.

† Vraye Narration, etc., 451.

by the Ghent treaty that certain points should be provisionally maintained and others settled by a speedy convocation of the states-general, the plainest course was to maintain the provisional points, and to summon the states-general at once.* This certainly was concise and logical. It is doubtful, however, whether he were really as anxious for the assembly-general as he appeared to be. Both parties were fencing at each other, without any real intention of carrying their points, for neither wished the convocation, while both affected an eagerness for that event.—The conversation proceeded.

"At least," said an envoy, "you can tell beforehand in what you are aggrieved, and what you have to propose."

"We are aggrieved in nothing, and we have nothing to propose," answered the Prince, "so long as you maintain the Pacification. We demand no other pledge, and are willing to refer everything afterwards to the assembly."

"But," asked Schetz, "what security do you offer us that you will yourselves maintain the Pacification?"

"We are not bound to give assurances," answered the Prince. "The Pacification is itself an assurance. 'Tis a provisional arrangement, to be maintained by both parties, until after the decision of the assembly. The Pacification must therefore be maintained or disavowed. Choose between the two. Only, if you mean still to acknowledge it, you must keep its articles. This *we* mean to do, and if up to the present time you have any complaint to make of our conduct, as we trust you have not, we are ready to give you satisfaction."†

"In short," said an envoy, "you mean, after we shall have placed in your hands the government of Utrecht, Amsterdam, and other places, to deny us any pledges on your part to maintain the Pacification."

"But," replied the Prince, "if we are already accomplishing the Pacification, what more do you wish?"

"In this fashion," cried the others, "after having got all

* Vraye Narration, etc., 452.

† Ibid., 452, 453.

that you ask, and having thus fortified yourselves more than you were ever fortified before, you will make war upon us."

"War?" cried the Prince, "what are you afraid of? We are but a handful of people; a worm compared to the King of Spain. Moreover, ye are fifteen provinces to two. What have you to fear?"*

"Ah," said Meetkercke, "we have seen what you could do, when you were masters of the sea. Don't make yourselves out quite so little."†

"But," said the Prince, "the Pacification of Ghent provides for all this. Your deputies were perfectly satisfied with the guarantees it furnished. As to making war upon you, 'tis a thing without foundation or appearance of probability. Had you believed then that you had anything to fear, you would not have forgotten to demand pledges enough. On the contrary, you saw how roundly we were dealing with you then, honestly disgarnishing the country, even before the peace had been concluded. For ourselves, although we felt the right to demand guarantees, we would not do it, for we were treating with you on terms of confidence. We declared expressly that had we been dealing with the King, we should have exacted stricter pledges. As to demanding them of us at the moment, 'tis nonsense. We have neither the means of assailing you, nor do we deem it expedient to do so."‡

"To say the truth," replied Schetz, "we are really confident that you will not make war upon us. On the other hand, however, we see you spreading your religion daily, instead of keeping it confined within your provinces. What assurance do you give us that, after all your demand shall have been accorded, you will make no innovation in religion."§

"The assurance which we give you," answered the Prince, "is that we will really accomplish the Pacification."

"But," persisted Schetz, "do you fairly promise to submit

---

* Vraye Narration, etc., 452, 453.

† "—— et pourtant ne vous faites pas si petits comme vous faictes."—Ibid.

‡ Vraye Narration, etc., 454.

§ Ibid.

to all which the states-general shall ordain, as well on this point of religious exercise in Holland and Zealand, as on all the others ?"*

This was a home thrust. The Prince parried it for a while. In his secret thoughts he had no expectation or desire that the states-general, summoned in a solemn manner by the Governor-General, on the basis of the memorable assembly before which was enacted the grand ceremony of the imperial abdication, would ever hold their session, and although he did not anticipate the prohibition by such assembly, should it take place, of the Reformed worship in Holland and Zealand, he did not intend to submit to it, even should it be made.

"I cannot tell," said he, accordingly, in reply to the last question, "for ye have yourselves already broken and violated the Pacification; having made an accord with Don John without our consent, and having already received him as Governor."

"So that you don't mean," replied Schetz, "to accept the decision of the states ?"†

"I don't say that," returned the Prince, continuing to parry; "it is possible that we might accept it; it is possible that we might not. We are no longer in our entire rights, as we were at the time of our first submission at Ghent."

"But we will make you whole," said Schetz.

"That you cannot do," replied the Prince, "for you have broken the Pacification all to pieces. We have nothing, therefore, to expect from the states, but to be condemned off-hand."‡

"You don't mean, then," repeated Schetz, "to submit to the estates touching the exercise of religion ?"

"No, we do not !" replied the Prince, driven into a corner at last, and striking out in his turn. "We certainly do not. To tell you the truth, we see that you intend our extirpation, and we don't mean to be extirpated."§

"Ho !" said the Duke of Aerschot, "there is nobody who wishes that."

* Vraye Narration, etc., 455.

† Ibid., 456.

‡ "Que d'estre condemnès à pur et à plain."—Ibid.

§ Ibid.

"Indeed, but you do," said the Prince. "We have submitted ourselves to you in good faith, and you now would compel us and all the world to maintain exclusively the Catholic religion. This cannot be done except by extirpating us."

A long, learned, vehement discussion upon abstract points, between Saint Aldegonde, Leoninus, and Doctor Gaill, then ensued, during which the Prince, who had satisfied himself as to the result of the conference, retired from the apartment. He afterwards had a private convention with Schetz and Leoninus, in which he reproached them with their inclination to reduce their fatherland to slavery.* He also took occasion to remark to Hierges, that it was a duty to content the people; that whatever might be accomplished for them was durable, whereas the will of kings was perishing. He told the Duke of Aerschot that if Utrecht were not restored, he would take it by force. He warned the Duke that to trust the King was to risk his head. He, at least, would never repose confidence in him, having been deceived too often. The King cherished the maxim, *hœreticis non est servanda fides;* as for himself he was *calbo y calbanista,* and meant to die so.†

The formal interchange of documents soon afterwards took place. The conversation thus held between the different parties shows, however, the exact position of affairs. There was no change in the intentions of either Reformers or Royalists. Philip and his representatives still contended for two points, and claimed the praise of moderation that their demands were so few in number. They were willing to concede everything, save the unlimited authority of the King and the exclusive maintenance of the Catholic religion. The Prince of Orange, on his side, claimed two points also—the ancient constitutions of the country and religious freedom. It was obvious

* Vraye Narration, etc., 459.

† Extracts from the MS. letters (28th and 29th of May, 1577) of Don John to the King, given by M. Gachard in the preface to the third vol. Correspondance de Guillaume le Tacit., p. lxiii.

enough that the contest was the same, in reality, as it had ever been. No approximation had been made towards reconciling absolutism with national liberty, persecution with toleration. The Pacification of Ghent had been a step in advance. That Treaty opened the door to civil and religious liberty,* but it was an agreement among the provinces, not a compact between the people and the monarch. By the casuists of Brussels and the licentiates of Louvain, it had, to be sure, been dogmatically pronounced orthodox, and had been confirmed by royal edict. To believe, however, that his Catholic Majesty had faith in the dogmas propounded, was as absurd as to believe in the dogmas themselves. If the Ghent Pacification really had made no breach in royal and Roman infallibility, then the efforts of Orange and the exultation of the Reformers had indeed been idle.

The envoys accordingly, in obedience to their instructions, made a formal statement to the Prince of Orange and the states of Holland and Zealand, on the part of Don John.† They alluded to the departure of the Spaniards, as if that alone had fulfilled every duty and authorized every claim. They therefore demanded the immediate publication in Holland and Zealand of the Perpetual Edict. They insisted on the immediate discontinuance of all hostile attempts to reduce Amsterdam to the jurisdiction of Orange; required the Prince to abandon his pretensions to Utrecht, and denounced the efforts making by him and his partisans to diffuse their heretical doctrines through the other provinces. They observed, in conclusion, that the general question of religion was not to be handled, because reserved for the consideration of the states-general, according to the treaty of Ghent.‡

---

* Even Tassis admits this fact, which is indeed indisputable.—"Abhorrebat Austriacus," says he (liii. p. 245), "a confirmatione Pacis Gandavensis, quod per eam tacite introducebatur libertas Religionis."

‡ See it in Bor, x. 816, 817.—Compare the letter of instruction published by Gachard, Correspondance de Guillaume le Tacit., iii. 438–446.

‡ Bor, x. 816–817. Gachard, Correspondance de Guillaume le Tacit., iii. 438–446.

The reply, delivered on the following day by the Prince of Orange and the deputies, maintained that the Perpetual Edict was widely different from the Pacification of Ghent, which it affected to uphold; that the promises to abstain from all violation of the ancient constitutions had not been kept, that the German troops had not been dismissed, that the property of the Prince in the Netherlands and Burgundy had not been restored, that his son was detained in captivity, that the government of Utrecht was withheld from him, that the charters and constitution of the country, instead of being extended, had been contracted, and that the Governor had claimed the right to convoke the states-general at his pleasure, in violation of the ancient right to assemble at their own. The document further complained that the adherents of the Reformed religion were not allowed to frequent the different provinces in freedom, according to the stipulations of Ghent; that Don John, notwithstanding all these short-comings, had been acknowledged as Governor-General, without the consent of the Prince; that he was surrounded with a train of Spaniards, Italians, and other foreigners—Gonzaga, Escovedo, and the like—as well as by renegade Netherlanders like Tassis, by whom he was unduly influenced against the country and the people, and by whom a "back door was held constantly open" to the admission of evils innumerable.* Finally, it was asserted that, by means of this last act of union, a new form of inquisition had been introduced, and one which was much more cruel than the old system; inasmuch as the Spanish Inquisition did not take information against men except upon suspicion, whereas, by the new process, all the world would be examined as to their conscience and religion, under pretence of maintaining the union.†

Such was the result of this second mission to the Prince of Orange on the part of the Governor-General. Don John

---

* "Dat Don Johan een achter deure open houd met de boven genoemde, en andere van gelijke stoffe," etc., etc.

† Reply of the States of Holland. Bor, x. 818ᵇ.

never sent another. The swords were now fairly measured between the antagonists, and the scabbard was soon to be thrown away. A few weeks afterwards, the Governor wrote to Philip that there was nothing in the world which William of Orange so much abhorred as his Majesty ; adding, with Castillian exaggeration, that if the Prince could drink the King's blood he would do so with great pleasure.*

Don John, being thus seated in the saddle, had a moment's leisure to look around him. It was but a moment, for he had small confidence in the aspect of affairs, but one of his first acts after assuming the government afforded a proof of the interpretation which he had adopted of the Ghent Pacification. An edict was issued, addressed to all bishops, "heretic-masters,"† and provincial councils, commanding the strict enforcement of the Canons of Trent, and other ecclesiastical decrees. These authorities were summoned instantly to take increased heed of the flocks under their charge, "and to protect them from the ravening wolves which were seeking to devour them."

The measure bore instant fruit. A wretched tailor of Mechlin, Peter Panis by name, an honest man, but a heretic, was arrested upon the charge of having preached or exhorted at a meeting in that city. He confessed that he had been present at the meeting, but denied that he had preached. He was then required to denounce the others who had been present, and the men who had actually officiated. He refused, and was condemned to death. The Prince of Orange, while the process was pending, wrote an earnest letter to the Council of Mechlin, imploring them not now to rekindle the fires of religious persecution.‡ His appeal was in vain. The poor tailor was beheaded at Mechlin on the 15th of June, the Conqueror

---

* Extract from MS. letter (28th of July, 1577) of Don John to the King, apud Gachard, preface to Correspondance de Guillaume le Tacit., iii. lxiv., notes, 112.

† "Ketter meesters."—See the edict, Bor, x. 819, 820.

‡ Bor, x. 820. Hoofd, xii. 507. Meteren, vii. 122ª.

of Lepanto being present at the execution,* and adding dignity to the scene. Thus, at the moment when William of Orange was protecting the Anabaptists of Middelburg in their rights of citizenship, even while they refused its obligations, the son of the Emperor was dipping his hands in the blood of a poor wretch who had done no harm but to listen to a prayer without denouncing the preacher. The most intimate friends of the Prince were offended with his liberality. The imperial shade of Don John's father might have risen to approve the son who had so dutifully revived his bloody edicts and his ruthless policy.

Three parties were now fairly in existence: the nobles, who hated the Spaniards, but who were disposed to hold themselves aloof from the people; the adherents of Don John, commonly called "Johanists;" and the partisans of the Prince of Orange—for William the Silent had always felt the necessity of leaning for support on something more substantial than the court party, a reed shaken by the wind, and failing always when most relied upon. His efforts were constant to elevate the middle class, to build up a strong third party which should unite much of the substantial wealth and intelligence of the land, drawing constantly from the people, and deriving strength from national enthusiasm—a party which should include nearly all the political capacity of the country; and his efforts were successful. No doubt the Governor and his Secretary were right when they said the people of the Netherlands were inclined to brook the Turk as easily as the Spaniard for their master, and that their hearts were in reality devoted to the Prince of Orange.

As to the grandees, they were mostly of those who "sought to swim between two waters," according to the Prince's expression. There were but few unswerving supporters of the Spanish rule, like the Berlaymont and the Tassis families. The rest veered daily with the veering wind. Aerschot, the great chief of the Catholic party, was but a cringing courtier,

* Bor, Hoofd, Meteren, ubi sup.

false and fawning both to Don John and the Prince. He sought to play a leading part in a great epoch; he only distinguished himself by courting and betraying all parties, and being thrown away by all. His son and brother were hardly more respectable. The Prince knew how little dependence could be placed on such allies, even although they had signed and sworn the Ghent Pacification. He was also aware how little it was the intention of the Governor to be bound by that famous Treaty. The Spanish troops had been, indeed, disbanded, but there were still between ten and fifteen thousand German mercenaries in the service of the King; these were stationed in different important places, and held firm possession of the citadels. The great keys of the country were still in the hands of the Spaniards. Aerschot, indeed, governed the castle of Antwerp, in room of Sancho d'Avila, but how much more friendly would Aerschot be than Avila, when interest prompted him to sustain Don John against the Prince?

Meanwhile, the estates, according to their contract, were straining every nerve to raise the requisite sum for the payment of the German troops. Equitable offers were made, by which the soldiers were to receive a certain proportion of the arrears due to them in merchandize, and the remainder in cash.* The arrangement was rejected, at the secret instance of Don John.† While the Governor affected an ingenuous desire to aid the estates in their efforts to free themselves from the remaining portion of this incumbrance, he was secretly tampering with the leading German officers, in order to prevent their acceptance of any offered terms.‡ He persuaded these military chiefs that a conspiracy existed, by which they were not only to be deprived of their wages but of their lives. He warned them to heed no promises, to accept no terms. Convincing them that he, and he only, was their friend, he arranged secret plans by which they should assist

---

* Bor, x. 820. † Meteren, vii. 122. Bor, x. 820, sqq. Hoofd, xii. 505.

‡ Meteren, Bor, Hoofd, ubi sup.

him in taking the fortresses of the country into still more secure possession,* for he was not more inclined to trust to the Aerschots and the Havrés than was the Prince himself.

The Governor lived in considerable danger, and in still greater dread of capture, if not of assassination. His imagination, excited by endless tales of ambush and half-discovered conspiracies, saw armed soldiers behind every bush, a pitfall in every street. Had not the redoubtable Alva been nearly made a captive? Did not Louis of Nassau nearly entrap the Grand Commander? No doubt the Prince of Orange was desirous of accomplishing a feat by which he would be placed in regard to Philip on the vantage ground which the King had obtained by his seizure of Count Van Buren, nor did Don John need for warnings coming from sources far from obscure. In May, the Viscount De Gand had forced his way to his bedside in the dead of night, and wakening him from his sleep, had assured him, with great solemnity, that his life was not worth a pin's purchase if he remained in Brussels. He was aware, he said, of a conspiracy by which both his liberty and his life were endangered, and assured him that in immediate flight lay his only safety.†

The Governor fled to Mechlin, where the same warnings were soon afterwards renewed, for the solemn sacrifice of Peter Panis, the poor preaching tailor of that city, had not been enough to strike terror to the hearts of all the Netherlanders. One day, toward the end of June, the Duke of Aerschot, riding out with Don John,‡ gave him a circumstantial account of plots, old and new, whose existence he had discovered or invented, and he showed a copy of a secret letter, written by the Prince of Orange to the estates, recommending the forcible seizure of his Highness. It is true that the Duke was, at that period and for long after, upon terms of the most "fraternal friendship" with the Prince, and was in the habit of signing himself "his

* Bor, Meteren, Hoofd.

† Vera et Simplex Narratio Eorum quæ ab Adventu D. Joannis Austriaci, etc., gesta sunt, p. 13.—Luxembergi, 1578.

‡ Ibid., p. 17.

very affectionate brother and cordial friend to serve him,"* yet this did not prevent him from accomplishing what he deemed his duty, in secretly denouncing his plans. It is also true that he, at the same time, gave the Prince private information concerning the government, and sent him intercepted letters from his enemies,† thus easing his conscience on both sides, and trimming his sails to every wind which might blow. The Duke now, however, reminded his Highness of the contumely with which he had been treated at Brussels, of the insolent threats with which the citizens had pursued his servants and secretaries even to the very door of his palace.‡ He assured him that the same feeling existed at Mechlin, and that neither himself nor family were much safer there than in the capital, a plot being fully organized for securing his person. The conspirators, he said, were openly supported by a large political party, who called themselves anti-Johanists, and who clothed themselves in symbolic costume, as had been done by the disaffected in the days of Cardinal Granvelle. He assured the Governor that nearly all the members of the states-general were implicated in these schemes. "And what becomes, then, of their promises?" asked Don John. "That for their promises!" cried the Duke, snapping his fingers;§ "no man in the land feels bound by engagements now." The Governor demanded the object of the states in thus seeking to deprive him of his liberty. The Duke informed him that it was to hold him in captivity until they had compelled him to sign every paper which they chose to lay before him. Such things had been done in the Netherlands in former days, the Duke observed, as he proceeded to narrate how a predecessor of his Highness and a prince of the land, after having been

---

* Archives et Correspondance, vi. 141–143.

† See the letter last quoted, Archives, etc., vi. 143, 144.

‡ Vera et Simplex Narratio, etc., p. 14.—Compare the Memoire de Grobbendonck, p. 172; Bull. Com. Roy., x.

§ Ibid., p. 19.—See also the letter of Don John to the states-general, dated August 24, 1577, in Bor, xi. 864, 865.—"Daerop hy antwoorde klickende mette fingern," etc.

compelled to sign innumerable documents, had been, in conclusion, tossed out of the windows of his own palace, with all his retinue, to perish upon the pikes of an insurgent mob below.* The Governor protested that it did not become the son of Charles the Fifth and the representative of his Catholic Majesty to hear such intimations a second time. After his return, he brooded over what had been said to him for a few days, and he then broke up his establishment at Mechlin, selling off his superfluous furniture and even the wine in his cellars.† Thus showing that his absence, both from Brussels and Mechlin, was to be a prolonged one, he took advantage of an unforeseen occurrence again to remove his residence.

* Vera Narratio, etc., p. 18, 19. Letter of Don John, ubi sup.

† Discours Sommier des Justes Causes, etc., etc., p. 17. Bor, x. 828.

CHAPTER III.

The city of Namur—Margaret of Valois—Her intrigues in Hainault in favour of Alençon—Her reception by Don John at Namur—Festivities in her honor—Seizure of Namur citadel by Don John—Plan for seizing that of Antwerp—Letter of the estates to Philip, sent by Escovedo—Fortunes and fate of Escovedo in Madrid—Repairing of dykes—The Prince's visit to Holland—His letter to the estates-general on the subject of Namur citadel—His visit to Utrecht—Correspondence and commissioners between Don John and the estates—Acrimonious and passionate character of these colloquies—Attempt of Treslong upon Antwerp citadel frustrated by De Bourse—Fortunate panic of the German mercenaries—Antwerp evacuated by the foreign troops—Renewed correspondence—Audacity of the Governor's demands—Letters of Escovedo and others intercepted—Private schemes of Don John not understood by the estates—His letter to the Empress Dowager—More correspondence with the estates—Painful and false position of the Governor—Demolition, in part, of Antwerp citadel, and of other fortresses by the patriots—Statue of Alva—Letter of estates-general to the King.

There were few cities of the Netherlands more picturesque in situation, more trimly built, and more opulent of aspect than the little city of Namur. Seated at the confluence of the Sombre with the Meuse, and throwing over each river a bridge of solid but graceful structure, it lay in the lap of a most fruitful valley. A broad crescent-shaped plain, fringed by the rapid Meuse, and enclosed by gently rolling hills cultivated to their crests, or by abrupt precipices of limestone crowned with verdure, was divided by numerous hedgerows, and dotted all over with corn-fields, vineyards, and flower-gardens. Many eyes have gazed with delight upon that well-known and most lovely valley, and many torrents of blood have mingled with those glancing waters since that long-buried and most sanguinary age which forms our theme ; and still placid as ever is the valley, brightly as ever flows the stream. Even now, as in that vanished, but never-forgotten time, nestles the little city in the angle of the two rivers ; still directly over its head seems to hang in mid-air the massive and frowning fortress, like the gigantic helmet in the fiction, as if ready to crush the pigmy town below.

It was this famous citadel, crowning an abrupt precipice five hundred feet above the river's bed, and placed near the frontier of France, which made the city so important, and which had now attracted Don John's attention in this hour of his perplexity. The unexpected visit of a celebrated personage, furnished him with the pretext which he desired. The beautiful Margaret of Valois, Queen of Navarre, was proceeding to the baths of Spa, to drink the waters.* Her health was as perfect as her beauty, but she was flying from a husband whom she hated, to advance the interest of a brother whom she loved with a more than sisterly fondness—for the worthless Duke of Alençon was one of the many competitors for the Netherland government ; the correspondence between himself and his brother with Orange and his agents being still continued. The hollow truce with the Huguenots in France had, however, been again succeeded by war. Henry of Valois had already commenced operations in Gascony against Henry of Navarre, whom he hated almost† as cordially as Margaret herself could do, and the Duke of Alençon was besieging Issoire.‡ Meantime, the beautiful Queen came to mingle the golden thread of her feminine intrigues with the dark woof of the Netherland destinies.

Few spirits have been more subtle, few faces so fatal as hers. True child of the Medicean mother, worthy sister of Charles, Henry, and Francis—princes for ever infamous in the

---

* Bor, x. 828. Meteren, vii. 122. Cabrera, xi. 929. Hoofd, xii. 508, et al.

† Mémoires de Marguerite de Valois, p. 123. Liege, 1714.

‡ De Thou, vii. 500, sqq., liv. 63.

annals of France—she possessed more beauty and wit than Mary of Scotland, more learning and accomplishments than Elizabeth of England. In the blaze of her beauty, according to the inflated language of her most determined worshiper, the wings of all rivals were melted. Heaven required to be raised higher and earth made wider, before a full sweep could be given to her own majestic flight.* We are further informed that she was a Minerva for eloquence, that she composed matchless poems which she sang most exquisitely to the sound of her lute, and that her familiar letters were so full of genius, that "poor Cicero" was but a fool to her in the same branch of composition.† The world has shuddered for ages at the dark tragedy of her nuptials. Was it strange that hatred, incest, murder, should follow in the train of a wedding thus hideously solemnized?

Don John, as in his Moorish disguise he had looked upon her perfections, had felt in danger of becoming really the slave he personated—"her beauty is more divine than human," he had cried, "but fitter to destroy men's souls than to bless them;"‡—and now the enchantress was on her way to his dominions. Her road led through Namur to Liege, and gallantry required that he should meet her as she passed. Attended by a select band of gentlemen and a few horsemen of his body-guard, the Governor came to Namur.§

Meantime the Queen crossed the frontier, and was courteously received at Cambray. The bishop—of the loyal house of Berlaymont—was a stanch supporter of the King, and although a Fleming, was Spanish to the core. On him the cajolery

* Eloge de Marguerite de Valois, Rayne de France et de Navarre, etc., par Brantome, p. 2, usâ.

† "—— Ses belles lettres—les mieux couchées soit pour estre graves, que pour estre familières —— il n'y a nul qui les voyant ne se mocque du pauvre Ciceron avec les siennes familières," etc., etc.—Eloge, etc., etc., p. 18.

‡ "Aunque la hermosura desta Reyna se mas divina que humana, es mas para perder y dañar los hombres que salvarlos."—Ibid., p. 4.

§ Bor, x. 828. Hoofd, xi. 508. Cabrera, xi. 929.

of the beautiful Queen was first essayed, but was found powerless. The prelate gave her a magnificent ball, but resisted her blandishments. He retired with the appearance of the confections, but the governor of the citadel, the Seigneur d'Inchy remained, with whom Margaret was more successful. She found him a cordial hater of Spain, a favorer of France, and very impatient under the authority of the bishop. He obtained permission to accompany the royal visitor a few stages of her journey, and returned to Cambray, her willing slave; holding the castle in future, neither for king nor bishop, but for Margaret's brother, Alençon, alone. At Mons she was received with great state by the Count Lalain, who was governor of Hainault, while his Countess governed him. A week of festivities graced the advent of the Queen, during which period the hearts of both Lalain and his wife were completely subjugated. They agreed that Flanders had been too long separated from the parental France to which it of right belonged. The Count was a stanch Catholic, but he hated Spain. He was a relative of Egmont, and anxious to avenge his death, but he was no lover of the people, and was jealous of Orange. Moreover, his wife had become entirely fascinated by the designing Queen. So warm a friendship had sprung up between the two fair ladies as to make it indispensable that Flanders and Hainault should be annexed to France. The Count promised to hold his whole government at the service of Alençon, and recommended that an attempt should be made to gain over the incorruptible Governor of Cambray. Margaret did not inform him that she had already turned that functionary round her finger, but she urged Lalain and his wife to seduce him from his allegiance, if possible.*

The Count, with a retinue of mounted men, then accompanied her on her way towards Namur, but turned as the distant tramp of Don John's cavalcade was heard approaching,

* Mémoires de Marguerite de Valois, ii. pp. 125, 129–134, sqq.

for it was not desirable for Lalain, at that moment, to find himself face to face with the Governor. Don John stood a moment awaiting the arrival of the Queen. He did not dream of her political intrigues, nor see in the fair form approaching him one mortal enemy the more. Margaret travelled in a splendid litter with gilt pillars, lined with scarlet velvet, and entirely enclosed in glass,* which was followed by those of the Princess de la Roche sur Yon, and of Madame de Tournon. After these came ten ladies of honor on horseback, and six chariots filled with female domestics. These, with the guards and other attendants, made up the retinue. On meeting the Queen's litter, Don John sprang from his horse and presented his greetings. The Queen returned his salutation, in the French fashion, by offering her cheek to his embrace, extending the same favor to the Duke of Aerschot and the Marquis of Havré.† The cavaliers then remounted and escorted the Queen to Namur, Don John riding by the side of the litter, and conversing with her all the way. It was late in the evening when the procession arrived in the city. The streets had, however, been brilliantly illuminated ; houses and shops, although it was near midnight, being in a blaze of light. Don John believing that no attentions could be so acceptable at that hour as to provide for the repose of his guest, conducted the Queen at once to the lodgings prepared for her. Margaret was astonished at the magnificence of the apartments into which she was ushered. A spacious and stately hall, most gorgeously furnished, opened into a series of chambers and cabinets, worthy, in their appointments, of a royal palace. The tent and bed coverings prepared for the Queen were exquisitely embroidered in needlework with scenes representing the battle of Lepanto.‡ The great hall was hung with gorgeous tapestry of satin and velvet, ornamented with columns of raised silver work, and with many figures in

* Mémoires de Marguerite de Valois, ii, 124–125, sqq.

† Ibid., ii. 135. Hoofd, xii. 508.

‡ Mémoires de Marguerite de Valois, 137.

antique costume, of the same massive embroidery. The rest of the furniture was also of satin, velvet, cloth of gold, and brocade. The Queen was dazzled with so much magnificence, and one of the courtiers could not help expressing astonishment at the splendor of the apartments and decorations, which, as he observed to the Duke of Aerschot, seemed more appropriate to the palace of a powerful monarch than to the apartments of a young bachelor prince.* The Duke replied by explaining that the expensive embroidery which they saw was the result, not of extravagance, but of valor and generosity. After the battle of Lepanto, Don John had restored, without ransom, the two sons, who had been taken prisoners, of a powerful Turkish bashaw. The father, in gratitude, had sent this magnificent tapestry as a present to the conqueror, and Don John had received it at Milan, in which city, celebrated for the taste of its upholsterers, it had been arranged for furniture.†

The next morning a grand mass with military music was performed, followed by a sumptuous banquet in the grand hall. Don John and the Queen sat at a table three feet apart from the rest, and Ottavio Gonzaga served them wine upon his knees.‡ After the banquet came, as usual, the ball, the festivities continuing till late in the night, and Don John scarcely quitting his fair guest for a moment. The next afternoon, a festival had been arranged upon an island in the river. The company embarked upon the Meuse, in a fleet of gaily scarfed and painted vessels, many of which were filled with musicians.§ Margaret reclined in her gilded barge, under a richly embroidered canopy. A fairer and falser Queen than "Egypt," had bewitched the famous youth who had triumphed, not lost the world, beneath the heights of Actium. The revellers landed

* "Ces meubles me semblent plustost d'un grand Roy que d'un jeune Prince à marier tel qu'est le Sgr. Dom Jean," etc.—Mémoires de Marguerite de Valois, ii. 136.

† Ibid.—Compare Van der Hammen y Leon, D. J. d'Austria, lib. ii.

‡ Mémoires de M. de Valois, p. 137. Hoofd, xii. 508.

§ Mémoires de Marguerite de Valois, ii. 137, 138. Hoofd, xii. 508.

on the island, where the banquet was already spread within a spacious bower of ivy, and beneath umbrageous elms. The dance upon the sward was protracted to a late hour, and the summer stars had been long in the sky when the company returned to their barges.

Don John, more than ever enthralled by the bride of St. Bartholomew, knew not that her sole purpose in visiting his dominion had been to corrupt his servants and to undermine his authority. His own purpose, however, had been less to pay court to the Queen than to make use of her presence to cover his own designs. That purpose he proceeded instantly to execute. The Queen next morning pursued her voyage by the river to Liege, and scarcely had she floated out of his sight than he sprang upon his horse and, accompanied by a few trusty attendants, galloped out of the gate and across the bridge which led to the citadel.* He had already despatched the loyal Berlaymont, with his four equally loyal sons, the Seigneurs de Meghen, Floyon, Hierges, and Haultepenne to that fortress. These gentlemen had informed the castellan that the Governor was about to ride forth hunting, and that it would be proper to offer him the hospitalities of the castle as he passed on his way. A considerable number of armed men had been concealed in the woods and thickets of the neighbourhood. The Seigneur de Froymont, suspecting nothing, acceded to the propriety of the suggestion made by the Berlaymonts. Meantime, with a blast of his horn, Don John appeared at the castle gate. He entered the fortress with the castellan, while one of the gentlemen watched outside, as the ambushed soldiers came toiling up the precipice. When all was ready the gentleman returned to the hall, and made a signal to Don John, as he sat at breakfast with the constable. The Governor sprang from the table and drew his sword; Berlaymont and

* Mémoires de Marguerite de Valois, 145, who relates the occurrence on the authority of the Marchioness of Havré. Hoofd, xii. 508.

his four sons drew their pistols, while at the same instant, the soldiers entered. Don John, exclaiming that this was the first day of his government, commanded the castellan to surrender. De Froymont, taken by surprise, and hardly understanding this very melo-dramatic attack upon a citadel by its own lawful governor, made not much difficulty in complying. He was then turned out of doors, along with his garrison, mostly feeble old men and invalids. The newly arrived soldiers took their places, at command of the Governor, and the stronghold of Namur was his own.*

There was little doubt that the representative of Philip had a perfect right to possess himself of any fortress within his government; there could be as little that the sudden stratagem by which he had thus made himself master of this citadel would prove offensive to the estates, while it could hardly be agreeable to the King; and yet it is not certain that he could have accomplished his purpose in any other way. Moreover, the achievement was one of a projected series by which he meant to re-vindicate his dwindling authority. He was weary of playing the hypocrite, and convinced that he and his monarch were both abhorred by the Netherlanders. Peace was impossible—war was forbidden him. Reduced almost to a nullity by the Prince of Orange, it was time for him to make a stand, and in this impregnable fastness his position at least was a good one. Many months before, the Prince of Orange had expressed his anxious desire that this most important town and citadel should be secured for the estates. "You know," he had written to Bossu in December, "the evil and the dismay which the loss of the city and fortress of Namur would occasion to us. Let me beseech you that all possible care be taken to preserve them."† Nevertheless,

---

* Hoofd, xii. 509.—"Stokouwde of verminkte soldaaten," etc. Bor, x. 832. Discours Sommier des Justes Causes, pp. 26, 27. Meteren, vii. 122. Bentivoglio, x. 194, 195.

† Archives de la Maison d'Orange, v. 571.

their preservation had been entrusted to a feeble-minded old constable, at the head of a handful of cripples.

We know how intense had been the solicitude of the Prince, not only to secure but to destroy these citadels, "nests of tyranny," which had been built by despots to crush, not protect, the towns at their feet. These precautions had been neglected, and the consequences were displaying themselves, for the castle of Namur was not the only one of which Don John felt himself secure. Although the Duke of Aerschot seemed so very much his humble servant, the Governor did not trust him, and wished to see the citadel of Antwerp in more unquestionable keeping. He had therefore withdrawn, not only the Duke, but his son, the Prince of Chimay, commander of the castle in his father's absence, from that important post, and insisted upon their accompanying him to Namur.* So gallant a courtier as Aerschot could hardly refuse to pay his homage to so illustrious a princess as Margaret of Valois, while during the absence of the Duke and Prince the keys of Antwerp citadel had been, at the command of Don John, placed in the keeping of the Seigneur de Treslong,† an unscrupulous and devoted royalist. The celebrated Colonel Van Ende, whose participation, at the head of his German cavalry, in the terrible sack of that city, which he had been ordered to defend, has been narrated, was commanded to return to Antwerp. He was to present himself openly to the city authorities, but he was secretly directed by the Governor-General to act in co-operation with the Colonels Fugger, Frondsberger, and Polwiller, who commanded the forces already stationed in the city.‡ These distinguished officers had been all summer in secret correspondence with Don John, for they were the instruments with which he meant by a bold stroke to recover his almost lost authority. While he had seemed to be seconding the efforts of the states-general

* Bor, x. 828. Meteren, vii. 122b.

† Bor, x. 828. Louis de Bloys, Seigneur de Treslon. Meteren, ubi sup. Discours Sommier des Justes Causes, etc. pp. 19, 20.

‡ Discours Sommier, etc. pp. 18, 19. See the original letters in the appendix to Discours Sommier, etc., p. 56, et sqq.; also in Bor, x. 848, sqq.—translated.

to pay off and disband these mercenaries, nothing had in reality been farther from his thoughts, and the time had now come when his secret plans were to be executed, according to the agreement between himself and the German colonels. He wrote to them, accordingly, to delay no longer the accomplishment of the deed*—that deed being the seizure of Antwerp citadel, as he had already successfully mastered that of Namur. The Duke of Aerschot, his brother, and son, were in his power, and could do nothing to prevent the co-operation of the colonels in the city with Treslong in the castle, so that the Governor would thus be enabled, laying his head tranquilly upon "the pillow of the Antwerp citadel,"† according to the reproachful expression subsequently used by the estates, to await the progress of events.

The current of his adventurous career was not, however, destined to run thus smoothly. It is true that the estates had not yet entirely lost their confidence in his character, but the seizure of Namur, and the attempt upon Antwerp, together with the contents of the intercepted letters written by himself and Escovedo to Philip, to Perez, to the Empress, to the Colonels Frondsberger and Fugger, were soon destined to open their eyes. In the meantime, almost exactly at the moment when Don John was executing his enterprise against Namur, Escovedo had taken an affectionate farewell of the estates at Brussels,‡ for it had been thought necessary, as already intimated, both for the apparent interests and the secret projects of Don John, that the Secretary should make a visit to Spain. At the command of the Governor-General he had offered to take charge of any communication for his Majesty which the estates might be disposed to entrust to him, and they had accordingly addressed a

---

* Letter of Don John, July 16, 1577, to the Colonels Frondsberger and Fugger. Discours Sommier, ubi sup. Bor, x. 843.

† "Et se reposant sur l'oreiller du Chasteau d'Anvers duquel il se tenoit entièrement asseuri," etc.—Discours Sommier, etc., p. 35.

‡ Bor, x. 825. Hoofd, xii. 507. Discours Sommier, etc., p. 47.

long epistle to the King, in which they gave ample expression to their indignation and their woe. They remonstrated with the King concerning the continued presence of the German mercenaries, whose knives were ever at their throats, whose plunder and insolence impoverished and tortured the people. They reminded him of the vast sums which the provinces had contributed in times past to the support of government, and they begged assistance from his bounty now. They recalled to his vision the melancholy spectacle of Antwerp, but lately the "nurse of Europe, the fairest flower in his royal garland, the foremost and noblest city of the earth,* now quite desolate and forlorn," and with additional instructions to Escovedo, that he should not fail, in his verbal communications, to represent the evil consequences of the course hitherto pursued by his Majesty's governors in the Netherlands, they dismissed him with good wishes, and with "crowns for convoy" in his purse to the amount of a revenue of two thousand yearly. His secret correspondence was intercepted and made known a few weeks after his departure for that terrible Spain whence so few travellers returned.†

For a moment we follow him thither. With a single word in anticipation, concerning the causes and the consummation of this celebrated murder, which was delayed till the following year, the unfortunate Escovedo may be dismissed from these pages. It has been seen how artfully Antonio Perez, Secretary of State, paramour of Princess Eboli, and ruling councillor at that day of Philip, had fostered in the King's mind the most extravagant suspicions as to the schemes of Don John, and of his confidential secretary.‡ He had represented it as their fixed and secret intention, after Don John should be finally established

* "—— voodster van geheel Europa, d'edelste bloeme van uwe majesteits krone en de vornaemste en rijxste van de wereld," etc., etc.—Letter of the States, Bor, 826, 827.

† Bor, x. 825. Hoofd, xii. 508. Discours Sommier, p. 47. Meteren, vii. 121. Bor, x. 827–842.

‡ Mem. de Ant. Perez, passim; particularly pages 284–317. Obras y Relaciones. Geneva, 1644.

on the throne of England, to attack Philip himself in Spain, and to deprive him of his crown, Escovedo being represented as the prime instigator and controller of this astounding plot, which lunatics only could have engendered, and which probably never had existence.

No proof of the wild design was offered. The language which Escovedo was accused by Perez of having held previously to his departure for Flanders—that it was the intention of Don John and himself to fortify the rock of Mogro, with which, and with the command of the city of Santander, they could make themselves masters of Spain after having obtained possession of England,*—is too absurd to have been uttered by a man of Escovedo's capacity. Certainly, had Perez been provided with the least scrap of writing from the hands of Don John or Escovedo which could be tortured into evidence upon this point, it would have been forthcoming, and would have rendered such fictitious hearsay superfluous. Perez, in connivance with Philip, had been systematically conducting his correspondence with Don John and Escovedo, in order to elicit some evidence of the imputed scheme. "'T was the only way," said Perez to Philip, "to make them unbare their bosoms to the sword." "I am quite of the same opinion," replied Philip to Perez, "for, according to my theology, you would do your duty neither to God nor the world, unless you did as you are doing."† Yet the excellent pair of conspirators at Madrid could wring no damning proofs from the lips of the supposititious conspirators in Flanders, save that Don John, after Escovedo's arrival in Madrid, wrote, impatiently and frequently, to demand that he should be sent back, together with the money which he had gone to Spain to procure. "Money, more money, and Escovedo,"‡ wrote the Governor, and Philip

* Mem. de Ant. Perez, 313.

† "Es menester de escrivir y oyr de aquella manera —— porque assy se meten porla espada," etc.—Billet of Ant. Perez to the King. "Y segun mi theologia yo entiendo lo mismo que vos —— Que no haviados para con Dios ni para con el mundo, sino lo hiziessedes ansy," etc.—Annotation in Philip's hand on the billet, Mem. de Perez, pp. 310, 311.

‡ "Dinero, y mas dinero, y Escovedo."—Ibid. 314.

was quite willing to accept this most natural exclamation as evidence of his brother's designs against his crown. Out of these shreds and patches—the plot against England, the Pope's bull, the desire expressed by Don John to march into France as a simple adventurer, with a few thousand men at his back—Perez, according to his own statement, drew up a protocol, afterwards formally approved by Philip, which concluded with the necessity of taking Escovedo's life, instantly but privately, and by poison. The Marquis de Los Velos, to whom the memorial was submitted for his advice, averred that if the death-bed wafer were in his own lips, he should vote for the death of the culprit ;* Philip had already jumped to the same conclusion ; Perez joyfully undertook the business, having received *carte blanche* from the King, and thus the unfortunate secretary was doomed. Immediately after the arrival of Escovedo in Madrid, he addressed a letter to the King. Philip filed it away among other despatches, with this annotation: "the *avant courier* has arrived—it is necessary to make great haste, and to despatch him before he murders us."†

The King, having been thus artfully inflamed against his brother and his unfortunate secretary, became clamorous for the blood of Escovedo. At the same time, that personage, soon after his return to Spain, was shocked by the discovery of the amour of Perez with the Princess Eboli.‡ He considered it his duty, both towards the deceased Prince and the living King, to protest against this perfidy. He threatened to denounce to the King, who seemed the only person about the court ignorant of the affair, this double treason of his mistress and his minister. Perez and Anna of Eboli, furious at Escovedo's insolence, and anxious lest he should execute his

* "Que con el Sacramento en la boca —— votara la (muerte) de Juan de Escovedo," etc., etc.—Mem. de Ant. Perez. 317.

† Cartas del S. D. Juan y del Sec. Escovedo, MS. of Royal Library, Hague.

‡ Mignet, Perez et Philippe II., pp. 28–33.—Compare Hoofd, xii. 512–515; Cabrera, xii. 972, who covers the name of the Princess with a vail which could have deceived no contemporary.

menace determined to disembarrass themselves of so meddlesome a person.* Philip's rage against Don John was accordingly turned to account, and Perez received the King's secret orders to procure Escovedo's assassination.† Thus an imaginary conspiracy of Don John against the crown of Philip was the pretext, the fears and rage of Eboli and her paramour were the substantial reason, for the crime now projected.

The details of the murder were arranged and executed by Perez,‡ but it must be confessed in justice to Philip, with much inferior nicety to that of his own performances in the same field. Many persons were privy to the plot. There was much blundering, there was great public scandal in Madrid, and no one ever had a reasonable doubt as to the instigators and the actual perpetrators of the crime. Two attempts to poison Escovedo were made by Perez, at his own table, through the agency of Antonio Enriquez, a confidential servant or page. Both were unsuccessful. A third was equally so, but suspicions were aroused. A female slave in the household of Escovedo, was in consequence arrested, and immediately hanged in the public square, for a pretended attempt to murder her master.§ A few days afterwards (on the 31st of March, 1578) the deed was accomplished at nightfall in the streets of Madrid, by six conspirators. They consisted of the majordomo of Perez, a page in his household, the page's

---

* Mignet, p. 32.

† Mem. de Ant. Perez, 314–317. Mignet, Ant. Perez, and Philippe II., pp. 32, 33. Hoofd, xii. 514.—Compare Cabrera, xii., 972—who seeking as usual to excuse the King, whose official panegyrist he is, narrates that Escovedo's death warrant was filled out on one of those blanks with the King's signature, such as ambassadors and viceroys have. He does not state why Perez (being neither viceroy nor ambassador) came to be provided with such documents. He admits, too, "que no desplaria al Rey su muerte violenta."—p. 972.

‡ The narrative of this assassination, so remarkable in its character, and so important in its remote consequences, has been given in a masterly manner by Mignet (Antonio Perez et Philippe II.), p. 34, sqq., from the MS. copy of the famous process belonging to the Foreign Office of France.

§ Mignet; from the MS. process, pp. 38, 39. Cabrera also narrates briefly the attempts at poisoning made by Perez at his own table, together with the execution of the slave.—xii. 972.

brother from the country, an ex-scullion from the royal kitchens, Juan Rubio by name, who had been the unsuccessful agent in the poisoning scheme, together with two professional bravos, hired for the occasion. It was Insausti, one of this last-mentioned couple, who despatched Escovedo with a single stab, the others aiding and abetting, or keeping watch in the neighbourhood.*

The murderers effected their escape, and made their report to Perez, who for the sake of appearances, was upon a visit in the country. Suspicion soon tracked the real culprits, who were above the reach of justice; nor, as to the motives which had prompted the murders, were many ignorant, save only the murderer himself. Philip had ordered the assassination, but he was profoundly deceived as to the causes of its accomplishment. He was the dupe of a subtler villain than himself, and thought himself sacrificing a conspirator against his crown, while he had really only crushed a poor creature who had been but too solicitous for what he thought his master's honor.

The assassins were, of course, protected from prosecution, and duly recompensed. Miguel Bosque, the country boy, received one hundred crowns in gold, paid by a clerk of Perez. Mesa, one of the bravos, was rewarded with a gold chain, fifty doubloons of eight, and a silver cup, besides receiving from the fair hand of Princess Eboli herself a certificate as under-steward upon her estates.† The second bravo, Insausti, who had done the deed, the page Enriquez, and the scullion, were *all appointed ensigns in his Majesty's army*, with twenty gold crowns of annual pension besides.‡ Their commissions were signed by Philip on the 19th of April, 1578. Such were the wages of murder at that day in Spain; gold chains, silver cups, doubloons, annuities, and commissions in the army! The reward of fidelity, as in poor Escovedo's case, was oftener the stiletto. Was it astonishing that murder was more common than fidelity?

---

* Mignet, p. 40.

† Mignet (from the MS. process), p. 41. ‡ Ibid.

With the subsequent career of Antonio Perez—his famous process, his banishment, his intrigues, his innuendos, his long exile, and his miserable death, this history has no concern. We return from our brief digression.

Before narrating the issue of the plot against Antwerp citadel, it is necessary to recur for a moment to the Prince of Orange. In the deeds and the written words of that one man are comprised nearly all the history of the Reformation in the Netherlands—nearly the whole progress of the infant Republic. The rest, during this period, is made up of the plottings and counter-plottings, the mutual wranglings and recriminations of Don John and the estates.

In the brief breathing-space now afforded them, the inhabitants of Holland and Zealand had been employing themselves in the extensive repairs of their vast system of dykes. These barriers, which protected their country against the ocean, but which their own hands had destroyed to preserve themselves against tyranny, were now thoroughly reconstructed, at a great expense, the Prince everywhere encouraging the people with his presence, directing them by his experience, inspiring them with his energy.* The task accomplished was stupendous and worthy, says a contemporary, of eternal memory.†

At the popular request, the Prince afterwards made a tour through the little provinces, honoring every city with a brief visit. The spontaneous homage which went up to him from every heart was pathetic and simple. There were no triumphal arches, no martial music, no banners, no theatrical pageantry—nothing but the choral anthem from thousands of grateful hearts. "Father William has come! Father William has come!" cried men, women, and children to each other, when the news of his arrival in town or village was announced.‡ He was a patriarch visiting his children, not a conqueror, nor a vulgar potentate displaying himself to his admirers. Happy were

---

* Bor, x. 819. Wagenaer, vii. 158. Hoofd, xii. 504.

† Bor, x. 819.

‡ Bor, x. 830. Hoofd, xii. 520. Wagenaer, vii. 159, 160.

they who heard his voice, happier they who touched his hands, for his words were full of tenderness, his hand was offered to all. There were none so humble as to be forbidden to approach him, none so ignorant as not to know his deeds. All knew that to combat in their cause he had descended from princely station, from luxurious ease, to the position of a proscribed and almost beggared outlaw. For them he had impoverished himself and his family, mortgaged his estates, stripped himself of jewels, furniture, almost of food and raiment. Through his exertions the Spaniards had been banished from their little territory, the Inquisition crushed within their borders, nearly all the sister provinces but yesterday banded into a common cause.

He found time, notwithstanding congratulating crowds who thronged his footsteps, to direct the labors of the states-general, who still looked more than ever to his guidance, as their relations with Don John became more complicated and unsatisfactory. In a letter addressed to them, on the 20th of June, from Harlem, he warned them most eloquently to hold to the Ghent Pacification as to their anchor in the storm. He assured them, if it was torn from them, that their destruction was inevitable. He reminded them that hitherto they had got but the shadow, not the substance of the Treaty; that they had been robbed of that which was to have been its chief fruit—union among themselves. He and his brothers, with their labor, their wealth, and their blood, had laid down the bridge over which the country had stepped to the Pacification of Ghent. It was for the nation to maintain what had been so painfully won; yet he proclaimed to them that the government were not acting in good faith, that secret preparations were making to annihilate the authority of the states, to restore the edicts, to put strangers into high places, and to set up again the scaffold and the whole machinery of persecution.*

In consequence of the seizure of Namur Castle, and the

* See the letter in Bor, x. 829, 830.

accusations made by Don John against Orange, in order to justify that act, the Prince had already despatched Taffin and Saint Aldegonde to the states-general with a commission to declare his sentiments upon the subject. He addressed, moreover, to the same body a letter full of sincere and simple eloquence. "The Seigneur Don John," said he, "has accused me of violating the peace, and of countenancing attempts against his life, and in endeavouring to persuade you into joining him in a declaration of war against me and against Holland and Zealand; but I pray you, most affectionately, to remember our mutal and solemn obligations to maintain the treaty of Ghent." He entreated the states, therefore, to beware of the artifices employed to seduce them from the only path which led to the tranquillity of their common country, and her true splendor and prosperity. "I believe there is not one of you," he continued, "who can doubt me, if he will weigh carefully all my actions, and consider closely the course which I am pursuing and have always pursued. Let all these be confronted with the conduct of Don John, and any man will perceive that all my views of happiness, both for my country and myself, imply a peaceable enjoyment of the union, joined with the legitimate restoration of our liberties, to which all good patriots aspire, and towards which all my designs have ever tended. As all the grandeur of Don John, on the contrary, consists in war, as there is nothing which he so much abhors as repose, as he has given ample proof of these inclinations in all his designs and enterprises, both before and after the Treaty of Marche en Famine, both within the country and beyond its borders, as it is most manifest that his purpose is, and ever has been, to embroil us with our neighbours of England and Scotland in new dissensions, as it must be evident to every one of you that his pretended accusations against me are but colors and shadows to embellish and to shroud his own desire for war, his appetite for vengeance, and his hatred not only to me but to yourselves, and as his determination is, in the words of Escovedo, to chastise some of us by means of the rest, and to excite the jealousy of one portion of the country against the other—therefore, gentlemen, do I most affectionately exhort you to found your decision, as to these matters, not upon words but upon actions. Examine carefully my conduct in the points concerning which the charges are made; listen attentively to what my envoys will communicate to you in my behalf; and then, having compared it with all the proceedings of Seigneur Don John, you will be able to form a resolution worthy the rank which you occupy, and befitting your obligations to the whole people, of whom you have been chosen chiefs and protectors by God and by men. Put away all considerations which might obscure your clear eye-sight; maintain with magnanimity, and like men, the safety of yourselves, your wives, your children, your estates, your liberties; see that this poor people, whose eyes are fixed upon you, does not perish; preserve them from the greediness of those who would grow great at your expense; guard them from the yoke of miserable servitude; let not all our posterity lament that, by our pusillanimity, they have lost the liberties which our ancestors had conquered for them, and bequeathed to them as well as to us, and that they have been subjugated by the proud tyranny of strangers.

"Trusting," said the Prince, in conclusion, "that you will accord faith and attention to my envoys, I will only add an expression of my sincere determination to employ myself incessantly in your service, and for the welfare of the whole people, without sparing any means in my power, nor my life itself."*

The vigilant Prince was indeed not slow to take advantage of the Governor's false move. While in reality intending peace, if it were possible, Don John had thrown down the gauntlet; while affecting to deal openly and manfully, like a warrior and an emperor's son, he had involved himself in

* This letter, of date August, 1577, the original of which is in French, has never been published. It is in a collection of MSS. in the Hague Archives, entitled, "Acta Statuum Belgii," tom. i. fol. 367, 368.—Compare Bor, x. 830.

petty stratagems and transparent intrigues, by all which he had gained nothing but the character of a plotter, whose word could not be trusted. Saint Aldegonde expressed the hope* that the seizure of Namur Castle would open the eyes of the people, and certainly the Prince did his best to sharpen their vision.

While in North Holland, William of Orange received an urgent invitation from the magistracy and community of Utrecht to visit that city. His authority, belonging to him under his ancient commission, had not yet been recognized over that province, but there was no doubt that the contemplated convention of "satisfaction" was soon to be arranged, for his friends there were numerous and influential. His princess, Charlotte de Bourbon, who accompanied him on his tour, trembled at the danger to which her husband would expose himself by venturing thus boldly into a territory which might be full of his enemies, but the Prince determined to trust the loyalty of a province which he hoped would be soon his own. With anxious forebodings, the Princess followed her husband to the ancient episcopal city. As they entered its gates, where an immense concourse was waiting to receive him, a shot passed through the carriage window, and struck the Prince upon the breast. The affrighted lady threw her arms about his neck, shrieking that they were betrayed, but the Prince, perceiving that the supposed shot was but a wad from one of the cannon, which were still roaring their welcome to him, soon succeeded in calming her fears.† The carriage passed slowly through the streets, attended by the vociferous greetings of the multitude; for the whole population had come forth to do him honor. Women and children clustered upon every roof and balcony, but a painful incident again marred the tranquillity of the occasion. An apothecary's child, a little girl of ten years, leaning eagerly from a lofty balcony, lost her balance

* Saint Aldegonde to Count John of Nassau.—Archives de la Maison d'Orange, vi. 116.

† Bor, x. 830. Hoofd, xii. 520.

and fell to the ground, directly before the horses of the Prince's carriage. She was killed stone dead by the fall. The procession stopped ; the Prince alighted, lifted the little corpse in his arms, and delivered it, with gentle words and looks of consolation, to the unhappy parents.* The day seemed marked with evil omens, which were fortunately destined to prove fallacious. The citizens of Utrecht became more than ever inclined to accept the dominion of the Prince, whom they honored and whom they already regarded as their natural chief. They entertained him with banquets and festivities during his brief visit, and it was certain before he took his departure that the treaty of "Satisfaction" would not be long delayed. It was drawn up, accordingly, in the autumn of the same year, upon the basis of that accepted by Harlem and Amsterdam—a basis wide enough to support both religions, with a nominal supremacy to the ancient Church.†

Meantime, much fruitless correspondence had taken place between Don John and the states. Envoys, despatched by the two parties to each other, had indulged in bitterness and recrimination. As soon as the Governor had taken possession of Namur Castle, he had sent the Seigneur de Rassinghem to the states-general. That gentleman carried with him copies of two anonymous letters, received by Don John upon the 19th and 21st of July, 1577, in which a conspiracy against his life and liberty was revealed. It was believed by the Governor that Count Lalain, who had secretly invited him to a conference, had laid an ambush for him. It was known that the country was full of disbanded soldiers, and the Governor asserted confidently that numbers of desperadoes were lying in wait for him in every village alehouse of Hainault and Flanders. He called on the states to ferret out these con-

* Bor. Hoofd, xii. 521.

† The articles of the "Satisfactie," dated October 9, 1577, are given in Bor, x. 893–896. Vera et Simplex Narratio, etc., p. 26.

‡ Bor, x. 832. Hoofd, xii. 509. Discours Sommier des Justes Causes, etc., 29.

spirators, and to inflict condign punishment upon their more guilty chiefs; he required that the soldiers, as well as the citizens, should be disarmed at Brussels and throughout Brabant, and he justified his seizure of Namur, upon the general ground that his life was no longer safe, except in a fortress.*

In reply to the letter of the Governor, which was dated the 24th of July, the states despatched Marolles, Archdeacon of Ypres, and the Seigneur de Bresse, to Namur, with a special mission to enter into the whole subject of these grievances.† These gentlemen, professing the utmost devotion to the cause of his Majesty's authority and the Catholic religion, expressed doubts as to the existence of the supposed conspiracy. They demanded that Don John should denounce the culprits, if any such were known, in order that proper chastisement might be instantly inflicted. The conversation which ensued was certainly unsatisfactory. The Governor used lofty and somewhat threatening language, assuring Marolles that he was at that moment in possession, not only of Namur but of Antwerp citadel; and the deputies accordingly departed, having accomplished very little by their journey. Their backs were scarcely turned, when Don John, on his part, immediately appointed another commission, consisting of Rassinghem and Grobbendonck, to travel from Namur to Brussels.‡ These envoys carried a long letter of grievances, enclosing a short list of demands.§ The letter reiterated his complaints about conspiracies, and his protestations of sincerity. It was full of censure upon the Prince of Orange; stigmatized his intrigues to obtain possession of Amsterdam without a proper "Satisfaction," and of Utrecht, to which he had no claim at all. It maintained that the Hollanders and Zealanders were bent upon utterly exterminating the Catholic religion, and that they avowed publicly their intention to refuse obedience to the assembly-general, should it decree the maintenance of the

* See the letter of Don John in Bor, x. 832.

† Bor, xi. 834.

‡ Bor, xi. 834, 835. Discours Sommier, etc., pp. 29, 30.

§ See the letter in Bor, xi. 836, 837.

ancient worship only. His chief demands were that the states should send him a list of persous qualified to be members of the general assembly, that he might see whether there were not individuals among them whom he might choose to reject. He further required that, if the Prince of Orange did not instantly fulfil the treaty of Ghent, the states should cease to hold any communication with him. He also summoned the states to provide him forthwith with a suitable body-guard.*

To these demands and complaints, the estates replied by a string of resolutions.† They made their usual protestations of attachment to his Majesty and the Catholic faith, and they granted willingly a foot-guard of three hundred archers. They, however, stoutly denied the Governor's right to make eliminations in their lists of deputies, because, from time immemorial, these representatives had been chosen by the clergy, nobles, cities, and boroughs. The names might change daily, nor were there any suspicious ones among them, but it was a matter with which the Governor had no concern. They promised that every effort should be made to bring about the execution of the treaty by the Prince of Orange. They begged Don John, however, to abandon the citadel of Namur, and gave him to understand that his secret practices had been discovered, a large packet of letters having recently been intercepted in the neighbourhood of Bourdeaux, and sent to the Prince of Orange.‡ Among them were some of the despatches of Don John and Escovedo, to his Majesty and to Antonio Perez, to which allusion has already been made.

Count Bossu, De Bresse, and Meetkercke were the envoys deputed to convey these resolutions to Namur. They had a long and bitter conversation with Don John, who complained more furiously than ever of the conspiracies against his person,

* Letter of Don John, July 27, 1577. Bor, ubi sup.

† In Bor, xi. 837, 838.

‡ They had fallen into the hands of Henry of Navarre, who had forwarded them to the Prince of Orange, by whom they were laid before the deputies of the states-general on the 28th of July.—Meteren, vii. 121. Hoofd, xii. 516. Compare Discours Sommier, etc., pp. 32, 33.

and of the intrigues of Orange. He insisted that this arch-traitor had been sowing the seed of his damnable doctrines broadcast through the Netherlands; that the earth was groaning with a daily ripening harvest of rebellion and heresy. It was time, he cried, for the states to abandon the Prince, and rally round their King. Patience had been exhausted. He had himself done all, and more than could have been demanded. He had faithfully executed the Ghent Pacification, but his conduct had neither elicited gratitude nor inspired confidence.*

The deputies replied, that to the due execution of the Ghent treaty it was necessary that he should disband the German troops, assemble the states-general, and carry out their resolutions. Until these things, now undone, had been accomplished, he had no right to plead his faithful fulfilment of the Pacification. After much conversation—in which the same grievances were repeated, the same statements produced and contradicted, the same demands urged and evaded, and the same menaces exchanged as upon former occasions—the deputies returned to Brussels.†

Immediately after their departure, Don John learned the result of his project upon Antwerp Castle. It will be remembered that he had withdrawn Aerschot, under pretext of requiring his company on the visit to Queen Margaret, and that he had substituted Treslong, an unscrupulous partisan of his own, in the government of the citadel. The temporary commander soon found, however, that he had undertaken more than he could perform. The troops under Van Ende were refused admittance into the town, although permission to quarter them there had been requested by the Governor-General.‡ The authorities had been assured that the troops were necessary for the protection of their city, but the magistrates had learned, but too recently, the nature of the protection which Van

* Bor, xi. 838, 839. † Ibid.

‡ Bor, xi. 852. Hoofd, xii. 517.

Ende, with his mercenaries, would afford. A detachment of states troops under De Vers, Champagny's nephew, encountered the regiment of Van Ende, and put it to flight with considerable loss. At the same time, an officer in the garrison of the citadel itself, Captain De Bours, undertook secretly to carry the fortress for the estates. His operations were secret and rapid. The Seigneur de Liedekerke had succeeded Champagny in the government of the city. This appointment had been brought about by the agency of the Greffier Martini, a warm partisan of Orange. The new Governor was known to be very much the Prince's friend, and believed to be at heart a convert to the Reformed religion. With Martini and Liedekerke, De Bours arranged his plot. He was supplied with a large sum of money, readily furnished in secret by the leading mercantile houses of the city. These funds were successfully invested in gaining over the garrison, only one company holding firm for Treslong. The rest, as that officer himself informed Don John, were ready at any moment "to take him by the throat."*

On the 1st of August, the day fixed upon in concert with the Governor and Greffier, he was, in fact, taken by the throat. There was but a brief combat, the issue of which became accidentally doubtful in the city. The white-plumed hat of De Bours had been struck from his head in the struggle, and had fallen into the foss. Floating out into the river, it had been recognized by the scouts sent out by the personages most interested, and the information was quickly brought to Liedekerke, who was lying concealed in the house of Martini, awaiting the result. Their dismay was great, but Martini, having more confidence than the Governor, sallied forth to learn the whole truth.† Scarcely had he got into the streets than he heard a welcome cry. "The Beggars have the

---

* Bor, Hoofd, ubi sup. Meteren, vii. 122. Discours Sommier, etc., p. 36, sqq. Cabrera, xi. 933, sqq. Letter of Treslong to Don John, August 1, 1577, in appendix to Discours Sommier, pp. 76, 77.

† Bor, xi. 853. Hoofd, xii. 518.

castle! the Beggars have the castle!" shouted a hundred voices.* He soon met a lieutenant coming straight from the fortress, who related to him the whole affair. Learning that De Bours was completely victorious, and that Treslong was a prisoner, Martini hastened with the important intelligence to his own home, where Liedekerke lay concealed. That functionary now repaired to the citadel, whither the magistrates, the leading citizens, and the chief merchants were instantly summoned. The castle was carried, but the city was already trembling with apprehension lest the German mercenaries quartered within its walls, should rise with indignation or panic, and repeat the horrid tragedy of The Antwerp Fury.†

In truth, there seemed danger of such a catastrophe. The secret correspondence of Don John with the colonels was already discovered,‡ and it was seen how warmly he had impressed upon the men with whom he had been tampering, "that the die was cast, and that all their art was necessary to make it turn up successfully.§ The castle was carried, but what would become of the city? A brief and eager consultation terminated in an immediate offer of three hundred thousand crowns by the leading merchants. This money was to be employed in amicably-satisfying, if possible, the German soldiers, who had meanwhile actually come to arms, and were assembled in the Place de Meer. Feeling unsafe, however, in this locality, their colonels had led them into the new town. Here, having barricaded themselves with gun-carriages, bales, and boxes, they awaited, instead of initiating, the events which the day might bring forth.|| A deputation soon arrived with a white

---

* "Het casteel is gies! het casteel is gies!"—Bor, xi. 854.

† Bor, xi. 854. Hoofd, xii. 518.

‡ It was discovered on the taking of the citadel by De Bours.—Bor, xi. 854. Hoofd, xii. 518.

§ "Y pues queda ya el dado fuera de la mano, es menester encaminarle a que corra buen."—Letter of Don John to Colonels Frondsberger and Fugger, July 23, 1577, appendix to Discours Sommier, p, 60. Bor, xi. 849.

|| Bor, xi. 854. Hoofd, xii. 518. Meteren, vii. 122.

flag from the castle, and commissioners were appointed by the commanding officers of the soldiery. The offer was made to pay over the arrears of their wages, at least to a very large amount, on condition that the troops should forthwith and for ever evacuate the city. One hundred and fifty thousand crowns were offered on the nail. The merchants stood on the bridge leading from the old town to the new, in full sight of the soldiers. They held in their hands their purses, filled with the glittering gold. The soldiers were frantic with the opportunity, and swore that they would have their officers' lives, if the tempting and unexpected offer should be declined. Nevertheless, the commissioners went to and fro, ever finding something to alter or arrange. In truth, the merchants had agreed to furnish, if necessary, three hundred thousand crowns ; but the thrifty negotiators were disposed, if diplomacy could do it, to save the moiety of that sum. Day began to sink, ere the bargain was completed, when suddenly sails were descried in the distance, and presently a large fleet of war vessels, with banner and pennon flying before a favoring breeze, came sailing up the Scheld.* It was a squadron of the Prince's ships, under command of Admiral Haultain. He had been sent against Tholen, but, having received secret intelligence, had, with happy audacity, seized the opportunity of striking a blow in the cause which he had served so faithfully. A shot or two fired from the vessels among the barricades had a quickening effect. A sudden and astounding panic seized the soldiers. "The Beggars are coming! the Beggars are coming!"† they yelled in dismay ; for the deeds of the ocean-beggars had not become less appalling since the memorable siege of Leyden. The merchants still stood on the bridge with their purses in their hand. The envoys from the castle still waved their white flags. It was too late. The horror inspired by the wild Zealanders overpowered the hope of wages, extinguished all confidence in the friendship of the

* Bor, xi. 855. Hoofd, xii. 519. Meteren, vii. 122.

† "Die guesen, die geusen, daar zynze!"—Hoofd, xii. 519. Bor, xi. 855.

citizens. The mercenaries, yielding to a violent paroxysm of fear, fled hither and thither, panting, doubling, skulking, like wolves before the hounds."* Their flight was ludicrous. Without staying to accept the money which the merchants were actually offering, without packing up their own property, in many cases even throwing away their arms, they fled, helter skelter, some plunging into the Scheld, some skimming-along the dykes, some rushing across the open fields.

A portion of them under Colonel Fugger, afterwards shut themselves up in Bergen op Zoom, where they were at once besieged by Champagny, and were soon glad to compromise the matter by surrendering their colonel and laying down their arms.† The remainder retreated to Breda, where they held out for two months, and were at length overcome by a neat stratagem of Orange. A captain, being known to be in the employment of Don John, was arrested on his way to Breda. Carefully sewed up in his waistband was found a letter, of a finger's breadth, written in cipher, and sealed with the Governor-General's seal. Colonel Frondsberger, commanding in Breda, was in this missive earnestly solicited to hold out two months longer, within which time a certain relief was promised. In place of this letter, deciphered with much difficulty, a new one was substituted, which the celebrated printer, William Sylvius, of Antwerp, prepared with great adroitness, adding the signature and seal of Don John.‡ In this counterfeit epistle, the Colonel was directed to do the best he could for himself, by reason that Don John was himself besieged, and unable to render him assistance. The same captain who had brought the real letter was bribed to deliver the counterfeit. This task he faithfully performed, spreading the fictitious intelligence besides, with such ardor through the town, that the troops rose upon their leader, and surrendered

---

* "Als wolven die nagejagt werden van de honden."—Bor, xi. 855*.

† Bor, xi. 856. Hoofd, xi. 522.

‡ Bor, xi. 856. Hoofd, xii. 522, 523.

him with the city and their own arms, into the custody of the estates. Such was the result of the attempt by Don John to secure the citadel of Antwerp. Not only was the fortress carried for the estates, but the city itself, for the first time in twelve years, was relieved from a foreign soldiery.*

The rage and disappointment of the Governor-General were excessive. He had boasted to Marolles a day too soon. The prize which he thought already in his grasp had slipped through his fingers, while an interminable list of demands which he dreamed not of, and which were likely to make him bankrupt, were brought to his door. To the states, not himself, the triumph seemed for the moment decreed. The "dice" had taken a run against him, notwithstanding his pains in loading and throwing. Nevertheless, he did not yet despair of revenge. "These rebels," he wrote to the Empress-dowager, his sister, "think that fortune is all smiles for them now, and that all is ruin for me. The wretches are growing proud enough, and forget that their chastisement, some fine morning, will yet arrive."†

On the 7th of August he addressed another long letter to the estates. This document was accompanied, as usual, by certain demands, drawn up categorically in twenty-three articles.‡ The estates considered his terms hard and strange, for in their opinion it was themselves, not the Governor, who were masters of the situation. Nevertheless, he seemed inclined to treat as if he had gained, not missed, the citadel of Antwerp; as if the troops with whom he had tampered were mustered in the field, not shut up in distant towns, and already at the mercy of the states party. The Governor demanded that all the forces of the country should be placed under his own immediate control; that Count Bossu, or some other person nominated by himself, should be appointed to the

---

* Bor, xi. 856, 857. Hoofd, xii. 523.

† Don John's letter to the Empress, August 14, 1577, appendix to Discours Sommier, p. 82.

‡ Bor, xi. 839, sqq.

government of Friesland; that the people of Brabant and Flanders should set themselves instantly to hunting, catching, and chastising all vagrant heretics and preachers. He required, in particular, that Saint Aldegonde and Theron, those most mischievous rebels, should be prohibited from setting their foot in any city of the Netherlands. He insisted that the community of Brussels should lay down their arms, and resume their ordinary handicrafts. He demanded that the Prince of Orange should be made to execute the Ghent treaty; to suppress the exercise of the Reformed religion in Harlem, Schoonhoven, and other places; to withdraw his armed vessels from their threatening stations, and to restore Nieuport, unjustly detained by him. Should the Prince persist in his obstinacy, Don John summoned them to take arms against him, and to support their lawful Governor. He, moreover, required the immediate restitution of Antwerp citadel, and the release of Treslong from prison.*

Although, regarded from the Spanish point of view, such demands might seem reasonable, it was also natural that their audacity should astonish the estates. That the man who had violated so openly the Ghent treaty should rebuke the Prince for his default—that the man who had tampered with the German mercenaries until they were on the point of making another Antwerp Fury, should now claim the command over them and all other troops—that the man who had attempted to gain Antwerp citadel by a base stratagem should now coolly demand its restoration, seemed to them the perfection of insolence. The baffled conspirator boldly claimed the prize which was to have rewarded a successful perfidy. At the very moment when the Escovedo letters and the correspondence with the German colonels had been laid before their eyes, it was a little too much that the double-dealing bastard of the double-dealing Emperor should read them a lecture upon sincerity. It was certain that the perplexed and outwitted

* Letter of Don John, 7 Aug., 1577.—Bor, xi. 839, 840.

warrior had placed himself at last in a very false position. The Prince of Orange, with his usual adroitness, made the most of his adversary's false moves. Don John had only succeeded in digging a pitfall for himself. His stratagems against Namur and Antwerp had produced him no fruit, saving the character, which his antagonist now fully succeeded in establishing for him, of an unscrupulous and artful schemer. This reputation was enhanced by the discovery of the intercepted letters, and by the ingenuity and eagerness with which they were turned to account against him by the Prince, by Saint Aldegonde, and all the anti-Catholic party. The true key to his reluctance against despatching the troops by land, the states had not obtained. They did not dream of his romantic designs upon England, and were therefore excusable in attributing a still deeper perfidy to his arrangements.

Even had he been sent to the Netherlands in the full possession of his faculties, he would have been no match in political combinations for his powerful antagonists. Hoodwinked and fettered, suspected by his master, baffled, bewildered, irritated by his adversary, what could he do but plunge from one difficulty to another and oscillate between extravagant menace and desponding concession, until his hopes and life were wasted quite away. His instructions came from Philip through Perez, and that most profound dissembler, as we have seen, systematically deceived* the Governor, with the view of eliciting treasonable matters, Philip wishing, if possible, to obtain proofs of Don John's secret designs against his own crown. Thus every letter from Spain was filled with false information and with lying persuasions.† No doubt the Governor considered himself entitled to wear a crown, and meant to win it, if not in Africa, then in England, or wherever fate might look propitiously upon him. He was of the stuff of which crusaders and dynasty founders had been made, at a

---

* Memorial de Ant. Perez, Obras y Relaciones, p. 309.

† Memorial of Antonio Perez, passim.—Compare Mignet, Antonio Perez et Philippe II., Bruxelles, 1845, pp. 16–21.

somewhat earlier epoch. Who could have conquered the holy sepulchre, or wrested a crown from its lawful wearer, whether in Italy, Muscovy, the Orient, or in the British Ultima Thule, more bravely than this imperial bastard, this valiant and romantic adventurer? Unfortunately, he came a few centuries too late. The days when dynasties were founded, and European thrones appropriated by a few foreign freebooters, had passed, and had not yet returned. He had come to the Netherlands desirous of smoothing over difficulties and of making a peaceful termination to that rebellion a stepping-stone to his English throne. He was doomed to a profound disappointment, a broken heart, and a premature grave, instead of the glittering baubles which he pursued. Already he found himself bitterly deceived in his hopes. The obstinate Netherlanders would not love him, notwithstanding the good wishes he had manifested. They would not even love the King of Spain, notwithstanding the blessings which his Majesty was declared to have heaped upon them. On the contrary, they persisted in wasting their perverse affections upon the pestilent Prince of Orange. That heretic was leading them to destruction, for he was showing them the road to liberty, and nothing, in the eyes of the Governor, could be more pitiable than to behold an innocent people setting forth upon such a journey. "In truth," said he, bitterly, in his memorable letter to his sister the Empress, "they are willing to recognize neither God nor king. They pretend to liberty in all things: so that 'tis a great pity to see how they are going on; to see the impudence and disrespect with which they repay his Majesty for the favors which he has shown them, and me for the labors, indignities, and dangers which I have undergone for their sakes."*

---

* "Porque estos aqui ni quieren conveer a su Dios ni obedeçer a su Rey como deven; antes pretenden libertad en todo. De manera que *es compassion grandissima ver como lo tratan* y las desverguenças y poco respeto con que pagan a su Majestad las *mercedes que les ha hecho; y a mi los trabajos*, indignidades y peligros que he passado por estas gentes."—Letter to the Empress, appendix to Discours Sommier, p. 81.

Nothing, indeed, in the Governor's opinion, could surpass the insolence of the Netherlanders, save their ingratitude. That was the serpent's tooth which was ever wounding the clement King and his indignant brother. It seemed so bitter to meet with thanklessness, after seven years of Alva and three of Requesens ; after the labors of the Blood Council, the massacres of Naarden, Zutphen, and Harlem, the siege of Leyden, and the Fury of Antwerp. "Little profit there has been," said the Governor to his sister, "or is like to be from all the good which we have done to these bad people. In short, they love and obey in all things the most perverse and heretic tyrant and rebel in the whole world, which *is this damned Prince of Orange*, while, on the contrary, without fear of God or shame before men, they abhor and dishonor the name and commandments of their natural sovereign."* Therefore, with a doubting spirit, and almost with a broken heart, had the warrior shut himself up in Namur Castle, to await the progress of events, and to escape from the snares of his enemies. "*God knows how much I desire to avoid extremities*," said he, "but I know not what to do with men who show themselves so obstinately rebellious."†

Thus pathetically Don John bewailed his fate. The nation had turned from God, from Philip, from himself; yet he still sat in his castle, determined to save them from destruction and his own hands from bloodshed, if such an issue were yet possible. Nor was he entirely deserted, for among the faithless a few were faithful still. Although the people were in open revolt, there was still a handful of nobles resolved to do their duty towards their God and King. "This little band," said the Governor, "has accompanied me hither, like gentlemen

* "Mire V. Mag[d]. quan poco que ha aprovechado in aprovecha para los malos el bien que se les haze. Al fin, ellos aman y obedecen de todo punto al mas perverso y tyranno hereje y rebelde de la tierra que *es este condenado del Principe de Oranges*: y aborrecen y desacatan el nombre y mandamientos de su principe y natural Señor: sin temor de Dios ni respeto o verguença de las gentes."—Ibid.

† Letter to the Empress, 81.

and chevaliers of honor."* Brave Berlaymont and his four sons were loyal to the last, but others of this limited number of gentlemen and chevaliers of honor were already deserting him. As soon as the result of the enterprise against Antwerp citadel was known, and the storm was gathering most darkly over the royal cause, Aerschot and Havré were first to spread their wings and flutter away in search of a more congenial atmosphere.† In September, the Duke was again as he had always professed himself to be, with some important intervals of exception—"the affectionate brother and cordial friend of the Prince of Orange."‡

The letter addressed by Don John to the states upon the 7th of August, had not yet been answered. Feeling, soon afterwards, more sensible of his position, and perhaps less inflamed with indignation, he addressed another communication to them, upon the 13th of the same month. In this epistle he expressed an extreme desire for peace, and a hearty desire to be relieved, if possible, from his most painful situation. He protested, before God and man, that his intentions were most honest, and that he abhorred war more than anything else in the world. He averred that, if his person was as odious to them as it seemed, he was only too ready to leave the land, as soon as the King should appoint his successor. He reminded them that the question of peace or war lay not with himself, but with them; and that the world would denounce as guilty those with whom rested the responsibility. He concluded with an observation which, in its humility, seemed sufficiently ironical, that if they had quite finished the perusal of the despatches from Madrid to his address, which they had intercepted, he should be thankful for an opportunity of reading them himself. He expressed a hope, therefore, that they would be forwarded to Namur.§

* "Como honradissimos cavalleros."—Ibid.

†. Hoofd, xii. 520. Aerschot was in such a hurry to escape, that he rode off from the castle upon a horse without a saddle.—Gachard, Bull. Com. Roy. ii. 135.

‡ Archives de la Maison d'Orange, vi. pp. 143, 144.

§ See the letter in Bor, xi. 857.

This letter was answered at considerable length, upon the second day. The states made their customary protestations of attachment to his Majesty, their fidelity to the Catholic church, their determination to maintain both the Ghent treaty and the Perpetual Edict. They denied all responsibility for the present disastrous condition of the relations between themselves and government, having disbanded nearly all their own troops, while the Governor had been strengthening his forces up to the period of his retreat into Namur. He protested, indeed, friendship and a sincere desire for peace, but the intercepted letters of Escovedo and his own had revealed to them the evil counsels to which he had been listening, and the intrigues which he had been conducting. They left it to his conscience whether they could reasonably believe, after the perusal of these documents, that it was his intention to maintain the Ghent treaty, or any treaty; and whether they were not justified in their resort to the natural right of self-defence.*

Don John was already fully aware of the desperate error which he had committed. In seizing Namur and attempting Antwerp, he had thrown down the gauntlet. Wishing peace, he had, in a panic of rage and anxiety, declared and enacted war. The bridge was broken behind him, the ships burned, a gulf opened, a return to peace rendered almost impossible. Yet it is painful to observe the almost passionate longings which at times seemed to possess him for accommodating the quarrel, together with his absolute incapacity to appreciate his position. The Prince was triumphant; the Governor in a trap. Moreover, it was a trap which he had not only entered voluntarily, but which he had set himself; he had played into the Prince's hands, and was frantic to see his adversary tranquilly winning the game. It was almost melancholy to observe the gradation of his tone from haughty indignation to dismal concession. In an elaborate letter which he addressed "to the particular states, bishops, coun-

* Bor, xi. 858.

cillors, and cities of the Netherlands," he protested as to the innocence of his intentions, and complained bitterly of the calumnies circulated to his discredit by the Prince of Orange. He denied any intention of recalling the troops which he had dismissed, except in case of absolute necessity. He affirmed that his Majesty sincerely desired peace. He averred that the country was either against the King, against the Catholic religion, against himself, or against all three together. He bitterly asked what further concessions were required. Had he not done all he had ever promised? Had he not discharged the Spaniards, placed the castles in the hands of natives, restored the privileges, submitted to insults and indecencies? Yet, in spite of all which had passed, he declared his readiness to resign, if another prince or princess of the blood more acceptable to them could be appointed.* The letter to the states was followed by a proposition for a cessation of hostilities, and for the appointment of a commission to devise means for faithfully executing the Ghent treaty. This proposition was renewed, a few days later, together with an offer for an exchange of hostages.†

It was not difficult for the estates to answer the letters of the Governor. Indeed, there was but little lack of argument on either side throughout this unhappy controversy. It is dismal to contemplate the interminable exchange of protocols, declarations, demands, apostilles, replications and rejoinders, which made up the substance of Don John's administration. Never was chivalrous crusader so out of place. It was not a soldier that was then required for Philip's exigency, but a scribe. Instead of the famous sword of Lepanto, the "barbarous pen" of Hopperus had been much more suitable for the work required. Scribbling Joachim in a war-galley, yard-arm and yard-arm with the Turkish capitan pacha, could have hardly felt less at ease than did the brilliant warrior thus condemned to scrawl and dissemble. While marching from concession to concession, he found the states conceiving daily more distrust,

* See the letter in Bor xi. 858–860. † Ibid., xi. 860, 861, 862.

and making daily deeper encroachments. Moreover, his deeds up to the time when he seemed desirous to retrace his steps had certainly been, at the least, equivocal. Therefore, it was natural for the estates, in reply to the questions in his letter, to observe that he had indeed dismissed the Spaniards, but that he had tampered with and retained the Germans; that he had indeed placed the citadels in the hands of natives, but that he had tried his best to wrest them away again; that he had indeed professed anxiety for peace, but that his intercepted letters proved his preparations for war.* Already there were rumors of Spanish troops returning in small detachments out of France. Already the Governor was known to be enrolling fresh mercenaries to supply the place of those whom he had unsuccessfully endeavoured to gain to his standard. As early as the 26th of July, in fact, the Marquis d'Ayamonte in Milan, and Don Juan de Idiaquez in Genoa, had received letters from Don John of Austria, stating that, as the provinces had proved false to their engagements, he would no longer be held by his own, and intimating his desire that the veteran troops which had but so recently been dismissed from Flanders, should forthwith return.† Soon afterwards, Alexander Farnese, Prince of Parma, received instructions from the King to superintend these movements, and to carry the aid of his own already distinguished military genius to his uncle in the Netherlands.‡

On the other hand, the states felt their strength daily more sensibly. Guided, as usual, by Orange, they had already assumed a tone in their correspondence which must have seemed often disloyal, and sometimes positively insulting, to the Governor. They even answered his hints of resignation in favor of some other prince of the blood, by expressing their hopes that his successor, if a member of the royal house at all, would at least be a legitimate one.§ This

---

* Bor, xi. 861, 862.

† Cabrera, xi. 937, 938.

‡ Ibid., xi. 940.

§ Bor, xi. 859.—Compare Meteren, vi. 119; Groen v. Prinst., Archives, vi. 170, note 1.

was a severe thrust at the haughty chieftain, whose imperial airs rarely betrayed any consciousness of Barbara Blomberg and the bend sinister on his shield. He was made to understand, through the medium of Brabantine bluntness, that more importance was attached to the marriage ceremony in the Netherlands than he seemed to imagine. The categorical demands made by the estates seemed even more indigestible than such collateral affronts, for they had now formally affirmed the views of Orange as to the constitutional government of the provinces. In their letter of 26th August, they expressed their willingness, notwithstanding the past delinquencies of the Governcr, to yield him their confidence again; but, at the same time, they enumerated conditions which, with his education and views, could hardly seem to him admissible. They required him to disband all the soldiers in his service, to send the Germans instantly out of the country, to dismiss every foreigner from office, whether civil or military, and to renounce his secret league with the Duke of Guise. They insisted that he should thenceforth govern only with the advice and consent of the State Council, that he should execute that which should by a majority of votes be ordained there, that neither measures nor despatches should be binding or authentic unless drawn up at that board.* These certainly were views of administration which, even if consonant with a sound historical view of the Netherland constitutions, hardly tallied with his monarch's instructions, his own opinions, or the practice under Alva and Requesens, but the country was still in a state of revolution, and the party of the Prince was gaining the upper hand.

It was the determination of that great statesman, according to that which he considered the legitimate practice of the government, to restore the administration to the State Council, which executive body ought of right to be appointed by the states-general. In the states-general, as in the states-particular, a constant care was to be taken towards strengthening the most

* Letter of Aug. 26, 1577, in Bor, xi. 861, 862.

popular element, the "community" of each city, the aggregate, that is to say, of its guild-representatives and its admitted burghers. This was, in the opinion of the Prince, the true theory of the government—republican in all but form—under the hereditary protection, not the despotic authority, of a family, whose rights were now nearly forfeited. It was a great step in advance that these views should come to be thus formally announced, not in Holland and Zealand only, but by the deputies of the states-general, although such a doctrine, to the proud stomach of Don John, seemed sufficiently repulsive. Not less so was the cool intimation with which the paper concluded, that if he should execute his threat of resigning, the country would bear his loss with fortitude, coupled as was that statement with a declaration that, until his successor should be appointed, the State Council would consider itself charged *ad interim* with the government. In the meantime, the Governor was requested not to calumniate the estates to foreign governments, as he had so recently done in his intercepted letter to the Empress-dowager.*

Upon receiving this letter, "Don John," says a faithful old chronicler, "found that the cranes had invited the fox to dinner."† In truth, the illustrious soldier was never very successful in his efforts, for which his enemies gave him credit, to piece out the skin of the lion with that of the fox.‡ He now felt himself exposed and outwitted, while he did not feel conscious of any very dark design. He answered the letter of the states by a long communication, dated from Namur Castle, 28th of August.§ In style, he was comparatively temperate, but the justification which he attempted of his past conduct was not very happy. He noticed the three different points which formed the leading articles of the accusation brought against him, the matter, namely, of the intercepted letters, of

* Letter of the states-general in Bor, xi. 861, 862.

† "—— en dat de Kraen, so de fabel seid, de Vos te gast genood hadde," etc. —Bor, xi. 862[b].

‡ Résponse à un petit livret, intitulé, Déclaration de l'Intention du Seign[r]. Don Jehan d'Austrice, p. 3.—Anvers, 1778.

§ Bor, xi. 862, 863.

the intrigues with the German colonels, and the seizure of Namur. He did not deny the authorship of the letters, but contented himself with a reference to their date, as if its priority to his installation as Governor furnished a sufficient palliation of the bad faith which the letters revealed.* As to the despatches of Escovedo, he denied responsibility for any statements or opinions which they might contain. As the Secretary, however, was known to be his most confidential friend, this attempt to shuffle off his own complicity was held to be both lame and unhandsome. As for the correspondence with the colonels, his defence was hardly more successful, and rested upon a general recrimination upon the Prince of Orange. As that personage was agitating and turbulent, it was not possible, the Governor urged, that he should himself remain quiet. It was out of his power to execute the treaty and the edict, in the face of a notorious omission on the part of his adversary to enforce the one or to publish the other. It comported neither with his dignity nor his safety to lay down his weapons while the Prince and his adherents were arming. He should have placed himself "in a very foolish position," had he allowed himself unarmed to be dictated to by the armed. In defence of himself on the third point, the seizure of Namur Castle, he recounted the various circumstances with which the reader is already acquainted. He laid particular stress upon the dramatic manner in which the Vicomte De Gand had drawn his curtains at the dead of night; he narrated at great length the ominous warning which he had likewise received from the Duke of Aerschot in Brussels, and concluded with a circumstantial account of the ambush which he believed to have been laid for him by Count De Lalain.† The letter concluded with a hope for an arrangement of difficulties, not yet admitted by the Governor to be insurmountable, and with a request for a formal conference, accompanied by an exchange of hostages.‡

---

* Bor, xi. 862, 863. Hoofd, xii. 521.

† Letter of Don John, Aug. 24, 1577. Bor, xi. 864.

‡ Letter of Don John, 24 August, 1577.

While this correspondence was proceeding between Namur and Brussels, an event was occurring in Antwerp which gave much satisfaction to Orange. The Spanish Fury, and the recent unsuccessful attempt of Don John to master the famous citadel, had determined the authorities to take the counsel which the Prince had so often given in vain, and the fortress of Antwerp was at length razed to the ground, on the side towards the city.* It would be more correct to say that it was not the authorities, but the city itself which rose at last and threw off the saddle by which it had so long been galled. More than ten thousand persons were constantly at work, morning, noon, and night, until the demolition was accomplished.† Grave magistrates, great nobles, fair ladies, citizens and their wives, beggars and their children, all wrought together pell-mell. All were anxious to have a hand in destroying the nest where so many murders had been hatched, whence so much desolation had flown. The task was not a long one for workmen so much in earnest, and the fortress was soon laid low in the quarter where it could be injurious to the inhabitants. As the work proceeded, the old statue of Alva was discovered in a forgotten crypt,‡ where it had lain since it had been thrown down by the order of Requesens. Amid the destruction of the fortress, the gigantic phantom of its founder seemed to start suddenly from the gloom, but the apparition added fresh fuel to the rage of the people. The image of the execrated Governor was fastened upon with as much fierceness as if the bronze effigy could feel their blows, or comprehend their wrath. It was brought forth from its dark hiding-place into the daylight. Thousands of hands were ready to drag it through the streets for universal inspection and outrage. A thousand sledge-hammers were ready to dash it to pieces, with a slight portion, at least, of the satisfaction with which those who wielded them would have dealt the same blows upon the head of the tyrant himself. It was soon reduced to a shape-

* Hoofd, xii. 323, 324. Bor, xi. 856.

† Hoofd, Bor, ubi sup. Strada ix. 443.

‡ Hoofd, xii. 523. Strada, ix. 443.

less mass. Small portions were carried away and preserved for generations in families as heirlooms of hatred. The bulk was melted again and reconverted, by a most natural metamorphosis, into the cannon from which it had originally sprung.*

The razing of the Antwerp citadel set an example which was followed in other places; the castle of Ghent, in particular, being immediately levelled, amid demonstrations of universal enthusiasm.† Meantime, the correspondence between Don John and the estates at Brussels dragged its slow length along, while at the same time, two elaborate letters were addressed to the King, on the 24th of August and the 8th of September, by the estates-general of the Netherlands. These documents, which were long and able, gave a vigorous representation of past evils and of the present complication of disorders under which the commonwealth was laboring. They asked, as usual, for a royal remedy ; and expressed their doubts whether there could be any sincere reconciliation so long as the present Governor, whose duplicity and insolence they represented in a very strong light, should remain in office. Should his Majesty, however, prefer to continue Don John in the government, they signified their willingness, in consideration of his natural good qualities, to make the best of the matter. Should, however, the estrangement between themselves and the Governor seem irremediable, they begged that another and a legitimate prince of the blood might be appointed in his place.‡

* Strada, ubi sup. Hoofd, xii. 524.

† Bor, xi. 856. Hoofd, xii. 524. Meteren, vii. 125.

‡ See the letters in Bor, xi. 867, 868. Meteren, vii. 123.

CHAPTER IV.

Orange invited to visit Brussels—His correspondence upon the subject with the estates-general—Triumphant journey of the Prince to the capital—Stop put by him to the negotiations with Don John—New and stringent demands made upon the Governor—His indignation—Open rupture—Intrigue of Netherland grandees with Archduke Matthias—Policy of Orange—Attitude of Queen Elizabeth—Flight of Matthias from Vienna—Anxiety of Elizabeth—Adroitness of the Prince—The office of Ruward—Election of Orange to that dignity—His complaints against the great nobles—Aerschot Governor of Flanders—A storm brewing in Ghent—Ryhove and Imbize—Blood-Councillor Hessels—Arrogance of the aristocratic party in Flanders—Ryhove's secret interview with Orange—Outbreak at Ghent—Arrest of Aerschot, Hessels, and others of the reactionary party—The Duke liberated at demand of Orange—The Prince's visit to Ghent—"Rhetorical" demonstrations—The new Brussels Union characterized—Treaty with England—Articles by which Matthias is nominally constituted Governor-General—His inauguration at Brussels—Brilliant and fantastic ceremonies—Letter of Don John to the Emperor—His anger with England—An army collecting—Arrival of Alexander Farnese—Injudicious distribution of offices in the States' army—The States' army fall back upon Gemblours, followed by Don John—Tremendous overthrow of the patriots—Wonderful disparity in the respective losses of the two armies.

While these matters were in progress, an important movement was made by the estates-general. The Prince of Orange was formally and urgently invited to come to Brussels to aid them with his counsel and presence.* The condemned traitor had not set foot in the capital for eleven years. We have narrated the circumstance of his departure, while the advancing trumpets of Alva's army were almost heard in the

* Bor, xi. 871. Meteren, vii. 125. Hoofd, xii. 526.

distance. His memorable and warning interview with Egmont has been described. Since that period, although his spirit had always been manifesting itself in the capital like an actual presence; although he had been the magnet towards which the states throughout all their oscillations had involuntarily vibrated, yet he had been ever invisible. He had been summoned by the Blood Council to stand his trial, and had been condemned to death by default. He answered the summons by a defiance, and the condemnation by two campaigns, unsuccessful in appearance, but which had in reality prostrated the authority of the sovereign.

Since that period, the representative of royalty had sued the condemned traitor for forgiveness. The haughty brother of Philip had almost gone upon his knees, that the Prince might name his terms, and accept the proffered hand of majesty. The Prince had refused, not from contumely, but from distrust. He had spurned the supplications, as he had defied the proscription of the King. There could be no friendship between the destroyer and the protector of a people. Had the Prince desired only the reversal of his death-sentence, and the infinite aggrandizement of his family, we have seen how completely he had held these issues in his power. Never had it been more easy, plausible, tempting, for a proscribed patriot to turn his back upon an almost sinking cause. We have seen how his brave and subtle Batavian prototype, Civilis,* dealt with the representative of Roman despotism. The possible or impossible Netherland Republic of the first century of our era had been reluctantly abandoned, but the modern Civilis had justly more confidence in his people.

And now again the scene was changed. The son of the Emperor, the King's brother, was virtually beleaguered; the proscribed rebel had arrived at victory through a long series of defeats. The nation everywhere acknowledged him master, and was in undisguised revolt against the anointed sovereign. The great nobles, who hated Philip on the one hand, and the

---

* Historical Introduction.

Reformed religion on the other, were obliged, in obedience to the dictates of a people with whom they had little sympathy, to accept the ascendency of the Calvinist Prince, of whom they were profoundly jealous. Even the fleeting and incapable Aerschot was obliged to simulate adhesion ; even the brave Champagny, cordial hater of Spaniards, but most devotedly Catholic, "the chiefest man of wysedome and stomach at that tyme in Brussels," so envoy Wilson wrote to Burghley,* had become "Brabantized," as his brother Granvelle expressed himself,† and was one of the commissioners to invite the great rebel to Brussels. The other envoys were the Abbot of Saint Gertrude, Dr. Leoninus, and the Seigneur de Liesvelt.‡ These gentlemen, on arriving at Gertruydenberg, presented a brief but very important memorial to the Prince.§ In that document they informed him that the states-general, knowing how efficacious would be his presence, by reason of his singular prudence, experience, and love for the welfare and repose of the country, had unanimously united in a supplication that he would incontinently transport himself to the city of Brussels, there to advise with them concerning the necessities of the land ; but, as the principal calumny employed by their adversaries was that all the provinces and leading personages intended to change both sovereign and religion, at the instigation of his Excellency, it was desirable to disprove such fictions. They therefore very earnestly requested the Prince to make some contrary demonstration, by which it might be manifest to all that his Excellency, together with the estates of Holland and Zealand, intended faithfully to keep what they had promised. They prayed, therefore, that the Prince, permitting the exercise of the Roman Catholic religion in the places which had recently accepted his authority, would also allow

---

* Elizabeth and her Times, a series of Original Letters, by Th. Wright, t. ii. 45.—London, 1838.

† "On disoit qu'ils avoient brabantisé M. de Champagney, ce qui ne me pleut quand je l'entendis," etc., etc.—Granvelle to M. de Bellefontaine, March 31, 1578, Archives de la Maison d'Orange, vi. 339.

‡ Bor, xi. 871. Hoofd, xii. 526. Meteren, vii. 125.

§ In Bor, xi. 872.—Compare Meteren, Hoofd, ubi sup.

its exercise in Holland and Zealand. They begged, further, that he would promise by a new and authentic act, that the provinces of Holland and Zealand would not suffer the said exercise to be impugned, or any new worship to be introduced, in the other provinces of the Netherlands.*

This letter might almost be regarded as a trap, set by the Catholic nobles. Certainly the Ghent Pacification forbade the Reformed religion in form, and as certainly winked at its exercise in fact. The proof was, that the new worship was spreading everywhere, that the exiles for conscience' sake were returning in swarms, and that the synod of the Reformed churches, lately held at Dort, had been publicly attended by the ministers and deacons of numerous dissenting churches established in many different places throughout all the provinces.† The pressure of the edicts, the horror of the inquisition being removed, the down-trodden religion had sprung from the earth more freshly than ever.

The Prince was not likely to fall into the trap, if a trap had really been intended. He answered the envoys loyally, but with distinct reservations.‡ He did not even accept the invitation, save on condition that his visit to Brussels should be expressly authorized by Holland and Zealand. Notwithstanding his desire once more to behold his dear country, and to enjoy the good company of his best friends and brothers, he felt it his duty to communicate beforehand with the states of those two provinces, between which and himself there had been such close and reciprocal obligations, such long-tried and faithful affection. He therefore begged to refer the question to the assembly of the said provinces about to be held at Gouda, where, in point of fact, the permission for his journey was, not without considerable difficulty, a few days afterwards obtained.

---

* Memorial in Bor, xi. 872. It is also published by Groen v. Prinst., Archives, etc., vi. 155–157.

† Groen v. Prinst., Archives, etc., vi. 148, 149. Languet, Ep. Sec., i. 2, 298.

‡ Answer of the Prince of Orange, in Bor, xi. 873[a], also in Groen v. Prinst., Archives, etc., vi. 157–161.—Compare Meteren, vii. 125, 126. Hoofd, xii. 527.

With regard to the more difficult requests addressed to him in the memorial, he professed generally his intention to execute the treaty of Ghent. He observed, however, that the point of permitting the exercise of the Roman Catholic religion in Holland and Zealand regarded principally the estates of these provinces, which had contracted for no innovation in this matter, at least till the assembling of the states-general. He therefore suggested that he neither could, nor ought to, permit any innovation, without the knowledge and consent of those estates. As to promising by authentic act, that neither he nor the two provinces would suffer the exercise of the Catholic religion to be in any wise impugned in the rest of the Netherlands, the Prince expressed himself content to promise that, according to the said Ghent Pacification, they would suffer no attempt to be made against the public repose or against the Catholic worship. He added that, as he had no intention of usurping any superiority over the states-general assembled at Brussels, he was content to leave the settlement of this point to their free-will and wisdom, engaging himself neither to offer nor permit any hindrance to their operations.*

With this answer the deputies are said to have been well pleased.† If they were so, it must be confessed that they were thankful for small favors. They had asked to have the Catholic religion introduced into Holland and Zealand. The Prince had simply referred them to the estates of these provinces. They had asked him to guarantee that the exercise of the Reformed religion should not be "procured" in the rest of the country. He had merely promised that the Catholic worship should not be prevented. The difference between the terms of the request and the reply was sufficiently wide.

The consent to his journey was with difficulty accorded by the estates of Holland and Zealand,‡ and his wife, with many tears

---

* Answer of the Prince of Orange to the Proposition of the states-general, Bor, Meteren, Hoofd, ubi sup.

† Bor, xi. 878. Hoofd, xii. 526.

‡ Bor, xi. 873.—"Hoewel ongeyrne."—Hoofd, xii. 527.

and anxious forebodings, beheld him depart for a capital where the heads of his brave and powerful friends had fallen, and where still lurked so many of his deadly foes. During his absence, prayers were offered daily for his safety in all the churches of Holland and Zealand, by command of the estates.*

He arrived at Antwerp on the 17th of September, and was received with extraordinary enthusiasm. The Prince, who had gone forth alone, without even a bodyguard, had the whole population of the great city for his buckler. Here he spent five days, observing, with many a sigh, the melancholy changes which had taken place in the long interval of his absence. The recent traces of the horrible "Fury," the blackened walls of the Hotel de Ville, the prostrate ruins of the marble streets, which he had known as the most imposing in Europe, could be hardly atoned for in his eyes even by the more grateful spectacle of the dismantled fortress.

On the 23rd of September he was attended by a vast concourse of citizens to the new canal which led to Brussels, where three barges were in waiting for himself and suite. In one a banquet was spread; in the second, adorned with emblematic devices and draped with the banners of the seventeen provinces, he was to perform the brief journey; while the third had been filled by the inevitable rhetoric societies, with all the wonders of their dramatic and plastic ingenuity. Rarely had such a complication of vices and virtues, of crushed dragons, victorious archangels, broken fetters, and resurgent nationalities, been seen before, within the limits of a single canal boat. The affection was, however, sincere, and the spirit noble, even though the taste which presided at these demonstrations may have been somewhat pedantic.†

The Prince was met several miles before the gates of Brussels by a procession of nearly half the inhabitants of the city, and thus escorted, he entered the capital in the afternoon of the 23rd of September.‡ It was the proudest day of

---

* Bor, xi. 873. † Bor, xi. 873. Hoofd, xii. 527.

‡ Bor, xi. 873. Hoofd, xii. 528. Meteren, vii. 126.

his life. The representatives of all the provinces, supported by the most undeniable fervor of the united Netherland people, greeted "Father William." Perplexed, discordant, hating, fearing, doubting, they could believe nothing, respect nothing, love nothing, save the "tranquil" Prince. His presence at that moment in Brussels was the triumph of the people and of religious toleration. He meant to make use of the crisis to extend and to secure popular rights, and to establish the supremacy of the states-general under the nominal sovereignty of some Prince, who was yet to be selected, while the executive body was to be a state-council, appointed by the states-general. So far as appears, he had not decided as to the future protector, but he had resolved that it should be neither himself nor Philip of Spain. The outlaw came to Brussels prepared at last to trample out a sovereignty which had worked its own forfeiture. So far as he had made any election within his breast, his choice inclined to the miserable Duke of Anjou, a prince whom he never came to know as posterity has known him, but whom he at least learned to despise. Thus far the worthless and paltry intriguer still wore the heroic mask, deceiving even such far-seeing politicians as Saint Aldegonde and the Prince.

William's first act was to put a stop to the negotiations already on foot with Don John.* He intended that they should lead to war, because peace was impossible, except a peace for which civil and religious liberty would be bartered, for it was idle, in his opinion, to expect the maintenance by the Spanish Governor of the Ghent Pacification, whatever promises might be extorted from his fears. A deputation, in the name of the states, had already been sent with fresh propositions to Don John, at Namur. The envoys were Caspar Schetz and the Bishop of Bruges.† They had nearly come to an amicable convention with the Governor,

---

* Bor, xi. 874, seq. Hoofd, xii. 528.

† Bor, xi. 874. Remigius Drutius, Bishop of Bruges. Hoofd, xii. 528. Cabrera, xi. 942.

the terms of which had been sent to the states-general for approval, at the very moment of the Prince's arrival in Brussels. Orange, with great promptness, prevented the ratification of these terms, which the estates had in reality already voted to accept. New articles were added to those which had originally been laid before Don John.* It was now stipulated that the Ghent treaty and the Perpetual Edict should be maintained. The Governor was required forthwith to abandon Namur Castle, and to dismiss the German troops. He was to give up the other citadels and strong places, and to disband all the soldiers in his service. He was to command the governors of every province to prohibit the entrance of all foreign levies. He was forthwith to release captives, restore confiscated property, and reinstate officers who had been removed; leaving the details of such restorations to the council of Mechlin and the other provincial tribunals. He was to engage that the Count Van Buren should be set free within two months. He was himself, while waiting for the appointment of his successor, to take up his residence in Luxemburg, and while there, he was to be governed entirely by the decision of the State Council, expressed by a majority of its members. Furthermore, and as not the least stinging of these sharp requisitions, the Queen of England—she who had been the secret ally of Orange, and whose crown the Governor had secretly meant to appropriate—was to be included in the treaty.†

It could hardly excite surprise that Don John, receiving these insolent propositions at the very moment in which he heard of the triumphant entrance into Brussels of the Prince,

* Mémoire et Recueil de ce qu'est passé entre le Seigneur don Jan d'Autriche, etc., depuis sa retraicte au chasteau de Namur—redigé par escript par le Seigneur de Grobbendonck, p. 220, seq. This very curious memoir, by one of the diplomatists engaged, has been republished, according to the original sketch, in the Bulletins de la Com. Roy., x. 172–223.—Compare Archives et Correspondance, vi. 166–170.

† These remarkable articles are to be found in Bor, xi. 874–876. A very meagre extract is given by Cabrera, xi. 942. Groen v. Prinst., vi. 166–170.—Compare the "Mémoire et Recueil" of Grobbendonck, passim.

should be filled with rage and mortification.* Never was champion of the Cross thus braved by infidels before. The Ghent treaty, according to the Orange interpretation, that is to say, heresy made legitimate, was to be the law of the land. His Majesty was to surrender—colors and cannon—to his revolted subjects. The royal authority was to be superseded by that of a State Council, appointed by the states-general, at the dictation of the Prince. The Governor-General himself, brother of his Catholic Majesty, was to sit quietly with folded arms in Luxemburg, while the arch heretic and rebel reigned supreme in Brussels. It was too much to expect that the choleric soldier would be content with what he could not help regarding as a dishonorable capitulation. The arrangement seemed to him about as reasonable as it would have been to invite Sultan Selim to the Escorial, and to send Philip to reside at Bayonne. He could not but regard the whole proposition as an insolent declaration of war. He was right. It was a declaration of war; as much so as if proclaimed by trump of herald. How could Don John refuse the wager of battle thus haughtily proffered?

Smooth Schetz, Lord of Grobbendonck, and his episcopal colleague, in vain attempted to calm the Governor's wrath, which now flamed forth, in defiance of all considerations.†

---

* "Mémoire et Recueil," passim.—According to Cabrera, xi. 944, a more cheerful view of the subject was taken by those who surrounded the Governor. The propositions only excited their laughter. The same historian, as well as all the Spanish writers, of course represent the Prince as influenced in his policy solely by self-interest, by his incapacity to pay his debts, and by his despair of obtaining a royal pardon, should a peace ensue. Peace for the country, so his enemies thought, was death for him; "doliendose un ministro de Orange, diziendo que ya se acabó el tratar de pazes aunque le fue nueva alegre, *con indignacion* respondio fuera *insigne par perder la vida el;* mostrando que su prosperidad no consistia en el bien publico, sino en la guerra: *que a esto le truxo la desesperacion del perdon de su pena no merecido,*" xi. 944. The reader is already competent to appreciate the calumnious nature of such statements, by a perusal of the correspondence and secret negotiations between Don John and Orange. The personal and unlimited offers of pardon and advancement, made to the Prince by the Governor-General, on his first arrival in the country, are a sufficient answer to these stupid accusations.

† Mémoire et Recueil par le Seigneur Grobbendonck.—Compare Bor, xi. 876. Hoofd, xii. 529.

They endeavored, without success, to palliate the presence of Orange, and the circumstances of his reception, for it was not probable that their eloquence would bring the Governor to look at the subject with their eyes. Three days were agreed upon for the suspension of hostilities, and Don John was highly indignant that the estates would grant no longer a truce. The refusal was, however, reasonable enough on their part, for they were aware that veteran Spaniards and Italians were constantly returning to him, and that he was daily strengthening his position. The envoys returned to Brussels, to give an account of the Governor's rage, which they could not declare to be unnatural, and to assist in preparations for the war, which was now deemed inevitable. Don John, leaving a strong garrison in the citadel of Namur, from which place he despatched a final communication to the estates-general, dated the 2nd of October, retired to Luxemburg. In this letter, without exactly uttering defiance, he unequivocally accepted the hostilities which had been pressed upon him, and answered their hollow professions of attachment to the Catholic religion and his Majesty's authority, by denouncing their obvious intentions to trample upon both. He gave them, in short, to understand that he perceived their intentions, and meant them to comprehend his own.*

Thus the quarrel was brought to an issue, and Don John saw with grim complacency, that the pen was at last to be superseded by the sword. A remarkable pamphlet was now published, in seven different languages, Latin, French, Flemish, German, Italian, Spanish, and English, containing a succinct account of the proceedings between the Governor and the estates, together with copies of the intercepted letters of Don John and Escovedo to the King, to Perez, to the German colonels, and to the Empress. This work, composed and published by order of the estates-general, was transmitted with an accompanying address to every potentate in Christendom.† It

* Bor, xi. 876. Hoofd, xii. 529, 530.

† Bor, xi. 881.—The quotations in the preceding pages from this pamphlet

was soon afterwards followed by a counter-statement, prepared by order of Don John, and containing his account of the same matters, with his recriminations against the conduct of the estates.*

Another important movement had, meanwhile, been made by the third party in this complicated game. The Catholic nobles, jealous of the growing influence of Orange, and indignant at the expanding power of the people, had opened secret negotiations with the Archduke Matthias, then a mild, easy-tempered youth of twenty, brother of the reigning emperor, Rudolph. After the matter had been discussed some time in secret, it was resolved, towards the end of September, to send a messenger to Vienna, privately inviting the young Prince to Brussels, but much to the surprise of these nobles, it was discovered that some fifteen or sixteen of the grandees of the land, among them Aerschot, Havré, Champagny, De Ville, Lalain, De Héze, and others, had already taken the initiative in the matter. On the 26th of August, the Seigneur de Maalsteede had set forth, by their appointment, for Vienna. There is no doubt that this step originated in jealousy felt towards Orange, but at the same time it is certain that several of the leaders in the enterprise were still his friends.† Some, like Champagny, and De Héze, were honestly so; others, like Aerschot, Havré, and De Ville, always traitors in heart to the national cause, loyal to nothing but their own advancement, were still apparently upon the best terms with

---

have been made from the original edition published in 1577 at Antwerp, by Silvius, under the title, "Discours Sommier des Justes Causes et Raisons qui ont contrainct les Estats Generaulx des Païs Bas de pourveoir à leur Deffence contre le Seigneur Don Jehan d'Austrice: avec plusieurs lettres interceptées en plus grand nombre," etc., etc. A Flemish translation is given in the Byvoegsel Auth. Stukh. i. 151 en 176 of Bor, under the title of "Kort Verhael van de rechte oorsaken en redenen," etc., etc.

* The edition of this pamphlet from which the citations in the text have been made, is the Latin one of Marchant, published at Luxemburg, anno 1578, under the title, "Vera et Simplex Narratio eorum quæ ab Adventu D. Joannis Austriaci Supremi in Belgio, etc., gesta sunt," etc., etc.

† Bor, xi. 898. Meteren. vii. 126. Hoofd, xii. 530. Cabrera, xi. 944, 945. Gr. v. Prinst., Archives, vi. 191.

him. Moreover, it is certain that he had been made aware of the scheme, at least, before the arrival of the Archduke in the Netherlands, for the Marquis Havré, on his way to England, as special envoy from the estates, had a conference with him at Gertruydenberg.* This was in the middle of September, and before his departure for Brussels. Naturally, the proposition seemed, at first, anything but agreeable; but the Marquis represented himself afterwards as having at last induced the Prince to look upon it with more favorable eyes.† Nevertheless, the step had been taken before the consultation was held, nor was it the first time that the advice of Orange had been asked concerning the adoption of a measure after the measure had been adopted.

Whatever may have been his original sentiments upon the subject, however, he was always less apt to complain of irrevocable events than quick to reconcile them with his own combinations, and it was soon to be discovered that the new stumbling-block which his opponents had placed in his path, could be converted into an additional stepping-stone towards his goal. Meanwhile, the secret invitation to the Archduke was regarded by the people and by foreign spectators as a plot devised by his enemies. Davison, envoy from Queen Elizabeth, was then in Brussels, and informed his royal mistress, whose sentiments and sympathies were unequivocally in favor of Orange, of the intrigues against the Prince.‡ The efforts of England were naturally to counteract the schemes of all who interfered with his policy, the Queen especially, with her customary sagacity, foreseeing the probable inclination of the Catholic nobles towards the protectorate of Alençon. She did not feel certain as to the precise plans of Orange, and there was no course better adapted to draw her from barren coquetry into positive engagements, than to arouse her jealousy of the French influence in the provinces. At this moment, she manifested the warmest friendship for the Prince.§

---

* Hoofd, xii. 520. † Bor, xi. 900. ‡ Ibid., 899.

§ Archives et Correspondance, vi. 190.

Costly presents were transmitted by her to his wife; among others, an ornament, of which a sculptured lizard formed a part. The Princess, in a graceful letter to her husband, desiring that her acknowledgments should be presented to her English Majesty, accepted the present as significative. "'Tis the fabled virtue of the lizard (she said) to awaken sleepers whom a serpent is about to sting. You are the lizard, and the Netherlands the sleepers,—pray Heaven they may escape the serpent's bite!"* The Prince was well aware, therefore, of the plots which were weaving against him. He had small faith in the great nobles, whom he trusted "as he would adders fanged," and relied only upon the communities, upon the mass of burghers. They deserved his confidence, and watched over his safety with jealous care. On one occasion, when he was engaged at the State Council till a late hour, the citizens conceived so much alarm, that a large number of them spontaneously armed themselves, and repaired to the palace. The Prince, informed of the circumstance, threw open a window and addressed them, thanking them for their friendship and assuring them of his safety. They were not satisfied, however, to leave him alone, but remained under arms below till the session was terminated, when they escorted him with affectionate respect to his own hotel.†

The secret envoy arrived in Vienna, and excited the ambition of the youthful Matthias.‡ It must be confessed that the offer could hardly be a very tempting one, and it excites our surprise that the Archduke should have thought the adventure worth the seeking. A most anomalous position in the Netherlands was offered to him by a slender and irresponsible faction of Netherlanders. There was a triple prospect before him: that of a hopeless intrigue against the first politician in Europe, a mortal combat with the most renowned conqueror of the age, a deadly feud with the most powerful and revengeful monarch

---

* Archives et Correspondance, vi. 190.

† Langueti, Epist. ad Aug. 125, 17 Oct., 1577, p. 324.

‡ Bor, xi. 898. Hoofd, xii. 531. Meteren, vii. 126.

in the world. Into this threefold enterprise he was about to plunge without any adequate resources, for the Archduke possessed no experience, power, or wealth.* He brought, therefore, no strength to a cause which was itself feeble. He could hope for no protection, nor inspire any confidence. Nevertheless, he had courage, pliability, and a turn for political adventure. Visions of the discomfited Philip conferring the hand of his daughter, with the Netherlands as her dowry, upon the enterprising youth who, at this juncture, should succeed in overturning the Spanish authority in that country, were conjured up by those who originated the plot,† and he was weak enough to consider such absurdities plausible, and to set forth at once to take possession of this castle in the air.

On the evening of October 3rd, 1577, he retired to rest at eight o'clock, feigning extreme drowsiness. After waiting till his brother Maximilian, who slept in another bed in the same chamber, was asleep, he slipped from his couch and from the room in his night apparel, without even putting on his slippers. He was soon after provided by the companions of his flight with the disguise of a servant, arrayed in which, with his face blackened, he made his escape by midnight from Vienna,‡ but it is doubtful whether Rudolph were as ignorant as he affected to be of the scheme.§ The Archduke arrived at Cologne, attended only by two gentlemen and a few servants. The Governor was beside himself with fury; the Queen of England was indignant; the Prince only, against whom

* Bor, xi. 899.

† Hoofd, xii. 530.

‡ Letter of Dr. Labbe to the Queen Mother of France, in Archives et Correspondance, vi. 202.

§ It was the opinion of Languet that the Emperor affected ignorance of the plot at its commencement, that he afterwards affected an original connivance, and that he was equally disingenuous in both pretences. "Pulchre sane instructa fabula," quoth shrewd Herbert, "sed caveant aucupes se suis retibus involvant;" and, again, six months later, "jam profitetur se fuisse authorem Matthiæ fratri, ut in Belgium iret. Quam caute id faciat, nescio, cum id antea constanter negaverit."—Huberti Langueti Epistolæ ad illustrem et generosum Dominum Philippum Sydnæum, Francof., 1633, lxii. 224, lxvi. 138.

the measure was mainly directed, preserved his usual tranquillity.*

Secretary Walsingham, as soon as the news reached England, sent for Meetkercke, colleague of Marquis Havré in the mission from the estates.† He informed that functionary of the great perplexity and excitement which, according to information received from the English resident, Davison, were then prevailing in Brussels, on account of the approach of the Archduke. Some, he said, were for receiving him at one place, some at another ; others were in favor of forbidding his entrance altogether. Things had been sufficiently complicated before, without this additional cause of confusion. Don John was strengthening himself daily, through the secret agency of the Duke of Guise and his party. His warlike genius was well known, as well as the experience of the soldiers who were fast rallying under his banner. On the other hand, the Duke of Alençon had come to La Fére, and was also raising troops, while to oppose this crowd of rival enemies, to deal with this host of impending disasters, there was but one man in the Netherlands. On the Prince of Orange alone could the distracted states rely. To his prudence and valor only could the Queen look with hopeful eyes. The Secretary proceeded to inform the envoy, therefore, that her Majesty would feel herself compelled to withdraw all succor from the states if the Prince of Orange were deprived of his leadership ; for it was upon that leadership only that she had relied for obtaining a successful result. She was quite indisposed to encounter indefinite risk with an impossibility of profit.‡

Meetkercke replied to the Secretary by observing, that the great nobles of the land had been unanimous in desiring a new Governor-General at this juncture. They had thought Matthias, with a strong Council of State, composed of native Netherlanders, to control him, likely to prove a serviceable candidate for the post. They had reason to believe that, after

* Bor, xi. 900. Meteren, vii. 126.

† Bor, xi. 899, 900.

‡ Ibid.

he should be received, the Emperor would be reconciled to the measure, and that by his intercession the King of Spain would be likewise induced to acquiesce.* He alluded, moreover, to the conference between the Marquis of Havré and Orange at Gertruydenberg, and quoted the opinion of the Prince that it would be unwise, after the invitation had been given, to insult the Archduke and his whole imperial house, by treating him with indignity upon his arrival. It was inevitable, said the envoy, that differences of opinion should exist in large assemblies, but according to information which he had recently received from Marquis Havré, then in Brussels, affairs had already become smooth again. At the conclusion of the conference, Walsingham repeated emphatically that the only condition upon which the Queen would continue her succor to the Netherlands was, that the Prince should be forthwith appointed Lieutenant-General for the Archduke.†

The immediate result of this movement was, that Matthias was received at Antwerp by Orange at the head of two thousand cavalry, and attended by a vast concourse of inhabitants.‡ Had the Prince chosen a contrary course, the Archduke might have been compelled to return, somewhat ridiculously, to Vienna; but, at the same time, the anger of the Emperor and of all Germany would have been aroused against Orange and the cause he served. Had the Prince, on the contrary, abandoned the field himself, and returned to Holland, he would have left the game in the hands of his adversaries. Ever since he had made what his brother John called that "dangerous gallows-journey" to Brussels,§ his influence had been culminating daily, and the jealousy of the great nobles rising as rapidly. Had he now allowed himself to be driven from his post, he would have exactly fulfilled their object. By remaining, he counteracted their schemes.

---

* Bor, xi. 899, 900. † Ibid., xi. 900. ‡ Ibid. Meteren, vii.

§ "—— wie man's achten mocht, zwar galgreisen, so des Hern Printz ahnhero und gehn Brussel—thun mussen," etc., etc.—Archives et Correspondance, vi. 215.

By taking Matthias wholly into his own possession, he obtained one piece the more in the great game which he was playing against his antagonist in the Escorial. By making adroit use of events as they arose, he made the very waves which were to sink him, carry his great cause triumphantly onward.

The first result of the invitation to Matthias was the election of Orange as Ruward of Brabant.* This office was one of great historical dignity, but somewhat anomalous in its functions. The province of Brabant, having no special governor, was usually considered under the immediate superintendence of the Governor-General. As the capital of Brabant was the residence of that functionary, no inconvenience from this course had been felt since the accession of the house of Burgundy. At present, however, the condition of affairs was so peculiar—the seat of government being empty without having been permanently vacated—that a special opportunity was offered for conferring both honor and power on the Prince. A Ruward was not exactly dictator, although his authority was universal. He was not exactly protector, nor governor, nor stadholder. His functions were unlimited as to time—therefore superior to those of an ancient dictator; they were commonly conferred on the natural heir to the sovereignty—therefore more lofty than those of ordinary stadholders. The individuals who had previously held the office in the Netherlands had usually reigned afterwards in their own right. Duke Albert, of the Bavarian line, for example, had been Ruward of Hainault and Holland, for thirty years, during the insanity of his brother, and on the death of Duke William had succeeded to his title.† Philip of Burgundy had declared himself Ruward of Brabant in 1425,‡ and had shortly afterwards deprived Jacqueline of all her titles and appropriated them to himself. In the one case the regent, in the second case the

* Hoofd, xii. 532. Wagenaer, vii. 171.

† Wagenaer, iii. 304 (in 1387, A.D.)

‡ Wagenaer, iii. 465.—Compare Groen, v. Prinsterer, vi. 208–210: Strada, ix. 440, 441; Wagenaer, vii. 171.

usurper, had become reigning prince. Thus the movement of the jealous nobles against the Prince had for its first effect his immediate appointment to an office whose chief characteristic was, that it conducted to sovereignty.

The election was accomplished thus. The "members," or estates of Brussels, together with the deans, guilds, and other of the principal citizens of Antwerp, addressed a request to the states of Brabant, that William of Orange should be appointed Ruward, and after long deliberation the measure was carried. The unsolicited honor was then solemnly offered to him. He refused, and was only, after repeated and urgent entreaties, induced to accept the office. The matter was then referred to the states-general, who confirmed the dignity, after some demur, and with the condition that it might be superseded by the appointment of a governor-general.* He was finally confirmed as Ruward on the 22d of October, to the boundless satisfaction of the people, who celebrated the event by a solemn holiday in Antwerp, Brussels, and other cities.† His friends, inspired by the intrigues of his enemies, had thus elevated the Prince to almost unlimited power; while a strong expression in favor of his government had been elicited from the most important ally of the Netherlands—England. It soon rested with himself only to assume the government of Flanders, having been elected stadholder, not once only, but many times, by the four estates of that important province, and having as constantly refused the dignity.‡ With Holland and Zealand devoted to him, Brabant and Flanders formally under his government, the Netherland capital lavishing testimonials of affection upon him, and the mass of the people almost worshipping him, it would not have been difficult for the Prince to play a game as selfish as it had hitherto been close and skilful. He might have proved to the grand seigniors that their suspicions were just, by assuming a crown which they had been intriguing to

* Groen, v. Prinst., vi. 208, 209. Bondam, iii. 319, sqq. (cited by Groen, v. Prinst.)

† Hoofd, xii. 522.

‡ Apologie du Prince d'Orange, pp. 108, 109.

push from his brows. Certainly the nobles deserved their defeat. They had done their best to circumvent Orange, in all ways and at all times. They had paid their court to power when it was most powerful, and had sought to swim on the popular tide when it was rising. He avenged himself upon their perfidy only by serving his country more faithfully than ever, but it was natural that he should be indignant at the conduct of these gentlemen, "children of good houses," (in his own words,) "issue of worthy sires," whose fathers, at least, he had ever loved and honored.*

"They serve the Duke of Alva and the Grand Commander like varlets," he cried; "they make war upon me to the knife. Afterwards they treat with me, they reconcile themselves with me, they are sworn foes of the Spaniard. Don John arrives, and they follow him; they intrigue for my ruin. Don John fails in his enterprise upon Antwerp citadel; they quit him incontinently and call upon me. No sooner do I come than, against their oath and without previous communication with the states or myself, they call upon the Archduke Matthias. Are the waves of the sea more inconstant—is Euripus more uncertain than the counsels of such men?"†

While these events were occurring at Brussels and Antwerp, a scene of a different nature was enacting at Ghent. The Duke of Aerschot had recently been appointed to the government of Flanders by the State Council,‡ but the choice was exceedingly distasteful to a large number of the inhabitants. Although, since the defeat of Don John's party in Antwerp, Aerschot had again become "the affectionate brother" of Orange, yet he was known to be the head of the cabal which had brought Matthias from Vienna. Flanders, moreover, swarmed with converts to the Reformed religion,§ and the Duke's strict Romanism was well known. The people, therefore, who hated the Pope and adored the Prince, were furious at the

* Apologie du P. d'Orange, pp. 106, 107. † Ibid., p. 107.

‡ Bor, xi. 903. Meteren, vii. 126. Van d. Vynckt, ii. 278.

§ Van d. Vynckt, ii. 276. Hoofd, xii. 533.

appointment of the new governor, but by dint of profuse promises regarding the instant restoration of privileges and charters which had long lain dormant, the friends of Aerschot succeeded in preparing the way for his installation.*

On the 20th of October, attended by twenty-three companies of infantry and three hundred horse, he came to Ghent.† That famous place was still one of the most powerful and turbulent towns in Europe. Although diminished in importance since the commercial decline which had been the inevitable result of Philip's bloody government, it was still swarming with a vigorous and dangerous population,‡ and it had not forgotten the days when the iron tongue of Roland could call eighty thousand fighting men to the city banner.§ Even now, twenty thousand were secretly pledged ‖ to rise at the bidding of certain chieftains resident among them, noble by birth, warmly attached to the Reformed religion, and devoted to Orange. These gentlemen were perfectly conscious that a reaction was to be attempted in favor of Don John and of Catholicism, through the agency of the newly-appointed governor of Flanders. Aerschot was trusted or respected by neither party. The only difference in the estimates formed of him was, that some considered him a deep and dangerous traitor; others that he was rather foolish than malicious,¶ and more likely to ruin a good cause than to advance the interests of a bad one. The leaders of the popular party at Ghent believed him dangerous. They felt certain that it was the deeply laid design of the Catholic nobles—foiled as they had been in the objects with which they had brought Matthias from Vienna, and enraged as they were that the only result of that movement had been to establish the

* Meteren, vii. 126. Van d. Vynckt, ii. 279.

† Meteren, Van d. Vynckt, ubi sup. Bor, xi. 903.

‡ Van d. Vynckt. ii. 276, 277.

§ Guicciardini-Gandavum, pp. 343, 344; see Introduction to this work. Tassis, iv. 916.

‖ Van d. Vynckt, ii. 277.

¶ "Sed plerique existimant eum stultitiâ potius quam malitiâ peccasse."—Languet. Ep. Sec., i. ii. 307.

power of Orange upon a firmer basis—to set up an opposing influence in Ghent. Flanders, in the possession of the Catholics, was to weigh up Brabant, with its recent tendencies to toleration. Aerschot was to counteract the schemes of Orange. Matthias was to be withdrawn from the influence of the great heretic, and be yet compelled to play the part set down for him by those who had placed him upon the stage. A large portion, no doubt, of the schemes here suggested, was in agitation, but the actors were hardly equal to the drama which they were attempting. The intrigue was, however, to be frustrated at once by the hand of Orange, acting as it often did from beneath a cloud.

Of all the chieftains possessing influence with the inhabitants of Ghent, two young nobles, named Ryhove and Imbize, were the most conspicuous.* Both were of ancient descent and broken fortunes, both were passionately attached to the Prince, both were inspired with an intense hatred for all that was Catholic or Spanish. They had travelled further on the reforming path than many had done in that day, and might even be called democratic in their notions. Their heads were filled with visions of Greece and Rome; the praise of republics was ever on their lips; and they avowed to their intimate associates that it was already feasible to compose a commonwealth like that of the Swiss Cantons out of the seventeen Netherlands.† They were regarded as dreamers by some, as desperadoes by others. Few had confidence in their capacity or their purity; but Orange, who knew mankind, recognized in them useful instruments for any hazardous enterprise. They delighted in stratagems and sudden feats of arms. Audacious and cruel by temperament, they were ever most happy in becoming a portion of the desolation which popular tumults engender.

There were several excited meetings of the four estates of Flanders immediately after the arrival of the Duke of Aerschot in Ghent.‡ His coming had been preceded by extensive

---

* Van d. Vynckt, ii. 274, sqq. † Ibid., ii. 284, 285.

‡ Van d. Vynckt, ii. 276, sqq. Meteren, vii. 126.

promises, but it soon became obvious that their fulfilment was to be indefinitely deferred. There was a stormy session on the 27th of October, many of the clergy and nobility being present, and comparatively few members of the third estate. Very violent speeches were made, and threats openly uttered, that the privileges, about which so much noise had been heard, would be rather curtailed than enlarged under the new administration. At the same session, the commission of Aerschot was formally presented by Champagny and Sweveghem, deputed by the State Council for that purpose.* Champagny was in a somewhat anomalous position. There was much doubt in men's minds concerning him. He had seemed lately the friend of Orange, but he was certainly the brother of Granvelle. His splendid but fruitless services during the Antwerp Fury had not been forgotten, but he was known to be a determined Catholic. He was a hater of Spaniards, but no lover of popular liberty. The nature of his sentiments towards Orange was perhaps unjustly suspected. At any rate, two or three days after the events which now occupy our attention, he wrote him a private letter, in which he assured him of his attachment. In reference to the complaints of the Prince, that he had not been seconded as he ought to have been, he said, moreover, that he could solemnly swear never to have seen a single individual who did not hold the Prince in admiration, and who was not affectionately devoted to him, not only by public profession, but by private sentiment.† There was little doubt entertained as to the opinions held by the rest of the aristocratic party, then commencing their manœuvres in Ghent. Their sentiments were uttered with sufficient distinctness in this remarkable session.

Hessels, the old Blood Councillor, was then resident in Ghent, where he discharged high governmental functions. It was he, as it will be remembered, who habitually fell asleep at that horrible council board, and could only start from his naps

* Meteren, vii. 126b. Hoofd, xii. 533.

† Archives de la Maison d'Orange, vi. 226.

to shout "ad patibulum," while the other murderers had found their work less narcotic. A letter from Hessels to Count de Reux, late royal governor of Flanders, was at the present juncture intercepted.* Perhaps it was invented, but genuine or fictitious, it was circulated extensively among the popular leaders, and had the effect of proving Madame de Hessels a true prophet. It precipitated the revolution in Flanders, and soon afterwards cost the Councillor his life. "We have already brought many notable magistrates of Flanders over to the side of his Highness Don John," wrote Hessels. "We hope, after the Duke of Aerschot is governor, that we shall fully carry out the intentions of his Majesty and the plans of his Highness. We shall also know *how to circumvent the scandalous heretic with all his adherents and followers.*"†

Certainly, if this letter were true, it was high time for the friends of the "scandalous heretic" to look about them. If it were a forgery,‡ which is highly probable, it was ingeniously imagined, and did the work of truth. The revolutionary party, being in a small minority in the assembly, were advised by their leaders to bow before the storm. They did so, and the bluster of the reactionary party grew louder as they marked the apparent discomfiture of their foes. They openly asserted that the men who were clamoring for privileges should obtain nothing but halters. The buried charters should never be resuscitated ; but the spirit of the dead Emperor, who had once put a rope around the necks of the insolent Ghenters, still lived in that of his son. There was no lack of denunciation. Don John and the Duke of Aerschot would soon bring the turbulent burghers to their senses, and there would then be an end to this renewed clamor about musty parchments.§ Much indignation was secretly excited in the

* Bor, xi. 905ª.

† Ibid., 905.

‡ Archives de la Maison d'Orange, vi. 220.—Compare the remarks of Groen v. Prinsterer; Bor, xi. 223.

§ Meteren, vii. 126. Bor, xi. 903, sqq.

assembly by such menaces. Without doors the subterranean flames spread rapidly, but no tumult occurred that night. Before the session was over, Ryhove left the city, pretending a visit to Tournay. No sooner had he left the gates, however, than he turned his horse's head in the opposite direction, and rode off post haste to Antwerp. There he had a conference with William of Orange,* and painted in lively colors the alarming position of affairs. "And what do you mean to do in the matter?" asked the Prince, rather drily.† Ryhove was somewhat disconcerted. He had expected a violent explosion; well as he knew the tranquil personage whom he was addressing. "I know no better counsel," he replied, at length, "than to take the Duke, with his bishops, councillors, lords, and the whole nest of them, by the throat, and thrust them all out together."‡

"Rather a desperate undertaking, however?" said the Prince, carelessly, but interrogatively.

"I know no other remedy," answered Ryhove; "I would rather make the attempt, relying upon God alone, and die like a man, if needful, than live in eternal slavery. Like an ancient Roman," continued the young republican noble, in somewhat bombastic vein, "I am ready to wager my life, where my fatherland's welfare is at stake."

"Bold words!" said the Prince, looking gravely at Ryhove; "but upon what force do you rely for your undertaking?"

"If I can obtain no assistance from your Excellency," was the reply, "I shall throw myself on the mass of the citizens. I can arouse them in the name of their ancient liberties, which must be redeemed now or never."

---

* Meteren, vi. 126b. Hoofd, xii. 533.—Bor merely observes that it was *supposed* that Ryhove had visited Orange during his brief absence from Ghent. Meteren, however gives a minute account of their interview, in which he is followed by Hoofd, who had additional sources of information.—Compare Groen v. Prinst., vi. 217, 218; Wagenaer, vii. 177; V. d. Vynckt, ii. 279, 280, et al.

† "Waer toe den Prince niet anders en wiste op te segghen dan vraeghde wat raedt?"—Meteren, vii. 126b. Hoofd, xii. 533.

‡ "—— met den geheele neste by den halse te vatten ende te verdrijven."—Meteren, vii. 126.—Compare Hoofd.

The Prince, believing probably that the scheme, if scheme there were, was but a wild one, felt little inclination to compromise himself with the young conspirator. He told him he could do nothing at present, and saying that he must at least sleep upon the matter, dismissed him for the night. Next morning, at daybreak, Ryhove was again closeted with him. The Prince asked his sanguine partisan if he were still determined to carry out his project, with no more definite support than he had indicated? Ryhove assured him, in reply, that he meant to do so, or to die in the attempt. The Prince shrugged his shoulders, and soon afterwards seemed to fall into a reverie.* Ryhove continued talking, but it was soon obvious that his Highness was not listening, and he therefore took his leave somewhat abruptly. Hardly had he left the house, however, when the Prince despatched Saint Aldegonde in search of him. That gentleman, proceeding to his hotel, walked straight into the apartment of Ryhove, and commenced a conversation with a person whom he found there, but to his surprise he soon discovered, experienced politician though he was, that he had made an egregious blunder. He had opened a dangerous secret to an entire stranger,† and Ryhove coming into the apartment a few minutes afterwards, was naturally surprised to find the Prince's chief councillor in close conversation about the plot with Van Rooyen, the burgomaster of Denremonde. The Flemish noble, however, always prompt in emergencies, drew his rapier, and assured the astonished burgomaster that he would either have his life on the instant, or his oath never to reveal a syllable of what he had heard. That functionary, who had neither desired the young noble's confidence, nor contemplated the honor of being run through the body as a consequence of receiving it, was somewhat aghast at the rapid manner in which these gentlemen

---

* "De Prince trok syn schouderen ende aenhoorde hem met doove ooren," etc.—Meteren, ubi sup. Hoofd, xii. 534.

† Meteren, vii. 126. Hoofd, xii. 534.

transacted business. He willingly gave the required pledge, and was permitted to depart.

The effect of the conference between Saint Aldegonde and Ryhove was to convince the young partisan that the Prince would neither openly countenance his project, nor be extremely vexed should it prove successful. In short, while, as in the case of the arrest of the State Council, the subordinates were left to appear the principals in the transaction, the persons most intimate with William of Orange were allowed to form satisfactory opinions as to his wishes, and to serve as instruments to his ends.* "*Vive qui vince!*" cried Saint Aldegonde, encouragingly, to Ryhove, shaking hands with him at parting. The conspirator immediately mounted, and rode off towards Ghent. During his absence there had been much turbulence, but no decided outbreak, in that city. Imbize had accosted the Duke of Aerschot in the street, and demanded when and how he intended to proclaim the restoration of the ancient charters. The haughty Duke had endeavoured to shake off his importunate questioner, while Imbize persisted, with increasing audacity, till Aerschot lost his temper at last. "Charters, charters!" he cried in a rage; "you shall learn soon, ye that are thus howling for charters, that we have still the old means of making you dumb, with a rope on your throats. I tell you this—were you ever so much hounded on by the Prince of Orange."†

The violence of the new governor excited the wrath of Imbize. He broke from him abruptly, and rushed to a rendezvous of his confederates, every man of whom was ready for a desperate venture. Groups of excited people were seen vocife-

* "Ryhove, ziende dat den Prince conniveerde ofte d'ooghe luyckte om sijn voorneemen in 't werk te stellen," etc.—Meteren, vii. 127. "Ryhove hieruit scheppende dat zyn Doorluchtigkeit door de vingeren zagh," etc.—Hoofd, xii. 533.—Compare Strada, ii. lib. i. p. 4; Groen v. Prinst., Archives, etc., vi. 217, 218.

† Meteren, vii. 127. Hoofd, xii, 534. Van d. Vynckt, ii. 280.

rating in different places. A drum was heard to rattle from time to time. Nevertheless, the rising tumult seemed to subside again after a season, owing partly to the exertions of the magistrates, partly to the absence of Ryhove. At four in the afternoon that gentleman entered the town, and riding directly to the head-quarters of the conspiracy, was incensed to hear that the work, which had begun so bravely, had been allowed to cool. "'Tis a time," he cried, "for vigilance. If we sleep now, we shall be dead in our beds before morning. Better to fan the fire which has begun to blaze in the people's heart. Better to gather the fruit while it is ripe. Let us go forward, each with his followers, and I pledge myself to lead the way. Let us scuttle the old ship of slavery; let us hunt the Spanish Inquisition, once for all, to the hell from whence it came!"*

"There spoke the voice of a man!"† cried the Flemish captain, Mieghem, one of the chief conspirators; "lead on, Ryhove, I swear to follow you as far as our legs will carry us." Thus encouraged, Ryhove, rushed about the city, calling upon the people everywhere to rise. They rose almost to a man. Arming and mustering at different points, according to previous arrangements, a vast number assembled by toll of bell, after nightfall, on the public square, whence, under command of Ryhove, they swept to the residence of Aerschot at Saint Bavon. The guards, seeing the fierce mob approaching, brandishing spears and waving torches, had scarce time to close the gates, as the people loudly demanded entrance and the delivery to them of the Governor. Both claims were refused. "Let us burn the birds in their nests," cried Ryhove, without hesitation.‡ Pitch, light wood, and other combustibles, were brought at his command, and in a few moments the palace would have been in flames, had not Aerschot, seeing

---

* Hoofd, Meteren, ubi sup. Bor, xi. 903, 904.

† Daar (zeyde Mieghem hierop) hoor ik een' man spreeken," etc.—Ibid. Meteren, vii. 127.

‡ Meteren, vii. 127. Hoofd, xii. 535. Bor, xi. 905.

that the insurgents were in earnest, capitulated. As soon as the gates were open, the foremost of the mob rushed upon him, and would have torn him limb from limb, had not Ryhove resolutely interfered, and twice protected the life of the governor, at the peril of his own.* The Duke was then made a prisoner, and, under a strong guard, was conveyed, still in his night-gown, and bare-footed, to the mansion of Ryhove. All the other leading members of the Catholic party were captured, the arrests proceeding till a late hour in the night. Rassinghem, Sweveghem, Fisch, De la Porta, and other prominent members of the Flemish estates or council, were secured, but Champagny was allowed to make his escape.† The Bishops of Bruges and Ypres were less fortunate. Blood-councillor Hessels, whose letter—genuine or counterfeited—had been so instrumental in hastening this outbreak, was most carefully guarded, and to him and to Senator Fisch the personal consequences of that night's work were to be very tragic.

Thus audaciously, successfully, and hitherto without bloodshed, was the anti-Catholic revolution commenced in Flanders. The event was the first of a long and most signal series. The deed was done. The provisional government was established, at the head of which was placed Ryhove, to whom oaths of allegiance were rendered, subject to the future arrangements of the states-general and Orange. On the 9th of November, the nobles, notables, and community of Ghent published an address, in which they elaborately defended the revolution which had been effected and the arrests which had taken place ; while the Catholic party, with Aerschot at its head, was declared to be secretly in league with Don John to bring back the Spanish troops, to overthrow the Prince of Orange, to deprive him of the protectorate of Brabant, to

---

* Hoofd, xii. 535. Meteren, vii. 127. Van d. Vynckt, ii. 282.

† "Zoo dat hy verreyst, verborghen, oft door gunste, verschoont moet geweest zyn."—Hoofd, xii. 535.

set at nought the Ghent treaty, and to suppress the Reformed religion.*

The effect of this sudden rising of the popular party was prodigious throughout the Netherlands. At the same time, the audacity of such extreme proceedings could hardly be countenanced by any considerable party in the states-general. Champagny wrote to the Prince of Orange that, even if the letter of Hessels were genuine, it proved nothing against Aerschot,† and he urged the necessity of suppressing such scene of licence immediately, through the influence of those who could command the passions of the mob. Otherwise, he affirmed that all legitimate forms of justice would disappear, and that it would be easy to set the bloodhounds upon any game whatever. Saint Aldegonde wrote to the Prince, that it would be a great point, but a very difficult one, to justify the Ghent transaction; for there was little doubt that the Hessels letter was a forgery.‡ It was therefore as well, no doubt, that the Prince had not decidedly committed himself to Ryhove's plot, and thus deprived himself of the right to interfere afterwards, according to what seemed the claims of justice and sound policy.

He now sent Arend Van Dorp to Ghent, to remonstrate with the leaders of the insurrection upon the violence of their measures, and to demand the liberation of the prisoners—a request which was only complied with in the case of Aerschot. That nobleman was liberated on the 14th of November, under the condition that he would solemnly pledge himself to forget and forgive the treatment which he had received, but the other prisoners were retained in custody for a much longer period. A few weeks afterwards, the Prince of Orange visited Ghent, at the earnest request of the four estates of Flanders, and it was hoped that his presence would contribute to the restoration of tranquillity.§

---

* Address of the Notables, in Bor. xi. 904, 905.

† Archives de la Maison d'Orange, vi. 224.

‡ Ibid., vi. 219, 220.

§ Bor, xi. 905, 916. The Prince came to the city on the 29th of December, 1577.

This visit was naturally honored by a brilliant display of "rhetorical" spectacles and *tableaux vivants;* for nothing could exceed the passion of the Netherlanders of that century for apologues and charades. In allegory they found an ever-present comforter in their deepest afflictions. The prince was escorted from the Town-gate to the Jacob's church amid a blaze of tar-barrels and torches, although it was mid-day, where a splendid exhibition had been arranged by that sovereign guild of rhetoric, "Jesus with the Balsam Flower." The drama was called Judas Maccabæus, in compliment to the Prince. In the centre of the stage stood the Hebrew patriot, in full armor, symbolizing the illustrious guest doing battle for his country. He was attended by the three estates of the country, ingeniously personified by a single individual, who wore the velvet bonnet of a noble, the cassock of a priest, and the breeches of a burgher.* Groups of allegorical personages were drawn up on the right and left;—Courage, Patriotism, Freedom, Mercy, Diligence, and other estimable qualities upon one side, were balanced by Murder, Rapine, Treason, and the rest of the sisterhood of Crime on the other. The Inquisition was represented as a lean and hungry hag. The "Ghent Pacification" was dressed in cramoisy satin, and wore a city on her head for a turban; while, tied to her apron-strings were Catholicism and Protestantism, bound in a loving embrace by a chain of seventeen links, which she was forging upon an anvil. Under the anvil was an individual in complete harness, engaged in eating his heart; this was Discord. In front of the scene stood History and Rhetoric, attired as "triumphant maidens, in white garments," each with a laurel crown and a burning torch. These personages, after holding a rhymed dialogue between themselves, filled with wonderful conceits

* "Beschrijvinghe van het gene dat vertoocht wierd ter inkomste Van der Excellentie, des Prinzen van Orangien, binnen der Stad van Ghendt."—Ghendt, 1578. For the history of art in Flanders and Europe this little volume, filled, not only with the poetry, but with the designs and architectural embellishments employed upon this occasion, is worthy of attention. The pamphlet is very rare. The one used by the writer is in the Duncan Collection of the Royal Library, Hague.

and quibbles, addressed the Prince of Orange and Maccabæus, one after the other, in a great quantity of very detestable verses.

After much changing of scenes and groups, and an enormous quantity of Flemish-woven poetry, the "Ghent Peace" came forward, leading a lion in one hand, and holding a heart of pure gold in the other. The heart, upon which was inscribed *Sinceritas*, was then presented to the real Prince, as he sat "reposing after the spectacle," and perhaps slightly yawning, the gift being accompanied by another tremendous discharge of complimentary verses.* After this, William of Orange was permitted to proceed towards the lodgings provided for him, but the magistrates and notables met him upon the threshold, and the pensionary made him a long oration. Even after the Prince was fairly housed, he had not escaped the fangs of allegory; for, while he sat at supper refreshing his exhausted frame after so much personification and metaphor, a symbolical personage, attired to represent the town corporation,† made his appearance, and poured upon him a long and particularly dull heroic poem. Fortunately, this episode closed the labors of the day.

On the 7th of December, 1577, the states-general formally declared that Don John was no longer Stadholder, Governor, nor Captain-General, but an infractor of the peace which he had sworn to maintain, and an enemy of the fatherland. All natives of the country who should show him favor or assistance were declared rebels and traitors; and by a separate edict, issued the same day, it was ordained that an inventory of the estates of such persons should forthwith be taken.‡

Thus the war, which had for a brief period been suspended during the angry, tortuous, and hopeless negotiations which succeeded the arrival of Don John, was once more to be let loose. To this point had tended all the policy of Orange—faithful as ever to the proverb with which he had broken off

* Beschrijvinghe, etc. † Ibid. ‡ Bor, xi. 916.

the Breda conferences, "that war was preferable to a doubtful peace." Even, however, as his policy had pointed to a war as the necessary forerunner of a solid peace with Spain, so had his efforts already advanced the cause of internal religious concord within the provinces themselves. On the 10th of December, a new act of union was signed at Brussels, by which those of the Roman Church and those who had retired from that communion bound themselves to respect and to protect each other with mutual guarantees against all enemies whatsoever.* Here was a step beyond the Ghent Pacification, and in the same direction. The first treaty tacitly introduced toleration by suppressing the right of persecution, but the new union placed the Reformed religion on a level with the old. This was the result of the Prince's efforts; and, in truth, there was no lack of eagerness among these professors of a faith which had been so long under ban, to take advantage of his presence. Out of dark alleys, remote thickets, subterranean conventicles, where the dissenters had so long been trembling for their lives, the oppressed now came forth into the light of day. They indulged openly in those forms of worship which persecution had affected to regard with as much holy horror as the Badahuennan or Hercynian mysteries of Celtic ages could inspire, and they worshipped boldly the common God of Catholic and Puritan, in the words most consonant to their tastes, without dreading the gibbet as an inevitable result of their audacity.

In truth, the time had arrived for bringing the northern and southern, the Celtic and German, the Protestant and Catholic, hearts together, or else for acquiescing in their perpetual divorce. If the sentiment of nationality, the cause

* Meteren, vii. 127d. Haraei Ann., iii. 268, 269.—It is singular that Bor, Reyd, Bentivoglio, Van der Vynckt, Grotius, and even the constitutional historian, Kluit, are all silent concerning this remarkable Act of Union. Hoofd alludes to it in exactly two lines; Strada, De Thou, and Wagenaer, are equally concise. The Archivarius de Jonghe has, however, left nothing to be desired in his interesting monography ("Verhandelingen en Onuitgegevene Stukken," pp. 163–204), besides publishing the original French text of the important document. The contemporary historians above cited (Meteren and Haraeus) had already given its substance.

of a common fatherland, could now overcome the attachment to a particular form of worship—if a common danger and a common destiny could now teach the great lesson of mutual toleration, it might yet be possible to create a united Netherland, and defy for ever the power of Spain. Since the Union of Brussels, of January, 1577, the internal cancer of religious discord had again begun to corrode the body politic. The Pacification of Ghent had found the door open to religious toleration. It had not opened, but had left it open. The union of Brussels had closed the door again. Contrary to the hopes of the Prince of Orange and of the patriots who followed in his track, the sanction given to the Roman religion had animated the Catholics to fresh arrogance and fresh persecution. In the course of a few months, the only fruits of the new union, from which so much had been hoped, were to be seen in imprisonments, confiscations, banishments, executions.* The Perpetual Edict, by which the fifteen provinces had united in acknowledging Don John while the Protestant stronghold of Holland and Zealand had been placed in a state of isolation by the wise distrust of Orange, had widened the breach between Catholics and Protestants. The subsequent conduct of Don John had confirmed the suspicions and demonstrated the sagacity of the Prince. The seizure of Namur and the open hostility avowed by the Governor once more forced the provinces together. The suppressed flames of nationality burst forth again. Catholic and Protestant, Fleming and Hollander, instinctively approached each other, and felt the necessity of standing once more shoulder to shoulder in defence of their common rights. The Prince of Orange was called for by the unanimous cry of the whole country. He came to Brussels. His first step, as already narrated, was to break off negotiations which had been already ratified by the votes of the states-general. The measure was reconsidered, under pretence of adding certain amendments. Those amendments were the unconditional

* "Die nieuwe oder nadere Unie van Brussell."—Doov J. C. Jonghe, Verhandelingen und Onuitg. Stukk., p. 184.

articles of surrender proposed for Don John's signature on the 25th of September—articles which could only elicit words of defiance from his lips.

Thus far the Prince's object was accomplished. A treacherous peace, which would have ensured destruction, was averted, but a new obstacle to the development of his broad and energetic schemes arose in the intrigue which brought the Archduke from Vienna. The cabals of Orange's secret enemies were again thwarted with the same adroitness to which his avowed antagonists were forced to succumb. Matthias was made the exponent of the new policy, the standard-bearer of the new union which the Prince now succeeded in establishing; for his next step was immediately to impress upon the provinces which had thus united in casting down the gauntlet to a common enemy the necessity of uniting in a permanent league. One province was already lost by the fall of Namur. The bonds of a permanent union for the other sixteen could be constructed of but one material—religious toleration, and for a moment, the genius of Orange, always so far beyond his age, succeeded in raising the mass of his countrymen to the elevation upon which he had so long stood alone.

The "new or nearer Union of Brussels" was signed on the 10th of December, eleven months after the formation of the first union. This was the third and, unfortunately, the last confederation of all the Netherlands. The original records have been lost, but it is known that the measure was accepted unanimously in the estates-general as soon as presented.* The leading Catholic nobles were with the army, but a deputation, sent to the camp, returned with their signatures and hearty approval; with the signatures and approval of such determined Catholics as the Lalains, Meluns, Egmont, and La Motte.† If such men could unite for the sake of the fatherland in an act of religious toleration, what lofty hopes for the future was not the Prince justified in forming; for it was the Prince alone‡ who accomplished this victory

* De Jonghe, p. 188.

† Ibid., pp. 188–190.

‡ De Jonghe, p. 185, seq. Meerbeck. Chronyk., p. 488.

of reason over passion. As a monument, not only of his genius, but of the elevated aspirations of a whole people in an age of intolerance, the "closer Union of Brussels" deserves especial place in the history of human progress. Unfortunately, it was destined to a brief existence. The battle of Gemblours was its death-blow, and before the end of a month, the union thus hopefully constructed was shattered for ever. The Netherland people was never united again. By the Union of Utrecht, seven states subsequently rescued their existence, and lived to construct a powerful republic. The rest were destined to remain for centuries in the condition of provinces to a distant metropolis, to be shifted about as make-weights in political balances, and only in our own age to come into the honorable rank of independent constitutional states.

The Prince had, moreover, strengthened himself for the coming struggle by an alliance with England. The thrifty but politic Queen, fearing the result of the secret practices of Alençon—whom Orange, as she suspected, still kept in reserve to be played off, in case of need, against Matthias and Don John—had at last consented to a treaty of alliance and subsidy. On the 7th of January, 1578, the Marquis Havré, envoy from the estates, concluded an arrangement in London, by which the Queen was to lend them her credit—in other words, to endorse their obligations, to the amount of one hundred thousand pounds sterling. The money was to be raised wherever the states might be able to negotiate the bills, and her liability was to cease within a year. She was likewise to be collaterally secured by pledges from certain cities in the Netherlands.* This amount was certainly not colossal, while the conditions were sufficiently parsimonious. At the same time a beginning was made, and the principle of subsidy was established. The Queen, furthermore, agreed to send five thousand infantry and one thousand cavalry to the provinces, under the command of an officer of high rank, who was to have a seat and vote in the Netherland Council of

* Meteren, vii. 127, 128. Bor, xi. 902, 903.

State.* These troops were to be paid by the provinces, but furnished by the Queen. The estates were to form no treaty without her knowledge, nor undertake any movement of importance without her consent. In case she should be herself attacked by any foreign power, the provinces were to assist her to the same extent as the amount of aid now afforded to themselves; and in case of a naval war, with a fleet of at least forty ships. It had already been arranged that the appointment of the Prince of Orange as Lieutenant-General for Matthias was a *sine qua non* in any treaty of assistance with England. Soon after the conclusion of this convention, Sir Thomas Wilkes was despatched on a special mission to Spain, and Mr. Leyton sent to confer privately with Don John.† It was not probable, however, that the diplomatic skill of either would make this new arrangement palatable to Philip or his Governor.

Within a few days after their signature of this important treaty, the Prince had, at length, wholly succeeded in conquering the conflicting passions in the states-general, and in reconciling them, to a certain extent, with each other. The closer union had been accepted, and now thirty articles, which had been prepared under his superintendence, and had already on the 17th of December been accepted by Matthias, were established as the fundamental terms, according to which the Archduke was to be received as Governor-General.‡ No power whatever was accorded to the young man, who had come so far with eager and ambitious views. As the Prince had neither solicited nor desired a visit which had, on the contrary, been the result of hostile machinations, the Archduke could hardly complain that the power accorded him was but shadowy, and that his presence was rendered superfluous. It

* Bor, xi. 902, 903. Meteren, vii. 128.

† Bor, xi. 900–903. Meteren, ubi sup.

‡ See the articles at full in Bor, xi. 727–929. In the notes of De Reiffenberg to Van d. Vynckt, ii. 368–383; and in Meteren, vii. 129, they are given with much less exactness.—Compare the remarks of Groen van Prinsterer Archives, vi. 259, 260.

was not surprising that the common people gave him the name of *Greffier*, or registering clerk to the Prince ;* for his functions were almost limited to the signing of acts which were countersigned by Orange. According to the stipulations of the Queen of England, and the views of the whole popular party, the Prince remained Ruward of Brabant, notwithstanding the appointment of a nominal Governor-General, by whom his own duties were to be superseded.

The articles which were laid down as the basis upon which the Archduke was to be accepted, composed an ample representative constitution, by which all the legislative and many of the executive powers of government were bestowed upon the states-general or upon the council by them to be elected. To avoid remaining in the condition of a people thus left without a head, the states declared themselves willing to accept Matthias as Governor-General, on condition of the King's subsequent approbation, and upon the general basis of the Ghent treaty. The Archduke, moreover, was to take an oath of allegiance to the King *and to the states-general* at the same time. He was to govern the land by the advice of a state council, the members of which were to be appointed by the states-general, and were "to be native Netherlanders, true patriots, and neither ambitious nor greedy."† In all matters discussed before the state council, a majority of votes was to decide. The Governor-General, with his Council of State, should conclude nothing concerning the common affairs of the nation—such as requests, loans, treaties of peace or declarations of war, alliances or confederacies with foreign nations—without the consent of the states-general. He was to issue no edict or ordinance, and introduce no law, without the consent of the same body duly assembled, and representing each individual province.‡ A majority of the members was declared necessary to a *quorum* of the council. All acts and despatches were to be drawn up by a member of the board. The states-general were to assemble

---

* Tassis, iv. 290.

† "Getrouvre en goede patriotten niet wesende ambitieus of gïerig.—Art. 4.

‡ Art. 8.

when, where, and as often as, and remain in session as long as, they *might think it expedient.** At the request of any individual province, concerning matters about which a convention of the generality was customary, the other states should be bound to assemble without waiting for directions from the Governor-General.† The estates of each particular province were to assemble at their pleasure. The governor and council, with advice of the states-general, were to appoint all the principal military officers. Troops were to be enrolled and garrisons established by and with the consent of the states. Governors of provinces were to be appointed by the Governor-General, with advice of his council, and with the consent of the estates of the province interested. All military affairs were to be conducted during war by the governor, with advice of his council, while the estates were to have absolute control over the levying and expenditure of the common funds of the country.‡

It is sufficiently plain from this brief summary, that the powers thus conferred upon Matthias alone, were absolutely null, while those which he might exercise in conjunction with the state council, were not much more extensive. The actual force of the government—legislative, executive, and administrative—was lodged in the general assembly, while no authority was left to the King, except the nominal right to approve these revolutionary proceedings, according to the statement in the preamble. Such a reservation in favor of his Majesty seemed a superfluous sarcasm. It was furthermore resolved that the Prince of Orange should be appointed Lieutenant-General for Matthias, and be continued in his office of Ruward.§ This constitution, drawn up under the superintendence of the Prince, had been already accepted by Matthias, while still at

---

* Article 13. † Art. 14.

‡ Art. 21.—"Le hizieron jurar," says Cabrera, "treinta i una condiciones," (one article more, by the way, than the actual number, which was thirty—Bor, xi. 927–929), "instituyendo el gobierno popular a la traça que Julio Cesar escrive de los antiguos Flamencos, que el pueblo tenia el mismo mando sobre el Rey, que el sobre pueblo: i el *Archiduque les serviria de estatua.*"—xii. 959[b].

§ Bor, xi. 927.

Antwerp, and upon the 18th of January, 1578, the ceremony of his inauguration took place.

It was the third triumphal procession which Brussels had witnessed within nine months. It was also the most brilliant of all; for the burghers, as if to make amends to the Archduke for the actual nullity to which he had been reduced, seemed resolved to raise him to the seventh heaven of allegory. By the rhetorical guilds he was regarded as the most brilliant constellation of virtues which had yet shone above the Flemish horizon. A brilliant cavalcade, headed by Orange, accompanied by Count John of Nassau, the Prince de Chimay and other notables, met him at Vilvoorde, and escorted him to the city gate. On an open field, outside the town, Count Bossu had arranged a review of troops, concluding with a sham-fight, which, in the words of a classical contemporary, seemed as "bloody a rencontre as that between Duke Miltiades of Athens and King Darius upon the plains of Attica."* The procession entered the Louvain gate, through a splendid triumphal arch, filled with a band of invisible musicians. "I believe that Orpheus had never played so melodiously on his harp," says the same authority, "nor Apollo on his lyre, nor Pan on his lute, as the city waits then performed."† On entering the gates, Matthias was at once delivered over to the hands of mythology, the burghers and rhetoricians taking possession of their illustrious captive, and being determined to outdo themselves in demonstrations of welcome. The representatives of the "nine nations" of Brussels met him in the Ritter-street, followed by a gorgeous retinue. Although it

* Bor, xi. 927.

† "Sommare Beschryvinghe van den triumphelijcke Incomst van den doorluchtigen Aertshoge Matthias binnen die Princelijcke Stadt van Brussele."—'t Antwerpen. Plantin, 1579. This little contemporary publication, drawn up by J. B. Houwaert, contains a detailed account of the festivities upon this occasion, together with all the poems sung and spoken, and well executed engravings of the decorations, temples, theatres, and triumphal arches. For the literary and artistic history of Flanders and Brabant, it is important. The copy used by the writer is in the "Collectio Duncaniana" of the Royal Library at the Hague.

was mid-day, all bore flaming torches. Although it was January, the streets were strewed with flowers. The houses were festooned with garlands, and hung with brilliant silks and velvets. The streets were thronged with spectators, and encumbered with triumphal arches. On the Grande Place always the central scene in Brussels, whether for comedies, or tournaments, or executions, the principal dramatic effects had been accumulated. The splendid front of the Hotel de Ville was wreathed with scarfs and banners; its windows and balconies, as well as those of the picturesque houses which formed the square, were crowded with gaily-dressed women. Upon the area of the place, twenty-four theatres had been erected, where a series of magnificent living pictures were represented by the most beautiful young females that could be found in the city. All were attired in brocades, embroideries, and cloth of gold. The subjects of the *tableaux vivants* were, of course, most classic, for the Netherlanders were nothing, if not allegorical; yet, as spectacles, provided by burghers and artisans for the amusement of their fellow-citizens, they certainly proved a considerable culture in the people who could thus be amused. All the groups were artistically arranged. Upon one theatre stood Juno with her peacock, presenting Matthias with the city of Brussels, which she held, beautifully modelled, in her hand. Upon another, Cybele gave him the keys, Reason handed him a bridle, Hebe a basket of flowers, Wisdom a looking-glass and two law books, Diligence a pair of spurs; while Constancy, Magnanimity, Prudence, and other virtues, furnished him with a helmet, corslet, spear, and shield. Upon other theatres, Bellona presented him with several men-at-arms, tied in a bundle; Fame gave him her trumpet, and Glory her crown. Upon one stage Quintus Curtius, on horseback, was seen plunging into the yawning abyss; upon six others Scipio Africanus was exhibited, as he appeared in the most picturesque moments of his career.* The beardless Archduke had never achieved anything, save his nocturnal

* Sommare Beschryvinghe, etc.

escape from Vienna in his night-gown; but the honest Flemings chose to regard him as a re-incarnation of those two eminent Romans. Carried away by their own learning, they already looked upon him as a myth; and such indeed he was destined to remain throughout his Netherland career. After surveying all these wonders, Matthias was led up the hill again to the ducal palace, where, after hearing speeches and odes till he was exhausted, he was at last allowed to eat his supper and go to bed.

Meantime the citizens feasted in the streets. Bonfires were blazing everywhere, at which the people roasted "geese, pigs, capons, partridges, and chickens," while upon all sides were the merriest piping and dancing. Of a sudden, a fiery dragon was seen flying through the air. It poised for a while over the heads of the revelling crowd in the Grande Place, and then burst with a prodigious explosion, sending forth rockets and other fireworks in every direction. This exhibition, then a new one, so frightened the people, that they all took to their heels, "as if a thousand soldiers had assaulted them," tumbling over each other in great confusion, and so dispersing to their homes.*

The next day Matthias took the oaths as Governor-General, to support the new constitution, while the Prince of Orange was sworn in as Lieutenant-General and Governor of Brabant. Upon the next a splendid banquet was given them in the grand hall of the Hotel de Ville, by the states-general, and when the cloth was removed, Rhetoric made her last and most ingenious demonstration, through the famous guild of "Mary with the Flower Garland."

Two individuals—the one attired as a respectable burgher, the other as a clerical personage in gown and bands—made their appearance upon a stage, opposite the seats of their Highnesses, and pronounced a long dialogue in rhyme. One of the speakers rejoiced in the appellation of the "Desiring Heart," the other was called "Common Comfort." Common

* Sommare Beschryvinghe, etc.

Sense might have been more to the purpose, but appeared to have no part in the play. Desiring Heart, being of an inquisitive disposition, propounded a series of puzzling questions, mythological in their nature, which seemed like classical conundrums, having reference, mainly, to the proceedings of Venus, Neptune, Juno, and other divinities.* They appeared to have little to do with Matthias or the matter in hand, but Common Comfort knew better. That clerical personage, accordingly, in a handsome allowance of rhymes, informed his despairing colleague that everything would end well; that Jupiter, Diana, Venus, and the rest of them would all do their duty, and that Belgica would be relieved from all her woes, at the advent of a certain individual. Whereupon cried Desiring Heart:

> Oh Common Comfort! who is he?
> His name, and of what family?

To which† Comfort responded by mentioning the Archduke,

---

* As for example—

> "Wanneer sal Jupiter Saturnum verdrijven?
> Wanneer sal Neptunus Phaethon verdrijncken,
> Wanneer sal Hercules Hydram ontlijven,
> Wanneer sal Vulcanus laten sijn hincken," etc., etc.
>
> Som. Beschryv.

Or, in the vernacular—

> When shall Jove his father follow,
> Or briny Neptune Phaethon swallow,
> Or Herc'les leave off Hydra crimping,
> Or honest Vulcan give up limping,
> Or Brontes cease to forge his thunder?
> All these are wonders upon wonder—etc., etc.

† "Hy is van Keyserlicken stamme gheboren,
> Aartshertoge Matthias is sijnen name,
> Die generale staten habben hem ghecoren,
> Voor Gouverneur, door sijne goete fame
> Hy is als Julius Cesar eersame," etc., etc. Som. Beschryv.

> He is formed of fine material,
> And is sprung of race imperial.
> He is brave as Julius Cæsar,
> Archduke Matthias is his name;
> He is chosen Governor-General
> By the states, for his great fame—etc., etc.

in a poetical and highly-complimentary strain, with handsome allusions to the inevitable Quintus Curtius and Scipio Africanus. The concluding words of the speech were not spoken, but were taken as the cue for a splendid charade; the long-suffering Scipio again making his appearance, in company with Alexander and Hannibal; the group typifying the future government of Matthias. After each of these heroic individuals had spouted a hundred lines or so, the play was terminated, and Rhetoric took her departure. The company had remained at table during this long representation, and now the dessert was served, consisting of a "richly triumphant banquet of confectionary, marmalade, and all kinds of genteelnesses in sugar."*

Meanwhile, Don John sat chafing and almost frenzied with rage at Namur. Certainly he had reasons enough for losing his temper. Never since the days of Maximilian had king's brother been so bearded by rebels. The Cross was humbled in the dust, the royal authority openly derided, his Majesty's representative locked up in a fortress, while "the accursed Prince of Orange" reigned supreme in Brussels, with an imperial Archduke for his private secretary.

The Governor addressed a long, private, and most bitter letter to the Emperor, for the purpose of setting himself right in the opinion of that potentate, and of giving him certain hints as to what was expected of the imperial court by Philip and himself. He expressed confidence that the imperial commissioners would have some effect in bringing about the pacification of the Netherlands, and protested his own strong desire for such a result, provided always that the two great points of the Catholic religion and his Majesty's authority were preserved intact. "In the hope that those articles would be maintained," said he, "I have emptied cities and important places of their garrisons, when I might easily have kept the soldiers, and with the soldiers the places, against all the world, instead of consigning them to the care of men who at this

---

* Sommare Beschryvinghe, etc., etc.

hour have arms in their hand against their natural prince." He declared vehemently that in all his conduct, since his arrival in the provinces, he had been governed exclusively by the interests of Philip, an object which he should steadily pursue to the end. He urged, too, that the Emperor, being of the same house as Philip, and therefore more obliged than all others to sustain his quarrel, would do well to espouse his cause with all the warmth possible. "The forgetfulness by vassals," said Don John, "of the obedience due to their sovereign is so dangerous, that all princes and potentates, even those at the moment exempt from trouble, should assist in preparing the remedy, in order that their subjects also may not take it into their heads to do the like, *liberty being a contagious disease, which goes on infecting one neighbour after another, if the cure be not promptly applied.*"* It was, he averred, a desperate state of things for monarchs, when subjects having obtained such concessions as the Netherlanders had obtained, nevertheless loved him and obeyed him so little. They showed, but too clearly, that the causes alleged by them had been but pretexts, in order to effect designs, long ago conceived, to overthrow the ancient constitution of the country, and to live thenceforward in unbridled liberty. So many indecent acts had been committed prejudicial to religion and to his Majesty's grandeur, that the Governor avowed his determination to have no farther communication with the provinces without fresh commands to that effect. He begged the Emperor to pay no heed to what the states *said*, but to observe what they *did*. He assured him that nothing could be more senseless than the reports that Philip and his Governor-General in the Netherlands were negotiating with France, for the purpose of alienating the provinces from the Austrian

* "—— Obéissance de leur Prince souverain, obly de laquelle est si dangereulx que tous princes et potentats voires ceulx qui présentement sont exempts de troubles en dérvoient soigner le remède affin que, a l'exemple de ceulx ci les leurs ne prennent quelque jour envye de f[re] le semblable, etant la liberté qu'ils cherchent comme ung mal contagieulx qui vast infectant au voisin si en temps et promptement ny est remèdié."

crown. Philip, being chief of the family, and sovereign of the Netherlands, could not commit the absurdity of giving away his own property to other people, nor would Don John choose to be an instrument in so foolish a transaction.* The Governor entreated the Emperor, therefore, to consider such fables as the invention of malcontents and traitors, of whom there were no lack at his court, and to remember that nothing was more necessary for the preservation of the greatness of his family than to cultivate the best relations with all its members. "Therefore," said he, with an absurd affectation of candor, "although I make no doubt whatever that the expedition hitherwards of the Archduke Matthias has been made with the best intentions; nevertheless, many are of opinion that it would have been better altogether omitted. If the Archduke," he continued, with hardly dissembled irony, "be desirous of taking charge of his Majesty's affairs, it would be preferable to employ himself in the customary manner. Your Majesty would do a laudable action by recalling him from this place, according to your Majesty's promise to me to that effect." In conclusion, Don John complained that difficulties had been placed in his way for making levies of troops in the Empire, while every facility had been afforded to the rebels. He therefore urgently insisted that so unnatural and unjust a condition of affairs should be remedied.†

Don John was not sorry in his heart that the crisis was at last come. His chain was broken. His wrath exploded in his first interview with Leyton, the English envoy, whom Queen Elizabeth had despatched to calm, if possible, his inevitable anger at her recent treaty with the states.‡ He knew nothing of England, he said, nor of France, nor of the

* "—— car estant icelle chef de la dite maison et Sgr des Pays Bas seroit chose absurde de lui attribuer une imprudence si grande que de donner le sien à autrui et à moi qu'en vouldrais estre l'instrument."

† This letter which has never been published, is in French, in the handwriting of John Baptist de Tassis, and signed by Don John. It is dated Luxembourg, 11th of January, 1578, and is in the collection of MSS. in the Brussels Archives, entitled, "Reconciliation des Provinces Wallones—t. i. 44–54.

‡ Bor, xi. 931.

Emperor. His Catholic Majesty had commissioned him now to make war upon these rebellious provinces. He would do it with all his heart. As for the Emperor, he would unchain the Turks upon him for his perfidy. As for the burghers of Brussels, they would soon feel his vengeance.*

It was very obvious that these were not idle threats. War had again broken loose throughout these doomed provinces. A small but well-appointed army had been rapidly collecting under the banner of Don John at Luxemburg, Peter Ernest Mansfeld had brought many well-trained troops from France, and Prince Alexander of Parma had arrived with several choice and veteran regiments of Italy and Spain.† The old schoolfellow, playmate and comrade of Don John, was shocked on his arrival, to witness the attenuated frame and care-worn features of his uncle.‡ The son of Charles the Fifth, the hero of Lepanto, seemed even to have lost the air of majesty which was so natural to him, for petty insults, perpetual crosses, seemed to have left their squalid traces upon his features. Nevertheless, the crusader was alive again, at the notes of warlike preparations which now resounded throughout the land.

On the 25th of January he issued a proclamation, couched in three languages—French, German, and Flemish. He declared in this document that he had not come to enslave the provinces, but to protect them. At the same time he meant to re-establish his Majesty's authority, and the down-trod religion of Rome. He summoned all citizens and all soldiers throughout the provinces to join his banners, offering them pardon for their past offences, and protection against heretics and rebels.§ This declaration was the natural consequence of the exchange of defiances which had already taken place, and it was evident also that the angry manifesto was soon to be followed up by vigorous blows. The army of Don John

* Bor, xi. 931. Hoofd, xiii. 546.

† Bor, xii. 932, 933. Hoofd, xiii. 546. Strada, ix. 460.

‡ "Attenuata non magis valetudine quam specie illa majestateque fortunatissimi Imperatoris."—Ibid.

§ Proclamation in Bor, xii. 932, 933.—Compare Cabrera, xii. 966.

already numbered more than twenty thousand well-seasoned and disciplined veterans.* He was himself the most illustrious chieftain in Europe. He was surrounded by lieutenants of the most brilliant reputation. Alexander of Parma, who had fought with distinction at Lepanto, was already recognised as possessing that signal military genius which was soon to stamp him as the first soldier of his age, while Mansfeld, Mondragon, Mendoza, and other distinguished officers, who had already won so much fame in the Netherlands, had now returned to the scene of their former achievements.†

On the other hand, the military affairs of the states were in confusion. Troops in nearly equal numbers to those of the royal army had been assembled, but the chief offices had been bestowed, by a mistaken policy, upon the great nobles. Already the jealousy of Orange, entertained by their whole order, was painfully apparent. Notwithstanding the signal popularity which had made his appointment as Lieutenant-general inevitable, it was not easy for him always to vindicate his authority over captious and rival magnates.‡ He had every wish to conciliate the affections of men whom he could not in his heart respect, and he went as far in gratifying their ambition as comported with his own dignity; perhaps farther than was consistent with the national interests. He was still willing to trust Lalain, of whose good affection to the country he felt sure. He had even been desirous of declining the office of Lieutenant-General, in order to avoid giving that nobleman the least occasion to think "that he would do him, or any other gentleman of the army, prejudice in any single matter in the world."§ This magnanimity had not been

* Bor, xii. 932. Hoofd, xiii. 546, 547, say 22,300, viz.—4000 Spanish, 4000 French, 5000 Germans, 6800 Walloons, 2500 cavalry; total, 22,300;—about 20,000 according to Strada, ix. 462. Cabrera asserts that there were but 10,000 in Don John's army, while the forces of the enemy amounted to double that number.—xii. 967[c].

† Strada, ix. 467.

‡ Ibid., 464.

§ Letter of Prince of Orange, Archives de la Maison d'Orange, vi. 279.

repaid with corresponding confidence. We have already seen that Lalain had been secretly in the interest of Anjou ever since his wife and himself had lost their hearts to Margaret of Navarre; yet the Count was chief commander of the infantry in the states' army then assembled. Robert Melun, Vicomte de Gand, was commander of the cavalry,* but he had recently been private envoy from Don John to the English Queen.† Both these gentlemen, together with Pardieu De la Motte, general of the artillery, were voluntarily absent from the forces, under pretext of celebrating the wedding of the Seigneur De Bersel with the niece and heiress of the unfortunate Marquis of Bergen.‡ The ghost of that ill-starred noble might almost have seemed to rise at the nuptial banquet of his heiress, to warn the traitors of the signal and bloody massacre which their treachery was soon to occasion. Philip Egmont, eldest son of the famous Lamoral, was with the army, as was the Seigneur de Héze, hero of the State Council's arrest, and the unstable Havré. But little was to be hoped from such leaders. Indeed, the affairs of the states continued to be in as perplexed a condition as that which honest John of Nassau had described some weeks before. "There were very few patriots," he had said, "but plenty of priests, with no lack of inexperienced lads—some looking for distinction, and others for pelf."§

The two armies had been mustered in the latter days of January. The Pope had issued a bull for the benefit of Don John, precisely similar to those formerly employed in the crusades against the Saracens.‖ Authority was given him to levy contributions upon ecclesiastical property, while full absolution, at the hour of death, for all crimes committed during a whole lifetime, was proclaimed to those who should now join the

---

* Archives de la Maison d'Orange, vi. 279. † Strada, ix. 463.

‡ Strada, ix. 464, 465. Hoofd, xiii. 548.

§ Letter to the Landgrave W. de Hesse.—Archives de la Maison d'Orange, vi. 227.

‖ See it in Bor, xii. 935[b].

standard of the Cross. There was at least no concealment. The Crescent-wearing Zealanders had been taken at their word, and the whole nation of Netherlanders were formally banned as unbelievers. The forces of Don John were mustered at Marche in Luxemburg; those of the states in a plain within a few miles of Namur.* Both armies were nearly equal in number, amounting to nearly twenty thousand each, including a force of two thousand cavalry on each side.† It had been the original intention of the patriots to attack Don John in Namur. Having learned, however, that he purposed marching forth himself to offer battle, they decided to fall back upon Gemblours, which was nine miles distant from that city.‡ On the last day of January, they accordingly broke up their camp at Saint Martius, before dawn, and marched towards Gemblours. The chief commander was De Goignies, an old soldier of Charles the Fifth, who had also fought at Saint Quintin. The states' army was disposed in three divisions. The van consisted of the infantry regiments of De Héze and Montigny, flanked by a protective body of light horse. The centre, composed of the Walloon and German regiments, with a few companies of French, and thirteen companies of Scotch and English under Colonel Balfour, was commanded by two most distinguished officers, Bossu and Champagny. The rear, which, of course, was the post of responsibility and honor, comprised all the heavy cavalry, and was commanded by Philip Egmont and Lumey de la Marck. The Marquis Havré and the General-in-chief, Goignies, rode to and fro, as the army proceeded, each attended by his staff.§

The troops of Don John broke up from before Namur with the earliest dawn, and marched in pursuit of the retiring foe. In front was nearly the whole of the cavalry—carabineers, lancers, and heavy dragoons. The centre, arranged in two

---

* Bor, xii. 932, sqq. Hoofd, xiii. 548.

† All the authorities agree as to the estimates of the forces of the states. Hoofd, xiii. 547. Cabrera, xii. 969. Strada, ix. 463, et mult. al.

‡ Bor, xii. 933. Hoofd, xiii. 547. Strada, ix. 464.

§ Bor, xii. 933, 934. Strada, ix. 464. Hoofd, xiii. 548.

squares, consisted chiefly of Spanish infantry, with a lesser number of Germans. In the rear came the Walloons, marching also in a square, and protecting the baggage and ammunition. Charles Mansfeld had been left behind with a reserved force, stationed on the Meuse; Ottavio Gonzaga commanded in front, Ernest Mansfeld brought up the rear; while in the centre rode Don John himself, attended by the Prince of Parma. Over his head streamed the crucifix-emblazoned banner, with its memorable inscription—*In hoc signo vici Turcos, in hoc Haereticos vincam.**

Small detachments of cavalry had been sent forward, under Olivera and Acosta, to scour the roads and forests, and to disturb all ambuscades which might have been prepared. From some stragglers captured by these officers, the plans of the retreating generals were learned. The winter's day was not far advanced, when the rearward columns of the states' army were descried in the distance. Don John, making a selection of some six hundred cavalry, all picked men, with a thousand infantry, divided the whole into two bodies, which he placed under command of Gonzaga and the famous old Christopher Mondragon.† These officers received orders to hang on the rear of the enemy, to harass him, and to do him all possible damage consistent with the possibility of avoiding a general engagement, until the main army under Parma and Don John should arrive. The orders were at first strictly obeyed. As the skirmishing grew hotter, however, Gonzaga observed that a spirited cavalry officer, named Perotti, had already advanced, with a handful of men, much further within the reach of the hostile forces than was deemed expedient. He sent hastily to recal the too eager chieftain. The order, delivered in a tone more peremptory than agreeable, was flatly disobeyed. "Tell Ottavio Gonzaga," said Perotti, "that I never yet turned my back on the enemy, nor shall I now begin. Moreover, were I ever so much inclined to do so, retreat is

* Bor, xii. 933. Hoofd, xiii. 549. Strada, ix. 465.

† Strada, ix. 465, 466. Hoofd, xiii. 549. Bor, xii. 933, sqq.

impossible."* The retiring army was then proceeding along the borders of a deep ravine, filled with mire and water, and as broad and more dangerous than a river.† In the midst of the skirmishing, Alexander of Parma rode up to reconnoitre. He saw at once that the columns of the enemy were marching unsteadily to avoid being precipitated into this creek. He observed the waving of their spears, the general confusion of their ranks, and was quick to take advantage of the fortunate moment. Pointing out to the officers about him the opportunity thus offered of attacking the retiring army unawares in flank, he assembled, with great rapidity, the foremost companies of cavalry already detached from the main body. Mounting a fresh and powerful horse, which Camillo Monte held in readiness for him, he signified his intention of dashing through the dangerous ravine, and dealing a stroke where it was least expected. "Tell Don John of Austria," he cried to an officer whom he sent back to the Commander-in-chief, "that Alexander of Parma has plunged into the abyss, to perish there, or to come forth again victorious."‡

The sudden thought was executed with lightning-like celerity. In an instant the bold rider was already struggling through the dangerous swamp; in another, his powerful charger had carried him across. Halting for a few minutes, lance in rest,§ till his troops had also forced their passage, gained the level ground unperceived, and sufficiently breathed their horses, he drew up his little force in a compact column. Then, with a few words of encouragement, he launched them at the foe. The violent and entirely unexpected shock was even more successful than the Prince had anticipated. The hostile cavalry reeled and fell into hopeless confusion, Egmont in vain striving to rally them to resistance. That name had lost its magic. Goignies also attempted, without success, to restore order among the panic-struck ranks. The sudden con-

* Strada, ix. 466. † Strada, ubi sup. Bor, xii. 934. Hoofd, xiii. 459.

‡ Strada, ix. 466, 467. Hoofd, xiii. 549.

§ "Con gran valor, la lança en puño," etc., etc.—Cabrera, xii. 968.

ception of Parma, executed as suddenly and in so brilliant a manner, had been decisive. Assaulted in flank and rear at the same moment, and already in temporary confusion, the cavalry of the enemy turned their backs and fled. The centre of the states' army thus left exposed, was now warmly attacked by Parma. It had, moreover, been already thrown into disorder by the retreat of its own horse, as they charged through them in rapid and disgraceful panic. The whole army broke to pieces at once,* and so great was the trepidation, that the conquered troops had hardly courage to run away. They were utterly incapable of combat. Not a blow was struck by the fugitives. Hardly a man in the Spanish ranks was wounded; while, in the course of an hour and a half, the whole force of the enemy was exterminated. It is impossible to state with accuracy the exact numbers slain. Some accounts spoke of ten thousand killed, or captive, with absolutely no loss on the royal side.† Moreover, this slaughter was effected, not by the army under Don John, but by so small a fragment of it, that some historians have even set down the whole number of royalists engaged at the commencement of the action, at six hundred, increased afterwards to twelve hundred. By this calculation, each Spaniard engaged must have killed ten enemies with his own hand; and that within an hour and a half's space!‡ Other historians more wisely omit the exact statistics of the massacre, and allow that a very few—ten or eleven, at most—were slain within the Spanish ranks. This, however, is the utmost that is claimed by even the Netherland historians, and it is, at

---

* Strada, Hoofd, Bor, ubi sup.—Compare Cabrera, xii. 968, 969; Meteren, viii. 133; Haraei Ann., iii. 273, 274; Tassis, iv. 293, 294, et mult. alt.

† "Dei vincitori *non mori quasi soldato alcuno*," says Bentivoglio, "pochi restaron feriti."—(Guerra di Fiandra x. 206). He however has the modesty to claim but three thousand killed on the states' side, with a large number of prisoners.

‡ "Siquidem à sexcentis equitibus (tot enim incepere aucti dein ad mille ac ducentos, confecere pugnam) peditum *millia omnino decem*, partim coesa, partim capta, ac reliquus exercitus non minor octo bellatorum millibus *sesquihoræ spatio* (!!); desideratis ex Regiis *tantum modo novem*, profligatus est."—Strada, ix. 468. Rather too warm work even for the 31st of January.

any rate, certain that the whole states' army was annihilated.* Rarely had a more brilliant exploit been performed by a handful of cavalry. To the distinguished Alexander of Parma, who improvised so striking and complete a victory out of a fortuitous circumstance, belonged the whole credit of the day, for his quick eye detected a passing weakness of the enemy, and turned it to terrible account with the promptness which comes from genius alone. A whole army was overthrown. Everything belonging to the enemy fell into the hands of the Spaniards. Thirty-four standards, many field-pieces, much camp equipage, and ammunition, besides some seven or eight thousand dead bodies, and six hundred living prisoners, were the spoils of that winter's day.† Of the captives, some were soon afterwards hurled off the bridge at Namur, and drowned like dogs in the Meuse,‡ while the rest were all hanged,§

---

* According to Tassis (iv. 294) seven thousand of the states' army were killed or captured (the prisoners afterwards having been drowned), while only ten royalists were killed or wounded. According to Haraeus (iii. 274), eight thousand of the states' army were slain by *two thousand* royalist troops (being four men apiece for each royalist). He does not state that any of the King's soldiers were slain, or even wounded. According to Cabrera (xii. 968), there were more than seven thousand of the Netherland army killed or taken (the number of the prisoners being nowhere stated at more than six hundred, *all* of whom were afterwards drowned or hanged), while of the Spanish troops two were killed, and five were wounded. According to Bor, thirty companies were slain, and six hundred men taken prisoners, on the states' side, while Don John lost but ten or twelve men. Hoofd accepts the absurd statistics of Strada; repeating, after that historian, that "twelve hundred Spaniards killed six, eight, nay even ten thousand of the states' army, within one hour and a half, with a loss of but ten men on their own side," (xiii. 550). Van Meteren, alone, in the teeth of all the evidence, doggedly maintains that it was not *much of a victory after all*, and that there were not many states' soldiers slain in the action.—"Het gethal der verslagenen war niet seer groot."—(viii. 133). A contemporary, and living near the spot, he certainly manifests his patriotism by so hardy an assertion; but we have often noticed the pertinacity of the distinguished chronicler upon such points.

† Bor, Strada, Hoofd, Haraeus, Meteren, Cabrera, ubi sup. et mult. al.

‡ Tassis, iv. 294.

§ Bor, xii. 934. Hoofd, xiii. 555.—The latter historian states that six hundred prisoners were hanged at Namur. Cabrera, on the contrary, asserts that Don John liberated the Scotch prisoners: "a Seiscientos Escoseses presos dio libertad Don Juan, mostrando su clemencia." To this very gratuitous assertion it is a sufficient answer that Tassis, who was on the spot, a leading privy

none escaping with life. Don John's clemency was not superior to that of his sanguinary predecessors.

And so another proof was added—if proofs were still necessary—of Spanish prowess. The Netherlanders may be pardoned if their foes seemed to them supernatural, and almost invulnerable. How else could these enormous successes be accounted for? How else could thousands fall before the Spanish swords, while hardly a single Spanish corpse told of effectual resistance? At Jemmingen, Alva had lost seven soldiers, and slain seven thousand; in the Antwerp Fury, two hundred Spaniards, at most, had fallen, while eight thousand burghers and states' troops had been butchered; and now at Gemblours, six, seven, eight, ten—Heaven knew how many—thousand had been exterminated, and hardly a single Spaniard had been slain! Undoubtedly, the first reason for this result was the superiority of the Spanish soldiers. They were the boldest, the best disciplined, the most experienced in the world. Their audacity, promptness, and ferocity made them almost invincible. In this particular action, at least half the army of Don John was composed of Spanish or Spanish-Italian veterans. Moreover, they were commanded by the most renowned captains of the age—by Don John himself, and Alexander of Parma, sustained by such veterans as Mondragon, the hero of the memorable submarine expeditions; Mendoza, the accomplished cavalry officer, diplomatist, and historian; and Mansfeld, of whom Don John had himself written to the King that his Majesty had not another officer of such account in all the Netherlands.* Such officers as these, besides Gonzaga, Camillo Monte, Mucio Pagano, at the head of such troops as fought that day under the banner

---

councillor of Don John, expressly states that of the captives the greater part, *who were Scotch*, were thrown off Namur bridge into the river. "Ac capti, quorum magna pars, qui Schoti erant, ex ponte Namuriensi in fluvium postea præcipitati," iv. 294.—Compare Haraei Ann., iii. 274, where it is stated that all the prisoners were hanged;—"extemplo suspendio necantur."

* "Y que no tiene aqui otro hombre de su estado."—Letter of Don John to Philip, Discours Sommier, p. 37, appendix.

of the Cross, might go far in accounting for this last and most tremendous victory of the Inquisition. On the other hand, although Bossu and Champagny were with the states' army, yet their hearts were hardly with the cause. Both had long been loyal, and had earned many laurels against the rebels, while Champagny was still devoutly a Papist, and wavered painfully between his hatred to heresy and to Spain. Egmont and De Hézé were raw, unpractised lads, in whom genius did not come to supply the place of experience. The Commander, De Goignies, was a veteran, but a veteran who had never gained much glory, and the chiefs of the cavalry, infantry, and artillery, were absent at the Brussels wedding. The news of this additional massacre inflicted upon a nation, for which Berghen and Montigny had laid down their lives, was the nuptial benediction for Berghen's heiress; for it was to the chief wedding guests upon that occasion that the disaster was justly attributed. The rank and file of the states' army were mainly mercenaries, with whom the hope of plunder was the prevailing motive; the chief commanders were absent; while those officers who were with the troops were neither heartily friendly to their own flag, nor sufficiently experienced to make it respected.

CHAPTER V.

Towns taken by Don John—Wrath excited against the aristocratic party by the recent defeat—Attempts upon Amsterdam—"Satisfaction" of Amsterdam and its effects—De Selles sent with royal letters from Spain—Terms offered by Philip—Proclamation of Don John—Correspondence between de Selles and the States-General—Between the King and the Governor-General—New forces raised by the States—St. Aldegonde at the Diet—Municipal revolution in Amsterdam—The Prince's letter on the subject of the Anabaptists of Middelburg—The two armies inactive—De la Noue—Action at Rijnemants—John Casimir—Perverse politics of Queen Elizabeth—Alençon in the Netherlands—Portrait of the Duke—Orange's position in regard to him—Avowed and supposed policy of the French court—Anger of Elizabeth—Terms arranged between Alençon and the Estates—Renewed negotiations with Don John—Severe terms offered him—Interview of the English envoys with the Governor—Despondency of Don John—Orange's attempts to enforce a religious peace—His isolation in sentiment—The malcontent party—Count John Governor of Gelderland—Proposed form of religious peace—Proclamation to that effect by Orange, in Antwerp—A petition in favor of the Roman Church presented by Champagny and other Catholic nobles to the States-General—Consequent commotion in Brussels—Champagny and others imprisoned—Indolence and poverty of the two armies—Illness and melancholy of Don John—His letters to Doria, to Mendoza, and to the King—Death of Don John—Suspicions of poison—Pompous burial—Removal of his body to Spain—Concluding remarks upon his character.

Don John having thus vindicated his own military fame and the amazing superiority of the Spanish arms, followed up his victory by the rapid reduction of many towns of second-rate importance. Louvain, Judoigne, Tirlemont, Aerschot, Bouvignes, Sichem, Nivelle, Roeux, Soignies, Binch, Beaumont, Walcourt, Maubeuge, and Chimay, either submitted to their conqueror, or were taken after short sieges. The usual atrocities were inflicted upon the unfortunate inhabitants of towns where resistance was attempted. The commandant of Sichem was hanged out of his own window, along with several chief burghers and officers, while the garrison was put to the sword, and the bodies cast into the Demer. The only crime committed by these unfortunates was to have ventured a blow or two in behalf of the firesides which they were employed to protect.*

In Brussels, on the other hand, there was less consternation excited by these events than boundless rage against the aristocratic party, for the defeat of Gemblours was attributed, with justice, to the intrigues and the incapacity of the Catholic magnates. It was with difficulty that Orange, going about by night from house to house, from street to street, succeeded in calming the indignation of the people, and in preventing them from sweeping in a mass to the residence of the leading nobles, in order to inflict summary vengeance on the traitors. All looked to the Prince as their only saviour, not a thought nor a word being wasted upon Matthias. Not a voice was raised in the assembly to vindicate the secret proceedings of the Catholic party, nor to oppose the measures which the Prince might suggest.† The terrible disaster had taught the necessity of union. All parties heartily joined in the necessary steps to place the capital in a state of complete defence, and to assemble forthwith new troops to take the place of the army just annihilated. The victor gained nothing by his victory, in comparison with the profit acquired by the states through their common misfortune. Nor were all the towns

* Bor, xii. 934, sqq. Hoofd, xiii. 551. Meteren, viii. 133. Strada, ix. 473. —"Alexander *omissa intempestira benignitate*," says the professed panegyrist of the Farnese family—"ex ipsa arce decem palam suspendi, reliquos (centum circiter ac septuaginta) noctu jugulatos in subjectum amnem projici jubet."

† Reidani Ann., ii. 22. "Ne quidem habuisse rationem Archiducis Matthiæ sed Orangius eum (populum) subtraxit periculo."—Languet, Ep. Secr. I., ii. p. 347. Bor, xii. 935. Languet ad Sydn., p. 314. 317, 329.

which had recently fallen into the hands of Don John at all comparable in importance to the city of Amsterdam, which now, by a most timely arrangement, furnished a rich compensation to the national party for the disaster of Gemblours.

Since the conclusion of the Ghent Pacification, it had been the most earnest wish of the Prince, and of Holland and Zealand, to recover possession of this most important city. The wish was naturally shared by every true patriot in the states-general. It had, however, been extremely difficult to arrange the terms of the "Satisfaction." Every fresh attempt at an amicable compromise was wrecked upon the obstinate bigotry of the leading civic authorities. They would make no agreement to accept the authority of Orange, except, as Saint Aldegonde expressed himself, upon terms which would enable them "to govern their governor."* The influence of the monks, who were resident in large numbers within the city, and of the magistrates, who were all stanch Catholics, had been hitherto sufficient to outweigh the efforts made by the large masses of the Reformed religionists composing the bulk of the population. It was, however, impossible to allow Amsterdam to remain in this isolated and hostile attitude to the rest of Holland. The Prince, having promised to use no coercion, and loyally adhering to his pledge, had only with extreme difficulty restrained the violence of the Hollanders and Zealanders, who were determined, by fair means or foul, to restore the capital city to its natural place within his stadholderate. He had been obliged, on various occasions, particularly on the 21st of October of the preceding year, to address a most decided and peremptory letter to the estates of Holland and Zealand, forbidding the employment of hostile measures against Amsterdam.† His commands had been reluctantly, partially, and only temporarily obeyed. The states desisted from their scheme of reducing the city by famine, but they did not the less encourage the secret and

* Archives et Correspondance, vi. 117.

† Bor, xi. 897, 898.

unofficial expeditions which were daily set on foot to accomplish the annexation by a sudden enterprise.

Late in November, a desperate attempt* had been made by Colonel Helling, in conjunction with Governor Sonoy, to carry the city by surprise. The force which the adventurer collected for the purpose was inadequate, and his plans were unskilfully arranged. He was himself slain in the streets, at the very commencement of the action; whereupon, in the quaint language of the contemporary chronicler, "the hearts of his soldiers sank in their shoes," and they evacuated the city with much greater rapidity than they had entered it.† The Prince was indignant at these violent measures, which retarded rather than advanced the desired consummation. At the same time it was an evil of immense magnitude—this anomalous condition of his capital. Ceaseless schemes were concerted by the municipal and clerical conspirators within its walls, and various attempts were known, at different times, to have been contemplated by Don John, to inflict a home-thrust upon the provinces of Holland and Zealand at the most vulnerable and vital point. The "Satisfaction" accepted by Utrecht,‡ in the autumn of 1577, had, however, paved the way for the recovery of Amsterdam; so that upon February the 8th, 1578, certain deputies from Utrecht succeeded at last in arranging terms, which were accepted by the sister city.§ The basis of the treaty was, as usual, the nominal supremacy of the Catholic religion, with toleration for the Reformed worship. The necessary effect would be, as in Harlem, Utrecht, and other places, to establish the new religion upon an entire equality with the old. It was arranged that no congregations were to be disturbed in their religious exercises in the places respectively assigned to them. Those of the

---

* Bor, xi. 906–908.

† "En het hert sonk de soldaaden in de schoen; so men seid," etc.—Bor, xi. 908ᵃ. Hoofd, xii. 537, 538.

‡ Bor, xi. 893–896.

§ The twenty-four articles of the "Satisfactie" are given at length in Bor, xi. 924–926.

Reformed faith were to celebrate their worship without the walls. They were, however, to enjoy the right of burying their dead within these precincts, and it is singular how much importance was attached at that day to a custom, at which the common sentiment and the common sense of modern times revolt. "To bury our dead within our own cities is a right hardly to be denied to a dog," said the Prince of Orange;* and accordingly this right was amply secured by the new Satisfaction of Amsterdam. It was, however, stipulated that the funerals should be modest, and attended by no more than twenty-four persons at once.† The treaty was hailed with boundless joy in Holland and Zealand, while countless benedictions were invoked upon the "blessed peace-makers," as the Utrecht deputies walked through the streets of Amsterdam.‡ There is no doubt that the triumph thus achieved by the national party far counterbalanced the Governor-General's victory at Gemblours.

Meantime, the Seigneur de Selles, brother of the deceased Noircarmes, had arrived from Spain.§ He was the special bearer of a letter from the King to the states-general, written in reply to their communications of the 24th of August and 8th of September of the previous year. The tone of the royal despatch ‖ was very affectionate, the substance such as entirely to justify the whole policy of Orange. It was obvious that the penetrating and steadfast statesman had been correct in refusing to be moved to the right or the left by the specious language of Philip's former letters, or by the apparent frankness of Don John. No doubt the Governor had been sincere in his desire for peace, but the Prince knew very well his incapacity to confer that blessing. The Prince knew—what no man else appeared fully to comprehend at that epoch—that the mortal combat between the Inquisition and the Reformation

---

* Bor, xi. 810ª,—"——die men schier den honden niet en soude konnen ontseggen," etc., etc.

† Satisfactie, in Bor, xii. 924, 926, Art. 1; also Hoofd, xiii. 554–558.

‡ Bor, xii. 926.

§ Bor, xii. 938. Hoofd, xiii. 558.

‖ See the letter in Bor, xii. 938.

was already fully engaged. The great battle between divine reason and right divine, on which the interests of unborn generations were hanging, was to be fought out, before the eyes of all Christendom, on the plain of the Netherlands.

Orange was willing to lay down his arms if he could receive security for the Reformed worship. He had no desire to exterminate the ancient religion, but he meant also to protect the new against extermination. Such security, he felt, would never be granted, and he had therefore resolutely refused to hearken to Don John, for he was sure that peace with him was impossible. The letters now produced by De Selles confirmed his positions completely. The King said not a word concerning the appointment of a new governor-general, but boldly insisted upon the necessity of maintaining the two cardinal points—his royal supremacy, and the Catholic religion *upon the basis adopted by his father*, the Emperor Charles the Fifth.*

This was the whole substance of his communication : the supremacy of royalty and of papacy as in the time of Charles the Fifth. These cabalistic words were repeated twice in the brief letter to the estates. They were repeated five times in the instructions furnished by his Majesty to De Selles.† The letter and the instructions indeed contained nothing else. Two simples were offered for the cure of the body politic, racked by the fever and convulsion of ten horrible years—two simples which the patient could hardly be so unreasonable as to reject—unlimited despotism and religious persecution. The whole matter lay in a nut-shell, but it was a nut-shell which enclosed the flaming edicts of Charles the Fifth, with their scaffolds, gibbets, racks, and funeral piles. The Prince and the states-general spurned such pacific overtures, and preferred rather to gird themselves for the combat.

That there might be no mistake about the matter, Don

---

* Letter of the King, December 18, 1577, in Bor, xii. 938.

† The instructions are likewise in Bor, xii. 939.

John, immediately after receiving the letter, issued a proclamation to enforce the King's command. He mentioned it as an acknowledged fact that the states-general had long ago sworn the maintenance of the two points of royal and Catholic supremacy, according to the practice under the Emperor Charles.* The states instantly published an indignant rejoinder, affirming the indisputable truth, that they had sworn to the maintenance of the Ghent Pacification, and proclaiming the assertion of Don John an infamous falsehood. It was an outrage upon common sense, they said, that the Ghent treaty could be tortured into sanctioning the placards and the Inquisition, evils which that sacred instrument had been expressly intended to crush.†

A letter was then formally addressed to his Majesty, in the name of the Archduke Matthias and of the estates, demanding the recal of Don John and the maintenance of the Ghent Pacification.‡ De Selles, in reply, sent a brief, deprecatory paper, enclosing a note from Don John, which the envoy acknowledged might seem somewhat harsh in its expressions. The letter contained, indeed, a sufficiently fierce and peremptory summons to the states to obey the King's commands with regard to the system of Charles the Fifth, according to their previous agreement, together with a violent declaration of the Governor's displeasure that they had dared to solicit the aid of foreign princes.§ On the 18th of February came a proposition from De Selles that the Prince of Orange should place himself in the hands of Don John, while the Prince of Parma, alone and without arms, would come before the assembly, to negotiate with them upon these matters.‖ The reply returned by the states-general to this absurd suggestion expressed their regret that the son of the Duchess Margaret should have taken part with the enemy of the Netherlanders, complained of the bull by which the Pope had invited war against them as if they had been Saracens, re-

* Proclamation, or Letters Patent, in Bor, xii. 940.

† Bor, xii. 939, 940.

‡ In Bor, xii. 940.

§ Bor, xii. 940, 941.

‖ In Bor, xii. 942.

peated their most unanswerable argument—that the Ghent Pacification had established a system directly the reverse of that which existed under Charles the Fifth—and affirmed their resolution never more to submit to Spanish armies, executioners, edicts, or inquisitions, and never more to return to the principles of the Emperor and of Alva.* To this diplomatic correspondence succeeded a war of words and of pamphlets, some of them very inflammatory and very eloquent. Meantime, the preparations for active hostilities were proceeding daily. The Prince of Orange, through his envoys in England, had arranged for subsidies in the coming campaign, and for troops which were to be led to the Netherlands, under Duke Casimir of the palatinate. He sent commissioners through the provinces to raise the respective contributions agreed upon, besides an extraordinary quota of four hundred thousand guilders monthly. He also negotiated a loan of a hundred and twenty thousand guilders from the citizens of Antwerp. Many new taxes were imposed by his direction, both upon income and upon consumption. By his advice, however, and with the consent of the states-general, the provinces of Holland and Zealand held no community of burthens with the other provinces, but of their own free will contributed more than the sums for which they would have been assessed. Mr. Leyton, who was about to return from his unsuccessful mission from Elizabeth to Don John, was requested by the states-general to convey to her Majesty a faithful report of the recent correspondence, and especially of the language held by the Governor-General. He was also urged to use his influence with the Queen, to the end that her promises of assistance might be speedily fulfilled.†

Troops were rapidly enrolled, and again, by the same honest but mistaken policy, the chief offices were conferred upon the great nobles—Aerschot, Champagny, Bossu, Egmont, Lalain, the Viscount of Ghent, Baron de Ville, and many others,

* Letter of states-general, Feb. 28, 1578, in Bor, xii. 942, sqq.

† Bor, xii. 948, 949.

most of whom were to desert the cause in the hour of its need. On the other hand, Don John was proceeding with his military preparations upon an extensive scale. The King had recently furnished him with one million nine hundred thousand dollars, and had promised to provide him with two hundred thousand more, monthly. With these funds his Majesty estimated that an army of thirty thousand foot, sixteen thousand cavalry, and thirty pieces of artillery, could be levied and kept on foot. If more remittances should prove to be necessary, it was promised that they should be forthcoming.*

This was the result of many earnest remonstrances made by the Governor concerning the dilatory policy of the King. Wearied with being constantly ordered "to blow hot and cold with the same breath,"† he had insisted that his Majesty should select the hot or the cold, and furnish him with the means of enforcing the choice. For himself, Don John assured his brother that the hottest measures were most to his taste, and most suitable to the occasion. Fire and sword could alone save the royal authority, for all the provinces had "abandoned themselves, body and soul, to the greatest heretic and tyrant that prince ever had for vassal."‡ Unceasing had been the complaints and entreaties of the Captain-General, called forth by the apathy or irresolution of Philip. It was only by assuring him that the Netherlands actually belonged to Orange, that the monarch could be aroused. "His they are, and none other's,"§ said the Governor, dolefully. The King had accordingly sent back De Billy, Don John's envoy, with decided injunctions to use force and energy to put down the revolt at once, and with an intimation that funds might be thenceforth more regularly depended upon, as the Indian fleets

* Letter of Philip, in Cabrera, xii. 978.

† "Sin encargar me que soplo frio y caliente, porque no lo comporta el negocio, sino que bien lo uno ó lo otro," etc., etc.—Carta del S. D. Juan al Rey, mano propria, MS. Bib. de Bourg., N°. xvii. 385.

‡ "Estas gentes sean dado y entregado ya de todo punto a la obediencia y sucesion del mayor herese y tiranno que truvo nunca principe por vasallo."—Ibid.

§ "—— Solamente del P. de Oranxes, que suyas son y no de otro," etc.—Ibid.

were expected in July. Philip also advised his brother to employ a portion of his money in purchasing the governors and principal persons who controlled the cities and other strong places belonging to the states.*

Meantime, Don John thundered forth a manifesto which had been recently prepared in Madrid, by which the estates, both general and particular, were ordered forthwith to separate, and forbidden to assemble again, except by especial licence. All commissions, civil or military, granted by states' authority, were moreover annulled, together with a general prohibition of any act of obedience to such functionaries, and of contribution to any imposts which might be levied by their authority.† Such thunders were now comparatively harmless, for the states had taken their course, and were busily engaged, both at home and abroad, in arming for the conflict. Saint Aldegonde was deputed to attend the Imperial diet, then in session at Worms, where he delivered an oration, which was very celebrated in its day as a composition, but which can hardly be said to have produced much practical effect. The current was setting hard in Germany against the Reformed religion and against the Netherland cause, the Augsburg Confessionists showing hardly more sympathy with Dutch Calvinists than with Spanish Papists.‡

Envoys from Don John also attended the diet, and requested Saint Aldegonde to furnish them with a copy of his oration. This he declined to do. While in Germany, Saint Aldegonde was informed by John Casimir that Duke Charles of Sweden had been solicited to furnish certain ships of war for a contemplated operation against Amsterdam.§ The Duke had himself given information of this plot to the Prince Palatine. It was therefore natural that Saint Aldegonde should forthwith despatch the intelligence to his friends in the Nether-

* Letter of Don John, MS. Bib. de Bourg.—Compare Cabrera, xii. 978.

† Proclamation in Bor, xii. 946, 947.—Compare Cabrera, xii. 978, 979; Hoofd, xii. 560.

‡ Bor, xii. 953–960.

§ Bor, xii. 952. Hoofd, xiii. 565.

lands, warning them of the dangers still to be apprehended from the machinations of the Catholic agents and functionaries in Amsterdam; for although the Reformation had made rapid progress in that important city since the conclusion of the Satisfaction, yet the magistracy remained Catholic.*

William Bardez, son of a former high-sheriff, a warm partisan of Orange and of the "religion," had already determined to overthrow that magistracy and to expel the friars who infested the city. The recent information despatched by Saint Aldegonde confirmed him in his purpose. There had been much wrangling between the Popish functionaries and those of the Reformed religion concerning the constitution of the burgher guard. The Calvinists could feel no security for their own lives, or the repose of the commonwealth of Holland, unless they were themselves allowed a full participation in the government of those important bands. They were, moreover, dissatisfied with the assignment which had been made of the churchyards to the members of their communion. These causes of discord had maintained a general irritation among the body of the inhabitants, and were now used as pretexts by Bardez for his design. He knew the city to be ripe for the overthrow of the magistracy, and he had arranged with Governor Sonoy to be furnished with a sufficient number of well-tried soldiers, who were to be concealed in the houses of the confederates. A large number of citizens were also ready to appear at his bidding with arms in their hands.†

On the 24th of May, he wrote to Sonoy, begging him to hold himself in readiness, as all was prepared within the city. At the same time, he requested the governor to send him forthwith a "morion and a buckler of proof;" for he intended to see the matter fairly through.‡ Sonoy answered encouragingly, and sent him the armor, as directed. On the 28th of May, Bardez, with four confederates, went to the council-room,

* Bor, xii. 952.

† Ibid., xii. 953. Hoofd, xiii. 569. Wagenaer, Vad. Hist., vii. 205.

‡ Bor, xii. 953. Hoofd, xiii. 570.

to remonstrate with the senate concerning the grievances which had been so often discussed. At about mid-day, one of the confederates, upon leaving the council-room, stepped out for a moment upon the balcony, which looked towards the public square. Standing there for a moment, he gravely removed his hat, and then as gravely replaced it upon his head. This was a preconcerted signal. At the next instant a sailor was seen to rush across the square, waving a flag in both hands. "All ye who love the Prince of Orange, take heart and follow me!" he shouted.* In a moment the square was alive. Soldiers and armed citizens suddenly sprang forth, as if from the bowels of the earth. Bardez led a strong force directly into the council-chamber, and arrested every one of the astonished magistrates. At the same time, his confederates had scoured the town and taken every friar in the city into custody. Monks and senators were then marched solemnly down towards the quay, where a vessel was in readiness to receive them. "To the gallows with them—to the gallows with them!" shouted the populace, as they passed along. "To the gibbet, whither they have brought many a good fellow before his time!" Such were the openly expressed desires of their fellow-citizens, as these dignitaries and holy men proceeded to what they believed their doom. Although treated respectfully by those who guarded them, they were filled with trepidation, for they believed the execrations of the populace the harbingers of their fate. As they entered the vessel, they felt convinced that a watery death had been substituted for the gibbet. Poor old Heinrich Dirckzoon, ex-burgomaster, pathetically rejected a couple of clean shirts which his careful wife had sent him by the hands of the housemaid. "Take them away; take them home again," said the rueful burgomaster; "I shall never need clean shirts again in this world."† He entertained no doubt that it was the intention of his captors to scuttle the vessel as

* Hoofd, xiii. 571. Wagenaer, vii. 206.

† Wagenaer, vii, 207.

soon as they had put a little out to sea, and so to leave them to their fate. No such tragic end was contemplated, however, and, in fact, never was a complete municipal revolution accomplished in so good-natured and jocose a manner. The Catholic magistrates and friars escaped with their fright. They were simply turned out of town, and forbidden, for their lives, ever to come back again. After the vessel had proceeded a little distance from the city, they were all landed high and dry upon a dyke, and so left unharmed within the open country.*

A new board of magistrates, of which stout William Bardez was one, was soon appointed; the train-bands were reorganized, and the churches thrown open to the Reformed worship—to the exclusion, at first, of the Catholics. This was certainly contrary to the Ghent treaty, and to the recent Satisfaction; it was also highly repugnant to the opinions of Orange. After a short time, accordingly, the Catholics were again allowed access to the churches, but the tables had now been turned for ever in the capital of Holland, and the Reformation was an established fact throughout that little province.

Similar events occurring upon the following day at Harlem, accompanied with some bloodshed—for which, however, the perpetrator was punished with death—opened the great church of that city to the Reformed congregations, and closed them for a time to the Catholics.†

Thus, the cause of the new religion was triumphant in Holland and Zealand, while it was advancing with rapid strides through the other provinces. Public preaching was of daily occurrence everywhere. On a single Sunday, fifteen different ministers of the Reformed religion preached in different places in Antwerp.‡ "Do you think this can be put down?" said Orange to the remonstrating burgomaster of that city. "'Tis for you to repress it," said the functionary, "I grant your Highness full power to do so." "And do you think," replied

* Hoofd, xiii. 571. Bor, xii. 953. Wagenaer, vii. 207.

† Bor, xii. 953. Hoofd, xiii. 572. Wagenaer, vii. 209, 210,

‡ Bor, Hoofd, ubi sup.

the Prince, "that I can do at this late moment, what the Duke of Alva was unable to accomplish in the very plenitude of his power?"* At the same time, the Prince of Orange was more than ever disposed to rebuke his own Church for practising persecution in her turn. Again he lifted his commanding voice in behalf of the Anabaptists of Middelburg. He reminded the magistrates of that city that these peaceful burghers were always perfectly willing to bear their part in all the common burthens, that their word was as good as their oath, and that as to the matter of military service, although their principles forbade them to bear arms, they had ever been ready to provide and pay for substitutes. "We declare to you therefore," said he, "that you have no right to trouble yourselves with any man's conscience, so long as nothing is done to cause private harm or public scandal. We therefore expressly ordain that you desist from molesting these Baptists, from offering hindrance to their handicraft and daily trade, by which they can earn bread for their wives and children, and that you permit them henceforth to open their shops and to do their work, according to the custom of former days. Beware, therefore, of disobedience and of resistance to the ordinance which we now establish."†

Meantime, the armies on both sides had been assembled, and had been moving towards each other. Don John was at the head of nearly thirty thousand troops, including a large proportion of Spanish and Italian veterans.‡ The states' army hardly numbered eighteen thousand foot and two thousand cavalry, under the famous François de la Noue, surnamed *Bras de Fer*, who had been recently appointed *Maréchal de Camp*, and, under Count Bossu, commander-in-chief.§ The

---

* Langueti, Ep. ad Aug. Sax., ep. 147, p. 744.

† This letter of the Prince to the Calvinist authorities of Middelburg is given by Bor, xii. 993, and by Brandt, Hist. der Ref., i. 609, 610.

‡ Bor, xii. 987. Meteren, viii. 140. Strada, Bentivoglio, and others allow only sixteen or seventeen thousand men.—Compare Hoofd, xiii. 581.

§ Hoofd, xiii. 581.

muster-place of the provincial forces was in the plains between Herenthals and Lier. At this point they expected to be reinforced by Duke Casimir, who had been, since the early part of the summer, in the country of Zutfen, but who was still remaining there inglorious and inactive, until he could be furnished with the requisite advance-money to his troops.*

Don John was determined if possible, to defeat the states' army, before Duke Casimir, with his twelve thousand Germans, should effect his juncture with Bossu. The Governor therefore crossed the Demer, near Aerschot, towards the end of July, and offered battle, day after day, to the enemy. A series of indecisive skirmishes was the result, in the last of which, near Rijnemants, on the first day of August, the royalists were worsted and obliged to retire, after a desultory action of nearly eight hours, leaving a thousand dead upon the field.† Their offer of "double or quits," the following morning was steadily refused by Bossu, who, secure within his intrenchments, was not to be induced at that moment to encounter the chances of a general engagement. For this he was severely blamed by the more violent of the national party.‡ His patriotism, which was of such recent origin, was vehemently suspected; and his death, which occurred not long afterwards, was supposed to have alone prevented his deserting the states to fight again under Spanish colours. These suspicions were probably unjust. Bossu's truth of character had been as universally recognized as was his signal bravery. If

* Hoofd, xiii. 581. Bor, xii. 987. Strada, x. 491.

† Bor, xii. 987. Meteren, viii. 140. Hoofd, xiii. 583.—The Spaniards, however, only allow twenty killed and fifty wounded.—Compare Hoofd, ubi sup. Not the least picturesque feature in this celebrated action is one reported by Strada. The heat of the day was so oppressive that a band of Scotch veterans under Robert Stuart thought it more comfortable to strip themselves to their shirts; and, at last, as the weather and the skirmish grew hotter, to lay aside even those integuments, and to fight all day long, in the costume of ancient Picts.—Strada, x. 497. The date of the battle in Strada, and in Bentivoglio, x. 213, is the first of August. The same date is given by Hoofd. Bor says 31st of July.

‡ Bor, xii. 987. Hoofd. xiii. 584.

he refused upon this occasion a general battle, those who reflected upon the usual results to the patriot banner of such engagements, might confess, perhaps, that one disaster the more had been avoided. Don John, finding it impossible to accomplish his purpose, and to achieve another Gemblours victory, fell back again to the neighbourhood of Namur.*

The states' forces remained waiting for the long-promised succor of John Casimir. It was the 26th of August, however, before the Duke led his twelve thousand men to the neighbourhood of Mechlin, where Bossu was encamped.† This young prince possessed neither the ability nor the generosity which were requisite for the heroic part which he was ambitious to perform in the Netherland drama. He was inspired by a vague idea of personal aggrandizement, although he professed at the same time the utmost deference to William of Orange. He expressed the hope that he and the Prince "should be but two heads under one hat;"‡ but he would have done well to ask himself whether his own contribution to this partnership of brains would very much enrich the silent statesman. Orange himself regarded him with respectful contempt, and considered his interference with Netherland matters but as an additional element of mischief. The Duke's right hand man, however, Peter Peutterich, the "equestrian doctor"—as Sir Philip Sydney called him—equally skilful with the sword as with the pen, had succeeded, while on a mission to England, in acquiring the Queen's favor for his master.§ To Casimir, therefore, had been entrusted the command of the levies, and the principal expenditure of the subsidies which she had placed at the disposition of the states. Upon Casimir she relied, as a counterweight to the Duke of Alençon, who, as she knew, had already entered the provinces at the secret solicitation of a large faction among the nobles. She had as much confidence as ever in Orange, but she imagined herself to be strengthening his cause by providing him with such a

* Bor, xii. 987. Hoofd, xiii. 584.

† Bor, xii. 997.

‡ Archives de la Maison d'Orange, vi. 377.

§ Groen v. Prinst., Archives, etc., vi. 376, 377, note 1.

lieutenant. Casimir's immediate friends had but little respect for his abilities. His father-in-law, Augustus of Saxony, did not approve his expedition. The Landgrave William, to whom he wrote for counsel, answered, in his quaint manner, that it was always difficult for one friend to advise another in three matters—to wit, in taking a wife, going to sea, and going to war; but that, nevertheless, despite the ancient proverb, he would assume the responsibility of warning Casimir not to plunge into what he was pleased to call the "*confusum chaos* of Netherland politics." The Duke felt no inclination, however, to take the advice which he had solicited. He had been stung by the sarcasm which Alva had once uttered, that the German potentates carried plenty of lions, dragons, eagles, and griffins on their shields; but that these ferocious animals were not given to biting or scratching. He was therefore disposed, once for all, to show that the teeth and claws of German princes could still be dangerous. Unfortunately, he was destined to add a fresh element of confusion to the chaos, and to furnish rather a proof than a refutation of the correctness of Alva's gibe.*

This was the hero who was now thrust, head and shoulders as it were, into the entangled affairs of the Netherlanders, and it was Elizabeth of England, more than ever alarmed at the schemes of Alençon, who had pushed forward this Protestant champion, notwithstanding the disinclination of Orange.

The Queen was right in her uneasiness respecting the French prince. The Catholic nobles, relying upon the strong feeling still rife throughout the Walloon country against the Reformed religion, and inflamed more than ever by their repugnance to Orange, whose genius threw them so completely

---

* Meteren, viii. 140. Hoofd, xiii. 584. Groen v. Prinst., Archives, etc., vi. 375, note. "Dann, zu weib nehmen, über mehr schiffen, undt zum Kriege, kein freundt dem andern, dem gemeynen Sprichwortt nach, rathen," etc.—Letter of Landgrave William, Archives de la Maison d'Orange, vi. 317. He adds that the Netherlanders were a wild, godless, and irresponsible crew, neither attached to the true religion, nor having any real regard for the Prince, etc., etc.—Ibid. See also Archives et Correspondance, vi. 300 and 427.

into the shade, had already drawn closer to the Duke. The same influences were at work to introduce Alençon, which had formerly been employed to bring Matthias from Vienna. Now that the Archduke, who was to have been the rival, had become the dependent of William, they turned their attention to the son of Catherine de' Medici, Orange himself having always kept the Duke in reserve, as an instrument to overcome the political coquetry of Elizabeth. That great Princess never manifested less greatness than in her earlier and most tormenting connexion with the Netherlands. Having allured them for years with bright but changeful face, she still looked coldly down upon the desolate sea where they were drifting. She had promised much ; her performance had been nothing. Her jealousy of French influence had at length been turned to account ; a subsidy and a levy extorted from her fears. Her ministers and prominent advisers were one and all in favor of an open and generous support to the provinces. Walsingham, Burleigh, Knollys, Davidson, Sidney, Leicester, Fleetwood, Wilson, all desired that she should frankly espouse their cause. A bold policy they believed to be the only prudent one in this case ; yet the Queen considered it sagacious to despatch envoys both to Philip and to Don John, as if after what they knew of her secret practices, such missions could effect any useful purpose. Better, therefore, in the opinion of the honest and intrepid statesmen of England, to throw down the gauntlet at once in the cause of the oppressed than to shuffle and palter until the dreaded rival should cross the frontier. A French Netherlands they considered even more dangerous than a Spanish, and Elizabeth partook of their sentiments, although incapable of their promptness. With the perverseness which was the chief blot upon her character, she was pleased that the Duke should be still a dangler for her hand, even while she was intriguing against his political hopes.* She listened with undisguised rapture to his propo-

* See, for example, a letter from Sir Amias Paulet to the Earl of Leicester, in Groen v. Prinst., vi. 421–423.

sals of love, while she was secretly thwarting the plans of his ambition.

Meanwhile, Alençon had arrived at Mons, and we have seen already the feminine adroitness with which his sister of Navarre had prepared his entrance. Not in vain had she cajoled the commandant of Cambray citadel ; not idly had she led captive the hearts of Lalain and his Countess, thus securing the important province of Hainault for the Duke. Don John might, indeed, gnash his teeth with rage, as he marked the result of all the feasting and flattery, the piping and dancing at Namur.

Francis Duke of Alençon, and—since the accession of his brother Henry to the French throne—Duke of Anjou was, upon the whole, the most despicable personage who had ever entered the Netherlands. His previous career at home had been so flagrantly false that he had forfeited the esteem of every honest man in Europe, Catholic or Lutheran, Huguenot or Malcontent. The world has long known his character. History will always retain him as an example, to show mankind the amount of mischief which may be perpetrated by a prince, ferocious without courage, ambitious without talent, and bigoted without opinions. Incapable of religious convictions himself, he had alternately aspired to be a commander of Catholic and of Huguenot zealots, and he had acquired nothing by his vacillating course, save the entire contempt of all parties and of both religions. Scared from the side of Navarre and Condé by the menacing attitude of the "league," fearing to forfeit the succession to the throne, unless he made his peace with the court, he had recently resumed his place among the Catholic commanders. Nothing was easier for him than to return shamelessly to a party which he had shamelessly deserted, save perhaps to betray it again, should his interest prompt him to do so, on the morrow. Since the peace of 1576, it had been evident that the Protestants could not count upon his friendship, and he had soon afterwards been placed at the head of the army which was besieging the Huguenots of

Issoire.* He sought to atone for having commanded the troops of the new religion by the barbarity with which he now persecuted its votaries. When Issoire fell into his hands, the luckless city was spared none of the misery which can be inflicted by a brutal and frenzied soldiery. Its men were butchered, its females outraged, its property plundered with a thoroughness which rivalled the Netherland practice of Alva, or Frederic Toledo, or Julian Romero. The town was sacked and burned to ashes by furious Catholics, under the command of Francis Alençon, almost at the very moment when his fair sister, Margaret, was preparing the way in the Netherlands for the fresh treason† which he already meditated to the Catholic cause. The treaty of Bergerac, signed in the autumn of 1577,‡ again restored a semblance of repose to France, and again afforded an opportunity for Alençon to change his politics, and what he called his religion. Reeking with the blood of the Protestants of Issoire, he was now at leisure to renew his dalliance with the Queen of Protestant England, and to resume his correspondence with the great chieftain of the Reformation in the Netherlands.

It is perhaps an impeachment upon the perspicacity of Orange, that he could tolerate this mischievous and worthless "son of France," even for the grave reasons which influenced him. Nevertheless, it must be remembered that he only intended to keep him in reserve, for the purpose of irritating the jealousy and quickening the friendship of the English Queen. Those who see anything tortuous in such politics must beware of judging the intriguing age of Philip and Catherine de' Medici by the higher standard of later, and possibly more candid times. It would have been puerile for a man of William the Silent's resources, to allow himself to be outwitted by the intrigues of all the courts and cabinets in Europe. Moreover, it must be remembered that, if he alone could guide himself and his country through the

* De Thou, vii. liv. lxiii. Mémoires de Marg. de Valois, liv. ii.

† But three men were spared, according to de Thou, vii. 502, liv. lxiii.

‡ De Thou, vii. 529, liv. lxiv.

perplexing labyrinth in which they were involved, it was because he held in his hand the clue of an honest purpose. His position in regard to the Duke of Alençon, had now become sufficiently complicated, for the tiger that he had led in a chain had been secretly unloosed by those who meant mischief. In the autumn of the previous year, the aristocratic and Catholic party in the states-general had opened their communications with a prince, by whom they hoped to be indemnified for their previous defeat.

The ill effects of Elizabeth's coquetry too plainly manifested themselves at last, and Alençon had now a foothold in the Netherlands. Precipitated by the intrigues of the party which had always been either openly or secretly hostile to Orange, his advent could no longer be delayed. It only remained for the Prince to make himself his master, as he had already subdued each previous rival. This he accomplished with his customary adroitness. It was soon obvious, even to so dull and so base a nature as that of the Duke, that it was his best policy to continue to cultivate so powerful a friendship. It cost him little to crouch, but events were fatally to prove at a later day, that there are natures too malignant to be trusted or to be tamed. For the present, however, Alençon professed the most friendly sentiments towards the Prince. Solicited by so ardent and considerable a faction, the Duke was no longer to be withheld from trying the venture,* and if he could not effect his entrance by fair means, was determined to do so by force.† He would obtrude his assistance, if it were declined. He would do his best to dismember the provinces, if only a portion of them would accept his proffered friendship. Under these circumstances, as the Prince could no longer exclude him from the country, it became necessary to accept his friendship, and to hold him in control. The Duke had formally offered his assistance to the states-general, di-

---

* See the remarks and citations of Groen v. Prinst., Archives, etc., vi. pp. 364–370.—Compare Apologie d'Orange, p. 107, and Bor, xii. 975.

† Rés. MSS. des Es. Gx., in Groen v. Prinst. vi. 370.

rectly after the defeat of Gemblours,* and early in July had made his appearance in Mons. Hence he despatched his envoys, Des Pruneaux and Rochefort, to deal with the states-general and with Orange, while he treated Matthias with contempt, and declared that he had no intention to negotiate with him. The Archduke burst into tears when informed of this slight, and feebly expressed a wish that succor might be found in Germany which would render this French alliance unnecessary. It was not the first nor the last mortification which the future Emperor was to undergo. The Prince was addressed with distinguished consideration; Des Pruneaux protesting that he desired but three things—the glory of his master, the glory of God, and the glory of William of Orange.†

The French King was naturally supposed to be privy to his brother's schemes, for it was thought ridiculous to suggest that Henry's own troops could be led by his own brother, on this foreign expedition, without his connivance.‡ At the same time, private letters, written by him at this epoch, expressed disapprobation of the schemes of Alençon, and jealousy of his aggrandizement. It was, perhaps, difficult to decide as to the precise views of a monarch who was too weak to form opinions for himself, and too false to maintain those with which he had been furnished by others. With the Medicean mother it was different, and it was she who was believed to be at the bottom of the intrigue. There was even a vague idea that the Spanish Sovereign himself might be privy to the plot, and that a possible marriage between Alençon and the Infanta might be on the cards.§ In truth, however, Philip felt himself outraged by the whole proceedings. He resolutely refused to accept the excuses proffered by the French court, or to doubt the complicity of the Queen Dowager, who, it was well known,

---

* Meteren, viii. 140ᵃ. Bor, xii. 950.

† Archives et Correspondance, vi. 404, sqq. Letter of Des Pruneaux, in Archives de la Maison d'Orange, vi. 399.

‡ This was Granvelle's opinion. See letter from Granvelle to Bellefontaine, Archives de la Maison d'Orange, vi. 426.

§ Remarks and citations of Groen v. Prinst., vi. 368, 424–427.—Compare De Thou, vii. 698.

governed all her sons. She had, to be sure, thought proper to read the envoys of the states-general a lecture upon the impropriety of subjects opposing the commands of their lawful Prince, but such artifices were thought too transparent to deceive. Granvelle scouted the idea of her being ignorant of Anjou's scheme, or opposed to its success.* As for William of Hesse, while he bewailed more than ever the luckless plunge into "*confusum chaos*" which Casimir had taken, he unhesitatingly expressed his conviction that the invasion of Alençon was a master-piece of Catherine. The whole responsibility of the transaction he divided, in truth, between the Dowager and the comet, which just then hung over the world, filling the soul of the excellent Landgrave with dismal apprehension.†

The Queen of England was highly incensed by the actual occurrence of the invasion which she had so long dreaded. She was loud in her denunciations of the danger and dishonor which would be the result to the provinces of this French alliance. She threatened not only to withdraw herself from their cause, but even to take arms against a commonwealth which had dared to accept Alençon for its master. She had originally agreed to furnish one hundred thousand pounds by way of loan. This assistance had been afterwards commuted into a levy of three thousand foot and two thousand horse, to be added to the forces of John Casimir, and to be placed under his command. It had been stipulated, also, that the Palatine should have the rank and pay of an English general-in-chief, and be considered as the Queen's lieutenant. The money had been furnished and the troops enrolled. So much had been already bestowed, and could not be recalled, but it was not probable that, in her present humor, the Queen would be induced to add to her favors.‡

---

* Letter of Granvelle to Bellefontaine.

† "—— Summa, der comett und die grosse *prodigia* so diesz jahr gesehenn wordenn, wollen ihre wirckung haben. Gott gebe dasz sie zu eynem guten ende lauffen."—Archives et Corresp., vi. 140—Compare Strada, ix. 463.

‡ Bor, xii. 948, 949, 975, sqq.—Compare Meteren, viii. 140.

The Prince, obliged by the necessity of the case, had prescribed the terms and the title under which Alençon should be accepted. Upon the 13th of August the Duke's envoy concluded a convention in twenty-three articles, which were afterwards subscribed by the Duke himself, at Mons, upon the twentieth of the same month.* The substance of this arrangement was that Alençon should lend his assistance to the provinces against the intolerable tyranny of the Spaniards and the unjustifiable military invasion of Don John. He was, moreover, to bring into the field ten thousand foot and two thousand horse for three months. After the expiration of this term, his forces might be reduced to three thousand foot and five hundred horse. The states were to confer upon him the title of "Defender of the Liberty of the Netherlands against the Tyranny of the Spaniards and their adherents." He was to undertake no hostilities against Queen Elizabeth. The states were to aid him, whenever it should become necessary, with the same amount of force with which he now assisted them. He was to submit himself contentedly to the civil government of the country, in everything regarding its internal polity. He was to make no special contracts or treaties with any cities or provinces of the Netherlands. Should the states-general accept another prince as sovereign, the Duke was to be preferred to all others, upon conditions afterwards to be arranged. All cities which might be conquered within the territory of the united provinces were to belong to the states. Such places not in that territory, as should voluntarily surrender, were to be apportioned, by equal division, between the Duke and the states. The Duke was to bring no foreign troops but French into the provinces. The month of August was reserved, during which the states were, if possible, to make a composition with Don John.†

These articles were certainly drawn up with skill. A high-sounding but barren title, which gratified the Duke's vanity

* Bor, xii. 976–978. Meteren, viii. 140, 141.

† See especially Articles 4, 5, 10, 14, 15, 16, 21.

and signified nothing, had been conferred upon him, while at the same time he was forbidden to make conquests or contracts, and was obliged to submit himself to the civil government of the country: in short, he was to obey the Prince of Orange in all things—and so here was another plot of the Prince's enemies neutralized. Thus, for the present at least, had the position of Anjou been defined.

As the month of August, during which it was agreed* that negotiations with the Governor-General should remain open, had already half expired, certain articles, drawn up by the states-general, were at once laid before Don John. Lord Cobham and Sir Francis Walsingham were then in the Netherlands, having been sent by Elizabeth for the purpose of effecting a pacification of the estates with the Governor, if possible. They had also explained—so far as an explanation was possible—the assistance which the English government had rendered to the rebels, upon the ground that the French invasion could be prevented in no other way.† This somewhat lame apology had been passed over in silence rather than accepted by Don John. In the same interview the envoys made an equally unsuccessful effort to induce the acceptance by the Governor of the terms offered by the states. A further proposition, on their part, for an "Interim,"‡ upon the plan attempted by Charles the Fifth in Germany, previously to the Peace of Passau, met with no more favor than it merited, for certainly that name—which became so odious in Germany that cats and dogs were called "Interim" by the common people, in derision—was hardly a potent word to conjure with, at that moment, in the Netherlands. They then expressed their intention of retiring to England, much grieved at the result of their mission. The Governor replied that they might do as they liked, but that he, at least, had done all in his power to

---

* Article 21 of the Convention.—See Bor, xii. 978; Meteren, viii. 141.

† "Y disculpando a la Reyna su ama de lo que avia hecho en favor de los Estados, y que avia sido por mejor y porque el frances no metiesse pie en ellos." —Lo que en substancia ha passado con su Alteza, 14 Agósto, 1578. Acta Stat. Belg. iii. MS. Hague Archives.

‡ Ibid.

bring about a peace, and that the King had been equally pacific in his intentions. He then asked the envoys what they themselves thought of the terms proposed. "Indeed, they *are too hard*, your Highness,"* answered Walsingham, "but 'tis only by *pure menace* that we have extorted them from the states, unfavorable though they seem."

"Then you may tell them," replied the Governor, "to keep their offers to themselves. Such terms will go but little way in any negotiation with me."

The envoys shrugged their shoulders.

"What is your own opinion on the whole affair?" resumed Don John. "Perhaps your advice may yet help me to a better conclusion."

The envoys continued silent and pensive.

"We can only answer," said Walsingham, at length, "by imitating the physician, who would prescribe no medicine until he was quite sure that the patient was ready to swallow it. 'Tis no use wasting counsel or drugs."†

The reply was not satisfactory, but the envoys had convinced themselves that the sword was the only surgical instrument likely to find favor at that juncture. Don John referred, in vague terms, to his peaceable inclinations, but protested that there was no treating with so unbridled a people as the Netherlanders. The ambassadors soon afterwards took their leave. After this conference, which was on the 24th of August, 1578, Walsingham and Cobham addressed a letter to the states-general, deploring the disingenuous and procrastinating conduct of the Governor, and begging that the failure to effect a pacification might not be imputed to them.‡ They then returned to England.

The Imperial envoy, Count Schwartzburg, at whose urgent solicitation this renewed attempt at a composition had been made, was most desirous that the Governor should accept the

---

* "Que in veritá erano troppo duri."—The conversation was carried on partly in Italian, partly in French, partly in Spanish.—MS. memorandum, dict. act.

† MS. Memorandum, dict. act.

‡ Acta Stat. Belg., iii. f. 71.—MS. Hague Archives.

articles.* They formed, indeed, the basis of a liberal, constitutional, representative government, in which the Spanish monarch was to retain only a strictly limited sovereignty.† The proposed convention required Don John, with all his troops and adherents, forthwith to leave the land after giving up all strongholds and cities in his possession. It provided that the Archduke Matthias should remain as Governor-general, *under the conditions according to which he had been originally accepted.* It left the question of religious worship to the decision of the states-general. It provided for the release of all prisoners, the return of all exiles, the restoration of all confiscated property. It stipulated that upon the death or departure of Matthias, his Majesty was not to appoint a governor-general *without the consent of the states-general.*‡

When Count Schwartzburg waited upon the Governor with these astonishing propositions—which Walsingham might well call somewhat hard—he found him less disposed to explode with wrath than he had been in previous conferences. Already the spirit of the impetuous young soldier was broken, both by the ill health which was rapidly undermining his constitution and by the helpless condition in which he had been left while contending with the great rebellion. He had soldiers, but no money to pay them withal; he had no means of upholding that supremacy of crown and church which he was so vigorously instructed to maintain; and he was heartily wearied of fulminating edicts which he had no power to enforce. He had repeatedly solicited his recal, and was growing daily more impatient that his dismissal did not arrive. Moreover, the horrible news of Escovedo's assassination had sickened him to the soul.§ The deed had flashed a sudden light into the abyss of dark duplicity in which his own fate was suspended. His most intimate and confidential friend had been

* Bor, xii. 979. Hoofd, xii. 587.

† See the thirteen articles in Bor, xii. 979, 980.

‡ Articles 5 and 12 of the proposed Convention, Bor, xii. 979.

§ That event had occurred, as already stated, upon the 31st of March of this year (1578).

murdered by royal command, while he was himself abandoned by Philip, exposed to insult, left destitute of defence. No money was forthcoming, in spite of constant importunities and perpetual promises.* Plenty of words were sent him; he complained, as if he possessed the art of extracting gold from them, or as if war could be carried on with words alone.†

Being in so desponding a mood, he declined entering into any controversy with regard to the new propositions, which, however, he characterized as most iniquitous. He stated merely that his Majesty had determined to refer the Netherland matters to the arbitration of the Emperor; that the Duke de Terra Nova would soon be empowered to treat upon the subject at the imperial court; and that, in the meantime, he was himself most anxiously awaiting his recal.‡

A synod of the Reformed churches had been held, during the month of June, at Dort. There they had laid down a platform of their principles of church government in one hundred and one articles.§ In the same month, the leading members of the Reformed Church had drawn up an ably reasoned address to Matthias and the Council of State on the subject of a general peace of religion for the provinces.‖

William of Orange did his utmost to improve the opportunity. He sketched a system of provisional toleration, which he caused to be signed by the Archduke Matthias, and which, at least for a season, was to establish religious freedom.¶ The brave, tranquil, solitary man still held his track across the raging waves, shedding as much light as one clear human soul could dispense; yet the dim lantern, so far in advance, was swallowed in the mist, ere those who sailed in his wake could shape their course by his example. No man understood him. Not even his nearest friends comprehended his views, nor saw that he strove to establish not freedom for Calvinism, but freedom for conscience. Saint Aldegonde complained that the

---

* See the letter of Philip in Cabrera, xii. 978.

† Strada, x. 502.

‡ Bor. xii. 981.—Compare Meteren, viii. 140, 141.

§ Given in Bor, xii. 981–986.

‖ In Bor, xii. 971.

¶ Bor, xii. 973.

Prince would not persecute the Anabaptists,* Peter Dathenus denounced him as an atheist, while even Count John, the only one left of his valiant and generous brothers, opposed the religious peace—except where the advantage was on the side of the new religion. Where the Catholics had been effectually put down, as in Holland and Zealand, honest John saw no reason for allowing them to lift themselves up again.† In the Popish provinces, on the other hand, he was for a religious peace. In this bigoted spirit he was followed by too many of the Reforming mass, while, on their part, the Walloons were already banding themselves together in the more southern provinces, under the name of Malcontents. Stigmatized by the Calvinists as "Paternoster Jacks,"‡ they were daily drawing closer their alliance with Alençon, and weakening the bonds which united them with their Protestant brethren. Count John had at length become a permanent functionary in the Netherlands. Urgently solicited by the leaders and the great multitude of the Reformers, he had long been unwilling to abandon his home, and to neglect the private affairs which his devotion to the Netherland cause had thrown into great confusion. The Landgrave, too, whose advice he had asked, had strongly urged him not to "dip his fingers into the *olla podrida*."§ The future of the provinces was, in his opinion, so big with disaster, that the past, with all its horrors, under Alva and Requesens, had only furnished the "*preludia*" of that which was to ensue.‖ For these desperate views his main reason, as usual, was the comet; that mischievous luminary still continuing to cast a lurid glare across the Landgrave's path.¶ Notwithstanding these direful warnings from a prince

* Hoofd, xiii. 575. Ev. Reyd. Ann. ii. 23.

† Groen v. Prinst., Archives, etc. vi. 434, 435.

‡ "Pater noster Knechten."—Meteren, viii. 143. Bor, xii. 998.—Compare Bentivoglio, x. 216.

§ Groen v. Prinst., Archives, vi. 317.

‖ Archives de la Maison d'Orange, vi. 256.

¶ Letters of Landgrave William, Archives et Correspondance, v. 34, ii. 256-269.

of the Reformation, notwithstanding the "*olla podrida*" and the "comet," Count John had nevertheless accepted the office of Governor of Gelderland, to which he had been elected by the estates of that province on the 11th of March.* That important bulwark of Holland, Zealand, and Utrecht on the one side, and of Groningen and Friesland on the other—the main buttress, in short, of the nascent republic, was now in hands which would defend it to the last.

As soon as the discussion came up in the states-general on the subject of the Dort petitions, Orange requested that every member who had formed his opinions should express them fully and frankly. All wished, however, to be guided and governed by the sentiments of the Prince. Not a man spoke, save to demand their leader's views, and to express adhesion in advance to the course which his wisdom might suggest.† The result was a projected convention, a draft for a religious peace,‡ which, if definitely established, would have healed many wounds and averted much calamity. It was not, however, destined to be accepted at that time by the states of the different provinces where it was brought up for discussion; and several changes were made, both of form and substance, before the system was adopted at all. Meantime, for the important city of Antwerp, where religious broils were again on the point of breaking out, the Prince preferred a provisional arrangement, which he forthwith carried into execution. A proclamation, in the name of the Archduke Matthias and of the State Council, assigned five special places in the city where the members of the "pretended Reformed religion" should have liberty to exercise their religious worship, with preaching, singing, and the sacraments.§ The churchyards of the parochial churches were to be opened for the burial of

* Archives et Correspondance, vi. 308.

† Langueti Ep. Sec. ad Aug. Sax. 147, p. 744.

‡ According to the 3rd and 4th Articles, the Catholic or the Reformed religion was to be re-established and freely exercised in any town or village where such re-establishment should be demanded by one hundred families.—Meteren, viii. 143[a].

§ See the document in Bor, xii. 974, 975. Hoofd, xiii. 575.

their dead, but the funerals were to be unaccompanied with exhortation, or any public demonstration which might excite disturbance. The adherents of one religion were forbidden to disturb, to insult, or in any way to interfere with the solemnities of the other. All were to abstain from mutual jeerings —by pictures, ballads, books, or otherwise—and from all injuries to ecclesiastical property. Every man, of whatever religion, was to be permitted entrance to the churches of either religion, and when there, all were to conform to the regulations of the church with modesty and respect. Those of the new religion were to take oaths of obedience to the authorities, and to abstain from meddling with the secular administration of affairs. Preachers of both religions were forbidden to preach out of doors, or to make use of language tending to sedition. All were to bind themselves to assist the magistrates in quelling riots, and in sustaining the civil government.*

This example of religious peace, together with the active correspondence thus occasioned with the different state assemblies, excited the jealousy of the Catholic leaders and of the Walloon population.† Champagny, who despite his admirable qualities and brilliant services, was still unable to place himself on the same platform of toleration with Orange, now undertook a decided movement against the policy of the Prince. Catholic to the core, he drew up a petition, remonstrating most vigorously against the draft for a religious peace, then in circulation through the provinces.‡ To this petition he procured many signatures among the more ardent Catholic nobles. De Héze, De Glimes, and others of the same stamp, were willing enough to follow the lead of so distinguished a chieftain. The

---

* Bor, xii. 974, 975. The principle of the religious peace was adopted, and churches accordingly allotted to the members of the Reformed Church, in the cities of Antwerp, Brussels, Mechlin, Bergen, Breda, Liere, Bruges, Ypres, and in many cities of Gelderland and Friesland.—Meteren, viii. 142.

† Bor, xii. 975. Hoofd, xiii. 575.

‡ See the Petition in Bor, xii. 989, 990.—Compare Hoofd, xiii. 578. Meteren, viii. 142.

remonstrance was addressed to the Archduke, the Prince of Orange, the State Council, and the States-general, and called upon them all to abide by their solemn promises to permit no schism in the ancient Church. Should the exercise of the new religion be allowed, the petitioners insisted that the godless licentiousness of the Netherlands would excite the contempt of all peoples and potentates. They suggested, in conclusion, that all the principal cities of France—and in particular the city of Paris—had kept themselves clear of the exercise of the new religion, and that repose and prosperity had been the result.*

This petition was carried with considerable solemnity by Champagny, attended by many of his confederates, to the Hotel de Ville, and presented to the magistracy of Brussels. These functionaries were requested to deliver it forthwith to the Archduke and Council. The magistrates demurred. A discussion ensued, which grew warmer and warmer as it proceeded. The younger nobles permitted themselves abusive language, which the civic dignitaries would not brook. The session was dissolved, and the magistrates, still followed by the petitioners, came forth into the street. The confederates, more inflamed than ever, continued to vociferate and to threaten. A crowd soon collected in the square. The citizens were naturally curious to know why their senators were thus browbeaten and insulted by a party of insolent young Catholic nobles. The old politician at their head, who, in spite of many services, was not considered a friend to the nation, inspired them with distrust.† Being informed of the presentation of the petition, the multitude loudly demanded that the document should be read. This was immediately done. The general drift of the remonstrance was anything but

---

* Petition in Bor, xii. 989, 990.

† Bor, xii. 988. Champagny was a Catholic and the brother of Granvelle; he was also one of the most patriotic and honourable—as he was unquestionably one of the bravest—of the Netherland nobles. His character is interesting, and his services were remarkable. It is said that he could not rise to the same tolerance in religious matters which the Prince of Orange had attained.

acceptable, but the allusion to Paris, at the close, excited a tempest of indignation. "Paris! Paris! Saint Bartholomew! Saint Bartholomew! Are we to have Paris weddings in Brussels also?" howled the mob, as is often the case, extracting but a single idea, and that a wrong one, from the public lecture which had just been made. "Are we to have a Paris massacre, a Paris blood-bath here in the Netherland capital? God forbid! God forbid! Away with the conspirators! Down with the Papists!"*

It was easily represented to the inflamed imaginations of the populace that a Brussels Saint Bartholomew had been organized, and that Champagny, who stood there before them, was its originator and manager. The ungrateful Netherlanders forgot the heroism with which the old soldier had arranged the defence of Antwerp against the "Spanish Fury" but two years before. They heard only the instigations of his enemies; they remembered only that he was the hated Granvelle's brother; they believed only that there was a plot by which, in some utterly incomprehensible manner, they were all to be immediately engaged in cutting each others throats and throwing each other out of the windows, as had been done half a dozen years before in Paris. Such was the mischievous intention ascribed to a petition, which Champagny and his friends had as much right to offer—however narrow and mistaken their opinions might now be considered—as had the synod of Dort to present their remonstrances. Never was a more malignant or more stupid perversion of a simple and not very alarming phrase. No allusion had been made to Saint Bartholomew, but all its horrors were supposed to be concealed in the sentence which referred to Paris. The nobles were arrested on the spot and hurried to prison, with the exception of Champagny, who made his escape at first, and lay concealed for several days.† He was, however, finally ferreted out of his hiding-place and carried off to Ghent. There he was thrown into strict

* Bor, xii. 988. Hoofd, xiii. 578, 579.

† Bor, xii. 988. Hoofd, xiii. 579. Meteren, viii. 142.

confinement, being treated in all respects as the accomplice of Aerschot and the other nobles who had been arrested in the time of Ryhove's revolution.* Certainly, this conduct towards a brave and generous gentleman was ill calculated to increase general sympathy for the cause, or to merit the approbation of Orange. There was, however, a strong prejudice against Champagny. His brother Granvelle had never been forgotten by the Netherlanders, and was still regarded as their most untiring foe, while Champagny was supposed to be in close league with the Cardinal. In these views the people were entirely wrong.

While these events were taking place in Brussels and Antwerp, the two armies of the states and of Don John were indolently watching each other. The sinews of war had been cut upon both sides. Both parties were cramped by the most abject poverty. The troops under Bossu and Casimir, in the camp near Mechlin, were already discontented, for want of pay. The one hundred thousand pounds of Elizabeth had already been spent, and it was not probable that the offended Queen would soon furnish another subsidy. The states could with difficulty extort anything like the assessed quotas from the different provinces. The Duke of Alençon was still at Mons, from which place he had issued a violent proclamation of war against Don John—a manifesto which had, however, not been followed up by very vigorous demonstrations. Don John himself was in his fortified camp at Bouge, within a league of Namur, but the hero was consuming with mental and with bodily fever. He was, as it were, besieged. He was left entirely without funds, while his royal brother obstinately refused compliance with his earnest demands to be recalled, and coldly neglected his importunities for pecuniary assistance.†

---

* Bor, xii. 988. Hoofd, xiii. 579. Meteren, viii. 142.—His captivity lasted several years.

† Bor, xii. 997, 998. Hoofd, xiv. 584, 585. The States had agreed to pay 600,000 guldens per month. The expenses of the army were estimated at 800,000 guldens per month.—Groen v. Prinst., Archives, vi. 397. Proclamation in Bor, xii. 996, 997.

Compelled to carry on a war against an armed rebellion with such gold only as could be extracted from royal words ; stung to the heart by the suspicion of which he felt himself the object at home, and by the hatred with which he was regarded in the provinces ; outraged in his inmost feelings by the murder of Escovedo ; foiled, outwitted, reduced to a political nullity by the masterly tactics of the "odious heretic of heretics" to whom he had originally offered his own patronage and the royal forgiveness, the high-spirited soldier was an object to excite the tenderness even of religious and political opponents. Wearied with the turmoil of camps without battle and of cabinets without counsel, he sighed for repose, even if it could be found only in a cloister or the grave. "I rejoice to see by your letter," he wrote, pathetically, to John Andrew Doria, at Genoa, "that your life is flowing on with such calmness, while the world around me is so tumultuously agitated. I consider you most fortunate that you are passing the remainder of your days for God and yourself; that you are not forced to put yourself perpetually in the scales of the world's events, nor to venture yourself daily on its hazardous games."* He proceeded to inform his friend of his own painful situation, surrounded by innumerable enemies, without means of holding out more than three months, and cut off from all assistance by a government which could not see that if the present chance were lost all was lost. He declared it impossible for him to fight in the position to which he was reduced, pressed as he was within half a mile of the point which he had always considered as his last refuge. He stated also that the French were strengthening themselves in Hainault, under Alençon, and that the King of France was in readiness to break in through Burgundy, should his brother obtain a firm foothold in the provinces. "I have besought his Majesty over and over again," he continued, "to send to me his orders ; if they come they shall be executed, unless they

* This remarkable and pathetic letter, as well as that addressed to Mendoza, is published in Bor, xii. 1004, 1005, and in Hoofd, xiv. 589, 590.

arrive too late. *They have cut off our hands, and we have now nothing for it but to stretch forth our heads also to the axe.* I grieve to trouble you with my sorrows, but I trust to your sympathy as a man and a friend. I hope that you will remember me in your prayers, for you can put your trust where, in former days, I never could place my own."*

The dying crusader wrote another letter, in the same mournful strain, to another intimate friend, Don Pedro Mendoza, Spanish envoy in Genoa. It was dated upon the same day from his camp near Namur, and repeated the statement that the King of France was ready to invade the Netherlands, so soon as Alençon should prepare an opening. "His Majesty," continued Don John, "is resolved upon nothing; at least, I am kept in ignorance of his intentions. *Our life is doled out to us here by moments.* I cry aloud, but it profits me little. Matters will soon be disposed, through our negligence, exactly as the Devil would best wish them. It is plain that we are left here to pine away till our last breath. God direct us all as He may see fit; in His hands are all things."†

Four days later he wrote to the King, stating that he was confined to his chamber with a fever, by which he was already as much reduced as if he had been ill for a month. "I assure your Majesty," said he, "that the work here is enough to destroy any constitution and any life." He reminded Philip how often he had been warned by him as to the insidious practices of the French. Those prophecies had now become facts. The French had entered the country, while some of the inhabitants were frightened, others disaffected. Don John declared himself in a dilemma. With his small force, hardly enough to make head against the enemy immediately in front, and to protect the places which required guarding, 'twas impossible for him to leave his position to attack the enemy in Burgundy. If he remained stationary, the communications were cut off through which his money and sup-

* Letter to Doria; Bor, Hoofd, ubi sup.

† Letter to Pedro de Mendoza; Bor, xii. 1005. Hoofd, xiv. 590.

plies reached him. "Thus I remain," said he, "perplexed and confused, desiring, more than life, some decision on your Majesty's part, for which I have implored so many times." He urged the King most vehemently to *send him instructions as to the course to be pursued*,* adding that it wounded him to the soul to find them so long delayed. He begged to be informed "whether he was to attack the enemy in Burgundy, whether he should await where he then was the succor of his Majesty, or whether he was to fight, and if so with which of his enemies: in fine, what he was to do; because, losing or winning, he meant to conform to his Majesty's will. He felt deeply pained, he said, at being disgraced and abandoned by the King, having served him, both as a brother, and a man, with love and faith and heartiness. "Our lives," said he, "are at stake upon this game, and all we wish is to lose them honorably."† He begged the King to send a special envoy to France, with remonstrances on the subject of Alençon, and another to the Pope to ask for the Duke's excommunication. He protested that he would give his blood rather than occasion so much annoyance to the King, but that he felt it his duty to tell the naked truth. The pest was ravaging his little army. Twelve hundred were now in hospital, besides those nursed in private houses, and he had no means or money to remedy the evil. Moreover, the enemy, seeing that they were not opposed in the open field, had cut off the passage into Liege by the Meuse, and had advanced to Nivelles and Chimay for the sake of communications with France, by the same river.‡

Ten days after these pathetic passages had been written, the writer was dead. Since the assassination of Escovedo, a con-

---

* "*La orden de como tengo de gobernar.*"—These words in Don John's letter were underlined by Philip, who made upon reading them the following most characteristic annotation: "The marked request I will not grant. I will not tell;" (lo rayado no yo le diré.)

† "Nos van las vidas en esto juego," etc., etc.

‡ Carta (descifrada) del Sor. D. Juan a Su Magd., 20 Sept., 1578. MS. Royal Library, Hague, f. 41–44vo

suming melancholy had settled upon his spirits, and a burning fever came, in the month of September, to destroy his physical strength. The house where he lay was a hovel, the only chamber of which had been long used as a pigeon-house. This wretched garret was cleansed, as well as it could be of its filth, and hung with tapestry emblazoned with armorial bearings. In that dovecot the hero of Lepanto was destined to expire. During the last few days of his illness, he was delirious. Tossing upon his uneasy couch, he again arranged in imagination, the combinations of great battles, again shouted his orders to rushing squadrons, and listened with brightening eye to the trumpet of victory. Reason returned, however, before the hour of death, and permitted him the opportunity to make the dispositions rendered necessary by his condition. He appointed his nephew, Alexander of Parma, who had been watching assiduously over his death-bed, to succeed him, provisionally, in the command of the army and in his other dignities, received the last sacraments with composure, and tranquilly breathed his last upon the first day of October, the month which, since the battle of Lepanto, he had always considered a festive and a fortunate one.*

It was inevitable that suspicion of poison should be at once excited by his decease. Those suspicions have been never set at rest, and never proved. Two Englishmen, Ratcliff and Gray by name, had been arrested and executed on a charge of having been employed by Secretary Walsingham to assassinate the Governor.† The charge was doubtless an infamous falsehood; but had Philip, who was suspected of being the real criminal, really compassed the death of his brother, it was none the less probable that an innocent victim or two would be executed, to save appearances. Now that time has unveiled to us many mysteries, now that we have learned from Philip's own lips and those of his accomplices the exact manner in which Montigny and Escovedo were put to

* Van der Hammen y Leon, vi. 324. Bor, xii. 1005. Cabrera, xii. 1008, 1009. Strada, x. 503, 505, 506. Hoofd, 591.

† De Thou, vii. 699.—Compare Cabrera, xii. 1006.

death, the world will hardly be very charitable with regard to other imputations. It was vehemently suspected that Don John had been murdered by the command of Philip, but no such fact was ever proved.

The body, when opened that it might be embalmed, was supposed to offer evidence of poison. The heart was dry, the other internal organs were likewise so desiccated as to crumble when touched, and the general color of the interior was of a blackish brown, as if it had been singed. Various persons were mentioned as the probable criminals; various motives assigned for the commission of the deed. Nevertheless, it must be admitted that there were causes, which were undisputed, for his death, sufficient to render a search for the more mysterious ones comparatively superfluous. A disorder called the pest was raging in his camp, and had carried off a thousand of his soldiers within a few days, while his mental sufferings had been acute enough to turn his heart to ashes. Disappointed, tormented by friend and foe, suspected, insulted, broken spirited, it was not strange that he should prove an easy victim to a pestilent disorder before which many stronger men were daily falling.*

On the third day after his decease, the funeral rites were celebrated. A dispute between the Spaniards, Germans, and Netherlanders in the army arose, each claiming precedence in

---

* "Namque in defuncti corpore extitisse non obscura veneni vestigia affirmant, qui viderunt."—Strada, x. 512. The Jesuit does not express any opinion as to the truth of the report.—Compare Cabrera, xii. 1009. Van d. Vynckt, ii. 253, 254. "—— hallaron la parte del coraçon seca i todo lo interior i lo esterior denegrido i come tostado, que se deshazia con el toque; i lo demas de color palido de natural difunto."—Cabrera, xii. 1009. The Seigneur de Brantome, after expressing his regrets that such a brave son of Mars should have died in his bed, ("—— comme si c'eust esté quelque mignon de Venus,") suggests that he was poisoned by *means of perfumed boots;* (certainly an original method, and one which was not likely to make his "interior" look as if "toasted,") "—— car on tient tout qu'il mourut empoissonné par des bottines parfumées."—Hommes Illust. et Gr., cap. ii. 140. The poisoning was attributed to various persons; to Philip, to the Prince of Orange, and to the Abbot of St. Gertrude, who is said to have effected the deed through one Guerin, a well-known poisoner of Marseilles.—V. Wyn Aanm. op Wagenaer, vii. 65. See also Hoofd, xiv. 591; Bor. xii. 1004.

the ceremony, on account of superior national propinquity to the illustrious deceased. All were, in truth, equally near to him, for different reasons, and it was arranged that all should share equally in the obsequies. The corpse disembowelled and embalmed, was laid upon a couch of state. The hero was clad in complete armor; his sword, helmet, and steel gauntlets lying at his feet, a coronet, blazing with precious stones, upon his head, the jewelled chain and insignia of the Golden Fleece about his neck, and perfumed gloves upon his hands. Thus royally and martially arrayed, he was placed upon his bier and borne forth from the house where he had died, by the gentlemen of his bedchamber. From them he was received by the colonels of the regiments stationed next his own quarters. These chiefs, followed by their troops with inverted arms and muffled drums, escorted the body to the next station, where it was received by the commanding officers, of other national regiments, to be again transmitted to those of the third. Thus by soldiers of the three nations, it was successively conducted to the gates of Namur, where it was received by the civic authorities. The pall-bearers, old Peter Ernest Mansfeld, Ottavio Gonzaga, the Marquis de Villa Franca, and the Count de Reux, then bore it to the church, where it was deposited until the royal orders should be received from Spain. The heart of the hero was permanently buried beneath the pavement of the little church, and a monumental inscription, prepared by Alexander Farnese, still indicates the spot where that lion heart returned to dust.*

It had been Don John's dying request to Philip that his remains might be buried in the Escorial by the side of his imperial father, and the prayer being granted, the royal order in due time arrived for the transportation of the corpse to Spain. Permission had been asked and given for the passage

* Strada, x. 515. Hoofd, xiv. 591. "Relacion de la enfermedad y muerte del S. D. Juan."—Documentos Inéditos, vii. 443–448.—Compare Tassis, iv. 326; Hoofd, xiv. 591; Haraeus (Ann. iii. 285.) The inscription on the tablet may yet be read at Namur, although a new church has replaced the one in which the heart was originally deposited.

of a small number of Spanish troops through France. The thrifty king had, however, made no allusion to the fact that those soldiers were to bear with them the mortal remains of Lepanto's hero, for he was disposed to save the expense which a public transportation of the body and the exchange of pompous courtesies with the authorities of every town upon the long journey would occasion. The corpse was accordingly divided into three parts, and packed in three separate bags; and thus the different portions, *to save weight*, being suspended at the saddle-bows of different troopers, the body of the conqueror was conveyed to its distant resting-place.*

> "Expende Hannibalem: quot libras in duce summo
> Invenies?" . . . . .

Thus irreverently, almost blasphemously, the disjointed relics of the great warrior were hurried through France;—France, which the romantic Saracen slave had traversed but two short years before, filled with high hopes, and pursuing extravagant visions. It has been recorded by classic historians,† that the different fragments, after their arrival in Spain, were re-united, and fastened together with wire; that the body was then stuffed, attired in magnificent habiliments, placed upon its feet, and supported by a martial staff, and that thus prepared for a royal interview, the mortal remains of Don John were presented to his Most Catholic Majesty. Philip is said to have manifested emotion at sight of the hideous spectre—for hideous and spectral, despite of jewels, balsams, and brocades, must

---

* Strada, x. 516, 519.—"Relacion de la enfermedad y muerte," pp. 443–448. Hoofd, xiv. 592.

† "—— ubi ossibus iterum commissis, æreique nexu fili colligatis, totam facile articulavere compagem corporis."—Strada, x. 519. "—— Quod tomento expletum, ac superindutis armis, pretiosis vestibus exornatum ita Regis obtulere oculis quasi pedibus innitens, Imperatorii videlicet baculi adjumento, *plane vivere ac spirare videretur.*"—Ibid. The story must be received, however, with extreme caution, as being perhaps only one of the imaginative embroideries of that genial Jesuit, Strada. There is no mention of the circumstance in the "Relacion de la enfermedad," etc., but, on the contrary, the body of the hero is there represented as having been wrapped decently in a shroud of "delicate Hollands," and placed in a coffin covered within and without with black velvet."—Documentos Inéditos, vii. 443–448.

have been that unburied corpse, aping life in attitude and vestment, but standing there only to assert its privilege of descending into the tomb. The claim was granted, and Don John of Austria at last found repose by the side of his imperial father.*

A sufficient estimate of his character has been apparent in the course of the narrative. Dying before he had quite completed his thirty-third year,† he excites pity and admiration almost as much as censure. His military career was a blaze of glory. Commanding in the Moorish wars at twenty-three, and in the Turkish campaigns at twenty-six, he had achieved a matchless renown before he had emerged from early youth ; but his sun was destined to go down at noon. He found neither splendor nor power in the Netherlands, where he was deserted by his king and crushed by the superior genius of the Prince of Orange. Although he vindicated his martial skill at Gemblours, the victory was fruitless. It was but the solitary spring of the tiger from his jungle, and after that striking conflict his life was ended in darkness and obscurity. Possessing military genius of a high order, with extraordinary personal bravery, he was the last of the paladins and the crusaders. His accomplishments were also considerable, and he spoke Italian, German, French, and Spanish with fluency. His beauty was remarkable ; his personal fascinations acknowledged by either sex ; but as a commander of men, excepting upon the battle-field, he possessed little genius. His ambition was the ambition of a knight-errant, an adventurer, a Norman pirate ; it was a personal and tawdry ambition. Vague and contradictory dreams of crowns, of royal marriages, of extemporized dynasties, floated ever before him ; but he was himself always the hero of his own romance. He sought a throne in Africa or in Britain ; he dreamed of espousing Mary of Scotland at the expense of Elizabeth, and was even thought to aspire secretly to the hand of the great English Queen her-

---

* Strada, x. 519.

† Tassis, iv. 326. Cabrera, xii. 1009. Strada, x. 503. Bentivoglio, x. 218.

self.* Thus, crusader and bigot as he was, he was willing to be reconciled with heresy, if heresy could furnish him with a throne.

It is superfluous to state that he was no match, by mental endowments, for William of Orange; but even had he been so, the moral standard by which each measured himself placed the Conqueror far below the Father of a people. It must be admitted that Don John is entitled to but small credit for his political achievements in the Netherlands. He was incapable of perceiving that the great contest between the Reformation and the Inquisition could never be amicably arranged in those provinces, and that the character of William of Orange was neither to be softened by royal smiles, nor perverted by appeals to sordid interests. It would have been perhaps impossible for him, with his education and temperament, to have embraced what seems to us the right cause, but it ought, at least, to have been in his power to read the character of his antagonist, and to estimate his own position with something like accuracy. He may be forgiven that he did not succeed in reconciling hostile parties, when his only plan to accomplish such a purpose was the extermination of the most considerable faction; but although it was not to be expected that he would look on the provinces with the eyes of William the Silent, he might have comprehended that the Netherland chieftain was neither to be purchased nor cajoled. The only system by which the two religions could live together in peace had been discovered by the Prince; but toleration, in the eyes of Catholics, and of many Protestants, was still thought the deadliest heresy of all.

* This project, among other visions, may have occupied the dreamy mind of Don John himself, but it seems astonishing that grave historians should record their opinion that such a scheme had ever been sanctioned by Elizabeth. Yet Cabrera, Bentivoglio, Strada, and even the more modern Van der Vynckt, allude to the report.—Vida Cabrera, xii. 971. Bentivoglio, x. 518. Strada, x. 503. Van d. Vynckt, ii. 254.—Compare Groen, v. Prinsterer, vi. 453.

PART VI.

ALEXANDER OF PARMA.

1578—1584.

CHAPTER I.

Birth, education, marriage, and youthful character of Alexander Farnese—His private adventures—Exploits at Lepanto and at Gemblours—He succeeds to the government—Personal appearance and characteristics—Aspect of affairs—Internal dissensions—Anjou at Mons—John Casimir's intrigues at Ghent—Anjou disbands his soldiers—The Netherlands ravaged by various foreign troops—Anarchy and confusion in Ghent—Imbize and Ryhove—Fate of Hessels and Visch—New Pacification drawn up by Orange—Representations of Queen Elizabeth—Remonstrance of Brussels—Riots and image-breaking in Ghent—Displeasure of Orange—His presence implored at Ghent, where he establishes a Religious Peace—Painful situation of John Casimir—Sharp rebukes of Elizabeth—He takes his departure—His troops apply to Farnese, who allows them to leave the country—Anjou's departure and manifesto—Elizabeth's letters to the states-general with regard to him—Complimentary addresses by the Estates to the Duke—Death of Bossu—Calumnies against Orange—Venality of the Malcontent grandees—La Motte's treason—Intrigues of the Prior of Renty—Saint Aldegonde at Arras—The Prior of St. Vaast's exertions—Opposition of the clergy in the Walloon provinces to the taxation of the general government—Triangular contest—Municipal revolution in Arras led by Gosson and others—Counter-revolution—Rapid trials and executions—"Reconciliation" of the malcontent chieftains—Secret treaty of Mount St. Eloi—Mischief made by the Prior of Renty—His accusations against the reconciled lords—Vengeance taken upon him—Counter movement by the liberal party—Union of Utrecht—The Act analyzed and characterized.

A FIFTH governor now stood in the place which had been successively vacated by Margaret of Parma, by Alva, by the Grand Commander, and by Don John of Austria. Of all the eminent personages to whom Philip had confided the reins of that most difficult and dangerous administration, the man who was now to rule was by far the ablest and the best fitted for his post. If there were living charioteer skilful enough to guide the wheels of state, whirling now more dizzily than ever through "*confusum chaos*," Alexander Farnese was the charioteer to guide—his hand the only one which could control.

He was now in his thirty-third year—his uncle Don John, his cousin Don Carlos, and himself, having all been born within a few months of each other. His father was Ottavio Farnese, the faithful lieutenant of Charles the Fifth, and grandson of Pope Paul the Third; his mother was Margaret of Parma, first Regent of the Netherlands after the departure of Philip from the provinces. He was one of the twins by which the reunion of Margaret and her youthful husband had been blessed, and the only one that survived. His great-grandfather, Paul, whose secular name of Alexander he had received, had placed his hand upon the new-born infant's head, and prophesied that he would grow up to become a mighty warrior.* The boy, from his earliest years, seemed destined to verify the prediction. Though apt enough at his studies, he turned with impatience from his literary tutors to military exercises and the hardiest sports. The din of arms surrounded his cradle. The trophies of Ottavio, returning victorious from beyond the Alps, had dazzled the eyes of his infancy, and when but six years of age he had witnessed the siege of his native Parma, and its vigorous defence by his martial father. When Philip was in the Netherlands—in the years immediately succeeding the abdication of the Emperor—he had received the boy from his parents as a hostage for their friendship. Although but eleven years of age, Alexander had begged earnestly to be allowed to serve as a volunteer on the memorable day of Saint Quentin, and had wept bitterly when the amazed monarch refused his request.† His education had been completed at Alcalá, and at Madrid, under the immediate supervision of his royal uncle, and in the companionship of the Infante Carlos and the brilliant Don John. The imperial

* Strada, ix. 451, x. 508.

† Ibid., ix. 458.

bastard was alone able to surpass, or even to equal the Italian prince in all martial and manly pursuits. Both were equally devoted to the chase and to the tournay ; both longed impatiently for the period when the irksome routine of monkish pedantry, and the fictitious combats which formed their main recreation, should be exchanged for the substantial delights of war. At the age of twenty he had been affianced to Maria of Portugal, daughter of Prince Edward, granddaughter of King Emanuel, and his nuptials with that peerless princess were, as we have seen, celebrated soon afterwards with much pomp in Brussels. Sons and daughters were born to him in due time, during his subsequent residence in Parma. Here, however, the fiery and impatient spirit of the future illustrious commander was doomed for a time to fret under restraint, and to corrode in distasteful repose. His father, still in the vigor of his years, governing the family duchies of Parma and Piacenza, Alexander had no occupation in the brief period of peace which then existed. The martial spirit, pining for a wide and lofty sphere of action, in which alone its energies could be fitly exercised, now sought delight in the pursuits of the duellist and gladiator. Nightly did the hereditary prince of the land perambulate the streets of his capital, disguised, well armed, alone, or with a single confidential attendant.* Every chance passenger of martial aspect whom he encountered in the midnight streets was forced to stand and measure swords with an unknown, almost unseen, but most redoubtable foe, and many were the single combats which he thus enjoyed, so long as his incognito was preserved. Especially, it was his wont to seek and defy every gentleman whose skill or bravery had ever been commended in his hearing. At last, upon one occasion it was his fortune to encounter a certain Count Torelli, whose reputation as a swordsman and duellist was well established in Parma. The blades were joined, and the fierce combat had already been engaged in the darkness, when the torch of an accidental passenger flashed full in the face of

---

* Strada, ix. 454, 455.

Alexander. Torelli, recognising thus suddenly his antagonist, dropped his sword and implored forgiveness,* for the wily Italian was too keen not to perceive that even if the death of neither combatant should be the result of the fray, his own position was, in every event, a false one. Victory would ensure him the hatred, defeat the contempt of his future sovereign. The unsatisfactory issue and subsequent notoriety of this encounter put a termination to these midnight joys of Alexander, and for a season he felt obliged to assume more pacific habits, and to solace himself with the society of that "phœnix of Portugal," who had so long sat brooding on his domestic hearth.

At last the holy league was formed, the new and last crusade proclaimed, his uncle and bosom friend appointed to the command of the united troops of Rome, Spain, and Venice. He could no longer be restrained. Disdaining the pleadings of his mother and of his spouse, he extorted permission from Philip, and flew to the seat of war in the Levant. Don John received him with open arms, just before the famous action of Lepanto, and gave him an excellent position in the very front of the battle, with the command of several Genoese galleys. Alexander's exploits on that eventful day seemed those of a fabulous hero of romance. He laid his galley alongside of the treasure-ship of the Turkish fleet, a vessel, on account of its importance, doubly manned and armed. Impatient that the Crescent was not lowered, after a few broadsides, he sprang on board the enemy alone, waving an immense two-handed sword—his usual weapon—and mowing a passage right and left through the hostile ranks for the warriors who tardily followed the footsteps of their vehement chief. Mustapha Bey, the treasurer and commander of the ship, fell before his sword, besides many others, whom he hardly saw or counted. The galley was soon his own, as well as another, which came to the rescue of the treasure-ship only to share its defeat. The booty which Alexander's crew secured was prodigious, individual soldiers obtaining two and three thousand ducats each.† Don John received his nephew after the battle with commendations,

* Strada, ix. 455.

† Ibid., ix. 456, 457.

not, however, unmingled with censure. The successful result alone had justified such insane and desperate conduct, for had he been slain or overcome, said the commander-in-chief, there would have been few to applaud his temerity. Alexander gaily replied by assuring his uncle that he had felt sustained by a more than mortal confidence, the prayers which his saintly wife was incessantly offering in his behalf since he went to the wars being a sufficient support and shield in even greater danger than he had yet confronted.*

This was Alexander's first campaign, nor was he permitted to reap any more glory for a few succeeding years. At last, Philip was disposed to send both his mother and himself to the Netherlands, removing Don John from the rack where he had been enduring such slow torture. Granvelle's intercession proved fruitless with the Duchess, but Alexander was all eagerness to go where blows were passing current, and he gladly led the reinforcements which were sent to Don John at the close of the year 1577. He had reached Luxemburg on the 18th of December of that year, in time, as we have seen, to participate, and, in fact, to take the lead in the signal victory of Gemblours. He had been struck with the fatal change which disappointment and anxiety had wrought upon the beautiful and haughty features of his illustrious kinsman.† He had since closed his eyes in the camp, and erected a marble tablet over his heart in the little church. He now governed in his stead.

His personal appearance corresponded with his character. He had the head of a gladiator, round, compact, combative, with something alert and snake-like in its movements. The black, closely-shorn hair was erect and bristling. The forehead was lofty and narrow. The features were handsome, the nose regularly aquiline, the eyes well opened, dark, piercing, but with something dangerous and sinister in their expression.‡ There was an habitual look askance, as of a man

* Strada, ix. 458.

† Ibid., ix. 460.

‡ "Een fel gesicht," says Bor, 3, xxix. 661, and the portraits confirm the statement.

seeking to parry or inflict a mortal blow—the look of a swordsman and professional fighter. The lower part of the face was swallowed in a bushy beard; the mouth and chin being quite invisible. He was of middle stature, well formed, and graceful in person, princely in demeanor, sumptuous and stately in apparel.* His high ruff of point lace, his badge of the Golden Fleece, his gold-inlaid Milan armor, marked him at once as one of high degree. On the field of battle he possessed the rare gift of inspiring his soldiers with his own impetuous and chivalrous courage. He ever led the way upon the most dangerous and desperate ventures, and, like his uncle and his imperial grandfather, well knew how to reward the devotion of his readiest followers with a poniard, a feather, a riband, a jewel, taken with his own hands from his own attire.†

His military abilities—now for the first time to be largely called into employment—were unquestionably superior to those of Don John, whose name had been surrounded with such splendor by the world-renowned battle of Lepanto. Moreover, he possessed far greater power for governing men, whether in camp or cabinet. Less attractive and fascinating, he was more commanding than his kinsman. Decorous and self-poised, he was only passionate before the enemy, but he rarely permitted a disrespectful look or word to escape condign and deliberate chastisement. He was no schemer or dreamer. He was no knight errant. He would not have crossed seas and mountains to rescue a captive queen, nor have sought to place her crown on his own head as a reward for his heroism. He had a single and concentrated kind of character. He knew precisely the work which Philip required, and felt himself to be precisely the workman that had so long been wanted. Cool, incisive, fearless, artful, he united the unscrupulous audacity of a *condottiere* with the wily patience of a Jesuit. He could coil unperceived through unsuspected paths,

---

* "Kostelijck en overdadig in kleederen."—Bor, loc. cit.

† Strada, 2, iii. 150.

could strike suddenly, sting mortally. He came prepared, not only to smite the Netherlanders in the open field, but to cope with them in tortuous policy; to outwatch and outweary them in the game to which his impatient predecessor had fallen a baffled victim. He possessed the art and the patience —as time was to prove—not only to undermine their most impregnable cities, but to delve below the intrigues of their most accomplished politicians. To circumvent at once both their negotiators and their men-at-arms was his appointed task. Had it not been for the courage, the vigilance, and the superior intellect of a single antagonist, the whole of the Netherlands would have shared the fate which was reserved for the more southern portion. Had the life of William of Orange been prolonged, perhaps the evil genius of the Netherlands might have still been exorcised throughout the whole extent of the country.

As for religion, Alexander Farnese was, of course, strictly Catholic, regarding all seceders from Romanism as mere heathen dogs. Not that he practically troubled himself much with sacred matters—for, during the life-time of his wife, he had cavalierly thrown the whole burden of his personal salvation upon her saintly shoulders. She had now flown to higher spheres, but Alexander was, perhaps, willing to rely upon her continued intercessions in his behalf. The life of a bravo in time of peace—the deliberate project in war to exterminate whole cities full of innocent people, who had different notions on the subject of image-worship and ecclesiastical ceremonies from those entertained at Rome, did not seem to him at all incompatible with the precepts of Jesus. Hanging, drowning, burning and butchering heretics were the legitimate deductions of his theology. He was no casuist nor pretender to holiness: but in those days every man was devout, and Alexander looked with honest horror upon the impiety of the heretics, whom he persecuted and massacred. He attended mass regularly—in the winter mornings by torch-light—and would as soon have foregone his daily tennis as his religious exercises. Romanism was the creed of his caste. It was the religion of princes and gentlemen of high degree. As for Lutheranism, Zwinglism, Calvinism, and similar systems, they were but the fantastic rites of weavers, brewers, and the like—an ignoble herd whose presumption in entitling themselves Christian, while rejecting the Pope, called for their instant extermination. His personal habits were extremely temperate. He was accustomed to say that he ate only to support life; and he rarely finished a dinner without having risen three or four times from table to attend to some public business which, in his opinion, ought not to be deferred.*

His previous connections in the Netherlands were of use to him, and he knew how to turn them to immediate account. The great nobles, who had been uniformly actuated by jealousy of the Prince of Orange, who had been baffled in their intrigue with Matthias, whose half-blown designs upon Anjou had already been nipped in the bud, were now peculiarly in a position to listen to the wily tongue of Alexander Farnese. The Montignys, the La Mottes, the Meluns, the Egmonts, the Aerschots, the Havrés, foiled and doubly foiled in all their small intrigues and their base ambition, were ready to sacrifice their country to the man they hated, and to the ancient religion which they thought that they loved. The Malcontents ravaging the land of Hainault and threatening Ghent, the "Paternoster Jacks" who were only waiting for a favorable opportunity and a good bargain to make their peace with Spain, were the very instruments which Parma most desired to use at this opening stage of his career. The position of affairs was far more favorable for him than it had been for Don John when he first succeeded to power. On the whole, there seemed a bright prospect of success. It seemed quite possible that it would be in Parma's power to reduce, at last, this chronic rebellion, and to re-establish the absolute supremacy of Church and King. The pledges of the Ghent treaty had been broken, while in the unions of Brussels which had succeeded, the fatal religious cause had turned the instru-

* Bor, xxix. 661[b]. d. iii.

ment of peace into a sword. The "religion-peace" which had been proclaimed at Antwerp had hardly found favor anywhere. As the provinces, for an instant, had seemingly got the better of their foe, they turned madly upon each other, and the fires of religious discord, which had been extinguished by the common exertions of a whole race trembling for the destruction of their fatherland, were now re-lighted with a thousand brands plucked from the sacred domestic hearth. Fathers and children, brothers and sisters, husbands and wives, were beginning to wrangle, and were prepared to persecute. Catholic and Protestant, during the momentary relief from pressure, forgot their voluntary and most blessed Pacification, to renew their internecine feuds. The banished Reformers, who had swarmed back in droves at the tidings of peace and good-will to all men, found themselves bitterly disappointed. They were exposed in the Walloon provinces to the persecutions of the Malcontents, in the Frisian regions to the still powerful coercion of the royal stadholders.

Persecution begat counter-persecution. The city of Ghent became the centre of a system of insurrection, by which all the laws of God and man were outraged under the pretence of establishing a larger liberty in civil and religious matters. It was at Ghent that the opening scenes in Parma's administration took place. Of the high-born suitors for the Netherland bride, two were still watching each other with jealous eyes. Anjou was at Mons, which city he had secretly but unsuccessfully attempted to master for his own purposes. John Casimir was at Ghent,* fomenting an insurrection which he had neither skill to guide, nor intelligence to comprehend. There was a talk of making him Count of Flanders,† and his paltry ambition was dazzled by the glittering prize. Anjou, who meant to be Count of Flanders himself, as well as Duke or Count of all the other Netherlands, was highly indignant at this report, which he chose to consider true. He wrote to the estates to express his indig-

* Bor, 3. xiii. 3.

† Ibid.

nation. He wrote to Ghent to offer his mediation between the burghers and the Malcontents. Casimir wanted money for his troops. He obtained a liberal supply, but he wanted more. Meantime, the mercenaries were expatiating on their own account throughout the southern provinces; eating up every green leaf, robbing and pillaging, where robbery and pillage had gone so often that hardly anything was left for rapine.* Thus dealt the soldiers in the open country, while their master at Ghent was plunging into the complicated intrigues spread over that unfortunate city by the most mischievous demagogues that ever polluted a sacred cause. Well had Cardinal Granvelle, his enemy, William of Hesse, his friend and kinsman, understood the character of John Casimir. Robbery and pillage were his achievements, to make chaos more confounded was his destiny. Anjou—disgusted with the temporary favor accorded to a rival whom he affected to despise—disbanded his troops in dudgeon, and prepared to retire to France.† Several thousand of these mercenaries took service immediately with the Malcontents‡ under Montigny, thus swelling the ranks of the deadliest foes to that land over which Anjou had assumed the title of protector. The states' army, meanwhile, had been rapidly dissolving. There were hardly men enough left to make a demonstration in the field, or properly to garrison the more important towns. The unhappy provinces, torn by civil and religious dissensions, were overrun by hordes of unpaid soldiers of all nations, creeds, and tongues—Spaniards, Italians, Burgundians, Walloons, Germans, Scotch and English; some who came to attack and others to protect, but who all achieved nothing and agreed in nothing save to maltreat and to outrage the defenceless peasantry and denizens of the smaller towns. The contemporary chronicles are full of harrowing domestic tragedies, in which the actors are always the insolent foreign soldiery and their desperate victims.§

Ghent—energetic, opulent, powerful, passionate, unruly

---

* Bor, 3, xiii. 3. † Ibid., 12. ‡ Ibid., Meteren, viii. 114^d.

§ Bor, b. xiii. Hoofd, b. xiv. Meteren, b. viii., passim.

Ghent—was now the focus of discord, the centre from whence radiated not the light and warmth of reasonable and intelligent liberty, but the bale-fires of murderous licence and savage anarchy. The second city of the Netherlands, one of the wealthiest and most powerful cities of Christendom, it had been its fate so often to overstep the bounds of reason and moderation in its devotion to freedom, so often to incur ignominious chastisement from power which its own excesses had made more powerful, that its name was already becoming a bye-word. It now, most fatally and for ever, was to misunderstand its true position. The Prince of Orange, the great architect of his country's fortunes, would have made it the keystone of the arch which he was laboring to construct. Had he been allowed to perfect his plan, the structure might have endured for ages, a perpetual bulwark against tyranny and wrong. The temporary and slender frame by which the great artist had supported his arch while still unfinished, was plucked away by rude and ribald hands; the keystone plunged into the abyss, to be lost for ever, and the great work of Orange remained a fragment from its commencem nt. The acts of demagogues, the conservative disgust at licence, the jealousy of rival nobles, the venality of military leaders, threw daily fresh stumbling-blocks in his heroic path. It was not six months after the advent of Farnese to power, before that bold and subtle chieftain had seized the double-edged sword of religious dissension as firmly as he had grasped his celebrated brand when he boarded the galley of Mustapha Bey, and the Netherlands were cut in twain, to be re-united nevermore. The separate treaty of the Walloon provinces was soon destined to separate the Celtic and Romanesque elements from the Batavian and Frisian portion of a nationality, which, thoroughly fused in all its parts, would have formed as admirable a compound of fire and endurance as history has ever seen.

Meantime, the grass was growing and the cattle were grazing in the streets of Ghent,* where once the tramp of

* Van d. Vynckt, iii. 3.

workmen going to and from their labor was like the movement of a mighty army.* The great majority of the burghers were of the Reformed religion, and disposed to make effectual resistance to the Malcontents, led by the disaffected nobles. The city, considering itself the natural head of all the southern country, was indignant that the Walloon provinces should dare to reassert that supremacy of Romanism which had been so effectually suppressed, and to admit the possibility of friendly relations with a sovereign who had been virtually disowned. There were two parties, however, in Ghent. Both were led by men of abandoned and dangerous character.† Imbize, the worse of the two demagogues, was inconstant, cruel, cowardly, and treacherous, but possessed of eloquence and a talent for intrigue. Ryhove was a bolder ruffian—wrathful, bitter, and unscrupulous. Imbize was at the time opposed to Orange, disliking his moderation, and trembling at his firmness. Ryhove considered himself the friend of the Prince. We have seen that he had consulted him previously to his memorable attack upon Aerschot, in the autumn of the preceding year, and we know the result of that conference.

The Prince, with the slight dissimulation which belonged less to his character than to his theory of politics, and which was perhaps not to be avoided, in that age of intrigue, by any man who would govern his fellow-men, whether for good or evil, had winked at a project which he would not openly approve. He was not thoroughly acquainted, however, with the desperate character of the man, for he would have scorned an instrument so thoroughly base as Ryhove subsequently proved. The violence of that personage on the occasion of the arrest of Aerschot and his colleagues was mildness compared with the deed with which he now disgraced the cause of freedom. He had been ordered out from Ghent to oppose a force of Malcontents which was gathering in the neighbourhood of Courtray;‡

* Guicciardini, Descript. Gandav.

† Van d. Vynckt, iii. 38, 39. Bor, xiii. 5, sqq. Hoofd, xiv. 589, 599.

‡ Bor, xiii. 5.

but he swore that he would not leave the gates so long as two of the gentlemen whom he had arrested on the twenty-eighth of the previous October, and who yet remained in captivity, were still alive.* These two prisoners were ex-procurator Visch and Blood-Councillor Hessels. Hessels, it seemed, had avowed undying hostility to Ryhove for the injury sustained at his hands, and he had sworn, "by his grey beard," that the ruffian should yet hang for the outrage. Ryhove, not feeling very safe in the position of affairs which then existed, and knowing that he could neither trust Imbize, who had formerly been his friend, nor the imprisoned nobles, who had ever been his implacable enemies, was resolved to make himself safe in one quarter at least, before he set forth against the Malcontents. Accordingly, Hessels and Visch, as they sat together in their prison, at chess, upon the 4th of October, 1578, were suddenly summoned to leave the house, and to enter a carriage which stood at the door. A force of armed men brought the order, and were sufficiently strong to enforce it. The prisoners obeyed, and the coach soon rolled slowly through the streets, left the Courtray gate, and proceeded a short distance along the road towards that city.†

After a few minutes a halt was made. Ryhove then made his appearance at the carriage-window, and announced to the astonished prisoners that they were forthwith to be hanged upon a tree which stood by the road-side. He proceeded to taunt the aged Hessels with his threat against himself, and with his vow "by his grey beard." "Such grey beard shalt thou never live thyself to wear, ruffian," cried Hessels, stoutly—furious rather than terrified at the suddenness of his doom. "There thou liest, false traitor!" roared Ryhove in reply; and to prove the falsehood, he straightway tore out a handful of the old man's beard, and fastened it upon his own cap like a plume. His action was imitated by several of his companions, who cut for themselves locks from the same grey beard, and decorated themselves as their leader

* Bor, xiii. 5.

† Hoofd, xiv. 593. Bor, xiii. 5.

had done. This preliminary ceremony having been concluded, the two aged prisoners were forthwith hanged on a tree, without the least pretence of trial or even sentence.*

Such was the end of the famous councillor who had been wont to shout "*ad patibulum*" in his sleep. It was cruel that the fair face of civil liberty showing itself after years of total eclipse, should be insulted by such bloody deeds on the part of her votaries. It was sad that the crimes of men like Imbize and Ryhove should have cost more to the cause of religious and political freedom than the lives of twenty thousand such ruffians were worth. But for the influence of demagogues like these, counteracting the lofty efforts and pure life of Orange, the separation might never have occurred between the two portions of the Netherlands. The Prince had not power enough, however, nor the nascent commonwealth sufficient consistency, to repress the disorganizing tendency of a fanatical Romanism on the one side, and a retaliatory and cruel ochlocracy on the other.

Such events, with the hatred growing daily more intense between the Walloons and the Ghenters, made it highly important that some kind of an accord should be concluded, if possible. In the country, the Malcontents, under pretence of protecting the Catholic clergy, were daily abusing and plundering the people, while in Ghent the clergy were maltreated, the cloisters pillaged, under the pretence of maintaining liberty.† In this emergency the eyes of all honest men turned naturally to Orange.

Deputies went to and fro between Antwerp and Ghent Three points were laid down by the Prince as indispensable to any arrangement—firstly, that the Catholic clergy should be allowed the free use of their property; secondly, that they should not be disturbed in the exercise of their religion; thirdly, that the gentlemen kept in prison since the memorable twenty-eighth of October should be released.‡ If these points

---

* Hoofd, xiv. 593, 594. Bor, xiii. 5, seq. Meteren, viii. 143. Wagenaer, Vad. Hist., vii. 234.

† Bor. xiii. Hoofd, xiv. Van der Vynckt, 3, iii. 33, sqq. ‡ Bor, xiii. 5.

should be granted, the Archduke Matthias, the states-general, and the Prince of Orange would agree to drive off the Walloon soldiery, and to defend Ghent against all injury.* The two first points were granted, upon condition that sufficient guarantees should be established for the safety of the Reformed religion. The third was rejected, but it was agreed that the prisoners, Champagny, Sweveghem, and the rest—who, after the horrid fate of Hessels and Visch, might be supposed to be sufficiently anxious as to their own doom—should have legal trial, and be defended in the meantime from outrage.†

On the 3rd of November, 1578, a formal act of acceptance of these terms was signed at Antwerp.‡ At the same time, there was murmuring at Ghent, the extravagant portion of the liberal party averring that they had no intention of establishing the "religious peace" when they agreed not to molest the Catholics. On the 11th of November, the Prince of Orange sent messengers to Ghent in the name of the Archduke and the states-general, summoning the authorities to a faithful execution of the act of acceptance. Upon the same day the English envoy, Davidson, made an energetic representation to the same magistrates, declaring that the conduct of the Ghenters was exciting regret throughout the world, and affording a proof that it was their object to protract, not suppress, the civil war which had so long been raging. Such proceedings, he observed, created doubts whether they were willing to obey any law or any magistracy. As, however, it might be supposed that the presence of John Casimir in Ghent at that juncture was authorized by Queen Elizabeth—inasmuch as it was known that he had received a subsidy from her—the envoy took occasion to declare that her Majesty entirely disavowed his proceedings. He observed further that, in the opinion of her Majesty, it was still possible to maintain peace by conforming to the counsels of the Prince of Orange and of the states-general. This, however,

---

* Bor, xiii. 5.

† See the Act of Acceptance; Bor, xiii. 5. sqq.

‡ Bor, xiii. 6, 7.

could be done only by establishing the three points which he had laid down. Her Majesty likewise warned the Ghenters that their conduct would soon compel her to abandon the country's cause altogether, and, in conclusion, she requested, with characteristic thriftiness, to be immediately furnished with a city bond for forty-five thousand pounds sterling.*

Two days afterwards, envoys arrived from Brussels to remonstrate, in their turn, with the sister city, and to save her, if possible, from the madness which had seized upon her. They recalled to the memory of the magistrates the frequent and wise counsels of the Prince of Orange. He had declared that he knew of no means to avert the impending desolation of the fatherland save union of all the provinces and obedience to the general government. His own reputation, and the honor of his house, he felt now to be at stake; for, by reason of the offices which he now held, he had been ceaselessly calumniated as the author of all the crimes which had been committed at Ghent. Against these calumnies he had avowed his intention of publishing his defence.† After thus citing the opinion of the Prince, the envoys implored the magistrates to accept the religious peace which he had proposed, and to liberate the prisoners as he had demanded. For their own part, they declared that the inhabitants of Brussels would never desert him; for, next to God, there was no one who understood their cause so entirely, or who could point out the remedy so intelligently.‡

Thus reasoned the envoys from the states-general and from Brussels, but even while they were reasoning, a fresh tumult occurred at Ghent. The people had been inflamed by demagogues, and by the insane howlings of Peter Dathenus, the unfrocked monk of Poperingen, who had been the servant and minister both of the Pope and of Orange, and who now hated each with equal fervor. The populace, under these influences, rose in its wrath upon the Catholics, smote all their

* Bor, xiii. 7.

† Bor, xiii. 8.

‡ "Als naest God niemand kennende die de gemeine sake en inwendigen nood beter verstaet en de remedien beter kan dirigeren."—Bor, ubi sup.

images into fragments, destroyed all their altar pictures, robbed them of much valuable property, and turned all the Papists themselves out of the city. The riot was so furious that it seemed, says a chronicler, as if all the inhabitants had gone raving mad.* The drums beat the alarm, the magistrates went forth to expostulate, but no commands were heeded till the work of destruction had been accomplished, when the tumult expired at last by its own limitation.

Affairs seemed more threatening than ever. Nothing more excited the indignation of the Prince of Orange than such senseless iconomachy. In fact, he had at one time procured an enactment by the Ghent authorities, making it a crime punishable with death.† He was of Luther's opinion, that idol-worship was to be eradicated from the heart, and that then the idols in the churches would fall of themselves. He felt too with Landgrave William, that "the destruction of such worthless idols was ever avenged by torrents of good human blood."‡ Therefore it may be well supposed that this fresh act of senseless violence, in the very teeth of his remonstrances, in the very presence of his envoys, met with his stern disapprobation. He was on the point of publishing his defence against the calumnies which his toleration had drawn upon him from both Catholic and Calvinist. He was deeply revolving the question, whether it were not better to turn his back at once upon a country which seemed so incapable of comprehending his high purposes, or seconding his virtuous efforts. From both projects he was dissuaded; and although bitterly wronged by both friend and foe, although feeling that even in his own Holland,§ there were whispers against his purity, since his favorable inclinations towards Anjou had become the general topic, yet he still preserved his majestic tranquillity,

* "Met sulken geraes, getier en gebaer datmen geseid soude hebben dat alle de inwoonders dol en rasende waren."—Bor, xiii. 9. Meteren, ix. 149.

† Gh. Gesch., ii. 39: cited by Groen, v. Prinst., vi. 465.

‡ Letter of Landgrave William of Hesse.—Groen, v. Prinst., Archives et Correspondance, vi. 451, sqq.

§ Groen, v. Prinst., Archives, etc., 481, 482.

and smiled at the arrows which fell harmless at his feet. "I admire his wisdom, daily more and more," cried Hubert Languet; "I see those who profess themselves his friends causing him more annoyance than his foes; while, nevertheless, he ever remains true to himself, is driven by no tempests from his equanimity, nor provoked by repeated injuries to immoderate action."*

The Prince had that year been chosen unanimously by the four "members" of Flanders to be governor of that province, but had again declined the office.† The inhabitants, notwithstanding the furious transactions at Ghent, professed attachment to his person, and respect for his authority. He was implored to go to the city. His presence, and that alone, would restore the burghers to their reason, but the task was not a grateful one. It was also not unattended with danger; although this was a consideration which never influenced him, from the commencement of his career to its close. Imbize and his crew were capable of resorting to any extremity or any ambush, to destroy the man whom they feared and hated. The presence of John Casimir was an additional complication; for Orange, while he despised the man, was unwilling to offend his friends. Moreover, Casimir had professed a willingness to assist the cause, and to defer to the better judgment of the Prince. He had brought an army into the field, with which, however, he had accomplished nothing except a thorough pillaging of the peasantry, while, at the same time, he was loud in his demands upon the states to pay his soldiers' wages. The soldiers of the different armies who now overran the country, indeed, vied with each other in extravagant insolence. "Their outrages are most execrable," wrote Marquis Havré; "they demand the most exquisite food, and drink Champagne and Burgundy by the bucketfull."‡ Nevertheless, on the 4th of December, the Prince came to Ghent.§ He held con-

* Letter to Sir P. Sidney.

† Bor, xiii. 9. Apologie d'Orange, pp. 108, 109.

‡ Kervyn de Volkersbeke et Diegerick, Documents Historiques, i. 156, 157.

§ Bor, xiii. 10.

stant and anxious conferences with the magistrates. He was closeted daily with John Casimir, whose vanity and extravagance of temper he managed with his usual skill. He even dined with Imbize, and thus, by smoothing difficulties and reconciling angry passions, he succeeded at last in obtaining the consent of all to a religious peace, which was published on the 27th of December, 1578. It contained the same provisions as those of the project prepared and proposed during the previous summer throughout the Netherlands. Exercise of both religions was established; mutual insults and irritations—whether by word, book, picture, song, or gesture—were prohibited, under severe penalties, while all persons were sworn to protect the common tranquillity by blood, purse, and life. The Catholics, by virtue of this accord, re-entered into possession of their churches and cloisters, but nothing could be obtained in favor of the imprisoned gentlemen.*

The Walloons and Malcontents were now summoned to lay down their arms; but, as might be supposed, they expressed dissatisfaction with the religious peace, proclaiming it hostile to the Ghent treaty and the Brussels union.† In short, nothing would satisfy them but total suppression of the Reformed religion; as nothing would content Imbize and his faction but the absolute extermination of Romanism. A strong man might well seem powerless in the midst of such obstinate and worthless fanatics.

The arrival of the Prince in Ghent was, on the whole, a relief to John Casimir. As usual, this addle-brained individual had plunged headlong into difficulties, out of which he was unable to extricate himself. He knew not what to do, or which way to turn. He had tampered with Imbize and his crew, but he had found that they were not the men for a person of his quality to deal with. He had brought a large army into the field, and had not a stiver in his coffers. He felt bitterly the truth of the Landgrave's warning—"that

* Groen, v. Prinst., Archives, etc., vi. 507, sqq. See the Accord in Bor, 2, xiii. 10, 11.

† Bor, xiii. 12

'twas better to have thirty thousand devils at one's back than thirty thousand German troopers, with no money to give them; it being possible to pay the devils with the sign of the cross, while the soldiers could be discharged only with money or hard knocks."* Queen Elizabeth, too, under whose patronage he had made this most inglorious campaign, was incessant in her reproofs, and importunate in her demands for reimbursement. She wrote to him personally, upbraiding him with his high pretensions and his shortcomings. His visit to Ghent, so entirely unjustified and mischievous; his failure to effect that junction of his army with the states' force under Bossu, by which the royal army was to have been surprised and annihilated; his having given reason to the common people to suspect her Majesty and the Prince of Orange of collusion with his designs, and of a disposition to seek their private advantage and not the general good of the whole Netherlands; the imminent danger, which he had aggravated, that the Walloon provinces, actuated by such suspicions, would fall away from the "generality" and seek a private accord with Parma; these and similar sins of omission and commission were sharply and shrewishly set forth in the Queen's epistle.† 'Twas not for such marauding and intriguing work that she had appointed him her lieutenant, and furnished him with troops and subsidies. She begged him forthwith to amend his ways, for the sake of his name and fame, which were sufficiently soiled in the places where his soldiers had been plundering the country which they came to protect.‡

The Queen sent Daniel Rogers with instructions of similar import to the states-general, repeatedly and expressly disavowing Casimir's proceedings and censuring his character. She also warmly insisted on her bonds. In short, never was unlucky prince more soundly berated by his superiors, more thoroughly disgraced by his followers. In this contemptible situation had Casimir placed himself by his rash ambition to

---

* Archives et Correspondance, vi. 479.

† Bor, 3, xiii. 13, sqq.

‡ Bor, xiii. 13.

prove before the world that German princes could bite and scratch like griffins and tigers as well as carry them in their shields. From this position Orange partly rescued him. He made his peace with the states-general. He smoothed matters with the extravagant Reformers, and he even extorted from the authorities of Ghent the forty-five thousand pounds bond, on which Elizabeth had insisted with such obduracy.* Casimir repaid these favors of the Prince in the coin with which narrow minds and jealous tempers are apt to discharge such obligations—ingratitude. The friendship which he openly manifested at first grew almost immediately cool. Soon afterwards he left Ghent and departed for Germany, leaving behind him a long and tedious remonstrance, addressed to the states-general, in which document he narrated the history of his exploits, and endeavored to vindicate the purity of his character. He concluded this very tedious and superfluous manifesto by observing that—for reasons which he thought proper to give at considerable length—he felt himself "neither too useful nor too agreeable to the provinces." As he had been informed, he said, that the states-general had requested the Queen of England to procure his departure, he had resolved, in order to spare her and them inconvenience, to return of his own accord, "leaving the issue of the war in the high and mighty hand of God."†

The estates answered this remonstrance with words of unlimited courtesy; expressing themselves "obliged to all eternity" for his services, and holding out vague hopes that the monies which he demanded on behalf of his troops should ere long be forthcoming.‡

Casimir having already answered Queen Elizabeth's reproachful letter by throwing the blame of his apparent misconduct upon the states-general, and having promised soon to appear before her Majesty in person, tarried accordingly but a brief season in Germany, and then repaired to England.

* Bor, xiii. 11, sqq.

† See the document at length in Bor, xiii. 13–17.

‡ Bor, 3, xiii. 17, (ii.)

Here he was feasted, flattered, caressed, and invested with the order of the Garter.* Pleased with royal blandishments, and highly enjoying the splendid hospitalities of England, he quite forgot the "thirty thousand devils" whom he had left running loose in the Netherlands, while these wild soldiers, on their part, being absolutely in a starving condition —for there was little left for booty in a land which had been so often plundered—now had the effrontery to apply to the Prince of Parma for payment of their wages.† Alexander Farnese laughed heartily at the proposition, which he considered an excellent jest. It seemed in truth, a jest, although but a sorry one. Parma replied to the messenger of Maurice of Saxony who had made the proposition, that the Germans must be mad to ask him for money, instead of offering to pay him a heavy sum for permission to leave the country. Nevertheless, he was willing to be so far indulgent as to furnish them with passports, provided they departed from the Netherlands instantly. Should they interpose the least delay, he would set upon them without further preface, and he gave them notice, with the arrogance becoming a Spanish general, that the courier was already waiting to report to Spain the number of them left alive after the encounter. Thus deserted by their chief, and hectored by the enemy, the mercenaries, who had little stomach for fight without wages, accepted the passports proffered by Parma.‡ They revenged themselves for the harsh treatment which they had received from Casimir and from the states-general, by singing, everywhere as they retreated, a doggerel ballad—half Flemish, half German—in which their wrongs were expressed with uncouth vigor.

Casimir received the news of the departure of his ragged soldiery on the very day which witnessed his investment with the Garter by the fair hands of Elizabeth herself.§ A few days afterwards he left England, accompanied by an escort of

* Bor, xiii. 34, 35. Hoofd, xiv. 609.

† Bor, xiii. 34, sqq. Strada, Dec. 2, i. 26, sqq.

‡ Strada, 2, i. 27, 28.

§ Ibid., 2, i. 28.

lords and gentlemen, especially appointed for that purpose by the Queen. He landed in Flushing, where he was received with distinguished hospitality, by order of the Prince of Orange, and on the 14th of February, 1579, he passed through Utrecht.* Here he conversed freely at his lodgings in the "German House" on the subject of his vagabond troops, whose final adventures and departure seemed to afford him considerable amusement; and he, moreover, diverted his company by singing, after supper, a few verses of the ballad already mentioned.†

The Duke of Anjou, meantime, after disbanding his troops, had lingered for a while near the frontier. Upon taking his final departure, he sent his resident minister, Des Pruneaux, with a long communication to the states-general, complaining that they had not published their contract with himself, nor fulfilled its conditions. He excused, as well as he could, the awkward fact that his disbanded troops had taken refuge with the Walloons, and he affected to place his own departure upon the ground of urgent political business in France, to arrange which his royal brother had required his immediate attendance. He furthermore most hypocritically expressed a desire for a speedy reconciliation of the provinces with their sovereign, and a resolution that—although for their sake he had made himself a foe to his Catholic Majesty—he would still interpose no obstacle to so desirable a result.‡

To such shallow discourse the states answered with infinite

---

* Languet. ad Sydnæum, 90; Groen v. Prinst., Archives, etc., vi. 571, 572. Bor, xiii. 34, (ii.)

† Bor—who heard the Duke sing the song at the "German House" in Utrecht, 3, xiii. 34.

A translation of a single verse may serve as a specimen of the song:—

"O, have you been in Brabant, fighting for the states?
O, have you brought back anything except your broken pates?
O, I have been in Brabant, myself and all my mates.
We'll go no more to Brabant, unless our brains were addle,
We're coming home on foot, we went there in the saddle;
For there's neither gold nor glory got, in fighting for the states,"
etc., etc.

‡ Bor, xii. 12, sqq.

urbanity, for it was the determination of Orange not to make enemies, at that juncture, of France and England in the same breath. They had foes enough already, and it seemed obvious at that moment, to all persons most observant of the course of affairs, that a matrimonial alliance was soon to unite the two crowns. The probability of Anjou's marriage with Elizabeth was, in truth, a leading motive with Orange for his close alliance with the Duke. The political structure, according to which he had selected the French Prince as protector of the Netherlands, was sagaciously planned ; but unfortunately its foundation was the shifting sandbank of female and royal coquetry. Those who judge only by the result, will be quick to censure a policy which might have had very different issue. They who place themselves in the period anterior to Anjou's visit to England, will admit that it was hardly human not to be deceived by the political aspects of that moment. The Queen, moreover, took pains to upbraid the states-general, by letter, with their disrespect and ingratitude towards the Duke of Anjou—behaviour with which he had been "justly scandalized." For her own part, she assured them of her extreme displeasure at learning that such a course of conduct had been held with a view to her especial contentment—"as if the person of Monsieur, son of France, brother of the King, were disagreeable to her, or as if she wished him ill ;" whereas, on the contrary, they would best satisfy her wishes by showing him all the courtesy to which his high degree and his eminent services entitled him.*

The estates, even before receiving this letter, had, however, acted in its spirit. They had addressed elaborate apologies and unlimited professions to the Duke. They thanked him heartily for his achievements, expressed unbounded regret at his departure, with sincere hopes for his speedy return, and promised "eternal remembrance of his heroic virtues."† They assured

* Archives, etc., de la Maison d'Orange, vi. 535, sqq.

† "Sijn bewesen bystand en sijne heroike deugt souden sy nimmermeer vergeten."—Bor, xiii. 12, sqq.

him, moreover, that should the first of the following March arrive without bringing with it an honorable peace with his Catholic Majesty, they should then feel themselves compelled to declare that the King had forfeited his right to the sovereignty of these provinces. In this case they concluded that, as the inhabitants would be then absolved from their allegiance to the Spanish monarch, it would then be in their power to treat with his Highness of Anjou concerning the sovereignty, according to the contract already existing.*

These assurances were ample, but the states, knowing the vanity of the man, offered other inducements, some of which seemed sufficiently puerile. They promised that "his statue, in copper, should be placed in the public squares of Antwerp and Brussels, for the eternal admiration of posterity," and that a "crown of olive-leaves should be presented to him every year."† The Duke—not inexorable to such courteous solicitations—was willing to achieve both immortality and power by continuing his friendly relations with the states, and he answered accordingly in the most courteous terms. The result of this interchange of civilities it will be soon our duty to narrate.

At the close of the year the Count of Bossu died, much to the regret of the Prince of Orange, whose party—since his release from prison by virtue of the Ghent treaty—he had warmly espoused. "We are in the deepest distress in the world," wrote the Prince to his brother, three days before the Count's death, "for the dangerous malady of M. de Bossu. Certainly, the country has much to lose in his death, but I hope that God will not so much afflict us."‡ Yet the calumniators of the day did not scruple to circulate, nor the royalist chroniclers to perpetuate, the most senseless and infamous fables on the subject of this nobleman's death. He died of poison, they said, administered to him "*in oysters*,"§ by com-

---

* Bor, xiii. 12, sqq.

† Meteren, ix. 145a.—"Accompanied, however, by substantial presents to the value of 100,000 livres Artois."—Meteren, ubi sup.

‡ Archives et Corresp., vi. 513. § J. B. Tassis, Comment., lib. v. 329.

mand of the Prince of Orange, who had likewise made a point of standing over him on his death-bed, for the express purpose of sneering at the Catholic ceremonies by which his dying agonies were solaced.* Such were the tales which grave historians have recorded concerning the death of Maximilian of Bossu, who owed so much to the Prince. The command of the states' army, a yearly pension of five thousand florins, granted at the especial request of Orange but a few months before, and the profound words of regret in the private letter just cited, are a sufficient answer to such slanders.†

The personal courage and profound military science of Parma were invaluable to the royal cause; but his subtle, unscrupulous, and subterranean combinations of policy were even more fruitful at this period. No man ever understood the art of bribery more thoroughly or practised it more skilfully. He bought a politician, or a general, or a grandee, or a regiment of infantry, usually at the cheapest price at which those articles could be purchased, and always with the utmost delicacy with which such traffic could be conducted. Men conveyed themselves to government for a definite price—fixed accurately in florins and groats, in places and pensions—while a decent gossamer of conventional phraseology was ever allowed to float over the nakedness of unblushing treason. Men high in station, illustrious by ancestry, brilliant in valor, huckstered themselves, and swindled a confiding country for as ignoble motives as ever led counterfeiters or bravoes to the gallows, but they were dealt with in public as if actuated only by the loftiest principles. Behind their ancient shields, ostentatiously emblazoned with fidelity to church and king, they thrust forth their itching palms with the mendicity which would be hardly credible, were it not attested by the monuments more perennial than brass, of their own letters and recorded conversations.

Already, before the accession of Parma to power, the true

* Strada, 2, i. 37.

† Compare Groen v. Prinst., vi. 511, 512. Bor, 2, xiii. 25b. Wagenaer, Vad. Hist., vii. 243, 244.

way to dissever the provinces had been indicated by the famous treason of the Seigneur de la Motte. This nobleman commanded a regiment in the service of the states-general, and was Governor of Gravelines. On promise of forgiveness for all past disloyalty, of being continued in the same military posts under Philip which he then held for the patriots, and of a "merced" large enough to satisfy his most avaricious dreams, he went over to the royal government.* The negotiation was conducted by Alonzo Curiel, financial agent of the King, and was not very nicely handled. The paymaster, looking at the affair purely as a money transaction—which in truth it was—had been disposed to drive rather too hard a bargain. He offered only fifty thousand crowns for La Motte and his friend Baron Montigny, and assured his government that those gentlemen, with the soldiers under their command, were very dear at the price.† La Motte higgled very hard for more, and talked pathetically of his services and his wounds—for he had been a most distinguished and courageous campaigner—but Alonzo was implacable.‡ Moreover, one Robert Bien-Aimé, Prior of Renty, was present at all the conferences. This ecclesiastic was a busy intriguer, but not very adroit. He was disposed to make himself useful to government, for he had set his heart upon putting the mitre of Saint Omer upon his head, and he had accordingly composed a very ingenious libel upon the Prince of Orange, in which production, "although the Prior did not pretend to be Apelles or Lysippus," he hoped that the Governor-General would recognize a portrait colored to the life.§ This accomplished artist was, however, not so successful as he was picturesque and

* Reconciliation des Provinces Wallones, i. 2–12, 202, 213–216, 227–234, 271, 272. Letters of La Motte and Don John of Austria, etc., MS., Royal Archives at Brussels.

† Lettres interceptées du Contador Alonzo Curiel au Pce de Parme. Plantin. Anvers, 1579.—"—— parece á me que son soldados comprados á muy alto precio."

‡ "—— con cien mil remonstraciones y historias de sus servicios y heridas," etc.—Ibid.

§ Renty to Prince of Parma, Rec. Prov. Wall., iii. 97. MS.

industrious. He was inordinately vain of his services, thinking himself, said Alonzo, splenetically, worthy to be carried in a procession like a little saint,* and as he had a busy brain, but an unruly tongue, it will be seen that he possessed a remarkable faculty of making himself unpleasant. This was not the way to earn his bishopric. La Motte, through the candid communications of the Prior, found himself the subject of mockery in Parma's camp and cabinet, where treachery to one's country and party was not, it seemed, regarded as one of the loftier virtues, however convenient it might be at the moment to the royal cause. The Prior intimated especially that Ottavio Gonzaga had indulged in many sarcastic remarks at La Motte's expense. The brave but venal warrior, highly incensed at thus learning the manner in which his conduct was estimated by men of such high rank in the royal service, was near breaking off the bargain. He was eventually secured, however, by still larger offers—Don John allowing him three hundred florins a month, presenting him with the two best horses in his stable, and sending him an open form, which he was to fill out in the most stringent language which he could devise, binding the government to the payment of an ample and entirely satisfactory "merced."† Thus La Motte's bargain was completed—a crime which, if it had only entailed the loss of the troops under his command, and the possession of Gravelines, would have been of no great historic importance. It was, however, the first blow of a vast and carefully sharpened treason, by which the country was soon to be cut in twain for ever—the first in a series of bargains by which the noblest names of the Netherlands were to be contaminated with bribery and fraud.

While the negotiations with La Motte were in progress, the government of the states-general at Brussels had sent Saint Aldegonde to Arras. The states of Artois, then assembled

---

* "—— que avia Va. Alteza de mandar traer en palmas o andas," etc. Lettres interceptées de Curiel.

† Don John to La Motte, Rec. Prov. Wall., MS. i. 271, 272. Lettres de Curiel.

in that city, had made much difficulty in acceding to an assessment of seven thousand florins laid upon them by the central authority. The occasion was skilfully made use of by the agents of the royal party to weaken the allegiance of the province, and of its sister Walloon provinces, to the patriot cause. Saint Aldegonde made his speech before the assembly, taking the ground boldly, that the war was made for liberty of conscience and of fatherland, and that all were bound, whether Catholic or Protestant, to contribute to the sacred fund. The vote passed, but it was provided that a moiety of the assessment should be paid by the ecclesiastical branch, and the stipulation excited a tremendous uproar. The clerical bench regarded the tax as both a robbery and an affront. "We came nearly to knife-playing," said the most distinguished priest in the assembly, "and if we had done so, the ecclesiastics would not have been the first to cry enough."* They all withdrew in a rage, and held a private consultation upon "these exorbitant and more than Turkish demands." John Sarrasin, Prior of Saint Vaast, the keenest, boldest, and most indefatigable of the royal partisans of that epoch, made them an artful harangue. This man—a better politician than the other prior—was playing for a mitre too, and could use his cards better. He was soon to become the most invaluable agent in the great treason preparing. No one could be more delicate, noiseless, or unscrupulous, and he was soon recognized both by Governor-General and King as the individual above all others to whom the re-establishment of the royal authority over the Walloon

* "—— les communs forcerent les ecclésiastiques d'en prendre la juste moitié a leur charge—et de fait la chose étoit venue jusques de venir aux mains et jouer des cousteaux pour veoir quy aurait belle amye—les eccléisastiques n'eussent fait joucq," etc.—MS. letter of the Prior of Saint Vaast, Rec. Prov. Wall., i. 76, 135, 136. The whole history of these Walloon intrigues is narrated in the numerous letters—entirely unpublished—of the Prior, with much piquancy and spirit. They are in the Collection of Correspondence between Don John, Parma, and others, and the Malcontent nobles, entitled "Reconciliation des Provinces Wallones," five vols., Royal Archives in Brussels. An examination of these most interesting documents is indispensable to a thorough understanding of the permanent separation of the Netherlands effected in the years 1578 and 1579.

provinces was owing. With the shoes of swiftness on his feet, the coat of darkness on his back, and the wishing purse in his hand, he sped silently and invisibly from one great Malcontent chieftain to another, buying up centurions, and captains, and common soldiers; circumventing Orangists, Ghent democrats, Anjou partisans; weaving a thousand intrigues, ventilating a hundred hostile mines, and passing unharmed through the most serious dangers and the most formidable obstacles. Eloquent, too, at a pinch, he always understood his audience, and upon this occasion unsheathed the most incisive, if not the most brilliant weapon which could be used in the debate. It was most expensive to be patriotic, he said, while silver was to be saved, and gold to be earned by being loyal. They ought to keep their money to defend themselves, not give it to the Prince of Orange, who would only put it into his private pocket on pretence of public necessities. The Ruward would soon be slinking back to his lair, he observed, and leave them all in the fangs of their enemies. Meantime, it was better to rush into the embrace of a bountiful king, who was still holding forth his arms to them. They were approaching a precipice, said the Prior; they were entering a labyrinth; and not only was the "sempiternal loss of body and soul impending over them, but their property was to be taken also, and the cat to be thrown against their legs." By this sudden descent into a very common proverbial expression, Sarrasin meant to intimate that they were getting themselves into a difficult position, in which they were sure to reap both danger and responsibility.*

The harangue had much effect upon his hearers, who were now more than ever determined to rebel against the government which they had so recently accepted, preferring, in the words of the Prior, "to be maltreated by their prince, rather than to be barbarously tyrannized over by a heretic." So much anger had been excited in celestial minds by a demand of thirty-five hundred florins.

Saint Aldegonde was entertained in the evening at a great

* Letter of Saint Vaast, before cited.

banquet, followed by a theological controversy, in which John Sarrasin complained that "he had been attacked upon his own dunghill." Next day the distinguished patriot departed on a canvassing tour among the principal cities; the indefatigable monk employing the interval of his absence in aggravating the hostility of the Artesian orders to the pecuniary demands of the general government. He was assisted in his task by a peremptory order which came down from Brussels, ordering, in the name of Matthias, a levy upon the ecclesiastical property, "rings, jewels, and reliquaries," unless the clerical contribution should be forthcoming. The rage of the bench was now intense, and by the time of Saint Aldegonde's return a general opposition had been organized. The envoy met with a chilling reception; there were no banquets any more—no discussions of any kind. To his demands for money, "he got a fine *nihil*," said Saint Vaast; and as for polemics, the only conclusive argument for the country would be, as he was informed on the same authority, the "finishing of Orange and of his minister along with him." More than once had the Prior intimated to government—as so many had done before him—that to "despatch Orange, author of all the troubles," was the best preliminary to any political arrangement. From Philip and his Governor-General, down to the humblest partisan, this conviction had been daily strengthening. The knife or bullet of an assassin was the one thing needful to put an end to this incarnated rebellion.*

Thus matters grew worse and worse in Artois. The Prior, busier than ever in his schemes, was one day arrested along with other royal emissaries, kept fifteen days "in a stinking cellar, where the scullion washed the dishes," and then sent to Antwerp to be examined by the states-general. He behaved

* "Ils commencent à desestimer leur Rouart et ont opinion que si lès affaires bastent mal, il se retirera en sa tasnière. Il semble aux bons que sy l'on peut dépescher le chef des troubles, que ce seroit le moyen pour réunir ce quy est tant divisé. Ste Aldegonde s'est bien apercheu que chacun se desgouste du Pce d'Orange. Et où auparavant tout le monde l'adorait et tenoit pour son saulveur, maintenant l'on ose bien dire qu'il le fault tuer et son ministre aussi."—MS. letters of Saint Vaast, before cited.

with great firmness, although he had good reason to tremble for his neck. Interrogated by Leoninus on the part of the central government, he boldly avowed that these pecuniary demands upon the Walloon estates, and particularly upon their ecclesiastical branches, would never be tolerated. "In Alva's time," said Sarrasin, "men were flayed, but not shorn." Those who were more attached to their skin than their fleece might have thought the practice in the good old times of the Duke still more objectionable. Such was not the opinion of the Prior and the rest of his order. After an unsatisfactory examination and a brief duresse, the busy ecclesiastic was released; and as his secret labors had not been detected, he resumed them after his return more ardently than ever.*

A triangular intrigue was now fairly established in the Walloon country. The Duke of Alençon's head-quarters were at Mons; the rallying-point of the royalist faction was with La Motte at Gravelines; while the ostensible leader of the states' party, Viscount Ghent, was governor of Artois, and supposed to be supreme in Arras. La Motte was provided by government with a large fund of secret-service money, and was instructed to be very liberal in his bribes to men of distinction; having a tender regard, however, to the excessive demands of this nature now daily made upon the royal purse.† The "little Count," as the Prior called Lalain, together with his brother, Baron Montigny, were considered highly desirable acquisitions for government, if they could be gained. It was thought, however, that they had the "*fleur-de-lys* imprinted too deeply upon their hearts,"‡ for the effect produced upon Lalain, governor of Hainault, by Margaret of Valois, had not yet been effaced. His brother also had been disposed to favor

* MS. letters of Saint Vaast, Rec. Prov. Wall., i. 269, 270, MS.

† Parma to La Motte, Rec. Prov. Wall., ii. 140–142, MS.

‡ Moncheaux to Parma, Rec. Prov. Wall., 216–218, MS. Emanuel de Lalain, Seigneur de Montigny, and afterwards Marquis de Renty, was brother to Count de Lalain, governor of Hainault, and cousin to Count Hoogstraaten and Count Renneberg. He was not related to the unfortunate Baron Montigny, whose tragical fate has been recorded in the second volume of this history, and who was a Montmorency.

the French prince, but his mind was more open to conviction. A few private conferences with La Motte, and a course of ecclesiastical tuition from the Prior—whose golden opinions had irresistible resonance—soon wrought a change in the Malcontent chieftain's mind. Other leading seigniors were secretly dealt with in the same manner. Lalain, Héze, Havré, Capres, Egmont, and even the Viscount of Ghent, all seriously inclined their ears to the charmer, and looked longingly and lovingly as the wily Prior rolled in his tangles before them—"to mischief swift." Few had yet declared themselves ; but of the grandees who commanded large bodies of troops, and whose influence with their order was paramount, none were safe for the patriot cause throughout the Walloon country.*

The nobles and ecclesiastics were ready to join hands in support of church and king, but in the city of Arras, the capital of the whole country, there was a strong Orange and liberal party. Gosson, a man of great wealth, one of the most distinguished advocates in the Netherlands, and possessing the gift of popular eloquence to a remarkable degree, was the leader of this burgess faction. In the earlier days of Parma's administration, just as a thorough union of the Walloon provinces in favor of the royal government had nearly been formed, these Orangists of Arras risked a daring stroke. Inflamed by the harangues of Gosson, and supported by five hundred foot soldiers and fifty troopers under one Captain Ambrose, they rose against the city magistracy, whose sentiments were unequivocally for Parma, and thrust them all into prison.† They then constituted a new board of fifteen,

* MS. correspondence of Parma with Saint Vaast, La Motte, Lalain, Montigny, Capres, Longueval, and others. Rec. Prov. Wall., ii. 3, 4, 19, 20, 31–42, 44, 61–77, 87, 88, 104, 105, 115, 116, 140–142.

† MS. anonymous letter from Arras (Oct. 26, 1578) in Rec. Prov. Wall., i. 440–442.—The whole episode is also most admirably related in a manuscript fragment by an eye-witness, entitled "Discours Véritable de ce que s'est passé en la ville d'Arras," Bibl. de Bourgogne, N°. 6042. The author was Pontus Payen, Seigneur des Essarts, a warm Catholic and partisan of the royal cause, whose larger work—also unpublished—upon the earlier troubles in the Nether-

some Catholics and some Protestants, but all patriots, of whom Gosson was chief. The stroke took the town by surprise, and was for a moment successful. Meantime, they depended upon assistance from Brussels. The royal and ecclesiastical party was, however, not so easily defeated, and an old soldier, named Bourgeois, loudly denounced Captain Ambrose, the general of the revolutionary movement, as a vile coward, and affirmed that with thirty good men-at-arms he would undertake to pound the whole rebel army to powder—"a pack of scarecrows," he said, "who were not worth as many owls for military purposes."

Three days after the imprisonment of the magistracy, a strong Catholic rally was made in their behalf in the Fish-market, the ubiquitous Prior of Saint Vaast flitting about among the Malcontents, blithe and busy as usual when storms were brewing. Matthew Doucet, of the revolutionary faction —a man both martial and pacific in his pursuits, being eminent both as a gingerbread baker and a sword-player*—swore he would have the little monk's life if he had to take him from the very horns of the altar ; but the Prior had braved sharper threats than these. Moreover, the grand altar would have been the last place to look for him on that occasion. While Gosson was making a tremendous speech in favor of conscience and fatherland at the Hotel de Ville, practical John Sarrasin, purse in hand, had challenged the rebel general, Ambrose to private combat. In half an hour, that warrior was routed, and fled from the field at the head of his scarecrows,† for there was no resisting the power before which the Montignys and the La Mottes had succumbed. Eloquent Gosson was left to his fate. Having the Catholic magistracy in durance, and with nobody to guard them, he felt, as was well observed

---

lands, has been often cited in the first and second volumes of this history. A chapter in the history of Renom de France is also devoted to this series of events; Troubles des P. B., iv. c. 3.

* "Faiseur des pains d'espices —— epicier et joueur d'espée."—Letter from Arras, before cited, P. Payen, Troubles d'Arras., MS.

† Letter from Arras, MS.

by an ill-natured contemporary, like a man holding a wolf by the ears, equally afraid to let go or to retain his grasp.

His dilemma was soon terminated. While he was deliberating with his colleagues—Mordacq, an old campaigner, Crugeot, Bertoul, and others—whether to stand or fly, the drums and trumpets of the advancing royalists were heard. In another instant the Hotel de Ville was swarming with men-at-arms, headed by Bourgeois, the veteran who had expressed so slighting an opinion as to the prowess of Captain Ambrose. The tables were turned, the miniature revolution was at an end, the counter-revolution effected. Gosson and his confederates escaped out of a back door, but were soon afterwards arrested. Next morning, Baron Capres, the great Malcontent seignior, who was stationed with his regiment in the neighbourhood, and who had long been secretly coquetting with the Prior and Parma, marched into the city at the head of a strong detachment, and straightway proceeded to erect a very tall gibbet in front of the Hotel de Ville.* This looked practical in the eyes of the liberated and reinstated magistrates, and Gosson, Crugeot, and the rest were summoned at once before them. The advocate thought, perhaps, with a sigh, that his judges, so recently his prisoners, might have been the fruit for another gallows-tree, had he planted it when the ground was his own; but taking heart of grace, he encouraged his colleagues—now his fellow-culprits. Crugeot, undismayed, made his appearance before the tribunal, arrayed in a corslet of proof, with a golden hilted sword, a scarf embroidered with pearls and gold, and a hat bravely plumaged with white, blue, and orange feathers—the colors of William the Silent—of all which finery he was stripped, however, as soon as he entered the court.†

The process was rapid. A summons from Brussels was expected every hour from the general government, ordering the cases to be brought before the federal tribunal, and as the Walloon provinces were not yet ready for open revolt, the order would be an inconvenient one. Hence the necessity for

---

* P. Payen, Troubles d'Arras, MS.

† Ibid.

haste. The superior court of Artois, to which an appeal from the magistrates lay, immediately held a session in another chamber of the Hotel de Ville while the lower court was trying the prisoners, and Bertoul, Crugeot, Mordacq, with several others, were condemned in a few hours to the gibbet. They were invited to appeal, if they chose, to the council of Artois, but hearing that the court was sitting next door, so that there was no chance of a rescue in the streets, they declared themselves satisfied with the sentence. Gosson had not been tried, his case being reserved for the morrow.

Meantime, the short autumnal day had drawn to a close. A wild, stormy, rainy night then set in, but still the royalist party—citizens and soldiers intermingled—all armed to the teeth, and uttering fierce cries, while the whole scene was fitfully illuminated with the glare of flambeaux and blazing tar-barrels, kept watch in the open square around the city hall. A series of terrible Rembrandt-like night-pieces succeeded—grim, fantastic, and gory. Bertoul, an old man, who for years had so surely felt himself predestined to his present doom that he had kept a gibbet in his own house to accustom himself to the sight of the machine, was led forth the first, and hanged at ten in the evening.* He was a good man, of perfectly blameless life, a sincere Catholic, but a warm partisan of Orange.

Valentine de Mordacq, an old soldier, came from the Hotel de Ville to the gallows at midnight. As he stood on the ladder, amid the flaming torches, he broke forth into furious execrations, wagging his long white beard to and fro, making hideous grimaces, and cursing the hard fate which, after many dangers on the battle-field and in beleaguered cities, had left him to such a death. The cord strangled his curses. Crugeot was executed at three in the morning, having obtained a few hours' respite in order to make his preparations, which he accordingly occupied himself in doing as tranquilly as if he had been setting forth upon an agreeable journey. He looked

* P. Payen, Troubles d'Arras, MS.

like a phantom, according to eye-witnesses, as he stood under the gibbet, making a most pious and Catholic address to the crowd.

The whole of the following day was devoted to the trial of Gosson. He was condemned at nightfall, and heard by appeal before the superior court directly afterwards. At midnight of the 25th of October, 1578, he was condemned to lose his head, the execution to take place without delay. The city guards and the infantry under Capres still bivouacked upon the square; the howling storm still continued, but the glare of fagots and torches made the place as light as day. The ancient advocate, with haggard eyes and features distorted by wrath, walking between the sheriff and a Franciscan monk, advanced through the long lane of halberdiers, in the grand hall of the Town House, and thence emerged upon the scaffold erected before the door. He shook his fists with rage at the released magistrates, so lately his prisoners, exclaiming that to his misplaced mercy it was owing that his head, instead of their own, was to be placed upon the block. He bitterly reproached the citizens for their cowardice in shrinking from dealing a blow for their fatherland, and in behalf of one who had so faithfully served them. The clerk of the court then read the sentence amid a silence so profound that every syllable he uttered, and every sigh and ejaculation of the victim, were distinctly heard in the most remote corner of the square. Gosson then, exclaiming that he was murdered without cause, knelt upon the scaffold. His head fell while an angry imprecation was still upon his lips.*

Several other persons of lesser note were hanged during the week—among others, Matthew Doucet, the truculent man of gingerbread, whose rage had been so judiciously but so unsuccessfully directed against the Prior of Saint Vaast. Captain Ambrose, too, did not live long to enjoy the price of his treachery. He was arrested very soon afterwards by the states' government in Antwerp, put to the torture, hanged and quar-

* P. Payen, Troubles d'Arras, MS.

tered.* In troublous times like those, when honest men found it difficult to keep their heads upon their shoulders, rogues were apt to meet their deserts, unless they had the advantage of lofty lineage and elevated position.

"Ille crucem sceleris pretium tulit, hic diadema."

This municipal revolution and counter-revolution, obscure though they seem, were in reality of very grave importance. This was the last blow struck for freedom in the Walloon country. The failure of the movement made that scission of the Netherlands certain, which has endured till our days, for the influence of the ecclesiastics in the states of Artois and Hainault, together with the military power of the Malcontent grandees, whom Parma and John Sarrasin had purchased, could no longer be resisted. The liberty of the Celtic provinces was sold, and a few high-born traitors received the price. Before the end of the year (1578) Montigny had signified to the Duke of Alençon that a prince who avowed himself too poor to pay for soldiers was no master for him.† The Baron, therefore, came to an understanding with La Motte and Sarrasin, acting for Alexander Farnese, and received the command of the infantry in the Walloon provinces, a merced of four thousand crowns a year, together with as large a slice of La Motte's hundred thousand florins for himself and soldiers, as that officer could be induced to part with.‡

Baron Capres, whom Sarrasin—being especially enjoined to purchase him—had, in his own language, "sweated blood and water" to secure, at last agreed to reconcile himself with the King's party upon condition of receiving the government-general of Artois, together with the particular government of Hesdin—very lucrative offices, which the Viscount of Ghent then held by commission of the states-general.* That

* Letter of Saint Vaast, Rec. Prov. Wall., ii. 41, 42, MS.

† Mémoire de ce qui s'est passé à l'entrevue entre le S[r]. de Montigny, Comte de Lalain, Duc d'Arschot, Marquis d'Havré, et al.; Rec. Prov. Wall., ii. 104, 105, MS.

‡ MS. letters of Parma, Saint Vaast, Montigny, La Motte, et al.; Rec. Prov. Wall., ii. 35–37, 115; iii. 120; iv. 221.

politic personage, however, whose disinclination to desert the liberty party which had clothed him with such high functions, was apparently so marked that the Prior had caused an ambush to be laid both for him and the Marquis Havré, in order to obtain bodily possession of two such powerful enemies,† now, at the last moment, displayed his true colors. He consented to reconcile himself also, on condition of receiving the royal appointment to the same government which he then held from the patriot authorities, together with the title of Marquis de Richebourg, the command of all the cavalry in the royalist provinces, and certain rewards in money besides. By holding himself at a high mark, and keeping at a distance, he had obtained his price. Capres, for whom Philip, at Parma's suggestion, had sent the commission as governor of Artois and of Hesdin, was obliged to renounce those offices, notwithstanding his earlier "reconciliation," and the "blood and water" of John Sarrasin.‡ Ghent was not even contented with these guerdons, but insisted upon the command of all the cavalry, including the band of ordnance which, with handsome salary, had been assigned to Lalain as a part of the wages for his treason,§ while the "little Count"—fiery as his small and belligerent cousin‖ whose exploits have been recorded in the earlier pages of this history—boldly taxed Parma and the King with cheating him out of his promised reward, in order to please a noble whose services had been less valuable than those of the Lalain family.¶ Having thus obtained the

* Rec. Prov. Wall., ii. 130–133, MS.

† Rec. Prov. Wall., ii., f. 73. MS.—Compare Corresp. Alex. Farnese, p. 61.—Parma to Philip II.

‡ MS. letters of Vicomte de Gand to Philip II., and of Philip II. to Vicomte de Gand, Marquis de Richebourg; Rec. Prov. Wall., ii. 197–210.—Compare Correspondance, Alex. Farnese, 81, 85, 89, 97.

§ Rec. Prov. Wall., iv. 223, Lalain to Parma, MS.

‖ Anthony, Count of Hoogstraaten, the friend of Orange.

¶ "——j'espère que S. M. ne jugera les services que j'ay fait et fais journellement à icelle moindres que ceulx du dit Marquis de Richebourg, et que pour son seul respect elle ne m'estimera si peu, de me frauder, de ce que le Comte de Mansfeld m'avait auparavant fait entendre de la part de V. E.," etc.—Lalain to Parma, Rec. Prov. Wall., iv. 278, MS. Parma to Lalain, Rec. Prov. Wall., ii. 75–77.

lion's share, due, as he thought, to his well known courage and military talents, as well as to the powerful family influence which he wielded—his brother, the Prince of Espinoy, hereditary seneschal of Hainault, having likewise rallied to the King's party—Ghent jocosely intimated to Parma his intention of helping himself to the two best horses in the Prince's stables in exchange for those lost at Gemblours,* in which disastrous action he had commanded the cavalry for the states. He also sent two terriers to Farnese, hoping that they would "prove more useful than beautiful."† The Prince might have thought, perhaps, as much of the Viscount's treason.

John Sarrasin, the all-accomplished Prior, as the reward of his exertions, received from Philip the abbey of Saint Vaast, the richest and most powerful ecclesiastical establishment in the Netherlands. At a subsequent period his grateful sovereign created him Archbishop of Cambray.‡

Thus the "troubles of Arras"—as they were called—terminated. Gosson, the respected, wealthy, eloquent, and virtuous advocate, together with his colleagues—all Catholics, but at the same time patriots and liberals—died the death of felons for their unfortunate attempt to save their fatherland from an ecclesiastical and venal conspiracy; while the actors in the plot, having all performed well their parts, received their full meed of prizes and applause.

The private treaty by which the Walloon provinces of Artois, Hainault, Lille, Douay, and Orchies, united themselves in a separate league was signed upon the 6th of January, 1579, but the final arrangements for the reconciliation of the Malcontent nobles and their soldiers were not completed until April 6th, upon which day a secret paper was signed at Mount Saint Eloi.

The secret current of the intrigue had not, however, flowed on with perfect smoothness until this placid termination. On the contrary, there had been much bickering, heart-burning,

* Rec. Prov. Wall., ii. 202–204, MS.

† Rec. Prov. Wall., iii. 127, Marquis de Richebourg to Parma, MS.

‡ Correspondance Alex. Farnese, 41, 46, 55.

and mutual suspicions and recriminations. There had been violent wranglings among the claimants of the royal rewards. Lalain and Capres were not the only Malcontents who had cause to complain of being cheated of the promised largess. Montigny, in whose favor Parma had distinctly commanded La Motte to be liberal of the King's secret-service money, furiously charged the Governor of Gravelines with having received a large supply of gold from Spain, and of "locking the rascal counters from his friends," so that Parma was obliged to quiet the Baron, and many other barons in the same predicament, out of his own purse. All complained bitterly, too, that the King, whose promises had been so profuse to the nobles while the reconciliation was pending, turned a deaf ear to their petitions and left their letters unanswered, after the deed was accomplished.*

The unlucky Prior of Renty, whose disclosures to La Motte concerning the Spanish sarcasms upon his venality, had so nearly caused the preliminary negotiation with that seignior to fail, was the cause of still further mischief through the interception of Alonzo Curiel's private letters. Such revelations of corruption, and of contempt on the part of the corrupters, were eagerly turned to account by the states' government. A special messenger was despatched to Montigny† with the intercepted correspondence, accompanied by an earnest prayer that he would not contaminate his sword and his noble name by subserviency to men who despised even while they purchased traitors. That noble, both confounded and exasperated, was for a moment inclined to listen to the voice of honor and patriotism, but reflection and solitude induced him to pocket up his wrongs and his "merced" together. The states-general also sent the correspondence to the Walloon provincial authorities, with an eloquent address, begging them to study well the pitiful part which La Motte had enacted in the private comedy then performing, and to

* Montigny to La Motte, Rec. Prov. Wall., iii. 120, and v. 145. MS. Mansfeld to Parma.—Compare Corresp. Alex. Farnese, 135.

† Groen v. Prinsterer, Archives, vi. 606.

behold as in a mirror their own position, if they did not recede ere it was too late.*

The only important effect produced by the discovery was upon the Prior of Renty himself. Ottavio Gonzaga, the intimate friend of Don John, and now high in the confidence of Parma, wrote to La Motte, indignantly denying the truth of Bien Aimé's tattle, and affirming that not a word had ever been uttered by himself or by any gentleman in his presence to the disparagement of the Governor of Gravelines. He added that if the Prior had worn another coat, and were of quality equal to his own, he would have made him eat his words or a few inches of steel. In the same vehement terms he addressed a letter to Bien Aimé himself.† Very soon afterwards, notwithstanding his coat and his quality, that unfortunate ecclesiastic found himself beset one dark night by two soldiers, who left him severely wounded and bleeding nearly to death upon the high road,‡ but escaping with life, he wrote to Parma, recounting his wrongs and the "sword-thrust in his left thigh," and made a demand for a merced.

The Prior recovered from this difficulty only to fall into another, by publishing what he called an apologue, in which he charged that the reconciled nobles were equally false to the royal and to the rebel government, and that, although "the fatted calf had been killed for them, after they had so long been feeding with perverse heretical pigs," they were, in truth, as mutinous as ever, being bent upon establishing an oligarchy in the Netherlands, and dividing the territory among themselves, to the exclusion of the sovereign. This naturally excited the wrath of the Viscount and others. The Seigneur d'Auberlieu, in a letter written in what the writer himself called the "gross style of a gendarme," charged the Prior with maligning honorable lords and—in the favorite colloquial phrase of the day

---

* MS. letter of the states-general to the estates of Artois, Hainault, Lille, Douay, and Orchies; Ord. Depêchen Boek der St. gl. A°. 1579, f. 200. Royal Archives at the Hague.

† Rec. Prov. Wall., ii. 270 and 270vo. MS. letters of Ottavio Gonzaga.

‡ Prieur de Renty to Parma, MS., Rec. Prov. Wall., iii. 140.

—with attempting "to throw the cat against their legs." The real crime of the meddling priest, however, was to have let that troublesome animal out of the bag. He was accordingly waylaid again, and thrown into prison by Count Lalain. While in durance he published an abject apology for his apologue, explaining that his allusions to "returned prodigals," "heretic swine," and to "Sodom and Gomorrah," had been entirely misconstrued. He was, however, retained in custody until Parma ordered his release on the ground that the punishment had been already sufficient for the offence. He then requested to be appointed Bishop of Saint Omer, that see being vacant. Parma advised the King by no means to grant the request—the Prior being neither endowed with the proper age nor discretion for such a dignity—but to bestow some lesser reward, in money or otherwise, upon the discomfited ecclesiastic, who had rendered so many services and incurred so many dangers.*

The states-general and the whole national party regarded, with prophetic dismay, the approaching dismemberment of their common country. They sent deputation on deputation to the Walloon states, to warn them of their danger, and to avert, if possible, the fatal measure. Meantime, as by the already accomplished movement, the "generality" was fast disappearing, and was indeed but the shadow of its former self, it seemed necessary to make a vigorous effort to restore something like unity to the struggling country. The Ghent Pacification had been their outer wall, ample enough and strong enough to enclose and to protect all the provinces. Treachery and religious fanaticism had undermined the bulwark almost as soon as reared. The whole beleaguered country was in danger of becoming utterly exposed to a foe who grew daily more threatening. As in besieged cities, a sudden breastwork is thrown up internally, when the outward defences are crumbling—so the energy of Orange had been silently pre-

* Rec. Prov. Wall., iv. 81–83, 264, 275, sqq., 336, v. 25. MS. letters of Renty, Auberlieu, and Parma.—Compare Corresp. Alex. Farnese, 74, 99.

paring the Union of Utrecht, as a temporary defence until the foe should be beaten back, and there should be time to decide on their future course of action.*

During the whole month of December, an active correspondence had been carried on by the Prince and his brother John with various agents in Gelderland, Friesland, and Groningen, as well as with influential personages in the more central provinces and cities.† Gelderland, the natural bulwark to Holland and Zealand, commanding the four great rivers of the country, had been fortunately placed under the government of the trusty John of Nassau, that province being warmly in favor of a closer union with its sister provinces, and particularly with those more nearly allied to itself in religion and in language.

Already, in December (1578), Count John, in behalf of his brother, had laid before the states of Holland and Zealand, assembled at Gorcum, the project of a new union with "Gelderland, Ghent, Friesland, Utrecht, Overyssel, and Groningen."‡ The proposition had been favorably entertained, and commissioners had been appointed to confer with other commissioners at Utrecht, whenever they should be summoned by Count John. The Prince, with the silence and caution which belonged to his whole policy, chose not to be the ostensible mover in the plan himself. He did not choose to startle unnecessarily the Archduke Matthias—the cipher who had been placed by his side, whose sudden subtraction would occasion more loss than his presence had conferred benefit. He did not choose to be cried out upon as infringing the Ghent Pacification, although the whole world knew that treaty to be hopelessly annulled. For these and many other weighty motives, he proposed that the new Union should be the apparent work of other hands, and only offered to him and to the country, when nearly completed.

After various preliminary meetings in December and

---

* Groen v. Prinsterer, vi. 537. † Ibid., vi. 479, sqq., 536, sqq.

‡ Ibid., vi. 479, sqq.

January, the deputies of Gelderland and Zutfen, with Count John, stadholder of these provinces, at their head, met with the deputies of Holland, Zealand, and the provinces between the Ems and the Lauwers, early in January, 1579, and on the 23rd of that month, without waiting longer for the deputies of the other provinces, they agreed provisionally upon a treaty of union which was published afterwards on the 29th, from the Town House of Utrecht.*

This memorable document—which is ever regarded as the foundation of the Netherland Republic—contained twenty-six articles.†

The preamble stated the object of the union. It was to strengthen, not to forsake the Ghent Pacification, already nearly annihilated by the force of foreign soldiery. For this purpose, and in order more conveniently to defend themselves against their foes, the deputies of Gelderland, Zutfen, Holland, Zealand, Utrecht, and the Frisian provinces, thought it desirable to form a still closer union. The contracting provinces agreed to remain eternally united, as if they were but one province. At the same time, it was understood that each was to retain its particular privileges, liberties, laudable and traditionary customs, and other laws. The cities, corporations, and inhabitants of every province were to be guaranteed as to their ancient constitutions. Disputes concerning these various statutes and customs were to be decided by the usual tribunals, by "good men," or by amicable compromise. The provinces, by virtue of the Union, were to defend each other "with life, goods, and blood," against all force brought against them in the King's name or behalf. They were also to defend each other against all foreign or domestic potentates, provinces, or cities, provided such defence were controlled by the "generality" of the union.‡ For the expense occasioned by

* Kluit, Hist. der Holl. Staatsreg., i. 170, sqq. Bor, xiii. 21, sqq.

† The whole document is given by Bor, xiii. 26–30, and, somewhat abridged, by Wagenaer, vii. 251–262; Meteren, ix. 151, 152; Tassis, v. 339, sqq.; Hoofd, xiv. 609–615.

‡ Articles, 1, 2, 3.

the protection of the provinces, certain imposts and excises were to be equally assessed and collected. No truce or peace was to be concluded, no war commenced, no impost established affecting the "generality," but by unanimous advice and consent of the provinces. Upon other matters the majority was to decide; the votes being taken in the manner then customary in the assembly of states-general. In case of difficulty in coming to a unanimous vote when required, the matter was to be referred to the stadholders then in office. In case of their inability to agree, they were to appoint arbitrators, by whose decision the parties were to be governed. None of the united provinces, or of their cities or corporations, were to make treaties with other potentates or states, without consent of their confederates. If neighbouring princes, provinces, or cities, wished to enter into this confederacy, they were to be received by the unanimous consent of the united provinces. A common currency was to be established for the confederacy. In the matter of divine worship, Holland and Zealand were to conduct themselves as they should think proper. The other provinces of the union, however, were either to conform to the religious peace already laid down by Archduke Matthias and his council, or to make such other arrangements as each province should for itself consider appropriate for the maintenance of its internal tranquillity—provided always that every individual should remain free in his religion, and that no man should be molested or questioned on the subject of divine worship, as had been already established by the Ghent Pacification.* As a certain dispute arose concerning the meaning of this important clause, an additional paragraph was inserted a few days afterwards. In this it was stated that there was no intention of excluding from the confederacy any province or city which was wholly Catholic, or in which the number of the Reformed was not sufficiently large to entitle them, by the religious peace, to public worship. On the contrary, the intention was to admit them, provided

* Articles, 5, 9, 10, 11, 12, 13.

they obeyed the articles of union, and conducted themselves as good patriots; it being intended that no province or city should interfere with another in the matter of divine service. Disputes between two provinces were to be decided by the others, or—in case the generality were concerned—by the provisions of the ninth article.

The confederates were to assemble at Utrecht whenever summoned by those commissioned for that purpose. A majority of votes was to decide on matters then brought before them, even in case of the absence of some members of the confederacy, who might, however, send written proxies. Additions or amendments to these articles could only be made by unanimous consent. The articles were to be signed by the stadholders, magistrates, and principal officers of each province and city, and by all the train-bands, fraternities, and sodalities which might exist in the cities or villages of the union.*

Such were the simple provisions of that instrument which became the foundation of the powerful Commonwealth of the United Netherlands. On the day when it was concluded, there were present deputies from five provinces only.† Count John of Nassau signed first, as stadholder of Gelderland and Zutfen. His signature was followed by those of four deputies from that double province; and the envoys of Holland, Zealand, Utrecht and the Frisian provinces, then signed the document.‡

The Prince himself, although in reality the principal

---

* Articles 16, 19, 22.

† Bor, 3. xiii. 26. Kluit, Holl. Staatsreg., i. 173, sqq. Wagenaer, Vad. Hist. vii. 263, sqq.

‡ Bor, Kluit, Wagenaer, ubi sup.—Count Renneberg, as stadholder of Friesland, Overyssel, Groningen, Drente, etc., did not give his final adhesion until June 11, 1579. His subsequent treason kept the city of Groningen out of the union, and it was not admitted till the year 1594.—(Wag. vii. 266.) On the other hand, several cities which were not destined eventually to form parts of the confederacy became members soon after its formation—as Ghent, on Feb. 4, 1579; Antwerp, July 28, 1579; Bruges, Feb. 1, 1580, etc.—Bor, xiii. 31, et sqq.

director of the movement, delayed appending his signature until May the 3rd, 1579.* Herein he was actuated by the reasons already stated, and by the hope which he still entertained that a wider union might be established, with Matthias for its nominal chief. His enemies, as usual, attributed this patriotic delay to baser motives. They accused him of a desire to assume the governor-generalship himself, to the exclusion of the Archduke—an insinuation which the states of Holland took occasion formally to denounce as a calumny.† For those who have studied the character and history of the man, a defence against such slander is superfluous. Matthias was but the shadow, Orange the substance. The Archduke had been accepted only to obviate the evil effects of a political intrigue, and with the express condition that the Prince should be his lieutenant-general in name, his master in fact. Directly after his departure in the following year, the Prince's authority, which nominally departed also, was re-established in his own person, and by express act of the states-general.‡

The Union of Utrecht was the foundation-stone of the Netherland Republic; but the framers of the confederacy did not intend the establishment of a Republic, or of an independent commonwealth of any kind. They had not forsworn the Spanish monarch. It was not yet their intention to forswear him. Certainly the act of union contained no allusion to such an important step. On the contrary, in the brief preamble they expressly stated their intention to strengthen the Ghent Pacification, and the Ghent Pacification acknowledged obedience to the King. They intended no political innovation of any kind. They expressly accepted matters as they were. All statutes, charters, and privileges of provinces, cities, or corporations were to remain untouched. They intended to form neither an independent state nor an independent federal system.§ No doubt the formal renunciation of allegiance,

* Bor, 2, xiii. 30.

† Resol. Holl., 8 Mei., f. 93. Kluit, Holl. Staatsreg., i. 180.

‡ Kluit, i. 180, 181, note 15.

§ Kluit, Holl. Staatsreg., i. 182, sqq.—Compare Groen v. Prinst., Archives, de la Maison d'Orange, vi. 536–564.

which was to follow within two years, was contemplated by many as a future probability; but it could not be foreseen with certainty.

The simple act of union was not regarded as the constitution of a commonwealth. Its object was a single one—defence against a foreign oppressor. The contracting parties bound themselves together to spend all their treasure and all their blood in expelling the foreign soldiery from their soil. To accomplish this purpose, they carefully abstained from intermeddling with internal politics and with religion. Every man was to worship God according to the dictates of his conscience. Every combination of citizens, from the provincial states down to the humblest rhetoric club, was to retain its ancient constitution. The establishment of a Republic, which lasted two centuries, which threw a girdle of rich dependencies entirely round the globe, and which attained so remarkable a height of commercial prosperity and political influence, was the result of the Utrecht Union; but it was not a premeditated result. A state, single towards the rest of the world, a unit in its external relations, while permitting internally a variety of sovereignties and institutions—in many respects the prototype of our own much more extensive and powerful union—was destined to spring from the act thus signed by the envoys of five provinces. Those envoys were acting, however, under the pressure of extreme necessity, and for what was believed an evanescent purpose. The future confederacy was not to resemble the system of the German empire, for it was to acknowledge no single head. It was to differ from the Achaian league, in the far inferior amount of power which it permitted to its general assembly, and in the consequently greater proportion of sovereign attributes which were retained by the individual states. It was, on the other hand, to furnish a closer and more intimate bond than that of the Swiss confederacy, which was only a union for defence and external purposes, of cantons otherwise independent.* It was,

* Compare Kluit, i. 193, 194.

finally, to differ from the American federal commonwealth in the great feature that it was to be merely a confederacy of sovereignties, not a representative Republic. Its foundation was a compact, not a constitution. The contracting parties were states and corporations, who considered themselves as representing small nationalities *de jure et de facto,* and as succeeding to the supreme power at the very instant in which allegiance to the Spanish monarch was renounced. The general assembly was a collection of diplomatic envoys, bound by instructions from independent states. The voting was not by heads, but by states. The deputies were not representatives of the people, but of the states; for the people of the United States of the Netherlands never assembled—as did the people of the United States of America two centuries later—to lay down a constitution, by which they granted a generous amount of power to the union, while they reserved enough of sovereign attributes to secure that local self-government which is the life-blood of liberty.

The Union of Utrecht, narrowed as it was to the nether portion of that country which, as a whole, might have formed a commonwealth so much more powerful, was in origin a proof of this lamentable want of patriotism. Could the jealousy of great nobles, the rancour of religious differences, the Catholic bigotry of the Walloon population on the one side, contending with the democratic insanity of the Ghent populace on the other, have been restrained within bounds by the moderate counsels of William of Orange, it would have been possible to unite seventeen provinces instead of seven, and to save many long and blighting years of civil war.

The Utrecht Union was, however, of inestimable value. It was time for some step to be taken, if anarchy were not to reign until the inquisition and absolutism were restored. Already, out of Chaos and Night, the coming Republic was assuming substance and form. The union, if it created nothing else, at least constructed a league against a foreign foe whose armed masses were pouring faster and faster into the territory of the provinces. Farther than this it did not propose to go. It maintained what it found. It guaranteed religious liberty, and accepted the civil and political constitutions already in existence. Meantime, the defects of those constitutions, although visible and sensible, had not grown to the large proportions which they were destined to attain.

Thus by the Union of Utrecht on the one hand, and the fast approaching reconciliation of the Walloon provinces on the other, the work of decomposition and of construction went hand in hand.

CHAPTER II.

Parma's feint upon Antwerp—He invests Maestricht—Deputation and letters from the states-general, from Brussels, and from Parma, to the Walloon provinces—Active negotiations by Orange and by Farnese—Walloon envoys in Parma's camp before Maestricht—Festivities—The Treaty of Reconciliation—Rejoicings of the royalist party—Comedy enacted at the Paris theatres—Religious tumults in Antwerp, Utrecht, and other cities—Religious Peace enforced by Orange—Philip Egmont's unsuccessful attempt upon Brussels—Siege of Maestricht—Failure at the Tongres gate—Mining and countermining—Partial destruction of the Tongres ravelin—Simultaneous attack upon the Tongres and Bois-le-Duc gates—The Spaniards repulsed with great loss—Gradual encroachments of the besiegers—Bloody contests—The town taken—Horrible massacre—Triumphal entrance and solemn thanksgiving—Calumnious attacks upon Orange—Renewed troubles in Ghent—Imbize and Dathenus—The presence of the Prince solicited—Coup d'état of Imbize—Order restored, and Imbize expelled by Orange.

THE political movements in both directions were to be hastened by the military operations of the opening season. On the night of the 2nd of March, 1579, the Prince of Parma made a demonstration against Antwerp. A body of three thousand Scotch and English, lying at Borgerhout, was rapidly driven in, and a warm skirmish ensued, directly under the walls of the city. The Prince of Orange, with the Archduke Matthias, being in Antwerp at the time, remained on the fortifications, superintending the action, and Parma was obliged to retire after an hour or two of sharp fighting, with a loss of four hundred men.* This demonstration was, however, only a

* Bor, xiii. 35, 36. Hoofd, xv. 620.

feint. His real design was upon Maestricht, before which important city he appeared in great force, ten days afterwards, when he was least expected.*

Well fortified, surrounded by a broad and deep moat, built upon both sides of the Meuse, upon the right bank of which river, however, the portion of the town was so inconsiderable that it was merely called the village of Wyk, this key to the German gate of the Netherlands was, unfortunately, in brave but feeble hands. The garrison was hardly one thousand strong; the trained bands of burghers amounted to twelve hundred more; while between three and four thousand peasants, who had taken refuge within the city walls, did excellent service as sappers and miners. Parma, on the other hand, had appeared before the walls with twenty thousand men, to which number he received constant reinforcements. The Bishop of Liege, too, had sent him four thousand pioneers—a most important service; for mining and countermining was to decide the fate of Maestricht.†

Early in January the royalists had surprised the strong chateau of Carpen, in the neighbourhood of the city, upon which occasion the garrison were all hanged by moonlight on the trees in the orchard. The commandant shared their fate; and it is a curious fact that he had, precisely a year previously, hanged the royalist captain, Blomaert, on the same spot, who, with the rope around his neck, had foretold a like doom to his destroyer.‡

The Prince of Orange, feeling the danger of Maestricht, lost no time in warning the states to the necessary measures, imploring them "not to fall asleep in the shade of a peace negotiation,"§ while meantime Parma threw two bridges over the Meuse, above and below the city, and then invested the

---

* Bor, xiii. 36. Hoofd, ubi sup. Strada, 2, ii. 58.

† Bentivoglio, 2, lib. i. 235. Bor, xiii. 36. According to Strada (2, ii. 81), 3000.

‡ Letter of G. de Merode, Ordinaris Depêchen Boek der Staten-gen., A°. 1579, f. 42. MS. Hague Archives.

§ Letter of Orange to States-general, Ord. Dep. Boek, 1579, f. 41vo, MS.

place so closely that all communication was absolutely suspended. Letters could pass to and fro only at extreme peril to the messengers, and all possibility of reinforcing the city at the moment was cut off.*

While this eventful siege was proceeding, the negotiations with the Walloons were ripening. The siege and the conferences went hand in hand. Besides the secret arrangements already described for the separation of the Walloon provinces, there had been much earnest and eloquent remonstrance on the part of the states-general and of Orange—many solemn embassies and public appeals. As usual, the Pacification of Ghent was the two-sided shield which hung between the parties to cover or to justify the blows which each dealt at the other. There is no doubt as to the real opinion entertained concerning that famous treaty by the royal party. "Through the peace of Ghent," said Saint Vaast, "all our woes have been brought upon us." La Motte informed Parma that it was necessary to pretend a respect for the Pacification, however, on account of its popularity, but that it was well understood by the leaders of the Walloon movement, that the intention was to restore the system of Charles the Fifth. Parma signified his consent to make use of that treaty as a basis, "provided always it were interpreted healthily, and not dislocated by cavillations and sinister interpolations, as had been done by the Prince of Orange." The Malcontent generals of the Walloon troops were inexpressibly anxious lest the cause of religion should be endangered ; but the arguments by which Parma convinced those military casuists as to the compatibility of the Ghent peace with sound doctrine have already been exhibited. The influence of the reconciled nobles was brought to bear with fatal effect upon the states of Artois, Hainault, and of a portion of French Flanders. The Gallic element in their blood, and an intense attachment to the Roman ceremonial, which distinguished the Walloon popula-

* Bor, xiii. 17–36, sqq. Hoofd, xv. 662–628. Strada, 2, i. 37, 57–61. Meteren, ix. 134.

tion from their Batavian brethren, were used successfully by the wily Parma to destroy the unity of the revolted Netherlands.* Moreover, the King offered good terms. The monarch, feeling safe on the religious point, was willing to make liberal promises upon the political questions. In truth, the great grievance of which the Walloons complained was the insolence and intolerable outrages of the foreign soldiers. This, they said, had alone made them malcontent.† It was, therefore, obviously the cue of Parma to promise the immediate departure of the troops. This could be done the more easily, as he had no intention of keeping the promise.

Meantime the efforts of Orange, and of the states-general, where his influence was still paramount, were unceasing to counteract the policy of Parma. A deputation was appointed by the generality to visit the estates of the Walloon provinces.‡ Another was sent by the authorities of Brussels. The Marquis of Havré, with several colleagues on behalf of the states-general, waited upon the Viscount of Ghent, by whom they were received with extreme insolence. He glared upon them, without moving, as they were admitted to his presence; "looking like a dead man, from whom the soul had entirely departed." Recovering afterwards from this stony trance of indignation, he demanded a sight of their instructions. This they courteously refused, as they were accredited not to him, but to the states of Artois. At this he fell into a violent passion, and threatened them with signal chastisement for daring to come thither with so treasonable a purpose. In short, according to their own expression, he treated them "as if they had been rogues and vagabonds."§ The Marquis of Havré, high-born though he was, had been sufficiently used to such conduct. The man who had successively served and betrayed every party, who had been the obsequious friend and

* Bor, Hoofd, Strada, ubi sup. Archives, etc., de la Maison d'Orange, vi. 610–613.

† Strada, 2, i. 50, 51.

‡ Bor, xiii. 37, 38. Hoofd, xv. 622, sqq. Meteren, ix. 150, 151.

§ Report of the Commissioners, Bor, xiii. 45.

the avowed enemy of Don John within the same fortnight, and who had been able to swallow and inwardly digest many an insult from that fiery warrior, was even fain to brook the insolence of Robert Melun.

The papers which the deputation had brought were finally laid before the states of Artois, and received replies as prompt and bitter as the addresses were earnest and eloquent. The Walloons, when summoned to hold to that ægis of national unity, the Ghent peace, replied that it was not they, but the heretic portion of the states-general, who were for dashing it to the ground. The Ghent treaty was never intended to impair the supremacy of the Catholic religion, said those provinces, which were already on the point of separating for ever from the rest. The Ghent treaty was intended expressly to destroy the inquisition and the placards, answered the national party. Moreover, the "very marrow of that treaty"* was the departure of the foreign soldiers, who were even then overrunning the land. The Walloons answered that Alexander had expressly conceded the withdrawal of the troops. "Believe not the fluting and the piping of the crafty foe," urged the patriots.† "Promises are made profusely enough—but only to lure you to perdition. Your enemies allow you to slake your hunger and thirst with this idle hope of the troops' departure, but you are still in fetters, although the chain be of Spanish pinchbeck, which you mistake for gold. "'Tis not we," cried the Walloons, "who wish to separate from the generality; 'tis the generality which separates from us. We had rather die the death than not maintain the union."‡ In the very same breath, however, they boasted of the excellent terms which the monarch was offering, and of their strong inclina-

---

* "De substantie en principael merg van selve pacificatie."—Bor, xiii. 39.

† "De vijand hem sal behelpen met het woord van de Religie aes met een bedriegelijk pijpken of fluijken om ons met de Tarre te vangen."—Address of the States-general, March 3, 1579, Bor, xiii. 41. "T gefluit en gepijp van de gene die komen van onser vijanden wegen—om namaels te gecken en te spotten met onse bederfenisse."—Ibid.

‡ Bor, xiii. 38.

tion to accept them. "Kings, struggling to recover a lost authority, always promise golden mountains and every sort of miracles," replied the patriots;* but the warning was uttered in vain.

Meantime the deputation from the city of Brussels arrived on the 28th of March at Mons, in Hainault, where they were received with great courtesy by Count de Lalain, governor of the province. The enthusiasm with which he had espoused the cause of Queen Margaret and her brother Anjou had cooled, but the Count received the Brussels envoys with a kindness in marked contrast with the brutality of Melun. He made many fine speeches—protesting his attachment to the union, for which he was ready to shed the last drop of his blood—entertained the deputies at dinner, proposed toasts to the prosperity of the united provinces, and dismissed his guests at last with many flowery professions. After dancing attendance for a few days, however, upon the estates of the Walloon provinces, both sets of deputies were warned to take their instant departure as mischief-makers and rebels. They returned, accordingly, to Brussels, bringing the written answers which the estates had vouchsafed to send.†

The states-general, too, inspired by William of Orange, addressed a solemn appeal to their sister provinces, thus about to abjure the bonds of relationship for ever.‡ It seemed right, once for all, to grapple with the Ghent Pacification for the last time, and to strike a final blow in defence of that large, statesmanlike interpretation, which alone could make the treaty live. This was done eloquently and logically. The Walloons were reminded that at the epoch of the Ghent peace the number of Reformers outside of Holland and Zealand was supposed small. Now the new religion had spread its roots through the whole land, and innumerable multitudes

---

* "Gewoont sijn te beloven goude berge en wonderlijke saken."—Address of the States-general, Bor, xiii. 44.

† Bor, xiii. 44, 45. Hoofd, xv. 622, sqq. Meteren, ix. 139, 150.

‡ Bor (xiii. 39–42), gives the text in full.

desired its exercise. If Holland and Zealand chose to re-establish the Catholic worship within their borders, they could manifestly do so without violating the treaty of Ghent. Why then was it not competent to other provinces, with equal allegiance to the treaty, to sanction the Reformed religion within their limits ?*

Parma, on his part, publicly invited the states-general, by letter, to sustain the Ghent treaty by accepting the terms offered to the Walloons, and by restoring the system of the Emperor Charles, of very lofty memory. To this superfluous invitation the states-general replied, on the 19th of March, that it had been the system of the Emperor Charles, of lofty memory, to maintain the supremacy of Catholicism and of Majesty in the Netherlands by burning Netherlanders—a custom which the states, with common accord, had thought it desirable to do away with.†

In various fervently-written appeals by Orange, by the states-general, and by other bodies, the wavering provinces were warned against seduction. They were reminded that the Prince of Parma was using this minor negotiation "as a second string to his bow;" that nothing could be more puerile than to suppose the Spaniards capable, after securing Maestricht, of sending away their troops—thus "deserting the bride in the midst of the honeymoon." They expressed astonishment at being invited to abandon the great and general treaty which had been made upon the theatre of the whole world by the intervention of the principal princes of Christendom, in order to partake in underhand negotiation with the commissioners of Parma—men, "who, it would not be denied, were felons and traitors." They warned their brethren not to embark on the enemy's ships in the dark, for that, while chaffering as to the price of the voyage, they would find that the false pilots had hoisted sail and borne them away in the night. In vain would they then seek to reach the

* Address of the States, apud Bor, 3, xiii. 40, sqq.

† Letter of the States-general.—Ibid., xiii. 48.

shore again. The example of La Motte and others, "bird-limed with Spanish gold," should be salutary for all—men who were now driven forward with a whip, laughed to scorn by their new masters, and forced to drink the bitter draught of humiliation along with the sweet poison of bribery. They were warned to study well the intercepted letters of Curiel, in order fully to fathom the deep designs and secret contempt of the enemy.*

Such having been the result of the negotiations between the states-general and the Walloon provinces, a strong deputation now went forth from those provinces, towards the end of April, to hold a final colloquy with Parma, then already busied with the investment of Maestricht. They were met upon the road with great ceremony, and escorted into the presence of Farnese with drum, trumpet, and flaunting banners.† He received them with stately affability, in a magnificently decorated pavilion, carelessly inviting them to a repast, which he called an afternoon's lunch, but which proved a most sumptuous and splendidly appointed entertainment.‡ This "trifling foolish banquet" finished, the deputies were escorted, with great military parade, to the lodgings which had been provided for them in a neighbouring village. During the period of their visit, all the chief officers of the army and the household were directed to entertain the Walloons with showy festivals, dinners, suppers, dances, and carousals of all kinds. At one of the most brilliant of these revels—a magnificent ball, to which all the matrons and maids of the whole country round had been bidden—the Prince of Parma himself unexpectedly made his appearance. He gently rebuked the entertainers for indulging in such splendid hospitality without, at least, permitting him to partake of it. Charmingly affable to the ladies assembled in the ball-room, courteous, but slightly

* Reponse des Etats-généraux sur les lettres des Etats d'Artois, Haynault, Lille, Douay et Orchies; Ord. Depêch. Boek der St.-gen., 1579, f. 35–51. MS. Hague Archives.

† Strada, 2, i. 49, sqq.

‡ "Regiis epulis quas extenuato ad superbiam vocabulo, pomeridianam gustationem appellabant, excepti sunt."—Strada, 2, i. 52.

reserved, towards the Walloon envoys, he excited the admiration of all by the splendid decorum of his manners. As he moved through the halls, modulating his steps in grave cadence to the music, the dignity and grace of his deportment seemed truly majestic ; but when he actually danced a measure himself the enthusiasm was at its height.* They should, indeed, be rustics, cried the Walloon envoys in a breath, not to give the hand of fellowship at once to a Prince so condescending and amiable.† The exclamation seemed to embody the general wish, and to foreshadow a speedy conclusion.

Very soon afterwards a preliminary accord was signed between the King's government and the Walloon provinces. The provisions on his Majesty's part were sufficiently liberal. The religious question furnishing no obstacle, it was comparatively easy for Philip to appear benignant. It was stipulated that the provincial privileges should be respected ; that a member of the King's own family, legitimately born, should always be Governor-General, and that the foreign troops should be immediately withdrawn.‡ The official exchange and ratification of this treaty were delayed till the 4th of the following September,§ but the news that the recon-

* Strada, 2, i. 53, who describes the scene with laughable gravity.

† Ibid.—"Agrestes se plus nimio visum iri, nisi adeo benigni amabilisque ingenii viro manus darent."

‡ The preliminary accord was signed May 17, 1579. A copy was sent by the Prince of Orange to the united states, on August 1, 1579.—Bor, xiii. 95-98. Tratado de Reconciliacion de las Provincias d'Artois, Haynau, Lille, Douay, y Orchies; Rec. Prov. Wall., iii. f. 289-296. MS. The terms of the treaty were not bad. The Ghent Pacification was to be maintained and the foreign troops were to be removed. Unfortunately the secret correspondence of the parties shows that the faithful observance of that pacification was very far from their thoughts, while the subsequent history of the country was to prove the removal of the troops to have been a comedy, in which the principal actor soon renounced the part which he had reluctantly consented to sustain.

§ Rec. Prov. Wall., iii. f. 179, 180. MS.—There is something almost comic in the preamble to the ratification. "Certain good personages in our provinces of Artois," etc., says Philip, "zealous in the service of God and desirous to escape danger to their property, and seeing the attempt to establish over the ecclesiastics, nobles, and good burgesses, a popular tyranny, which, by exorbitant contributions, is gnawing the nation to the bone, having at length opened their own eyes, have done their best to awaken their neighbours," etc.

ciliation had been definitely settled soon spread through the country. The Catholics were elated, the patriots dismayed. Orange—the "Prince of Darkness,"* as the Walloons of the day were fond of calling him—still unwilling to despair, reluctant to accept this dismemberment, which he foresaw was to be a perpetual one, of his beloved country, addressed the most passionate and solemn adjurations to the Walloon provinces, and to their military chieftains. He offered all his children as hostages for his good faith in keeping sacredly any covenant which his Catholic countrymen might be willing to close with him. It was in vain. The step was irretrievably taken; religious bigotry, patrician jealousy, and wholesale bribery, had severed the Netherlands in twain for ever. The friends of Romanism, the enemies of civil and religious liberty, exulted from one end of Christendom to the other, and it was recognized that Parma had, indeed, achieved a victory which although bloodless, was as important to the cause of absolutism as any which even his sword was likely to achieve.

The joy of the Catholic party in Paris manifested itself in a variety of ways. At the principal theatre† an uncouth pantomime was exhibited, in which his Catholic Majesty was introduced upon the stage, leading by a halter a sleek cow, typifying the Netherlands. The animal by a sudden effort, broke the cord, and capered wildly about. Alexander of Parma hastened to fasten the fragments together while sundry personages, representing the states-general, seized her by the horns, some leaping upon her back, others calling upon the bystanders to assist in holding the restive beast. The Emperor, the King of France, and the Queen of England—which last personage was observed now to smile upon one party, now to affect deep sympathy with the other—remained stationary; but the Duke of Alençon rushed upon the stage, and caught the cow by the tail. The Prince of Orange and

* "Le Prince d'Orenges, qu'ils nommérent en ce temps Prince des Tenèbres," etc.—Renom de France, iv. c. xii., MS. At least, in poor Tom's phrase, "the prince of darkness was a gentleman."

† Strada, 2, i. 55.

Hans Casimir then appeared with a bucket, and set themselves busily to milk her, when Alexander again seized the halter. The cow gave a plunge, upset the pail, prostrated Casimir with one kick and Orange with another, and then followed Parma with docility as he led her back to Philip.* This seems not very "admirable fooling," but it was highly relished by the polite Parisians of the sixteenth century, and has been thought worthy of record by classical historians.

The Walloon accord was an auspicious prelude, in the eyes of the friends of absolutism, to the negotiations which were opened in the month of May, at Cologne. Before sketching, as rapidly as possible, those celebrated but barren conferences, it is necessary, for the sake of unity in the narrative, to cast a glance at certain synchronical events in different parts of the Netherlands.

The success attained by the Catholic party in the Walloon negotiations had caused a corresponding bitterness in the hearts of the Reformers throughout the country. As usual, bitterness had begot bitterness; intolerance engendered intolerance. On the 28th of May, 1579, as the Catholics of Antwerp were celebrating the *Ommegang*—the same festival which had been the exciting cause of the memorable tumults of the year sixty-five—the irritation of the populace could not be repressed.† The mob rose in its wrath to put down these demonstrations—which, taken in connection with recent events, seemed ill-timed and insolent—of a religion whose votaries then formed but a small minority of the Antwerp citizens. There was a great tumult. Two persons were killed. The Archduke Matthias, who was himself in the Cathedral of Nôtre Dame assisting at the ceremony, was in danger of his life. The well known cry of "*paapen uit*" (out with the papists) resounded through the streets, and the priests and monks were all hustled out of town amid a tempest of execrations.‡ Orange did his utmost to quell the mutiny, nor were his efforts fruit-

* Strada, 2, i. 55, 56.

† Bor, xiii. 67.

‡ Ibid. Meteren, ix. 153ª.

less—for the uproar, although seditious and disgraceful, was hardly sanguinary. Next day the Prince summoned the magistracy, the Monday council, the guild officers, with all the chief municipal functionaries, and expressed his indignation in decided terms. He protested that if such tumults, originating in that very spirit of intolerance which he most deplored, could not be repressed for the future, he was determined to resign his offices, and no longer to affect authority in a city where his counsels were derided. The magistrates, alarmed at his threats, and sympathizing with his anger, implored him not to desert them, protesting that if he should resign his offices, they would instantly lay down their own. An ordinance was then drawn up and immediately proclaimed at the Town House, permitting the Catholics to re-enter the city, and to enjoy the privileges of religious worship. At the same time, it was announced that a new draft of a religious peace would be forthwith issued for the adoption of every city.*

A similar tumult, arising from the same cause, at Utrecht, was attended with the like result.† On the other hand, the city of Brussels was astonished by a feeble and unsuccessful attempt‡ at treason, made by a youth who bore an illustrious name. Philip, Count of Egmont, eldest son of the unfortunate Lamoral, had command of a regiment in the service of the states. He had, besides, a small body of cavalry in immediate attendance upon his person. He had for some time felt inclined—like the Lalains, Meluns, La Mottes, and others—to reconcile himself with the Crown, and he wisely thought that the terms accorded to him would be more liberal if he could bring the capital of Brabant with him as a peace-offering to his Majesty. His residence was in Brussels. His regiment was stationed outside the gates, but in the immediate neighbourhood of the city. On the morning of the 4th of June he despatched his troopers—as had been frequently his

* Bor, xiii. 68.

† Ibid., 70–73.

‡ Ibid., xiii. 66, sqq. Meteren, ix. 153. Hoofd, xv. 637, sqq.

custom—on various errands into the country. On their return, after having summoned the regiment, they easily mastered and butchered the guard at the gate through which they had re-entered, supplying their place with men from their own ranks. The Egmont regiment then came marching through the gate in good order—Count Philip at their head—and proceeded to station themselves upon the Grande Place in the centre of the city. All this was at dawn of day. The burghers, who looked forth from their houses, were astounded and perplexed by this movement at so unwonted an hour, and hastened to seize their weapons. Egmont sent a detachment to take possession of the palace. He was too late. Colonel Van der Tympel, commandant of the city, had been beforehand with him, had got his troops under arms, and now secured the rebellious detachment. Meantime, the alarm had spread. Armed burghers came from every house, and barricades were hastily thrown up across every one of the narrow streets leading to the square. Every issue was closed. Not a man of Egmont's adherents—if he indeed had adherents among the townsmen—dared to show his face. The young traitor and his whole regiment, drawn up on the Grande Place, were completely entrapped. He had not taken Brussels, but assuredly Brussels had taken him. All day long he was kept in his self-elected prison and pillory, bursting with rage and shame. His soldiers, who were without meat or drink, became insolent and uproarious, and he was doomed also to hear the bitter and well-merited taunts of the towns-people. A thousand stinging gibes, suggested by his name and the locality, were mercilessly launched upon him. He was asked if he came thither to seek his father's head. He was reminded that the morrow was the anniversary of that father's murder—upon that very spot—by those with whom the son would now make his treasonable peace. He was bidden to tear up but a few stones from the pavement beneath his feet, that the hero's blood might cry out against him from the very ground.*

* Bor, xiii. 66. Hoofd, xv. 638.

Tears of shame and fury sprang from the young man's eyes* as he listened to these biting sarcasms, but the night closed upon that memorable square, and still the Count was a prisoner. Eleven years before, the summer stars had looked down upon a more dense array of armed men within that place. The preparations for the pompous and dramatic execution, which on the morrow was to startle all Europe, had been carried out in the midst of a hushed and overawed population; and now, on the very anniversary of the midnight in which that scaffold had risen, should not the grand spectre of the victim have started from the grave to chide his traitorous son?

Thus for a whole day and night was the baffled conspirator compelled to remain in the ignominious position which he had selected for himself. On the morning of the 5th of June he was permitted to depart, by a somewhat inexplicable indulgence, together with all his followers. He rode out of the gate at early dawn, contemptible and crest-fallen, at the head of his regiment of traitors, and shortly afterwards—pillaging and levying black mail as he went—made his way to Montigny's quarters.†

It might have seemed natural, after such an exhibition, that Philip Egmont should accept his character of renegade, and confess his intention of reconciling himself with the murderers of his father. On the contrary, he addressed a letter to the magistracy of Brussels, denying with vehemence "any intention of joining the party of the pernicious Spaniards," warmly protesting his zeal and affection for the states, and denouncing the "perverse inventors of these calumnies against him as the worst enemies of the poor afflicted country." The magistrates replied by expressing their inability to comprehend how the Count, who had suffered villanous wrongs from the Spaniards, such as he could never sufficiently deplore

---

* Meteren, ix. 153.—"Sulcx dat de tranen hem van passie ontopronghen," etc. —Bor, Hoofd, ubi sup.

† Bor, Hoofd, Meteren, ubi sup.

or avenge, should ever be willing to enslave himself to those tyrants. Nevertheless, exactly at the moment of this correspondence, Egmont was in close negotiation with Spain, having fifteen days before the date of his letter to the Brussels senate, conveyed to Parma his resolution to "embrace the cause of his Majesty and the ancient religion"—an intention which he vaunted himself to have proved "by cutting the throats of three companies of states' soldiers at Nivelle, Grandmont, and Ninove." Parma had already written to communicate the intelligence to the King, and to beg encouragement for the Count. In September, the monarch wrote a letter to Egmont, full of gratitude and promises, to which the Count replied by expressing lively gratification that his Majesty was pleased with his little services, by avowing profound attachment to Church and King, and by asking eagerly for money, together with the government of Alost. He soon became singularly importunate for rewards and promotion, demanding, among other posts, the command of the "band of ordnance," which had been his father's. Parma, in reply, was prodigal of promises, reminding the young noble "that he was serving a sovereign who well knew how to reward the distinguished exploits of his subjects." Such was the language of Philip the Second and his Governor to the son of the headless hero of Saint Quentin ; such was the fawning obsequiousness with which Egmont could kiss that royal hand reeking with his father's blood.*

Meanwhile the siege of Maestricht had been advancing with steady precision. To military minds of that epoch—perhaps of later ages—this achievement of Parma seemed a masterpiece of art. The city commanded the Upper Meuse, and was the gate into Germany. It contained thirty-four thousand inhabitants. An army, numbering almost as many souls, was brought against it ; and the number of deaths by

---

* Ordin. Depêchen Boek der Staten-gen., A°. 1579, f. 287. Hague Archives, MS. Reconciliation des Provinces Wallones, iv. f. 110, 116. Brussels Royal Archives, MS.—Compare Correspondance d'Alexandre Farnese avec Phil. II, Gachard, 1853. Kervyn und Diegerich, Documents Inédits, i. 428.

which its capture was at last effected, was probably equal to that of a moiety of the population.* To the technical mind, the siege no doubt seemed a beautiful creation of human intelligence. To the honest student of history, to the lover of human progress, such a manifestation of intellect seems a sufficiently sad exhibition. Given, a city with strong walls and towers, a slender garrison and a devoted population on one side ; a consummate chieftain on the other, with an army of veterans at his back, no interruption to fear, and a long season to work in ; it would not seem to an unsophisticated mind a very lofty exploit for the soldier to carry the city at the end of four months' hard labor.

The investment of Maestricht was commenced upon the 12th of March, 1579. In the city, besides the population, there were two thousand peasants, both men and women, a garrison of one thousand soldiers, and a trained burgher guard, numbering about twelve hundred.† The name of the military commandant was Melchior. Sebastian Tappin, a Lorraine officer of much experience and bravery, was next in command, and was, in truth, the principal director of the operations. He had been despatched thither by the Prince of Orange, to serve under La Noue, who was to have commanded in Maestricht, but had been unable to enter the city.‡ Feeling that the siege was to be a close one, and knowing how much depended upon the issue, Sebastian lost no time in making every needful preparation for coming events. The walls were strengthened everywhere ; shafts were sunk, preparatory to the countermining operations which were soon to become necessary ; the moat was deepened and cleared, and the forts near the gates were put in thorough repair. On the other hand, Alexander had encircled the city, and had thrown two bridges,

* Strada, 2, iii. 59, 130. At the termination of the siege, the army of Parma was estimated at twenty thousand men, and four thousand had fallen in the two assaults of April alone—Bor, ubi sup.

† Bor, xiii. 36. Hoofd, xv. 628. Meteren, ix. 154.—Compare Strada, 2, ii. 59, who reckons the civic guards at six thousand, and the boors at as many more.

‡ Strada, 2, ii. 59. Hoofd, xv. 628.

well fortified, across the river. There were six gates to the town, each provided with ravelins, and there was a doubt in what direction the first attack should be made. Opinions wavered between the gate of Bois-le-Duc, next the river, and that of Tongres on the south-western side, but it was finally decided to attempt the gate of Tongres.

Over against that point the platforms were accordingly constructed, and after a heavy cannonade from forty-six great guns continued for several days, it was thought, by the 25th of March, that an impression had been made upon the city. A portion of the brick curtain had crumbled, but through the breach was seen a massive terreplein, well moated, which, after six thousand shots already delivered on the outer wall—still remained uninjured.* It was recognized that the gate of Tongres was not the most assailable, but rather the strongest portion of the defences, and Alexander therefore determined to shift his batteries to the gate of Bois-le-Duc. At the same time, the attempt upon that of Tongres was to be varied, but not abandoned. Four thousand miners, who had passed half their lives in burrowing for coal in that anthracite region, had been furnished by the Bishop of Liege, and this force was now set to their subterranean work.† A mine having been opened at a distance, the besiegers slowly worked their way towards the Tongres gate, while at the same time the more ostensible operations were in the opposite direction. The besieged had their miners also, for the peasants in the city had been used to work with mattock and pickaxe. The women, too, enrolled themselves into companies, chose their officers—or "mine-mistresses," as they were called‡—and did good service daily in the caverns of the earth. Thus a whole army of gnomes were noiselessly at work to destroy and defend the beleaguered city. The mine advanced towards the gate ; the besieged delved deeper, and intersected it with a transverse excavation, and the contending forces met daily, in deadly encounter, within these

* Strada, ii. 65, 66.

† Bor, xiii. 36. Hoofd, xv. 628. Strada.

‡ "Magistras cunicularias appellabant."—Strada, 70.

sepulchral gangways. Many stratagems were mutually employed. The citizens secretly constructed a dam across the Spanish mine, and then deluged their foe with hogsheads of boiling water. Hundreds were thus scalded to death. They heaped branches and light fagots in the hostile mine, set fire to the pile, and blew thick volumes of smoke along the passage with organ-bellows brought from the churches for the purpose. Many were thus suffocated. The discomfited besiegers abandoned the mine where they had met with such able countermining, and sunk another shaft, at midnight, in secret, at a long distance from the Tongres gate. Still towards that point, however, they burrowed in the darkness; guiding themselves to their destination with magnet, plumb-line and level, as the mariner crosses the trackless ocean with compass and chart. They worked their way, unobstructed, till they arrived at their subterranean port, directly beneath the doomed ravelin. Here they constructed a spacious chamber, supporting it with columns, and making all their architectural arrangements with as much precision and elegance as if their object had been purely æsthetic. Coffers full of powder, to an enormous amount, were then placed in every direction across the floor, the train was laid, and Parma informed that all was ready. Alexander, having already arrayed the troops destined for the assault, then proceeded in person to the mouth of the shaft, and gave orders to spring the mine. The explosion was prodigious; a part of the tower fell with the concussion, and the moat was choked with heaps of rubbish. The assailants sprang across the passage thus afforded, and mastered the ruined portion of the fort. They were met in the breach, however, by the unflinching defenders of the city, and, after a fierce combat of some hours, were obliged to retire; remaining masters, however, of the moat, and of the ruined portion of the ravelin. This was upon the 3rd of April.*

Five days afterwards, a general assault was ordered.

---

* Strada, 2, ii. 666–671.

A new mine having been already constructed towards the Tongres ravelin, and a faithful cannonade having been kept up for a fortnight against the Bois-le-Duc gate, it was thought advisable to attack at both points at once. On the 8th of April, accordingly, after uniting in prayer, and listening to a speech from Alexander Farnese, the great mass of the Spanish army advanced to the breach. The moat had been rendered practicable in many places by the heaps of rubbish with which it had been encumbered, and by the fagots and earth with which it had been filled by the besiegers. The action at the Bois-le-Duc gate was exceedingly warm. The tried veterans of Spain, Italy, and Burgundy, were met face to face by the burghers of Maestricht, together with their wives and children. All were armed to the teeth, and fought with what seemed superhuman valor. The women, fierce as tigresses defending their young, swarmed to the walls, and fought in the foremost rank. They threw pails of boiling water on the besiegers, they hurled firebrands in their faces, they quoited blazing pitch-hoops with unerring dexterity about their necks. The rustics too, armed with their ponderous flails, worked as cheerfully at this bloody harvesting as if thrashing their corn at home. Heartily did they winnow the ranks of the royalists who came to butcher them, and thick and fast fell the invaders, fighting bravely, but baffled by these novel weapons used by peasant and woman, coming to the aid of the sword, spear, and musket of trained soldiery. More than a thousand had fallen at the Bois-le-Duc gate, and still fresh besiegers mounted the breach, only to be beaten back, or to add to the mangled heap of the slain.* At the Tongres gate, meanwhile, the assault had fared no better. A herald had been despatched thither in hot haste, to shout at the top of his lungs, "Santiago! Santiago! the Lombards have the gate of Bois-le-Duc!" while the same stratagem was employed to persuade the invaders on the other side of the town that their comrades had forced the gate of Tongres.† The soldiers, animated by this fiction, and advancing

* Strada, 2, ii. 68–71.

† Hoofd, xv. 629. Meteren, ix. 154. Strada, 2, ii. 75.

with fury against the famous ravelin, which had been but partly destroyed, were received with a broadside from the great guns of the unshattered portion, and by a rattling discharge of musketry from the walls. They wavered a little. At the same instant the new mine—which was to have been sprung between the ravelin and the gate, but which had been secretly countermined by the townspeople, exploded with a horrible concussion, at a moment least expected by the besiegers. Five hundred royalists were blown into the air. Ortiz, a Spanish captain of engineers, who had been inspecting the excavations, was thrown up bodily from the subterranean depth. He fell back again instantly into the same cavern, and was buried by the returning shower of earth which had spouted from the mine. Forty-five years afterwards, in digging for the foundations of a new wall, his skeleton was found. Clad in complete armor, the helmet and cuirass still sound, with his gold chain around his neck, and his mattock and pickaxe at his feet, the soldier lay* unmutilated, seeming almost capable of resuming his part in the same war which—even after his half century's sleep—was still ravaging the land.

Five hundred of the Spaniards, perished by the explosion,† but none of the defenders were injured, for they had been prepared. Recovering from the momentary panic, the besiegers again rushed to the attack. The battle raged. Six hundred and seventy officers, commissioned or non-commissioned, had already fallen, more than half mortally wounded. Four thousand royalists, horribly mutilated, lay on the ground.‡ It was time that the day's work should be finished, for Maestricht was not to be carried upon that occasion. The best and bravest of the surviving officers besought Parma to put an end to the carnage by recalling the troops; but the gladiator-

* Strada, 2, ii. 76.

† Five to six hundred, according to a letter written between the 12th and 16th of April, 1579, by a citizen of Maestricht, and quoted by Bor, xiii. 51, 52.

‡ Letter from Maestricht above cited.—Compare Strada, 2, ii. 79. Hoofd, xv. 629, who puts the number of Spaniards slain in this assault at two thousand.—Meteren, ix. 154. Haraeus (Tumult. Belg.), t. iii. 299.

heart of the commander was heated, not softened, by the savage spectacle. "Go back to the breach," he cried, "and tell the soldiers that Alexander is coming to lead them into the city in triumph, or to perish with his comrades."* He rushed forward with the fury which had marked him when he boarded Mustapha's galley at Lepanto; but all the generals who were near him threw themselves upon his path, and implored him to desist from such insensate rashness. Their expostulations would have probably been in vain, had not his confidential friend, Serbelloni, interposed with something like paternal authority, reminding him of the strict commands contained in his Majesty's recent letters, that the Governor-General, to whom so much was entrusted, should refrain, on pain of the royal displeasure, from exposing his life like a common fighter.†

Alexander reluctantly gave the signal of recal at last, and accepted the defeat. For the future he determined to rely more upon the sapper and miner,‡ and less upon the superiority of veterans to townsmen and rustics in open fight. Sure to carry the city at last, according to line and rule, determined to pass the whole summer beneath the walls, rather than abandon his purpose, he calmly proceeded to complete his circumvallations. A chain of eleven forts upon the left, and five upon the right side of the Meuse, the whole connected by a continuous wall,§ afforded him perfect security against interruptions, and allowed him to continue the siege at leisure. His numerous army was well housed and amply supplied, and he had built a strong and populous city in order to destroy another. Relief was impossible. But a few thousand men were now required to defend Farnese's improvised town, while the bulk of his army could be marched at any moment against an advancing foe. A force of seven thousand, painfully collected by the Prince of Orange, moved towards the place, under command of Hohenlo and John of Nassau,

* Strada, 2. ii. 77.

† Ibid. The letter of Philip is partly given by the historian.

‡ Strada, 2, ii. 80 Bor, xiii. 52.

§ Strada, 2, ii. 83.

but struck with wonder at what they saw, the leaders recognized the hopelessness of attempting relief. Maestricht was surrounded by a second Maestricht.

The efforts of Orange were now necessarily directed towards obtaining, if possible, a truce of a few weeks from the negotiators at Cologne. Parma was too crafty, however, to allow Terranova* to consent, and as the Duke disclaimed any power over the direct question of peace and war, the siege proceeded. The gates of Bois-le-Duc and Tongres having thus far resisted the force brought against them, the scene was changed to the gate of Brussels. This adjoined that of Tongres, was farthest from the river, and faced westwardly towards the open country. Here the besieged had constructed an additional ravelin, which they had christened, in derision, "Parma," and against which the batteries of Parma were now brought to bear. Alexander erected a platform of great extent and strength directly opposite the new work, and after a severe and constant cannonade from this elevation, followed by a bloody action, the "Parma" fort was carried. One thousand, at least, of the defenders fell, as, forced gradually from one defence to another, they saw the triple walls of their ravelin crumble successively before their eyes. The tower was absolutely annihilated before they abandoned its ruins, and retired within their last defences. Alexander being now master of the foss and the defences of the Brussels gate, drew up a large force on both sides of that portal, along the margin of the moat, and began mining beneath the inner wall of the city.†

Meantime, the garrison had been reduced to four hundred soldiers, nearly all of whom were wounded. Wearied and driven to despair, these soldiers were willing to treat. The townspeople, however, answered the proposition with a shout of fury, and protested that they would destroy the garrison

* See a remarkable letter from Parma to the Duke of Terranova, dated Camp before Maestricht, May 21, 1579, in Bor, xiii. 57, 58.

† Bor, xiii. 64. Strada, iii. 113–117.

with their own hands if such an insinuation were repeated. Sebastian Tappin, too, encouraged them with the hope of speedy relief, and held out to them the wretched consequences of trusting to the mercy of their foes. The garrison took heart again, while that of the burghers and their wives had never faltered. Their main hope now was in a fortification which they had been constructing inside the Brussels gate—a demilune of considerable strength. Behind it was a breastwork of turf and masonry, to serve as a last bulwark when every other defence should be forced. The whole had been surrounded by a foss thirty feet in depth, and the besiegers, as they mounted upon the breaches which they had at last effected in the outer curtain, near the Brussels gate, saw for the first time this new fortification.*

The general condition of the defences, and the disposition of the inhabitants, had been revealed to Alexander by a deserter from the town. Against this last fortress the last efforts of the foe were now directed. Alexander ordered a bridge to be thrown across the city moat. As it was sixty feet wide and as many deep, and lay directly beneath the guns of the new demilune, the enterprise was sufficiently hazardous. Alexander led the way in person, with a mallet in one hand and a mattock in the other. Two men fell dead instantly, one on his right hand and his left, while he calmly commenced, in his own person, the driving of the first piles for the bridge. His soldiers fell fast around him. Count Berlaymont† was shot dead, many officers of distinction were killed or wounded, but no soldier dared recoil while their chieftain wrought amid the bullets like a common pioneer. Alexander, unharmed, as by a miracle, never left the spot till the bridge had been constructed, and till ten great guns had been carried across it,

* Strada, 2, iii. 117, 118.

† Better known as Baron Hierges, eldest son of the celebrated royalist, afterwards Count Berlaymont. Hierges had not long before succeeded to the title on the death of his father.—Strada, 2, iii. 119.—Compare Bor, xiii. 64. Hoofd, xv. 630; Meteren, ix. 154e; Archives de la Maison d'Orange, vi. 622; Tassis, v. 338.

and pointed against the demilune.* The battery was opened, the mines previously excavated were sprung, a part of the demilune was blown into the air, and the assailants sprang into the breach. Again a furious hand-to-hand conflict succeeded; again, after an obstinate resistance, the townspeople were forced to yield. Slowly abandoning the shattered fort, they retired behind the breastwork in its rear—their innermost and last defence. To this barrier they clung as to a spar in shipwreck, and here at last they stood at bay, prepared dearly to sell their lives.

The breastwork, being still strong, was not attempted upon that day. The assailants were recalled, and in the mean time a herald was sent by Parma, highly applauding the courage of the defenders, and begging them to surrender at discretion. They answered the messenger with words of haughty defiance, and, rushing in a mass to the breastwork, began with spade, pickax, and trowel, to add to its strength. Here all the able-bodied men of the town took up their permanent position, and here they ate, drank, and slept upon their posts, while their food was brought to them by the women and children.†

A little letter, "written in a fine neat handwriting," now mysteriously arrived in the city, encouraging them in the name of the Archduke and the Prince of Orange, and assuring them of relief within fourteen days.‡ A brief animation was thus produced, attended by a corresponding languor upon the part of the besiegers, for Alexander had been lying ill with a fever since the day when the demilune had been carried. From his sick bed he rebuked his officers severely that a temporary breastwork, huddled together by boors and burghers in the midst of a siege, should prove an insurmountable obstacle to men who had carried everything before them. The morrow was the festival§ of Saint Peter and Saint Paul,

* Strada, 2, iii. 118.

† Bor, xiii. 64. Hoofd, xv. 630. Strada, 2, iii. 120, 121.

‡ This letter is still preserved in the Archives of Holland.—Groen v. Prinst. Archives de la Maison d'Orange, vi. 622, note. Bor, xiii. 65.

§ 29th of June, 1579.

and it was meet that so sacred a day should be hallowed by a Christian and Apostolic victory. Saint Peter would be there with his keys to open the gate ; Saint Paul would lead them to battle with his invincible sword. Orders were given accordingly, and the assault was assigned for the following morning.

Meantime, the guards were strengthened and commanded to be more than usually watchful. The injunction had a remarkable effect. At the dead of night, a soldier of the watch was going his rounds on the outside of the breastwork, listening, if perchance he might catch, as was not unusual, a portion of the conversation among the beleaguered burghers within. Prying about on every side, he at last discovered a chink in the wall, the result, doubtless, of the last cannonade, and hitherto overlooked. He enlarged the gap with his fingers, and finally made an opening wide enough to admit his person. He crept boldly through, and looked around in the clear starlight.* The sentinels were all slumbering at their posts. He advanced stealthily in the dusky streets. Not a watchman was going his rounds. Soldiers, burghers, children, women, exhausted by incessant fatigue, were all asleep. Not a footfall was heard ; not a whisper broke the silence ; it seemed a city of the dead. The soldier crept back through the crevice, and hastened to apprise his superiors of his adventure.†

Alexander, forthwith instructed as to the condition of the city, at once ordered the assault, and the last wall was suddenly stormed before the morning broke. The soldiers forced their way through the breach or sprang over the breastwork, and surprised at last—in its sleep—the city which had so long and vigorously defended itself. The burghers, startled from their slumber, bewildered, unprepared, found themselves engaged in unequal conflict with alert and savage foes. The battle, as usual when Netherland towns were surprised by Philip's

---

* Strada, 2, iii. 121.

† Ibid.—Compare Bor, xiii. 65, sqq. Hoofd, xv. 632, 633. Meteren, ix. 155, sqq.

soldiers, soon changed to a massacre. The townspeople rushed hither and thither, but there was neither escape, nor means of resisting an enemy who now poured into the town by thousands upon thousands. An indiscriminate slaughter succeeded. Women, old men, and children, had all been combatants; and all, therefore, had incurred the vengeance of the conquerors. A cry of agony arose which was distinctly heard at the distance of a league. Mothers took their infants in their arms, and threw themselves by hundreds into the Meuse—and against women the blood-thirst of the assailants was especially directed. Females who had fought daily in the trenches, who had delved in mines and mustered on the battlements, had unsexed themselves in the opinion of those whose comrades they had helped to destroy. It was nothing that they had laid aside the weakness of women in order to defend all that was holy and dear to them on earth. It was sufficient that many a Spanish, Burgundian, or Italian mercenary had died by their hands. Women were pursued from house to house, and hurled from roof and window. They were hunted into the river; they were torn limb from limb in the streets. Men and children fared no better; but the heart sickens at the oft-repeated tale. Horrors, alas, were commonplaces in the Netherlands. Cruelty too monstrous for description, too vast to be believed by a mind not familiar with the outrages practised by the soldiers of Spain and Italy upon their heretic fellow-creatures, were now committed afresh in the streets of Maestricht.*

On the first day four thousand men and women were slaughtered.† The massacre lasted two days longer; nor would it be an exaggerated estimate, if we assume that the amount of victims upon the two last days was equal to half the number sacrificed on the first.‡ It was said that not four

* Bentivoglio, 2, i. 239. Haraei, Ann. Brab., iii. 299. Hoofd. xv. 633. Bor, xiii. 66. Meteren, ix. 155. Strada, 2, iii. 124.

† This is the estimate of the Jesuit Strada.

‡ Strada puts the total number of inhabitants of Maestricht, slain during the four months' siege, at eight thousand, of whom seventeen hundred were women. —P. 127

hundred citizens were left alive after the termination of the siege.* These soon wandered away, their places being supplied by a rabble rout of Walloon sutlers and vagabonds. Maestricht was depopulated as well as captured. The booty obtained after the massacre was very large, for the city had been very thriving, its cloth manufacture extensive and important. Sebastian Tappin, the heroic defender of the place, had been shot through the shoulder at the taking of the Parma ravelin, and had been afterwards severely injured at the capture of the demilune. At the fall of the city he was mortally wounded, and carried a prisoner to the hostile camp, only to expire. The governor, Swartsenberg, also lost his life.†

Alexander, on the contrary, was raised from his sick bed with the joyful tidings of victory, and as soon as he could be moved, made his appearance in the city. Seated in a splendid chair of state, borne aloft on the shoulders of his veterans, with a golden canopy above his head to protect him from the summer's sun, attended by the officers of his staff, who were decked by his special command in their gayest trappings, escorted by his body-guard, followed by his "plumed troops," to the number of twenty thousand, surrounded by all the vanities of war, the hero made his stately entrance into the town.‡ His way led through deserted streets of shattered houses. The pavement ran red with blood. Headless corpses, mangled limbs—an obscene mass of wretchedness and corruption, were spread on every side, and tainted the summer air. Through the thriving city which, in the course of four months

* Not more than three or four hundred, says Bor, xiii. 65. Not more than four hundred, says Hoofd, xv. 633. Not three hundred, says Meteren, ix. This must of course be an exaggeration, for the population had numbered thirty-four thousand at the commencement of the siege. At any rate, the survivors were but a remnant, and they all wandered away. The place, which had been so recently a very thriving and industrious town, remained a desert. During the ensuing winter most of the remaining buildings were torn down, that the timber and woodwork might be used as firewood by the soldiers and vagabonds who from time to time housed there.—Meteren, Hoofd, Bor, ubi sup.

† Strada, 2, iii. 126.

‡ Strada, 2, iii. 130.—Compare Tassis, v. 339.

Alexander had converted into a slaughter-house and a solitude, the pompous procession took its course to the church of Saint Servais.* Here humble thanks were offered to the God of Love, and to Jesus of Nazareth, for this new victory. Especially was gratitude expressed to the Apostles Paul and Peter, upon whose festival, and by whose sword and key the crowning mercy had been accomplished,† and by whose special agency eight thousand heretics now lay unburied in the streets. These acts of piety performed, the triumphal procession returned to the camp, where, soon afterwards, the joyful news of Alexander Farnese's entire convalescence was proclaimed.

The Prince of Orange, as usual, was blamed for the tragical termination to this long drama. All that one man could do, he had done to awaken his countrymen to the importance of the siege. He had repeatedly brought the subject solemnly before the assembly, and implored for Maestricht, almost upon his knees. Lukewarm and parsimonious, the states had responded to his eloquent appeals with wrangling addresses and insufficient votes. With a special subsidy obtained in April and May, he had organized the slight attempt at relief, which was all which he had been empowered to make, but which proved entirely unsuccessful. Now that the massacre to be averted was accomplished, men were loud in reproof, who had been silent, and passive while there was yet time to speak and to work. It was the Prince, they said, who had delivered so many thousands of his fellow-countrymen to butchery. To save himself, they insinuated he was now plotting to deliver the land into the power of the treacherous Frenchman, and he alone, they asserted, was the insuperable obstacle to an honorable peace with Spain.‡

A letter, brought by an unknown messenger, was laid

* Strada, 2, iii. 130.—Compare Tassis, v. 339.

† According to Father Strada, Alexander considered this ceremony as a payment of wages due to his divine comrades, Peter and Paul: "Petro et Paulo gratias *quasi stipendium persolvit commilitonibus Divis.*"—P. 130.

‡ Groen v. Prinst., Archives, etc., vi. 621, 622; vii. 41, 42. Bor, xiii. Hoofd, xvi., passim.

before the states' assembly, in full session, and sent to the clerk's table, to be read aloud. After the first few sentences, that functionary faltered in his recital. Several members also peremptorily ordered him to stop ; for the letter proved to be a violent and calumnious libel upon Orange, together with a strong appeal in favor of the peace propositions then under debate at Cologne. The Prince alone, of all the assembly, preserving his tranquillity, ordered the document to be brought to him, and forthwith read it aloud himself, from beginning to end. Afterwards, he took occasion to express his mind concerning the ceaseless calumnies of which he was the mark. He especially alluded to the oft-repeated accusation that he was the only obstacle to peace, and repeated that he was ready at that moment to leave the land, and to close his lips for ever, if by so doing he could benefit his country, and restore her to honorable repose. The outcry, with the protestations of attachment and confidence which at once broke from the assembly, convinced him, however, that he was deeply rooted in the hearts of all patriotic Netherlanders, and that it was beyond the power of slanderers to loosen his hold upon their affection.*

Meantime, his efforts had again and again been demanded to restore order in that abode of anarchy, the city of Ghent. After his visit during the previous winter, and the consequent departure of John Casimir to the palatinate, the pacific arrangements made by the Prince had for a short time held good. Early in March, however, that master of misrule, John van Imbize, had once more excited the populace to sedition. Again the property of Catholics, clerical and lay, was plundered; again the persons of Catholics, of every degree, were maltreated. The magistrates, with first senator Imbize at their head, rather encouraged than rebuked the disorder; but Orange, as soon as he received official intelligence of the event, hastened to address them in the words of earnest warning and wisdom.† He allowed that the inhabi-

* Archives, etc., vii. 42, 43. † Ibid., vi. 586, sqq.

tants of the province had reason to be discontented with the presence and the misconduct of the Walloon soldiery. He granted that violence and the menaces of a foreign tyranny made it difficult for honest burghers to gain a livelihood. At the same time he expressed astonishment that reasonable men should seek a remedy for such evils in tumults which would necessarily bring utter destruction upon the land. "It was," he observed, "as if a patient should from impatience, tear the bandages from his wounds, and, like a maniac, instead of allowing himself to be cured, plunge a dagger into his own heart."*

These exhortations exerted a wholesome effect for a moment, but matters soon went from bad to worse. Imbize, fearing the influence of the Prince, indulged in open-mouthed abuse of a man whose character he was unable even to comprehend. He accused him of intriguing with France for his own benefit, of being a Papist in disguise, of desiring to establish what he called a "religious peace," merely to restore Roman idolatry. In all these insane ravings, the demagogue was most ably seconded by the ex-monk. Incessant and unlicensed were the invectives hurled by Peter Dathenus from his pulpit upon William the Silent's head. He denounced him—as he had often done before—as an atheist in heart; as a man who changed his religion as easily as his garments; as a man who knew no God but state expediency, which was the idol of his worship; a mere politician who would tear his shirt from his back and throw it in the fire, if he thought it were tainted with religion.†

Such witless but vehement denunciation from a preacher who was both popular and comparatively sincere, could not but affect the imagination of the weaker portion of his hearers. The faction of Imbize became triumphant. Ryhove—the ruffian whose hands were stained with the recent blood of Visch and Hessels—rather did damage than service to the

* Archives, etc., vi. 589.

† Gh. Gesch., ii. 199, cited in Gr. v. Prinst., Archives, etc., vii. 81, note.

cause of order. He opposed himself to the demagogue who was prating daily of Greece, Rome, and Geneva, while his clerical associate was denouncing William of Orange, but he opposed himself in vain. An attempt to secure the person of Imbize failed,* but by the influence of Ryhove, however, a messenger was despatched to Antwerp in the name of a considerable portion of the community of Ghent. The counsel and the presence of the man to whom all hearts in every part of the Netherlands instinctively turned in the hour of need, were once more invoked.*

The Prince again addressed them in language which none but he could employ with such effect. He told them that his life, passed in service and sacrifice, ought to witness sufficiently for his fidelity. Nevertheless, he thought it necessary—in view of the calumnies which were circulated—to repeat once more his sentiment that no treaty of peace, war, or alliance, ought to be negotiated, save with the consent of the people.† His course in Holland and Zealand had proved, he said, his willingness always to consult the wishes of his countrymen. As for the matter of religion it was almost incredible that there should be any who doubted the zeal which he bore the religion for which he had suffered so much. "I desire," he continued, fervently, "that men should compare that which has been done by my accusers during ten years past with that which I have done. In that which touches the true advancement of religion, I will yield to no man. They *who so boldly accuse me have no liberty of speech*, save that which has been acquired for them by the blood of my kindred, by my labors, and my excessive expenditures. To me they owe it that they dare speak at all." This letter (which was dated on the 24th of July, 1579) contained an assurance that the writer was about to visit Ghent.‡

* Archives, etc., vi. 586, sqq. and vii. 18. Van der Vynckt, iii. 29, sqq.

† "Dieu merci, je ne suis pas si peu cognoissant que je ne sache bien qu'il faut nécessairement traicter, soit de paix, soit de guerre, soit d'alliance, avec le gré du peuple," etc.—Letter of Orange, Archives, etc., vii 20, sqq.

‡ Ibid.—The whole of this noble document should be read again and again by all who feel interested in the character of William of Orange.

On the following day, Imbize executed a *coup d'état.* Having a body of near two thousand soldiers at his disposal, he suddenly secured the persons of all the magistrates and other notable individuals not friendly to his policy, and then, in violation of all law, set up a new board of eighteen irresponsible functionaries, according to a list prepared by himself alone. This was his way of enforcing the democratic liberty of Greece, Rome, and Geneva, which was so near to his heart. A proclamation, in fourteen articles, was forthwith issued, justifying this arbitrary proceeding. It was declared that the object of the somewhat irregular measure "was to prevent the establishment of the religious peace, which was merely a method of replanting uprooted papistry and the extirpated tyranny of Spain." Although the arrangements had not been made in strict accordance with formal usage and ceremony, yet they were defended upon the ground that it had been impossible, by other means, to maintain their ancient liberties and their religious freedom. At the same time a pamphlet, already prepared for the occasion by Dathenus, was extensively circulated. In this production the arbitrary revolution effected by a demagogue was defended with effrontery, while the character of Orange, was loaded with customary abuse. To prevent the traitor from coming to Ghent, and establishing what he called his religious peace, these irregular measures, it was urged, had been wisely taken.*

Such were the efforts of John Imbize—such the calumnies of Peter Dathenus—in order to counteract the patriotic endeavors of the Prince; but neither the ruffianism of John nor the libels of Peter were destined upon this occasion to be successful. William the Silent treated the slanders of the scolding monk with dignified contempt. "Having been informed," said he to the magistrates of Ghent, "that Master Peter Dathenus has been denouncing me as a man without religion or fidelity, and full of ambition, with other propositions hardly becoming

* Archives et Correspondance, vii. 31. Van der Vynckt, iii. 38, sqq. Meteren, ix. 161, sqq. Bor, xiii. 84, 85.

his cloth, I do not think it worth while to answer more at this time than that I willingly refer myself to the judgment of all who know me."*

The Prince came to Ghent, great as had been the efforts of Imbize and his partisans to prevent his coming. His presence was like magic. The demagogue and his whole flock vanished like unclean birds at the first rays of the sun. Imbize dared not look the Father of his country in the face. Orange rebuked the populace in the strong and indignant language that public and private virtue, energy, and a high purpose enabled such a leader of the people to use. He at once set aside the board of eighteen—the Grecian-Roman-Genevese establishment of Imbize—and remained in the city until the regular election, in conformity with the privileges, had taken place. Imbize, who had shrunk at his approach, was meantime discovered by his own companions. He had stolen forth secretly on the night before the Prince's arrival, and was found cowering in the cabin of a vessel, half dead with fear, by an ale-house keeper who had been his warm partisan. "No skulking," cried the honest friend, seizing the tribune of the people by the shoulder; "no sailing away in the night-time. You have got us all into this bog, and must come back, and abide the issue with your supporters."†

In this collapsed state was the windy demagogue, who had filled half Flanders with his sound and fury, conveyed before the patriot Prince. He met with grave and bitter rebukes, but felt sufficiently relieved when allowed to depart unharmed.‡ Judging of his probable doom by the usual practice of himself and his fellows in similar cases, he had anticipated nothing short of the gibbet. That punishment, however, was to be inflicted at a later period, by other hands, and not until he had added treason to his country and a shameless recantation of all his violent professions in favor of civil and religious

---

* Archives, et Corresp., vii. 33, 34.

† Bor, xiii. 85, sqq. Meteren, ix. 161, sqq. Van der Vynckt, iii. 38, sqq.

‡ Bor, Meteren, Van der Vynckt, ubi sup.

liberty to the list of his crimes. On the present occasion he was permitted to go free. In company with his clerical companion, Peter Dathenus, he fled to the abode of his excellent friend, John Casimir, who received both with open arms, and allowed them each a pension.*

Order being thus again restored in Ghent by the exertions of the Prince, when no other human hand could have dispelled the anarchy which seemed to reign supreme, William the Silent, having accepted the government of Flanders, which had again and again been urged upon him, now returned to Antwerp.†

---

* Van der Vynckt, iii. 38–42.—Compare Hoofd, xv. 145–150.

† Archives, vii. 60, and Meteren, ix. 163[b], but the Prince says, in his Apologie, published eighteen months later (Dec., 1580), that he had hitherto, although often urged to accept, refused the government of Flanders.—Apologie, etc., 108, 109. It is probable that his acceptance was only conditional, as, indeed, Meteren observes.

CHAPTER III.

The Cologne conferences—Intentions of the parties—Preliminary attempt by government to purchase the Prince of Orange—Offer and rejection of various articles among the plenipotentiaries—Departure of the imperial commissioners—Ultimatum of the States compared with that of the royal government—Barren negotiations terminated—Treason of De Bours, Governor of Mechlin—Liberal theories concerning the nature of government—Abjuration of Philip imminent—Self-denial of Orange—Attitude of Germany—of England—Marriage negotiations between Elizabeth and Anjou—Orange favors the election of the Duke as sovereign—Address and speeches of the Prince—Parsimony and interprovincial jealousy rebuked—Secret correspondence of Count Renneberg with the royal government—His treason at Groningen.

Since the beginning of May, the Cologne negotiations had been dragging their slow length along. Few persons believed that any good was likely to result from these stately and ponderous conferences; yet men were so weary of war, so desirous that a termination might be put to the atrophy under which the country was languishing, that many an eager glance was turned towards the place where the august assembly was holding its protracted session. Certainly, if wisdom were to be found in mitred heads—if the power to heal angry passions and to settle the conflicting claims of prerogative and conscience were to be looked for among men of lofty station, then the Cologne conferences ought to have made the rough places smooth and the crooked paths straight throughout all Christendom. There was the Archbishop of Rossano, afterwards Pope Urban VII., as plenipotentiary from Rome; there was Charles of Aragon, Duke of Terranova, supported by five councillors, as ambassador from his Catholic Majesty; there were the Duke of Aerschot, the Abbot of Saint Gertrude, the Abbot of Marolles, Doctor Bucho Aytta, Caspar Schetz, Lord of Grobbendonck, that learned Frisian, Aggeus van Albada, with seven other wise men, as envoys from the states-general. There were their Serene Highnesses the Elector and Archbishops of Cologne and Treves, with the Bishop of Wurtzburg. There was also a numerous embassy from his Imperial Majesty, with Count Otto de Schwartzenburg at its head.*

Here then were holiness, serenity, dignity, law, and learning in abundance. Here was a pope *in posse*, with archbishops, princes, dukes, jurisconsults, and doctors of divinity *in esse*, sufficient to remodel a world, if worlds were to be remodelled by such instruments. If protocols, replications, annotations, apostilles, could heal a bleeding country, here were the physicians to furnish those drugs in unlimited profusion. If reams of paper, scrawled over with barbarous technicalities, could smother and bury a quarrel which had its origin in the mutual antagonism of human elements, here were the men to scribble unflinchingly, till the reams were piled to a pyramid. If the same idea presented in many aspects could acquire additional life, here were the word-mongers who could clothe one shivering thought in a hundred thousand garments, till it attained all the majesty which decoration could impart. In truth, the envoys came from Spain, Rome, and Vienna, provided with but two ideas. Was it not a diplomatic masterpiece, that from this frugal store they could contrive to eke out seven mortal months of negotiation? Two ideas—the supremacy of his Majesty's prerogative, the exclusive exercise of the Roman Catholic religion—these were the be-all and the end-all of their commission. Upon these two strings they were to harp, at least till the walls of Maestricht had fallen. The envoys did their duty well; they were sent to enact a solemn comedy, and in the most stately manner did they walk

* Bor, xiii. 52. Meteren, ix. 155.

through their several parts. Not that the King was belligerent; on the contrary, he was heartily weary of the war. Prerogative was weary—Romanism was weary—Conscience was weary—the Spirit of Freedom was weary—but the Prince of Orange was not weary. Blood and treasure had been pouring forth so profusely during twelve flaming years, that all but that one tranquil spirit were beginning to flag.

At the same time, neither party had more disposition to concede than stomach to fight. Certainly the royal party had no inclination to yield. The King had granted easy terms to the Walloons, because upon the one great point of religion there was no dispute, and upon the others there was no intention of keeping faith.* With regard to the present negotiation, it was desirable to gain a little time. It was thought probable that the religious difference, judiciously managed at this juncture, might be used to effect a permanent severance of the provinces so lately banded together in a common union. "To divide them," wrote Tassis, in a very confidential letter, "no better method can be found than to amuse them with this peace negotiation. Some are ready for a pacification from their desire of repose, some from their fear of war, some from the differences which exist among themselves, and which it is especially important to keep alive."† Above all things, it was desirable to maintain the religious distraction till Maestricht had been taken. That siege was the key to the whole situation. If the separate Walloon accord could be quietly made in a corner, while Parma was battering that stronghold on the Meuse, and while decorous negotiation was smoothly holding its course on the Rhine, much disorganization, it was

---

* This is most evident from the correspondence of Parma, both before and after the treaty of Arras.—Rec. Prov. Wallones, MS., Brussels Archives, particularly vols. iv. and v.

† Archives de la Maison d'Orange, vii. 30. So also Du Plessis Mornay, in writing to a friend three years afterwards, observed: "Le traité de Cologne a suffisament monstré quelle a esté l'intention de l'ennemi en proposant ce beau nom de Paix, à scavoir de diviser et rompre les provinces et suborner les villes." —Mem. de Mornay, i. p. 75.

hoped, would be handsomely accomplished before the end of the year.

"As for a suspension of arms," wrote Alexander to Terranova, on the 21st of May, "the longer 'tis deferred the better. With regard to Maestricht, everything depends upon it that we possess, or desire to possess. Truly, if the Prince of Orange can relieve the city he will do it. If he does so, neither will this expedition of ours, nor any other expedition, be brought to a good end. As soon as men are aware that our affairs are looking badly, they will come again to a true union, and all will join together, in hope to accomplish their boasts."* Therefore, it was natural that the peace-wrights of Cologne should industriously ply their task.

It is not desirable to disturb much of that learned dust, after its three centuries' repose. A rapid sketch of the course of the proceedings, with an indication of the spirit which animated the contending parties, will be all that is necessary. They came and they separated with precisely opposite views. "The desires of Terranova and of the estates," says the royalist, Tassis, "were diametrically contrary to each other. The King wished that the exercise of the Roman Catholic religion should be exclusively established, and the absolute prerogative preserved in its integrity."† On the other hand, the provinces desired their charters and a religious peace. In these perpetual lines and curves ran the asymptotical negotiation from beginning to end—and so it might have run for two centuries, without hope of coincidence. Neither party was yet vanquished. The freshly united provinces were no readier now than before to admit that the Holy Office formed part of their national institutions. The despotic faction was not prepared to renounce that establishment. Foiled, but not disheartened, sat the Inquisition, like a beldame, upon the border, impotently threatening the land whence she had been for ever excluded; while industrious as the Parcæ,

* Letter of Parma, May 21, 1579, from his camp before Maestricht, apud Bor, 2, xiii. 57.

† Com. de Tum. Belg., v. 367.

distaff in hand, sat, in Cologne, the inexorable three—Spain, the Empire, and Rome—grimly spinning and severing the web of mortal destinies.

The first step in the proceedings had been a secret one. If by any means the Prince of Orange could be detached from his party—if by bribery, however enormous, he could be induced to abandon a tottering cause, and depart for the land of his birth—he was distinctly but indirectly given to understand that he had but to name his terms. We have seen the issue of similar propositions made by Don John of Austria. Probably there was no man living who would care to make distinct application of this dishonorable nature to the Father of his country. The Aerschots, the Meluns, the Lalains, and a swarm of other nobles, had their price, and were easily transferable from one to another, but it was not easy to make a direct offer to William of Orange. They knew—as he said shortly afterwards in his famous Apology—that "neither for property nor for life, neither for wife nor for children, would he mix in his cup a single drop of treason."* Nevertheless, he was distinctly given to understand that "there was nothing he could demand for himself personally that would not be granted." All his confiscated property, restoration of his imprisoned son, liberty of worship for himself, payment of all his debts, reimbursement of all his past expenses, and anything else which he could desire, were all placed within his reach. If he chose to retire into another land, his son might be placed in possession of all his cities, estates, and dignities, and himself indemnified in Germany; with a million of money over and above as a gratuity. The imperial envoy, Count Schwartzenburg, pledged his personal honor and reputation that every promise which might be made to the Prince should be most sacredly fulfilled.†

---

* "Si je ne veuille ni pour les biens ni pour la vie, ni pour femme ni pour enfans, mesler en mon breuvage une seule goutte de venin de trahison."—Apologie, p. 127.

† "—— Que je n'eusse rien sçeu demander pour mon particulier, qu'on ne m'eust accordé, et me donner comptant un million."—Ibid.—Compare Strada,

It was all in vain. The indirect applications of the imperial commissioners made to his servants and his nearest relations were entirely unsuccessful. The Prince was not to be drawn into a negotiation in his own name or for his own benefit. If the estates were satisfied, he was satisfied. He wanted no conditions but theirs ; " nor would he directly, or indirectly," he said, " separate himself from the cause on which hung all his evil or felicity." He knew that it was the object of the enemy to deprive the country of its head, and no inducements were sufficient to make him a party to the plot.* At the same time, he was unwilling to be an obstacle, in his own person, to the conclusion of an honorable peace. He would resign his offices which he held at the solicitation of the whole country, if thus a negotiation were likely to be more successful. " The Prince of Parma and the *disunited* provinces," said he to the states-general, " affect to consider this war as one waged against me and in my name—as if the question alone concerned the name and person of the general. If it be so, I beg you to consider whether it is not because I have been ever faithful to the land. Nevertheless, if I am an obstacle, I am ready to remove it. If you, therefore, in order to deprive the enemy of every right to inculpate us, think proper to choose another head and conductor of your affairs, *I promise you to serve and to be obedient to him with all my heart.* Thus shall we leave the enemy no standing-place to work dissensions among us."† Such was his language to friend and foe, and here, at least, was one man in history whom kings were not rich enough to purchase.

On the 18th of May, the states' envoys at Cologne presented fourteen articles, demanding freedom of religion and the ancient political charters. Religion, they said, was to be

---

who wrote with all the secret papers of the Farnese family before him, —— si hæc omnia abituro homini adhuc non sufficiant, neque hanc neque quamcumque persimilem conditionem repudiandam," etc.—2, ii. 86.—Compare, particularly, Ev. Reidani, Ann., ii. 29. Compare Gachard, Correspondance de Guillaume le Tacit., vol. iv., preface.

* Apologie, pp. 127, 128. Ev. Reidani, ii. 29.

† See the letter in Bor, xiii. 95–98.

referred, not to man, but to God. To him the King was subject as well as the people. Both King and people—"and *by people was meant every individual in the land*"—were bound to serve God according to their conscience.*

The imperial envoys found such language extremely reprehensible, and promptly refused, as umpires, to entertain the fourteen articles. Others drawn up by Terranova and colleagues, embodying the claims of the royal and Roman party, were then solemnly presented, and as promptly rejected. Then the imperial umpires came forward with two bundles of propositions—approved beforehand by the Spanish plenipotentiaries. In the political bundle, obedience due to the King was insisted upon, "as in the time of the Emperor Charles." The religious category declared that "the Roman religion—*all others excluded*—should thenceforth be exercised in all the provinces." Both these categories were considered more objectionable by the states' envoys than the terms of Terranova, and astonishment was expressed that "mention should again be made of the edicts—as if blood enough had not been shed already in the cause of religion."†

The Netherland envoys likewise gave the imperial commissioners distinctly to understand that—in case peace were not soon made—"the states would forthwith declare the King fallen from his sovereignty;" would for ever dispense the people from their oaths of allegiance to him, and would probably accept the Duke of Anjou in his place. The states-general, to which body the imperial propositions had been sent, also rejected the articles in a logical and historical argument of unmerciful length.‡

An appeal secretly made by the imperial and Spanish commissioners, from the states' envoys to the states themselves, and even to the people of the various provinces, had excited the anger of the plenipotentiaries. They complained loudly of this violation of all diplomatic etiquette, and the answer of

* See the document in Bor, xiii. 54, sqq.—Compare Meteren, ix. 156, sqq.

† Bor, xiii. 58, 59.

‡ Ibid., 3, xiii. 58[a], 115–118.

the states-general, fully confirming the views of their ambassadors, did not diminish their wrath.

On the 13th of November, 1579, the states' envoys were invited into the council chamber of the imperial commissioners, to hear the last solemn commonplaces of those departing functionaries. Seven months long they had been waiting in vain, they said, for the states' envoys to accede to moderate demands. Patience was now exhausted. Moreover, their mediatory views had been the subject of bitter lampooning throughout the country, while the authorities of many cities had publicly declared that all the inhabitants would rather die the death than accept such terms. The peace-makers, accordingly, with endless protestations as to their own purity, wisdom, and benevolence, left the whole "in the hands of God and the parties concerned."*

The reply to this elaborate farewell was curt and somewhat crusty. "Had they known," said the states' envoys, "that their transparencies and worthinesses had no better intention, and the Duke of Terranova no ampler commission, the whole matter might have been despatched, not in six months, but in six days."†

Thus ended the conferences, and the imperial commissioners departed. Nevertheless, Schwartzenburg remained yet a little time at Cologne, while five of the states' envoys also protracted their stay, in order to make their private peace with the King. It is hardly necessary to observe that the chief of these penitents was the Duke of Aerschot.‡ The ultimatum of the states was deposited by the departing envoys with Schwartzenburg,§ and a comparison of its terms with those offered by the imperial mediators, as the best which could be obtained from Spain, shows the hopelessness of the pretended negotiation. Departure of the foreign troops, restitution of all confiscated property, unequivocal recognition of the Ghent treaty and the perpetual edict, appointment to office

* Bor, xiii. 101, sqq. Meteren, ix. 157, sqq.

† Ibid.—Compare Strada, 2, ii. 110, 111.

‡ Bor, xiii. 108.

§ Apud Bor, 2, xiii. 108–110.

of none but natives, oaths of allegiance to the King and the states-general, exercise of the Reformed religion and of the Confession of Augsburg in all places where it was then publicly practised: such were the main demands of the patriot party.

In the secret instructions* furnished by the states to their envoys, they were told to urge upon his Majesty the absolute necessity, if he wished to retain the provinces, of winking at the exercise of the Reformed and the Augsburg creeds. "The new religion had taken too deep root," it was urged, "ever to be torn forth, save with the destruction of the whole country."

Thus, after seven dreary months of negotiation, after protocols and memoranda in ten thousand folia, the august diplomatists had travelled round to the points from which they had severally started. On the one side, unlimited prerogative and exclusive Catholicism; on the other, constitutional liberty, with freedom of conscience for Catholic and Protestant alike: these were the claims which each party announced at the commencement, and to which they held with equal firmness at the close ot the conferences.†

The congress had been expensive. Though not much had been accomplished for the political or religious advancement of mankind, there had been much excellent eating and drinking at Cologne during the seven months. Those drouthy deliberations had needed moistening. The Bishop of Wurtzburg had consumed "eighty hogsheads of Rhenish wine and twenty great casks of beer."† The expense of the states' envoys were

* Apud Bor, xiii. 110–113.

† All the most important documents of this elaborate but sterile negotiation are given in full by Bor, iii. 13, sqq. The whole mass of the protocols and arguments is also to be found in a volume entitled, "Acta pacificationis quæ coram sac. ces. maj. inter ser. reg. Hisp. et Princip. Matth. ordinumque Belg. leg. Coloniæ habita sunt." Leyden, 1580.—Compare Strada, 2, ii. 82–112; Haraei, Tum. Belg., iii. 295–298; Tassis, Com. Tum. Belg., v. 348–385; Meteren, ix. 155–161; Wagenaer, Vad. Hist., vii. 278–285, and 310–316; Hoofd, xv. 631, 632, and xvi. 658–672, et mult. al.

‡ Bor, xiii. 114.

twenty-four thousand guldens. The Archbishop of Cologne had expended forty thousand thalers.* The deliberations were, on the whole, excessively detrimental to the cause of the provinces, "and a great personage" wrote to the states-general, that the King had been influenced by no motive save to cause dissension.† This was an exaggeration, for his Majesty would have been well pleased to receive the whole of the country on the same terms which had been accepted by the Walloons. Meantime, those southern provinces had made their separate treaty, and the Netherlands were permanently dissevered. Maestricht had fallen. Disunion and dismay had taken possession of the country.

During the course of the year other severe misfortunes had happened to the states. Treachery, even among the men who had done good service to the cause of freedom, was daily showing her hateful visage. Not only the great chieftains who had led the Malcontent Walloon party, with the fickle Aerschot and the wavering Havré besides, had made their separate reconciliation with Parma, but the epidemic treason had mastered such bold partisans as the Seigneur de Bours, the man whose services in rescuing the citadel of Antwerp had been so courageous and valuable. He was governor of Mechlin; Count Renneberg was governor of Friesland. Both were trusted implicitly by Orange and by the estates; both were on the eve of repaying the confidence reposed in them by the most venal treason.

It was already known that Parma had tampered with De Bours; but Renneberg was still unsuspected. "The Prince," wrote Count John, "is deserted by all the noblemen, save the stadholder of Friesland and myself, and has no man else in whom he can repose confidence."‡ The brothers were doomed to be rudely awakened from the repose with regard to Renneberg, but previously the treason of a less important functionary was to cause a considerable but less lasting injury to the national party.

---

* Bor, xiii. 114. † Ibid.

‡ Archives de la Maison d'Orange, vii. 36, 37; letter of July 31, 1579.

In Mechlin was a Carmelite friar, of audacious character and great eloquence; a man who, "with his sweet, poisonous tongue, could ever persuade the people to do his bidding."* This dangerous monk, Peter Lupus, or Peter Wolf, by name, had formed the design of restoring Mechlin to the Prince of Parma, and of obtaining the bishopric of Namur as the reward of his services. To this end he had obtained a complete mastery over the intellect of the bold but unprincipled De Bours. A correspondence was immediately opened between Parma and the governor, and troops were secretly admitted into the city. The Prince of Orange, in the name of the Archduke and the estates, in vain endeavoured to recal the infatuated governor to his duty. In vain he conjured him, by letter after letter, to be true to his own bright fame so nobly earned. An old friend of De Bours, and like himself a Catholic, was also employed to remonstrate with him. This gentleman, De Fromont by name, wrote him many letters;† but De Bours expressed his surprise that Fromont, whom he had always considered a good Catholic and a virtuous gentleman, should wish to force him into a connection with the Prince of Orange and his heretic supporters. He protested that his mind was quite made up, and that he had been guaranteed by Parma not only the post which he now held, but even still farther advancement.‡

De Fromont reminded him, in reply, of the frequent revolutions of fortune's wheel, and warned him that the advancement of which he boasted would probably be an entire degradation. He bitterly recalled to the remembrance of the new zealot for Romanism his former earnest efforts to establish Calvinism. He reproached him, too, with having melted up the silver images of the Mechlin churches, including even the renowned shrine of Saint Rombout, which the Prince of Orange had always respected. "I don't say how much you

* "En konde met sijn soete fenijnige tonge het volk luiden en bewegen daer hy toe wilde."—Bor, xiii. 80.

† Bor, xiii. 80–83. Hoofd, xv. 636, 637.

‡ Letter of Pontus de Noyelles, Seigneur de Bours, apud Bor, xiii. 83.

took of that plunder for your own share," continued the indignant De Fromont, "for the very children cry it in your ears as you walk the streets. 'Tis known that if God himself had been changed into gold you would have put him in your pocket."*

This was plain language, but as just as it was plain. The famous shrine of Saint Rombout—valued at seventy thousand guldens, of silver gilt, and enriched with precious stones—had been held sacred alike by the fanatical iconoclasts and the greedy Spaniards who had successively held the city. It had now been melted up, and appropriated by Peter Lupus, the Carmelite, and De Bours, the Catholic convert, whose mouths were full of devotion to the ancient Church and of horror for heresy.†

The efforts of Orange and of the states were unavailing. De Bours surrendered the city, and fled to Parma, who received him with cordiality, gave him five thousand florins—the price promised for his treason, besides a regiment of infantry—but expressed surprise that he should have reached the camp alive.‡ His subsequent career was short, and he met his death two years afterwards, in the trenches before Tournay.§ The archiepiscopal city was thus transferred to the royal party, but the gallant Van der Tympel, governor of Brussels, retook it by surprise within six months of its acquisition by Parma, and once more restored it to the jurisdiction of the states. Peter Lupus, the Carmelite, armed to the teeth, and fighting fiercely at the head of the royalists, was slain in the street, and thus forfeited his chance for the mitre of Namur.‖

---

* Letter of J. v. Bourgoigne, Sr. de Fromont, apud Bor, 2, xii. 83.

† Meteren, x. 172. Bor, ubi sup. Hoofd, xv. 636.

‡ Bor (xiii. 84) states that he was treated with great contempt by Parma, and deprived of his posts. In this the faithful old chronicler is mistaken; as it appears from the manuscript letters of the Prince that he received the traitor with many caresses and with much greater respect than he deserved. Reports to the contrary were very current, however, in consequence of the Seigneur de Rossignol having been appointed by Parma governor of Mechlin in place of De Bours.—Letter of Prince of Parma to Mansfeld, Rec. Prov. Wall. iv. f. 324–328, MS., Royal Archives, Brussels.

§ Bor, xv. 288.

‖ Ibid., xiv. 175.

During the weary progress of the Cologne negotiations, the Prince had not been idle, and should this august and slow-moving congress be unsuccessful in restoring peace, the provinces were pledged to an act of abjuration. They would then be entirely without a head. The idea of a nominal Republic was broached by none. The contest had not been one of theory, but of facts ; for the war had not been for revolution, but for conservation, so far as political rights were concerned. In religion, the provinces had advanced from one step to another, till they now claimed the largest liberty—freedom of conscience—for all. Religion, they held, was God's affair, not man's, in which neither people nor king had power over each other, but in which both were subject to God alone. In politics it was different. Hereditary sovereignty was acknowledged as a fact, but at the same time, the spirit of freedom was already learning its appropriate language. It already claimed boldly the natural right of mankind to be governed according to the laws of reason and of divine justice. If a prince were a shepherd, it was at least lawful to deprive him of his crook when he butchered the flock which he had been appointed to protect.

"What reason is there," said the states-general, "why the provinces should suffer themselves to be continually oppressed by their sovereign, with robbings, burnings, stranglings, and murderings ?* Why, being thus oppressed, should they still give their sovereign—exactly *as if he were well conducting himself*†—the honor and title of lord of the land ?" On the other hand, if hereditary rule were an established fact, so also were ancient charters. To maintain, not to overthrow, the political compact, was the purpose of the states. "*Je maintiendrai*" was the motto of Orange's escutcheon. That a compact existed between prince and people, and that the

---

* "Wat reden is dat de Landen altijd sollen van hunnen Heere getraivalleert, bedorven en met roven, branden, worgen en moorden continuelijk overvallen en verkracht worden, etc., etc.—Address of States-general, July, 1579, Bor, xiii. 93b.

† "Gelijk als ob hij wel dede," etc.—Ibid.

sovereign held office only on condition of doing his duty, were startling truths which men were beginning, not to whisper to each other in secret, but to proclaim in the market-place. "'Tis well known to all," said the famous Declaration of Independence, two years afterwards, "that if a prince is appointed by God over the land, 'tis to protect them from harm, even as a shepherd to the guardianship of his flock. The subjects are not appointed by God for the behoof of the prince, but the prince for his subjects, without whom he is no prince. Should he violate the laws, he is to be forsaken by his meanest subject, and to be recognized no longer as prince."*

William of Orange always recognized these truths, but his scheme of government contemplated a permanent chief, and as it was becoming obvious that the Spanish sovereign would soon be abjured, it was necessary to fix upon a substitute. "As to governing these provinces in the form of a republic," said he, speaking for the states-general, "those who know the condition, privileges, and ordinances of the country, can easily understand that 'tis hardly possible to dispense with a head or superintendent."† At the same time, he plainly intimated that this "head or superintendent" was to be, not a monarch—a one-ruler—but merely the hereditary chief magistrate of a free commonwealth.

Where was this hereditary chief magistrate to be found? His own claims he absolutely withdrew. The office was within his grasp, and he might easily have constituted himself sovereign of all the Netherlands.‡ Perhaps it would have been better at that time had he advanced his claims and accepted the sovereignty which Philip had forfeited. As he did not believe in the possibility of a republic, he might honestly

---

* Bor, xv. 277.

† Ibid., xiii. 93.

‡ "U nog moet erkend worden dat er gelegenheiden waren in welke zijne *verkiezinge met eene groote meer de rheid* doorgegaan zoude zijn—en *mischien zonder tegensprack*, indien hij deze eerzucht gehad had. Echter verneemt men niet dat noch hij noch zijne aanhangelingen daartoe immer het voorstel gewaagd hebben," etc.—Van der Vynckt, iii. 72, sqq.

have taken into his own hands the sceptre which he considered indispensable. His self-abnegation was, however, absolute. Not only did he decline sovereignty, but he repeatedly avowed his readiness to lay down all the offices which he held, if a more useful substitute could be found. "Let no man think," said he, in a remarkable speech to the states-general, "that my good-will is in any degree changed or diminished. I agree to obey—as the least of the lords or gentlemen of the land could do—whatever person it may please you to select. You have but to command my services wheresoever they are most wanted; to guard a province or a single city, or in any capacity in which I may be found most useful. I promise to do my duty, with all my strength and skill, as God and my conscience are witnesses that I have done it hitherto."*

The negotiations pointed to a speedy abjuration of Philip; the Republic was contemplated by none; the Prince of Orange absolutely refused to stretch forth his own hand;—who then was to receive the sceptre which was so soon to be bestowed? A German Prince had been tried—in a somewhat abnormal position—but had certainly manifested small capacity for aiding the provinces. Nothing could well be more insignificant than the figure of Matthias; and, moreover, his imperial brother was anything but favorably disposed. It was necessary to manage Rudolph. To treat the Archduke with indignity, now that he had been partly established in the Netherlands, would be to incur the Emperor's enmity. His friendship, however, could hardly be secured by any advancement bestowed upon his brother; for Rudolph's services against prerogative and the Pope were in no case to be expected. Nor was there much hope from the Protestant princes of Germany. The day had passed for generous sympathy with those engaged in the great struggle which Martin Luther had commenced. The present generation of German Protestants were more inclined to put down the Calvinistic schism at home than to save it from oppression abroad. Men were more

* Bor, xiv. 143. Speech of Nov. 26, 1579.

disposed to wrangle over the thrice-gnawed bones of ecclesiastical casuistry, than to assist their brethren in the field. "I know not," said Gaultherus, "whether the calamity of the Netherlands, or the more than bestial stupidity of the Germans, be most deplorable. To the insane contests on theological abstractions we owe it that many are ready to breathe blood and slaughter against their own brethren. The hatred of the Lutherans has reached that point that they can rather tolerate Papists than ourselves."*

In England, there was much sympathy for the provinces, and there—although the form of government was still arbitrary—the instincts for civil and religious freedom, which have ever characterized the Anglo-Saxon race, were not to be repressed. Upon many a battle-field for liberty in the Netherlands, "men whose limbs were made in England" were found contending for the right. The blood and treasure of Englishmen flowed freely in the cause of their relatives by religion and race, but these were the efforts of individuals. Hitherto but little assistance had been rendered by the English Queen, who had, on the contrary, almost distracted the provinces by her fast-and-loose policy, both towards them and towards Anjou. The political rivalry between that Prince and herself in the Netherlands had, however, now given place to the memorable love-passage from which important results were expected, and it was thought certain that Elizabeth would view with satisfaction any dignity conferred upon her lover.†

Orange had a right to form this opinion. At the same time, it is well known that the chief councillors of Elizabeth—while they were all in favor of assisting the provinces—looked with anything but satisfaction upon the Anjou marriage. "The Duke," wrote Davidson to Walsingham (in July, 1579),

---

* Groen v. Prinst., Archives, etc., vii. 7. Hubert Languet, too, lamented the coldness of Germany towards her brethren in blood and creed. "Germania suo more," he writes to Sir Philip Sydney, "est otiosa spectatrix tragœdiarum, quæ apud vicinas ipsi gentes aguntur et ex alienis incommodis sua commoda capit."—Ep. 71, p. 254.

† Letter of Orange to the "Nearer-united states," apud Bor, 3, xiv. 132.

"seeks, forsooth, under a pretext of marriage with her Highness, the rather to espouse the Low Countries—the chief ground and object of his pretended love, howsoever it be disguised." The envoy believed both Elizabeth and the provinces in danger of taking unto themselves a very bad master. "Is there any means," he added, "so apt to sound the very bottom of our estate, and to hinder and breake the neck of all such good purpose as the necessity of the tyme shall set abroch?"*

The provinces of Holland and Zealand, notwithstanding the love they bore to William of Orange, could never be persuaded by his arguments into favoring Anjou. Indeed, it was rather on account of the love they bore the Prince—whom they were determined to have for their sovereign—that they refused to listen to any persuasion in favor of his rival, although coming from his own lips. The states-general, in a report to the states of Holland, drawn up under the superintendence of the Prince, brought forward all the usual arguments for accepting the French duke, in case the abjuration should take place.† They urged the contract with Anjou (of August 13th, 1578), the great expenses he had already incurred in their behalf; the danger of offending him; the possibility that in such case he would ally himself with Spain; the prospect that, in consequence of such a result, there would be three enemies in the field against them—the Walloons, the Spaniards, and the French, all whose forces would eventually be turned upon Holland and Zealand alone. It was represented that the selection of Anjou would, on the other hand, secure the friendship of France—an alliance which would inspire both the Emperor and the Spanish monarch with fear; for they could not contemplate without jealousy a possible incorporation of the provinces with that kingdom. Moreover, the geographical situation of France made its friendship inexpressibly desirable. The states of Holland and Zealand were, therefore, earnestly

* Archives de la Maison d'Orange, etc., vi. 646, sqq.

† Report in Bor, xiii. 92–95.

invited to send deputies to an assembly of the states-general, in order to conclude measures touching the declaration of independence to be made against the King, and concerning the election of the Duke of Anjou.*

The official communications by speech or writing of Orange to the different corporations and assemblies, were at this period of enormous extent. He was moved to frequent anger by the parsimony, the inter-provincial jealousy, the dull perception of the different estates, and he often expressed his wrath in unequivocal language. He dealt roundly with all public bodies. His eloquence was distinguished by a bold, uncompromising, truth-telling spirit, whether the words might prove palatable or bitter to his audience. His language rebuked his hearers more frequently than it caressed them, for he felt it impossible, at all times, to consult both the humors and the high interests of the people, and he had no hesitation, as guardian of popular liberty, in denouncing the popular vices by which it was endangered.†

By both great parties, he complained, his shortcomings were all noted, the good which he had accomplished passed over in silence.‡ He solemnly protested that he desired, out of his whole heart, the advancement of that religion which he

---

* Bor, xiii. 95ª.

† "Artes ad regendam plebem," says one who knew him well, "in eo omnes; quam licet præfracti obstinati animi, tandem ad obsequium flexit: nunc blanda aspera nunc ac violenta oratione *cujus frequentior illi usus, quam lenociniorum.* Libertatis atque autoritatis sane adsiduus custos, ut liberé plebi sua objicere vitia posset."—Ev. Reidan., Ann. Belg., ii. 59.

‡ Letter to the States-general, August, 1579, apud Bor, xiv. 97, sqq. This was the opinion frequently expressed by Languet: "Cherish the friendship of the Prince, I beseech you," he writes to Sir Philip Sydney, "for there is no man like him in all Christendom. Nevertheless, his is the lot of all men of prudence—to be censured by all parties. The people complain that he despises them; the nobility declare that it is their order which he hates; and this is as sensible as if you were to tell me that you were the son of a clown: (quasi v. dicebat nihi, ego sim patre rustico natus)."—Ep. ad Sydn., ep. 76, p. 270. "Ego non possum satis admirari Auriaci prudentiam et æquanimitatem," he continues, "in tanta negotiorum mole sustinenda et ferendis tot injuriis. Obsecro respice ejus virtutem et ne deterreat a colenda cum eo amicitia ejus fortuna, quæ tandem etiam forte magis laeta fulgebit."—Ibid.

publicly professed, and with God's blessing, hoped to profess to the end of his life,* but nevertheless, he reminded the states that he had sworn, upon taking office as Lieutenant-General, to keep "all the subjects of the land equally under his protection," and that he had kept his oath. He rebuked the parsimony which placed the accepted chief of the provinces in a sordid and contemptible position. "The Archduke has been compelled," said he, in August, to the states-general, "to break up housekeeping, for want of means. How shameful and disreputable for the country, if he should be compelled, for very poverty, to leave the land!" He offered to lay down all the power with which he had himself been clothed, but insisted, if he were to continue in office, upon being provided with larger means of being useful. "'Twas impossible," he said, "for him to serve longer on the same footing as heretofore; finding himself without power or authority, without means, without troops, without money, without obedience."* He reminded the states-general that the enemy—under pretext of peace negotiations—were ever circulating calumnious statements to the effect that he was personally the only obstacle to peace. The real object of these hopeless conferences was to sow dissension through the land, to set burgher against burgher, house against house. As in Italy, Guelphs and Ghibellines—as in Florence, the Neri and Bianchi—as in Holland, the Hooks and Cabbeljaws had, by their unfortunate quarrels, armed fellow countrymen and families against each other—so also, nothing was so powerful as religious difference to set friend against friend, father against son, husband against wife.†

He warned the states against the peace propositions of the enemy. Spain had no intention to concede, but was resolved to

* "——hoewel dat wy niet en willen ontkennen dat wy niet uit ganscher herten en souden begeert hebben de vorderinge van der Religie van de welke wy God lof openbare professie doen en verhopen 't selve te doen tot den einde onser leevens," etc.—Letter to the States-general, ubi sup.

† Letter to the States-general, Sept. 18 1579, Bor, 2, xiv. 131, sqq.

extirpate. For himself, he had certainly everything to lose by continued war. His magnificent estates were withheld, and—added he with simplicity—there is no man who does not desire to enjoy his own.* The liberation of his son, too, from his foreign captivity, was, after the glory of God and the welfare of the fatherland, the dearest object of his heart. Moreover, he was himself approaching the decline of life. Twelve years he had spent in perpetual anxiety and labor for the cause. As he approached old age, he had sufficient reason to desire repose. Nevertheless, considering the great multitude of people who were leaning upon him, he should account himself disgraced if, for the sake of his own private advantage, he were to recommend a peace which was not perfectly secure. As regarded his own personal interests, he could easily place himself beyond danger—yet it would be otherwise with the people. The existence of the religion which, through the mercy of God he professed, would be sacrificed, and countless multitudes of innocent men would, by his act, be thrown bodily into the hands of the blood-thirsty inquisitors who, in times past, had murdered so many persons, and so utterly desolated the land. In regard to the ceaseless insinuations against his character which men uttered "over their tables and in the streets," he observed philosophically, that "mankind were naturally inclined to calumny, particularly against those who exercised government over them. His life was the best answer to those slanders. Being overwhelmed with debt, he should doubtless do better in a personal point of view to *accept the excellent and profitable* offers which were daily made to him by the enemy."† He might be justified in such a course, when it was remembered how many had deserted him and forsworn their religion. Nevertheless, he had ever refused, and should ever refuse to listen to offers by which only his own personal interests were secured. As to the

* "Daer is niemand hy soude wel begeren het sijne te gebruiken."—Letter to the States-general.

† "Om alsulke goede vorderlijke condition aen te nemen als de zelve zijn gepresenteert en aengeboden even verre hy daer na hadde willen luisteren en gedurende desen vredenhandel tot eenig particulier accord verstaen."—Ibid.

defence of the country, he had thus far done all in his power, with the small resources placed at his command. He was urged by the "nearer-united states" to retain the post of Lieutenant-General. He was ready to consent. He was, however, not willing to hold office a moment, unless he had power to compel cities to accept garrisons, to enforce the collection of needful supplies throughout the provinces, and in general to do everything which he judged necessary for the best interests of the country.*

Three councils were now established—one to be in attendance upon the Archduke and the Prince of Orange, the two others to reside respectively in Flanders and in Utrecht. They were to be appointed by Matthias and the Prince, upon a double nomination from the estates of the united provinces. Their decisions were to be made according to a majority of votes, and there was to be no secret cabinet behind and above their deliberations.† It was long, however, before these councils were put into working order. The fatal jealousy of the provincial authorities, the small ambition of local magistrates, interposed daily obstacles to the vigorous march of the generality.‡ Never was jealousy more mischievous, never circumspection more misapplied. It was not a land nor a crisis in which there was peril of centralization. Local municipal government was in truth the only force left. There was no possibility of its being merged in a central authority which did not exist. The country was without a centre. There was small chance of apoplexy where there was no head. The danger lay in the mutual repulsiveness of these atoms of sovereignty—in the centrifugal tendencies which were fast resolving a nebulous commonwealth into chaos. Disunion and dissension would soon bring about a more fatal centralization—that of absorption in a distant despotism.

At the end of November, 1579, Orange made another

* Letter to the States-general, Sept. 18, 1579. Bor, 2, xiv. 131, sqq.

† Bor, xiv. 135. Archives de la M. d'Orange, vii. 107.

‡ Archives, etc., vii. 94.

remarkable speech in the states-general at Antwerp.* He handled the usual topics with his customary vigor, and with that grace and warmth of delivery which always made his eloquence so persuasive and impressive.† He spoke of the countless calumnies against himself, the chaffering niggardliness of the provinces, the slender result produced by his repeated warnings. He told them bluntly the great cause of all their troubles. It was the absence of a broad patriotism; it was the narrow power grudged rather than given to the deputies who sat in the general assembly. They were mere envoys, tied by instructions. They were powerless to act, except after tedious reference to the will of their masters, the provincial boards. The deputies of the Union came thither, he said, as advocates of their provinces or their cities, not as councillors of a commonwealth—and sought to further those narrow interests, even at the risk of destruction to their sister states. The contributions, he complained, were assessed unequally, and expended selfishly. Upon this occasion, as upon all occasions, he again challenged inquiry into the purity of his government, demanded chastisement, if any act of mal-administration on his part could be found, and repeated his anxious desire either to be relieved from his functions, or to be furnished with the means of discharging them with efficiency.

On the 12th of December, 1579, he again made a powerful speech in the states-general.‡ Upon the 9th of January, 1580, following, he made an elaborate address upon the state of the country, urging the necessity of raising instantly a considerable army of good and experienced soldiers. He fixed the indispensable number of such a force at twelve thousand foot, four thousand horse, and at least twelve hundred pioneers. "Weigh well the matters," said he, in

* In Bor, xiv. 141–143.

† "Avec un accent propre," says one of his most bitter enemies, "et action convenable, en quoi le Prince d'Oranges excelloit—donnant à l'assemblée si grande impression et persuasion qu'il remporta le fruict qu'il desiroit," etc.—Renom de France, MS., t. iv. c. xi.

‡ Bor, xiv. 150–151.

conclusion, "which I have thus urged, and which are of the most extreme necessity. Men in their utmost need are daily coming to me for refuge, *as if I held power over all things in my hand.*" At the same time he complained that by reason of the dilatoriness of the states, he was prevented from alleviating misery when he knew the remedy to be within reach. "I beg you, however, my masters," he continued, "to believe that this address of mine is no simple discourse. 'Tis a faithful presentment of matters which, if not reformed, will cause the speedy and absolute ruin of the land. Whatever betide, however, I pray you to hold yourselves assured, that with God's help, I am determined to live with you or to die with you."*

Early in the year 1580, the Prince was doomed to a bitter disappointment, and the provinces to a severe loss, in the treason of Count Renneberg, governor of Friesland. This young noble was of the great Lalain family. He was a younger brother of Anthony, Count of Hoogstraaten—the unwavering friend of Orange. He had been brought up in the family of his cousin, the Count de Lalain, governor of Hainault, and had inherited the title of Renneberg from an uncle, who was a dignitary of the church.† For more than a year there had been suspicions of his fidelity. He was supposed to have been tampered with by the Duke of Terranova, on the first arrival of that functionary in the Netherlands.‡ Nevertheless, the Prince of Orange was unwilling to listen to the whispers against him. Being himself the mark of calumny, and having a tender remembrance of the elder brother, he persisted in reposing confidence in a man who was in

---

* Bor, xiv. 153–156. The estimated expenses of the states' army for the year 1580, to be assessed upon all the provinces, was, per month, 518,000 florins. This provided for 225 infantry companies, amounting to 32,162 men, at a monthly pay of 359,240 florins; 3,750 cavalry at 80,590 florins monthly wages, besides 1,200 German reiters at 40,000 florins per month, with other incidental expenses. A captain received 90 florins per month, a lieutenant 45, a sergeant 12, a surgeon 12, etc., etc. —Renom de France, MS., t. iv. c. 37.

† Bor, xv. 276. ‡ Bor, xiv. 162, sqq. Meteren, x. 168. Hoofd, xvi. 681.

reality unworthy of his friendship. George Lalain, therefore, remained stadholder of Friesland and Drenthe, and in possession of the capital city, Groningen.

The rumors concerning him proved correct. In November, 1579, he entered into a formal treaty with Terranova, by which he was to receive—as the price of "the virtuous resolution which he contemplated"—the sum of ten thousand crowns in hand, a further sum of ten thousand crowns within three months, and a yearly pension of ten thousand florins. Moreover, his barony of Ville was to be erected into a marquisate, and he was to receive the order of the Golden Fleece at the first vacancy. He was likewise to be continued in the same offices under the King which he now held from the estates.* The bill of sale, by which he agreed with a certain Quislain le Bailly to transfer himself to Spain, fixed these terms with the technical scrupulousness of any other mercantile transaction. Renneberg sold himself as one would sell a yoke of oxen, and his motives were no whit nobler than the cynical contract would indicate. "See you not," said he in a private letter to a friend, "that this whole work is brewed by the Nassaus for the sake of their own greatness, and that they are everywhere provided with the very best crumbs? They are to be stadholders of the principal provinces; we are to content ourselves with Overyssel and Drente. Therefore I

* Reconciliation de Groningen et du Comte de Renneberg, MS., i. f. 59, 69, 75. Under this euphemism, by way of title, the original agreements of Renneberg, together with a large mass of correspondence relative to his famous treason, are arranged in the royal archives at Brussels, in two folio vols. of MS.—Compare Byvoegsel Auth. Stukk. tot P. Bor, ii. 3, 4. The terms of the bargain thus coldly set forth, are worthy attention, as showing the perfectly mercantile manner in which these great nobles sold themselves. An honest attachment, such as was manifested by cavaliers like Berlaymont and his four brave sons, to the royal and Catholic cause, can be respected, even while we regret that so much bravery should have been expended in support of so infamous a tyranny. But while their fanaticism can be forgiven, no language is strong enough to stigmatize the men who deserted the cause of liberty and conscience for hire. It must be remembered that Renneberg was much more virtuous than a large number of his distinguished compeers, many of whom were transferred so often from one side to the other, that they at last lost all convertible value.

have thought it best to make my peace with the King, from whom more benefits are to be got."*

Jealousy and selfishness, then, were the motives of his "virtuous resolution." He had another, perhaps a nobler incentive. He was in love with the Countess Meghen, widow of Lancelot Berlaymont, and it was privately stipulated that the influence of his Majesty's government should be employed to bring about his marriage with the lady. The treaty, however, which Renneberg had made with Quislain le Bailly was not immediately carried out. Early in February, 1580, his sister and evil genius, Cornelia Lalain, wife of Baron Monceau, made him a visit at Groningen. She implored him not to give over his soul to perdition by oppressing the Holy Church. She also appealed to his family pride, which should keep him, she said, from the contamination of companionship with "base-born weavers and furriers." She was of opinion that to contaminate his high-born fingers with base bribes were a lower degradation. The pension, the crowns in hand, the marquisate, the collar of the Golden Fleece, were all held before his eyes again. He was persuaded, moreover, that the fair hand of the wealthy widow would be the crowning prize of his treason, but in this he was destined to disappointment. The Countess was reserved for a more brilliant and a more bitter fate. She was to espouse a man of higher rank, but more worthless character, also a traitor to the cause of freedom, to which she was herself devoted, and who was even accused of attempting her life in her old age, in order to supply her place with a younger rival.†

The artful eloquence of Cornelia de Lalain did its work, and Renneberg entered into correspondence with Parma. It is singular with how much indulgence his conduct and character were regarded both before and subsequently to his treason. There was something attractive about the man. In an age

* Kluit. Holl. Staatsreg., i. 176, note 5.

† Meteren, x. 168. Bor, xiv. 161, and Hoofd, xviii. 423.

when many German and Netherland nobles were given to drunkenness and debauchery, and were distinguished rather for coarseness of manner and brutality of intellect* than for refinement or learning, Count Renneberg, on the contrary, was an elegant and accomplished gentleman—the Sydney of his country in all but loyalty of character. He was a classical scholar, a votary of music and poetry, a graceful troubadour, and a valiant knight.† He was "sweet and lovely of conversation,"‡ generous and bountiful by nature. With so many good gifts, it was a thousand pities that the gift of truth had been denied him. Never did treason look more amiable, but it was treason of the blackest die. He was treacherous, in the hour of her utmost need, to the country which had trusted him. He was treacherous to the great man who had leaned upon his truth, when all others had abandoned him.§ He was treacherous from the most sordid of motives—jealousy of his friend and love of place and pelf; but his subsequent remorse and his early death have cast a veil over the blackness of his crime.

While Cornelia de Lalain was in Groningen, Orange was in Holland. Intercepted letters left no doubt of the plot, and it was agreed that the Prince, then on his way to Amsterdam, should summon the Count to an interview. Renneberg's trouble at the proximity of Orange could not be suppressed.|| He felt that he could never look his friend in the face again. His plans were not ripe; it was desirable to dissemble for a season longer; but how could he meet that tranquil eye which "looked quite through the deeds of men?" It was obvious to

* See the letters of Count John of Nassau and of the Landgrave William, in Archives, etc., vols. vi. and vii., passim.

† Hoofd, xviii. 773.

‡ "Soet en lieflijk van conversatie."—Bor, xvi. 276[a].

§ "Je me suis trouvé," wrote the Prince in March, 1580, to Lazarus Schwendi, "et trouve encore à présent abandonné non seulement de secours et assistance, mais mesme de communication et de conseil, en la plus grande difficulté du temps et dangereuses occurrences qui me tombent sur les bras."—Archives, vii. 231.

|| Bor, xiv. 167.

Renneberg that *his* deed was to be done forthwith, if he would escape discomfiture. The Prince would soon be in Groningen, and his presence would dispel the plots which had been secretly constructed.

On the evening of March the 3rd, 1580, the Count entertained a large number of the most distinguished families of the place at a ball and banquet. At the supper-table, Hildebrand, chief burgomaster of the city, bluntly interrogated his host concerning the calumnious reports which were in circulation, expressing the hope that there was no truth in these inventions of his enemies. Thus summoned, Renneberg, seizing the hands of Hildebrand in both his own, exclaimed, "Oh, my father! you whom I esteem as my father, can you suspect me of such guilt? I pray you, trust me, and fear me not!"*

With this he restored the burgomaster and all the other guests to confidence. The feast and dance proceeded, while Renneberg was quietly arranging his plot. During the night all the leading patriots were taken out of their beds, and carried to prison, notice being at the same time given to the secret adherents of Renneberg. Before dawn, a numerous mob of boatmen and vagrants, well armed, appeared upon the public square. They bore torches and standards, and amazed the quiet little city with their shouts. The place was formally taken into possession, cannon were planted in front of the Town House to command the principal streets, and barricades erected at various important points. Just at daylight, Renneberg himself, in complete armor, rode into the square, and it was observed that he looked ghastly as a corpse.† He was followed by thirty troopers, armed like himself, from head to foot. "Stand by me now," he cried to the assembled throng; "fail me not at this moment, for now I am for the first time your stadholder."

---

* Bor, 167. Meteren, x. 169. Hoofd, xvi. 682.

† Van 't hooft ten voete gewapent."—Bor, ubi sup. "In vollen harnas."—Hoofd, xvi. 682. "Hy sag anders niet dan een dood mensch."—Bor, xiv. 168b. "Heel bestorven om de kaaken."—Hoofd, ubi sup.

While he was speaking, a few citizens of the highest class forced their way through the throng and addressed the mob in tones of authority. They were evidently magisterial persons endeavoring to quell the riot. As they advanced, one of Renneberg's men-at-arms discharged his carabine at the foremost gentleman, who was no other than burgomaster Hildebrand. He fell dead at the feet of the stadholder—of the man who had clasped his hands a few hours before, called him father, and implored him to entertain no suspicions of his honor. The death of this distinguished gentleman created a panic, during which Renneberg addressed his adherents, and stimulated them to atone by their future zeal in the King's service for their former delinquency. A few days afterwards the city was formally reunited to the royal government, but the Count's measures had been precipitated to such an extent, that he was unable to carry the province with him, as he had hoped. On the contrary, although he had secured the city, he had secured nothing else. He was immediately beleaguered by the states' force in the province under the command of Barthold Entes, Hohenlo, and Philip Louis Nassau, and it was necessary to send for immediate assistance from Parma.*

The Prince of Orange, being thus bitterly disappointed by the treachery of his friend, and foiled in his attempt to avert the immediate consequences, continued his interrupted journey to Amsterdam. Here he was received with unbounded enthusiasm.†

---

* MS. holographic letter of Renneberg to Prince of Parma, March 3, 1580.—Rec. Groning, et Renneberg, i. 69. Bor, Meteren, Hoofd.—Compare Apologie d'Orange, p. 121. Groen v. Prinst., Archives, vii. 243–248; Strada, 2, iii, 135, 136. Ev. Reidani, ii. 30.

† Bor, xiv. 170. Hoofd, xvi. 684.

CHAPTER IV.

Captivity of La Noue—Cruel propositions of Philip—Siege of Groningen—Death of Barthold Entes—His character—Hohenlo commands in the north—His incompetence—He is defeated on Hardenberg Heath—Petty operations—Isolation of Orange—Dissatisfaction and departure of Count John—Remonstrance of Archduke Matthias—Embassy to Anjou—Holland and Zealand offer the sovereignty to Orange—Conquest of Portugal—Granvelle proposes the Ban against the Prince—It is published—The document analyzed—The Apology of Orange analyzed and characterized—Siege of Steenwyk by Renneberg—Forgeries—Siege relieved—Death of Renneberg—Institution of the "Land-Council"—Duchess of Parma sent to the Netherlands—Anger of Alexander—Prohibition of Catholic worship in Antwerp, Utrecht, and elsewhere—Declaration of Independence by the United Provinces—Negotiations with Anjou—The sovereignty of Holland and Zealand provisionally accepted by Orange—Tripartition of the Netherlands—Power of the Prince described—Act of Abjuration analyzed—Philosophy of Netherland politics—Views of the government compact—Acquiescence by the people in the action of the estates—Departure of Archduke Matthias.

THE war continued in a languid and desultory manner in different parts of the country. At an action near Ingelmunster, the brave and accomplished De la Noue was made prisoner.* This was a severe loss to the states, a cruel blow to Orange, for he was not only one of the most experienced soldiers, but one of the most accomplished writers of his age. His pen was as celebrated as his sword.† In exchange for the

---

* Bor, xv. 194, 195. Hoofd, xvi. 690.

† "Che egli habbia saputo," says Bentivoglio, "cosi ben maneggiare la penna come la spada; e valere in pace non punto meno che in guerra."—Guerra di Fiandra, 2, i. 249.

illustrious Frenchman the states in vain offered Count Egmont, who had been made prisoner a few weeks before, and De Selles, who was captured shortly afterwards. Parma answered, contemptuously, that he would not give a lion for two sheep.* Even Champagny was offered in addition, but without success. Parma had written to Philip, immediately upon the capture, that, were it not for Egmont, Selles, and others, then in the power of Orange, he should order the execution of La Noue. Under the circumstances, however, he had begged to be informed as to his Majesty's pleasure, and in the meantime had placed the prisoner in the castle of Limburg, under charge of De Billy.† His Majesty, of course, never signified his pleasure, and the illustrious soldier remained for five years in a loathsome dungeon more befitting a condemned malefactor than a prisoner of war. It was in the donjon keep of the castle, lighted only by an aperture in the roof, and was therefore exposed to the rain and all inclemencies of the sky, while rats, toads, and other vermin housed in the miry floor.‡ Here this distinguished personage, Francis with the Iron Arm, whom all Frenchmen, Catholic or Huguenot, admired for his genius, bravery, and purity of character, passed five years of close confinement. The government was most anxious to take his life, but the captivity of Egmont and others prevented the accomplishment of their wishes. During this long period, the wife and numerous friends of La Noue were unwearied in their efforts to effect his ransom or exchange,§ but none of the prisoners in the hands of the patriots were considered a fair equivalent. The hideous proposition was even made by Philip the Second to La Noue, that he should receive his liberty if he would *permit his eyes to be put out*, as a preliminary condition. The fact is attested by several letters

* Ev. Reidan., Ann. ii. 39.

† Strada, d. 2, iii. 155, 156. Parma is said to have hinted to Philip that De Billy would willingly undertake the private assassination of La Noue.—Popelinière, Hist. des Pays Bas, 1556–1584.

‡ Moyse Amirault: La Vie de François, Seigneur de la Nouë dit Bras de Fer (Leyde, 1661), pp. 267–277.

§ Amirault, 267–298.

written by La Noue to his wife. The prisoner, wearied, shattered in health, and sighing for air and liberty, was disposed and even anxious to accept the infamous offer, and discussed the matter philosophically in his letters. That lady, however, horror-struck at the suggestion, implored him to reject the condition, which he accordingly consented to do. At last, in June, 1585, he was exchanged, on extremely rigorous terms, for Egmont. During his captivity in this vile dungeon, he composed not only his famous political and military discourses, but several other works, among the rest, Annotations upon Plutarch and upon the Histories of Guicciardini.*

The siege of Groningen proceeded, and Parma ordered some forces under Martin Schenck to advance to its relief. On the other hand, the meagre states' forces under Sonoy, Hohenlo, Entes, and Count John of Nassau's young son, William Louis, had not yet made much impression upon the city.† There was little military skill to atone for the feebleness of the assailing army, although there was plenty of rude valor. Barthold Entes, a man of desperate character, was impatient at the dilatoriness of the proceedings. After having been in disgrace with the states, since the downfall of his friend and patron, the Count De la Marck, he had recently succeeded to a regiment in place of Colonel Ysselstein, "dismissed for a homicide or two."‡ On the 17th of May, he had been dining at Rolda, in company with Hohenlo and the young Count of Nassau. Returning to the trenches in a state of wild intoxication, he accosted a knot of superior officers, informing

---

* "Enfin on en vint jusques à ce degré de barbarie que de luy faire suggerer sous main, que pour donner une suffisante caution de ne porter jamais les armes contre le Roy Catholicque, il falloit qu'il se laissast crever les yeux. A peine l'eusse-je creu si je ne l'avois sçeu que par la lecture des histoires et par le rapport d'un tiers. *Mais 7 ou 8 lettres* qu'il en a faites de sa propre main à sa femme m'ont rendu *la chose si indubitable*, que sur sa foy je la donne icy pour telle."—Amirault, pp. 280, 281–298.—Compare Strada, 2, iii. 156.

† Bor, xv. 203–205. Hoofd, xvi. 691, sqq. Meteren, x. 169, 170.

‡ Hoofd, xvi. 691.

them that they were but boys, and that he would show them how to carry the faubourg of Groningen on the instant. He was answered that the faubourg, being walled and moated, could be taken only by escalade or battery. Laughing loudly, he rushed forward toward the counterscarp, waving his sword, and brandishing on his left arm the cover of a butter firkin, which he had taken instead of his buckler. He had advanced, however, but a step, when a bullet from the faubourg pierced his brain, and he fell dead without a word.*

So perished one of the wild founders of the Netherland commonwealth—one of the little band of reckless adventurers who had captured the town of Brill in 1572, and thus laid the foundation stone of a great republic, which was to dictate its laws to the empire of Charles the Fifth. He was in some sort a type. His character was emblematical of the worst side of the liberating movement. Desperate, lawless, ferocious—a robber on land, a pirate by sea—he had rendered great service in the cause of his fatherland, and had done it much disgrace. By the evil deeds of men like himself, the fair face of liberty had been profaned at its first appearance. Born of a respectable family, he had been noted, when a student in this very Groningen where he had now found his grave, for the youthful profligacy of his character. After dissipating his partrimony, he had taken to the sea, the legalized piracy of the mortal struggle with Spain offering a welcome refuge to spendthrifts like himself. In common with many a banished noble of ancient birth and broken fortunes, the riotous student became a successful corsair, and it is probable that his prizes were made as well among the friends as the enemies of his country. He amassed in a short time one hundred thousand crowns—no contemptible fortune in those days. He assisted La Marck in the memorable attack upon Brill, but behaved badly and took to flight when Mondragon made his memorable expedition to relieve Tergoes.† He had subsequently been

* Hoofd, ubi sup. Meteren, x. 170[a].—Compare Bor, 3, xv. 205.

† Meteren, x. 170[a].

imprisoned with La Marck for insubordination, and during his confinement had dissipated a large part of his fortune. In 1576, after the violation of the Ghent treaty, he had returned to his piratical pursuits, and having prospered again as rapidly as he had done during his former cruises, had been glad to exchange the ocean for more honorable service on shore. The result was the tragic yet almost ludicrous termination which we have narrated. He left a handsome property, the result of his various piracies, or, according to the usual euphemism, prizes. He often expressed regret at the number of traders whom he had cast into the sea, complaining, in particular, of one victim whom he had thrown overboard, who would never sink, but who for years long ever floated in his wake, and stared him in the face whenever he looked over his vessel's side. A gambler, a profligate, a pirate, he had yet rendered service to the cause of freedom, and his name—sullying the purer and nobler ones of other founders of the commonwealth—"is enrolled in the capitol."*

Count Philip Hohenlo, upon whom now devolved the entire responsibility of the Groningen siege and of the Friesland operations, was only a few degrees superior to this northern corsair. A noble of high degree, nearly connected with the Nassau family, sprung of the best blood in Germany, handsome and dignified in appearance, he was, in reality only a debauchee and a drunkard. Personal bravery was his main qualification for a general; a virtue which he shared with many of his meanest soldiers. He had never learned the art of war, nor had he the least ambition to acquire it. Devoted to his pleasures, he depraved those under his command, and injured the cause for which he was contending.† Nothing but defeat and disgrace were expected by the purer patriots from such guidance. "The benediction of God," wrote

---

* Meteren, x. 170. Bor, xv. 205. Hoofd, xvi. 691. Archives de la Maison d'Orange, vii. 370. The names of the band of adventurers who seized Brill are all carefully preserved in the old records of the Republic.

† Letter of Albada, Archives et Correspondance, vii. 370. Ev. Reidani Ann. Belg., ii. 34.

Albada, "cannot be hoped for under this chieftain, who by life and manners is fitter to drive swine than to govern pious and honorable men."*

The event justified the prophecy. After a few trifling operations before Groningen, Hohenlo was summoned to the neighbourhood of Coewerden, by the reported arrival of Martin Schenck, at the head of a considerable force. On the 15th of June, the Count marched all night and a part of the following morning, in search of the enemy. He came up with them upon Hardenberg Heath, in a broiling summer forenoon. His men were jaded by the forced march, overcome with the heat, tormented with thirst, and unable to procure even a drop of water. The royalists were fresh, so that the result of the contest was easily to be foreseen. Hohenlo's army was annihilated in an hour's time, the whole population fled out of Coewerden, the siege of Groningen was raised, Renneberg was set free to resume his operations on a larger scale, and the fate of all the north-eastern provinces was once more swinging in the wind.† The boors of Drenthe and Friesland rose again. They had already mustered in the field at an earlier season of the year, in considerable force. Calling themselves "the desperates," and bearing on their standard an eggshell with the yolk running out—to indicate that, having lost the meat they were yet ready to fight for the shell—they had swept through the open country, pillaging and burning. Hohenlo had defeated them in two encounters, slain a large number of their forces, and reduced them for a time to tranquillity.‡ His late overthrow once more set them loose. Renneberg, always apt to be over-elated in prosperity, as he was unduly dejected in adversity, now assumed all the airs of a conqueror. He had hardly eight thousand men under his orders,§ but his strength lay in the weakness of his

---

* "—— qui porcis regendis vita et moribus magis est idoneus quam bonis piisque defendendis."—Archives et Correspondance, vii. 370.

† Bor, xv. 207. Meteren, x. 170, 171. Hoofd, xvi. 693, 694. Strada, 2. iv. 169–172.

‡ Bor, xiv. 177–178.

§ Bor, xv. 221[a].

adversaries. A small war now succeeded, with small generals, small armies, small campaigns, small sieges. For the time, the Prince of Orange was even obliged to content himself with such a general as Hohenlo. As usual, he was almost alone. "Donec eris felix," said he, emphatically—

"multos numerabis amicos,
Tempora cum erunt nubila, nullus erit,"*

and he was this summer doomed to a still harder deprivation by the final departure of his brother John from the Netherlands.

The Count had been wearied out by petty miseries.† His stadholderate of Gelderland had overwhelmed him with annoyance, for throughout the north-eastern provinces there was neither system nor subordination. The magistrates could exercise no authority over an army which they did not pay, or a people whom they did not protect. There were endless quarrels between the various boards of municipal and provincial government—particularly concerning contributions and expenditures.‡ During this wrangling, the country was exposed to the forces of Parma, to the private efforts of the

* Archives, vii. 231, Letter to Lazarus Schwendi.

† See the letters of Count John in Archives, vol. vii. passim; particularly letters 929, 930, 931, 932, 974, 1019, and the Memoir on pages 510–530.

‡ When the extraordinary generosity of the Count himself, and the altogether unexampled sacrifices of the Prince are taken into account, it may well be supposed that the patience of the brothers would be sorely tried by the parsimony of the states. It appears by a document laid before the states-general in the winter of 1580–1581, that the Count had himself advanced to Orange 570,000 florins in the cause. The total of money spent by the Prince himself for the sake of Netherland liberty was 2,200,000. These vast sums had been raised in various ways and from various personages. His estates were deeply hypothecated, and his creditors so troublesome, that, in his own language, he was unable to attend properly to public affairs, so frequent and so threatening were the applications made upon him for payment. Day by day he felt the necessity advancing more closely upon him of placing himself personally in the hands of his creditors and making over his estates to their mercy until the uttermost farthing should be paid. In his two campaigns against Alva (1568 and 1572) he had spent 1,050,000 florins. He owed the Elector Palatine 150,000 florins, the Landgrave 60,000, Count John 570,000, and other sums to other individuals.—Staat ende kort begrip van het geen, M. E. Heere den P. van Orange betalt mag hebben mitsgaders het geene syne V. G. schuldig is gebleeven, etc. Ordin. Depechen Boek, A°. 1580, 1581, f. 245vo, sqq., MS. Hague Archives.

Malcontents, to the unpaid soldiery of the states, to the armed and rebellious peasantry. Little heed was paid to the admonitions of Count John, who was of a hotter temper than was the tranquil Prince. The stadholder gave way to fits of passion at the meanness and the insolence to which he was constantly exposed. He readily recognized his infirmity, and confessed himself unable to accommodate his irascibility to the "humores" of the inhabitants. There was often sufficient cause for his petulance. Never had prætor of a province a more penurious civil list. "The baker has given notice," wrote Count John, in November, "that he will supply no more bread after to-morrow, unless he is paid." The states would furnish no money to pay the bill. It was no better with the butcher. "The cook has often no meat to roast," said the Count, in the same letter, "so that we are often obliged to go supperless to bed." His lodgings were a half-roofed, half-finished, unfurnished barrack, where the stadholder passed his winter days and evenings in a small, dark, freezing-cold chamber, often without fire-wood.* Such circumstances were certainly not calculated to excite envy. When in addition to such wretched parsimony, it is remembered that the Count was perpetually worried by the quarrels of the provincial authorities with each other and with himself, he may be forgiven for becoming thoroughly exhausted at last. He was growing "grey and grizzled" with perpetual perplexity. He had been fed with annoyance, as if—to use his own homely expression—"he had eaten it with a spoon." Having already loaded himself with a debt of six hundred thousand florins, which he had spent in the states' service, and having struggled manfully against the petty tortures of his situation, he cannot be severely censured for relinquishing his post.† The affairs of his own Countship were in great confusion. His children—boys and girls—were many, and needed their fathers' guidance, while the eldest, William Louis, was already in arms

* Archives et Correspondance, vii. 109, 113, 328, 329.

† Ibid., vii. 334, 487.

for the Netherlands, following the instincts of his race. Distinguished for a rash valor, which had already gained the rebuke of his father and the applause of his comrades, he had commenced his long and glorious career by receiving a severe wound at Coewerden, which caused him to halt for life.* Leaving so worthy a representative, the Count was more justified in his departure.

His wife, too, had died in his absence, and household affairs required his attention. It must be confessed, however, that if the memory of his deceased spouse had its claims, the selection of her successor was still more prominent among his anxieties. The worthy gentleman had been supernaturally directed as to his second choice, ere that choice seemed necessary, for before the news of his wife's death had reached him, the Count dreamed that he was already united in second nuptials to the fair Cunigunda, daughter of the deceased Elector Palatine—a vision which was repeated many times. On the morrow he learned, to his amazement, that he was a widower, and entertained no doubt that he had been specially directed towards the princess seen in his slumbers, whom he had never seen in life.† His friends were in favor of his marrying the Electress Dowager, rather than her daughter, whose years numbered less than half his own. The honest Count, however, "after ripe consideration," decidedly preferred the maid to the widow. "I confess," he said, with much gravity, "that the marriage with the old Electress, in respect of her God-fearing disposition, her piety, her virtue, and the like, would be much more advisable. Moreover, as she hath borne her cross, and knows how to deal with gentlemen, so much the better would it be for me. Nevertheless, inasmuch as she has already had two husbands, is of a tolerable

---

* Bor, xv. 216. Archives, etc., vii. 383–386. Hoofd, xvii. 707.

† Archives, etc., vii. 323, sqq. This conviction of divine interposition was inserted in the marriage contract.—Vide Memorial von Gr. Ernst zu Schawenburg and Dr. Jacob Schwartz. Archives et Correspondance, vii. 361, sqq.

age, and is *taller of stature than myself*, my inclination is less towards her than towards her daughter."*

For these various considerations, Count John, notwithstanding the remonstrances of his brother, definitely laid down his government of Gelderland, and quitted the Netherlands about midsummer.† Enough had not been done, in the opinion of the Prince, so long as aught remained to do, and he could not bear that his brother should desert the country in the hour of its darkness, or doubt the Almighty when his hand was veiled in clouds. "One must do one's best," said he, "and believe that when such misfortunes happen, God desires to prove us. If He sees that we do not lose our courage, He will assuredly help us. Had we thought otherwise, we should never have pierced the dykes on a memorable occasion, for it was an uncertain thing and a great sorrow for the poor people; yet did God bless the undertaking. He will bless us still, for his arm hath not been shortened."‡

On the 22nd of July, 1580, the Archduke Matthias, being fully aware of the general tendency of affairs, summoned a meeting of the generality in Antwerp. He did not make his appearance before the assembly, but requested that a deputation might wait upon him at his lodgings, and to this committee he unfolded his griefs. He expressed his hope that the states were not—in violation of the laws of God and man—about to throw themselves into the arms of a foreign prince. He reminded them of their duty to the holy Catholic religion, and to the illustrious house of Austria, while he also pathetically called their attention to the necessities of his own household, and hoped that they would, at least, provide for the arrears due to his domestics.§

The states-general replied with courtesy as to the personal

---

* Archives et Correspondance, vii. 325 and 364, note.—"Item:" says the marriage memorial already cited, "the widow is a tolerably stout person, which would be almost derogatory to his Grace. When they should be in company of other gentlemen and ladies, or should be walking together in the streets, his Grace would seem almost little at her side."—Memoir of Dr. Schwartz.

† Archives, etc., vii. 390.

‡ Archives et Correspondance, vii. 316.

§ Bor, xv. 212, 213.

claims of the Archduke. For the rest, they took higher grounds, and the coming declaration of independence already pierced through the studied decorum of their language. They defended their negotiation with Anjou on the ground of necessity, averring that the King of Spain had proved inexorable to all intercession, while, through the intrigues of their bitterest enemies, they had been entirely forsaken by the Empire.*

Soon afterwards, a special legation, with Saint Aldegonde at its head, was despatched to France to consult with the Duke of Anjou, and settled terms of agreement with him by the treaty of Plessis les Tours (on the 29th of September, 1580), afterwards definitely ratified by the convention of Bordeaux, signed on the 23rd of the following January.†

The states of Holland and Zealand, however, kept entirely aloof from this transaction, being from the beginning opposed to the choice of Anjou. From the first to the last, they would have no master but Orange, and to him, therefore, this year they formally offered the sovereignty of their provinces; but they offered it in vain.

The conquest of Portugal had effected a diversion in the affairs of the Netherlands. It was but a transitory one. The provinces found the hopes which they had built upon the necessity of Spain for large supplies in the peninsula—to their own consequent relief—soon changed into fears, for the rapid success of Alva in Portugal gave his master additional power to oppress the heretics of the north. Henry, the Cardinal King, had died in 1580, after succeeding to the youthful adventurer, Don Sebastian, slain during his chivalrous African campaign (4th of August, 1578). The contest for the succession which opened upon the death of the aged monarch was brief, and in fifty-eight days, the bastard Antonio, Philip's only formidable competitor, had been utterly defeated and driven forth to lurk, like a hunted wild beast, among rugged mountain caverns, with a price of a hundred thousand crowns upon his head.‡ In the course of the suc-

* Bor, xv. 212, 213.

† Ibid., 214.

‡ Cabrera, xii. cap. 29; xiii. cap. 1, 2, 5, 6, pp. 1095–1139. Bor, xiv. 178 sqq. Archives de la Maison d'Orange, vii. 398, sqq.

ceeding year, Philip received homage at Lisbon as King of Portugal.* From the moment of this conquest, he was more disposed, and more at leisure than ever, to vent his wrath against the Netherlands, and against the man whom he considered the incarnation of their revolt.

Cardinal Granvelle had ever whispered in the King's ear the expediency of taking off the Prince by assassination. It has been seen how subtly distilled, and how patiently hoarded, was this priest's venom against individuals, until the time arrived when he could administer the poison with effect. His hatred of Orange was intense and of ancient date. He was of opinion, too, that the Prince might be scared from the post of duty, even if the assassin's hand were not able to reach his heart. He was in favor of publicly setting a price upon his head—thinking that if the attention of all the murderers in the world were thus directed towards the illustrious victim, the Prince would tremble at the dangers which surrounded him. "A sum of money would be well employed in this way," said the Cardinal, "and, as the Prince of Orange *is a vile coward*, fear alone will throw him into confusion."† Again, a few months later, renewing the subject, he observed, "'twould be well to offer a reward of thirty or forty thousand crowns to any one who will deliver the Prince, dead or alive; since from very fear of it—as he is pusillanimous—it would not be unlikely that *he should die of his own accord*."‡

It was insulting even to Philip's intelligence to insinuate that the Prince would shrink before danger, or die of fear.

---

* He wore on the occasion of the ceremony "a cassock of cramoisy brocade, with large folds." With his sceptre grasped in his right hand, and his crown upon his head, he looked, says his enthusiastic biographer, "like King David—red, handsome, and venerable." "Parecia al Rey David, rojo, hermoso à la vista, i venerable en la Majestad que representaba."—Cabrera, xiii. 1126.

† Archives, etc., vii. 166.—"Y qualquier dinero seria muy bien empleado —— y como es vil y cobarde, el miedo le pondria en confusion."—Letter of the Cardinal to Philip, August 8, 1579.

‡ "Tambien se podria al Principe d'Oranges poner talla de 30 o 40 mil escudos, á quien le matasse o diésse vivo, como hazen todos los potentados de Italia, pues con miedo solo desto *como es pusillanime*, no seria mucho moriésse de suyo," etc.—Ibid.

Had Orange ever been inclined to bombast, he might have answered the churchman's calumny, as Cæsar the soothsayer's warning :—

> "————Danger knows full well
> That Cæsar is more dangerous than he—"

and in truth, Philip had long trembled on his throne before the genius of the man who had foiled Spain's boldest generals and wiliest statesmen. The King, accepting the priest's advice, resolved to fulminate a ban against the Prince, and to set a price upon his head. "It will be well," wrote Philip to Parma, "to offer thirty thousand crowns or so to any one who will deliver him dead or alive. Thus the country may be rid of a man so pernicious ; or at any rate he will be held in perpetual fear, and therefore prevented from executing leisurely his designs."*

In accordance with these suggestions and these hopes, the famous ban was accordingly drawn up, and dated on the 15th of March, 1580. It was, however, not formally published in the Netherlands until the month of June of the same year.†

This edict wlll remain the most lasting monument to the memory of Cardinal Granvelle. It will be read when all his other state-papers and epistles—able as they incontestably are—shall have passed into oblivion. No panegyric of friend, no palliating magnanimity of foe, can roll away this rock of infamy from his tomb. It was by Cardinal Granvelle and by Philip that a price was set upon the head of the foremost man of his age, as if he had been a savage beast, and that admission into the ranks of Spain's haughty nobility was made the additional bribe to tempt the assassin.

The ban‡ consisted of a preliminary narrative to justify the penalty with which it was concluded. It referred to the favors conferred by Philip and his father upon the Prince ; to his signal ingratitude and dissimulation. It accused him of

---

* Archives, vii. 165–170. Letter of Philip to the Prince of Parma, Nov. 30, 1579. The letter, says Groen v. Prinsterer, was doubtless dictated by Granvelle.

† Wagenaer, Vad. Hist., vii. 345, 346.

‡ It is appended to the "Apologie," in the edition of Sylvius, pp. 145–160.

originating the Request, the image-breaking, and the public preaching. It censured his marriage with an abbess—even during the lifetime of his wife; alluded to his campaigns against Alva, to his rebellion in Holland, and to the horrible massacres committed by Spaniards in that province—as the necessary consequences of his treason. It accused him of introducing liberty of conscience, of procuring his own appointment as Ruward, of violating the Ghent treaty, of foiling the efforts of Don John, and of frustrating the counsels of the Cologne commissioners by his perpetual distrust. It charged him with a newly-organized conspiracy, in the erection of the Utrecht Union; and for these and similar crimes—set forth with involutions, slow, spiral, and cautious as the head and front of the indictment was direct and deadly—it denounced the chastisement due to the "wretched hypocrite" who had committed such offences.

"For these causes," concluded the ban, "we declare him traitor and miscreant, enemy of ourselves and of the country. As such we banish him perpetually from all our realms, forbidding all our subjects, of whatever quality, to communicate with him openly or privately—to administer to him victuals, drink, fire, or other necessaries. We allow all to injure him in property or life. We expose the said William Nassau as an enemy of the human race—giving his property to all who may seize it. And if any one of our subjects or any stranger should be found sufficiently generous of heart to rid us of this pest, delivering him to us, alive or dead, or taking his life, we will cause to be furnished to him immediately after the deed shall have been done, the sum of twenty-five thousand crowns in gold. *If he have committed any crime, however heinous, we promise to pardon him; and if he be not already noble, we will ennoble him for his valor.*"

Such was the celebrated ban against the Prince of Orange. It was answered before the end of the year by the memorable "Apology of the Prince of Orange" one of the most startling documents in history. No defiance was ever thundered forth in the face of a despot in more terrible tones. It had become sufficiently manifest to the royal party that the Prince was not to be purchased by "millions of money," or by unlimited family advancement—not to be cajoled by flattery or offers of illustrious friendship. It had been decided, therefore, to terrify him into retreat, or to remove him by murder. The Government had been thoroughly convinced that the only way to finish the revolt, was to "finish Orange," according to the ancient advice of Antonio Perez. The mask was thrown off. It had been decided to forbid the Prince bread, water, fire, and shelter ; to give his wealth to the fisc, his heart to the assassin, his soul, as it was hoped, to the Father of Evil. The rupture being thus complete, it was right that the "wretched hypocrite" should answer ban with ban, royal denunciation with sublime scorn. He had ill-deserved, however, the title of hypocrite, he said. When the friend of government, he had warned them that by their complicated and perpetual persecutions they were twisting the rope of their own ruin. Was that hypocrisy ? Since becoming their enemy, there had likewise been little hypocrisy found in him—unless it were hypocrisy to make open war upon government, to take their cities, to expel their armies from the country.

The proscribed rebel, towering to a moral and even social superiority over the man who affected to be his master by right divine, swept down upon his antagonist with crushing effect. He repudiated the idea of a king in the Netherlands. The word might be legitimate in Castille, or Naples, or the Indies, but the provinces knew no such title. Philip had inherited in those countries only the power of Duke or Count—a power closely limited by constitutions more ancient than his birthright. Orange was no rebel then—Philip no legitimate monarch. Even were the Prince rebellious, it was no more than Philip's ancestor, Albert of Austria, had been towards *his* anointed sovereign, Emperor Adolphus of Nassau, ancestor of William. The ties of allegiance and conventional authority being severed, it had become idle for the King to affect superiority of lineage to the man whose family had occupied illustrious stations when the Habsburgs were obscure squires in Switzerland, and had ruled as sovereign in the Netherlands before that overshadowing house had ever been named.

But whatever the hereditary claims of Philip in the country, he had forfeited them by the violation of his oaths, by his tyrannical suppression of the charters of the land ; while by his personal crimes he had lost all pretension to sit in judgment upon his fellow man. Was a people not justified in rising against authority when all their laws had been trodden under foot, "not once only, but a million of times?"—and was William of Orange, lawful husband of the virtuous Charlotte de Bourbon, to be denounced for moral delinquency by a lascivious, incestuous, adulterous, and murderous king? With horrible distinctness he laid before the monarch all the crimes of which he believed him guilty, and having thus told Philip to his beard, "thus diddest thou," he had a withering word for the priest who stood at his back. "Tell me," he cried, "by whose command Cardinal Granvelle administered poison to the Emperor Maximilian? I know what the Emperor told me, and how much fear he felt afterwards for the King and for all Spaniards."

He ridiculed the effrontery of men like Philip and Granvelle, in charging "distrust" upon others, when it was the very atmosphere of their own existence. He proclaimed that sentiment to be the only salvation for the country. He reminded Philip of the words which his namesake of Macedon—a schoolboy in tyranny, compared to himself—had heard from the lips of Demosthenes—that the strongest fortress of a free people against a tyrant was *distrust*. That sentiment, worthy of eternal memory, the Prince declared that he had taken from the "divine philippic," to engrave upon the heart of the nation, and he prayed God that he might be more readily believed than the great orator had been by his people.

He treated with scorn the price set upon his head, ridiculing this project to terrify him, for its want of novelty, and asking the monarch if he supposed the rebel ignorant of the various bargains which had frequently been made before with cut-throats and poisoners to take away his life. "I am in the hand of God," said William of Orange; "my worldly goods and my life have been long since dedicated to His service. He will dispose of them as seems best for His glory and my salvation."

On the contrary, however, if it could be demonstrated, or even hoped, that his absence would benefit the cause of the country, he proclaimed himself ready to go into exile. "Would to God," said he, in conclusion, "that my perpetual banishment, or even my death, could bring you a true deliverance from so many calamities. Oh, how consoling would be such banishment—how sweet such a death! For why have I exposed my property? Was it that I might enrich myself? Why have I lost my brothers? Was it that I might find new ones? Why have I left my son so long a prisoner? Can you give me another? Why have I put my life so often in danger? What reward can I hope after my long services, and the almost total wreck of my earthly fortunes, if not the prize of having acquired, perhaps at the expense of my life, your liberty? If then, my masters, you judge that my absence or my death can serve you, behold me ready to obey. Command me—send me to the ends of the earth—I will obey. Here is my head, over which no prince, no monarch, has power but yourselves. Dispose of it for your good, for the preservation of your Republic, but if you judge that the moderate amount of experience and industry which is in me, if you judge that the remainder of my property and of my life can yet be of service to you, I dedicate them afresh to you and to the country."*

His motto—most appropriate to his life and character—"*Je maintiendrai*," was the concluding phrase of the document. His arms and signature were also formally appended, and the Apology, translated into most modern languages, was sent to nearly every potentate in Christendom.† It had been previously, on the 13th of December, 1580, read before the

---

* Apologie, pp. 140, 141.

† Wagenaer, vii. 354.

assembly of the united states at Delft, and approved as cordially as the ban was indignantly denounced.*

During the remainder of the year 1580, and the half of the following year, the seat of hostilities was mainly in the north-east—Parma, while waiting the arrival of fresh troops, being inactive. The operations, like the armies and the generals, were petty. Hohenlo was opposed to Renneberg. After a few insignificant victories, the latter laid siege to Steenwyk,† a city in itself of no great importance, but the key to the province of Drenthe. The garrison consisted of six hundred soldiers, and half as many trained burghers. Renneberg, having six thousand foot and twelve hundred horse, summoned the place to surrender, but was answered with defiance. Captain Cornput, who had escaped from Groningen, after unsuccessfully warning the citizens of Renneberg's meditated treason, commanded in Steenwyk, and his courage and cheerfulness sustained the population of the city during a close winter siege. Tumultuous mobs in the streets demanding that the place should be given over ere it was too late, he denounced to their faces as "flocks of gabbling geese," unworthy the attention of brave men. To a butcher who, with the instinct of his craft, begged to be informed what the population were to eat when the meat was all gone, he coolly observed, "We will eat you, villain, first of all, when the time comes; so go home and rest assured that you, at least, are not to die of starvation."‡

* Ibid. Archives et Correspondance, vii. 480.—The "Apologie" was drawn up by Villiers, a clergyman of learning and talent. (Vide Duplessis Mornay, note to De Thou, v. 813, La Haye, 1740.) No man, however, at all conversant with the writings and speeches of the Prince, can doubt that the entire substance of the famous document was from his own hand. The whole was submitted to him for his final emendations, and it seems by no means certain that it derived anything from the hand of Villiers, save the artistic arrangement of the parts, together with certain inflations of style, by which the severe sublimity of the general effect is occasionally marred. The appearance of the Apology created both admiration and alarm among the friends of its author. "Now is the Prince a dead man," cried Saint Aldegonde, when he read it in France.—Hoofd, xvii. 735.

† Bor, xv. 219, 221. Hoofd, xvii. 710. Meteren, x. 176, sqq.

‡ Hoofd, xvii. 715. Meteren, x. 178a.

With such rough but cheerful admonitions did the honest soldier, at the head of his little handful, sustain the courage of the beleaguered city. Meantime Renneberg pressed it hard. He bombarded it with red-hot balls, a new invention introduced five years before by Stephen Bathor, King of Poland, at the siege of Dantzig.* Many houses were consumed, but still Cornput and the citizens held firm. As the winter advanced, and the succor which had been promised still remained in the distance, Renneberg began to pelt the city with sarcasms, which, it was hoped, might prove more effective than the red-hot balls. He sent a herald to know if the citizens had eaten all their horses yet; a question which was answered by an ostentatious display of sixty starving hacks—all that could be mustered—upon the heights. He sent them on another occasion, a short letter, which ran as follows :—

"MOST HONORABLE, MOST STEADFAST,—As, during the present frost, you have but little exercise in the trenches—as you cannot pass your time in twirling your finger-rings, seeing that they have all been sold to pay your soldiers' wages—as you have nothing to rub your teeth upon, nor to scour your stomachs withal, and as, nevertheless, you require something if only to occupy your minds, I send you the enclosed letter, in hope it may yield amusement.—January 15, 1581."†

The enclosure was a letter from the Prince of Orange to the Duke of Anjou, which, as it was pretended, had been intercepted. It was a clumsy forgery, but it answered the purpose of more skilful counterfeiting, at a period when political and religious enmity obscured men's judgment. "As to the point of religion," the Prince was made to observe, for example, to his illustrious correspondent, "that is all plain and clear. No sovereign who hopes to come to any great advancement ought to consider religion, or hold it in regard. Your Highness, by means of the garrisons, and fortresses, will be easily master of

* Meteren, x. 169[d]. Wagenear, vii. 359.

† Meteren, x. 178[e].

the principal cities in Flanders and Brabant, even if the citizens were opposed to you. Afterwards you will compel them without difficulty to any religion which may seem most conducive to the interests of your Highness."*

Odious and cynical as was the whole tone of the letter, it was extensively circulated. There were always natures base and brutal enough to accept the calumny and to make it current among kindred souls. It may be doubted whether Renneberg attached faith to the document; but it was natural that he should take a malicious satisfaction in spreading this libel against the man whose perpetual scorn he had so recently earned. Nothing was more common than such forgeries, and at that very moment a letter, executed with equal grossness, was passing from hand to hand, which purported to be from the Count himself to Parma.† History has less interest in contradicting the calumnies against a man like Renneberg. The fictitious epistle of Orange, however, was so often republished, and the copies so carefully distributed, that the Prince had thought it important to add an express repudiation of its authorship, by way of appendix to his famous Apology. He took the occasion to say, that if a particle of proof could be brought that he had written the letter, or any letter resembling it, he would forthwith leave the Netherlands, never to show his face there again.‡

Notwithstanding this well known denial, however, Renneberg thought it facetious to send the letter into Steenwyk, where it produced but small effect upon the minds of the burghers. Meantime, they had received intimation that succor was on its way. Hollow balls containing letters were shot

---

* The whole letter is given by Bor, of course as a forgery, xvi. 239–241. It was probably prepared by Assonleville.—Ibid. Compare Groen v. Prinst., Archives, vii. 380.

† This letter, the fictitious character of which is as obvious as that of the forged epistle of Orange, is given at length by Bor, xv. 211, 212. It is amusing to see the gravity with which the historian introduces the ridiculous document, evidently without entertaining a doubt as to its genuineness.

‡ Bor, xvi. 239b.

into the town, bringing the welcome intelligence that the English colonel, John Norris, with six thousand states' troops, would soon make his appearance for their relief, and the brave Cornput added his cheerful exhortations to heighten the satisfaction thus produced. A day or two afterwards, three quails were caught in the public square, and the commandant improved the circumstance by many quaint homilies. The number three, he observed, was typical of the Holy Trinity, which had thus come symbolically to their relief. The Lord had sustained the fainting Israelites with quails. The number three indicated three weeks, within which time the promised succor was sure to arrive. Accordingly, upon the 22nd of February, 1581, at the expiration of the third week, Norris succeeded in victualling the town, the merry and steadfast Cornput was established as a true prophet, and Count Renneberg abandoned the siege in despair.*

The subsequent career of that unhappy nobleman was brief. On the 19th of July his troops were signally defeated by Sonoy and Norris, the fugitive royalists retreating into Groningen at the very moment when their general, who had been prevented by illness from commanding them, was receiving the last sacraments. Remorse, shame, and disappointment had literally brought Renneberg to his grave. "His treason," says a contemporary, "was a nail in his coffin," and on his deathbed he bitterly bemoaned his crime. "Groningen! Groningen! would that I had never seen thy walls!" he cried repeatedly in his last hours. He refused to see his sister, whose insidious counsels had combined with his own evil passions to make him a traitor; and he died on the 23rd of July, 1581, repentant and submissive.† His heart, after his decease, was found "shrivelled to the dimensions of a walnut,"‡ a circumstance attributed to poison

* Strada, 2, iv. 172. Meteren, x. 179. Bor, xvi. 238. Hoofd, xvii. 717, 718.

† Bor, xvi. 276. Hoofd, xviii. 773. Meteren, x. 184.

‡ "So verdorret en kleen als een walse note."—Bor, xvi. 276.

by some, to remorse by others. His regrets, his early death, and his many attractive qualities, combined to save his character from universal denunciation, and his name, although indelibly stained by treason, was ever mentioned with pity rather than with rancor.*

Great changes, destined to be perpetual, were steadily preparing in the internal condition of the provinces. A preliminary measure of an important character had been taken early this year by the assembly of the united provinces held in the month of January at Delft. This was the establishment of a general executive council. The constitution of the board was arranged on the 13th of the month, and was embraced in eighteen articles. The number of councillors was fixed at thirty, all to be native Netherlanders; a certain proportion to be appointed from each province by its estates. The advice and consent of this body as to treaties with foreign powers were to be indispensable, but they were not to interfere with the rights and duties of the states-general, nor to interpose any obstacle to the arrangements with the Duke of Anjou.†

While this additional machine for the self-government of the provinces was in the course of creation, the Spanish monarch, on the other hand, had made another effort to recover the authority which he felt slipping from his grasp. Philip was in Portugal, preparing for his coronation in that new kingdom—an event to be nearly contemporaneous with his deposition from the Netherland sovereignty, so solemnly conferred upon him a quarter of a century before in Brussels; but although thus distant, he was confident that he could more wisely govern the Netherlands than the inhabitants could do, and unwilling as ever to confide in the abilities of those to whom he had delegated his authority. Provided, as he

* His death was attributed by the royalists to regret at his ill success in accomplishing the work for which he had received so large a price.—MS. letter of Henri de Nebra to Prince of Parma, July 22, 1581, Rec. Gron. und Renneberg, ii. f. 184, Royal Archives, Brussels.

† The Constitution of the "Land Raed" is given in full by Bor, xvi. 241–243.

unquestionably was at that moment, with a more energetic representative than any who had before exercised the functions of royal governor in the provinces, he was still disposed to harass, to doubt, and to interfere. With the additional cares of the Portuguese Conquest upon his hands, he felt as irresistibly impelled as ever to superintend the minute details of provincial administration. To do this was impossible. It was, however, not impossible, by attempting to do it, to produce much mischief. "It gives me pain," wrote Granvelle, "to see his Majesty working as before—choosing to understand everything and to do everything. By this course, as I have often said before, he really accomplishes much less." The King had, moreover, recently committed the profound error of sending the Duchess Margaret of Parma to the Netherlands again. He had the fatuity to believe her memory so tenderly cherished in the provinces as to ensure a burst of loyalty at her reappearance, while the irritation which he thus created in the breast of her son he affected to disregard. The event was what might have been foreseen. The Netherlanders were very moderately excited by the arrival of their former regent, but the Prince of Parma was furious. His mother actually arrived at Namur in the month of August, 1580, to assume the civil administration of the provinces,† and he was himself, according to the King's request, to continue in the command of the army. Any one who had known human nature at all, would have recognized that Alexander Farnese was not the man to be put into leading strings. A sovereign who was possessed of any administrative sagacity, would have seen the absurdity of taking the reins of government at that crisis from the hands of a most determined and energetic man, to confide them to the keeping of a woman. A king who was willing to reflect upon the consequences of his own acts, must have foreseen the scandal likely to result from an open quarrel for precedence between such a mother and son. Mar-

* Archives, etc., vii. 568.

† Wagenaer, vii. 344, 345. Strada, 2, iii. 156.

garet of Parma was instantly informed, however, by Alexander, that a divided authority like that proposed was entirely out of the question. Both offered to resign; but Alexander was unflinching in his determination to retain all the power or none. The Duchess, as docile to her son after her arrival as she had been to the King on undertaking the journey, and feeling herself unequal to the task imposed upon her, implored Philip's permission to withdraw, almost as soon as she had reached her destination. Granvelle's opinion was likewise opposed to this interference with the administration of Alexander, and the King at last suffered himself to be overruled. By the end of the year 1581, letters arrived confirming the Prince of Parma in his government, but requesting the Duchess of Parma to remain privately in the Netherlands. She accordingly continued to reside there under an assumed name until the autumn of 1583, when she was at last permitted to return to Italy.*

During the summer of 1581, the same spirit of persecution which had inspired the Catholics to inflict such infinite misery upon those of the Reformed faith in the Netherlands, began to manifest itself in overt acts against the Papists by those who had at last obtained political ascendency over them. Edicts were published in Antwerp, in Utrecht, and in different cities of Holland, suspending the exercise of the Roman worship. These statutes were certainly a long way removed in horror from those memorable placards which sentenced the Reformers by thousands to the axe, the cord, and the stake, but it was still melancholy to see the persecuted becoming persecutors in their turn. They were excited to these stringent measures by the noisy zeal of certain Dominican monks in Brussels, whose extravagant discourses† were daily inflaming the passions of the Catholics to a dangerous degree. The authorities of the city accordingly thought it necessary to suspend, by proclamation, the public exercise of the ancient

* Strada, 2, iii. 156–165. Wagenaer, vii. 344, 345.—Compare Meteren, x. 174, who states, erroneously, that the Duchess retired during the year following her arrival.

† Bor, xvi. 260.

religion, assigning, as their principal reason for this prohibition, the shocking jugglery by which simple-minded persons were constantly deceived. They alluded particularly to the practice of working miracles by means of relics, pieces of the holy cross, bones of saints, and the perspiration of statues. They charged that bits of lath were daily exhibited as fragments of the cross; that the bones of dogs and monkeys were held up for adoration as those of saints; and that oil was poured habitually into holes drilled in the heads of statues, that the populace might believe in their miraculous sweating. For these reasons, and to avoid the tumult and possible bloodshed to which the disgust excited by such charlatanry might give rise, the Roman Catholic worship was suspended until the country should be restored to greater tranquillity.* Similar causes led to similar proclamations in other cities. The Prince of Orange lamented the intolerant spirit thus showing itself among those who had been its martyrs, but it was not possible at that moment to keep it absolutely under control.

A most important change was now to take place in his condition, a most vital measure was to be consummated by the provinces. The step, which could never be retraced was, after long hesitation, finally taken upon the 26th of July, 1581, upon which day the united provinces, assembled at the Hague, solemnly declared their independence of Philip, and renounced their allegiance for ever.†

This act was accomplished with the deliberation due to its gravity. At the same time it left the country in a very divided condition. This was inevitable. The Prince had done all that one man could do to hold the Netherlands together and unite them perpetually into one body politic, and perhaps, if he had been inspired by a keener personal ambition, this task might have been accomplished. The seventeen provinces might have accepted his dominion, but they would agree to

* See the Proclamation in Bor, xiv. 260, 261.

† Bor. xvi. 276. Meteren, x. 187. Strada, 2, iv. 178, sqq.

that of no other sovereign. Providence had not decreed that the country, after its long agony, should give birth to a single and perfect commonwealth. The Walloon provinces had already fallen off from the cause, notwithstanding the entreaties of the Prince. The other Netherlands, after long and tedious negotiation with Anjou, had at last consented to his supremacy, but from this arrangement Holland and Zealand held themselves aloof. By a somewhat anomalous proceeding, they sent deputies along with those of the other provinces, to the conferences with the Duke, but it was expressly understood that they would never accept him as sovereign. They were willing to contract with him and with their sister provinces—over which he was soon to exercise authority—a firm and perpetual league, but as to their own chief, their hearts were fixed. The Prince of Orange should be their lord and master, and none other. It lay only in his self-denying character that he had not been clothed with this dignity long before. He had, however, persisted in the hope that all the provinces might be brought to acknowledge the Duke of Anjou as their sovereign, under conditions which constituted a free commonwealth with an hereditary chief, and in this hope he had constantly refused concession to the wishes of the northern provinces. He in reality exercised sovereign power over nearly the whole population of the Netherlands. Already in 1580, at the assembly held in April, the states of Holland had formally requested him to assume the full sovereignty over them, with the title of Count* of Holland and Zealand forfeited by Philip. He had not consented, and the proceedings had been kept comparatively secret. As the negotiations with Anjou advanced, and as the corresponding abjuration of Philip was more decisively indicated, the consent of the Prince to this request was more warmly urged. As it was evident that the provinces, thus bent upon placing him at their head, could by no possibility

* Groen v. Prinst., Archives, etc., vii. 307. Kluit. Holl. Staatsreg., i. 308, and note 42. Correspondence between Prince of Orange and States of Holland, in Bor, xv. 182, sqq., 186ª. particularly.

be induced to accept the sovereignty of Anjou—as, moreover, the act of renunciation of Philip could no longer be deferred, the Prince of Orange reluctantly and provisionally accepted the supreme power over Holland and Zealand. This arrangement was finally accomplished upon the 24th of July, 1581,* and the act of abjuration took place two days afterwards. The offer of the sovereignty over the other united provinces had been accepted by Anjou six months before.

Thus, the Netherlands were divided into three portions—the reconciled provinces, the united provinces under Anjou, and the northern provinces under Orange; the last division forming the germ, already nearly developed, of the coming republic. The constitution, or catalogue of conditions, by which the sovereignty accorded to Anjou was reduced to such narrow limits as to be little more than a nominal authority, while the power remained in the hands of the representative body of the provinces, will be described, somewhat later, together with the inauguration of the Duke. For the present it is necessary that the reader should fully understand the relative position of the Prince and of the northern provinces. The memorable act of renunciation—the Netherland declaration of independence—will then be briefly explained.

On the 29th of March, 1580, a resolution passed the assembly of Holland and Zealand never to make peace or enter into any negotiations with the King of Spain on the basis of his sovereignty. The same resolution provided that his name—hitherto used in all public acts—should be for ever discarded, that his seal should be broken, and that the name and seal of the Prince of Orange should be substituted in all commissions and public documents. At almost the same time the states of Utrecht passed a similar resolution. These offers were, however, not accepted, and the affair was preserved profoundly secret.† On the 5th of July, 1581, "the knights, nobles, and cities of Holland and Zealand," again, in an urgent and solemn manner, requested the Prince to

* Bor, xv. 185, 186.

† Bor, xv. 181, 182.

accept the "entire authority as sovereign and chief of the land, *as long as the war should continue*."* This limitation as to time was inserted *most reluctantly* by the states, and because it was perfectly well understood that without it the Prince would not accept the sovereignty at all.† The act by which this dignity was offered, conferred full power to command all forces by land and sea, to appoint all military officers, and to conduct all warlike operations, without the control or advice of any person whatsoever. It authorized him, with consent of the states, to appoint all financial and judicial officers, created him the supreme executive chief, and fountain of justice and pardon, and directed him "to maintain the exercise only of the Reformed evangelical religion, without, however, permitting that inquiries should be made into any man's belief or conscience, or that any injury or hindrance should be offered to any man on account of his religion."‡

The sovereignty thus pressingly offered, and thus limited as to time, was finally accepted by William of Orange, according to a formal act dated at the Hague, 5th of July, 1581,§ but it will be perceived that no powers were conferred by this new instrument beyond those already exercised by the Prince. It was, as it were, a formal continuance of the functions which he had exercised since 1576 as the King's stadholder, according to his old commission of 1555, although a vast difference existed in reality. The King's name was now discarded and his sovereignty disowned, while the proscribed rebel stood in his place, exercising supreme functions, not vicariously, but in his own name. The *limitation as to time* was, moreover, soon afterwards *secretly, and without the knowledge of Orange, cancelled by the states*.‖ They were determined that the Prince should be their sovereign—if they could make him so—for the term of his life.

---

* Bor, xv. 184, 185.

† Ibid.—Compare Kluit, Holl. Staatsreg., i. 213, sqq; Groen v. Prinst., Archives, vii. 304–309.

‡ Bor, xv. 183, 184.

§ Ibid.

‖ Kluit, i. 213, 214.

The offer having thus been made and accepted upon the 5th of July, oaths of allegiance and fidelity were exchanged between the Prince and the estates upon the 24th of the same month. In these solemnities, the states, as representing the provinces, declared that because the King of Spain, contrary to his oath as Count of Holland and Zealand, had not only not protected these provinces, but had sought with all his might to reduce them to eternal slavery, it had been found necessary to forsake him. They therefore proclaimed every inhabitant absolved from allegiance, while at the same time, in the name of the population, they swore fidelity to the Prince of Orange, as representing the supreme authority.*

Two days afterwards, upon the 26th of July, 1581, the memorable declaration of independence was issued by the deputies of the united provinces, then solemnly assembled at the Hague. It was called the Act of Abjuration.† It deposed Philip from his sovereignty, but was not the proclamation of a new form of government, for the united provinces were not ready to dispense with an hereditary chief. Unluckily, they had already provided themselves with a very bad one to succeed Philip in the dominion over most of their territory, while the northern provinces were fortunate enough and wise enough to take the Father of the country for their supreme magistrate.

The document by which the provinces renounced their allegiance was not the most felicitous of their state papers. It was too prolix and technical. Its style had more of the formal phraseology of legal documents than befitted this great appeal to the whole world and to all time. Nevertheless, this is but matter of taste. The Netherlanders were so eminently

* Bor, xv. 185, 186.

† The document is given in full by Bor, xvi. 276–280, by Meteren, x. 187–190. The nature and consequences of the measure are commented upon by Kluit, the constitutional historian of Holland, in a masterly manner (x. Hoofdt, vol. i. 198–280). See also Wagenaer, vii. 391.—Compare Strada, who introduces his account of the abjuration with sepulchral solemnity: "Jam mihi dicendum est facinus, cujus a commemoratione, quasi abhorrente animo, hactenus supersedi," etc.—Bell, Belg., 2, iv. 178, sqq.

a law-abiding people, that, like the American patriots of the eighteenth century, they on most occasions preferred punctilious precision to florid declamation. They chose to conduct their revolt according to law. At the same time, while thus decently wrapping herself in conventional garments, the spirit of Liberty revealed none the less her majestic proportions.

At the very outset of the Abjuration, these fathers of the Republic laid down wholesome truths, which at that time seemed startling blasphemies in the ears of Christendom. "All mankind know," said the preamble, "that a prince is appointed by God to cherish his subjects, even as a shepherd to guard his sheep. When, therefore, the prince does not fulfil his duty as protector; when he oppresses his subjects, destroys their ancient liberties, and treats them as slaves, he is to be considered, not a prince, but a tyrant. As such, the estates of the land may lawfully and reasonably depose him, and elect another in his room."*

Having enunciated these maxims, the estates proceeded to apply them to their own case, and certainly never was an ampler justification for renouncing a prince since princes were first instituted. The states ran through the history of the past quarter of a century, patiently accumulating a load of charges against the monarch, a tithe of which would have furnished cause for his dethronement. Without passion or exaggeration, they told the world their wrongs. The picture was not highly colored. On the contrary, it was rather a feeble than a striking portrait of the monstrous iniquity which had so long been established over them. Nevertheless, they went through the narrative conscientiously and earnestly. They spoke of the King's early determination to govern the Netherlands, not by natives but by Spaniards; to treat them not as constitutional countries, but as conquered provinces; to regard the inhabitants not as liege subjects, but as enemies; above all, to supersede their ancient liberty by the Spanish Inquisition, and they alluded to the first great step in this

---

* Act of Abjuration.

scheme—the creation of the new bishoprics, each with its staff of inquisitors.*

They noticed the memorable Petition, the mission of Berghen and Montigny, their imprisonment and taking off, in violation of all national law, even that which had ever been held sacred by the most cruel and tyrannical princes.† They sketched the history of Alva's administration; his entrapping the most eminent nobles by false promises, and delivering them to the executioner; his countless sentences of death, outlawry, and confiscation; his erection of citadels to curb, his imposition of the tenth and twentieth penny to exhaust the land; his Blood Council and its achievements; and the immeasurable woe produced by hanging, burning, banishing, and plundering, during his seven years of residence. They adverted to the Grand Commander, as having been sent, not to improve the condition of the country, but to pursue the same course of tyranny by more concealed ways. They spoke of the horrible mutiny which broke forth at his death; of the Antwerp Fury; of the express approbation rendered to that great outrage by the King, who had not only praised the crime, but promised to recompense the criminals. They alluded to Don John of Austria and his duplicity; to his pretended confirmation of the Ghent treaty; to his attempts to divide the country against itself; to the Escovedo policy; to the intrigues with the German regiments. They touched upon the Cologne negotiations, and the fruitless attempt of the patriots upon that occasion to procure freedom of religion, while the object of the royalists was only to distract and divide the nation. Finally, they commented with sorrow and despair upon that last and crowning measure of tyranny—the ban against the Prince of Orange.

They calmly observed, after this recital, that they were

---

* "—— en door de voorsz Canoniken de Spaense Inquisitie ingebrocht de welke in dese altijt so schrickelijk en odieus als de uitterste slavernye," etc.—Act of Abjuration.

† "Ook onder de wreetste en tyrannigste Princen altijd onverbrekelijik onderhouden."—Ibid.

sufficiently justified in forsaking a sovereign who for more than twenty years had forsaken them.* Obeying the law of nature—desirous of maintaining the rights, charters, and liberties of their fatherland—determined to escape from slavery to Spaniards—and making known their decision to the world, they declared the King of Spain deposed from his sovereignty, and proclaimed that they should recognize thenceforth neither his title nor jurisdiction. Three days afterwards, on the 29th of July, the assembly adopted a formula, by which all persons were to be required to signify their abjuration.†

Such were the forms by which the united provinces threw off their allegiance to Spain, and *ipso facto* established a republic, which was to flourish for two centuries. This result, however, was not exactly foreseen by the congress which deposed Philip. The fathers of the commonwealth did not baptize it by the name of Republic. They did not contemplate a change in their form of government. They had neither an aristocracy nor a democracy in their thoughts.‡ Like the actors in our own great national drama, these Netherland patriots were struggling to sustain, not to overthrow; unlike them, they claimed no theoretical freedom for humanity—promulgated no doctrine of popular sovereignty: they insisted merely on the fulfilment of actual contracts, signed, sealed, and sworn to by many successive sovereigns. Acting upon the principle that government should be for the benefit of the governed, and in conformity to the dictates of reason and justice, they examined the facts by those divine lights, and

* "—— te meer dat in al sulken desordre en overlaet de Landen bet dan 20 jaren van haren Coning sijn verlaten geweest," etc.—Act of Abjuration.

† Bor, xvi. 280.—It ran as follows: "I solemnly swear that I will henceforward not respect, nor obey, nor recognize the King of Spain as my prince and master; but that I renounce the King of Spain, and abjure the allegiance by which I may have formerly been bound to him. At the same time I swear fidelity to the United Netherlands—to wit, the provinces of Brabant, Flanders, Gueldres, Holland, Zealand, etc., etc., and also to the national council established by the estates of these provinces; and promise my assistance according to the best of my abilities against the King of Spain and his adherents."

‡ Kluit, i. 199.

discovered cause to discard their ruler. They did not object to being ruled. They were satisfied with their historical institutions, and preferred the mixture of hereditary sovereignty with popular representation, to which they were accustomed. They did not devise an *à priori* constitution. Philip having violated the law of reason and the statutes of the land, was deposed, and a new chief magistrate was to be elected in his stead. This was popular sovereignty in fact, but not in words. The deposition and election could be legally justified only by the inherent right of the people to depose and to elect; yet the provinces, in their Declaration of Independence, spoke of the divine right of kings, even while dethroning, by popular right, their own King!

So also, in the instructions given by the states to their envoys charged to justify the abjuration before the Imperial diet held at Augsburg,* twelve months later, the highest ground was claimed for the popular right to elect or depose the sovereign, while at the same time, kings were spoken of as "appointed by God." It is true that they were described, in the same clause, as "chosen by the people"—which was, perhaps, as exact a concurrence in the maxim of *Vox populi, vox Dei*, as the boldest democrat of the day could demand. In truth, a more democratic course would have defeated its own ends. The murderous and mischievous pranks of Imbize, Ryhove, and such demagogues, at Ghent and elsewhere, with their wild theories of what they called Grecian, Roman, and Helvetian republicanism, had inflicted damage enough on the cause of freedom, and had paved the road for the return of royal despotism. The senators assembled at the Hague gave more moderate instructions to their delegates at Augsburg. They were to place the King's tenure upon contract—not an implied one, but a contract as literal as the lease of a farm. The house of Austria, they were to maintain, had come into the possession of the seventeen Netherlands upon certain express conditions,

* The instructions are given in Bor, xvii. 324–327.

and with the understanding that its possession was to cease with the first condition broken. It was a question of law and fact, not of royal or popular right. They were to take the ground, not only that the contract had been violated, but that the foundation of perpetual justice upon which it rested, had likewise been undermined. It was time to vindicate both written charters and general principles. "*God has given absolute power to no mortal man*," said Saint Aldegonde, "*to do his own will against all laws and all reason.*"* "The contracts which the King has broken are no pedantic fantasies," said the estates, "but laws planted by nature in the universal heart of mankind, and expressly acquiesced in by prince and people."† All men, at least, who speak the English tongue, will accept the conclusion of the provinces, that when laws which protected the citizen against arbitrary imprisonment and guaranteed him a trial in his own province—which forbade the appointment of foreigners to high office—which secured the property of the citizen from taxation, except by the representative body—which forbade intermeddling on the part of the sovereign with the conscience of the subject in religious matters—when such laws had been subverted by blood tribunals, where drowsy judges sentenced thousands to stake and scaffold without a hearing—by excommunication, confiscation, banishment—by hanging, beheading, burning, to such enormous extent and with such terrible monotony that the executioner's sword came to be looked upon as the only symbol of justice—then surely it might be said, without exaggeration, that the complaints of the Netherlanders were "no pedantic fantasies," and that the King had ceased to perform his functions as dispenser of God's justice.

The Netherlanders dealt with facts. They possessed a body of laws, monuments of their national progress, by which as good a share of individual liberty was secured to the citizen as was then enjoyed in any country of the world. Their insti-

---

* Archives et Correspondance, vii. 277.

† Instructions to the envoys, etc.; apud Bor, 3 xvii. 324-327.

tutions admitted of great improvement, no doubt; but it was natural that a people so circumstanced should be unwilling to exchange their condition for the vassalage of "Moors or Indians."

At the same time it may be doubted whether the instinct for political freedom only would have sustained them in the long contest, and whether the bonds which united them to the Spanish Crown would have been broken, had it not been for the stronger passion for religious liberty, by which so large a portion of the people was animated. Boldly as the united states of the Netherlands laid down their political maxims, the quarrel might perhaps have been healed if the religious question had admitted of a peaceable solution. Philip's bigotry amounting to frenzy, and the Netherlanders of "the religion" being willing, in their own words, "to die the death" rather than abandon the Reformed faith, there was upon this point no longer room for hope. In the act of abjuration, however, it was thought necessary to give offence to no class of the inhabitants, but to lay down such principles only as enlightened Catholics would not oppose. All parties abhorred the Inquisition, and hatred to that institution is ever prominent among the causes assigned for the deposition of the monarch. "Under pretence of maintaining the Roman religion," said the estates, "the King has sought by evil means to bring into operation the whole strength of the placards and of the Inquisition—*the first and true cause of all our miseries.*"*

Without making any assault upon the Roman Catholic faith, the authors of the great act by which Philip was for ever

* Transactions between the envoys of the States-general and the Duke of Anjou.—Bor, 3, xvii. 304–307. So also in the remarkable circular addressed in the year 1583 (May 6) by the States of Holland to those of Utrecht and other provinces, the same intolerable grievance is described in the strongest language. "Under pretext of the new bishoprics," say the estates, "the Inquisition and Council of Trent have been established. Thus the Spaniards and their adherents have been empowered to accuse all persons who are known to be not of their humor, to bring them into the snares of the Inquisition, and to rob them of life, honor, and property."—Bor, 3, xv. 188.

expelled from the Netherlands showed plainly enough that religious persecution had driven them at last to extremity. At the same time, they were willing—for the sake of conciliating all classes of their countrymen—to bring the political causes of discontent into the foreground, and to use discreet language upon the religious question.*

Such, then, being the spirit which prompted the provinces upon this great occasion, it may be asked who were the men who signed a document of such importance? In whose name and by what authority did they act against the sovereign? The signers of the declaration of independence acted in the name and by the authority of the Netherland people. The estates were the constitutional representatives of that people. The statesmen of that day discovering, upon cold analysis of facts, that Philip's sovereignty was legally forfeited, formally proclaimed that forfeiture. Then inquiring what had become of the sovereignty, they found it not in the mass of the people, but in the representative body, which actually personated the people. The estates of the different provinces—consisting of the knights, nobles, and burgesses of each—sent, accordingly, their deputies to the general assembly at the Hague, and by this congress the decree of abjuration was issued. It did not occur to any one to summon the people in their primary assemblies, nor would the people of that day have comprehended the objects of such a summons. They were accustomed to the action of the estates, and those bodies represented as large a number of political capacities as could be expected of assemblies chosen *then* upon general principles. The hour had not arrived for more profound analysis of the social compact. Philip was accordingly deposed justly, legally, formally—justly, because it had become necessary to abjure a monarch who was determined not only to oppress but to exterminate his people; legally, because he had habitually violated the constitutions which he had sworn to support; formally, because the act was done in the name of the people, by the body historically representing the people.

* Groen v. Prinst., Archives. vii. 588.

What, then, was the condition of the nation, after this great step had been taken? It stood, as it were, with its sovereignty in its hand, dividing it into two portions, and offering it, thus separated, to two distinct individuals. The sovereignty of Holland and Zealand had been reluctantly accepted by Orange. The sovereignty of the united provinces had been offered to Anjou, but the terms of agreement with that Duke had not yet been ratified. The movement was therefore triple, consisting of an abjuration and of two separate elections of hereditary chiefs; these two elections being accomplished in the same manner, by the representative bodies respectively of the united provinces, and of Holland and Zealand. Neither the abjuration nor the elections were acted upon beforehand by the communities, the train-bands, or the guilds of the cities—all represented, in fact, by the magistrates and councils of each; nor by the peasantry of the open country—all supposed to be represented by the knights and nobles. All classes of individuals, however, arranged in various political or military combinations, gave their acquiescence afterwards, together with their oaths of allegiance. The people approved the important steps taken by their representatives.*

Without a direct intention on the part of the people or its leaders to establish a republic, the Republic established itself. Providence did not permit the whole country, so full of wealth intelligence, healthy political action—so stocked with powerful cities and an energetic population, to be combined into one free and prosperous commonwealth. The factious ambition of a few grandees, the cynical venality of many nobles, the frenzy of the Ghent democracy, the spirit of religious intolerance, the consummate military and political genius of Alexander Farnese, the exaggerated self-abnegation and the tragic fate of Orange, all united to dissever this group of flourishing and kindred provinces.

The want of personal ambition on the part of William the Silent inflicted perhaps a serious damage upon his country.

* Kluit, i. 247–250.

He believed a single chief requisite for the united states; he might have been, but always refused to become that chief; and yet he has been held up for centuries by many writers as a conspirator and a self-seeking intriguer. "It seems to me," said he, with equal pathos and truth, upon one occasion, "that I was born in this bad planet that all which I do might be misinterpreted."* The people worshipped him, and there was many an occasion when his election would have been carried with enthusiasm.† "These provinces," said John of Nassau, "are coming very unwillingly into the arrangement with the Duke of Alençon. The majority feel much more inclined *to elect the Prince, who is daily, and without intermission, implored to give his consent.* His Grace, however, will in no wise agree to this; not because he fears the consequences, such as loss of property or increased danger, for therein he is plunged as deeply as he ever could be;—on the contrary, if he considered only the interests of his race and the grandeur of his house, he could expect nothing but increase of honor, gold, and gear, with all other prosperity. *He refuses only on this account—that it may not be thought that, instead of religious freedom for the country, he has been seeking a kingdom for himself and his own private advancement.* Moreover, he believes that the connexion with France will be of more benefit to the country and to Christianity than if a peace should be made with Spain, or than if he should himself accept the sovereignty, as he is desired to do."‡

The unfortunate negotiations with Anjou, to which no man was more opposed than Count John, proceeded therefore. In the meantime, the sovereignty over the united provinces was provisionally held by the national council, and, at the urgent solicitation of the states-general, by the Prince.§ The Archduke Matthias, whose functions were most unceremoniously brought to an end by the transactions which we have been recording, took his leave of the states, and departed in the

* Archives et Corresp., vii. 387.

† Bor, xix. 455ᵇ.—Compare Van d. Vynckt, iii. 73.

‡ Archives, etc., vii. 332, 333.

§ Ibid., vii. 589.

month of October.* Brought to the country a beardless boy, by the intrigues of a faction who wished to use him as a tool against William of Orange, he had quietly submitted, on the contrary, to serve as the instrument of that great statesman. His personality during his residence was null, and he had to expiate, by many a petty mortification, by many a bitter tear, the boyish ambition which brought him to the Netherlands. He had certainly had ample leisure to repent the haste with which he had got out of his warm bed in Vienna to take his bootless journey to Brussels. Nevertheless, in a country where so much baseness, cruelty, and treachery was habitually practised by men of high position, as was the case in the Netherlands, it is something in favor of Matthias that he had not been base, or cruel, or treacherous.† The states voted him, on his departure, a pension of fifty thousand guldens annually,‡ which was probably not paid with exemplary regularity.§

* Bor, xvi. 282. Meteren, x. 190. Wagenaer, vii. 414, 415.

† He is, however, accused by Meteren of having entered at last into secret intrigues with the King of Spain against William of Orange.—Nederl. Hist., x. 190c. Hoofd repeats the story.—Nederl. Hist., xviii. 779. Wagenaer discredits it: vii. 414.

‡ Bor, xvi. 282. Meteren, Hoofd, Wagenaer, ubi sup.

§ Wagenaer, vii. 414, 415. Groen v. Prinst., Archives, vii. 588.

CHAPTER V.

Policy of electing Anjou as sovereign—Commoda et incommoda—Views of Orange—Opinions at the French Court—Anjou relieves Cambray—Parma besieges Tournay—Brave defence by the Princess of Espinoy—Honorable capitulation—Anjou's courtship in England—The Duke's arrival in the Netherlands—Portrait of Anjou—Festivities in Flushing—Inauguration at Antwerp—The conditions or articles subscribed to by the Duke—Attempt upon the life of Orange—The assassin's papers—Confession of Venero—Gaspar Anastro—His escape—Execution of Venero and Zimmermann—Precarious condition of the Prince—His recovery—Death of the Princess—Premature letters of Parma—Further negotiations with Orange as to the sovereignty of Holland and Zealand—Character of the revised Constitution—Comparison of the positions of the Prince before and after his acceptance of the countship.

Thus it was arranged that, for the present, at least, the Prince should exercise sovereignty over Holland and Zealand; although he had himself used his utmost exertions to induce those provinces to join the rest of the United Netherlands in the proposed election of Anjou.* This, however, they sternly refused to do. There was also a great disinclination felt by many in the other states to this hazardous offer of their allegiance,† and it was the personal influence of Orange that eventually carried the measure through. Looking at the position of affairs and at the character of Anjou, as they appear to us now, it seems difficult to account for the Prince's

* Bor, xiv. 183.

† See, in particular, two papers from the hand of Count John upon the subject. Archives et Correspondance, vii. 48–51, and 162–165.

policy. It is so natural to judge only by the result, that we are ready to censure statesmen for consequences which beforehand might seem utterly incredible, and for reading falsely human characters whose entire development only a late posterity has had full opportunity to appreciate.* Still, one would think that Anjou had been sufficiently known to inspire distrust.

There was but little, too, in the aspect of the French court to encourage hopes of valuable assistance from that quarter. It was urged, not without reason, that the French were as likely to become as dangerous as the Spaniards; that they would prove nearer and more troublesome masters; that France intended the incorporation of the Netherlands into her own kingdom; that the provinces would therefore be dispersed for ever from the German Empire; and that it was as well to hold to the tyrant under whom they had been born, as to give themselves voluntarily to another of their own making.† In short, it was maintained, in homely language, that "France and Spain were both under one coverlid."‡ It might have been added that only extreme misery could make the provinces take either bedfellow. Moreover, it was asserted, with reason,

* Saint Aldegonde, for instance, wrote from Paris to an intimate friend, that after a conversation with Anjou of an hour and a half's duration, he had formed the very highest estimate of his talents and character. He praised to the skies the elegance of his manners, the liveliness of his mind, his remarkable sincerity—in which last gifts he so particularly resembled the Netherlanders themselves. Above all, he extolled the Duke's extreme desire to effect the liberation of the provinces. He added, that if the opportunity should be let slip of securing such a prince, "posterity would regret it with bitter tears for a thousand years to come."—Hoofd, xvii. 736. The opinion expressed by Henry the Fourth to Sully is worth placing in juxtaposition with this extravagant eulogium of Marnix: "Il me trompera bien s'il ne trompe tous ceux qui se fieront en luy, et surtout s'il aime jamais ceux de la Religion, ny leur fait aucuns advantages; car je scay pour lui avoir ouy dire plus d'une fois, *qu'il les hait comme le diable dans son cœur*, et puis il a le cœur si double et si malin, a le courage si lasche, le corps si mal basty, et est tant inhabile à toutes sortes de vertueux exercices, que je ne me sçaurois persuader qu'il fasse jamais rien ne généreux."—Mem. de Sully, i. 102.—Compare Groen v. Prinsterer, Archives, etc., vii. 4–13.

† "Incommoda et commoda," etc.—Archives et Correspondance, vii. 48.

‡ "Dasz Franckreich und Spanien mit einander under einer decke liegen."—Ibid.

that Anjou would be a very expensive master, for his luxurious and extravagant habits were notorious—that he was a man in whom no confidence could be placed, and one who would grasp at arbitrary power by any means which might present themselves.* Above all, it was urged that he was not of the true religion, that he hated the professors of that faith in his heart, and that it was extremely unwise for men whose dearest interests were their religious ones, to elect a sovereign of opposite creed to their own. To these plausible views the Prince of Orange and those who acted with him, had, however, sufficient answers. The Netherlands had waited long enough for assistance from other quarters. Germany would not lift a finger in the cause ; on the contrary, the whole of Germany, whether Protestant or Catholic, was either openly or covertly hostile. It was madness to wait till assistance came to them from unseen sources. It was time for them to assist themselves, and to take the best they could get ; for when men were starving they could not afford to be dainty. They might be bound hand and foot, they might be overwhelmed a thousand times before they would receive succor from Germany, or from any land but France. Under the circumstances in which they found themselves, hope delayed was but a cold and meagre consolation.†

"To speak plainly," said Orange, "asking us to wait is very much as if you should keep a man three days without any food in the expectation of a magnificent banquet, should persuade him to refuse bread, and at the end of three days should tell him that the banquet was not ready, but that a still better one was in preparation. Would it not be better, then, that the poor man, to avoid starvation, should wait no longer, but accept bread wherever he might find it ? Such is our case at present."‡

It was in this vein that he ever wrote and spoke. The Netherlands were to rely upon their own exertions, and to

---

* Archives, etc., vii. 48.

† "Une froide et bien maigre consolation."—Archives, vii. 240.

‡ Archives, etc., vii. 240 and 235; Letter to Lazarus Schwendi.

procure the best alliance, together with the most efficient protection possible. They were not strong enough to cope single-handed with their powerful tyrant, but they were strong enough if they used the instruments which Heaven offered. It was not trusting but tempting Providence to wait supinely, instead of grasping boldly at the means of rescue within reach. It became the character of brave men to act, not to expect. "Otherwise," said the Prince, "we may climb to the tops of trees, like the Anabaptists of Munster, and expect God's assistance to drop from the clouds."* It is only by listening to these arguments so often repeated, that we can comprehend the policy of Orange at this period. "God has said that he would furnish the ravens with food, and the lions with their prey," said he; "but the birds and the lions do not, therefore, sit in their nests and their lairs waiting for their food to descend from heaven, but they seek it where it is to be found."† So also, at a later day, when events seemed to have justified the distrust so generally felt in Anjou, the Prince, nevertheless, held similar language. "I do not," said he, "calumniate those who tell us to put our trust in God. That is my opinion also. But it *is* trusting God to use the means which he places in our hands, and to ask that his blessings may come upon them."‡

There was a feeling entertained by the more sanguine that the French King would heartily assist the Netherlands, after his brother should be fairly installed. He had expressly written to that effect, assuring Anjou that he would help him with all his strength, and would enter into close alliance with those Netherlands which should accept him as prince and sovereign.§ In another and more private letter to the Duke,

* Archives, etc., vii. 576.

† Letter to Count John, Archives et Corresp., vii. 576.

‡ Letter to States-general, apud Bor, xvii. 349–354 (one of the noblest State papers that ever came from his hand).

§ The letter, dated Blois, Dec. 26, 1580, is given by Hoofd, xviii. 754. According to Duplessis Mornay, the Duke had, however, been expressly instructed by his royal brother to withdraw the letter as soon as the deputies had seen it. He was always commanded never to importune his Majesty on the subject.—V. Borgnet, Philippe II. et la Belgique, p. 147.

the King promised to assist his brother, "even to his last shirt."* There is no doubt that it was the policy of the statesmen of France to assist the Netherlands, while the "*mignons*" of the worthless King were of a contrary opinion. Many of them were secret partizans of Spain, and found it more agreeable to receive the secret pay of Philip than to assist his revolted provinces. They found it easy to excite the jealousy of the monarch against his brother—a passion which proved more effective than the more lofty ambition of annexing the Low Countries, according to the secret promptings of many French politicians.† As for the Queen Mother, she was fierce in her determination to see fulfilled in this way the famous prediction of Nostradamus. Three of her sons had successively worn the crown of France. That she might be "the mother of four kings," without laying a third child in the tomb, she was greedy for this proffered sovereignty to her youngest and favorite son. This well-known desire of Catharine de Medici was duly insisted upon by the advocates of the election; for her influence, it was urged, would bring the whole power of France to support the Netherlands.‡

At any rate, France could not be worse—could hardly be so bad—as their present tyranny. "Better the government of the Gaul, though suspect and dangerous," said Everard Reyd, "than the truculent dominion of the Spaniard. Even thus will the partridge fly to the hand of man, to escape the talons of the hawk."§ As for the individual character of Anjou, proper means would be taken, urged the advocates of his sovereignty, to keep him in check, for it was intended so closely to limit the power conferred upon him, that it would be only supreme in name. The Netherlands were to be, in reality, a republic, of which Anjou was to be a kind of Italian or Frisian podesta. "The Duke is not to act according to his pleasure," said one of the negotiators, in a private letter to

* Quotation in Archives, etc., vii. 403.

† De Thou, ix. 28–33.

‡ Renom de France, MS., tom. v. c. 5.—Compare Strada, ii. 214, 215.

§ Reidani, Ann. Belg., ii. 31.

Count John; "we shall take care to provide a good muzzle for him."* How conscientiously the "muzzle" was prepared, will appear from the articles by which the states soon afterwards accepted the new sovereign. How basely he contrived to slip the muzzle—in what cruel and cowardly fashion he bathed his fangs in the blood of the flock committed to him, will also but too soon appear.

As for the religious objection to Anjou, on which more stress was laid than upon any other, the answer was equally ready. Orange professed himself "not theologian enough" to go into the subtleties brought forward. As it was intended to establish most firmly a religious peace, with entire tolerance for all creeds, he did not think it absolutely essential to require a prince of the Reformed faith. It was bigotry to dictate to the sovereign, when full liberty in religious matters was claimed for the subject. Orange was known to be a zealous professor of the Reformed worship himself; but he did not therefore reject political assistance, even though offered by a not very enthusiastic member of the ancient Church.

"If the priest and the Levite pass us by when we are fallen among thieves," said he, with much aptness and some bitterness, "shall we reject the aid proffered by the Samaritan, because he is of a different faith from the worthy fathers who have left us to perish?"† In short, it was observed with perfect truth that Philip had been removed, not because he was a Catholic, but because he was a tyrant; not because his faith was different from that of his subjects, but because he was resolved to exterminate all men whose religion differed from his own It was not, therefore, inconsistent to choose another Catholic for a sovereign, if proper guarantees could be obtained that he would protect and not oppress the Reformed churches. "If the Duke have the same designs as the King," said Saint Aldegonde, "it would be a great piece of folly to change one tyrant and persecutor for another. If, on the contrary, instead of oppressing our liberties, he will maintain

* Archives et Corresp., vii. 290.

† Ibid. vii. 573.

them, and in place of extirpating the disciples of the true religion, he will protect them, then are all the reasons of our opponents without vigor."*

By midsummer the Duke of Anjou made his appearance in the western part of the Netherlands. The Prince of Parma had recently come before Cambray with the intention of reducing that important city. On the arrival of Anjou, however, at the head of five thousand cavalry—nearly all of them gentlemen of high degree, serving as volunteers—and of twelve thousand infantry, Alexander raised the siege precipitately, and retired towards Tournay. Anjou victualled the city, strengthened the garrison, and then, as his cavalry had only enlisted for a summer's amusement, and could no longer be held together, he disbanded his forces. The bulk of the infantry took service for the states under the Prince of Espinoy, governor of Tournay. The Duke himself, finding that, notwithstanding the treaty of Plessis les Tours and the present showy demonstration upon his part, the states were not yet prepared to render him formal allegiance, and being, moreover, in the heyday of what was universally considered his prosperous courtship of Queen Elizabeth, soon afterwards took his departure for England.†

Parma, being thus relieved of his interference, soon afterwards laid siege to the important city of Tournay. The Prince of Espinoy was absent with the army in the north, but the Princess commanded in his absence. She fulfilled her duty in a manner worthy of the house from which she sprang, for the blood of Count Horn was in her veins. The daughter of Mary de Montmorency, the admiral's sister, answered the summons of Parma to surrender at discretion with defiance. The garrison was encouraged by her steadfastness. The Princess appeared daily among her troops, superintending the defences, and personally directing the officers. During one of

* Archives et Corresp., vii., 278.

† Bor, xvi. 287. Strada, 2, iv. 185–193. Tassis, vi. 428. Hoofd, xviii. 785.

the assaults, she is said, but perhaps erroneously, to have been wounded in the arm, notwithstanding which she refused to retire.*

The siege lasted two months. Meantime, it became impossible for Orange and the estates, notwithstanding their efforts, to raise a sufficient force to drive Parma from his entrenchments. The city was becoming gradually and surely undermined from without, while at the same time the insidious art of a Dominican friar, Father Géry by name, had been as surely sapping the fidelity of the garrison from within. An open revolt of the Catholic population being on the point of taking place, it became impossible any longer to hold the city. Those of the Reformed faith insisted that the place should be surrendered; and the Princess, being thus deserted by all parties, made an honorable capitulation with Parma. She herself, with all her garrison, was allowed to retire with personal property, and with all the honors of war, while the sack of the city was commuted for one hundred thousand crowns, levied upon the inhabitants. The Princess, on leaving the gates, was received with such a shout of applause from the royal army that she seemed less like a defeated commander than a conqueror. Upon the 30th November, Parma accordingly entered the place which he had been besieging since the 1st of October.†

By the end of the autumn, the Prince of Orange, more than ever dissatisfied with the anarchical condition of affairs, and with the obstinate jealousy and parsimony of the different provinces, again summoned the country in the most earnest language to provide for the general defence, and to take measures for the inauguration of Anjou. He painted in sombre colors the prospect which lay before them, if nothing was done to arrest the progress of the internal disorders and of

---

* Bor, xvi., 287, 288. Meteren, x. 190. Hoofd, xviii. 785, 786. Strada, 2, iv. 195–213, et al.

† Bor, Hoofd, Meteren, Strada, Bentivoglio.

the external foe, whose forces were steadily augmenting. Had the provinces followed his advice, instead of quarreling among themselves, they would have had a powerful army on foot to second the efforts of Anjou, and subsequently to save Tournay. They had remained supine and stolid, even while the cannonading against these beautiful cities was in their very ears. No man seemed to think himself interested in public affairs, save when his own province or village was directly attacked.* The general interests of the commonwealth were forgotten in local jealousy. Had it been otherwise, the enemy would have long since been driven over the Meuse. "When money," continued the Prince, "is asked for to carry on the war, men answer as if they were talking with the dead Emperor.† To say, however, that they will pay no more, is as much as to declare that they will give up their land and their religion both. I say this, not because I have any desire to put my hands into the common purse. You well know that I have never touched the public money, but it is important that you should feel that there is no war in the country except the one which concerns you all."

The states, thus shamed and stimulated, set themselves in earnest to obey the mandates of the Prince, and sent a special mission to England, to arrange with the Duke of Anjou for his formal installation as sovereign. Saint Aldegonde and other commissioners were already there. It was the memorable epoch in the Anjou wooing, when the rings were exchanged between Elizabeth and the Duke, and when the world thought that the nuptials were on the point of being celebrated. Saint Aldegonde wrote to the Prince of Orange on the 22nd of November, that the marriage had been finally settled upon that day.‡ Throughout the Netherlands, the

---

* Remonstrance to the States-general, Dec. 1, 1581, in Bor, xvi. 289, 290.

† "——So varen sy in de sake voort en antwoorden daer op als sy spraken met den doden Kayser."—Ibid.

‡ Strada, 2, iv. 214, sqq. Bor, xvi. 290. De Thou, viii. 536, sqq.

auspicious tidings were greeted with bonfires, illuminations, and cannonading,* and the measures for hailing the Prince, thus highly favored by so great a Queen, as sovereign master of the provinces, were pushed forward with great energy.

Nevertheless, the marriage ended in smoke. There were plenty of tournays, pageants, and banquets; a profusion of nuptial festivities, in short, where nothing was omitted but the nuptials. By the end of January, 1582, the Duke was no nearer the goal than upon his arrival three months before. Acceding, therefore, to the wishes of the Netherland envoys, he prepared for a visit to their country, where the ceremony of his joyful entrance as Duke of Brabant and sovereign of the other provinces was to take place. No open rupture with Elizabeth occurred. On the contrary, the Queen accompanied the Duke, with a numerous and stately retinue, as far as Canterbury, and sent a most brilliant train of her greatest nobles and gentlemen to escort him to the Netherlands, communicating at the same time, by special letter, her wishes to the estates-general, that he should be treated with as much honor "as if he were her second self."†

On the 10th of February, fifteen large vessels cast anchor at Flushing. The Duke of Anjou, attended by the Earl of Leicester, the Lords Hunsdon, Willoughby, Sheffield, Howard, Sir Philip Sidney, and many other personages of high rank and reputation,‡ landed from this fleet. He was greeted on his arrival by the Prince of Orange, who, with the Prince of Espinoy and a large deputation of the states-general, had been

---

* Bor, De Thou, ubi sup. Hoofd xviii. 788.

† "Oblectatus distractusque juvenis, —— videt se in mediis nuptiis celebrare omnia præter nuptias."—Strada, 2, iv. 217.—Compare De Thou, viii. 600, sqq. Hoofd, xix. 795. "—— qu'il allast accompagné de la recommendation d'une Princesse —— qui estime avoir tel interest en vous que vous en serez poussés d'avantage à honnorer un Prince qui lui est si cher qu'elle fait autant de lui comme d'un autre soi-même," etc., etc.—Lettre de la Serenissime Reine d'Angleterre aux Etats-généraux, Fev. 6, 1581, MS. Ordinaris Depêchen Boek der Staten-general, A°, 1582–1583, f. 1vo, Hague Archives.

‡ De Thou, Hoofd, ubi sup. Bor, xvii. 296. Meteren, xi. 192.

for some days waiting to welcome him. The man whom the Netherlands had chosen for their new master stood on the shores of Zealand. Francis Hercules, Son of France, Duke of Alençon and Anjou, was at that time just twenty-eight years of age; yet not even his flatterers, or his "minions," of whom he had as regular a train as his royal brother, could claim for him the external graces of youth or of princely dignity. He was below the middle height, puny and ill-shaped. His hair and eyes were brown, his face was seamed with the small-pox, his skin covered with blotches, his nose so swollen and distorted that it seemed to be double. This prominent feature did not escape the sarcasms of his countrymen, who, among other gibes, were wont to observe that the man who always wore two faces, might be expected to have two noses also. It was thought that his revolting appearance was the principal reason for the rupture of the English marriage, and it was in vain that his supporters maintained that if he could forgive her age, she might, in return, excuse his ugliness. It seemed that there was a point of hideousness beyond which even royal princes could not descend with impunity, and the only wonder seemed that Elizabeth, with the handsome Robert Dudley ever at her feet, could even tolerate the addresses of Francis Valois.*

His intellect was by no means contemptible. He was not without a certain quickness of apprehension and vivacity of expression which passed current among his admirers for wit and wisdom. Even the experienced Saint Aldegonde was deceived in his character, and described him after an hour and half's interview, as a Prince overflowing with bounty, intelligence, and sincerity. That such men as Saint Aldegonde and the Prince of Orange should be at fault in their judgment, is evidence not so much of their want of discernment, as of the difference between the general reputation of the

* Bor, xvii. 296. Meteren, xi. 192. Hoofd, ubi sup. Mem. de Sully, loc. cit. "Fu piccioli di statura e poco ben fatto della persona."—Bentivoglio, G. di Fiandra, 2, ii. 275. "Pusillo ac deformi in corpore."—Ev. Reidan., Ann. Belg., ii. 34; iii. 42. Van der Vynckt, iii. 69. Strada, 2, iv. 215.

Duke at that period, and that which has been eventually established for him in history. Moreover, subsequent events were to exhibit the utter baseness of his character more signally than it had been displayed during his previous career, however vacillating. No more ignoble yet more dangerous creature had yet been loosed upon the devoted soil of the Netherlands. Not one of the personages who had hitherto figured in the long drama of the revolt had enacted so sorry a part. Ambitious but trivial, enterprising but cowardly, an intriguer and a dupe, without religious convictions or political principles, save that he was willing to accept any creed or any system which might advance his own schemes, he was the most unfit protector for a people who, whether wrong or right, were at least in earnest, and who were accustomed to regard truth as one of the virtues. He was certainly not deficient in self-esteem. With a figure which was insignificant, and a countenance which was repulsive, he had hoped to efface the impression made upon Elizabeth's imagination by the handsomest man in Europe. With a commonplace capacity, and with a narrow political education, he intended to circumvent the most profound statesman of his age. And there, upon the pier at Flushing, he stood between them both; between the magnificent Leicester, whom he had thought to outshine, and the silent Prince of Orange, whom he was determined to outwit. Posterity has long been aware how far he succeeded in the one and the other attempt.

The Duke's arrival was greeted with the roar of artillery, the ringing of bells, and the acclamations of a large concourse of the inhabitants; suitable speeches were made by the magistrates of the town, the deputies of Zealand, and other functionaries,* and a stately banquet was provided, so remarkable "for its sugar-work and other delicacies, as to entirely astonish the French and English lords who partook thereof."† The Duke visited Middelburg, where he was received with

* Bor, xvii. 296. Hoofd, xix. 795.

† Bor, xvii. 297.

great state, and to the authorities of which he expressed his gratification at finding two such stately cities situate so close to each other on one little island.*

On the 17th of February, he set sail for Antwerp. A fleet of fifty-four vessels, covered with flags and streamers, conveyed him and his retinue, together with the large deputation which had welcomed him at Flushing, to the great commercial metropolis. He stepped on shore at Kiel within a bowshot of the city—for, like other Dukes of Brabant, he was not to enter Antwerp until he had taken the oaths to respect the constitution—and the ceremony of inauguration was to take place outside the walls. A large platform had been erected for this purpose, commanding a view of the stately city, with its bristling fortifications and shady groves.† A throne, covered with velvet and gold, was prepared, and here the Duke took his seat, surrounded by a brilliant throng, including many of the most distinguished personages in Europe.

It was a bright winter's morning. The gaily bannered fleet lay conspicuous in the river, while an enormous concourse of people were thronging from all sides to greet the new sovereign. Twenty thousand burgher troops, in bright uniforms, surrounded the platform, upon the tapestried floor of which stood the magistrates of Antwerp, the leading members of the Brabant estates, with the Prince of Orange at their head, together with many other great functionaries. The magnificence everywhere displayed, and especially the splendid costumes of the military companies, excited the profound astonishment of the French, who exclaimed that every soldier seemed a captain, and who regarded with vexation their own inferior equipments.‡

Andrew Hessels, *doctor utriusque juris*, delivered a saluta-

---

* Bor, xvii. 297.

† "La joyeuse et magnifique entrée du Monseign[r] François, Fils de France, Duc d'Anjou, etc., en sa très renommée ville d'Anvers."—Anvers. Plantin., 1582.—Compare Bor, xvii. 297. Hoofd, xix. 795.

‡ Renom de France, MS., v. 2.

tory oration, in which, among other flights of eloquence, he expressed the hope of the provinces that the Duke, with the beams of his greatness, wisdom, and magnanimity, would dissipate all the mists, fogs, and other exhalations which were pernicious to their national prosperity, and that he would bring back the sunlight of their ancient glory.*

Anjou answered these compliments with equal courtesy, and had much to say of his willingness to shed every drop of his blood in defence of the Brabant liberties; but it might have damped the enthusiasm of the moment could the curtain of the not very distant future have been lifted. The audience, listening to these promises, might have seen that it was not so much his blood as theirs which he was disposed to shed, and less, too, in defence than in violation of those same liberties which he was swearing to protect.

Orator Hessels then read aloud the articles of the Joyous Entry, in the Flemish language, and the Duke was asked if he required any explanations of that celebrated constitution. He replied that he had thoroughly studied its provisions, with the assistance of the Prince of Orange, during his voyage from Flushing, and was quite prepared to swear to maintain them. The oaths, according to the antique custom, were then administered. Afterwards, the ducal hat and the velvet mantle, lined with ermine, were brought, the Prince of Orange assisting his Highness to assume this historical costume of the Brabant dukes, and saying to him, as he fastened the button at the throat, "I must secure this robe so firmly, my lord, that no man may ever tear it from your shoulders."†

Thus arrayed in his garment of sovereignty, Anjou was compelled to listen to another oration from the pensionary of Antwerp, John Van der Werken. He then exchanged oaths with the magistrates of the city, and received the keys, which he returned for safe-keeping to the burgomaster. Meanwhile the trumpets sounded, largess of gold and silver coins

* The oration is given in full by Bor, xvii. 297, 298.

† Bor, xvii. 298. Hoofd, xix. 796. Meteren, xi. 192.

was scattered among the people, and the heralds cried aloud, "Long live the Duke of Brabant."*

A procession was then formed to escort the new Duke to his commercial capital. A stately and striking procession it was. The Hanseatic merchants in ancient German attire, the English merchants in long velvet cassocks, the heralds in their quaint costume, the long train of civic militia with full bands of music, the chief functionaries of city and province in their black mantles and gold chains, all marching under emblematical standards or time-honored blazons, followed each other in dignified order. Then came the Duke himself, on a white Barbary horse, caparisoned with cloth of gold. He was surrounded with English, French, and Netherland grandees, many of them of world-wide reputation. There was the stately Leicester; Sir Philip Sidney, the mirror of chivalry; the gaunt and imposing form of William the Silent; his son; Count Maurice of Nassau, destined to be the first captain of his age, then a handsome, dark-eyed lad of fifteen; the Dauphin of Auvergne; the Maréchal de Biron and his sons; the Prince of Espinoy; the Lords Sheffield, Willoughby, Howard, Hunsdon, and many others of high degree and distinguished reputation.† The ancient guilds of the crossbow-men and archers of Brabant, splendidly accoutred, formed the bodyguard of the Duke, while his French cavaliers, the life-guardsmen of the Prince of Orange, and the troops of the line, followed in great numbers, their glittering uniforms all gaily intermingled, "like the flowers de luce upon a royal mantle." The procession, thus gorgeous and gay, was terminated by a dismal group of three hundred malefactors, marching in fetters, and imploring pardon of the Duke, a boon which was to be granted at evening. Great torches, although it was high noon, were burning along the road, at intervals of four or five feet,

* "La joyeuse et magnifique entrée," etc., Bor, xvii. 297, sqq., who conscientiously gives all the long speeches at full length. Meteren, xi. 192. Tassis, vi. 429.

† "La joyeuse et magnifique entrée," etc., Bor, xvii. 300, sqq. Hoofd, xix. 797, 898.

in a continuous line reaching from the platform at Kiel to the portal of Saint Joris, through which the entrance to the city was to be made.

Inside the gate a stupendous allegory was awaiting the approach of the new sovereign.* A huge gilded car, crowded with those emblematical and highly bedizened personages so dear to the Netherlanders, obstructed the advance of the procession. All the virtues seemed to have come out for an airing in one chariot, and were now waiting to offer their homage to Francis Hercules Valois. Religion in "red satin," holding the gospel in her hand, was supported by Justice, "in orange velvet," armed with blade and beam. Prudence and Fortitude embraced each other near a column enwreathed by serpents "with their tails in their ears to typify deafness to flattery;" while Patriotism as a pelican, and Patience as a brooding hen, looked benignantly upon the scene. This greeting duly acknowledged, the procession advanced into the city. The streets were lined with troops and with citizens; the balconies were filled with fair women; "the very gables," says an enthusiastic contemporary, "seemed to laugh with ladies' eyes."† The market-place was filled with waxen torches and with blazing tar barrels, while in its centre stood the giant Antigonus—founder of the city thirteen hundred years before the Christian era—the fabulous personage who was accustomed to throw the right hands of all smuggling merchants into the Scheld.‡ This colossal individual, attired in a "surcoat of sky-blue," and holding a banner emblazoned with the arms of Spain, turned its head

---

* "La joyeuse et magnifique entrée," etc., in which contemporary pamphlet are many beautifully executed engravings of the wonders exhibited on this occasion.—Bor, xvii. 300, 301.

† Hoofd, xix. 798.

‡ "La joyeuse entrée," etc.

> "Hic fuit Antigoni castrum insigne Gigantis,
> Quem Brabo devicit, de quo Brabonica tellus," etc., etc.

Ancient verses quoted by Ludov. Guicciardini, in his description of Antwerp, "but by whom written," says that author, "*novit Deus.*"—Tot. Belg. Descript., 131.

as the Duke entered the square, saluted the new sovereign, and then dropping the Spanish scutcheon upon the ground, raised aloft another bearing the arms of Anjou.*

And thus, amid exuberant outpouring of confidence, another lord and master had made his triumphal entrance into the Netherlands. Alas! how often had this sanguine people greeted with similar acclamations the advent of their betrayers and their tyrants! How soon were they to discover that the man whom they were thus receiving with the warmest enthusiasm was the most treacherous tyrant of all.

It was nightfall before the procession at last reached the palace of Saint Michael, which had been fitted up for the temporary reception of the Duke.† The next day was devoted to speech-making; various deputations waiting upon the new Duke of Brabant with congratulatory addresses. The Grand Pensionary delivered a pompous oration upon a platform hung with sky-blue silk, and carpeted with cloth of gold. A committee of the German and French Reformed Churches made a long harangue, in which they expressed the hope that the Lord would make the Duke "as valiant as David, as wise as Solomon, and as pious as Hezekiah."‡ A Roman Catholic deputation informed his Highness that for eight months the members of the Ancient Church had been forbidden all religious exercises, saving baptism, marriage, visitation of the sick, and burials. A promise was therefore made that this prohibition, which had been the result of the disturbances recorded in a preceding chapter, should be immediately modified, and on the 15th of March, accordingly, it was arranged, by command of the magistrates, that all Catholics should have permission to attend public worship, according to the ancient ceremonial, in the church of Saint Michael, which had been originally designated for the use of

---

* "La joyeuse entrée," etc., Bor, xvii. 301.

† Bor, ubi sup. Hoofd, xix. 798, 199. "Maer de geheele stadt was vol Tortsen, Fackelen ende Vyeren op alle de straden, ende op de kerck torens, dat de stadt scheen in een vyer te staen."—Meteren, xi. 193c.

‡ Bor, xvii. 303

the new Duke of Brabant. It was, however, stipulated that all who desired to partake of this privilege should take the oath of abjuration beforehand, and go to the church without arms."*

Here then had been oaths enough, orations enough, compliments enough, to make any agreement steadfast, so far as windy suspirations could furnish a solid foundation for the social compact. Bells, trumpets, and the brazen throats of men and of cannons had made a sufficient din, torches and tar-barrels had made a sufficient glare, to confirm—so far as noise and blazing pitch could confirm—the decorous proceedings of church and town-house, but time was soon to show the value of such demonstrations. Meantime, the "muzzle" had been fastened with solemnity and accepted with docility. The terms of the treaty concluded at Plessis les Tours and Bordeaux were made public. The Duke had subscribed to twenty-seven articles, which made as stringent and sensible a constitutional compact as could be desired by any Netherland patriot. These articles, taken in connection with the ancient charters which they expressly upheld, left to the new sovereign no vestige of arbitrary power. He was merely the hereditary president of a representative republic. He was to be Duke, Count, Margrave, or Seignior of the different provinces on the same terms which his predecessors had accepted. He was to transmit the dignities to his children. If there were more than one child, the provinces were to select one of the number for their sovereign. He was to maintain all the ancient privileges, charters, statutes, and customs, and to forfeit his sovereignty at the first violation. He was to assemble the states-general at least once a year. He was always to reside in the Netherlands. He was to permit none but natives to hold office. His right of appointment to all important posts was limited to a selection from three candidates, to be proposed by the estates of the province concerned, at each vacancy. He was to main-

* Bor, xvii. 303. † The articles are given in full by Bor, 3, xvii. 307–309.

tain "the Religion" and the religious peace in the same state in which they then were, or as should afterwards be ordained by the estates of each province, without making any innovation on his own part.* Holland and Zealand were to remain as they were, both in the matter of religion *and otherwise.*† His Highness was not to permit that any one should be examined or molested in his house, or otherwise, in the matter or under pretext of religion.‡ He was to procure the assistance of the King of France for the Netherlands. He was to maintain a perfect and a perpetual league, offensive and defensive, between that kingdom and the provinces; without, however, permitting any incorporation of territory. He was to carry on the war against Spain with his own means and those furnished by his royal brother, in addition to a yearly contribution by the estates of two million four hundred thousand guldens.§ He was to dismiss all troops at command of the states-general. He was to make no treaty with Spain without their consent.

It would be superfluous to point out the great difference between the notions entertained upon international law in the sixteenth century and in our own. A state of nominal peace existed between Spain, France and England; yet here was the brother of the French monarch, at the head of French troops, and attended by the grandees of England, solemnly accepting the sovereignty over the revolted provinces of Spain.‖ It is also curious to observe that the constitutional compact by which the new sovereign of the Netherlands was admitted to the government, would have been repudiated as revolutionary and republican by the monarchs of France or England, if an attempt had been

---

* Article 12.

† Holland en Zeland sullen blijven als sy tegenwoordlijk sijn in 't stuk van den Religie *en andersins.*—Art. 13.

‡ Art. 14.

§ Art. 18.

‖ On the other hand, the denial by England of an asylum to the refugees, in 1572, and their forcible expulsion from her shores, led to the occupation of Brill and the foundation of the Dutch Republic.

made to apply it to their own realms, for the ancient charters —which in reality constituted a republican form of government—had all been re-established by the agreement with Anjou.

The first-fruits of the ban now began to display themselves. Sunday, 18th of March, 1582, was the birthday of the Duke of Anjou, and a great festival had been arranged, accordingly, for the evening, at the palace of Saint Michael, the Prince of Orange as well as all the great French lords being of course invited. The Prince dined, as usual, at his house in the neighbourhood of the citadel, in company with the Counts Hohenlo and Laval, and the two distinguished French commissioners, Bonnivet and Des Pruneaux. Young Maurice of Nassau, and two nephews of the Prince, sons of his brother John, were also present at table. During dinner the conversation was animated, many stories being related of the cruelties which had been practised by the Spaniards in the provinces. On rising from the table, Orange led the way from the dining-room to his own apartments, showing the noblemen in his company as he passed along, a piece of tapestry upon which some Spanish soldiers were represented. At this moment, as he stood upon the threshold of the ante-chamber, a youth of small stature, vulgar mien, and pale dark complexion, appeared from among the servants and offered him a petition. He took the paper, and as he did so, the stranger suddenly drew a pistol and discharged it at the head of the Prince. The ball entered the neck under the right ear, passed through the roof of the mouth, and came out under the left jaw-bone, carrying with it two teeth.* The pistol had been held so

* Hoofd, xix. 804. Bor, xvii. 313. Meteren, xi. 194c. Tassis, vi. 431. Strada, 2, iv. 219. "Korte Verhaal van den moorddadigen aanslag, bedreven op den persoon van den zeer doorluchtigen vorst, den heere Prins van Oranje, door Jan Jauregui, een Spanjard."—This is the title of a pamphlet published at the time with authentic documents, by Plantin, at Antwerp. There is also a French edition, printed simultaneously with that in Flemish, intituled, "Bref Recueil de l'Assassinat," etc.—Reiffenberg has republished it in his edition of Van der Vynckt. Letter of Derens, March, 27, 1582, in Archives et Correspondance, viii. 77.

near, that the hair and beard of the Prince were set on fire by the discharge. He remained standing, but blinded, stunned, and for a moment entirely ignorant of what had occurred. As he afterwards observed, he thought perhaps that a part of the house had suddenly fallen. Finding very soon that his hair and beard were burning, he comprehended what had occurred, and called out quickly, "Do not kill him—I forgive him my death!" and turning to the French noblemen present, he added, "Alas! what a faithful servant does his Highness lose in me!"*

These were his first words, spoken when, as all believed, he had been mortally wounded. The message of mercy came, however, too late; for two of the gentlemen present, by an irresistible impulse, had run the assassin through with their rapiers. The halberdiers rushed upon him immediately afterwards, so that he fell pierced in thirty-two vital places.† The Prince, supported by his friends, walked to his chamber, where he was put to bed, while the surgeons examined and bandaged the wound. It was most dangerous in appearance, but a very strange circumstance gave more hope than could otherwise have been entertained. The flame from the pistol had been so close that it had actually cauterized the wound inflicted by the ball. But for this, it was supposed that the flow of blood from the veins which had been shot through would have proved fatal before the wound could be dressed. The Prince, after the first shock, had recovered full possession of his senses, and believing himself to be dying, he expressed the most unaffected sympathy for the condition in which the Duke of Anjou would be placed by his death. "Alas, poor Prince!" he cried frequently; "alas, what troubles will now beset thee!"‡ The surgeons enjoined and implored his silence, as

* "Doodt hem niet, ik vergeef hem mijen dood!"—Korte Verhaal. Bor, xvii. 312. Hoofd, xix. 804. Meteren, xi. 194.

† Ibid. Letter of Herle, Archives et Correspondance, supplément, pp. 220, sqq. Letter of Derens, Archives et Correspondance, viii. 78.

‡ "Ach arme vorst, arme vorst! wat zult gij nog moeijelijkheden ont moeten!" —Korte Verhaal. Bor, xvii. 313. Meteren, xi. 194c. Hoofd, xix. 805.

speaking might cause the wound to prove immediately fatal. He complied, but wrote incessantly.* As long as his heart could beat, it was impossible for him not to be occupied with his country.

Lion Petit, a trusty Captain of the city guard, forced his way to the chamber, it being absolutely necessary, said the honest burgher, for him to see with his own eyes that the Prince was living, and report the fact to the townspeople: otherwise, so great was the excitement, it was impossible to say what might be the result. It was in fact believed that the Prince was already dead, and it was whispered that he had been assassinated by the order of Anjou. This horrible suspicion was flying through the city, and producing a fierce exasperation,† as men talked of the murder of Coligny, of Saint Bartholomew, of the murderous propensities of the Valois race. Had the attempt taken place in the evening, at the birth-night banquet of Anjou, a horrible massacre would have been the inevitable issue. As it happened, however, circumstances soon occurred to remove the suspicion from the French, and to indicate the origin of the crime. Meantime, Captain Petit was urged by the Prince, in writing, to go forth instantly with the news that he yet survived, but to implore the people, in case God should call him to Himself, to hold him in kind remembrance, to make no tumult, and to serve the Duke obediently and faithfully.‡

Meantime, the youthful Maurice of Nassau was giving proof of that cool determination which already marked his character. It was natural that a boy of fifteen should be somewhat agitated at seeing such a father shot through the head before his eyes. His situation was rendered doubly grave by the suspicions which were instantly engendered as to the probable origin of the attempt. It was already whispered in the hall that the gentlemen who had been so officious in

---

* Korte Verhaal, etc.—"Met eene vaste handen vlug schreef."

† Korte Verhaal, 591. Bor, ubi sup. Meteren, xi. 194. Hoofd, xix. 804. Strada, 2, iv. 219. Bor, xvii. 313.

‡ Bor, Meteren, Hoofd, ubi sup. Korte Verhaal.

slaying the assassin, were his accomplices, who—upon the principle that dead men would tell no tales—were disposed, now that the deed was done, to preclude inconvenient revelations as to their own share in the crime. Maurice, notwithstanding these causes for perturbation, and despite his grief at his father's probable death, remained steadily by the body of the murderer. He was determined, if possible, to unravel the plot, and he waited to possess himself of all papers and other articles which might be found upon the person of the deceased.*

A scrupulous search was at once made by the attendants, and everything placed in the young Count's own hands. This done, Maurice expressed a doubt lest some of the villain's accomplices might attempt to take the articles from him,† whereupon a faithful old servant of his father came forward, who with an emphatic expression of the importance of securing such important documents, took his young master under his cloak, and led him to a retired apartment of the house. Here, after a rapid examination, it was found that the papers were all in Spanish, written by Spaniards to Spaniards, so that it was obvious that the conspiracy, if one there were, was not a French conspiracy. The servant, therefore, advised Maurice to go to his father, while he would himself instantly descend to the hall with this important intelligence. Count Hohenlo had, from the instant of the murder, ordered the doors to be fastened, and had permitted no one to enter or to leave the apartment without his permission. The information now brought by the servant as to the character of the papers caused great relief to the minds of all; for, till that moment, suspicion had even lighted upon men who were the firm friends of the Prince.‡

Saint Aldegonde, who had meantime arrived, now proceeded,

---

* Korte Verhaal, etc. Bor, xvii. 313. Hoofd, xix. 805. Meteren, xi. 194.

† Korte Verhaal.—"Helas," said the boy, "ik ben zoo bevreest dat hier eenig andere booswicht zij, die mij die papieren afneemt."

‡ Korte Verhaal, Bor, Meteren, Hoofd, ubi sup. Strada, 2, iv. 219.

in company of the other gentlemen, to examine the papers and other articles taken from the assassin. The pistol with which he had done the deed was lying upon the floor; a naked poniard, which he would probably have used also, had his thumb not been blown off by the discharge of the pistol, was found in his trunk hose. In his pockets were an *Agnus Dei*, a taper of green wax, two bits of hareskin, two dried toads—which were supposed to be sorcerer's charms—a crucifix, a Jesuit catechism, a prayer-book, a pocket-book containing two Spanish bills of exchange—one for two thousand, and one for eight hundred and seventy-seven crowns—and a set of writing tablets.* These last were covered with vows and pious invocations, in reference to the murderous affair which the writer had in hand. He had addressed fervent prayers to the Virgin Mary, to the Angel Gabriel, to the Saviour, and *to the Saviour's Son*—"as if," says the Antwerp chronicler, with simplicity, "the Lord Jesus had a son"†—that they might all use their intercession with the Almighty towards the certain and safe accomplishment of the contemplated deed. Should he come off successful and unharmed, he solemnly vowed to fast a week on bread and water. Furthermore, he promised to Christ a "new coat of costly pattern;" to the Mother of God, at Guadalupe, a new gown; to Our Lady of Montserrat, a crown, a gown, and a lamp; and so on through a long list of similar presents thus contemplated for various shrines.‡ The poor fanatical fool had been taught by deeper villains than himself that his pistol was to rid the world

* Korte Verhaal, etc., 589, 590. Strada, 2, iv. 219.—Compare Haraei, Tum. Belg., iii. 336.—"Twee stukken huid, zoo het scheen van eenen haas; het geen velen aanleiding gaf om te zeggen, dat hij padden en toovery bij zich had." Korte Verhaal, etc. Bor, Hoof, Meteren, ubi sup.

† "Als of Christus noch eenen sonne hadde."—Meteren, xi. 194. The following extracts from the assassin's memorandum-book are worthy of attention. The papers were published by authority, immediately after the deed. "Al Angel Gabriel me encomiendo con todo mi spiritu y coraçon para que agora y siempre me sea mi intercessor á nuestro Señor Jesu Christo *y a su hijo preciosissimo*, y a la Virgen Sancta Maria y a todos los sanctos y sanctas de la corte del cielo de guardarme," etc., etc.—Korte Verhaal.

‡ Korte Verhaal. Meteren. Bor, xvii. 313.

of a tyrant, and to open his own pathway to Heaven, if his career should be cut short on earth. To prevent so undesirable a catastrophe to himself, however, his most natural conception had been to bribe the whole heavenly host, from the Virgin Mary downwards, for he had been taught that absolution for murder was to be bought and sold like other merchandise. He had also been persuaded that, after accomplishing the deed, *he would become invisible.**

Saint Aldegonde hastened to lay the result of this examination before the Duke of Anjou. Information was likewise instantly conveyed to the magistrates at the Town House, and these measures were successful in restoring confidence throughout the city as to the intentions of the new government. Anjou immediately convened the State Council, issued a summons for an early meeting of the states-general, and published a proclamation that all persons having information to give concerning the crime which had just been committed, should come instantly forward, upon pain of death. The body of the assassin was forthwith exposed upon the public square, and was soon recognized as that of one Juan Jaureguy, a servant in the employ of Gaspar d'Anastro, a Spanish merchant of Antwerp. The letters and bills of exchange had also, on nearer examination at the Town House, implicated Anastro in the affair. His house was immediately searched, but the merchant had taken his departure, upon the previous Tuesday, under pretext of pressing affairs at Calais. His cashier, Venero, and a Dominican friar, named Antony Zimmermann, both inmates of his family, were, however, arrested upon suspicion. On the following day the watch stationed at the gate carried the foreign post-bags, as soon as they arrived, to the magistracy, when letters were found from Anastro to Venero, which made the affair quite plain.† After they had been thoroughly studied, they were shown to Venero, who, seeing

---

* Letter of P. van Reigersberg, March 19, 1582; apud Van Wyn op Wagenaer, 7, iii. 112. Letter of Herle, before cited.

† Korte Verhaal. Bor, xvii. 313. Hoofd, xix. 805. Meteren, xi. 194.

himself thus completely ruined, asked for pen and ink, and wrote a full confession.

It appeared that the crime was purely a commercial speculation on the part of Anastro. That merchant, being on the verge of bankruptcy, had entered with Philip into a mutual contract, which the King had signed with his hand and sealed with his seal, and according to which Anastro, within a certain period, was to take the life of William of Orange, and for so doing was to receive eighty thousand ducats, and the cross of Santiago.* To be a knight companion of Spain's proudest order of chivalry was the guerdon, over and above the eighty thousand pieces of silver, which Spain's monarch promised the murderer, if he should succeed. As for Anastro himself, he was too frugal and too wary to risk his own life, or to lose much of the premium. With tears streaming down his cheeks, he painted to his faithful cashier the picture which his master would present, when men should point at him and say, "Behold yon bankrupt!" protesting, therefore, that he would murder Orange and secure the reward, or perish in the attempt. Saying this, he again shed many tears. Venero, seeing his master thus disconsolate, wept bitterly likewise, and begged him not to risk his own precious life.‡ After this pathetic commingling of their grief, the merchant and his book-keeper became more composed, and it was at last concerted between them that John Jaureguy should be entrusted with the job. Anastro had intended—as he said in a letter afterwards intercepted—"to accomplish the deed with his own hand; but, as God had probably reserved him for other things, and particularly to be of service to his very affectionate friends, he had thought best to entrust the execution of the design to his servant."§ The price paid by the master to the man, for the

---

* Korte Verhaal. Bor, xvii. 313. Hoofd, xix. 802. Meteren, xi. 194b.

† "Mirad aquel hombre que ha hecho bancarote," etc.—Confession of Venero in Bref. Recueil.

‡ "Todo lo dezia llorando e yo viendole tan desconsolado llorava mucho."—Ibid.

§ "—— Doch het mag wesen dat God mij noch heeft willen bewaren om dienst

work, seems to have been but two thousand eight hundred and seventy-seven crowns. The cowardly and crafty principal escaped. He had gone post haste to Dunkirk, pretending that the sudden death of his agent in Calais required his immediate presence in that city. Governor Sweveseel, of Dunkirk, sent an orderly to get a passport for him from La Motte, commanding at Gravelingen. Anastro being on tenter-hooks lest the news should arrive that the projected murder had been consummated before he had crossed the border, testified extravagant joy on the arrival of the passport, and gave the messenger who brought it thirty pistoles. Such conduct naturally excited a vague suspicion in the mind of the governor, but the merchant's character was good, and he had brought pressing letters from Admiral Treslong. Sweveseel did not dare to arrest him without cause, and he neither knew that any crime had been committed, nor that the man before him was the criminal. Two hours after the traveller's departure, the news arrived of the deed, together with orders to arrest Anastro, but it was too late. The merchant had found refuge within the lines of Parma.*

Meanwhile, the Prince lay in a most critical condition. Believing that his end was fast approaching, he dictated letters to the states-general, entreating them to continue in their obedience to the Duke, than whom he affirmed that he knew no better prince for the government of the provinces. These letters were despatched by Saint Aldegonde to the assembly, from which body a deputation, in obedience to the wishes of Orange, was sent to Anjou, with expressions of condolence and fidelity.†

---

en vrundschap te mogen doen mijn geaffectioneerde vrienden, gelijk ik die hebbe op *sekere lijste*."—Letter of Anastro to the "very magnificent Lord, Martin Drogue, Sea-captain in Flushing," dated March 28, 1582, in Bor, xvii. 315. It must have been disagreeable to the very magnificent Drogue—and to Admiral Treslong, who received a letter of similar purport from Anastro—to find themselves inscribed on the list of "his affectionate friends" by this consummate villain.

* Bor, xvii. 314. Hoofd, xix. 803, 804.

† Korte Verhaal.

On Wednesday a solemn fast was held, according to proclamation, in Antwerp, all work and all amusements being prohibited, and special prayers commanded in all the churches for the recovery of the Prince. "Never, within men's memory," says an account published at the moment, in Antwerp, "had such crowds been seen in the churches, nor so many tears been shed."*

The process against Venero and Zimmermann was rapidly carried through, for both had made a full confession of their share in the crime. The Prince had enjoined from his sick bed, however, that the case should be conducted with strict regard to justice, and, when the execution could no longer be deferred, he had sent a written request, by the hands of Saint Aldegonde, that they should be put to death in the least painful manner. The request was complied with, but there can be no doubt that the criminals, had it not been made, would have expiated their offence by the most lingering tortures. Owing to the intercession of the man who was to have been their victim, they were strangled, before being quartered, upon a scaffold erected in the market-place, opposite the Town House. This execution took place on Wednesday, the 28th of March.†

The Prince, meanwhile, was thought to be mending, and thanksgivings began to be mingled with the prayers offered almost every hour in the churches; but for eighteen days he lay in a most precarious state. His wife hardly left his bedside, and his sister, Catharine Countess of Schwartzburg, was

---

* Korte Verhaal.

† Bor, xvii. 314.—The following is the text of this most interesting letter:—"Monsieur de Saint Aldegonde: j'ay entendu que l'on doibt demain faire justice de deux prisonniers, estans complices de celuy qui m'a tiré le coup, De ma part, je leur pardonne tres volontiers de ce qu'ils me peuvent avoir offensé, et s'ils ont peut etre merité un chastoy et rigoureux, je vous prie vouloir tenir la main devers Messrs du Magistrat qu'ils ne les veuillent faire souffrir grand tourment et se contenter, s'ils l'ont merité d'une courte mort. Votre bien bon amy à vous faire service, Guillaume de Nassau."—Bref Recueil de l'Assassinat commis en la personne du tres illustre Prince d'Orange (Anvers. Chr. Plantin. 1582).

indefatigable in her attentions. The Duke of Anjou visited him daily, and expressed the most filial anxiety for his recovery, but the hopes, which had been gradually growing stronger, were on the 5th of April exchanged for the deepest apprehensions. Upon that day the cicatrix by which the flow of blood from the neck had been prevented, almost from the first infliction of the wound, fell off. The veins poured forth a vast quantity of blood ; it seemed impossible to check the hæmorrhage, and all hope appeared to vanish. The Prince resigned himself to his fate, and bade his children "good night for ever," saying calmly, "it is now all over with me."*

It was difficult, without suffocating the patient, to fasten a bandage tightly enough to staunch the wound, but Leonardo Botalli, of Asti, body physician of Anjou, was nevertheless fortunate enough to devise a simple mechanical expedient, which proved successful. By his advice, a succession of attendants, relieving each other day and night, prevented the flow of blood by keeping the orifice of the wound slightly but firmly compressed with the thumb. After a period of anxious expectation, the wound again closed, and by the end of the month the Prince was convalescent. On the 2nd of May he went to offer thanksgiving in the Great Cathedral, amid the joyful sobs of a vast and most earnest throng.†

The Prince was saved, but unhappily the murderer had yet found an illustrious victim. The Princess of Orange, Charlotte de Bourbon—the devoted wife who for seven years had so faithfully shared his joys and sorrows—lay already on her death-bed. Exhausted by anxiety, long watching, and the

---

* Bor, xvii. 314. Korte Verhaal. Bor, xvii. 316. Hoofd, xix. 806. Meteren, xi. 194. Letter of Mary of Orange to Count John, Archives et Corresp., viii. 88.

† Hoofd, xix. 806, ascribes the superintendence of the cure to Botalli (as stated in the text). Bor and Meteren, however, only mention the name of Joseph Michaeli, of Lucca. Bor does not speak at all of the singular expedient employed to stop the effusion of blood; Hoofd, Meteren, and others, allude to it.

alternations of hope and fear during the first eighteen days, she had been prostrated by despair at the renewed hæmorrhage. A violent fever seized her, under which she sank on the 5th of May, three days after the solemn thanksgiving for her husband's recovery.* The Prince, who loved her tenderly, was in great danger of relapse upon the sad event, which, although not sudden, had not been anticipated. She was laid in her grave on the 9th of May, amid the lamentations of the whole country,† for her virtues were universally known and cherished. She was a woman of rare intelligence, accomplishment, and gentleness of disposition, whose only offence had been to break, by her marriage, the Church vows to which she had been forced in her childhood, but which had been pronounced illegal by competent authority, both ecclesiastical and lay. For this, and for the contrast which her virtues afforded to the vices of her predecessor, she was the mark of calumny and insult. These attacks, however, had cast no shadow upon the serenity of her married life, and so long as she lived she was the trusted companion and consoler of her husband. "His Highness," wrote Count John in 1580, "is in excellent health, and, in spite of adversity, incredible labor, perplexity, and dangers, is in such good spirits that it makes me happy to witness it. No doubt a chief reason is the consolation he derives from the pious and highly-intelligent wife whom the Lord has given him—a woman who ever conforms to his wishes, and is inexpressibly dear to him."‡

The Princess left six daughters—Louisa Juliana, Elizabeth, Catharina Belgica, Flandrina, Charlotta Brabantica, and Emilia Secunda.§

Parma received the first intelligence of the attempt from the mouth of Anastro himself, who assured him that the deed had been entirely successful, and claimed the promised reward.

---

* Hoofd, Meteren, Bor, ubi sup.

† "With a stately procession of two thousand mourning mantles," says Hoofd, xix. 807.

‡ Apologie d'Orange. Archives, etc., vii. 333.

§ Bor, xvii. 316. Meteren, xi. 195.

Alexander, in consequence, addressed circular letters to the authorities of Antwerp, Brussels, Bruges, and other cities, calling upon them, now that they had been relieved of their tyrant and their betrayer, to return again to the path of their duty and to the ever open arms of their lawful monarch.* These letters were premature. On the other hand, the states of Holland and Zealand remained in permanent session, awaiting with extreme anxiety the result of the Prince's wound. "With the death of his Excellency, if God should please to take him to himself," said the magistracy of Leyden, "in the death of the Prince we all foresee our own death." It was, in truth, an anxious moment, and the revulsion of feeling consequent on his recovery was proportionately intense.†

In consequence of the excitement produced by this event, it was no longer possible for the Prince to decline accepting the countship of Holland and Zealand, which he had refused absolutely two years before, and which he had again rejected, except for a limited period, in the year 1581.‡ It was well understood, as appears by the treaty with Anjou, and afterwards formally arranged, "that the Duke was never to claim sovereignty over Holland and Zealand,"§ and the offer of the sovereign countship of Holland was again made to the Prince of Orange in most urgent terms. It will be recollected that he had accepted the sovereignty on the 5th of July, 1581, only for the term of the war. In a letter, dated Bruges, 14th of August, 1582, he accepted the dignity without limitation.|| This offer and acceptance, however, constituted but the preliminaries, for it was further necessary that the letters of "*Renversal*" should be drawn up, that they should be formally

---

* Bor (xvii. 314, 315) gives the letters. Meteren, xi. 195.

† Bor, xvii. 316. Kluit, i. 292.

‡ Ibid., i. 262; 201, sqq. § Ibid., i. 246, 247. Bor, xv. 182, 183.

|| Ibid., xv. 183, 184, 185.—Compare Kluit, i. 213, 214. The deeds of offer and of acceptance were dated July 5th, 1581. The oaths were exchanged between the estates and the Prince, July 24th, two days before the act of abjuration. The letter of August 14th, 1582, is given in Bor, xv. 186, 187.

delivered, and that a new constitution should be laid down, and confirmed by mutual oaths. After these steps had been taken, the ceremonious inauguration or rendering of homage was to be celebrated.

All these measures were duly arranged, except the last. The installation of the new Count of Holland was prevented by his death, and the northern provinces remained a Republic, not only in fact but in name.*

In political matters, the basis of the new constitution was the "Great Privilege" of the Lady Mary, the Magna Charta of the country. That memorable monument in the history

---

* As the measures therefore were, after all, inchoate, a brief indication of these dates and objects will suffice to show the relative position of the Prince and the people of Holland and Zealand. The act of acceptance by William the Silent of the proffered sovereignty, was dated August 12, 1582.—(Bor, xv. 186, 187.) The letters patent, or the Renversal, as they were technically called, were drawn up and signed and sealed by the "three eldest nobles."—(Bor, xv. 187. Kluit, i. 311, 312.) They were then sent to all the cities, and received their twenty-five separate seals at different dates.—(Kluit, i. 311, 312, and Bijlagen, 451–463.) The original was afterwards delivered to the Prince, and still exists, with its twenty-eight seals, among the Archives of the now royal family of Orange Nassau.—(Kluit, i. 316.) On the 6th of May, 1583, the States of Holland addressed a remarkable circular (Bor, xv. 187–190), who states that it was addressed only to the States of Utrecht, while Kluit (i. 322) shows that it was a general circular to the States of Utrecht, Friesland, Overyssel, Brabant, Flanders, Gelderland, and to the States-general also, giving an historical sketch of the life and services of William the Silent, together with the weighty reason which had induced them to urge the ancient Countship of Holland upon his acceptance. This step they declared themselves to have taken, "after frequent communication with our cities, and each of them; after ripe deliberation and council; after having heard the advice of the colleges and communities of the cities, as well as that of the magistracies and senates, and of all other persons whom it behoved to consult, and whose counsel in matters of consequence is usually asked."—(See the Commentary of Kluit, i. 322–326.) They moreover expressed the hope that the measure would meet with the approval of all their sister provinces and with the especial co-operation of those estates with which they were accustomed to act. On the 15th of November, 1583, the Deputies of Zealand and Utrecht, thus especially alluded to, formally declared their intention to remain in their ancient friendship and union with Holland, "under one sovereignty and government."—(Kluit, i. 329, 330.) An act to this effect was drawn up, to be referred for ratification to their principals at the next assembly.—It had, however, not been ratified when the proceedings were for ever terminated by the Prince's death.—(Kluit, 330, 351, 352, 353. Bor, xv.

of the Netherlands and of municipal progress had been overthrown by Mary's son, with the forced acquiescence of the states, and it was therefore stipulated by the new article, that even such laws and privileges as had fallen into disuse should be revived. It was furthermore provided that the little state should be a free Countship, and should thus silently sever its connexion with the Empire.*

With regard to the position of the Prince, as hereditary chief of the little commonwealth, his actual power was rather diminished than increased by his new dignity. What was his position at the moment? He was sovereign *during the war*, on the general basis of the authority originally bestowed upon him by the King's commission of stadholder. In 1581, his Majesty had been abjured and the stadholder had become sovereign. He held in his hands the supreme power, *legislative, judicial, executive.* The Counts of Holland—and Philip as their successor—were the great fountains of that triple stream. Concessions and exceptions had become so extensive, no doubt, that the provincial charters constituted a vast body of "liberties" by which the whole country was reasonably well supplied. At the same time, all the power not expressly granted away remained in the breast of the Count.† If ambition, then, had been William's ruling principle, he had exchanged substance for shadow, for the new state now constituted was a free commonwealth—a republic in all but name.

By the new constitution he ceased to be the source of

186.) Holland accepted this formality as sufficient, and the act of Renversal was accordingly delivered on the 7th of December, 1583.—(Kluit, i. 330.) On the 30th of the same month, forty-nine articles (they are given in full by Bor, xv. 191–194), containing as sensible a plan for a free Commonwealth as had ever been drawn up previously to that day in Christendom, were agreed upon by the Prince and the estates, as the fundamental conditions under which he should be invested with the Countship. The Prince, however, accepted the dignity and the articles, only upon the further condition that the whole proceeding should be once more approved and confirmed by the senates of the cities.—(Kluit, i. 335.—Compare Bor, iii. xv. 194[b]).

* Kluit, i. 346, 347. See Introduction to this work. Article 5. Kluit, i. 337, note 63.

† Kluit, i. 11–16 and 346, sqq.

governmental life, or to derive his own authority from above by right divine. The sacred oil which had flowed from Charles the Simple's beard was dried up. Orange's sovereignty was from the estates, as legal representatives of the people, and, instead of exercising all the powers not otherwise granted away, he was content with those especially conferred upon him. He could neither declare war nor conclude peace without the co-operation of the representative body. The appointing power was scrupulously limited. Judges, magistrates, governors, sheriffs, provincial and municipal officers, were to be nominated by the local authorities or by the estates, on the triple principle. From these triple nominations he had only the right of selection by advice and consent of his council. He was expressly enjoined to see that the law was carried to every man's door, without *any distinction* of persons, to submit himself to its behests, to watch against all impediments to the even flow of justice, to prevent false imprisonments, and to secure trials for every accused person by the local tribunals. This was certainly little in accordance with the arbitrary practice of the past quarter of a century.

With respect to the great principle of taxation, stricter bonds even were provided than those which already existed. Not only the right of taxation remained with the states, but the Count was to see that, except for war purposes, every impost was levied by a unanimous vote. He was expressly forbidden to tamper with the currency. As executive head, save in his capacity as Commander-in-chief by land or sea, the new sovereign was, in short, strictly limited by self-imposed laws. It had rested with him to dictate or to accept a constitution. He had in his memorable letter of August, 1582, from Bruges, laid down generally the articles prepared at Plessis and Bourdeaux, for Anjou—together with all applicable provisions of the Joyous Entry of Brabant—as the outlines of the constitution for the little commonwealth then forming in the north. To these provisions he was willing to add any others which, after ripe deliberation, might be thought beneficial to the country.

Thus limited were his executive functions. As to his judicial authority it had ceased to exist. The Count of Holland was now the guardian of the laws, but the judges were to administer them. He held the sword of justice to protect and to execute, while the scales were left in the hands which had learned to weigh and to measure.

As to the Count's legislative authority, it had become coordinate with, if not subordinate to, that of the representative body. He was strictly prohibited from interfering with the right of the separate or the general states to assemble as often as they should think proper; and he was also forbidden to summon them outside their own territory.* This was one immense step in the progress of representative liberty, and the next was equally important. It was now formally stipulated that the estates were to deliberate upon all measures which "concerned justice and polity," and that no change was to be made—that is to say, no new law was to pass—without their consent as well as that of the council.† Thus, the principle was established of two legislative chambers, with the right, but not the exclusive right, of initiation on the part of government, and in the sixteenth century one would hardly look for broader views of civil liberty and representative government. The foundation of a free commonwealth was thus securely laid, which had William lived, would have been a representative monarchy, but which his death converted into a federal republic. It was necessary for the sake of unity to give a connected outline of these proceedings with regard to the sovereignty of Orange. The formal inauguration only remained, and this, as will be seen, was for ever interrupted.

---

* Kluit, i. 347.

† Article 20.—Compare Kluit, i. 348.

CHAPTER VI.

Parma recals the foreign troops—Siege of Oudenarde—Coolness of Alexander—Capture of the city and of Ninove—Inauguration of Anjou at Ghent—Attempt upon his life and that of Orange—Lamoral Egmont's implication in the plot—Parma's unsuccessful attack upon Ghent—Secret plans of Anjou—Dunkirk, Ostend, and other towns surprised by his adherents—Failure at Bruges—Suspicions at Antwerp—Duplicity of Anjou—The "French Fury"—Details of that transaction—Discomfiture and disgrace of the Duke—His subsequent effrontery—His letters to the magistracy of Antwerp, to the Estates, and to Orange—Extensive correspondence between Anjou and the French Court with Orange and the Estates—Difficult position of the Prince—His policy—Remarkable letter to the States-general—Provisional arrangement with Anjou—Marriage of the Archbishop of Cologne—Marriage of Orange with Louisa de Coligny—Movements in Holland, Brabant, Flanders, and other provinces, to induce the Prince to accept sovereignty over the whole country—His steady refusal—Treason of Van den Berg in Gueldres—Intrigues of Prince Chimay and Imbize in Flanders—Counter efforts of Orange and the patriot party—Fate of Imbize—Reconciliation of Bruges—Death of Anjou.

During the course of the year 1582, the military operations on both sides had been languid and desultory, the Prince of Parma, not having a large force at his command, being comparatively inactive. In consequence, however, of the treaty concluded between the united states and Anjou, Parma had persuaded the Walloon provinces that it had now become absolutely necessary for them to permit the entrance of fresh Italian and Spanish troops.* This, then, was the end of the famous provision against foreign soldiery in the Walloon

---

* Bor, xvii. 320, 321.

treaty of reconciliation. The Abbot of Saint Vaast was immediately despatched on a special mission to Spain, and the troops, by midsummer, had already begun to pour into the Netherlands.*

In the meantime, Farnese, while awaiting these reinforcements, had not been idle, but had been quietly picking up several important cities. Early in the spring he had laid siege to Oudenarde, a place of considerable importance upon the Scheld, and celebrated as the birthplace of his grandmother, Margaret van Geest.† The burghers were obstinate; the defence was protracted; the sorties were bold; the skirmishes frequent and sanguinary. Alexander commanded personally in the trenches, encouraging his men by his example, and often working with the mattock, or handling a spear in the assault, like a private pioneer or soldier. Towards the end of the siege, he scarcely ever left the scene of operation, and he took his meals near the outer defences, that he might lose no opportunity of superintending the labors of his troops. One day his dinner was laid for himself and staff in the open air, close to the entrenchment.‡ He was himself engaged in planting a battery against a weak point in the city wall, and would on no account withdraw for an instant. The tablecloth was stretched over a number of drum-heads, placed close together, and several nobles of distinction—Aremberg, Montigny, Richebourg, La Motte, and others, were his guests at dinner. Hardly had the repast commenced, when a ball came flying over the table, taking off the head of a young Walloon officer who was sitting near Parma, and who was earnestly requesting a foremost place in the morrow's assault. A portion of his skull struck out the eye of another gentleman present. A second ball from the town fortifications, equally

---

* Bor, xvii. 320, 321.—Compare Reconc. Prov. Wall., t. v., MS.

† Bor, vii. 322. Strada, 2, iv. 225–234. Meteren, xi. 195. The city is in Flanders, on the Scheld, in the country of the ancient Nervii, from which valiant tribe, according to Meteren, it derived its name, Oude-narde, Oude Naarden, old Nervii.—xi. 195[b].

‡ Bor, ubi sup. Strada, 2, iv. 225–234.

well directed, destroyed two more of the guests as they sat at the banquet—one a German captain, the other the Judge-Advocate-General. The blood and brains of these unfortunate individuals were strewn over the festive board, and the others all started to their feet, having little appetite left for their dinner. Alexander alone remained in his seat, manifesting no discomposure. Quietly ordering the attendants to remove the dead bodies, and to bring a clean tablecloth,* he insisted that his guests should resume their places at the banquet which had been interrupted in such ghastly fashion. He stated with very determined aspect that he could not allow the heretic burghers of Oudenarde the triumph of frightening him from his dinner, or from the post of danger. The other gentlemen could, of course, do no less than imitate the impassibility of their chief, and the repast was accordingly concluded without further interruption. Not long afterwards, the city, close pressed by so determined a commander, accepted terms, which were more favorable by reason of the respect which Alexander chose to render to his mother's birthplace. The pillage was commuted for thirty thousand crowns, and on the 5th of July the place was surrendered to Parma almost under the very eyes of Anjou, who was making a demonstration of relieving the siege.†

Ninove, a citadel then belonging to the Egmont family, was next reduced. Here, too, the defence was more obstinate than could have been expected from the importance of the place, and as the autumn advanced, Parma's troops were nearly starved in their trenches, from the insufficient supplies furnished them. They had eaten no meat but horseflesh for weeks, and even that was gone. The cavalry horses were all consumed, and even the chargers of the officers were not respected. An aide-camp of Parma fastened his steed one day at the door of

* "—— solus Alexander nec sedem nec vultum mutavit —— jubet auferri illinc, humarique cadavera, alia induci in *mensam lintea, alias dapes.*"—Strada, 2, v. 233.

† Strada, 2, v. 232–234.—Compare Bor, xvii. 322. Hoofd, xix. 812.

the Prince's tent, while he entered to receive his commander's instructions. When he came out again, a few minutes afterwards, he found nothing but the saddle and bridle hanging where he had fastened the horse. Remonstrance was useless, for the animal had already been cut into quarters, and the only satisfaction offered to the aid-de-camp was in the shape of a steak. The famine was long familiarly known as the "Ninove starvation," but notwithstanding this obstacle, the place was eventually surrendered.*

An attempt upon Lochum, an important city in Gelderland, was unsuccessful, the place being relieved by the Duke of Anjou's forces, and Parma's troops forced to abandon the siege. At Steenwyk, the royal arms were more successful, Colonel Tassis, conducted by a treacherous Frisian peasant, having surprised the city which had so long and so manfully sustained itself against Renneberg during the preceding winter. With this event the active operations under Parma closed for the year. By the end of the autumn, however, he had the satisfaction of numbering, under his command, full sixty thousand well-appointed and disciplined troops, including the large reinforcements recently despatched from Spain and Italy.† The monthly expense of this army—half of which was required for garrison duty, leaving only the other moiety for field operations—was estimated at six hundred and fifty thousand florins.‡ The forces under Anjou and the united provinces were also largely increased, so that the marrow of the land was again in fair way of being thoroughly exhausted by its defenders and its foes.§

The incidents of Anjou's administration, meantime, during the year 1582, had been few and of no great importance. After the pompous and elaborate "homage-making" at Antwerp, he had, in the month of July, been formally accepted, by

---

* Strada, 2, v. 242.

† 56,550 infantry and 3537 cavalry—total 60,087.—Meteren, xi. 198ª.

‡ 654,356 guldens.—Ibid.

§ Meteren, xi. 197. Tassis, vi. 433. Strada, 2, v. 244, 245.

writing, as Duke of Guelders and Lord of Friesland. In the same month he had been ceremoniously inaugurated at Bruges as Count of Flanders—an occasion upon which the Prince of Orange had been present. In that ancient and stately city there had been, accordingly, much marching about under triumphal arches, much cannonading and haranguing, much symbol work of suns dispelling fogs, with other cheerful emblems, much decoration of ducal shoulders with velvet robes lined with weasel skin, much blazing of tar-barrels and torches.* In the midst of this event, an attempt was made upon the lives both of Orange and Anjou. An Italian, named Basa, and a Spaniard, called Salseda, were detected in a scheme to administer poison to both princes, and when arrested, confessed that they had been hired by the Prince of Parma to compass this double assassination. Basa destroyed himself in prison. His body was, however, gibbeted, with an inscription that he had attempted, at the instigation of Parma, to take the lives of Orange and Anjou. Salseda, less fortunate, was sent to Paris, where he was found guilty, and executed by being torn to pieces by four horses. Sad to relate, Lamoral Egmont, younger son and namesake of the great general, was intimate with Salseda, and implicated in this base design.† His mother, on her death-bed, had especially recommended the youth to the kindly care of Orange.‡ The Prince had ever recognized the claim, manifesting uniform tenderness for the son of his ill-starred friend; and now the youthful Lamoral—as if the name of

* Bor, xvii. 328, 329, 332. Meteren, xi. 196. A rising sun, with the motto "fovet et discutit," was the favorite device of Anjou.

† Bor, xvii. 331. Hoofd, xix. 814, 815. Meteren, xi. 196. Egmont pretended to be studying alchemy with Salseda.

‡ Meteren, Hoofd, ubi sup. See a letter of Orange to Josse Borluut, October 11, 1580, requesting him to furnish young Lamoral with needful funds, adding, "le principal point pour se faire valoir au chemin de la vertu pour auquel continuer au bien en mieulx, ay donné ordre qu'il soit guidé de personnes à ce bien propres et qualifiés."—Documents Inédits, par Kervyn de Volkaersbeke et J. Diegerick, ii. 158.

Egmont had not been sufficiently contaminated by the elder brother's treason at Brussels—had become the comrade of hired conspirators against his guardian's life. The affair was hushed up, but the story was current and generally believed that Egmont had himself undertaken to destroy the Prince at his own table by means of poison which he kept concealed in a ring. Saint Aldegonde was to have been taken off in the same way, and a hollow ring filled with poison was said to have been found in Egmont's lodgings.*

The young noble was imprisoned; his guilt was far from doubtful; but the powerful intercessions of Orange himself, combined with Egmont's near relationship to the French Queen, saved his life, and he was permitted, after a brief captivity, to take his departure for France.†

The Duke of Anjou, a month later, was received with equal pomp, in the city of Ghent. Here the ceremonies were interrupted in another manner. The Prince of Parma, at the head of a few regiments of Walloons, making an attack on a body of troops by which Anjou had been escorted into Flanders, the troops retreated in good order, and without much loss, under the walls of Ghent, where a long and sharp action took place, much to the disadvantage of Parma. The Prince of Orange and the Duke of Anjou were on the city walls during the whole skirmish, giving orders and superintending the movements of their troops, and at nightfall Parma was forced to retire, leaving a large number of dead behind him.‡

The 15th day of December, in this year was celebrated—according to the new ordinance of Gregory the Thirteenth—as Christmas.§ It was the occasion of more than usual merry-

---

* "Wreede Turkshe wonderlijcke verhaalinge van dit leste verraet teghen Ducks Dangu (sic) en tegen den edelen P. v. Orangien," etc., etc.—Leyden, 1582. This curious pamphlet, in the Duncan collection, consists of a letter from Bruges of 25th July, and another from Antwerp, of 27th July, 1582.

† Louise de Vaudemont, wife of Henry III., was daughter of the great Count Egmont's sister. She was consequently first cousin to young Lamoral.

‡ Bor, xvii. 334. Strada, 2, v. 240, 241. Meteren, xi. 197.

§ Bor, xvii. 338. Meteren, xi. 198, sqq. Hoofd, xix. 827. Strada, 2, v. 245.

making among the Catholics of Antwerp, who had procured, during the preceding summer, a renewed right of public worship from Anjou and the estates. Many nobles of high rank came from France, to pay their homage to the new Duke of Brabant. They secretly expressed their disgust, however, at the close constitutional bonds in which they found their own future sovereign imprisoned by the provinces. They thought it far beneath the dignity of the "Son of France" to play the secondary part of titular Duke of Brabant, Count of Flanders, Lord of Friesland, and the like, while the whole power of government was lodged with the states. They whispered that it was time to take measures for the incorporation of the Netherlands into France, and they persuaded the false and fickle Anjou that there would never be any hope of his royal brother's assistance, except upon the understanding that the blood and treasure of Frenchmen were to be spent to increase the power, not of upstart and independent provinces, but of the French crown.*

They struck the basest chords of the Duke's base nature by awakening his jealousy of Orange. His whole soul vibrated to the appeal. He already hated the man by whose superior intellect he was overawed, and by whose pure character he was shamed. He stoutly but secretly swore that he would assert his own rights, and that he would no longer serve as a shadow, a statue, a zero, a Matthias.† It is needless to add, that neither in his own judgment nor in that of his *mignons,* were the constitutional articles which he had recently sworn to support, or the solemn treaty which he had signed and sealed at Bordeaux, to furnish any obstacles to his seizure of unlimited power, whenever the design could be cleverly accomplished. He rested not, day or night, in the elaboration of his plan.

Early in January, 1583, he sent one night for several of his

---

* Bor, xvii. 339, sqq. Strada, 2, v. 246, sqq. Meteren, xi. 199, 200. Hoofd, xix. 837, 838.

† Bor, xvii. 339. Hoofd, xix. 837. Strada, 2, v. 247.

intimate associates, to consult with him after he had retired to bed. He complained of the insolence of the states, of the importunity of the council which they had forced upon him, of the insufficient sums which they furnished both for him and his troops, of the daily insults offered to the Catholic religion. He protested that he should consider himself disgraced in the eyes of all Christendom, should he longer consent to occupy his present ignoble position. But two ways were open to him, he observed; either to retire altogether from the Netherlands, or to maintain his authority with the strong hand, as became a prince. The first course would cover him with disgrace. It was therefore necessary for him to adopt the other. He then unfolded his plan to his confidential friends, La Fougère, De Fazy, Valette, the sons of Maréchal Biron, and others. Upon the same day, if possible, he was determined to take possession, with his own troops, of the principal cities in Flanders. Dunkirk, Dixmuyde, Denremonde, Bruges, Ghent, Vilvoorde, Alost, and other important places, were to be simultaneously invaded, under pretext of quieting tumults artfully created and encouraged between the burghers and the garrisons, while Antwerp was reserved for his own especial enterprise. That important capital he would carry by surprise at the same moment in which the other cities were to be secured by his lieutenants.*

The plot was pronounced an excellent one by the friends around his bed—all of them eager for Catholic supremacy, for the establishment of the right divine on the part of France to the Netherlands, and for their share in the sacking of so many wealthy cities at once. These worthless *mignons* applauded their weak master to the echo; whereupon the Duke leaped from his bed, and kneeling on the floor in his night-gown, raised his eyes and his clasped hands to heaven, and piously invoked the blessing of the Almighty upon the project which

---

* Bor, xvii. 339, 340. Meteren, xi. 200, 201. Hoofd, xix. 837, 838. Strada, 2, v. 248, 249.

he had thus announced.* He added the solemn assurance that, if favored with success in his undertaking, he would abstain in future from all unchastity, and forego the irregular habits by which his youth had been stained. Having thus bribed the Deity, and received the encouragement of his flatterers, the Duke got into bed again. His next care was to remove the Seigneur du Plessis, whom he had observed to be often in colloquy with the Prince of Orange, his suspicious and guilty imagination finding nothing but mischief to himself in the conjunction of two such natures. He therefore dismissed Du Plessis, under pretext of a special mission to his sister, Margaret of Navarre; but in reality, that he might rid himself of the presence of an intelligent and honorable countryman.†

On the 15th January, 1583, the day fixed for the execution of the plot, the French commandant of Dunkirk, Captain Chamois, skilfully took advantage of a slight quarrel between the citizens and the garrison, to secure that important frontier town. The same means were employed simultaneously, with similar results, at Ostend, Dixmuyde, Denremonde, Alost, and Vilvoorde, but there was a fatal delay at one important city. La Fougère, who had been with Chamois at Dunkirk, was arrested on his way to Bruges by some patriotic citizens who had got wind of what had just been occurring in the other cities, so that when Valette, the provost of Anjou, and Colonel la Rebours, at the head of fifteen hundred French troops, appeared before the gates, entrance was flatly refused. De Grijse, burgomaster of Bruges, encouraged his fellow townsmen by words and stout action, to resist the nefarious project then on foot against religious liberty and free government, in favor of a new foreign tyranny.‡ He spoke to men who could sympathize with, and second his courageous resolution, and the delay of twenty-four hours,

---

* Deposition of La Fougère, the Duke's maître d'hôtel, in Bor, xvii. 340. Hoofd, xix. 838.

† Ibid. Strada, 2, v. 248.

‡ Bor, xvii. 340. Hoofd, xix. 834.

during which the burghers had time to take the alarm, saved the city. The whole population was on the alert, and the baffled Frenchmen were forced to retire from the gates, to avoid being torn to pieces by the citizens whom they had intended to surprise.

At Antwerp, meanwhile, the Duke of Anjou had been rapidly maturing his plan, under pretext of a contemplated enterprise against the city of Endhoven, having concentrated what he esteemed a sufficient number of French troops at Borgerhout, a village close to the walls of Antwerp.

On the 16th of January, suspicion was aroused in the city. A man in a mask entered the mainguard-house in the night, mysteriously gave warning that a great crime was in contemplation, and vanished before he could be arrested. His accent proved him to be a Frenchman. Strange rumors flew about the streets. A vague uneasiness pervaded the whole population as to the intention of their new master, but nothing was definitely known, for of course there was entire ignorance of the events which were just occurring in other cities. The colonels and captains of the burgher guard came to consult the Prince of Orange. He avowed the most entire confidence in the Duke of Anjou, but, at the same time, recommended that the chains should be drawn, the lanterns hung out, and the drawbridge raised an hour earlier than usual, and that other precautions, customary in the expectation of an attack, should be duly taken. He likewise sent the Burgomaster of the interior, Dr. Alostanus, to the Duke of Anjou, in order to communicate the suspicions created in the minds of the city authorities by the recent movements of troops.*

---

* Corte Verclaering, ghedaen by Burgemeesteren, Schepenen ende Raedt der Stadt Antwerpen, nopende den aenslaeg tegen de selve stadt aengerichtet den xvii deser maendt, Jan. 1583.—Antwerp. Christ. Plantin, 1583. This is the official account—published by authority immediately after the event—and the source whence Bor, Meteren, and other contemporary chroniclers have derived the details of this important transaction.—Compare Bor, xvii. 341, sqq.; Meteren, xi. 201, sqq. Hoofd, xix. 838, 839, sqq. Reid., iii. 46.

Anjou, thus addressed, protested in the most solemn manner that nothing was farther from his thoughts than any secret enterprise against Antwerp. He was willing, according to the figure of speech which he had always ready upon every emergency, "to shed every drop of his blood in her defence." He swore that he would signally punish all those who had dared to invent such calumnies against himself and his faithful Frenchmen, declaring earnestly, at the same time, that the troops had only been assembled in the regular course of their duty. As the Duke was so loud and so fervent; as he, moreover, made no objections to the precautionary measures which had been taken; as the burgomaster thought, moreover, that the public attention thus aroused would render all evil designs futile, even if any had been entertained; it was thought that the city might sleep in security for that night at least.*

On the following morning, as vague suspicions were still entertained by many influential persons, a deputation of magistrates and militia officers waited upon the Duke, the Prince of Orange—although himself still feeling a confidence which seems now almost inexplicable—consenting to accompany them. The Duke was more vehement than ever in his protestations of loyalty to his recent oaths, as well as of deep affection for the Netherlands—for Brabant in particular, and for Antwerp most of all, and he made use of all his vivacity to persuade the Prince, the burgomasters, and the colonels, that they had deeply wronged him by such unjust suspicions. His assertions were accepted as sincere, and the deputation withdrew, Anjou having first solemnly promised—at the suggestion of Orange—not to leave the city during the whole day, in order that unnecessary suspicion might be prevented.†

This pledge the Duke proceeded to violate almost as

* Corte Verclaering. Bor, Hoofd, Meteren, ubi sup. Ev. Reidani, iii. 46, 47.

† Bor, xvii. 342. Corte Verclaering, etc.

soon as made. Orange returned with confidence to his own house, which was close to the citadel, and therefore far removed from the proposed point of attack, but he had hardly arrived there when he received a visit from the Duke's private secretary, Quinsay, who invited him to accompany his Highness on a visit to the camp. Orange declined the request, and sent an earnest prayer to the Duke not to leave the city that morning. The Duke dined as usual at noon. While at dinner he received a letter, was observed to turn pale on reading it, and to conceal it hastily in a muff which he wore on his left arm. The repast finished, the Duke ordered his horse. The animal was restive, and so strenuously resisted being mounted that, although it was his usual charger, it was exchanged for another. This second horse started in such a flurry that the Duke lost his cloak, and almost his seat. He maintained his self-possession, however, and placing himself at the head of his body-guard and some troopers, numbering in all three hundred mounted men, rode out of the palace-yard towards the Kipdorp gate.*

This portal opened on the road towards Borgerhout, where his troops were stationed, and at the present day bears the name of that village. It is on the side of the city farthest removed from and exactly opposite the river. The town was very quiet, the streets almost deserted; for it was one o'clock, the universal dinner-hour, and all suspicion had been disarmed by the energetic protestations of the Duke. The guard at the gate looked listlessly upon the cavalcade as it approached, but as soon as Anjou had crossed the first drawbridge, he rose in his stirrups and waved his hand. "There is your city, my lads," said he to the troopers behind him; "go and take possession of it!"†

At the same time he set spurs to his horse, and galloped off towards the camp at Borgerhout. Instantly afterwards, a

* Hoofd, xix. 839–843. Meteren, xi. 201. Bor, xvii. 342.

† Corte Verclaering, etc. Bor, Meteren, Hoofd, ubi sup. Strada, 2, v. 249. Ev. Reid., iii. 47.

gentleman of his suite, Count Rochepot,* affected to have broken his leg through the plunging of his horse, a circumstance by which he had been violently pressed against the wall as he entered the gate. Kaiser, the commanding officer at the guard-house, stepped kindly forward to render him assistance, and his reward was a desperate thrust from the Frenchman's rapier. As he wore a steel cuirass, he fortunately escaped with a slight wound.†

The expression, "broken leg," was the watch-word, for at one and the same instant, the troopers and guardsmen of Anjou set upon the burgher watch at the gate, and butchered every man. A sufficient force was left to protect the entrance thus easily mastered, while the rest of the Frenchmen entered the town at full gallop, shrieking "*Ville gaignée, ville gaignée! vive la messe! vive le Duc d'Anjou!*" They were followed by their comrades from the camp outside, who now poured into the town at the preconcerted signal, at least six hundred cavalry and three thousand musketeers, all perfectly appointed, entering Antwerp at once. From the Kipdorp gate two main arteries—the streets called the Kipdorp and the Meer—led quite through the heart of the city, towards the townhouse and the river beyond. Along these great thoroughfares the French soldiers advanced at a rapid pace; the cavalry clattering furiously in the van, shouting "*Ville gaignée, ville gaignée! vive la messe, vive la messe! tue, tue, tue!*"‡

The burghers coming to door and window to look for the cause of all this disturbance, were saluted with volleys of musketry. They were for a moment astonished, but not appalled, for at first they believed it to be merely an accidental tumult. Observing, however, that the soldiers, meeting

---

* "Dont le nom est enseveli dans l' oubli," says De Thou, adding, "et plût à Dieu que l'infamie de son action le fût aussi!"—Tom. ix. liv. 77, p. 37. Reyd, however, says it was Count Rochepot.—Ann. Belg. 347. De Weert's MS. Journal also gives the name and the incident.

† De Thou, Reyd, Bor, Meteren, Hoofd.

‡ Corte Verclaering, etc. Bor, xvii. 343. Hoofd, xix. 841, sqq. Meteren, Reyd, ubi sup. Strada, 2, v. 249, sqq.

with but little effective resistance, were dispersing into dwellings and warehouses, particularly into the shops of the goldsmiths and lapidaries, the citizens remembered the dark supicions which had been so rife, and many recalled to mind that distinguished French officers had during the last few days been carefully examining the treasures of the jewellers, under pretext of purchasing, but, as it now appeared, with intent to rob intelligently.*

The burghers, taking this rapid view of their position, flew instantly to arms. Chains and barricades were stretched across the streets; the trumpets sounded through the city; the municipal guards swarmed to the rescue. An effective rally was made, as usual, at the Bourse, whither a large detachment of the invaders had forced their way. Inhabitants of all classes and conditions, noble and simple, Catholic and Protestant, gave each other the hand, and swore to die at each other's side in defence of the city against the treacherous strangers. The gathering was rapid and enthusiastic. Gentlemen came with lance and cuirass, burghers with musket and bandoleer, artisans with axe, mallet, and other implements of their trade. A bold baker, standing by his oven—stark naked, according to the custom of bakers at that day—rushed to the street as the sound of the tumult reached his ear. With his heavy bread shovel, which he still held in his hand, he dealt a French cavalry officer, just riding and screaming by, such a hearty blow that he fell dead from his horse. The baker seized the officer's sword, sprang all unattired as he was, upon his steed, and careered furiously through the streets, encouraging his countrymen everywhere to the attack, and dealing dismay through the ranks of the enemy. His services in that eventful hour were so signal that he was publicly thanked afterwards by the magistrates for his services, and rewarded with a pension of three hundred florins for life.†

* Strada, 2, v. 252. Ev. Reidani, ii. 53.

† Corte Verclaering. Bor, xvii. 343. Meteren, xi. 201. Hoofd, xix. 841, 842. Strada, 2, v. 250. Tassis, vi. 435.

The invaders had been forced from the Bourse, while another portion of them had penetrated as far as the Market-place. The resistance which they encountered became every instant more formidable, and Fervacques, a leading French officer, who was captured on the occasion, acknowledged that no regular troops could have fought more bravely than did these stalwart burghers.* Women and children mounted to roof and window, whence they hurled, not only tiles and chimney pots, but tables, ponderous chairs, and other bulky articles, upon the heads of the assailants,† while such citizens as had used all their bullets, loaded their pieces with the silver buttons from their doublets, or twisted gold and silver coins with their teeth into ammunition. With a population so resolute, the four thousand invaders, however audacious, soon found themselves swallowed up. The city had closed over them like water, and within an hour nearly a third of their whole number had been slain. Very few of the burghers had perished, and fresh numbers were constantly advancing to the attack. The Frenchmen, blinded, staggering, beaten, attempted to retreat. Many threw themselves from the fortifications into the moat. The rest of the survivors struggled through the streets—falling in large numbers at every step—towards the point at which they had so lately entered the city. Here at the Kipdorp gate was a ghastly spectacle, the slain being piled up in the narrow passage full ten feet high, while some of the heap, not quite dead, were striving to extricate a hand or foot, and others feebly thrust forth their heads to gain a mouthful of air.‡

From the outside, some of Anjou's officers were attempting to climb over this mass of bodies in order to enter the city; from the interior, the baffled and fugitive remnant of their comrades were attempting to force their passage through the

* Ev. Reid., iii. 48.

† Bor, Hoofd, Meteren, Strada.

‡ Bor, xvii. 343, 344. Meteren, xi. 201. Hoofd, xix. 841, 842, 843. Strada, 2, v. 250. "Ut duorum altitudinem hominum exaequaret cadaverum strues."

same horrible barrier; while many dropped at every instant upon the heap of slain, under the blows of the unrelenting burghers.* On the other hand, Count Rochepot himself, to whom the principal command of the enterprise had been entrusted by Anjou, stood directly in the path of his fugitive soldiers, not only bitterly upbraiding them with their cowardice, but actually slaying ten or twelve of them with his own hands,† as the most effectual mode of preventing their retreat. Hardly an hour had elapsed from the time when the Duke of Anjou first rode out of the Kipdorp gate, before nearly the whole of the force which he had sent to accomplish his base design was either dead or captive. Two hundred and fifty nobles of high rank and illustrious name were killed; recognized at once as they lay in the streets by their magnificent costume. A larger number of the gallant chivalry of France had been sacrificed—as Anjou confessed—in this treacherous and most shameful enterprise, than had often fallen upon noble and honorable fields. Nearly two thousand of the rank and file had perished, and the rest were prisoners. It was at first asserted that exactly fifteen hundred and eighty-three Frenchmen had fallen, but this was only because this number happened to be the date of the year, to which the lovers of marvellous coincidences struggled very hard to make the returns of the dead correspond. Less than one hundred burghers lost their lives.‡

Anjou, as he looked on at a distance, was bitterly reproached for his treason by several of the high-minded gentlemen about his person, to whom he had not dared to confide his plot. The Duke of Montpensier protested vehemently that he washed his hands of the whole transaction, whatever might be the

---

* Meteren, xi. 201, sqq., who had his information from eyewitnesses.—Compare Hoofd, Bor, Meteren, Strada, loc. cit.

† Hoofd, xix. 843. Reidani, iii. 47.

‡ According to a statement made by a French prisoner, more than fifty gentlemen had been killed, of whom the poorest had six thousand livres annual income. Bor, xvii. 343.—Compare Meteren, xi. 202. Ev. Reid., iii. 48. Strada, 2, v. 252. Hoofd, xix. 843.

issue.* He was responsible for the honor of an illustrious house, which should never be stained, he said, if he could prevent it, with such foul deeds. The same language was held by Laval, by Rochefoucauld, and by the Maréchal de Biron, the last gentleman, whose two sons were engaged in the vile enterprise, bitterly cursing the Duke to his face, as he rode through the gate after revealing his secret undertaking.†

Meanwhile, Anjou, in addition to the punishment of hearing these reproaches from men of honor, was the victim of a rapid and violent fluctuation of feeling. Hope, fear, triumph, doubt, remorse, alternately swayed him. As he saw the fugitives leaping from the walls, he shouted exultingly, without accurately discerning what manner of men they were, that the city was his, that four thousand of his brave soldiers were there, and were hurling the burghers from the battlements. On being made afterwards aware of his error, he was proportionably depressed; and when it was obvious at last that the result of the enterprise was an absolute and disgraceful failure, together with a complete exposure of his treachery, he fairly mounted his horse, and fled conscience-stricken from the scene.‡

The attack had been so unexpected, in consequence of the credence that had been rendered by Orange and the magistracy to the solemn protestations of the Duke, that it had been naturally out of any one's power to prevent the catastrophe. The Prince was lodged in a part of the town remote from the original scene of action, and it does not appear that information had reached him that anything unusual was occurring, until the affair was approaching its termination. Then there was little for him to do. He hastened, however, to the scene, and mounting the ramparts, persuaded the citizens to cease cannonading the discomfited and retiring foe. He felt the full gravity of the situation, and the necessity of diminishing the rancor of the inhabitants against their

* De Thou, ix. 37, and xxvii.

† Hoofd, xix. 834. Bentivoglio, 2, ii. 268, 271. De Thou, loc. cit.

‡ Corte Verclaering. Meteren, xi. 201d. Bor, xvii. 343. Hoofd, xix. 842.

treacherous allies, if such a result were yet possible.* The burghers had done their duty, and it certainly would have been neither in his power nor his inclination to protect the French marauders from expulsion and castigation.

Such was the termination of the French Fury, and it seems sufficiently strange that it should have been so much less disastrous to Antwerp than was the Spanish Fury of 1576, to which men could still scarcely allude without a shudder. One would have thought the French more likely to prove successful in their enterprise than the Spaniards in theirs. The Spaniards were enemies against whom the city had long been on its guard. The French were friends in whose sincerity a somewhat shaken confidence had just been restored. When the Spanish attack was made, a large force of defenders was drawn up in battle array behind freshly strengthened fortifications. When the French entered at leisure through a scarcely guarded gate, the whole population and garrison of the town were quietly eating their dinners. The numbers of the invading forces on the two occasions did not materially differ; but at the time of the French Fury there was not a large force of regular troops under veteran generals to resist the attack. Perhaps this was the main reason for the result, which seems at first almost inexplicable. For protection against the Spanish invasion, the burghers relied on mercenaries, some of whom proved treacherous, while the rest became panic-struck. On the present occasion the burghers relied on themselves. Moreover, the French committed the great error of despising their enemy. Recollecting the ease with which the Spaniards had ravished the city, they believed that they had nothing to do but to enter and take possession. Instead of repressing their greediness, as the Spaniards had done, until they had overcome resistance, they dispersed almost immediately into by-streets, and entered warehouses to search for plunder. They seemed actuated by a fear that they should not have time to rifle the city before additional troops should

* Meteren, xi. 201[d]. Hoofd, xix. 843.—Compare Bentivoglio, 2, ii. 271.

be sent by Anjou to share in the spoil.* They were less used to the sacking of Netherland cities than were the Spaniards, whom long practice had made perfect in the art of methodically butchering a population at first, before attention should be diverted to plundering, and supplementary outrages. At any rate, whatever the causes, it is certain that the panic, which upon such occasions generally decides the fate of the day, seized upon the invaders and not upon the invaded, almost from the very first. As soon as the marauders faltered in their purpose and wished to retreat, it was all over with them. Returning was worse than advance, and it was the almost inevitable result that hardly a man escaped death or capture.

The Duke retreated the same day in the direction of Denremonde, and on his way met with another misfortune, by which an additional number of his troops lost their lives. A dyke was cut by the Mechlin citizens to impede his march, and the swollen waters of the Dill, liberated and flowing across the country which he was to traverse, produced such an inundation, that at least a thousand of his followers were drowned.†

As soon as he had established himself in a camp near Berghem, he opened a correspondence with the Prince of Orange, and with the authorities of Antwerp. His language was marked by wonderful effrontery. He found himself and soldiers suffering for want of food; he remembered that he had left much plate and valuable furniture in Antwerp; and he was therefore desirous that the citizens, whom he had so basely outraged, should at once send him supplies and restore his property. He also reclaimed the prisoners who still remained in the city, and to obtain all this he applied to the man whom he had bitterly deceived, and whose life would have been sacrificed by the Duke, had the enterprise succeeded.‡

It had been his intention to sack the city, to re-establish

* Strada, 2, v. 252. Reidani, ii. 53.

† Meteren, xi. 202b. Hoofd, xx. 848. Strada, 2, v. 251.

‡ Hoofd, xix. 844.—Compare De Thou, t. ix. l. 77.

exclusively the Roman Catholic worship, to trample upon the constitution which he had so recently sworn to maintain, to deprive Orange, by force, of the Renversal by which the Duke recognized the Prince as sovereign of Holland, Zealand, and Utrecht,* yet notwithstanding that his treason had been enacted in broad daylight, and in a most deliberate manner, he had the audacity to ascribe the recent tragic occurrences to chance. He had the farther originality to speak of himself as an aggrieved person, who had rendered great services to the Netherlands, and who had only met with ingratitude in return. His envoys, Messieurs Landmater and Escolières, despatched on the very day of the French Fury to the burgomasters and senate of Antwerp, were instructed to remind those magistrates that the Duke had repeatedly exposed his life in the cause of the Netherlands. The affronts, they were to add, which he had received, and the approaching ruin of the country, which he foresaw, had so altered his excellent nature, as to engender the present calamity, which he infinitely regretted. Nevertheless, the senate was to be assured that his affection for the commonwealth was still so strong, as to induce a desire on his part to be informed what course was now to be pursued with regard to him. Information upon that important point was therefore to be requested, while at the same time the liberation of the prisoners at Antwerp, and the restoration of the Duke's furniture and papers, were to be urgently demanded.†

Letters of similar import were also despatched by the Duke to the states of the Union, while to the Prince of Orange, his application was brief but brazen. "You know well, my cousin," said he, "the just and frequent causes of offence which this people has given me. The insults which I this morning experienced cut me so deeply to the heart, that they are *the only reasons* of the misfortune which has happened to-

* Bor, xvii. 344.

† Bor (xvii. 344, sqq.) gives the instructions, together with the whole correspondence.

day. Nevertheless, to those who desire my friendship I shall show equal friendship and affection. Herein I shall follow the counsel you have uniformly given me, since I know it comes from one who has always loved me. Therefore I beg that you will kindly bring it to pass, that I may obtain some decision, and that no injury may be inflicted upon my people. Otherwise the land shall pay for it dearly."*

To these appeals, neither the Prince nor the authorities of Antwerp answered immediately in their own names. A general consultation was, however, immediately held with the estates-general, and an answer forthwith despatched to the Duke by the hands of his envoys. It was agreed to liberate the prisoners, to restore the furniture, and to send a special deputation for the purpose of making further arrangements with the Duke by word of mouth, and for this deputation his Highness was requested to furnish a safe conduct.†

Anjou was overjoyed when he received this amicable communication. Relieved for a time from his fears as to the result of his crime, he already assumed a higher ground. He not only spoke to the states in a paternal tone, which was sufficiently ludicrous, but he had actually the coolness to *assure them of his forgiveness.* "He felt hurt," he said, "that they should deem a safe conduct necessary for the deputation which they proposed to send. If they thought that *he had reason* on account of the past, to feel offended, he begged them to believe that he had forgotten it all, and that he had buried the past in its ashes, even as if it had never been." He furthermore begged them—and this seemed the greatest insult of all—*in future to trust to his word,* and to believe that if any thing should be attempted to their disadvantage, he would be the very first to offer himself for their protection."‡

It will be observed that in his first letters the Duke had not affected to deny his agency in the outrage—an agency so flagrant that all subterfuge seemed superfluous. He in fact avowed that the attempt had been made by his command, but

* See the letter in Bor, xvii. 345[a]. † Ibid., xvii. 345. ‡ Ibid.

sought to palliate the crime on the ground that it had been the result of the ill-treatment which he had experienced from the states. "The affronts which I have received," said he, both to the magistrates of Antwerp and to Orange, "have engendered the present calamity." So also, in a letter written at the same time to his brother, Henry the Third, he observed that "the indignities which were put upon him, and the manifest intention of the states to make a Matthias of him, had been the cause of the catastrophe."*

He now, however, ventured a step farther. Presuming upon the indulgence which he had already experienced, and bravely assuming the tone of injured innocence, he ascribed the enterprise partly to accident, and partly to the insubordination of his troops. This was the ground which he adopted in his interviews with the states' commissioners. So also, in a letter addressed to Van der Tympel, commandant of Brussels, in which he begged for supplies for his troops, he described the recent invasion of Antwerp as entirely unexpected by himself, and beyond his control. He had been intending, he said, to leave the city and to join his army. A tumult had accidentally arisen between his soldiers and the guard at the gate. Other troops rushing in from without, had joined in the affray, so that to his great sorrow, an extensive disorder had arisen. He manifested the same Christian inclination to forgive, however, which he had before exhibited. He observed that "good men would never grow cold in his regard, or find his affection diminished." He assured Van der Tympel, in particular, of his ancient good-will, as he knew him to be a lover of the common weal.†

In his original communications he had been both cringing and threatening—but, at least, he had not denied truths which were plain as daylight. His new position considerably damaged his cause. This forgiving spirit on the part of the malefactor was a little more than the states could bear, disposed as they felt, from policy, to be indulgent, and to smooth

* Bor gives the letter, xvii. 348.

† See the letter to V. der Tympel in Bor, xvii. 345, 346.

over the crime as gently as possible. The negotiations were interrupted, and the authorities of Antwerp published a brief and spirited defence of their own conduct. They denied that any affront or want of respect on their part could have provoked the outrage of which the Duke had been guilty. They severely handled his self-contradiction, in ascribing originally the recent attempt to his just vengeance for past injuries, and in afterwards imputing it to accident or sudden mutiny, while they cited the simultaneous attempts at Bruges, Denremonde, Alost, Dixmuyde, Newport, Ostend, Vilvoorde, and Dunkirk, as a series of damning proofs of a deliberate design.*

The publication of such plain facts did not advance the negotiations when resumed. High and harsh words were interchanged between his Highness and the commissioners, Anjou complaining, as usual, of affronts and indignities, but when pushed home for particulars, taking refuge in equivocation. "He did not wish," he said, "to re-open wounds which had been partially healed." He also affected benignity, and wishing to forgive and to forget, he offered some articles as the basis of a fresh agreement. Of these it is sufficient to state that they were entirely different from the terms of the Bordeaux treaty, and that they were rejected as quite inadmissible.†

He wrote again to the Prince of Orange,‡ invoking his influence to bring about an arrangement. The Prince, justly indignant at the recent treachery and the present insolence of the man whom he had so profoundly trusted, but feeling certain that the welfare of the country depended at present upon avoiding, if possible, a political catastrophe, answered the Duke in plain, firm, mournful, and appropriate language. He had ever manifested to his Highness, he said, the most uniform and sincere friendship. He had, therefore, the right to tell him that affairs were now so changed that his greatness and glory had departed. Those men in the Netherlands,

* Bor, vii. 346, 347.

† Ibid., xvii. 347.

‡ From Vilvoorde, Jan. 25, 1583. Bor, xvii. 347, 348.

who, but yesterday, had been willing to die at the feet of his Highness, were now so exasperated that they avowedly preferred an open enemy to a treacherous protector. He had hoped, he said, that after what had happened in so many cities at the same moment, his Highness would have been pleased to give the deputies a different and a more becoming answer. He had hoped for some response which might lead to an arrangement. He, however, stated frankly, that the articles transmitted by his Highness were so unreasonable that no man in the land would dare open his mouth to recommend them. His Highness, by this proceeding, had much deepened the distrust. He warned the Duke accordingly, that he was not taking the right course to reinstate himself in a position of honor and glory, and he begged him, therefore, to adopt more appropriate means. Such a step was now demanded of him, not only by the country, but by all Christendom.*

This moderate but heartfelt appeal to the better nature of the Duke, if he had a better nature, met with no immediate response.

While matters were in this condition, a special envoy arrived out of France, despatched by the King and Queen-mother, on the first reception of the recent intelligence from Antwerp.† M. de Mirambeau, the ambassador, whose son had been killed in the Fury, brought letters of credence to the states of the Union and to the Prince of Orange.‡ He delivered also a short confidential note, written in her own hand, from Catherine de Medici to the Prince, to the following effect:—

"My Cousin,—The King, my son, and myself, send you Monsieur de Mirambeau, to prove to you that we do not believe—for we esteem you an honorable man—that you would manifest ingratitude to my son, and to those who have followed him for the welfare of your country. We feel that you have too much affection for one who has the support of so

* The letter is given in Bor, xvii. 348.

† Bor, xvii. 349. Meteren, xi. 202[d].

‡ Bor, Meteren, ubi sup. Hoofd, xx. 849.

powerful a prince as the King of France, as to play him so base a trick. Until I learn the truth, I shall not renounce the good hope which I have always indulged—that you would never have invited my son to your country, without intending to serve him faithfully. As long as you do this, you may ever reckon on the support of all who belong to him.

"Your good Cousin,

"CATHERINE."*

It would have been very difficult to extract much information or much comfort from this wily epistle. The menace was sufficiently plain, the promise disagreeably vague. Moreover, a letter from the same Catherine de Medici, had been recently found in a casket at the Duke's lodgings in Antwerp. In that communication, she had distinctly advised her son to re-establish the Roman Catholic religion, assuring him that by so doing, he would be enabled to marry the Infanta of Spain.† Nevertheless, the Prince, convinced that it was his duty to bridge over the deep and fatal chasm which had opened between the French Prince and the provinces, if an honorable reconciliation were possible, did not attach an undue importance either to the stimulating or to the upbraiding portion of the communication from Catherine. He was most anxious to avert the chaos which he saw returning. He knew that while the tempers of Rudolph, of the English Queen, and of the Protestant princes of Germany, and the internal condition of the Netherlands remained the same, it were madness to provoke the government of France, and thus gain an additional enemy, while losing their only friend. He did not renounce the hope of forming all the Netherlands—excepting of course the Walloon provinces already reconciled to Philip—into one

* Archives et Correspondance, viii. 148. Bor, xvii, 349.

† Hoofd is the authority for the anecdote, having heard it related by old inhabitants of the place. "Replantez la Religion Catholique dans Anvers," said Catherine, "et je me fais fort que vous vous marierez avec l'Infante d'Espagne."—xx. 846.—Compare Strada, 2, v. 258, who alludes to the rumour which was spread "either by Anjou or by Orange," that a marriage between the Duke and the Infanta was in contemplation, and that Parma was privy to the scheme.

independent commonwealth, freed for ever from Spanish tyranny. A dynasty from a foreign house he was willing to accept, but only on condition that the new royal line should become naturalized in the Netherlands, should conform itself to the strict constitutional compact established, and should employ only natives in the administration of Netherland affairs. Notwithstanding, therefore, the recent treachery of Anjou, he was willing to treat with him upon the ancient basis. The dilemma was a very desperate one, for whatever might be his course, it was impossible that it should escape censure. Even at this day, it is difficult to decide what might have been the result of openly braving the French government, and expelling Anjou. The Prince of Parma—subtle, vigilant, prompt with word and blow—was waiting most anxiously to take advantage of every false step of his adversary. The provinces had been already summoned in most eloquent language, to take warning by the recent fate of Antwerp, and to learn by the manifestation just made by Anjou, of his real intentions, that their only salvation lay in a return to the King's arms.* Anjou himself, as devoid of shame as of honor, was secretly holding interviews with Parma's agents, Acosta and Flaminio Carnero,† at the very moment when he was alternately expressing to the states his resentment that they dared to doubt his truth, or magnanimously extending to them his pardon for their suspicions. He was writing letters full of injured innocence to Orange and to the states, while secretly cavilling over the terms of the treaty by which he was to sell himself to Spain. Scruples as to enacting so base a part did not trouble the "Son of France." He did not hesitate at playing this doubly and trebly false game with the provinces, but he was anxious to drive the best possible bargain for himself with Parma. He offered to restore Dunkirk, Dixmuyde, and the other cities which he had so recently filched from the states, and to enter into a strict alliance with Philip; but he claimed that certain

* Bor, xvii. 348, sqq. Meteren, xi. 202[d]. Hoofd, xx. 849.

† Strada, ii. 257.

Netherland cities on the French frontier, should be made over to him in exchange. He required, likewise, ample protection for his retreat from a country which was likely to be sufficiently exasperated. Parma and his agents smiled, of course, at such exorbitant terms.* Nevertheless, it was necessary to deal cautiously with a man who, although but a poor baffled rogue to-day, might to-morrow be seated on the throne of France. While they were all secretly haggling over the terms of the bargain, the Prince of Orange discovered the intrigue.† It convinced him of the necessity of closing with a man whose baseness was so profound, but whose position made his enmity, on the whole, more dangerous than his friendship. Anjou, backed by so astute and unscrupulous a politician as Parma, was not to be trifled with. The feeling of doubt and anxiety was spreading daily through the country : many men, hitherto firm, were already wavering, while at the same time the Prince had no confidence in the power of any of the states, save those of Holland and Utrecht, to maintain a resolute attitude of defiance, if not assisted from without.

He therefore endeavored to repair the breach, if possible, and thus save the Union. Mirambeau, in his conferences with the estates, suggested, on his part, all that words could effect. He expressed the hope that the estates would use their discretion "in compounding some sweet and friendly medicine" for the present disorder ; and that they would not judge the Duke too harshly for a fault which he assured them did not come from his natural disposition. He warned them that the enemy would be quick to take advantage of the present occasion to bring about, if possible, their destruction, and he added that he was commissioned to wait upon the Duke of Anjou, in order to assure him that, however alienated he might then be from the Netherlands, his Majesty was determined to effect an entire reconciliation.‡

The envoy conferred also with the Prince of Orange, and

* Strada, ii. 255–257. † Ibid., 257.

‡ Bor, xvii. 349.—Compare Meteren, xi. 202, 203. Hoofd, xx. 850.

urged him most earnestly to use his efforts to heal the rupture. The Prince, inspired by the sentiments already indicated, spoke with perfect sincerity. His Highness, he said, had never known a more faithful and zealous friend than himself. He had begun to lose his own credit with the people by reason of the earnestness with which he had ever advocated the Duke's cause, and he could not flatter himself that his recommendation would now be of any advantage to his Highness. It would be more injurious than his silence. Nevertheless, he was willing to make use of all the influence which was left to him for the purpose of bringing about a reconciliation, provided that the Duke were acting in good faith. If his Highness were now sincerely desirous of conforming to the *original treaty*, and willing to atone for the faults *committed by him on the same day in so many cities*—offences which could not be excused upon the ground of any affronts which he might have received from the citizens of Antwerp—it might even now be possible to find a remedy for the past. He very bluntly told the envoy, however, that the frivolous excuses offered by the Duke caused more bitterness than if he had openly acknowledged his fault. It were better, he said, to express contrition, than to excuse himself by laying blame on those to whom no blame belonged, but who, on the contrary, had ever shown themselves faithful servants of his Highness.*

The estates of the Union, being in great perplexity as to their proper course, now applied formally, as they always did in times of danger and doubt, to the Prince, for a public expression of his views.† Somewhat reluctantly, he complied with their wishes in one of the most admirable of his state papers.‡

He told the states that he felt some hesitation in expressing his views. The blame of the general ill success was always laid upon his shoulders; as if the chances of war could be controlled even by a great potentate with ample means at his

* Bor, xvii. 349. † Ibid. Meteren, xi. 203b. Hoofd, xx. 851.

‡ It is given in full by Bor, xvii. 349–354, and abridged by Meteren, xi. 203–205, and by Hoofd, xx. 851–856.

disposal. As for himself, with so little actual power that he could never have a single city provided with what he thought a sufficient garrison, it could not be expected that he could command fortune. His advice, he said, was always asked, but ever judged good or evil according to the result, as if the issue were in any hands but God's. It did not seem advisable for a man of his condition and years, who had so often felt the barb of calumny's tongue, to place his honor again in the judgment scale of mankind, particularly as he was likely to incur fresh censure for another man's crime.* Nevertheless, he was willing, for the love he bore the land, once more to encounter this danger.

He then rapidly reviewed the circumstances which had led to the election of Anjou, and reminded the estates that they had employed sufficient time to deliberate concerning that transaction. He recalled to their remembrance his frequent assurances of support and sympathy if they would provide any other means of self-protection than the treaty with the French Prince. He thought it, therefore, unjust, now that calamity had sprung from the measure, to ascribe the blame entirely to him, even had the injury been greater than the one actually sustained. He was far from palliating the crime, or from denying that the Duke's rights under the Treaty of Bordeaux had been utterly forfeited. He was now asked what was to be done. Of three courses, he said, one must be taken: they must make their peace with the King, or consent to a reconciliation with Anjou, or use all the strength which God had given them to resist, single-handed, the enemy. With regard to the first point, he resumed the argument as to the hopelessness of a satisfactory arrangement with the monarch of Spain. The recent reconciliation of the Walloon provinces

* The Prince was always keenly sensitive to attacks upon his honor. On the other hand, he was singularly exempt from "the last infirmity of noble minds." "To reply to what men tell me—*namely, that I have rendered my name sufficiently famous*," he observed in a remarkable letter to his brother, at this period, "seems quite superfluous, *since never did such vanity* move me to so much labor, so many losses, and to confront such dangerous enmities."—Archives et Correspondance, viii. 354, 355.

and its shameful infraction by Parma in the immediate recal of large masses of Spanish and Italian troops, showed too plainly the value of all solemn stipulations with his Catholic Majesty. Moreover, the time was unpropitious. It was idle to look, after what had recently occurred, for even fair promises. It was madness then to incur the enmity of two such powers at once. The French could do the Netherlands more harm as enemies than the Spaniards. The Spaniards would be more dangerous as friends, for in cases of a treaty with Philip, the Inquisition would be established in the place of a religious peace. For these reasons the Prince declared himself entirely opposed to any negotiations with the Crown of Spain.

As to the second point, he admitted that Anjou had gained little honor by his recent course, and that it would be a mistake on their part to stumble a second time over the same stone. He foresaw, nevertheless, that the Duke—irritated as he was by the loss of so many of his nobles, and by the downfall of all his hopes in the Netherlands—would be likely to inflict great injuries upon their cause. Two powerful nations like France and Spain would be too much to have on their hands at once. How much danger, too, would be incurred by braving at once the open wrath of the French King and the secret displeasure of the English Queen. She had warmly recommended the Duke of Anjou. She had said that honors to him were rendered to herself, and she was now entirely opposed to their keeping the present quarrel alive.* If France became their enemy, the road was at once opened through that kingdom for Spain. The estates were to ponder well

* Discourse of Orange, apud Bor, loc. cit.—"—— vous conseiller et vous admonestrer," wrote Elizabeth to the states-general, "que vous donnez bien garde d'offencer un Prince de sa qualité —— aijant déjà par *le mépris passé refroidi beaucoup en lui la première affection* qu'il vous portoit. (!) Car vous pourriez aisement penser que s'il est *si avant irrité par telles façons* de faire qu'il en devienne votre ennemi. Celui sera chose assez facile de se venger sur vous avec les moyens et la force que son frère lui pourra mettre en main," etc.—Lettre de la Serme Roine d'Anglet. MS., 20 Ap., 1583. Ord. Dep. Boek der St.-gl., Ao. 1582–1583, f. 557vo.—Compare Elizabeth's instructions to Sir John Somers, special envoy to the Duke of Anjou; Meteren, xi. 203.

whether they possessed the means to carry on such a double war without assistance. They were likewise to remember how many cities still remained in the hands of Anjou, and their possible fate if the Duke were pushed to extremity.

The third point was then handled with vigor. He reminded the states of the perpetual difficulty of raising armies, of collecting money to pay for troops, of inducing cities to accept proper garrisons, of establishing a council which could make itself respected. He alluded briefly and bitterly to the perpetual quarrels of the states among themselves; to their mutual jealousy; to their obstinate parsimony; to their jealousy of the general government; to their apathy and inertness before impending ruin. He would not calumniate those, he said, who counselled trust in God. That was his sentiment also. To attempt great affairs, however, and, through avarice, to withhold sufficient means, was not trusting, but tempting God. On the contrary, it was trusting God to use the means which He offered to their hands.

With regard, then, to the three points, he rejected the first. Reconciliation with the King of Spain was impossible. For his own part, he would much *prefer the third course.* He had always been in favor of their maintaining independence by their own means and the assistance of the Almighty. He was obliged, however, in sadness, to confess that the narrow feeling of individual state rights, the general tendency to disunion, and the constant wrangling, had made this course a hopeless one. There remained, therefore, only the second, and they must effect an honorable reconciliation with Anjou. Whatever might be their decision, however, it was meet that it should be a speedy one. Not an hour was to be lost. Many fair churches of God, in Anjou's power, were trembling on the issue, and religious and political liberty was more at stake than ever. In conclusion, the Prince again expressed his determination, whatever might be their decision, to devote the rest of his days to the services of his country.*

* Discourse of Orange, etc.

The result of these representations by the Prince—of frequent letters from Queen Elizabeth,* urging a reconciliation—and of the professions made by the Duke and the French envoys, was a provisional arrangement, signed on the 26th and 28th of March. According to the terms of this accord, the Duke was to receive thirty thousand florins for his troops, and to surrender the cities still in his power. The French prisoners were to be liberated, the Duke's property at Antwerp was to be restored, and the Duke himself was to await at Dunkirk the arrival of plenipotentiaries to treat with him as to a new and perpetual arrangement.†

The negotiations, however, were languid. The quarrel was healed on the surface, but confidence so recently and violently uprooted was slow to revive. On the 28th of June, the Duke of Anjou left Dunkirk for Paris, never to return to the Netherlands, but he exchanged on his departure affectionate letters with the Prince and the estates. M. des Pruneaux remained as his representative, and it was understood that the arrangements for re-installing him as soon as possible in the sovereignty which he had so basely forfeited, were to be pushed forward with earnestness.‡

In the spring of the same year, Gerard Truchses, Archbishop of Cologne, who had lost his see for the love of Agnes Mansfeld, whom he had espoused in defiance of the Pope, took refuge with the Prince of Orange at Delft.§ A civil war in Germany broke forth, the Protestant princes undertaking to support the Archbishop, in opposition to Ernest of Bavaria, who had been appointed in his place. The Palatine, John Casimir, thought it necessary to mount and ride as usual. Making his appearance at the head of a hastily collected force, and prepared for another plunge into chaos, he suddenly heard, however, of his elder brother's death at Heidelberg. Leaving his men, as was his habit, to shift for themselves, and Baron

* Meteren, xi. 203.

† See the Accord, in twenty-one articles, in Bor, xvii. 355–357.

‡ Bor, xviii. 371, 372, sqq. Meteren, xi. 206c.

§ Bor, xviii. 360, 361.

Truchses, the Archbishop's brother, to fall into the hands of the enemy, he disappeared from the scene with great rapidity, in order that his own interests in the palatinate and in the guardianship of the young palatines might not suffer by his absence.*

At this time, too, on the 12th of April, the Prince of Orange was married, for the fourth time, to Louisa, widow of the Seigneur de Teligny, and daughter of the illustrious Coligny.†

In the course of the summer, the states of Holland and Zealand, always bitterly opposed to the connection with Anjou, and more than ever dissatisfied with the resumption of negotiations since the Antwerp catastrophe, sent a committee to the Prince in order to persuade him to set his face against the whole proceedings. They delivered at the same time a formal remonstrance, in writing (25th of August, 1583), in which they explained how odious the arrangement with the Duke had ever been to them. They expressed the opinion that even the wisest might be sometimes mistaken, and that the Prince had been bitterly deceived by Anjou and by the French court. They besought him to rely upon the assistance of the Almighty, and upon the exertions of the nation, and they again hinted at the propriety of his accepting that supreme sovereignty over all the united provinces which would be so gladly conferred, while, for their own parts, they voluntarily offered largely to increase the sums annually contributed to the common defence.‡

Very soon afterwards, in August, 1583, the states of the united provinces assembled at Middelburg formally offered the general government—which under the circumstances was the general sovereignty—to the Prince, warmly urging his acceptance of the dignity. He manifested, however, the same reluctance which he had always expressed, demanding that the project should beforehand be laid before the councils of all the large cities, and before the estates of certain provinces

---

* Bor, ubi sup.

† Bor, xviii. 366. Meteren, xi. 205. Hoofd, xx. 864.

‡ Bor, xviii. 397, 398.

which had not been represented at the Middelburg diet. He also made use of the occasion to urge the necessity of providing more generously for the army expenses and other general disbursements. As to ambitious views, he was a stranger to them, and his language at this moment was as patriotic and self-denying as at any previous period. He expressed his thanks to the estates for this renewed proof of their confidence in his character, and this additional approbation of his course, —a sentiment which he was always ready "as a good patriot to justify by his most faithful service." He reminded them, however, that he was no great monarch, having in his own hands the means to help and the power to liberate them; and that even were he in possession of all which God had once given him, he should be far from strong enough to resist, single-handed, their powerful enemy. All that was left to him, he said, was an "honest and moderate experience in affairs." With this he was ever ready to serve them to the utmost; but they knew very well that the means to make that experience available were to be drawn from the country itself. With modest simplicity, he observed that he had been at work fifteen or sixteen years, doing his best, with the grace of God, to secure the freedom of the fatherland and to resist tyranny of conscience; that he alone—assisted by his brothers and some friends and relatives—had borne the whole burthen in the beginning, and that he had afterwards been helped by the states of Holland and Zealand, so that he could not but render thanks to God for His great mercy in thus granting His blessing to so humble an instrument, and thus restoring so many beautiful provinces to their ancient freedom and to the true religion. The Prince protested that this result was already a sufficient reward for his labors—a great consolation in his sufferings. He had hoped, he said, that the estates, "taking into consideration his long-continued labors, would have been willing to excuse him from a new load of cares, and would have granted him some little rest in his already advanced age;" that they would have selected "some other person more fitted for the labor, whom he would himself faithfully promise to assist to the best of his abilities, rendering him willing obedience proportionate to the authority conferred upon him."*

Like all other attempts to induce the acceptance, by the Prince, of supreme authority, this effort proved ineffectual, from the obstinate unwillingness of his hand to receive the proffered sceptre.

In connection with this movement, and at about the same epoch, Jacob Swerius, member of the Brabant Council, with other deputies, waited upon Orange, and formally tendered him the sovereign dukedom of Brabant,† forfeited and vacant by the late crime of Anjou. The Prince, however, resolutely refused to accept the dignity, assuring the committee that he had not the means to afford the country as much protection as they had a right to expect from their sovereign. He added that "he would never give the King of Spain the right to say that the Prince of Orange had been actuated by no other motives in his career than the hope of self-aggrandizement, and the desire to deprive his Majesty of the provinces in order to appropriate them to himself."‡

Accordingly, firmly refusing to heed the overtures of the United States, and of Holland in particular, he continued to further the re-establishment of Anjou—a measure in which, as he deliberately believed, lay the only chance of union and independence.

The Prince of Parma, meantime, had not been idle. He had been unable to induce the provinces to listen to his wiles, and to rush to the embrace of the monarch whose arms he described as ever open to the repentant. He had, however, been busily occupied in the course of the summer in taking

* Message of Orange to the states-general, MS.—"Ghe exhibeert by sijne Exe[tie] den vi. Sept., 1583." Ordinaris Depêchen Boek der St.-gl. A°. 1583, 1584, f. 21, 22, Hague Archives. This very important and characteristic document has never been published.

† Bor, xix. 455[b], who had his information from Jacob Swerius himself.—Compare Wagenaer, vii. 484.

‡ "Maer dat het syne Excellentie afsloeg seggende den middel van sich selven niet te hebben om dat te beschermen en dat hy ook de Koning van Spangien geen oorsake wilde geven te seggen dat hy anders niet hadde gesocht dan hem alle sijne landen of te nemen."—Bor, loc. cit.

up many of the towns which the treason of Anjou had laid open to his attacks.*

Eindhoven, Diest, Dunkirk, Newport, and other places, were successively surrendered to royalist generals.† On the 22nd of September, 1583, the city of Zutfen, too, was surprised by Colonel Tassis, on the fall of which most important place, the treason of Orange's brother-in-law, Count Van den Berg, governor of Gueldres, was revealed. His fidelity had been long suspected, particularly by Count John of Nassau, but always earnestly vouched for by his wife and by his sons.‡ On the capture of Zutfen, however, a document was found and made public, by which Van den Berg bound himself to deliver the principal cities of Gueldres and Zutfen, beginning with Zutfen itself, into the hands of Parma, on condition of receiving the pardon and friendship of the King.§

Not much better could have been expected of Van den Berg. His pusillanimous retreat from his post in Alva's time will be recollected; and it is certain that the Prince had never placed implicit confidence in his character. Nevertheless, it was the fate of this great man to be often deceived by the friends whom he trusted, although never to be outwitted by his enemies. Van den Berg was arrested, on the 15th of November, carried to the Hague, examined and imprisoned for a time in Delftshaven. After a time he was, however, liberated, when he instantly, with all his sons, took service under the King.||

* Strada, 2, v. 259, sqq.

† Bor, xviii. 366, 367, 371, 372. Strada, 2, v. 259–266. Meteren, xi. 206, 207. Hoofd, xx. 866–872. Tassis, vi. 436, 437, 440.

‡ See the letters of the various members of the family in Archives et Correspondance, vii., passim.

§ See the Agreement (signed and sealed upon the 25th of August, 1583), apud Bor, 3, xviii. 402. He had succeeded Count John in the stadholderate of Gueldres in 1581, but the appointment had never been particularly agreeable to the Prince of Orange. When applied to by Van den Berg for a recommendation, he had thus addressed the estates of Gueldres, "My brother-in-law, desirous of obtaining the government of your province, has asked for my recommendation. He professes the greatest enthusiasm for the service and the just cause of the fatherland. I could wish that he had shown it sooner. Nevertheless, 'tis better late than never."—Ev. Reid., 37. Hoofd, xx. 875.

|| Bor, xviii. 402. Hoofd, xx. 875. Archives et Corresp., viii. 288, sqq.

While treason was thus favoring the royal arms in the north, the same powerful element, to which so much of the Netherland misfortunes had always been owing, was busy in Flanders.

Towards the end of the year 1583, the Prince of Chimay, eldest son of the Duke of Aerschot, had been elected governor of that province.* This noble was as unstable in character, as vain, as unscrupulous, and as ambitious as his father and uncle. He had been originally desirous of espousing the eldest daughter of the Prince of Orange, afterwards the Countess of Hohenlo, but the Duchess of Aerschot was too strict a Catholic to consent to the marriage,† and her son was afterwards united to the Countess of Meghem, widow of Lancelot Berlaymont.‡

As affairs seemed going on prosperously for the states in the beginning of this year, the Prince of Chimay had affected a strong inclination for the Reformed religion, and as governor of Bruges, he had appointed many members of that Church to important offices, to the exclusion of Catholics. By so decided a course, he acquired the confidence of the patriot party and at the end of the year he became governor of Flanders. No sooner was he installed in this post, than he opened a private correspondence with Parma, for it was his intention to make his peace with the King, and to purchase pardon and advancement by the brilliant service which he now undertook, of restoring this important province to the royal authority. In the arrangement of his plans he was assisted by Champagny, who, as will be recollected, had long been a prisoner in Ghent, but whose confinement was not so strict as to prevent frequent intercourse with his friends without.§ Champagny was indeed believed to be the life of the whole intrigue. The plot was, however, forwarded by Imbize, the roaring

* Bor, xviii. 406, sqq. Meteren, xi. 206, 207. † Meteren, xii. 209.

‡ The same lady whose charms and whose dower had so fatal an influence upon the career of Count Renneberg.

§ Bor, xviii. 406. Meteren, xii. 211. Ev. Reidani, iii. 55.

demagogue whose republicanism could never reconcile itself with what he esteemed the aristocratic policy of Orange, and whose stern puritanism could be satisfied with nothing short of a general extermination of Catholics. This man, after having been allowed to depart, infamous and contemptible, from the city which he had endangered, now ventured after five years, to return, and to engage in fresh schemes which were even more criminal than his previous enterprises. The uncompromising foe to Romanism, the advocate of Grecian and Genevan democracy, now allied himself with Champagny and with Chimay, to effect a surrender of Flanders to Philip and to the Inquisition. He succeeded in getting himself elected chief senator in Ghent, and forthwith began to use all his influence to further the secret plot.* The joint efforts and intrigues of Parma, Champagny, Chimay, and Imbize, were near being successful. Early in the spring of 1584 a formal resolution was passed by the government of Ghent, to open negotiations with Parma. Hostages were accordingly exchanged, and a truce of three weeks was agreed upon, during which an animated correspondence was maintained between the authorities of Ghent and the Prince of Chimay on the one side, and the United States-general, the magistracy of Antwerp, the states of Brabant, and other important bodies on the other.

The friends of the Union and of liberty used all their eloquence to arrest the city of Ghent in its course, and to save the province of Flanders from accepting the proposed arrangement with Parma. The people of Ghent were reminded that the chief promoter of this new negotiation was Champagny,† a man

---

* Bor, xviii. 407. Meteren, xii. 211, 212. Hoofd, xx. 885, 886. Van der Vynckt, iii. 104–110.

† Bor, xviii. 407, 410–419.—"There is a report," wrote the Prince of Orange to the magistracy of Ghent, "that a passport has been given to one of our most especial enemies (eenen van onse partiaelste vyanden) to come within the city of Ghent in order to converse with Champagny by word of mouth (mondelinge met Champigny te spreecken)."—Letter of 31 May, in de Jonge, Onuitgegevene Stukken. 's Gravenhage und Amsterdam, 1827. "'Tis Champagny who is at the bottom of all these proceedings," wrote the states of Brabant to the magistrates of Ghent.—Letter of March 14, in Bor, xviii. 415, 416.

who owed a deep debt of hatred to their city, for the long, and as he believed, the unjust confinement which he had endured within its walls. Moreover, he was the brother of Granvelle, source of all their woes. To take counsel with Champagny, was to come within reach of a deadly foe, for "he who confesses himself to a wolf," said the burgomasters of Antwerp, "will get wolf's absolution." The Flemings were warned by all their correspondents that it was puerile to hope for faith in Philip ; a monarch whose first principle was, that promises to heretics were void. They were entreated to pay no heed to the "sweet singing of the royalists," who just then affected to disapprove of the practice adopted by the Spanish Inquisition, that they might more surely separate them from their friends. "Imitate not," said the magistrates of Brussels, "the foolish sheep who made with the wolves a treaty of perpetual amity, from which the faithful dogs were to be excluded." It was affirmed—and the truth was certainly beyond peradventure—that religious liberty was dead at the moment when the treaty with Parma should be signed. "To look for political privilege or evangelical liberty," said the Antwerp authorities, "in any arrangement with the Spaniards, is to look for light in darkness, for fire in water." "Philip is himself the slave of the Inquisition," said the states-general, and has but one great purpose in life—to cherish the institution everywhere, and particularly in the Netherlands. Before Margaret of Parma's time, one hundred thousand Netherlanders had been burned or strangled, and Alva had spent seven years in butchering and torturing many thousands more." The magistrates of Brussels used similar expressions.* "The King of Spain," said they to their brethren of Ghent, "is fastened to the Inquisition. Yea, he is so much in its power, that even if he desired, he is unable to maintain his promises."† The Prince of Orange

* Letter of the burgomasters of Antwerp to the authorities of Ghent, in Bor, xviii. 417. Letter from the magistrates of Brussels to those of Ghent, March 16, 1584.—Bor, xviii. 414. Letter of states-general to Prince of Chimay and the bailiffs of Bruges, March 17, 1584.—Bor, 3, xviii. 410b.

† Letter of magistrates of Brussels.—Bor, xviii. 414.

too, was indefatigable in public and private efforts to counteract the machinations of Parma and the Spanish party in Ghent. He saw with horror the progress which the political decomposition of that most important commonwealth was making, for he considered the city the keystone to the union of the provinces, for he felt with a prophetic instinct that its loss would entail that of all the southern provinces, and make a united and independent Netherland state impossible. Already in the summer of 1583, he addressed a letter full of wisdom and of warning to the authorities of Ghent, a letter in which he set fully before them the iniquity and stupidity of their proceedings, while at the same time he expressed himself with so much dexterity and caution as to avoid giving offence, by accusations which he made, as it were, hypothetically, when, in truth, they were real ones.*

These remonstrances were not fruitless, and the authorities and citizens of Ghent once more paused ere they stepped from the precipice. While they were thus wavering, the whole negotiation with Parma was abruptly brought to a close by a new incident, the demagogue Imbize having been discovered in a secret attempt to obtain possession of the city of Denremonde, and deliver it to Parma.† The old acquaintance, ally, and enemy of Imbize, the Seigneur de Ryhove, was commandant of the city, and information was privately conveyed to him of the design, before there had been time for its accomplishment. Ryhove, being thoroughly on his guard, arrested his old comrade, who was shortly afterwards brought to trial, and executed at Ghent.‡ John van Imbize had returned to the city from which the contemptuous mercy of Orange had permitted him formerly to depart, only to expiate fresh turbulence and fresh treason by a felon's death. Meanwhile the

* The letter is published, together with others of great interest, by De Jonge, Onuitgegevene Stukken., 84–92.

† Bor, xviii. 420. Meteren, xi. 212. Hoofd, xx. 886. Van der Vynckt, iii. 105–110.

‡ Van der Vynckt, iii. 110. Meteren, xii. 213. In the month of August. 1584.

citizens of Ghent, thus warned by word and deed, passed an earnest resolution to have no more intercourse with Parma, but to abide faithfully by the union.* Their example was followed by the other Flemish cities, excepting, unfortunately, Bruges, for that important town, being entirely in the power of Chimay, was now surrendered by him to the royal government. On the 20th of May, 1584, Baron Montigny, on the part of Parma, signed an accord with the Prince of Chimay, by which the city was restored to his Majesty, and by which all inhabitants not willing to abide by the Roman Catholic religion were permitted to leave the land. The Prince was received with favor by Parma, on conclusion of the transaction, and subsequently met with advancement from the King, while the Princess, who had embraced the Reformed religion, retired to Holland.†

The only other city of importance gained on this occasion by the government was Ypres, which had been long besieged, and was soon afterwards forced to yield. The new Bishop, on taking possession, resorted to instant measures for cleansing a place which had been so long in the hands of the infidels, and as the first step in this purification, the bodies of many heretics who had been buried for years were taken from their graves, and publicly hanged in their coffins. All living adherents to the Reformed religion were instantly expelled from the place.‡

Ghent and the rest of Flanders were, for the time, saved from the power of Spain, the inhabitants being confirmed in their resolution of sustaining their union with the other provinces by the news from France. Early in the spring the negotiations between Anjou and the states-general had been earnestly renewed, and Junius, Mouillerie, and Asseliers, had been despatched on a special mission to France, for the purpose of arranging a treaty with the Duke. On the 19th of April, 1584, they arrived in Delft, on their return, bringing warm letters from the French court, full of promises to assist the Netherlands ; and it was understood that a constitution, upon

---

* Bor, xviii. 420. † Ibid., xviii. 420–423. ‡ Ibid., 425. Hoofd, xx. 887.

the basis of the original arrangement of Bordeaux, would be accepted by the Duke.* These arrangements were, however, for ever terminated by the death of Anjou, who had been ill during the whole course of the negotiations. On the 10th of June, 1584, he expired at Chateau Thierry, in great torture, sweating blood from every pore, and under circumstances which, as usual, suggested strong suspicions of poison.†

* Bor, xviii. 423.

† Bor, xviii. 426. Meteren, xii. 214. Hoofd, xx. 890, 891. Ev. Reidani, iii. 54. De Thou, ix. 181–184.

CHAPTER VII.

Various attempts upon the life of Orange—Delft—Mansion of the Prince described—Francis Guion or Balthazar Gérard—His antecedents—His correspondence and interviews with Parma and with d'Assonleville—His employment in France—His return to Delft and interview with Orange—The crime—The confession—The punishment—The consequences—Concluding remarks.

It has been seen that the Ban against the Prince of Orange had not been hitherto without fruits, for although unsuccessful, the efforts to take his life and earn the promised guerdon had been incessant. The attempt of Jaureguy, at Antwerp, of Salseda and Baza at Bruges, have been related, and in March, 1583, moreover, one Pietro Dordogno was executed in Antwerp for endeavoring to assassinate the Prince. Before his death, he confessed that he had come from Spain solely for the purpose, and that he had conferred with La Motte, governor of Gravelines, as to the best means of accomplishing his design.* In April, 1584, Hans Hanzoon, a merchant of Flushing, had been executed for attempting to destroy the Prince by means of gunpowder, concealed under his house in that city, and under his seat in the church. He confessed that he had deliberately formed the intention of performing the deed, and that he had discussed the details of the enterprise with the Spanish ambassador in Paris.† At about the

* Meteren, xi. 205d.

† Ibid. Bor, xviii. 423. Hoofd, xx. 892.

same time, one Le Goth, a captive French officer, had been applied to by the Marquis de Richebourg, on the part of Alexander of Parma, to attempt the murder of the Prince. Le Goth had consented, saying that nothing could be more easily done ; and that he would undertake to poison him in a dish of eels, of which he knew him to be particularly fond. The Frenchman was liberated with this understanding ; but being very much the friend of Orange, straightway told him the whole story, and remained ever afterwards a faithful servant of the states.* It is to be presumed that he excused the treachery to which he owed his escape from prison on the ground that faith was no more to be kept with murderers than with heretics. Thus within two years there had been five distinct attempts to assassinate the Prince, all of them with the privity of the Spanish government. A sixth was soon to follow.

In the summer of 1584, William of Orange was residing at Delft,† where his wife, Louisa de Coligny, had given birth, in the preceding winter, to a son, afterwards the celebrated stadholder, Frederic Henry. The child had received these names from his two godfathers, the Kings of Denmark and of Navarre, and his baptism had been celebrated with much rejoicing on the 12th of June, in the place of his birth.‡

It was a quiet, cheerful, yet somewhat drowsy little city, that ancient burgh of Delft. The placid canals by which it was intersected in every direction were all planted with

---

* Meteren, xi. 205, 206. Hoofd, xx. 891, 892. He is sometimes called Gott.

† He had removed thither from Antwerp on the 22nd July, 1583. His departure from the commercial metropolis had been hastened by an indignity offered to him by a portion of the populace, on the occasion of some building which had been undertaken in the neighbourhood of the citadel. A senseless rumor had been circulated that the Prince had filled the castle with French troops, and was about to surrender it to Anjou. Although the falsehood of the report had been publicly demonstrated, and although the better portion of the citizens felt indignant at its existence, yet the calumniators had not been punished. The Prince, justly aggrieved, retired accordingly from the city.—Meteren, xi. 207, 208.

‡ Bor, xviii. 407[b]. Hoofd. xx. 883

whispering, umbrageous rows of limes and poplars, and along these watery highways the traffic of the place glided so noiselessly that the town seemed the abode of silence and tranquillity. The streets were clean and airy, the houses well built, the whole aspect of the place thriving.

One of the principal thoroughfares was called the old Delft-street. It was shaded on both sides by lime trees, which in that midsummer season covered the surface of the canal which flowed between them with their light and fragrant blossoms. On one side of this street was the "old kirk," a plain, antique structure of brick, with lancet windows, and with a tall, slender tower, which inclined, at a very considerable angle, towards a house upon the other side of the canal. That house was the mansion of Wiliam the Silent. It stood directly opposite the church, being separated by a spacious courtyard from the street, while the stables and other offices in the rear extended to the city wall. A narrow lane, opening out of Delft-street, ran along the side of the house and court, in the direction of the ramparts. The house was a plain, two-storied edifice of brick, with red-tiled roof, and had formerly been a cloister dedicated to Saint Agatha, the last prior of which had been hanged by the furious Lumey de la Marck.

The news of Anjou's death had been brought to Delft by a special messenger from the French court. On Sunday morning, the 8th of July, 1584, the Prince of Orange, having read the despatches before leaving his bed, caused the man who had brought them to be summoned, that he might give some particular details by word of mouth concerning the last illness of the Duke.* The courier was accordingly admitted to the Prince's bed-chamber, and proved to be one Francis Guion, as he called himself. This man had, early in the spring, claimed and received the protection of Orange, on the ground of being the son of a Protestant at Besançon, who had suffered death for his religion, and of his own ardent attachment to the

* Bor, xviii. 427, sqq. Meteren, xii. 214, sqq. Hoofd, xx. 892–894, sqq. Wagenaer, vii. 529, sqq. Le Petit, Grande Chronique des P. B., liv. v.

Reformed faith.* A pious, psalm-singing, thoroughly Calvinistic youth he seemed to be, having a bible or a hymn-book under his arm whenever he walked the street, and most exemplary in his attendance at sermon and lecture. For the rest, a singularly unobtrusive personage, twenty-seven years of age, low of stature, meagre, mean-visaged, muddy complexioned, and altogether a man of no account—quite insignificant in the eyes of all who looked upon him. If there were one opinion in which the few who had taken the trouble to think of the puny, somewhat shambling stranger from Burgundy at all coincided, it was that he was inoffensive, but quite incapable of any important business. He seemed well educated, claimed to be of respectable parentage, and had

* The main source from which the historians cited in the last note, and all other writers, have derived their account of Balthazar Gérard, his crime and punishment, is the official statement drawn up by order of the States-general, entitled, "Verhaal van de moort ghedaen aen den personne des doorluchtigen fursten ende heeren Wilhelms Prince van Oraengien," etc., etc., Delft, A°. 1584, of which a copy may be found in the Duncan collection in the Royal Library at the Hague. The basis of this account was the confession of Balthazar, written in the convent of Saint Agatha (or Prinzen Hof, the residence of Orange) immediately after his arrest, together with his answers to the interrogatories between the 10th and 14th of July. The confession has been recently published by M. Gachard (Acad. Roy. de Belg. t. xx. N°. 9, Bulletins) from an old and probably contemporaneous MS. copy. A very curious pamphlet—a copy of which also may be found in the Duncan Collection—should also be consulted, called "Historie Balthazars Geraert, alias Serach, die den Tyran van 't Nederlandt den Princen van Orangie doorschoten heeft: ende is darom duer grouwelijcke ende vele tormenten binnen de stadt van Delft openbaerlijck ghedoodt, 1584," (with no name of place or publisher.) This account, by a very bitter royalist and papist—perhaps a personal acquaintance of Gérard—extols the deed to the skies, and depicts the horrible sufferings of the malefactor as those of a blessed martyr. A manuscript in the Bibliothèque de Bourgogne (now the MS. section of the Royal Library at Brussels), entitled, "Particularités touchant Balthazar Gérard," No. 17,386, contains many important documents, letters of Parma, of Gérard, and of Cornelius Aertsens. The fifth volume of the MS. history of Renom de France has a chapter devoted to the subject, important because he wrote from the papers of d'Assonleville, who was Parma's agent in the preliminary negotiations with Gérard. Part of these documents have been published by Dewez (Hist. Gen. de la Belg., tom. vi.), by Reiffenberg, and still more recently by Professor Arent ("Recherches Critiques et Historiques sur la Confession de B. Gérard, Bruxelles, 1854,") who has ably demonstrated the authenticity of the "Confession" published by M. Gachard.

considerable facility of speech, when any person could be found who thought it worth while to listen to him ; but on the whole he attracted little attention.

Nevertheless, this insignificant frame locked up a desperate and daring character ; this mild and inoffensive nature had gone pregnant seven years with a terrible crime, whose birth could not much longer be retarded. Francis Guion, the Calvinist, son of a martyred Calvinist, was in reality Balthazar Gérard, a fanatical Catholic, whose father and mother were still living at Villefans in Burgundy. Before reaching man's estate, he had formed the design of murdering the Prince of Orange, "who, so long as he lived, seemed like to remain a rebel against the Catholic King, and to make every effort to disturb the repose of the Roman Catholic Apostolic religion."

When but twenty years of age, he had struck his dagger with all his might into a door, exclaiming, as he did so, "Would that the blow had been in the heart of Orange!" For this he was rebuked by a bystander, who told him it was not for him to kill princes, and that it was not desirable to destroy so good a captain as the Prince, who, after all, might one day reconcile himself with the King.*

As soon as the Ban against Orange was published, Balthazar, more anxious than ever to execute his long-cherished design, left Dôle and came to Luxemburg. Here he learned that the deed had already been done by John Jaureguy. He received this intelligence at first with a sensation of relief, was glad to be excused from putting himself in danger,† and believing the Prince dead, took service as clerk with one John Duprel, secretary to Count Mansfeld, governor of Luxemburg. Ere long, the ill success of Jaureguy's attempt becoming known, the "inveterate determination" of Gérard aroused itself more fiercely than ever. He accordingly took models of Mansfeld's official seals in wax, in order that he might make

* Confession de B. Gérard.—Bor, Meteren, Hoofd, Le Petit, ubi sup. et al.

† "—— des quelles nouvelles je fus fort aise, tant pour estre (comme j'estimois) la justice faite, que pour avoir excuse de me mettre au danger."—Conf. de Gérard.

use of them as an acceptable offering to the Orange party, whose confidence he meant to gain.

Various circumstances detained him, however. A sum of money was stolen, and he was forced to stay till it was found, for fear of being arrested as the thief. Then his cousin and employer fell sick, and Gérard was obliged to wait for his recovery. At last, in March, 1584, "the weather, as he said, appearing to be fine," Balthazar left Luxemburg and came to Tréves. While there, he confided his scheme to the regent of the Jesuit college—a "red-haired man" whose name has not been preserved.* That dignitary expressed high approbation of the plan, gave Gérard his blessing, and promised him that, if his life should be sacrificed in achieving his purpose, he should be enrolled among the martyrs.† Another Jesuit, however, in the same college, with whom he likewise communicated, held very different language, making great efforts to turn the young man from his design, *on the ground of the inconveniences which might arise from the forging of Mansfeld's seals*—adding, that neither he nor any of the Jesuits liked to meddle with such affairs, but advising that the whole matter should be laid before the Prince of Parma.‡ It does not appear that this personage, "an excellent man and a learned," attempted to dissuade the young man from his project by arguments drawn from any supposed criminality in the assassination itself, or from any danger, temporal or eternal, to which the perpetrator might expose himself.

Not influenced, as it appears, except on one point, by the advice of this second ghostly confessor, Balthazar came to

* Verhaal van de Moordt, etc.—Compare Bor, ubi sup.

† Ibid.—Compare Meteren, Le Petit, ubi sup.

‡ This curious fact was disingenuously suppressed in the official account, "Verhaal van de Moordt," etc., and is consequently not mentioned by the previously cited authors. The statement appears in the copy of the Confession published by M. Gachard; "—— et s'efforça le dit père de m'oster de teste ceste mienne délibération, pour les dangers et inconvéniens qu'il m'allégoit en pourroient survenir, au préjudice de Dieu et du Roy, par le moyen des cachets vollans; disant, au reste, qu'il ne se mesloit pas voluntiers de telz affaires, ny pareillement tous ceulx de leur dicte compagnie."

Tournay, and held council with a third—the celebrated Franciscan, Father Géry—by whom he was much comforted and strengthened in his determination.* His next step was to lay the project before Parma, as the "excellent and learned" Jesuit at Tréves had advised. This he did by a letter, drawn up with much care, and which he evidently thought well of as a composition. One copy of this letter he deposited with the guardian of the Franciscan convent at Tournay; the other he presented with his own hand to the Prince of Parma.† "The vassal," said he, "ought always to prefer justice and the will of the king to his own life." That being the case, he expressed his astonishment that no man had yet been found to execute the sentence against William of Nassau, "except the gentle Biscayan, since defunct."‡ To accomplish the task, Balthazar observed, very judiciously, that it was necessary to have access to the person of the Prince—wherein consisted the difficulty. Those who had that advantage, he continued, were therefore bound to extirpate the pest at once, without obliging his Majesty to send to Rome for a chevalier, because not one of them was willing to precipitate himself into the venomous gulf, which by its contagion infected and killed the souls and bodies of all poor abused subjects, exposed to its influence. Gérard avowed himself to have been so long goaded and stimulated by these considerations—so extremely nettled with displeasure and bitterness at seeing the obstinate wretch still escaping his just judgment—as to have formed the design of baiting a trap for the fox, hoping thus to gain access to him, and to take him unawares.§ He added—without explaining the nature of the trap and the bait—that he

---

* Verhaal van de Moordt, etc. Bor, Meteren, Le Petit, ubi sup.

† This letter, with several others relative to the subject, is contained in a manuscript of the Bib. de Bourgogne, N°. 17,386, entitled, "Particularités touchant Balthazar Gérard."

‡ "Hormis le gentil Biscayen défunct."

§ "Estant de long temps durement piqué et stimulé par ces deux points et poinçonné extrêment de déplaisir et amertume —— si finalement me suis advisé de donner une amorce à ce renard pour avoir accés chez-lui, afin de le prendre au trébuchet en momens opportuns, et si proprement qu'il n'en puisse échapper."

deemed it his duty to lay the subject before the most serene Prince of Parma, protesting at the same time that he did not contemplate the exploit for the sake of the reward mentioned in the sentence, and that he preferred trusting in that regard to the immense liberality of his Majesty.*

Parma had long been looking for a good man to murder Orange,† feeling—as Philip, Granvelle, and all former governors of the Netherlands had felt—that this was the only means of saving the royal authority in any part of the provinces. Many unsatisfactory assassins had presented themselves from time to time, and Alexander had paid money in hand to various individuals—Italians, Spaniards, Lorrainers, Scotchmen, Englishmen, who had generally spent the sums received without attempting the job. Others were supposed to be still engaged in the enterprise, and at that moment there were four person—each unknown to the others, and of different nations—in the city of Delft, seeking to compass the death of William the Silent.‡ Shag-eared, military, hirsute ruffians—ex-captains of free companies and such marauders—were daily offering their services; there was no lack of them, and they had done but little. How should Parma, seeing this obscure, under-sized, thin-bearded, runaway clerk before him, expect pith and energy from *him?* He thought him quite unfit for an enterprise of moment, and declared as much to his secret councillors and to the King.§

* "—— et moins encore être vue si présompteux que de préférer la liberalité immense de S. M.," etc.

† "Y porque tal enemigo tuviese castigo, andava el Principe de Parma buscando maneras como quitarle del mundo."—Herrera, Hist. del mundo en el reynado del Rey D. Phelipe II., xiv. 10, tom. ii. 550.

‡ "—— aulcuns Italiens et soldats avoient paravant obtenu certaines sommes au mesme effet sans avoir riens attenté."—Renom de France MS., tom. v. c. 26.—Compare Strada, 2, v. 287.

§ "—— le dit jeune homme," wrote Parma to the King, "m'avait communiqué sa résolution de la quelle pour dire la verité je tenois *peu de compte*, pour ce que la disposition du personnaige ne sembloit promettre emprinse de si grande importance. Touttefois je le laisaye aller, après l'avoir fait exorter par quelques ungz de ceux qui servent ici."—Relation du Duc de Parma au Roy. Phil. II.; in the manuscript entitled, "Particularités touchant B. Gérard." Bib. de Bourgogne, No. 17,386.

He soon dismissed him, after receiving his letters, and it may be supposed that the bombastic style of that epistle would not efface the unfavorable impression produced by Balthazar's exterior. The representations of Haultepenne and others induced him so far to modify his views as to send his confidential councillor, d'Assonleville, to the stranger, in order to learn the details of the scheme.* Assonleville had accordingly an interview with Gérard, in which he requested the young man to draw up a statement of his plan in writing, and this was done upon the 11th of April, 1584.

In this letter Gérard explained his plan of introducing himself to the notice of Orange, at Delft, as the son of an executed Calvinist; as himself warmly, though secretly, devoted to the Reformed faith, and as desirous, therefore, of placing himself in the Prince's service, in order to avoid the insolence of the Papists. Having gained the confidence of those about the Prince, he would suggest to them the great use which might be made of Mansfeld's signet in forging passports for spies and other persons whom it might be desirous to send into the territory of the royalists. "With these or similar feints and frivolities," continued Gérard, "he should soon obtain access to the person of the said Nassau," repeating his protestation that nothing had moved him to his enterprise "save the good zeal which he bore to the faith and true religion guarded by the Holy Mother Church Catholic, Apostolic, and Roman, and to the service of his Majesty." He begged pardon for having purloined the impressions of the seals—a turpitude which he would never have committed, but would sooner have suffered a thousand deaths, except for the great end in view. He particularly wished forgiveness for that crime before going to his task, "in order that he might confess, and receive the holy communion at the coming Easter, without scruples of conscience." He likewise begged the Prince of Parma to obtain for him absolution from his

* Renom de France MS., loc. cit., who wrote his history from the papers of Councillor d'Assonleville.

Holiness for this crime of pilfering—the more so "as he was about to keep company for some time with heretics and atheists, and in some sort to conform himself to their customs."*

From the general tone of the letters of Gérard, he might be set down at once as a simple, religious fanatic, who felt sure that, in executing the command of Philip publicly issued to all the murderers of Europe, he was meriting well of God and his King. There is no doubt that he was an exalted enthusiast, but not purely an enthusiast. The man's character offers more than one point of interest, as a psychological phenomenon. He had convinced himself that the work which he had in hand was eminently meritorious, and he was utterly without fear of consequences. He was, however, by no means so disinterested as he chose to represent himself in letters which, as he instinctively felt, were to be of perennial interest. On the contrary, in his interviews with Assonleville, he urged that he was a poor fellow, and that he had undertaken this enterprise in order to acquire property—to make himself rich†—and that he depended upon the Prince of Parma's influence in obtaining the reward promised by the Ban to the individual who should put Orange to death.

This second letter decided Parma so far that he authorized Assonleville to encourage the young man in his attempt, and to promise that the reward should be given to him in case of success, and to his heirs in the event of his death.‡ Assonleville, in the second interview, accordingly made known these assurances in the strongest manner to Gérard, warning him, at the same time, on no account, if arrested, to inculpate the Prince of Parma. The councillor, while thus exhorting the stranger, according to Alexander's commands, confined him-

* The letter is contained in the MS. before cited, "Particularités touchant B. Gérard."

† "Estant povre compagnon," etc.—Verhaal van de Moordt, etc. Le Petit. Bor, loc. cit.

‡ "—— qu'on procurevoit en sa faveur ou de ses proches héritiers les mercedes et récompenses promises par l'édict qui fut toute la consolation qu'il réceut, plus propre pour le retirer et divertir que pour l'encourager à une emprinse si hazardeuse."—Renom de France MS., loc. cit.

self, however, to generalities, refusing even to advance fifty crowns, which Balthazar had begged from the Governor-General in order to provide for the necessary expenses of his project.* Parma had made similar advances too often to men who had promised to assassinate the Prince and had then done little, and he was resolute in his refusal to this new adventurer, of whom he expected absolutely nothing. Gérard, notwithstanding this rebuff, was not disheartened. "I will provide myself out of my own purse," said he to Assonleville, "and within six weeks you will hear of me." "Go forth, my son," said Assonleville, paternally, upon this spirited reply, "and if you succeed in your enterprise, the King will fulfil all his promises, and you will gain an immortal name beside."†

The "inveterate deliberation," thus thoroughly matured, Gérard now proceeded to carry into effect. He came to Delft, obtained a hearing of Villers, the clergyman and intimate friend of Orange, showed him the Mansfeld seals, and was, somewhat against his will, sent to France, to exhibit them to Maréchal Biron, who, it was thought, was soon to be appointed governor of Cambray. Through Orange's recommendation, the Burgundian was received into the suite of Noel de Caron, Seigneur de Schoneval, then setting forth on a special mission to the Duke of Anjou.‡ While in France, Gérard could rest neither by day nor night, so tormented was he by the desire of accomplishing his project,§ and at length he obtained permission, upon the death of the Duke, to carry this important intelligence to the Prince of Orange. The despatches having been entrusted to him, he travelled post-haste to Delft, and, to his astonishment, the letters had hardly been delivered before he was summoned in person to

* "—— et aianct d'Assonleville traicté la dessus avec le Prince de Parme fut conclud que on n'avanceroit riens à Balthazar Gérard, non pas les 50 escus ausquels il se restraindoit," etc.—Ibid.

† Ibid. Verhaal van de Moordt. Bor, Meteren, Le Petit.

‡ Confession de Gérard. Verhaal van de Moordt. Bor, Meteren, Le Petit, Hoofd, ubi sup.

§ Verhaal van de Moordt.

the chamber of the Prince. Here was an opportunity such as he had never dared to hope for. The arch-enemy to the Church and to the human race, whose death would confer upon his destroyer wealth and nobility in this world, besides a crown of glory in the next, lay unarmed, alone, in bed, before the man who had thirsted seven long years for his blood.

Balthazar could scarcely control his emotions sufficiently to answer the questions which the Prince addressed to him concerning the death of Anjou,* but Orange, deeply engaged with the despatches, and with the reflections which their deeply-important contents suggested, did not observe the countenance of the humble Calvinist exile, who had been recently recommended to his patronage by Villers. Gérard, had, moreover, made no preparation for an interview so entirely unexpected, had come unarmed, and had formed no plan for escape. He was obliged to forego his prey when most within his reach, and after communicating all the information which the Prince required, he was dismissed from the chamber.

It was Sunday morning, and the bells were tolling for church. Upon leaving the house he loitered about the court-yard, furtively examining the premises, so that a sergeant of halberdiers asked him why he was waiting there. Balthazar meekly replied that he was desirous of attending divine worship in the church opposite, but added, pointing to his shabby and travel-stained attire, that, without at least a new pair of shoes and stockings, he was unfit to join the congregation. Insignificant as ever, the small, pious, dusty stranger excited no suspicion in the mind of the good-natured sergeant. He forthwith spoke of the wants of Gérard to an officer, by whom they were communicated to Orange himself, and the Prince instantly ordered a sum of money to be given him.† Thus Balthazar obtained from William's charity what Parma's thrift had denied—a fund for carrying out his purpose!

Next morning, with the money thus procured he purchased

* Verhaal, etc. Bor, Meteren, Le Petit.

† Verhaal van de Moordt. Bor, Meteren, Hoofd, loc. cit.

a pair of pistols, or small carabines, from a soldier, chaffering long about the price because the vender could not supply a particular kind of chopped bullets or slugs which he desired. Before the sunset of the following day that soldier had stabbed himself to the heart, and died despairing, on hearing for what purpose the pistols had been bought.*

On Tuesday, the 10th of July, 1584, at about half-past twelve, the Prince, with his wife on his arm, and followed by the ladies and gentlemen of his family, was going to the dining-room. William the Silent was dressed upon that day, according to his usual custom, in very plain fashion. He wore a wide-leaved, loosely-shaped hat of dark felt, with a silken cord round the crown—such as had been worn by the Beggars in the early days of the revolt. A high ruff encircled his neck, from which also depended one of the Beggar's medals, with the motto, "*Fidèles au roy jusqu'à la besace*," while a loose surcoat of grey frieze cloth, over a tawny leather doublet, with wide, slashed underclothes completed his costume.† Gérard presented himself at the doorway, and demanded a passport. The Princess, struck with the pale and agitated countenance of the man, anxiously questioned her husband concerning the stranger. The Prince carelessly observed that "it was merely a person who came for a passport," ordering, at the same time, a secretary forthwith to prepare one. The Princess, still not relieved, observed in an under-tone that "she had never seen so villanous a countenance."‡ Orange, however, not at all impressed with the appearance of Gérard, conducted himself at table with his usual cheerfulness, conversing much with the burgomaster of Leewarden, the only guest present at the family dinner, concerning the political and religious aspects of Friesland.§ At two o'clock the

* "—— zig op 't hooren van 't gruuwzaam gebruik, 't geen er de Booswigt van gemacht hadt, uit wanhoop, met twee of drie poignaard steeken om 't leven bragt."—Van Wyn op Wagenaer, vii. 116.

† The whole dress worn by the Prince on this tragical occasion is still to be seen at the Hague in the National Museum.

‡ Bor, Meteren, Hoofd, ubi sup.

§ Historie Balth. Geraerts alias Serach, etc.

company rose from table. The Prince led the way, intending to pass to his private apartments above. The dining-room, which was on the ground floor, opened into a little square vestibule, which communicated, through an arched passage-way, with the main entrance into the court-yard. This vestibule was also directly at the foot of the wooden staircase leading to the next floor, and was scarcely six feet in width.* Upon its left side, as one approached the stairway, was an obscure arch, sunk deep in the wall, and completely in the shadow of the door. Behind this arch a portal opened to the narrow lane at the side of the house. The stairs themselves were completely lighted by a large window, half way up the flight. The Prince came from the dining-room, and began leisurely to ascend. He had only reached the second stair, when a man emerged from the sunken arch, and, standing within a foot or two of him, discharged a pistol full at his heart. Three balls entered his body, one of which, passing quite through him, struck with violence against the wall beyond. The Prince exclaimed in French, as he felt the wound, "O my God, have mercy upon my soul! O my God, have mercy upon this poor people!"†

* The house (now called the Prinsen Hof, but used as a barrack) still presents nearly the same appearance as it did in 1584.

† Korte Verhaal van den Moordt, etc.—Bor, Meteren, Hoofd. Doubts have been expressed by some writers as to the probability of the Prince, thus mortally wounded, having been able to speak so many words distinctly. (See Wagenaer, Vad. Hist., vii. 532, and note.) There can, however, be no doubt on the subject. The circular letter of the States-general to the respective provinces, dated Delft, July 12, 1584, has this passage: "Die corts daervan t'onser grooten leedwesen ende verdriete overleden, segghende deselve ont faen hebbende, Mon Dieu, ayez pitié de mon âme; Mon Dieu, ayez pitié de ce pouvre peuple!" (Brieven van de Gen.-staten., etc., nopende de dood van heere P. van Orangien. Ordinaris Dep. Boek, MS., 1584, f. 162, Hague Archives.) This is conclusive evidence. See also a letter from young Maurice of Nassau to the magistracy of Ghent, relating the death and last words of his father in similar terms, but in the Flemish tongue. "Maer alzoo de leste woorden van zijne Exc[ie] waeren, myn Godt! ontfermt U. mynder ziele, myn Godt! ontfermt uwer ghemeente." (De Jonge Onuitg. Stukken., 100–103.—Compare Regist. der Resolut. Holl., July 10, 1584; Bor, Auth. Stukk., ii. 58). The Greffier Cornelius Aertsens, writing to Brussels on the 11th of July from Delft, uses precisely the same language: "Son Ex[ce] est

These were the last words he ever spoke, save that when his sister, Catherine of Schwartzburg, immediately afterwards asked him if he commended his soul to Jesus Christ, he faintly answered, "Yes." His master of the horse, Jacob van Maldere, had caught him in his arms as the fatal shot was fired. The Prince was then placed on the stairs for an instant, when he immediately began to swoon. He was afterwards laid upon a couch in the dining-room, where in a few minutes, he breathed his last in the arms of his wife and sister.*

The murderer succeeded in making his escape through the side door, and sped swiftly up the narrow lane. He had almost reached the ramparts, from which he intended to spring into the moat, when he stumbled over a heap of rubbish. As he rose, he was seized by several pages and halberdiers, who had pursued him from the house. He had dropped his pistols upon the spot where he had committed the crime, and upon his person were found a couple of bladders, provided with a piece of pipe with which he had intended to assist himself across the moat, beyond which a horse was waiting for him. He made no effort to deny his identity, but boldly avowed himself and his deed. He was brought back to the house, where he immediately underwent a preliminary examination before the city magistrates. He was afterwards subjected to excruciating tortures; for the fury against the wretch who had destroyed the Father of the country was uncontrollable, and William the Silent was no longer alive to intercede—as he had often done before—in behalf of those who assailed his life.

The organization of Balthazar Gérard would furnish a subject of profound study, both for the physiologist and the metaphysician. Neither wholly a fanatic, nor entirely a ruffian, he combined the most dangerous elements of both

---

trespassé et fini en Dieu, n'aiant parlé autre chose que ces mots bien hauts—Mon Dieu, ayez pitié de mon âme; et après, Ayez pitié de ce pauvre peuple, demeurans les deux derniers mots quasi en sa bouche."—Relation au Mag. de Brux., N°. 17,386, Bib. de Bourg., MS.

* Bor, Meteren, Hoofd, ubi sup. Historie B. Geraerts alias Serach.

characters. In his puny body and mean exterior were enclosed considerable mental powers and accomplishments, a daring ambition, and a courage almost superhuman. Yet those qualities led him only to form upon the threshold of life a deliberate determination to achieve greatness by the assassin's trade. The rewards held out by the Ban, combining with his religious bigotry and his passion for distinction, fixed all his energies with patient concentration upon the one great purpose for which he seemed to have been born, and after seven years' preparation, he had at last fulfilled his design.

Upon being interrogated by the magistrates, he manifested neither despair nor contrition, but rather a quiet exultation. "Like David," he said, "he had slain Goliath of Gath."* When falsely informed that his victim was not dead, he showed no credulity or disappointment. He had discharged three poisoned balls into the Prince's stomach, and he knew that death must have already ensued.† He expressed regret, however, that the resistance of the halberdiers had prevented him from using his second pistol, and avowed that if he were a thousand leagues away he would return in order to do the deed again, if possible. He deliberately wrote a detailed confession of his crime, and of the motives and manner of its commission, taking care, however, not to implicate Parma in the transaction. After sustaining day after day the most horrible tortures, he subsequently related his interviews with Assonleville and with the president of the Jesuit college at Tréves, adding that he had been influenced in his work by the assurance of obtaining the rewards promised by the Ban.‡ During the intervals of repose from the rack he conversed with ease, and even eloquence, answering all questions addressed to him with apparent sincerity. His constancy in suffering so astounded

* Haraei Annales, iii. 363.

† "—— j'ai ce jourd'hui tiré et débendé celle portant les trois balles contre l'estomach dudict Prince d'Orange," etc.—Confession de Gérard. "—— en heeft hem also met een pistolet onder zijne mantel met drij fenijnige ende geketende looten aen een gehecht geladen zijnde aen die treppen vander eetplatsen verwacht," etc.—Historie B. Geraerts alias Serach.

‡ Verhaal van de Moordt. Bor, Meteren.

his judges that they believed him supported by witchcraft. "Ecce homo!" he exclaimed, from time to time, with insane blasphemy, as he raised his blood-streaming head from the bench. In order to destroy the charm which seemed to render him insensible to pain, they sent for the shirt of a hospital patient, supposed to be a sorcerer. When clothed in this garment, however, Balthazar was none the less superior to the arts of the tormentors, enduring all their inflictions, according to an eye-witness, "without once exclaiming, Ah me!" and avowing that he would repeat his enterprise, if possible, were he to die a thousand deaths in consequence. Some of those present refused to believe that he was a man at all. Others asked him how long since he had sold himself to the Devil? to which he replied, mildly, that he had no acquaintance whatever with the Devil. He thanked the judges politely for the food which he received in prison, and promised to recompense them for the favor. Upon being asked how that was possible, he replied, that he would serve as their advocate in Paradise.*

The sentence pronounced against the assassin was execrable —a crime against the memory of the great man whom it professed to avenge. It was decreed that the right hand of Gérard should be burned off with a red-hot iron, that his flesh should be torn from his bones with pincers in six different places, that he should be quartered and disembowelled alive, that his heart should be torn from his bosom and flung in his face, and that, finally, his head should be taken off. Not even his horrible crime, with its endless consequences, nor the natural frenzy of indignation which it had excited, could justify

* Verhaal van de Mooodt, Bor, Meteren.—"—— mais je n'ay ouy de ma vie une plus grande resolution d'homme ny constance, il n'a oncques dit 'Ay my,' mais en tous tourmens s'est tenu sans dire mot, et sur tous interrogatories a repondu bien àpropos et avec bonne suite, quelquefois que voulez-vous faire de moy? je suis resolu de mourir aussy d'une mort cruelle que je n'eusse laissé mon entreprinse ni encore si j'étois libre la laisseroie, comme que je deusse mourir mille morts," etc.—Extrait d'une Relation faite à ceux du Magistrat de Bruxelles, par Corneille Aertsens alors leur Greffier, 11 Juillet, 1584. Bib. de Bourg. MS., N°. 17,386, Historie B. Geraerts alias Serach.

this savage decree, to rebuke which the murdered hero might have almost risen from the sleep of death. The sentence was literally executed on the 14th of July, the criminal supporting its horrors with the same astonishing fortitude. So calm were his nerves, crippled and half roasted as he was ere he mounted the scaffold, that when one of the executioners was slightly injured in the ear by the flying from the handle of the hammer with which he was breaking the fatal pistol in pieces, as the first step in the execution—a circumstance which produced a general laugh in the crowd—a smile was observed upon Balthazar's face in sympathy with the general hilarity. His lips were seen to move up to the moment when his heart was thrown in his face—"Then," said a looker-on, "he gave up the ghost."*

The reward promised by Philip to the man who should murder Orange was paid to the heirs of Gérard. Parma informed his sovereign that the "poor man" had been executed, but that *his father and mother* were still living, to whom he recommended the payment of that "merced" which "the laudable and generous deed had so well deserved."† This was accordingly done, and the excellent parents, ennobled and enriched by the crime of their son, received instead of the twenty-five thousand crowns promised in the Ban, the three seignories of Lievremont, Hostal, and Dampmartin, in the Franche Comté, and took their place at once among the landed aristocracy.‡ Thus the bounty of the Prince had furnished the weapon by which his life was destroyed, and his estates supplied the fund out of which the assassin's family

* Extrait d'une Relation de Corneille Aertsens (14 Juillet, 1584). He was present at all the tortures and at the execution, and drew up his report the same day. Manuscript before cited.—Compare Meteren, Bor, Le Petit, Historie B. Geraerts alias Serach.

† Relation du Duc de Parme au Roy Phil. II., 12 Août, 1584.—"Le pauvre homme est demeuré prisonnier. L'acte est tel qu'il mérite grande louange, et je me vais informant des parens du deffunt, duquel j'entends le père et la mère être encoires vivans, pour après supplier V. M. leur faire le mercède qu'une si généreuse résolution mérite."—MS. before cited.

‡ MS. before cited.

received the price of blood. At a later day, when the unfortunate eldest son of Orange returned from Spain after twenty-seven years' absence, a changeling and a Spaniard, the restoration of those very estates was offered to him by Philip the Second, provided he would continue to pay a *fixed proportion of their rents to the family of his father's murderer*. The education which Philip William had received, under the King's auspices, had however, not entirely destroyed all his human feelings, and he rejected the proposal with scorn.* The estates remained with the Gérard family, and the patents of nobility which they had received were used to justify their exemption from certain taxes, until the union of Franche Comté, with France, when a French governor tore the documents in pieces and trampled them under foot.†

William of Orange, at the period of his death, was aged fifty-one years and sixteen days. He left twelve children. By his first wife, Anne of Egmont, he had one son, Philip, and one daughter, Mary, afterwards married to Count Hohenlo. By his second wife, Anna of Saxony, he had one son, the celebrated Maurice of Nassau, and two daughters, Anna, married afterwards to her cousin, Count William Louis, and Emilie, who espoused the Pretender of Portugal, Prince Emanuel. By Charlotte of Bourbon, his third wife, he had six daughters; and by his fourth, Louisa de Coligny, one son, Frederic William, afterwards stadholder of the Republic in her most palmy days.‡ The Prince was entombed on the 3rd of August, at Delft, amid the tears of a whole nation.§ Never was a more extensive, unaffected, and legitimate sorrow felt at the death of any human being.

---

* Van Kampen, i. 545.

† Van d. Vynct, iii.—Notes of Tarte and Reiffenberg.

‡ Bor, ubi sup. Archives, ubi sup. Meteren, xii. 216.

§ Bor, xviii. 433. Meteren, xii. 215. Hoofd, xx. 896.

THE life and labors of Orange had established the emancipated commonwealth upon a secure foundation, but his death rendered the union of all the Netherlands into one republic hopeless. The efforts of the Malcontent nobles, the religious discord, the consummate ability, both political and military, of Parma, all combined with the lamentable loss of William the Silent to separate for ever the southern and Catholic provinces from the northern confederacy. So long as the Prince remained alive, he was the Father of the whole country; the Netherlands—saving only the two Walloon provinces—constituting a whole. Notwithstanding the spirit of faction and the blight of the long civil war, there was at least one country, or the hope of a country, one strong heart, one guiding head, for the patriotic party throughout the land. Philip and Granvelle were right in their estimate of the advantage to be derived from the Prince's death; in believing that an assassin's hand could achieve more than all the wiles which Spanish or Italian statesmanship could teach, or all the armies which Spain or Italy could muster. The pistol of the insignificant Gérard destroyed the possibility of a united Netherland state, while during the life of William there was union in the policy, unity in the history of the country.

In the following year, Antwerp, hitherto the centre around which all the national interests and historical events group themselves, fell before the scientific efforts of Parma. The city which had so long been the freest, as well as the most opulent, capital in Europe, sank for ever to the position of a provincial town. With its fall, combined with other circumstances, which it is not necessary to narrate in anticipation, the final separation of the Netherlands was completed. On the other hand, at the death of Orange, whose formal inauguration as sovereign Count had not yet taken place, the states of Holland and Zealand reassumed the sovereignty. The commonwealth which William had liberated for ever from Spanish tyranny continued to exist as a great and flourishing republic during more than two centuries, under the successive stadholderates of his sons and descendants.

His life gave existence to an independent country—his death defined its limits. Had he lived twenty years longer, it is probable that the seven provinces would have been seventeen; and that the Spanish title would have been for ever extinguished both in Nether Germany and Celtic Gaul. Although there was to be the length of two human generations more of warfare ere Spain acknowledged the new government, yet before the termination of that period the United States had become the first naval power and one of the most considerable commonwealths in the world; while the civil and religious liberty, the political independence of the land, together with the total expulsion of the ancient foreign tyranny from the soil, had been achieved ere the eyes of William were closed. The republic existed, in fact, from the moment of the abjuration in 1581.

The most important features of the polity which thus assumed a prominent organization have been already indicated. There was no revolution, no radical change. The ancient rugged tree of Netherland liberty—with its moss-grown trunk, gnarled branches, and deep-reaching roots—which had been slowly growing for ages, was still full of sap, and was to deposit for centuries longer its annual rings of consolidated and concentric strength. Though lopped of some luxuriant boughs, it was sound at the core, and destined for a still larger life than even in the healthiest moments of its mediæval existence.

The history of the rise of the Netherland Republic has been at the same time the biography of William the Silent. This, while it gives unity to the narrative, renders an elaborate description of his character superfluous. That life was a noble Christian epic; inspired with one great purpose from its commencement to its close; the stream flowing ever from one fountain with expanding fulness, but retaining all its original purity. A few general observations are all which are necessary by way of conclusion.

In person, Orange was above the middle height, perfectly well made and sinewy, but rather spare than stout. His eyes, hair, beard, and complexion were brown. His head was small, symmetrically-shaped, combining the alertness and compactness characteristic of the soldier, with the capacious brow furrowed prematurely with the horizontal lines of thought, denoting the statesman and the sage. His physical appearance was, therefore, in harmony with his organization, which was of antique model. Of his moral qualities, the most prominent was his piety. He was more than anything else a religious man. From his trust in God, he ever derived support and consolation in the darkest hours. Implicitly relying upon Almighty wisdom and goodness, he looked danger in the face with a constant smile, and endured incessant labors and trials with a serenity which seemed more than human. While, however, his soul was full of piety, it was tolerant of error. Sincerely and deliberately himself a convert to the Reformed Church, he was ready to extend freedom of worship to Catholics on the one hand, and to Anabaptists on the other, for no man ever felt more keenly than he, that the Reformer who becomes in his turn a bigot is doubly odious.

His firmness was allied to his piety. His constancy in bearing the whole weight of struggle as unequal as men have ever undertaken, was the theme of admiration even to his enemies. The rock in the ocean, "tranquil amid raging billows," was the favorite emblem by which his friends expressed their sense of his firmness. From the time when, as a hostage in France, he first discovered the plan of Philip to plant the Inquisition in the Netherlands, up to the last moment of his life, he never faltered in his determination to resist that iniquitous scheme. This resistance was the labor of his life. To exclude the Inquisition, to maintain the ancient liberties of his country, was the task which he appointed to himself when a youth of three-and-twenty. Never speaking a word concerning a heavenly mission, never deluding himself or others with the usual phraseology of enthusiasts, he accomplished the task, through danger, amid toils, and with sacrifices such as few men have ever been able to make on their country's altar;—for the disinterested benevolence of the man was as prominent as his fortitude. A prince of high rank and with royal revenues, he stripped himself of station, wealth, almost at times of the common necessaries of life, and became, in his country's cause, nearly a beggar as well as an outlaw. Nor was he forced into his career by an accidental impulse from which there was no recovery. Retreat was ever open to him. Not only pardon but advancement was urged upon him again and again. Officially and privately, directly and circuitously, his confiscated estates, together with indefinite and boundless favors in addition, were offered to him on every great occasion. On the arrival of Don John, at the Breda negotiations, at the Cologne conferences, we have seen how calmly these offers were waved aside, as if their rejection was so simple that it hardly required many words for its signification, yet he had mortgaged his estates so deeply that his heirs hesitated at accepting their inheritance,* for fear it should involve them in debt. Ten years after his death, the account between his executors and his brother John amounted to one million four hundred thousand florins† due to the Count, secured by various pledges of real and personal property, and it was finally settled upon this basis. He was besides largely indebted to every one of his powerful relatives, so that the payment of the incumbrances upon his estate very nearly justified the fears of his children. While on the one hand, therefore, he poured out these enormous sums like water, and firmly refused a hearing to the tempting offers of the royal government, upon the other hand he proved the disinterested nature of his services by declining, year after year, the sovereignty over the provinces; and by only accepting, in the last days of his life, when refusal had become almost impossible, the limited, constitutional supremacy over that portion of them which now makes the realm of his descendants. He lived and died, not for himself, but for his country: "God pity this poor people!" were his dying words.

His intellectual faculties were various and of the highest order. He had the exact, practical, and combining qualities which make the great commander, and his friends

* Ev. Reyd, iii. 59.

† Bor, xviii. 438.

claimed that, in military genius, he was second to no captain in Europe.* This was, no doubt, an exaggeration of partial attachment, but it is certain that the Emperor Charles had an exalted opinion of his capacity for the field. His fortification of Philippeville and Charlemont, in the face of the enemy—his passage of the Meuse in Alva's sight—his unfortunate but well-ordered campaign against that general—his sublime plan of relief, projected and successfully directed at last from his sick bed, for the besieged city of Leyden—will always remain monuments of his practical military skill.

Of the soldier's great virtues—constancy in disaster, devotion to duty, hopefulness in defeat—no man ever possessed a larger share. He arrived, through a series of reverses, at a perfect victory. He planted a free commonwealth under the very battery of the Inquisition, in defiance of the most powerful empire existing. He was therefore a conqueror in the loftiest sense, for he conquered liberty and a national existence for a whole people. The contest was long, and he fell in the struggle, but the victory was to the dead hero, not to the living monarch. It is to be remembered, too, that he always wrought with inferior instruments. His troops were usually mercenaries, who were but too apt to mutiny upon the eve of battle, while he was opposed by the most formidable veterans of Europe, commanded successively by the first captains of the age. That, with no lieutenant of eminent valor or experience, save only his brother Louis, and with none at all after that chieftain's death, William of Orange should succeed in baffling the efforts of Alva, Requesens, Don John of Austria, and Alexander Farnese—men whose names are among the most brilliant in the military annals of the world—is in itself sufficient evidence of his warlike ability. At the period of his death he had reduced the number of obedient provinces to two; only Artois and Hainault acknowledging Philip, while the other fifteen were in open revolt, the greater part having solemnly forsworn their sovereign.

* "Belli artibus neminem suo tempore parem habuit," says Ev. Reyd, Ann. iii. 59.

The supremacy of his political genius was entirely beyond question. He was the first statesman of the age. The quickness of his perception was only equalled by the caution which enabled him to mature the results of his observations. His knowledge of human nature was profound. He governed the passions and sentiments of a great nation as if they had been but the keys and chords of one vast instrument; and his hand rarely failed to evoke harmony even out of the wildest storms. The turbulent city of Ghent, which could obey no other master, which even the haughty Emperor could only crush without controlling, was ever responsive to the master-hand of Orange. His presence scared away Imbize and his bat-like crew, confounded the schemes of John Casimir, frustrated the wiles of Prince Chimay, and while he lived, Ghent was what it ought always to have remained, the bulwark, as it had been the cradle, of popular liberty. After his death it became its tomb.

Ghent, saved thrice by the policy, the eloquence, the self-sacrifices of Orange, fell within three months of his murder into the hands of Parma. The loss of this most important city, followed in the next year by the downfall of Antwerp, sealed the fate of the Southern Netherlands. Had the Prince lived, how different might have been the country's fate! If seven provinces could dilate, in so brief a space, into the powerful commonwealth which the Republic soon became, what might not have been achieved by the united seventeen; a confederacy which would have united the adamantine vigor of the Batavian and Frisian races with the subtler, more delicate, and more graceful national elements in which the genius of the Frank, the Roman, and the Romanized Celt were so intimately blended. As long as the Father of the country lived, such a union was possible. His power of managing men was so unquestionable, that there was always a hope, even in the darkest hour, for men felt implicit reliance, as well on his intellectual resources as on his integrity.

This power of dealing with his fellow-men he manifested in the various ways in which it has been usually exhibited by statesmen. He possessed a ready eloquence—sometimes impassioned, oftener argumentative, always rational. His influence over his audience was unexampled in the annals of that country or age; yet he never condescended to flatter the people. He never followed the nation, but always led her in the path of duty and of honor, and was much more prone to rebuke the vices than to pander to the passions of his hearers. He never failed to administer ample chastisement to parsimony, to jealousy, to insubordination, to intolerance, to infidelity, wherever it was due, nor feared to confront the states or the people in their most angry hours, and to tell them the truth to their faces. This commanding position he alone could stand upon, for his countrymen knew the generosity which had sacrificed his all for them, the self-denial which had eluded rather than sought political advancement, whether from king or people, and the untiring devotion which had consecrated a whole life to toil and danger in the cause of their emancipation. While, therefore, he was ever ready to rebuke, and always too honest to flatter, he at the same time possessed the eloquence which could convince or persuade. He knew how to reach both the mind and the heart of his hearers. His orations, whether extemporaneous or prepared—his written messages to tho states-general, to the provincial authorities, to the municipal bodies—his private correspondence with men of all ranks, from emperors and kings down to secretaries, and even children—all show an easy flow of language, a fulness of thought, a power of expression rare in that age, a fund of historical allusion, a considerable power of imagination, a warmth of sentiment, a breadth of view, a directness of purpose—a range of qualities, in short, which would in themselves have stamped him as one of the master-minds of his century, had there been no other monument to his memory than the remains of his spoken or written eloquence. The bulk of his performances in this department was prodigious. Not even Philip was more industrious in the cabinet. Not even Granvelle held a more facile pen. He wrote and spoke equally well in French German, or Flemish; and he possessed, besides, Spanish, Italian, Latin. The weight of his correspondence alone would have almost sufficed for the common industry of a lifetime, and although many volumes of his speeches and letters have been published, there remain in the various archives of the Netherlands and Germany many documents from his hand which will probably never see the light. If the capacity for unremitted intellectual labor in an honorable cause be the measure of human greatness, few minds could be compared to the "large composition" of this man. The efforts made to destroy the Netherlands by the most laborious and painstaking of tyrants were counteracted by the industry of the most indefatigable of patriots.

Thus his eloquence, oral or written, gave him almost boundless power over his countrymen. He possessed, also, a rare perception of human character, together with an iron memory which never lost a face, a place, or an event, once seen or known. He read the minds even the faces of men, like printed books. No man could overreach him, excepting only those to whom he gave his heart. He might be mistaken where he had confided, never where he had been distrustful or indifferent. He was deceived by Renneberg, by his brother-in-law Van den Berg, by the Duke of Anjou. Had it been possible for his brother Louis or his brother John to have proved false, he might have been deceived by them. He was never outwitted by Philip, or Granvelle, or Don John, or Alexander of Parma. Anna of Saxony was false to him, and entered into correspondence with the royal governors and with the King of Spain; Charlotte of Bourbon or Louisa de Coligny might have done the same had it been possible for their natures also to descend to such depths of guile.

As for the Aerschots, the Havrés, the Chimays, he was never influenced either by their blandishments or their plots. He was willing to use them when their interest made them friendly, or to crush them when their intrigues against his policy rendered them dangerous. The adroitness with which he converted their schemes in behalf of Matthias, of Don John, of Anjou, into so many additional weapons for his own cause, can never be too often studied. It is instructive to observe the wiles of the Macchiavelian school employed by a master of the craft, to frustrate, not to advance, a knavish purpose. This character, in a great measure, marked his whole policy. He was profoundly skilled in the subtleties of Italian statesmanship, which he had learned as a youth at the Imperial court, and which he employed in his manhood in the service, not of tyranny, but of liberty. He fought the Inquisition with its own weapons. He dealt with Philip on his own ground. He excavated the earth beneath the King's feet by a more subtle process than that practised by the most fraudulent monarch that ever governed the Spanish empire, and Philip, chain-mailed as he was in complicated wiles, was pierced to the quick by a keener policy than his own.

Ten years long the King placed daily his most secret letters in hands which regularly transmitted copies of the correspondence to the Prince of Orange, together with a key to the ciphers and every other illustration which might be required.* Thus the secrets of the King were always as well known to Orange as to himself; and the Prince being as prompt as Philip was hesitating, the schemes could often be frustrated before their execution had been commenced. The crime of the unfortunate clerk, John de Castillo, was discovered in the autumn of the year 1581, and he was torn to pieces by four horses.† Perhaps his treason to the monarch whose bread he was eating, while he received a regular salary from the King's most determined foe, deserved even this horrible punishment, but casuists must determine how much guilt attaches to the Prince for his share in the transaction. This history is not the eulogy of Orange, although, in discussing his character, it is difficult to avoid the monotony of panegyric. Judged by a severe moral standard, it cannot be called virtuous or honorable to suborn treachery or any other crime, even to accomplish a lofty purpose; yet the universal practice of mankind in all ages has tolerated the artifices of war, and no

* Bor, xvi. 288[b]. Hoofd, xviii. 791.

† Meteren, Bor, ubi sup.

people has ever engaged in a holier or more mortal contest than did the Netherlands in their great struggle with Spain. Orange possessed the rare quality of caution, a characteristic by which he was distinguished from his youth. At fifteen he was the confidential counsellor, as at twenty-one he became the general-in-chief, to the most politic, as well as the most warlike potentate of his age, and if he at times indulged in wiles which modern statesmanship, even while it practises, condemns, he ever held in his hand the clue of an honorable purpose to guide him through the tortuous labyrinth.

It is difficult to find any other characteristic deserving of grave censure, but his enemies have adopted a simpler process. They have been able to find few flaws in his nature, and therefore have denounced it in gross. It is not that his character was here and there defective, but that the eternal jewel was false. The patriotism was counterfeit ; the self-abnegation and the generosity were counterfeit. He was governed only by ambition—by a desire of personal advancement. They never attempted to deny his talents, his industry, his vast sacrifices of wealth and station ; but they ridiculed the idea that he could have been inspired by any but unworthy motives.* God

* "A man born to the greatest fame," says Bentivoglio, "if, content with his fortunes, he had not sought amid precipices for a still greater one." While paying homage to the extraordinary genius of the Prince, to his energy, eloquence, perspicacity in all kinds of affairs, his absolute dominion over the minds and hearts of men, and his consummate skill in improving his own positions and taking advantage of the false moves of his adversary, the Cardinal proceeds to accuse him of "ambition, fraud, audacity, and rapacity." The last qualification seems sufficiently absurd to those who have even superficially studied the life of William the Silent. Of course, the successive changes of religion by the Prince are ascribed to motives of interest—"Videsi variare di Religione secondo che vario d'interessi. Da fanciullo in Germania fú Luterano. Passato in Fiandra mostrossi Cattolico. Al principio della rivolte si dichiara fautore delle nuove sette ma non professore manifesto d'alcuna; sinche finalmente gli parve di seguitar quella de' Calvinisti, come la piú contraria di tutte alla Religione Cattolica sostenuta dal Ré di Spagna."—(Guerra di Fiandra, p. 2, l. ii. 276.) The Cardinal does *not* add that the conversion of the Prince to the Reformed religion was at the blackest hour of the Reformation. Cabrera is cooler and coarser. According to him the Prince was a mere impostor. The Emperor even had been often cautioned as to his favorite's arrogance, deceit and ingratitude, and warned that the Prince was "a fox who would eat up all his

alone knows the heart of man. He alone can unweave the tangled skein of human motives, and detect the hidden springs of human action, but as far as can be judged by a careful observation of undisputed facts, and by a diligent collation of public and private documents, it would seem that no man—not even Washington—has ever been inspired by a purer patriotism. At any rate, the charge of ambition and self-seeking can only be answered by a reference to the whole picture which these volumes have attempted to portray. The words, the deeds of the man are there. As much as possible, his inmost soul is revealed in his confidential letters, and he who looks in a right spirit will hardly fail to find what he desires.

Whether originally of a timid temperament or not, he was certainly possessed of perfect courage at last. In siege and battle—in the deadly air of pestilential cities—in the long exhaustion of mind and body which comes from unduly pro-

Majesty's chickens." While acknowledging that he "could talk well of public affairs," and that he "entertained the ambassadors and nobility with splendor and magnificence," the historian proclaims him, however, "faithless and mendacious, a flatterer and a cheat."—(Cabrera. v. 233.) We have seen that Tassis accused the Prince of poisoning Count Bossu with oysters, and that Strada had a long story of his attending the deathbed of that nobleman in order to sneer at the viaticum. We have also seen the simple and heartfelt regret which the Prince expressed in his private letters for Bossu's death and the solid service which he rendered to him in life. Of false accusations of this nature there was no end. One of the most atrocious has been recently resuscitated. A certain Christophe de Holstein accused the Prince in 1578 of having instigated him to murder Duke Eric of Brunswick. The assassin undertook the job, but seems to have been deterred by a mysterious bleeding at his nose from proceeding with the business. As this respectable witness, by his own confession, had murdered his own brother, for money, and two merchants besides, had moreover been concerned in the killing or plundering of a "curate, a monk, and two hermits," and had been all his life a professional highwayman and assassin, it seems hardly worth while to discuss his statements. Probably a thousand such calumnies were circulated at different times against the Prince. Yet the testimony of this wretched malefactor is gravely reproduced, at the expiration of near three centuries, as if it were admissible in any healthy court of historical justice. Truly says the adage: "calomniez toujours, il en restera quelque chose."—See Compte Rendu de la Com. Roy. d'Hist., tom. xi., Bruxelles, 1846. Notice sur les aveux de Chr. de Holstein, etc., etc., par le D[r]. Coremans, pp. 10–18.

tracted labor and anxiety—amid the countless conspiracies of assassins—he was daily exposed to death in every shape. Within two years, five different attempts against his life had been discovered. Rank and fortune were offered to any malefactor who would compass the murder. He had already been shot through the head, and almost mortally wounded. Under such circumstances even a brave man might have seen a pitfall at every step, a dagger in every hand, and poison in every cup. On the contrary, he was ever cheerful, and hardly took more precaution than usual. "God in his mercy," said he, with unaffected simplicity, "will maintain my innocence and my honor during my life and in future ages. As to my fortune and my life, I have dedicated both, long since, to His service. He will do therewith what pleases Him for His glory and my salvation."* Thus his suspicions were not even excited by the ominous face of Gérard, when he first presented himself at the dining-room door. The Prince laughed off his wife's prophetic apprehension at the sight of his murderer, and was as cheerful as usual to the last.

He possessed, too, that which to the heathen philosopher seemed the greatest good—the sound mind in the sound body. His physical frame was after death found so perfect that a long life might have been in store for him, notwithstanding all which he had endured. The desperate illness of 1574, the frightful gunshot wound inflicted by Jaureguy in 1582, had left no traces. The physicians pronounced that his body presented an aspect of perfect health.† His temperament was cheerful. At table, the pleasures of which, in moderation, were his only relaxation, he was always animated and merry, and this jocoseness was partly natural, partly intentional. In the darkest hours of his country's trial, he affected a serenity which he was far from feeling, so that his apparent gaiety at momentous epochs was even censured by dullards, who

---

* Apologie, p. 133.

† Reydani, iii. 59.

could not comprehend its philosophy, nor applaud the flippancy of William the Silent.*

He went through life bearing the load of a people's sorrows upon his shoulders with a smiling face. Their name was the last word upon his lips, save the simple affirmative, with which the soldier who had been battling for the right all his lifetime, commended his soul in dying "to his great captain, Christ." The people were grateful and affectionate, for they trusted the character of their "Father William," and not all the clouds which calumny could collect ever dimmed to their eyes the radiance of that lofty mind to which they were accustomed, in their darkest calamities, to look for light. As long as he lived, he was the guiding-star of a whole brave nation, and when he died the little children cried in the streets.†

---

* "Imprimis inter cibos hilaris et velut omnium securus: quâ re et tetricos atque arrogantiores nonnullos offendit, qui simulatam saepe et coactam eam laetitiam haud capiebant: cum illius aspectu cuncti refoverentur, illius ex vultu spei quisque aut desperationsi caussam sumeret."—Ev. Reyd., ubi sup.

† Literal expression in the official report made by the Greffier Corneille Aertsens: "dont par toute la ville l'on est en si grand duil tellement que les petits enfans en pleurent par les rues."—Relation faite a ceux du Magistrat de Bruxelles, 11 Juillet, 1584, MS., Bib. de Bourg., No. 17,386.

INDEX.

The Roman numerals refer to the volume; the figures to the pages.

THE END.

www.ingramcontent.com/pod-product-compliance
Lightning Source LLC
LaVergne TN
LVHW021051110826
845150LV00001B/41

* 9 7 8 1 4 2 5 5 6 7 8 7 3 *